FREE MARKET ECONOMICS:
A BASIC READER

Free Market ECONOMICS
A Basic Reader

Compiled by Bettina Bien Greaves

THE FOUNDATION FOR
ECONOMIC EDUCATION, INC.
IRVINGTON-ON-HUDSON, NEW YORK 10533

ACKNOWLEDGMENTS

Thanks are due the more than 50 authors, living and dead, whose thoughts and efforts made this volume possible. Special appreciation is given the individuals and publishers who originally granted permission to the Foundation for Economic Education (referred to in this basic reader as FEE) to reproduce the many titles appearing here from its early pamphlets and other publications—*Ideas on Liberty, The Freeman* and *Notes From FEE.* Hopefully all persons and organizations who contributed have been adequately recognized in the footnote identifying each essay. However, any omissions or errors which may have occurred must be laid at the door of the compiler.

ABOUT THE PUBLISHER

The Foundation for Economic Education is a nonpolitical, nonprofit, educational institution. Its senior staff and numerous writers are students as well as teachers of the free market, private ownership, limited government rationale. Sample copies of the Foundation's monthly study journal, *The Freeman,* are available on request.

Published 1975
2nd Printing 1977
3rd Printing 1979
4th Printing 1984
5th Printing 1989
ISBN 0-910614-56-3

PREFACE

The 81 readings in this BASIC READER have been selected to accompany and to supplement FREE MARKET ECONOMICS: A SYLLABUS. They are arranged here in broad subject categories so that they form in effect a "course of study" in and of themselves. A substantial understanding of free market economics may be gained by reading this volume systematically from beginning to end. However, anyone seriously interested in a full and logical explanation of the theories illustrated by these readings should also refer to the SYLLABUS.

The compiler of this anthology studied for many years with the leading spokesman of the so-called "Austrian School of Economics," Ludwig von Mises, and acknowledges a tremendous intellectual debt to him personally as well as to his many works. Several excerpts from his writings are included in this collection, along with those by many other authors. Each reading was chosen to help explain or to illustrate some aspect of the theory of free market economics.

The majority of these readings have been reprinted from *The Freeman,* the monthly journal of The Foundation for Economic Education (FEE). This may be explained not only by the compiler's long association with FEE (since 1951) but also by the fact that FEE, since its founding in 1946, has been one of the major consistent publishers of materials dealing with the free market, individual freedom, private property and the detrimental effects of governmental intervention.

A glossary of terms used here and in the SYLLABUS appear in the back of this volume.

Bettina Bien Greaves

TABLE OF CONTENTS

General Introduction

1. ECONOMICS FOR BOYS AND GIRLS*

Leonard E. Read

> *Train up a child in the way he should go: and when he is old, he will not depart from it.*
> PROVERBS 22:6

Time and again we have been asked to devise economic instruction for the youngsters, the thought being that it's the oncoming generation that counts. And, just as often, we have shaken our heads, pleading ignorance of how to go about it.

Trying to devise economic lessons for grownups has seemed difficult enough, for only now and then is there an adult who shows any interest in or aptitude for the subject. But we have tried, and over the years of trial and error, it has seemed that our best approach to adults is to leave them alone until they seek such instruction or light as we may come to possess. In other words, our job, as we now see it, is to concentrate on improving our own understanding and practice of freedom, with faith that others will be attracted precisely to the extent that we are able to show self-improvement.

Thus, we are constantly striving to better understand and explain and apply the economics of specialization and the division of labor, freedom in transactions, the marginal utility theory of value, and reliance on the orderliness of the free market as a guide to creativities and exchange.

Is there a way to present such complex ideas to children so that they might be attracted toward the free market way of social behavior? Perhaps. But first, let us consider our raw material, the youngsters we would teach.

There are those who contend that every baby starts life as a little savage; that he is equipped, among other things, with organs and muscles over which he has no control, with an urge for self-preservation, with aggressive drives and emotions like anger, fear, and love over which he likewise has practically no control, and that in the process of growing up, it is normal for every child to be dirty, to fight, to talk back, to disobey, to evade. "*Every child has to grow out of delinquent behavior.*" So runs this argument. For my part, however, I take small comfort in this Freudian view of the genesis of the human race. I would much prefer to think of the child as a budding plant with all the potential for beauty and happiness which such a growing organism portends. In each case, of course, there may be from the adult point of view, apparent disorganization, lack of coordination, and disharmony. Yet, the potential for harmony and beauty is there.

Whether the child be considered a brutal barbarian or a budding beauty, the challenge is to help him emerge from a state of ignorance as to his relationship with others and into harmony with the universal laws which govern the human situation. The child is an extension of the parent's responsibility, and that responsibility includes pointing the child in the direction of sound economic under-

**Notes from FEE*, September 1965

standing. I shall hint at, but by no means exhaust, the possibilities:

If You Drop Something, Pick it Up

This is easily taught, especially by parents who observe this dictum themselves. It is elementary training in assuming a responsibility for one's own actions, that is, of not burdening others with one's behaviors. A child who takes this simple first step in self-control—should the steps continue and become habitual—will likely, when attaining adulthood, look to himself rather than to the rest of us to bail him out of economic difficulties brought on by his own mistakes. He will, more than likely, not be a burden on society.

A genuine mastery of self-control tends to develop a rare and valuable faculty: the ability to will one's own actions. Such a person will not be tempted to shift his position by reason of pressures, fickle opinions, popular notions, and the like. He will become his own man.

Picking up what you drop has its reward in orderliness of mind. When it becomes second nature, it is a joyous habit and on occasion leads to picking up after others. Projected into adult life, this shows up as a charitable attitude—in the Judeo-Christian sense—one's personal duty toward the less fortunate.

If You Open a Door, Close It

This is a sequel to the above; it is merely another practice that confirms the wisdom of completing each of life's transactions.

> An inevitable dualism bisects nature, so that each thing is a half, and suggests another thing to make it whole; as spirit, matter; man, woman; subjective, objective; in, out; upper, under; motion, rest; yea, nay.[1]

For child training, I would add: drop, pick up; open, close; and others.

If You Make a Promise, Keep It

Social chaos has no better ally than broken promises. Children not brought up to keep their word will be the authors of treaties written not to be observed; they'll run for office on bogus platforms, cancel gold contracts, use the political means to expropriate property; they'll sell their souls to gain fame or fortune or power. Not only will they fail to be honest with their fellow men; they will not even heed the dictates of their own conscience. On the other hand, children brought up to keep their promises will not go back on their bond, come hell or high water. Integrity will be their mark of distinction!

Whatever You Borrow, Pay Back

This is an extension of promise keeping. An adherence to these admonitions develops a respect for private property, a major premise in sound economic doctrine. No person, thus brought up, would think of feathering his own nest at the expense of others. Welfare statists and social planners are not born of this training, that is, if the training really sinks in. True, a socialist will honor debts incurred in his own name but will disregard any indebtedness he sponsors in the name of "the public." He has not been brought up to understand that the principle of compensation applies "across the board."

Play the Thank-You Game

It will take a brilliant parent and a mighty perceptive child to get anywhere with this one. I can set forth the idea but not how to teach it. The idea, once grasped, is simple enough, yet so evasive that, in spite of the 33,000 years since Cro-Magnon man, it was only discovered a bare century ago: The value of a good or service is determined not *objectively* by cost of production, *but subjectively* by what others will give in willing exchange. Economic science has no more important concept than this; the free market has no other economic genesis than this subjective or marginal utility theory of value. Indeed, it is most accurately identified as the free market theory of value.

To repeat an illustration used earlier: When mother exchanges 30¢ for a can of beans, she values the beans more than the 30¢ and the grocer values the 30¢ more than the beans. If mother valued the 30¢ more than the beans, she wouldn't trade. If the grocer valued his beans more than the 30¢, he wouldn't trade. The value of both the 30¢ and the beans (excluding other considerations) is determined by the two subjective judgments. The amount of effort exerted (cost) to obtain the 30¢ or to acquire the beans has nothing to do with the value of either the beans or the 30¢.

I repeat, the value of any good or service is determined by what it will bring in willing, *not forcible* or unwilling, exchange.[2] When the 30¢ is exchanged for the beans, the grocer concludes the transaction with "Thank you," for, in his judgment, he has gained. There is precisely the same justification for the mother to say, "Thank you," for, in her judgment, she has gained. It wouldn't be at all amiss to describe this as "the thank-you way of economic life."

This concept of value, be it remembered, was practiced off and on by the common man ages before economic theorists identified it as the efficacious way of mutually advancing economic well-being. And, by the same token, the child can be taught to practice it before he can possibly grasp the theory. In exchanging toys or marbles or jacks or whatever with another, can he not play the thank-you game? Can he not be taught to express the same "thank you" himself as he expects from his playmate? That something is wrong with the trade if this is not the case? That both have gained when each says, "Thank you"? Accomplish this with a boy or girl and you have laid the groundwork for sound economic thinking.

Do Nothing to a Playmate You Wouldn't Enjoy Having Him Do to You

Moral philosophy is the investigation into and the study of what's right and wrong. Economics is a division of this discipline: the study of right and wrong in economic affairs.

The free market is the Golden Rule in its economic application, thus free market economics is dependent on the practice of the Golden Rule.

That the Golden Rule can be phrased and taught so as to be completely perceived prior to adolescence is doubtful. Its apprehension requires a moral nature, a faculty rarely acquired earlier than teen-age—in many instances, never!

But the effort to teach the Golden Rule to boys and girls will, at a minimum, result in a better observation of it on the parent's part. Children—highly impressionable—are far more guided by parental conduct than by parental admonishments. Thus, the attempt to teach this fundamental principle of morality and justice, *resulting in highly exemplary behavior*, may lead the child first to imitation and then to habitual observance and practice.

Writing the above, which only hints at how boys and girls may get off to a good start in economic thinking, has supplied the missing explanation to something I have known for several years: *women are more hopeful prospects than men in the contest between free market and authoritarian ideas!* In our seminar activities, we have found the distaffers better students than the mill run of males, as well as more idealistic and less compromising. Beyond this, it is the mothers, rather than the fathers, in whose care the citizens of tomorrow are largely committed. It is primarily the mothers who will refine the methods for getting boys and girls on the track of sound thinking.

But mothers or fathers, it is the parents who are responsible for the generations to come and who also are responsible for the kinds of people who assist in teaching their children.

Notes

[1] Excerpted from *Compensation* by Ralph Waldo Emerson.

[2] TVA, Post Office, and a thousand and one other deficits, are paid for by forcible exchange. Moon specialists are paid by forcible, not willing, exchange. This goes, also, for all governmental subsidies.

What is Economics?

2. SOMETHING FOR NOTHING?*

Mark C. Schinnerer

The writer of this editorial practices what he preaches. I know because I am well acquainted with him and his career. He has always given at least as much, and usually more, than he expected to receive. He is a stalwart American citizen. It is fortunate for all of us when men like Mark Schinnerer occupy important positions of leadership, especially in education. Dr. Schinnerer is a valued member of the National Advisory Council for Scholastic Magazines.

—John W. Studebaker
Chairman, Editorial Board

This is about economics. This is about the teaching of economics, not directed just to teachers of economics, but to all teachers. It is directed to all teachers because the job that needs to be done cannot be done by just the teachers of economics.

There is a colossal oversupply of people in my country who either never discovered some of the basic principles of economics or think that the economic laws have been repealed. We hear much wailing that the schools have failed in this regard and the cry is for required courses in economics. We have failed—in school and out—but the answer is not in required courses. The answer, in my opinion, lies in a continuous effort to inculcate in children, from kindergarten through high school, some basic and very simple facts.

There are three things which almost anyone can be brought to understand and if these three are ingrained, we can leave the more complicated principles to the experts.

1. You can't get something for nothing. Too many think they can. That is the basis of gambling and most speculation. Giving a higher mark in school than is earned is proving that the student can get something for nothing. That is bad business. When parents urge no homework, they somehow expect something for nothing. One gets out of school work about what he puts into it. Only parasites get something for nothing.

2. You can't spend more than you have and remain solvent. The longer such a system is followed, the more impossible it becomes to keep afloat. Know anyone who trades in a mortgaged car on a new one and has both a newer car and a bigger mortgage? The woods are full of such people. It is bad economics. It's somewhat like drug addiction. This applies equally to a person, a business, or a government.

3. You cannot equalize ability by a handicap system. It is wrong to expect as much from a youngster with a low I. Q. as is expected from a youngster with a high I. Q. It is also wrong to set up handicaps so that they come out even. Leave that for the exclusive use of the racing stewards. Competition still has a place in America, thank goodness, and I don't want it any other way.

In every school day, there are numerous incidents in each student's school experience when these three fundamentals are present. Just repeatedly bringing them to the pupil's consciousness will work wonders. If all our people accepted these three economic axioms and lived by them, we would live in an economic paradise.

Clipping of Note No. 61 (FEE, 1954). Reprinted from *Scholastic Magazines*, January 6, 1954

3. THE BROKEN WINDOW*

Henry Hazlitt

It is often sadly remarked that the bad economists present their errors to the public better than the good economists present their truths. The reason is that the bad economists are presenting half-truths. They are speaking only of the immediate effect of a proposed policy or its effect upon a single group. The answer consists in supplementing and correcting the half-truth with the other half.

But the lesson will not be driven home, and the fallacies will continue to go unrecognized, unless both are illustrated by examples. Let us begin with the simplest illustration possible: let us, emulating Bastiat,[1] choose a broken pane of glass.

A young hoodlum, say, heaves a brick through the window of a baker's shop. The shopkeeper runs out furious, but the boy is gone. A crowd gathers, and begins to stare with quiet satisfaction at the gaping hole in the window and the shattered glass over the bread and pies. After a while the crowd feels the need for philosophic reflection. And several of its members are almost certain to remind each other or the baker that, after all, the misfortune has its bright side. It will make business for some glazier. As they begin to think of this they elaborate upon it. How much does a new plate glass window cost? Fifty dollars? That will be quite a sum. After all, if windows were never broken, what would happen to the glass business? Then, of course, the thing is endless. The glazier will have $50.00 more to spend with other merchants, and these in turn will have $50.00 more to spend with still other merchants, and so ad infinitum. The smashed window will go on providing money and employment in ever-widening circles. The logical conclusion from all this would be, if the crowd drew it, that the little hoodlum who threw the brick, far from being a public menace, was a public benefactor.

Now let us take another look. The crowd is at least right in its first conclusion. This little act of vandalism will in the first instance mean more business for some glazier. The glazier will be no more unhappy to learn of the incident than an undertaker to learn of a death. But the shopkeeper will be out $50.00 that he was planning to spend for a new suit. Because he has had to replace a window, he will have to go without the suit (or some equivalent need or luxury). Instead of having a window and $50.00, he now has merely a window. Or, as he was planning to buy the suit that very afternoon, instead of having both a window and a suit, he must be content with the window and no suit. If we think of him as a part of the community, the community has lost a new suit that might otherwise have come into being, and is just that much poorer.

The glazier's gain of business, in short, is merely the tailor's loss of business. No new "employment" has been added. The people in the crowd were thinking only of two parties to the transaction, the baker and the glazier. They had forgotten the potential third party involved, the tailor. They forgot him precisely because he will not now enter the scene. They will see the new window in the next day or two. They will never see the extra suit, precisely because it will never be made. They see only what is immediately visible to the eye.

So we have finished with the broken window. An elementary fallacy. Anybody, one would think, would be able to avoid it after a few moments' thought. Yet the broken-window fallacy, under a hundred disguises, is the most persistent in the history of economics. It is more rampant now than at any time in the past.

*Clipping of Note No. 95 (FEE, 1959). Excerpted from *Economics in One Lesson* (Harper, 1946)

Note

[1]Frederic Bastiat, 1801-1850, French economist, statesman, writer.

4. THE INDIVIDUAL IN SOCIETY*

Ludwig von Mises

The words freedom and liberty signified for the most eminent representatives of mankind one of the most precious and desirable goods. Today it is fashionable to sneer at them. They are, trumpets the modern sage, "slippery" notions and "bourgeois" prejudices.

Freedom and liberty are not to be found in nature. In nature there is no phenomenon to which these terms could be meaningfully applied. Whatever man does, he can never free himself from the restraints which nature imposes upon him. If he wants to succeed in acting, he must submit unconditionally to the laws of nature.

Freedom and liberty always refer to interhuman relations. A man is free as far as he can live and get on without being at the mercy of arbitrary decisions on the part of other people. In the frame of society everybody depends upon his fellow citizens. Social man cannot become independent without forsaking all the advantages of social cooperation.

The fundamental social phenomenon is the division of labor and its counterpart—human cooperation.

Experience teaches man that cooperative action is more efficient and productive than isolated action of self-sufficient individuals. The natural conditions determining man's life and effort are such that the division of labor increases output per unit of labor expended. These natural facts are: (1) the innate inequality of men with regard to their ability to perform various kinds of labor, and (2) the unequal distribution of the nature-given, non-human opportunities of production on the surface of the earth. One may as well consider these two facts as one and the same fact, namely, the manifoldness of nature which makes the universe a complex of infinite varieties.

*FEE, 1952. Extracted and reprinted with permission of the publisher from 1st ed. of *Human Action* (Yale, 1949)

Innate Inequality

The division of labor is the outcome of man's conscious reaction to the multiplicity of natural conditions. On the other hand, it is itself a factor bringing about differentiation. It assigns to the various geographic areas specific functions in the complex of the processes of production. It makes some areas urban, others rural; it locates the various branches of manufacturing, mining, and agriculture in different places. Still more important, however, is the fact that it intensifies the innate inequality of men. Exercise and practice of specific tasks adjust individuals better to the requirements of their performance; men develop some of their inborn faculties and stunt the development of others. Vocational types emerge, people become specialists.

The division of labor splits the various processes of production into minute tasks, many of which can be performed by mechanical devices. It is this fact that made the use of machinery possible and brought about the amazing improvements in technical methods of production. Mechanization is the fruit of the division of labor, its most beneficial achievement, not its motive and fountain spring. Power-driven specialized machinery could be employed only in a social environment under the division of labor. Every step forward on the road toward the use of more specialized, more refined, and more productive machines requires a further specialization of tasks.

Within Society

Seen from the point of view of the individual, society is the great means for the attainment of all his ends. The preservation of society is an essential condition of any plans an individual may want to realize by any action whatever. Even the refractory delinquent who fails to adjust his conduct to the requirements of life within the societal system of cooperation does not want to miss any of the advantages derived from the division of labor. He does not consciously aim at the destruction of society. He wants to lay his hands on a greater portion of the jointly produced wealth than the social order assigns to him. He would feel miserable if antisocial behavior were to become universal and its inevitable outcome, the return to primitive indigence, resulted.

Liberty and freedom are the conditions of man within a contractual society. Social cooperation under a system of private ownership of the means of production means that within the range of the market the individual is not bound to obey and to serve an overlord. As far as he gives and serves other people, he does so of his own accord in order to be rewarded and served by the receivers. He exchanges goods and services, he does not do compulsory labor and does not pay tribute. He is certainly not independent. He depends on the other members of society. But this dependence is mutual. The buyer depends on the seller and the seller on the buyer.

Self-Interest

The main concern of many writers of the nineteenth and twentieth centuries was to misrepresent and to distort this obvious state of affairs. The workers, they said, are at the mercy of their employers. Now, it is true that the employer has the right to fire the employee. But if he makes use of this right in order to indulge in his whims, he hurts his own interests. It is to his own disadvantage if he discharges a better man in order to hire a less efficient one. The market does not directly prevent anybody from arbitrarily inflicting harm on his fellow citizens; it only puts a penalty upon such conduct. The shopkeeper is free to be rude to his customers provided he is ready to bear the consequences. The consumers are free to boycott a purveyor provided they are ready to pay the costs. What impels every man to the utmost exertion in the service of his fellow men and curbs innate tendencies toward arbitrariness and malice is, in the market, not compulsion and coercion on the part of gendarmes, hangmen, and penal courts; it is self-interest. The member of a contractual society is free because he serves others only in serving himself. What restrains him is only the inevitable natural phenomenon of scarcity. For the rest he is free in the range of the market.

In the market economy the individual is free to act within the orbit of private property and the market. His choices are final. For his fellow men his actions are data which they must take into account in their own acting. The coordination of the autonomous actions of all individuals is accomplished by the operation of the market. Society does not tell a man what to do and what not to do. There is no need to enforce cooperation by special orders or prohibitions. Non-cooperation penalizes itself. Adjustment to the requirements of society's productive effort and the pursuit of the individual's own concerns are not in conflict. Consequently no agency is required to settle such conflicts. The system can work and accomplish its tasks without the interference of an authority issuing special orders and prohibitions and punishing those who do not comply.

Compulsion and Coercion

Beyond the sphere of private property and the market lies the sphere of compulsion and coercion; here are the dams which organized society has built for the protection of private property and the market against violence, malice, and fraud. This is the realm of constraint as distinguished from the realm of freedom. Here are rules discriminating between what is legal and what is illegal, what is permitted and what is prohibited. And here is a grim machine of arms, prisons, and gallows and the men operating it, ready to crush those who dare to disobey.

It is important to remember that government interference always means either violent action or the threat of such action. Government is in the last resort the employment of armed men, of policemen, gendarmes, soldiers, prison guards, and hangmen. The essential feature of government is the enforcement of its decrees by beating, killing, and imprisoning. Those who are asking for more government interference are asking ultimately for more compulsion and less freedom.

Liberty and freedom are terms employed for the description of the social conditions of the individual members of a market society in which the power of the indispensable hegemonic bond, the state, is curbed lest the operation of the market be endangered. In a totalitarian system there is nothing to which the attribute "free" could be attached but the unlimited arbitrariness of the dictator.

There would be no need to dwell upon this obvious fact if the champions of the abolition of liberty had not purposely brought about a semantic confusion. They realized that it was hopeless for them to fight openly and sincerely for restraint and servitude. The notions liberty and freedom had such prestige that no propaganda could shake their popularity. Since time immemorial in the realm of Western civilization liberty has been considered as the most precious good. What gave to the West its eminence was precisely its concern about liberty, a social ideal foreign to the oriental peoples. The social philosophy of the Occident is essentially a philosophy of freedom. The main content of the history of Europe and the communities founded by European emigrants and their descendants in other parts of the world was the struggle for liberty. "Rugged" individualism is the signature of our civilization. No open attack upon the freedom of the individual had any prospect of success.

New Definitions

Thus the advocates of totalitarianism chose other tactics. They reversed the meaning of words. They call true or genuine liberty the condition of the individuals under a system in which they have no right other than to obey orders. They call themselves true *liberals* because they strive after such a social order. They call democracy the Russian methods of dictatorial government. They call the labor union methods of violence and coercion "industrial democracy." They call freedom of the press a state of affairs in which only the government is free to publish books and newspapers. They define liberty as the opportunity to do the "right" things, and, of course, they arrogate to themselves the determination of what is right and what is not. In their eyes government omnipotence means full liberty. To free the police power from all restraints is the true meaning of their struggle for freedom.

The market economy, say these self-styled liberals, grants liberty only to a parasitic class of exploiters, the bourgeoisie; that these scoundrels enjoy the freedom to enslave the masses; that the wage earner is not free; that he must toil for the sole benefit of his masters, the employers; that the capitalists appropriate to themselves what according to the inalienable rights of man should belong to the worker; that under socialism the worker will enjoy freedom and human dignity because he will no longer have to slave for a capitalist; that socialism means the emancipation of the common man, means freedom for all; that it means, moreover, riches for all.

These doctrines have been able to triumph because they did not encounter effective rational criticism. It is useless to stand upon an alleged "natural" right of individuals to own property if other people assert that the foremost "natural" right is that of income equality. Such disputes can never be settled. It is beside the point to criticize nonessential, attendant features of the socialist program. One does not refute socialism by attacking the socialists' stand on religion, marriage, birth control, and art.

A New Subterfuge

In spite of these serious shortcomings of the defenders of economic freedom it was impossible to fool all the people all the time about the essential features of socialism. The most fanatical planners were forced to admit that their projects involve the abolition of many freedoms people enjoy under capitalism and "plutodemocracy." Pressed hard, they resorted to a new subterfuge. The freedom to be abolished, they emphasize, is merely the spurious "economic" freedom of the capitalists that harms the common man; that outside the "economic sphere" freedom will not only be fully preserved, but considerably expanded. "Planning for Freedom" has lately become the most popular slogan of the champions of totalitarian government and the Russification of all nations.

The fallacy of this argument stems from the spurious distinction between two realms of human life and action, the "economic" sphere and the "noneconomic" sphere. Strictly speaking, people do not long for tangible goods as such, but for the services which these goods are fitted to render them. They want to attain the increment in well-being which these services are able to convey. It is a fact that people, in dealing on the market, are motivated not only by the desire to get food, shelter, and sexual enjoyment, but also by manifold "ideal" urges. Acting man is always concerned both with "material" and "ideal" things. He chooses between various alternatives, no matter whether they are to be classified as material or ideal. In the actual scales of value, material and ideal things are jumbled together.

Preserving the Market

Freedom, as people enjoyed it in the democratic countries of Western civilization in the years of the old liberalism's triumph, was not a product of constitutions, bills of rights, laws, and statutes. Those documents aimed only at safeguarding liberty and freedom, firmly established by the operation of the market economy, against encroachments on the part of officeholders. No government and no civil law can guarantee and bring about freedom otherwise than by supporting and defending the fundamental institutions of the market economy. Government means always coercion and compulsion and is by necessity the opposite of liberty. Government is a guarantor of liberty and is compatible with liberty only if its range is adequately restricted to the preservation of economic freedom. Where there is no market economy, the best-intentioned provisions of constitutions and laws remain a dead letter.

Competition

The freedom of man under capitalism is an effect of competition. The worker does not depend on the good graces of an employer. If his employer discharges him, he finds another employer. The consumer is not at the mercy of the shopkeeper. He is free to patronize another shop if he likes. Nobody must kiss other people's hands or fear their disfavor. Interpersonal relations are businesslike. The exchange of goods and services is mutual; it is not a favor to sell or to buy, it is a transaction dictated by selfishness on either side.

It is true that in his capacity as a producer every man depends either directly, as does the entrepreneur, or indirectly, as does the hired worker, on the demands of the consumers. However, this dependence upon the supremacy of the consumers is not unlimited. If a man has a weighty reason for defying the sovereignty of the consumers, he can try it. There is in the range of the market a very substantial and effective right to resist oppression. Nobody is forced to go into the liquor industry or into a gun factory if his conscience objects. He may have to pay a price for his conviction; there are in this world no ends the attainment of which is gratuitous. But it is left to a man's own decision to choose between a material advantage and the call of what he believes to be his duty. In the market economy the individual alone is the supreme arbiter in matters of his satisfaction.

Capitalist society has no means of compelling a man to change his occupation or his place of work other than to reward those complying with the wants of the consumers by higher pay. It is precisely this kind of pressure which many people consider as unbearable and hope to see abolished under socialism. They are too dull to realize that the only alternative is to convey to the authorities full power to determine in what branch and at what place a man should work.

In his capacity as a consumer man is no less free. He alone decides what is more and what is less important for him. He chooses how to spend his money according to his own will.

The substitution of economic planning for the market economy removes all freedom and leaves to the individual merely the right to obey. The authority directing all economic matters controls all aspects of a man's life and activities. It is the only employer. All labor becomes compulsory labor because the employee must accept what the chief deigns to offer him. The economic tsar determines what and how much of each the consumer may consume. There is no sector of human life in which a decision is left to the individual's value judgments. The authority assigns a definite task to him, trains him for this job, and employs him at the place and in the manner it deems expedient.

The "Planned" Life Is not Free

As soon as the economic freedom which the market economy grants to its members is removed, all political liberties and bills of rights become humbug. Habeas corpus and trial by jury are a sham if, under the pretext of economic expediency, the authority has full power to relegate every citizen it dislikes to the arctic or to a desert and to assign him "hard labor" for life. Freedom of the press is a mere blind if the authority controls all printing offices and paper plants. And so are all the other rights of men.

A man has freedom as far as he shapes his life according to his own plans. A man whose fate is determined by the plans of a superior authority, in which the exclusive power to plan is vested, is not free in the sense in which the term "free" was used and understood by all people until the semantic revolution of our day brought about a confusion of tongues.

The Nature of the Individual—Values and Actions

5. THE BIOLOGY OF BEHAVIOR*

Roger J. Williams

The prevalence of student rebellions throughout the world makes one wonder just how effectively modern education relates to real human problems. To approach the problems of generic man from a biological standpoint may be far too superficial in this scientific age with its tremendous advances in technology; yet, could not the general weakness of human science be the basis for the comment by Robert Frost: "Poets like Shakespeare knew more about psychiatry than any $25-an-hour man"?

Biologically, each member of the human family possesses inborn differences based on his brain structure and on his vast mosaic of endocrine glands—in fact, on every aspect of his physical being. Each of us has a distinctive set of drives—for physical activity, for food, for sexual expression, for power. Each one has his own mind qualities: abilities, ways of thinking, and patterns of mental conditions. Each one has his own emotional setup and his leanings toward music and art in its various forms, including literature. All these leanings are subject to change and development, but there is certainly no mass movement toward uniformity. No one ever "recovers" from the fact that he was born an individual.

When a husband and wife disagree on the temperature of the soup or on the amount of bed coverings, or if their sleep patterns do not jibe, this is evidence of inborn differences in physiology. If one child loves to read or is interested in science and another has strong likings for sports or for art, this is probably due to inborn differences in makeup. If two people disagree about food or drink, they should not disregard the fact that taste and smell reactions often widely differ and are inherited. If we see a person wearing loud clothing without apparent taste, we need to remember, in line with the investigations of Pickford in England, that each individual has a color vision all his own; some may deviate markedly from the pack.

The inborn leanings of Mozart were evident by age three, and he began composing when he was four. Capablanca was already a good chess player —good enough to beat his father—when at age five he played his first game. For many centuries, Indian philosophers have recognized innate individuality, which they explain on the basis of experience in previous incarnations.

Biology has always recognized inborn individuality. If this inborn distinctiveness had not always been the rule in biology, evolution could never have happened. It is a commonplace fact in biology that every living organism needs a heredity and a suitable environment. Unfortunately, in the minds of most intellectuals biological considerations have been pushed aside.

Professor Jerry Hirsch, a psychologist at the University of Illinois, has protested in *Science* that "the opinion makers of two generations have literally excommunicated heredity from the behavioral sciences." This neglect of the study of heredity has effectively produced a wide gap between biology and psychology. Biology deals with living things, and psychology is logically an important phase of biology.

Bernard Rimland, director of the Institute for

*From *The Freeman*, April 1971. Reprinted by permission from *Saturday Review*, January 30, 1971. Copyright 1971, *Saturday Review, Inc.*

Child Behavior Research in San Diego, in reviewing my book, *You Are Extraordinary* in *American Psychologist,* wrote: "Since between-group differences are commonly a small fraction of the enormous, important, and very interesting within-group (individual) difference, psychology's focus on average values for heterogeneous groups represents, as Williams indicates, a chronic case of throwing out the babies with the bath water. 'Throwing out the babies' is bad enough, but we psychologists have the dubious distinction of making this error not only repeatedly but *on purpose.*"

Social solidarity exists and social problems are pressing, but we cannot hope to deal with these successfully by considering only generic man, that is, average values for heterogeneous groups. We need a better understanding of *men.*

A Firm Foundation

The basic problem of generic man is how to achieve "life, liberty, and the pursuit of happiness." The writers of our Declaration of Independence were on solid ground, biologically speaking, when they took the position that each human being has inalienable rights and that no one has, by virtue of his imagined "royal blood," the right to rule over another. In their emphasis on mankind as individuals, Jefferson and his co-authors were closer to biological reality than are those of our time who divorce psychology from biology and center their attention on that statistical artifact, the average man.

Because each of us is distinctive, we lean in different directions in achieving life, liberty, and the pursuit of happiness. Happiness may come to individual people in vastly different ways, and so the human problem of achieving life and the pursuit of happiness resolves itself, more than it is comfortable to admit, into a series of highly individual human problems. We need to take this consideration into account in attempting to build an advanced society.

In understanding the scope of human desires, it is worthwhile to consider briefly the problems that real—as opposed to theoretical—people face. These may be grouped under four headings: 1) making a livelihood; 2) maintaining health; 3) getting along with others; and 4) getting along with one's self. These four categories, singly or in combination, cover most of the familiar human problems—marriage and divorce, crime, disease, war, housing, air and water pollution, urban congestion, race relations, poverty, the population explosion, the all-pervading problem of education, and the building of an abundant life.

The importance of approaching the problem of making a livelihood from the individual's standpoint lies in the fact that in our complex society a multitude of ways exist—an estimated 23,000—in which people can make a living. People are not by any means interchangeable parts in society. While some might function well in any one of a large number of capacities, many others might be highly restricted in their capabilities and yet be extremely valuable members of society. The idea that it is all a matter of education and training cannot possibly be squared with the hard biological facts of inborn individuality. This perversion of education perpetuates the banishment of heredity—an ever present biological fact—from our thinking. Fitting together people and jobs is just as real and compelling as fitting shoes to people. People sometimes suffer from ill-fitting shoes; they suffer more often from ill-fitting jobs.

The maintenance of health—both physical and mental—involves individual problems to such a degree that it is difficult to exaggerate their role. Ever since the days of Hippocrates it has been known in a vague way that "different sorts of people have different maladies," but we are only beginning to learn how to sort people on the basis of their inborn individual characteristics. When we have become expert in this area, vast progress will result, particularly in the prevention of metabolic and psychosomatic diseases, i.e., those not resulting from infection. As long as we dodge the biological fact of inborn individuality, we remain relatively impotent in the handling of diseases that arise from within individual constitutions.

The problem of getting along with others is a very broad one, in which individual problems are basic. If husbands and wives and members of the same family always get along well together, we would have some reason to be surprised when squabbles break out within business, religious, or political groups. If all these kinds of squabbles were nonexistent, we would have a basis for being surprised at the phenomenon of war.

Distinctive Qualities

While self-interest and differences in training are vital factors in these common conflicts, another factor should not be overlooked: the inborn individuality of the participants. There is a mass of evidence to support the thesis that every individual, by virtue of his or her unique brain structure and peripheral nervous system, is psychologically conditionable in a distinctive manner. Thus, a person's unique nervous system picks up distinctive sets of impulses, and because his interpretive apparatus is also unique he learns different things and interprets the world in a distinctive manner. Even if two individuals were to have exactly the same learning opportunities, each would think differently and not quite like anyone else. This is the basis for the observation by Santayana: "Friendship is almost always the union of a part of one mind with another; people are friends in spots."

In spite of our attempts to do so, individual minds cannot be compared on a quantitative basis. The minds of Shakespeare and Einstein cannot be weighed one against the other; there were many facets to the minds of each. At birth the two minds were equally blank, but as they matured, each saw, perceived, and paid attention to different aspects of the world around it. Each was conditionable in a unique way.

Each Mind Unique

The recognition of the uniqueness of human minds is essential to human understanding. By developing expertness in this area, psychology will eventually become far more valuable. In an advanced society with a growing population and closer associations, it is obviously essential that we learn better how to get along with each other. When we are unaware of the innate differences that reside within each of us, it becomes very easy to think of one who disagrees with us as a "nitwit" or a "jerk," or perhaps as belonging to the "lunatic fringe." When we appreciate the existence of innate differences, we are far more likely to be understanding and charitable. Strife will not be automatically eliminated, but tensions can be decreased immeasurably.

Individual problems are at the root of the problem of crime. Many years ago, James Devon placed his finger on the crucial point. "There is only one principle in penology that is worth any consideration: It is to find out why a man does wrong and make it not worth his while." The question, "Why does a particular man commit crime?" is a cogent one; the question, "Why does man turn to crime?" is relatively nonsensical.

Since all human beings are individual by nature, they do not tick in a uniform way nor for the same reasons. Broadly speaking, however, many doubtless turn to crime because society has not provided other outlets for their energies. If we could find a suitable job for every individual, the problem of crime would largely vanish. The problem of crime is thoroughly permeated with individual problems; it cannot be blamed solely on social conditions, because as the studies of Sheldon and Eleanor Glueck have shown, highly respected citizens may come from areas where these conditions are the worst.

A Race of Individuals

Racial relations would ease tremendously if we faced squarely the biological facts of individuality. If we were all educated to *know* that all whites are not the same, that all Negroes do not fit in the same pattern, that all Latins are not identical, that all American Indians are individuals, and that all Jews do not fit a stereotype, it would help us to treat every member of the human race as an individual.

It is no denial of the existence of racial problems to assert that individual problems need to be stressed more than they are. For individual Negroes and individual whites, the pursuit of happiness is by no means a uniform pursuit. Doubtless, although there are whites and Negroes who would think they had reached utopia if they had a decent shelter and were assured three meals a day, this would not satisfy millions of others for whom striving and a sense of accomplishment are paramount. "The Negro problem" or "the white problem"—depending on one's point of view—is shot through with a host of individual problems.

Learning to live with one's self is certainly an individual problem, and will be greatly eased by recognition of inborn individuality. Much unhappiness and many suicides can be traced to misguided desire to be something other than one's self. Each of us as an individual has the problem of finding his way through life as best he can. Knowing one's self as a distinctive individual should be an important goal of education; it will help pave the road each of us travels in his pursuit of happiness.

Dangers of Oversimplification

Why have these facts of individuality not been generally accepted as a backdrop in every consideration of human problems? For one thing, many people, including scholars, like being grandiose and self-inflationary. To make sweeping pronouncements about "man" sounds more impressive than to express more limited concerns. Simplicity, too, has an attractiveness; if life could be made to fit a simple formula, this might be regarded as a happy outcome.

One excuse for excommunicating inheritance from the behavioral sciences for two generations has been the fact that inheritance in mammals is recognized by careful students as being exceedingly complex and difficult to interpret. It is true that some few characteristics may be inherited through the operation of single genes or a few recognizable ones. But other characteristics—those that differ in quantity—are considered to be inherited in obscure and indefinable ways commonly ascribed to multiple genes of indefinite number and character. These multiple-gene characteristics include, to quote the geneticists Snyder and David, "the more deep-seated characters of a race, such as form, yield, intelligence, speed, fertility, strength, development of parts, and so on." To say that a particular characteristic is inherited through the mediation of multiple genes is to admit that we are largely ignorant of how this inheritance comes about.

Identical Twins?

Recently, some light has been thrown on this problem by experiments carried out in our laboratories. These experiments involved armadillos, which are unusual mammals in that they commonly produce litters of four monozygous ("identical") quadruplets that are necessarily all males or all females.

By making measurements and studying sixteen sets of these animals at birth, it became evident that although they develop from identical genes, they are not identical at all. Organ weights may differ by as much as twofold, the free amino acids in the brain may vary fivefold, and certain hormone levels may vary as much as seven-, sixteen-, or even thirty-two-fold. These findings clearly suggest that inheritance comes not by genes alone but by cytoplasmic factors that help govern the size of organs (including endocrine glands) and the cellular makeup of the central nervous system. "Identical" twins are not identical except with respect to the genes in the nucleus of the egg cell from which they developed.

One of the most interesting suggestions arising out of this study is the probability that individual brain structures, which have been known to have "enormous" differences since the investigations of Lashley more than twenty years ago, are made distinctive by the same mechanisms that make for differences in organ weights. The size, number, and distributions of neurons in normal brains vary greatly; this is biologically in line with the uniqueness of human minds. The further elucidation of this type of inheritance should help to focus more attention on heredity.

If this line of thought is valid it makes even more ridiculous the invitation issued by the Ford Foundation to the biological sciences to stay out of the precinct of human behavior. The expression "behavioral science" came into being many years ago as a result of the formulation of the Ford Foundation-supported programs. Biochemistry and genetics, for example, were kept apart from the "scientific activities designed to increase knowledge of factors which influence or determine human conduct."

What can be done to bridge the gap between psychology and biology? More importantly, how can we develop expertise in dealing with the human problems that plague us but at present go unsolved?

Differential Psychology

A broad, long-range, and practical strategy for learning how to deal more effectively with human problems is to explore, problem by problem, the inborn human characteristics that are pertinent to each one. Differential psychology, for example, needs to be intensified and greatly expanded; this can probably be done most effectively in connection with a series of problem-centered explorations.

Some of the specific problem-areas that require study from the standpoint of how inborn characteristics come into play are: delinquency and crime, alcoholism, drug addiction, unemployability, accident proneness, cancer, heart disease, arthritic disease, mental disease, and broadest of all, education. Each of these problems could be vastly better understood as the result of interdisciplinary study of the influences of inborn characteristics. Such study would include differential psychology when applicable, combined with extensive and intensive biochemical and physiological examinations, for example, of blood, saliva, urine, and biopsy materials. To expedite these investigations, automated equipment and computer techniques would be used extensively to help interpret the complex data.

It is not likely that these explorations will find that some individuals are born criminals, others alcoholics, etc. Once we recognize the unique leanings that are a part of each of us, we will see how, by adjusting the environment, these leanings can be turned toward ends that are socially constructive. Every inherited factor can be influenced by an appropriate adjustment of the environment. All this should not be made to sound too easy; it may be more difficult than going to the moon, but it will be far more worthwhile.

One of these specific problems—alcoholism—has been of special interest to me. After about twenty-five years of study, I am convinced that inborn biochemical characteristics are basic to this disease, but that expert application of knowledge about cellular nutrition (which is not far off) will make it scientifically possible to prevent the disease completely and to correct the condition if the application of corrective measures is not too long delayed.

Inborn inherited characteristics have a direct bearing on the current revolt against the Establishment. If biology had not been banished from behavioral science, and if students and other intellectuals were well aware of the biological roots of their existence, it would be taken for granted that conformity is not a rule of life.

If all that we human beings inherit is our humanity, then we all should be reaching for the same uniform goal: becoming a thoroughly representative and respectable specimen of Homo sapiens. There is rebellion against this idea. Revolters want to do "their thing." The revolt takes on many forms because many unique individuals are involved.

If nonconformity had a better status in the eyes of the Establishment (and it would have if our thinking were more biologically oriented), exhibitionism would be diminished and the desire of each individual to live his own life could be fostered in a natural way.

Human beings are not carbon copies of one another. Students and others who are in revolt have found this out. Perhaps without fully recognizing it, they are pleading for a recognition of inborn individuality. This is essentially a legitimate plea, but it can take the form of disastrous anarchy. A peaceful means of helping resolve the ideological mess we are in is to recognize heredity by having a happy marriage of biology and behavioral science.

6. THE ONLY KIND OF PEOPLE THERE ARE*

Roger J. Williams

If Socrates were resurrected, I suspect he would call attention again to what was written about 25 centuries ago: Know thyself; if you know a lot about other things and are ignorant of yourself, this is ridiculous.

We in this advanced and scientific age have never taken Socrates seriously on this point. I maintain that we are being ridiculous; we seek to plan and yet are not informed about ourselves for whom we plan. Of course, we know *something* about ourselves, but science has never undertaken a serious job of understanding people—a multidisciplinary undertaking. We have not tackled the job of understanding ourselves with one-tenth of the fervor we have shown in our research in outer space.

One of the most important facts about ourselves we have not grasped: All of us are basically and inevitably individuals in many important and striking ways. Our individuality is as inescapable as our humanity. If we are to plan for people, we must plan for individuals, because that's the only kind of people there are.

In what ways are we individuals? First as to our bodies. These ways are tangible and not subject to argument. Each of us has a distinctive stomach, a distinctive heart and circulatory system. Each of us has a distinctive muscular system, distinctive breathing apparatus, and an endocrine system all our own. Most surprising and significant perhaps, each of us has a distinctive set of nerve receptors, trunk nerves, and a brain that is distinctive in structure and not like other brains.

We are individuals also with respect to our minds. We do not all think with equal facility about the various things that can be thought about. Einstein was an extremely precocious student of mathematics, but on the other hand, he learned language so slowly that his parents were concerned about his learning to talk. William Lyon Phelps, the famous English professor at Yale, on the other hand, confessed that in mathematics he was "slow but not sure." There are at least forty facets to human minds. Each of us may be keen in some ways and stupid in others.

The importance of this individuality in minds would be hard to exaggerate. Because of it two or more people agree with each other only *in spots*, never totally. The grandiose idea that all workers of the world can unite and speak and act as a unit is wholly untenable because of individuality in the minds of the individual workers. Nor can all capitalists unite, and for the same reason. Neither can all Negroes, all Latins, all Chinese, all Jews, all Europeans, or all English-speaking peoples.

It is often assumed that people disagree only because of self-interest and differences in their education. They also disagree because their minds do not grasp the same ideas with equal facility. Sometimes an individual has a specific idea which seems to him perfectly clear and potent. To him it seems certain that once this idea is expressed it will gain automatic acceptance. Practical trial shows, however, that it does not. To other individuals, because the patterns of their minds are different, this supposedly clear and potent idea may appear foggy, dubious, or even unsound.

Failure to recognize individuality in minds is widespread and is a revelation of the fact that we are ignorant about the people for whom we plan.

"Environmental Determinism"

I do not know that anyone else has ever expressed it this way, but on a long walk with Aldous Huxley about a year before he died, he decried to me the fact that the prevailing philos-

*From *The Freeman*, January 1969. Slightly condensed and published by permission from an address before the American Institute of Planners at Hot Springs, Arkansas, July 12-19, 1968

ophy today may be described as "environmental determinism." Environment is assumed to be the only factor in our lives; inborn individuality in body and mind are completely neglected. According to this philosophy, every child who is placed in a slum environment becomes a delinquent and a criminal. This, from the work of the Gluecks at Harvard and others, is manifestly untrue. Neither is it true that every child who is furnished with plenty becomes for this reason an honorable and upright citizen.

Our "social studies" and "social science" teaching in all our schools and universities is permeated with environmental determinism which shows no interest in the crucial facts of individuality and quite inevitably tends to destroy all moral responsibility. A delinquent cannot help being a delinquent, we are told. Society should take all the blame. A criminal is that way because society has made him so, so society is to blame. This is blatant oversimplification in the name of social science! It disregards how human beings are built—their fundamental nature—and can by its short-sightedness lead to a breakdown of our civilization.

What I have been saying does not in any sense deny the importance of environment. Environments are what we can control, and to study how to improve them is the essence of planning. But we, the people, are not putty; we are individuals, and *we* need to be understood.

Individuality is Crucial

To me it seems certain that the facts of individuality need to be taken into account. There are three areas, related to planning, in which I have some special knowledge. In all these areas individuality is crucial.

Take for instance the area of nutrition and health. It would be relatively easy to produce economically in factories a "man-chow" which would supposedly be the perfect food for the average man. Laboratory experiences as well as wide observations show, however, that this "man-chow" idea is completely unrealistic. It will not work. Because of biochemical individuality we do not all like the same foods nor can we thrive on the same mixture. Many human beings are so built that they derive a substantial part of the satisfaction of life out of eating. Taking variety and choices from them would be depriving them of their pursuit of happiness. The best food planning devised involves supermarkets where thousands of kinds of foods in great variety are available.

The Food and Drug Administration in Washington has, at least until very recently, done its planning on the basis of the hypothetical average man and has sought to regulate the marketing of medicinal substances, vitamins, and the like on this basis. This cannot work because of the hard facts of biochemical individuality. Real people—individuals—do not react in a uniform manner either to drugs or to nutritional factors such as amino acids, minerals, and vitamins.

No planning in the area of nutrition and health can work on a long range basis unless the facts of individuality are taken into account. If we plan for people, we must plan for individuals, because that is the only kind of people there are.

Another area of planning in which I have some special knowledge is that of education. I have recently completed my fiftieth year as a teacher. While I have in mind no pet schemes for reorganizing schools or universities, I have had for years a growing consciousness that no successful long-range planning can be done unless we recognize fully that every mind is a distinctive one and that every young person is endowed with peculiar aptitudes which need to be recognized, developed, and used. One of the worst lacks in modern education is the failure of youngsters to know themselves and to recognize their own strengths as well as weaknesses. Education for the hypothetical average child is no good. We must plan for individual children; that's the only kind there are.

Closely related to the problem of planning education is planning to curb crime, violence, racial hatred, and war. As Clement Attlee aptly pointed out years ago, the roots of war are to be found in the minds and hearts of men. The late Robert Kennedy pointed out when he was Attorney-General that peaceful relations between people cannot be enforced with guns and bayonets.

In my opinion, we will get nowhere in planning to curb violence by thinking in terms of the city of Dallas killing John F. Kennedy, the city of Memphis killing Martin Luther King, or the city of Los Angeles killing Robert Kennedy. Of course, social factors enter into violence, but there are important individual factors, too.

No informed person can think that curbing crime and violence is a simple problem. Because it is difficult, it is all the more important that we seek out—thoroughly—the root causes. I maintain that a great weakness which we exhibit in this modern scientific age is *ignorance about ourselves*.

Finally, let me say that our love of liberty and

freedom is based upon this individuality. If we all had the same kinds of stomachs, the same kinds of muscles, nerves, and endocrine glands, the same kinds of brains, planning would be simple. We would all like exactly the same things. We would all be satisfied to read the same books, have the same amusements, eat the same food, and go to the same church. In short, we would all live happily in the same rut.

Planning is not that simple. We must plan for individuals—that's the only kind of people there are.

7. THE UNKNOWN QUANTITY*

Madelyn Shepard Hyde

Perhaps one of the best arguments against attempts to equalize the fruits of human labor under a collectivist society is the infinite variety of human nature. It should be obvious that each person's desires and aspirations defy measurement—in both quality and quantity—by any other person. And since *it is impossible to equate what cannot be measured,* the collectivist society must fail in this announced objective.

It is perfectly possible, of course, to divide a pound of steak equally between two persons. That is a task requiring only a pound of steak, a set of scales, and a knife—and someone to do the dividing. It is also possible to decree that the two individuals shall have a certain number of leisure hours each day. But it is quite another matter to measure the relative value that two persons will place upon steak and upon leisure, for one is certain to be more fond of steak—or leisure—than the other. What satisfies the soul of one person may have little or no appeal to another—certainly not to the same degree.

Now suppose the purveyor of equality realizes that equal portions of steak will not accomplish this equality which he has set out to attain. He might then undertake to divide the steak *un*equally by weight, and to reapportion the total number of leisure hours, so that both individuals would be satisfied to exactly the same degree. By what means could he determine what quantity of leisure for one is equal to a certain quantity of steak for the other? At this point, he will have to abdicate from his collectivist throne, realizing that he has no scale by which he can measure any value for any other person.

If it is impossible for a third party to solve even this one simple equation for two persons, it is fantastic to believe that he could solve the infinitely more complex problem of equally satisfying all the desires of all the people. This egalitarian objective could be attained only if all people wanted the same quantities of all things in life. But they do not. Our forefathers sought to preserve the freedom of each individual to pursue, to the best of his ability, the satisfaction of his own particular set of desires—known only to himself. They had the wisdom to realize that in designing a society in harmony with this variation in human wants they were working with, rather than against, a principle of nature.

*Clipping of Note No. 44 (FEE, 1951)

8. FREEDOM'S THEORY OF VALUE*

Leonard E. Read

Those of us who wish to assist in a reversal of the present trend away from individual liberty must, among other refinements of the mind, understand, believe in, and be able to explain the subjective theory of value, as forbidding as that term sounds. Except as we understand and apply this correct theory of value, individual liberty is out of the question.

The possessions one accumulates are a reflection of his values. What a man owns—what is his own—is what he is. One's personality and property reflect his subjective values.

But few of us care to live in isolation. We prefer to exchange ideas and goods and services with others. And the problem is to work our strictly personal values into a price or value structure for purposes of peaceful trade. The question to be answered is, how does the subjective theory of value determine the market price?

Here it is: *The exchange value of any loaf of bread, of any painting, of any day's work, or of any good or service is whatever another or others will offer in willing exchange.*

When Mrs. Smith swaps a shawl for Mrs. Jones' goose, the value of that shawl is that goose and vice versa. Yet, each lady gains in her own (subjective) judgment. Were this not a fact, neither would have willingly exchanged.

Value can make no sense except as it is subjectively determined, that is, as utility or gain is judged by self. Gain or value cannot be determined for anyone by another. What has value for one may have more or less value to someone else: there are those who prefer a chinchilla coat to a college education and vice versa, a freedom library to a vacation and vice versa, the theater to a TV performance and vice versa, ad infinitum.

Assume that I am an artist and do a painting each month. Unfortunately for me, no one wants "a Read." The value of my work? Zero! Now, assume that a change occurs in the minds of buyers (in each instance, subjective); "Reads" become a popular whim to the point that each will bring $1,000. The value of my work? $1,000! For the sake of this illustration, there was no change in the quality of the paintings. Buyers changed their minds and, thus, the value of my work.

It is perfectly plain that the practice of subjective evaluations is the practice of individual liberty or, if you prefer, personal freedom of choice.

It is also easily demonstrable that freedom of the press, freedom of religion, freedom of speech, freedom of assembly are impossible in the absence of economic freedom.[1]

This correct theory of value is opposed by the objective theory, that is, by arrangements where someone else, by some standard of evaluation other than your own, attempts to determine the value of goods and services to you. An understanding of the fallacious objective theory and an ability to identify it in its many manifestations helps to accent the importance and the validity of the subjective theory in practice.

Prior to 1870 no one had formulated the subjective theory. Nor was it invented. Three economists—Menger, Jevons, and Walras—from different countries and without collaboration, formulated the theory almost simultaneously. Their enlightenment came by merely observing how common people behave—produce and exchange—in the absence of governmental or other interference. Thus, before 1870 when there was no understanding of the subjective theory, objective methods of arriving at value predominated.

The classical example of the objective theory of value is the labor theory of value. This theory merely affirms that value is determined by cost of production or, stated another way, by the amount

*From *The Freeman*, October 1967

of energy expended. While some classical economists knew the theory to be wrong, they were not certain as to what was right.

Pursuing the labor theory to its logical and absurd conclusion, a mud pie would have the same value as a mince pie, provided that they were produced by equal expenditures of energy. If a pearl diver came up with a pearl in one hand and a pebble in the other, they would be of equal value!

Of course, people will not exchange as much for a mud pie or a pebble as for a mince pie or a pearl. So, how does this theory find expression in practice? Simply use the power of government to take from the mince pie makers and give to the mud pie makers! Karl Marx gave the formula: "from each according to his ability, to each according to his need."

However, even the Russians no longer are strictly addicted to the labor theory of value. Yet, they largely rely upon objective standards of one kind or another. That is, self-determination is at a minimum; the government arbitrarily prices nearly everything. Willing exchange is not the mode; individual freedom of choice is substantially taboo; the subjective theory is less used in Russia than elsewhere.

Note that there is no freedom of the press, of speech, of religion, of assembly in Russia. It is because economic freedom is denied; and economic freedom is impossible unless subjective value judgments are respected.

One of the most important points to keep in mind is that the amount of effort exerted or the cost of production does not determine exchange value. It is determined by individual evaluations of personal utility. The market price or value is somewhere within the range of these evaluations.

We who are interested in individual liberty and, thus, in the observance of subjective value judgments, must know that the objective theory is antithetical to our welfare, and we should be able to identify its many practices, regardless of how cleverly disguised they are.

Actually, we need only keep our eyes on unwilling as distinguished from willing exchanges. All unwilling exchanges rest on objective and not on subjective value judgments.

Would you willingly exchange your income or capital for farmers not to grow tobacco, to rebuild someone else's downtown, to put men on the moon, to underwrite power and light for the people of the Tennessee Valley, to pay people not to work? If your answers are negative, you can take the political applications of the objective theory from there. Examples abound by the thousands.[2]

It is a gross understatement of the case to say that freedom rests on the practice of the subjective theory; subjective value judgments, when honored, *are* freedom!

Notes

[1] See "Freedom Follows the Free Market" by Dean Russell, *The Freeman*, January, 1963.

[2] See *Encyclopedia of U.S. Government Benefits* (Union City, N. J.: William H. Wise and Co., Inc., 1965). This tome of more than 1,000 pages lists over 10,000 benefits.

Private Property and Exchange

9. PROPERTY*

James Madison

This term, in its particular application, means "that dominion which one man claims and exercises over the external things of the world, in exclusion of every other individual."

In its larger and juster meaning, it embraces everything to which a man may attach a value and have a right, and *which leaves to every one else the like advantage.*

In the former sense, a man's land, or merchandise, or money, is called his property.

In the latter sense, a man has a property in his opinions and the free communication of them.

He has a property of peculiar value in his religious opinions, and in the profession and practice dictated by them.

He has a property very dear to him in the safety and liberty of his person.

He has an equal property in the free use of his faculties, and free choice of the objects on which to employ them.

In a word, as a man is said to have a right to his property, he may be equally said to have a property in his rights.

Where an excess of power prevails, property of no sort is duly respected. No man is safe in his opinions, his person, his faculties, or his possessions.

Where there is an excess of liberty, the effect is the same, though from an opposite cause.

Government is instituted to protect property of every sort; as well that which lies in the various rights of individuals, as that which the term particularly expresses. This being the end of government, that alone is a *just government* which *impartially* secures to every man whatever is his *own.*

According to this standard of merit, the praise of affording a just security to property should be sparingly bestowed on a government which, however scrupulously guarding the possessions of individuals, does not protect them in the enjoyment and communication of their opinions, in which they have an equal, and, in the estimation of some, a more valuable property.

More sparingly should this praise be allowed to a government where a man's religious rights are violated by penalties, or fettered by tests, or taxed by a hierarchy.

Conscience is the most sacred of all property; other property depending in part on positive law, the exercise of that being a natural and unalienable right. To guard a man's house as his castle, to pay public and enforce private debts with the most exact faith, can give no title to invade a man's conscience, which is more sacred than his castle, or to withhold from it that debt of protection for which the public faith is pledged by the very nature and original conditions of the social pact.

That is not a just government, nor is property secure under it, where the property which a man has in his personal safety and personal liberty is violated by arbitrary seizures of one class of citizens for the service of the rest. A magistrate issuing his warrants to a press-gang would be in his proper functions in Turkey or Indostan, under appellations proverbial of the most complete despotism.

That is not a just government, nor is property

*March 27, 1792. From *Letters and Other Writings* of James Madison, Vol. IV, pp. 478-480 secure under it, where arbitrary restrictions, exemptions, and monopolies deny to part of its citizens that free use of their faculties and free choice of their occupations which not only constitute their property in the general sense of the word, but are the means of acquiring property strictly so called.

What must be the spirit of legislation where a manufacturer of linen cloth is forbidden to bury his own child in a linen shroud, in order to favour his neighbour who manufactures woolen cloth; where the manufacturer and weaver of woolen cloth are again forbidden the economical use of buttons of that material, in favor of the manufacturer of buttons of other materials!

A just security to property is not afforded by that government, under which unequal taxes oppress one species of property and reward another species; where arbitrary taxes invade the domestic sanctuaries of the rich, and excessive taxes grind the faces of the poor; where the keenness and competitions of want are deemed an insufficient spur to labor, and taxes are again applied by an unfeeling policy, as another spur, in violation of that sacred property which Heaven, in decreeing man to earn his bread by the sweat of his brow, kindly reserved to him in the small repose that could be spared from the supply of his necessities.

If there be a government, then, which prides itself in maintaining the inviolability of property; which provides that none shall be taken *directly*, even for public use, without indemnification to the owner, and yet *directly* violates the property which individuals have in their opinions, their religion, their passions, and their faculties—nay, more, which *indirectly* violates their property in their actual possessions, in the labor that acquires their daily subsistence, and in the hallowed remnant of time which ought to relieve their fatigues and soothe their cares—the inference will have been anticipated that such a government is not a pattern for the United States.

If the United States mean to obtain or deserve the full praise due to wise and just governments, they will equally respect the rights of property and the property in rights; they will rival the government that most sacredly guards the former, and by repelling its example in violating the latter, will make themselves a pattern to that and all other governments.

10. LETTER TO HIS STEPBROTHER*

Abraham Lincoln

Pioneer life was hard for a man with two children but no woman to care for them, nor to help with the chores at home. Thus Thomas Lincoln remarried about a year after the death (1818) of his first wife, Nancy Hanks, Abraham's mother. The new "mother" was a widow, Sarah Bush Johnston, with three youngsters of her own. According to historians, Abraham Lincoln's stepbrother, John D. Johnston, five years Lincoln's junior, turned out to be shiftless and lazy. The following letter was written to his young stepbrother when Lincoln was 39 years old and a U. S. Congressman from Illinois.

*Reproduced from the original manuscript with slight changes only in style and form

Washington, December 24, 1848

Dear Johnston: Your request for eighty dollars I do not think it best to comply with now. At the various times when I have helped you a little, you have said to me, "We can get along very well now," but in a very short time I find you in the same difficulty again. Now this can only happen by some defect in your conduct. What that defect is, I think I know. You are not lazy, and still you are an idler. I doubt whether since I saw you, you have done a good whole day's work, in any one day. You do not very much dislike to work; and still you do not work much, merely because it does not seem to you that you could get much for it. This habit of needlessly wasting time, is the whole difficulty; and it is vastly important to you, and still more so to your children, that you should break this habit. It is more important to them, because they have longer to live, and can keep out of an idle habit before they are in it, easier than they can get out after they are in.

You are now in need of some money; and what I propose is, that you shall go to work, "tooth and nails," for somebody who will give you money for it. Let father and your boys take charge of things at home—prepare for a crop, and make the crop; and you go to work for the best money wages, or in discharge of any debt you owe, that you can get. And to secure you a fair reward for your labor, I now promise you that for every dollar you will, between this and the first of next May, get for your own labor, either in money, or on your own indebtedness, I will then give you one other dollar. By this, if you hire yourself at ten dollars a month, from me you will get ten more, making twenty dollars a month for your work. In this, I do not mean you shall go off to St. Louis, or the lead mines, or the gold mines in California, but I [mean for you to go at it for the best wages you] can get close to home in Coles County. Now if you will do this, you will be soon out of debt, and what is better, you will have a habit that will keep you from getting in debt again. But if I should now clear you out, next year you would be just as deep in as ever. You say you would almost give your place in Heaven for $70 or $80. Then you value your place in Heaven very cheaply, for I am sure you can with the offer I make you get the seventy or eighty dollars for four or five months work. You say if I furnish you the money you will deed me the land, and, if you don't pay the money back, you will deliver possession. Nonsense! If you can't now live with the land, how will you then live without it? You have always been [kind] to me, and I do not now mean to be unkind to you. On the contrary, if you will but follow my advice, you will find it worth more than eight times eighty dollars to you.

Affectionately your brother,
A. Lincoln

11. PROPERTY RIGHTS AND HUMAN RIGHTS*

Paul L. Poirot

It is not the right of property which is protected, but the right to property. Property, per se, has no rights; but the individual—the man—has three great rights, equally sacred from arbitrary interference: the right to his life, the right to his liberty, the right to his property. . . . The three rights are so bound together as to be essentially one right. To give a man his life but deny him his liberty, is to take from him all that makes his life worth living. To give him his liberty but take from him the property which is the fruit and badge of his liberty, is to still leave him a slave.

U.S. Supreme Court Justice
GEORGE SUTHERLAND

Tricky phrases with favorable meanings and emotional appeal are being used today to imply a distinction between *property* rights and *human* rights.

By implication, there are two sets of rights—one belonging to human beings and the other to property. Since human beings are more important, it is natural for the unwary to react in favor of *human* rights.

Actually, there is no such distinction between property rights and human rights. The term *property* has no significance except as it applies to something owned by someone. Property itself has neither rights nor value, save only as human interests are involved. There are no rights but human rights, and what are spoken of as property rights are only the human rights of individuals to property.

Expressed more accurately, the issue is not one of property rights versus human rights, but of the

*FEE, 1952, as excerpted from the July 1952 *Monthly Letter* of the National City Bank and the October 1952 *Guaranty Survey* of the Guaranty Trust Company

human rights of one person in the community versus the human rights of another.

Those who talk about two sets of rights apparently want to discriminate between property income and labor income—with the implication that the rights to rental and investment income are inferior, as a class, to the rights to income from wages and salaries. Actually, this is an unwarranted assumption. It must be evident that all persons have rights which are entitled to respect. Safeguarding such rights is essential to the well-being of all. This is the only just principle. Thus, the problem is not to establish priorities on human rights in the community, but rather to determine what the respective rights are in the particular cases under dispute. This is the real problem in human relations, and it is one that calls for the exercise of wisdom, restraint, and true administration of justice under law.

What Are "Property Rights"?

What are the property rights thus disparaged by being set apart from human rights? They are among the most ancient and basic of human rights, and among the most essential to freedom and progress. They are the privileges of private ownership, which give meaning to the right to the product of one's labor—privileges which men have always regarded instinctively as belonging to them almost as intimately and inseparably as their own bodies.

The ownership of property is the right for which, above all others, the common man has struggled in his slow ascent from serfdom. It is the right for which he struggles today in countries emerging from feudalism. The sense of this right is so deep-rooted in human nature, so essential as a stimulant of productive effort, that even totalitarian regimes have been unable to abolish it entirely.

It is a mistake to belittle the importance of property rights. Respect for these rights is basic to organized society, and the instinct of individuals to acquire property is at the root of all economic progress. Unless people can feel secure in their ability to retain the fruits of their labor, there is little incentive to save and to expand the fund of capital—the tools and equipment for production and for better living. The industrial development of this country, which has given us the highest standard of living in the world and has made possible a miracle of production in war and peace, is dependent upon the observance of property rights. Who is going to work and save if these rights are not recognized and protected?

The right to own property means the right to use it, to save it, to invest it for gain, and to transmit it to others. It means freedom from unreasonable search and seizure and from deprivation without due process of law or without just compensation. It might also be fairly taken to imply a limitation upon taxation because "the power to tax involves the power to destroy." For a like reason, it should imply assurance against governmental dilution of the money whereby the government takes property which otherwise could be claimed by wage and salary checks and other credit instruments. Further, it should insure against other measures so burdensome or restrictive as to prevent the employment of savings in legitimate productive enterprise with a reasonable prospect of gain. Violation of any of these rights can nullify, in whole or in part, the right to property.

The Bill of Rights in the United States Constitution recognizes no distinction between property rights and other human rights. The ban against unreasonable search and seizure covers "persons, houses, papers, and effects," without discrimination. No person may, without due process of law, be deprived of "life, liberty, or property"; all are equally inviolable. The right of trial by jury is assured in criminal and civil cases alike. Excessive bail, excessive fines, and cruel and unusual punishments are grouped in a single prohibition. The founding fathers realized what some present-day politicians seem to have forgotten: A man without property rights—without the right to the product of his own labor—is not a free man. He can exist only through the generosity or forbearance of others.

These constitutional rights all have two characteristics in common. First, they apply equally to all persons. Second, they are, without exception, guarantees of freedom or immunity from governmental interference. They are not assertions of claims against others, individually or collectively. They merely say, in effect, that there are certain human liberties, including some pertaining to property, which are essential to free men and upon which the state shall not infringe. . . .

What Are "Human Rights"?

Now what about the so-called human rights that are represented as superior to property rights? What about the "right" to a job, the "right" to a standard of living, the "right" to a minimum wage or a maximum workweek, the "right" to a "fair" price, the "right" to bargain collectively, the "right" to security against the adversities and hazards of life, such as old age and disability?

The framers of the Constitution would have been astonished to hear these things spoken of as rights. They are not immunities from governmental compulsion; on the contrary, they are demands for new forms of governmental compulsion. They are not claims to the product of one's own labor; they are, in some if not in most cases, claims to the products of other people's labor.

These "human rights" are indeed different from property rights, for they rest on a denial of the basic concept of property rights. They are not freedoms or immunities assured to all persons alike. They are special privileges conferred upon some persons at the expense of others. The real distinction is not between property rights and human rights, but between equality of protection from governmental compulsion on the one hand and demands for the exercise of such compulsion for the benefit of favored groups on the other.

The "Right" to a Job

To point out these characteristics of the so-called human rights is not to deny the reality nor belittle the importance of the social problems they represent. Some of these problems are real and important. They are also complex, and in this further respect they are different from the rights guaranteed by the Constitution.

There is no great difficulty nor danger in declaring that certain individual rights shall not be tampered with by the government—and in adhering to that principle. It is quite another matter to say that the government shall seize the property or curtail the freedom of some of its citizens for the benefit, or the supposed benefit, of others. To adopt this view is to cast both the government and the citizen in radically new roles, with far-reaching effects on economic behavior, political practices, and individual character.

Consider, for example, the so-called *right to a job*. This is a fine-sounding phrase that evokes an emotional response. It creates a mental image of an unemployed worker and his family suffering hardship through no fault of their own. No one would deny the reality nor the seriousness of that, especially when the unemployed worker is multiplied by millions. To find the best remedy, however, is a difficult matter, and it is not made easier by the use of such misleading catchwords as the "right" to a job. One man's "right" to a job implies an obligation on the part of someone else to give him a job. Who has any such obligation?

An economy of private enterprise functions by means of voluntary contracts entered into for the sake of mutual advantage. Jobs arise from such contracts. The obligation to fulfill his contract is the only right any person can have to a job. Both sides of the contract have to be fulfilled. The employer's job—his side of the contract—is to anticipate what the consumers will want in the market place. His capacity to offer jobs to employees depends upon how well he understands the market pattern of consumer preferences. He has no right of control over the market. There is a limit to his capacity to provide jobs. And in the final analysis, an employee's so-called *right to a job* is determined by what consumers think the product or service is worth to them.

As with the "right" to a job, so with the other so-called human rights. These are not rights in the constitutional sense of respect for privacy; they are, instead, social programs which the government has undertaken or has been asked to promote. These programs, unlike true rights, are selective, coercive, complex, and experimental. Hence, they need to be carefully considered each on its own merits with due regard to the serious threats they may involve to the real and basic human rights that have enabled free men to build a society with the highest level of material well-being ever achieved anywhere.

Triple Threats to Private Property

On the economic side, the gravest threat is that productive enterprise will be so burdened and impeded by high taxes, prohibitions, red tape, and controls that industry will stagnate. Without the products of industry, social programs of any kind become empty promises. New political powers and functions increase the cost of government and drain manpower from farms and factories into administrative bureaus. The great bulk of the money for benefit payments to favored groups must be taken from those who produce by putting forth their own efforts or by investing their savings. Minimum-wage rates wipe out the entire lower range of job opportunities in the business world. Only the government, with the power to tax, can pay more for labor than it is worth. Maximum-hour laws further limit the opportunity to be productive. Artificially pegged prices and wage rates interfere with the normal market process of gearing production to the maximum satisfaction of consumer wants.

On the political side, the increase of power multiplies the opportunities for the abuse of power and the harm that can be done by such abuse. High tax rates expose taxpayers and collectors to strong temptations. The disbursement of billions of dollars in public funds opens new avenues for favoritism and corruption. This system of political distribution of the wealth of a nation encourages government by pressure groups, with the favors flowing toward the groups with the most votes. Demands for more liberal benefits on the one hand and for tax relief on the other converge upon the public treasury. Deficit financing and currency depreciation tend to become national habits which feed upon the savings of individuals and wipe out the means of production and progress.

On the human side, the individual citizen discovers that it is increasingly difficult to get ahead by enterprise and thrift—increasingly profitable to join in the scramble for governmental favors and handouts. The sense of relationship between services rendered and payment received grows weaker. Personal initiative and self-reliance give way to an attitude of: let the government do it. Free citizens tend to degenerate into wards of the state.

These are not imaginary effects, but real ones. They are visible here and now. They are the consequences of placing social programs, mislabeled "human rights," above the *real* human rights, disparagingly called "property rights," which underlie the productive strength of free men.

12. WHO CONSERVES OUR RESOURCES?*

Ruth Shallcross Maynard

"Who should conserve our resources?" If a poll were taken, a large majority probably would answer: "Our federal and state governments." And if one were to ask why this view is so widely held, he would find among other "reasons" the following:

(1) that the free market is chaotic, gives profits to the few, and is unmindful of the great "waste" of our diminishing limited resources;

(2) that "people's rights" are above "private or special interests" and only the government can properly serve the public interest;

(3) that government has access to more funds;

(4) that government has the power and facilities to obtain all the necessary data and to do the research needed for the best "scientific" decisions on resource conservation;

(5) that the price system does not operate in the interests of conservation because of the "unrestrained pursuit of self-interest";

(6) that the concentration of power in some corporations further threatens our dwindling resources and must be regulated by government.

*From *The Freeman*, July 1962

These "reasons," of course, do not indicate how a government agency would go about attempting a solution to the conservation problem—this is always just assumed—but consider them briefly:

(1a) The free market is anything but chaotic. Competing natural market forces reflect in prices the wishes of both buyers and sellers—millions of individuals, separately accountable and responsible for their own actions in their own field of economic activity. All persons seek their own advantage when allowed a choice, but in the free market a producer cannot profit unless he pleases consumers better than his competitor does. Since he must think of efficiency and lowered costs in order to survive, it is false to assume that he alone profits from the use of natural resources from which are made the products wanted by consumers. All gain who use the resulting products.

(2a) Can there be "people's rights" superior to the rights of individuals? All individuals have special and private interests and rights. Therefore, the "people" cannot have rights except individually; and the right to life carries with it the right to maintain it by private and special means.

(3a) The government has no funds that have not been taken from the people by force, whereas many a large private undertaking has come forth from voluntarily contributed funds. In fact, the entire industrial development in this country has been a continuous example of this voluntary way of creating the facilities for production by giving the consumer what he wants at the price he is willing to pay in competition.

(4a) Offhand it would seem that a government might have access to more data about scarce resources than would a private enterpriser. But government cannot bring forth the detailed information so vital to sound decision. The kind of detailed knowledge needed simply isn't "given to anyone in its totality," as Hayek has pointed out.[1] "Knowledge of the circumstances of which we must make use never exists in concentrated or integrated form," he states, "but solely as dispersed bits of incomplete and frequently contradictory knowledge which all the separate individuals possess." Yet, producers need such information before they can decide how to act. The chief communicator of this knowledge is free price movements. If the price of a given resource continues upward, this tells producers all they need to know about its increasing scarcity and signals them to conserve it, to use it sparingly and for the most valuable products. Advocates of government planning never seem to grasp how this works, for they are constantly tampering with market forces, distorting the delicate price signals that could otherwise guide them. Thus, government planners must rely on using *general* data obtained by crude polling methods which are unreliable for action in specific economic areas and are out of date before they can be collected, analyzed, and summarized. Moreover, such studies cannot tell the government controller as much as free price movements tell individuals acting in a particular market as buyers or sellers.

(5a) The role that prices play in the free economy is so little understood that many people believe government must set prices lest they reflect only the "selfish interests" of the producers. The price system not only tells producers and consumers when scarcity of a product exists (prices rise) or when it has become more plentiful (prices drop); it also supplies the incentive to act in the interests of conservation by seeking a substitute for the high-priced scarce material. Competitive prices allocate scarce resources to those who will *pay* more (not those who *have* more, as is alleged) for the right to try to serve consumers efficiently and profitably.

(6a) If concentration of power in corporations is too great to be permitted, what about the ultimate concentration of power in a government institution beyond the regulation of market forces? Government is unaccountable in the sense that it is not obliged to please consumers in order to stay in business. If it does not show a profit, its losses can be covered by tax money. Big corporations can behave in monopolistic fashion only if they enjoy government privileges of some kind. Potential competition, substitution, and elasticity of demand force them to keep prices close to the competitive level.[2]

When Government Controls

The foregoing arguments, however, do not touch upon the basic problem involved in the conservation of resources. Let us assume that Congress passes a conservation law setting up "The Federal Bureau of Conservation." Tax money must then be appropriated for this Bureau. The director, a political appointee, must find a building and hire a staff large enough to justify his salary. To investigate and collect data on what is being done is a time- and tax-consuming job.

Turning the conservation problems over to an agency with police power does not mean solution, however. It only means that the director has been given the authority to find a solution and to force it on those individuals who are in the market for natural resources. This does not assure the public that the director has any special grant of wisdom concerning the problems involved, or that he will even know what they are. This appointment would lead him to assume that individual enterprisers were not doing their jobs well. He would undoubtedly define his task as one of finding what individual enterprisers are doing wrong and stopping it. Such interference could only prevent private individuals from utilizing their creativity and energy in seeking a solution to both immediate and long-run conservation problems. Having stopped this flow of creative endeavor, he would need to find a "positive" solution—such as stockpiling by force certain quantities of those materials deemed most scarce.

Difficult Decisions

But for whom would the director be stockpiling? Would he sacrifice the present generation to future ones? And, if so, which ones? The next generation, the one after that, those living a hundred years from now, or whom? And how could he possibly know what those generations would want or need? Moreover, he would have the problem of what quantities to stockpile and what grades (best or worst) to save. Would some items have alternative uses? Would he plan for possible added or new uses in the future? These questions never seem to be asked by the authors of books and articles on conservation, whose specialty is to condemn private enterprise.

Stockpiling only aggravates the very scarcity given as the reason for stockpiling. The more scarce a stockpiled item, the higher the price, and the more complaints to be heard from the users. Whereupon, the director probably would seek power to fix prices lower than market levels. This, of course, could only lead to increased demand and pressure on prices, leading to black markets or government rationing, or both. Allocation by rationing would present the problem of whom to favor and whom to slight. His authority to discriminate would subject the director to strong political pressures. If not by political favoritism, the director could select by personal preference, or first come, first favored. Any system is discriminatory. The system of government planning implies arbitrary discrimination by one man with police power who decides who shall get what. Without personal favoritism, the free market "discriminates" *against* those who would waste scarce materials—it lets their businesses fail—and "discriminates" *for* those who would most efficiently use the resource to serve consumers—their profit depends on their capacity to conserve the scarce resource.

The government system is based on arbitrary decisions of man over man, with strong probability of political influence; the free market system is influenced by nonpolitical and nonpersonal forces. There is no other alternative. The first system leads to static conditions which cannot meet the changing needs and desires of consumers, the "people" most involved and presumably those whom a conservation agency ought to protect. The business way encourages search for substitutes when price rises indicate growing scarcity. This not only aids conservation but also affords the consuming public more reasonably priced alternatives in times of scarcity. When prices are fixed below market levels by the government director, this discourages conservation and gives a false signal as to the degree of scarcity all the way from the natural resource level to the final consumer.

Private Enterprisers Conserve What Is Worth Saving

Until someone discovers that a resource has a specific use, it has no value for which it should be conserved. Alexander the Great had no use for the reservoir of oil beneath his domain. The underdeveloped countries do not lack resources. But they have not yet found the key (personal saving and competitive private enterprise) by which to utilize the resources to meet the people's needs. Private enterprisers are constantly trying to find new materials and new uses for known resources, always looking ahead to see which ones will be available and how efficiently they can be utilized. Pick up any trade journal and note the articles on how to cut costs, utilize waste materials, be more efficient. Because the government told them to? No. The hope of profits acts as a powerful compulsion to be efficient, to improve, to conserve. The following examples show how private enterprisers eliminate waste and utilize natural resources to meet the needs of the consuming public.

Until natural gas was known to be useful as a fuel, petroleum producers burned it to get rid of it. Until ways were found of storing and transporting gas with safety, it had only local use. Competition forced the search for further uses and wider markets, and profits rewarded those who best served consumers. As ways were found to handle gas beyond local markets, consumers elsewhere gained a wider choice of fuel, and other fuels were thereby conserved.

Reliance on Hindsight

Accusations of waste in private industry are always based on hindsight. Any statistics of inadequate use of natural resources are history. When a new method or new use is discovered, it is easy to point out past waste and misuse. The assumption is that industrialists are wasteful if they haven't seen in advance all possible uses for all materials.

The meat-packing industry over the last century has used all but the squeal of the pig. But this did not come all at once. Nor did or could it have come from government decrees. It came slowly through individual efforts to cut costs and increase profits in competition with others.

In the lumber and pulp-paper industries, uses have been found for virtually all of a tree, including the bark, branches, and sawdust which were formerly "wasted." The "waste" lignin, after removal of the carbohydrates, has been the concern of many a pulp company as well as scientists at The Institute of Paper Chemistry, who have yet to find a use that will meet adequately the competitive market test of consumer choice.

With the increasing scarcity of pure water, the pulp and paper industry has used less and less of it per ton of product. When wood became scarce in Wisconsin, the "Trees-for-Tomorrow" program was instigated, encouraging farmers to grow trees as an added cash crop. As salt cake from Saskatchewan grew scarce, the Southern kraft-pulp mills learned how to reclaim it and cut the amount needed per ton of pulp by two-thirds or more. Could such a conservation measure have been forced by government decree? It is most doubtful.

In the agricultural field are many illustrations of continuous improvement: of tools (the history of the plow alone would make an impressive volume); of methods of utilizing land, fertilizers, insecticides, and seeds; of knowledge of genetics, hydroponics, and radioactive materials. All of these have played a vital part in getting better farm products to the people with fewer man-hours and at less cost. These all conserve time.

Time also is a resource. Conserving time can save lives from starvation, give relief from backbreaking jobs, enable individuals to further achieve their respective purposes. Improved tools have won time for more leisure, for increasing recreational, cultural, educational, and religious activities.

Individual Improvement

Improvement of the well-being of individuals, rather than conservation, is the chief goal in the utilization of resources. Absolute conservation could lead to the absurdity of not utilizing our resources at all, and thus conserving to no purpose—no freedom and no improvement of our lives. J. S. Mill has expressed it thus: "The only unfailing and permanent source of improvement is liberty, since by it there are as many possible independent centers of improvement as there are individuals." The energy of the police force of a government agency must by its very nature be negative. Enterprisers are positive, constantly trying to solve specific problems. It is impossible to force the release of the creative energy of millions of individuals who, if free, are each highly motivated to release it in trying to improve their status. Thus, force only inhibits the real sources of improvement.

Because individuals have been free to find the best use of land resources, the American farmer today feeds himself and at least 25 others. In our early history food production was the principal occupation, and in some countries today as high as 90 per cent of the population still spends long hours of backbreaking work farming for a bare subsistence.

Who Is Responsible for Waste?

The real waste in resources comes from government policies. It is seen especially in wartime, but more and more in peacetime programs. The government farm program has encouraged waste of land, seeds, fertilizers, labor, and capital by subsidizing the production of surpluses to be stored in bins that dot the countryside. The foreign aid program has wasted various resources, sending them to countries where little if any use has been or could be made of them. Waste occurs in such projects as the TVA that floods permanently many fertile acres which formerly provided millions of dollars worth of food products and which the Army Engineers have estimated would not be flooded by the natural forces of the Tennessee River in 500 years.

Rising taxes also promote waste. The corporate income tax of 52 per cent of earnings, for example, encourages industrialists to engage in questionable and wasteful projects which appear justified only when purchased with a 48-cent dollar. This is not in the interests of conservation.

However, the errors individuals make and their waste of resources are small and inconsequential compared with those made by government agents in controlling a major supply of a scarce resource. Those in civil service positions are rarely dismissed or otherwise held accountable for their errors. A private individual stands to lose personally if he wastes resources in his field of economic activity, and has a built-in motivation for attempting to correct his mistakes as soon as they are reflected in rising costs or decreasing demand. A government agent, however, risks no personal loss when he misuses resources, he cannot recognize mistakes by rising costs when prices are fixed arbitrarily, nor is he motivated to correct his mistakes even when recognized.

Natural resources are best utilized and conserved where they meet specific economic requirements in the most efficient way as determined by competition in the free market. Government control of natural resources reduces the freedom of choice of producers in using these materials and this affects adversely the freedom of choice of consumers who buy the final products made from them. There is no effective method of determining the economic requirements of the people when the free market is not allowed to reflect them, nor can force solve the problem of conservation. It is a false panacea that is centuries old, advocated by those who desire power over others whom they neither trust nor respect. Conservation will take place in the best sense where individuals are allowed to seek solutions to their own personal problems as they arise. Necessity is the mother not only of invention but of conservation as well.

Notes

[1]F. A. Hayek, "The Use of Knowledge in Society," *The American Economic Review*, Vol. XXXV, No. 4, September 1945; reprinted in *The Freeman*, May 1961.

[2]Hans Sennholz, "The Phantom Called Monopoly" (Reading No. 53).

13. THE WAR ON PROPERTY*

Paul L. Poirot

The results, after more than 30 years of Federal "war on poverty" in America, suggest that the campaign has failed. "Instead of temporary aid, relief has become a permanent way of life for millions. Second and third generations of families now live on relief."[1] Nor is it that the millions in this new class of poverty-stricken are simply destitute of the material manifestations of private property. Far worse; many have lost their self-respect and the respect of their fellow men; they have lost their human dignity. What can these persons claim as their own?

Respect for the dignity of an individual presumes him to be responsible for the development and use of his faculties, his qualities, his properties. The personal freedom of choice that is liberty depends upon self-control and possession or ownership in the form of private property. And consistent with this concept of human dignity and private property is the right of the individual to make his own mistakes, if he so chooses, and to abide by the consequences—to know the penalties of improper choice and action as well as the fruits of success.

*From *The Freeman*, October 1967

"Property is desirable, is a positive good in the world," said Abraham Lincoln. "That some should be rich shows that others may become rich and hence is just encouragement to industry and enterprise. Let not him who is houseless pull down the house of another, but let him work diligently to build one for himself, thus by example assuring that his own shall be safe from violence."

Lincoln understood that poverty is not to be overcome by warlike or compulsory measures, but by peaceful example. Not by pulling down the house of another, not by destroying another's life or character or estate, but by each man working diligently to build one for himself.

A property owner, of course, might be able to live upon his own resources. But few of us nowadays would be content with such a subsistence level of living. We have grown accustomed to the advantages of specialized production and peaceful exchange of goods and services. Such voluntary exchange also depends on private property. Every trader is a property owner and his own man. Something to offer is his ticket of admission to the market—his purchasing power.

This requirement for trade gives rise to a common complaint about the so-called tyranny of the market economy: that it tends to be exclusive—for property owners only. The fact that a buyer's purchasing power depends upon what he has to offer is said to be undemocratic and unfair; it doesn't afford everyone everything he wants. Some even argue that "property is theft," in the belief that any accumulations of private property must have impoverished other people.

Such beliefs might have been justified under various conditions of the past—might be justified in some parts of the world today. A slave owner, for example, acquires and holds his slaves by force, and thus impoverishes them. Tribal wars for territory or other property leave the losers poorer to the extent of the victors' spoils. But in a trading society as we know it, property required for production and marketing can only be accumulated and retained by an owner insofar as he uses it as consumers want him to. Otherwise, he's out of business.

The complaint that not everyone can have everything he wants should be leveled, not against the market and the private ownership of property, but against the nature of things. The real world is characterized by unlimited human wants and limited means, not the other way round. Any realistic social system must consider not only the boundless appetites of consumers but also the conservation and efficient use of scarce resources.

Ours is not a world that affords abundance for consumption without productive effort or other thought for the source of supply. This is why it is important to understand the basic principles and practices of private ownership and control of scarce resources. These are essential features of any peaceful society.

Regulated by Competition

To say that a prosperous market economy depends upon respect for private property is the truth but not the whole truth. Private ownership and control, of itself, does not assure the most efficient use of scarce resources in service to others. That assurance comes as a result of competition. This is not to say that competitors are solely interested in pleasing customers. But catering to the wishes of customers is the surest and easiest way to have and to hold valuable, scarce items. The fact that two or more businessmen bid for possession and use of the same resource is the consumer's guarantee that it will be used efficiently to serve him. Consumers pay handsomely for efficient service and thus determine who, among various competitors, is to own and control the means of production.

Competition for property is the great moderator or regulator of temptations to abuse the privileges of private ownership. Competition, of course, cannot force anyone to buy or sell at a price unacceptable to him. But competitors can make trading difficult for those who expect something for nothing. Competition is truly the life of trade—a powerful, peaceful influence for honest and efficient service by those who hope to own and control the use of property.

Nor is the moderating force of competition confined to the supplier side of the exchange process. Consumers also compete against one another for available supplies. The resultant level of market prices tempers appetites, rations scarce items, requires responsible performance by those who are to receive goods and services in exchange for their own. The market will no more serve consumers who demand something for nothing than it will tolerate the false advertising of fraudulent suppliers. So, competition is a form of peaceful "policing" of the market. It tends to keep buyers and sellers honest in their trading and efficient in their use of ever-scarce resources.

Voluntary or Compulsory

Let it be clear that our discussion thus far pertains to the so-called "private sector" of the economy—the production, the saving and investment, the trading of goods and services, and the personal consumption practices that result from voluntary choices of buyers and sellers in open competition. And it bears repeating that the "private sector" market is a voluntary association of property owners for the purpose of trading to their mutual advantage. Admittance to the market is gained by having something to offer. True, such offerings constitute the means for the satisfaction of the wants of consumers. But the expressed wants of consumers do not necessarily constitute a market situation. A combination of consumers to satisfy their wants could very well be a den of thieves.

When the power of government is invoked to plunder property, in the name of war on poverty, any receiver of such loot must recognize that he possesses it at his own risk. The "human right" to plunder is a denial of the right to own and control property. It simply proclaims that might makes right; and that's a rough game for the meek and weak. That is precisely how thieves operate: non-owners deciding how an owner may or may not use his property.

The more we observe and become involved in the government war on poverty, the clearer comes the message: *War against poverty is war against property, and war against property is war against the poor.*

Monetary Misunderstanding

Much of the confusion about all this may be traced to the love of money, under the illusion that money as such is wealth. True, at a given moment, a quantity of money given to a poor person will enable him to buy goods and services otherwise beyond his reach. But his level of living depends upon the goods and services rather than the money. And redistributing the money supply does nothing as such to increase the total available supply of goods and services. It simply transfers buying power from one person to another. Such transfer, however, has important consequences.

Who buys *what* affects price and consumption and saving and production patterns throughout the economy. When money is taxed from one person and given to another, to equalize wealth, there is the strong probability that goods and services will be diverted from productive use to immediate consumption. Taxing the fruits of saving and productive effort discourages thrift and work. Subsidizing idleness increases it. This is the reason why compulsory socialism has failed to relieve poverty when and wherever it has been tried. It redistributes the money supply, but with consequences that waste resources and lives and lead relentlessly toward famine.

The formula, "from each according to his ability and to each according to his need," simply empties the breadbasket faster than it can be filled. Within our lifetimes we have seen this happening in Russia, Red China, India, Cuba, and other nations willing to accept every gift the free world has offered—but not willing to practice freedom. And perhaps the most dramatic of all examples was afforded by the history of the Plymouth Colony in the New World. The first years of communal effort, pooling the harvest and sharing "according to need," were marked by dissension, dearth, and death. Fortunately, the settlers then tried private ownership of the land and the fruits of each owner's labor; and hunger and famine have been unknown in the land since that change.

The reason why socialism fails to relieve poverty comes clearer if one looks behind the monetary screen. Then it may be seen that material wealth is comprised of hoes and rakes and wheelbarrows, among other things.

Taking from a worker half the tools he needs to do a decent job (or taking them from that worker's employer) and dividing the proceeds among the poor in the form of consumer goods lowers the production potential of such a society. It's a grasshopper's way of high living for the moment and no thought for the morrow. The industrial revolution, that makes for a high level of production and a high level of living for all industrious and thrifty members of society, is contingent upon respect for private property in the hands of those who have earned and saved it for a purpose. Owners of tools are in a position to hire others to help them use those tools for productive purposes. As previously discussed, competition obliges the owners of resources to use them efficiently and in a responsible manner.

The public-sector war on property includes various governmental programs of a socialistic nature such as outlined by Marx and Engels in *The Communist Manifesto.* And these may be studied at close range without traveling to Russia or Red China or Cuba. What country today lacks experience with price supports and price ceilings, rent controls, minimum wage and maximum profit laws, rate regulations and other controls over interest, electricity, gas, water, housing, garbage disposal, communications, travel, insurance, banking, and what not? Where in today's world is a person free to assume his own risks against the vicissitudes of old age, illness, illiteracy, illegitimacy, indigence, and unemployment instead of being taxed for everybody else's benefit? What country is free of such protectionist measures as tariffs, quotas, embargoes, and similar restraints of trade? All these are forms of plunder, war on property, class warfare in the Marxian sense.

Helping the Aged

Most of us readily recognize plunder when it takes the form of force applied to a person or to his property by an authoritarian dictator or by some unlicensed crook. But what do we make of a proposition like this from President Johnson's "Message on Older Americans" addressed to Congress last January?

"We should look upon the growing number of older citizens, not as a problem or a burden for our democracy, but as an opportunity to enrich their lives, and, through them, the lives of all of us."

The President was advocating further expansion of the social security program originally enacted in 1935. After all these years, who could possibly question so worthy a goal as helping ourselves by helping the aged? Yet, compulsory social security is a plundering game, perhaps more harmful in the long run simply because its ultimate impact was so dimly foreseen in the beginning.

The social security tax bill has doubled on the average every six years since the first collections in 1937. It amounted to $20 billion in 1966 and threatens, under new proposals, to double again by 1974. A younger worker, facing the prospect of an annual social security tax of $1,000 or more, surely must suspect that this could become "a burden for our democracy." Every taxpayer knows that taxes are a burden.

But is the taxpayer the only victim of the social security plunder game? What of the harm done the recipients of such handouts? Are their lives truly enriched by relieving them of the responsibility and the opportunity to grow out of their own errors and misfortunes? Can a life be enriched, except as it becomes more useful? Just how does a government promise of old age assistance help anyone to help himself?

We know the harmful consequences of paternalism beyond the call of duty within the family. And we also should understand the danger of paternalistic practices on a societal scale. That danger lies in the moral and economic impoverishment of the victims of such intervention.

Urban Renewal

Another campaign front in the general war on poverty has been that of Federal urban renewal. Professor Martin Anderson has admirably documented the failure of that program.[2] More homes were destroyed than have been built under the program; and those destroyed were predominantly low-rent homes while those built were predominantly high-rent homes. Many of the small business firms displaced by urban renewal went out of business, while others relocated in higher-rent and higher-cost areas; very few have ever moved back into the urban renewal area. Most renewal programs decrease the tax revenues flowing into the cities' tax coffers, placing added tax burdens on presumably unaffected properties. And all programs involve the use of the power of eminent domain to take the property of some for redistribution or use by others. So, urban renewal is a form of the war against property; and the major victims have been the families of the very persons—the poor—in whose interests the program supposedly was initiated.

Not all of the various welfare programs of compulsory intervention and redistribution have been as clearly cost-accounted and measured in their impact as the Federal urban renewal program has been weighed by Professor Anderson. But there is no reason to expect any other result from any of the other seizures or controls of private property intended to overcome poverty. The noblest of intentions may go unrealized. But the unforeseen and inevitable consequences are quite real.

When government sets the price of bread below the market level, there are two victims: the producer of bread who is driven out of business, and the consumer who is left waiting in line for the bread that was not produced. The victims of rent control are as much the tenants who cannot find housing space as the landlords who cannot supply it at that fixed price. Minimum wage laws injure not only the employers who cannot afford to hire at such wages but also the employees incapable of earning them. The same tariff that bars a producer from the market also bars a consumer. Every consumer subsidy is a tax upon producers, a war against property that injures the poor.

The Key to Jobs

The private ownership of resources by persons most capable of using them productively is the key to job opportunities and more abundant living for the poor. The "lower third" and the "upper third" and the "middle class" have a common interest in protecting the private ownership of property. The jobs and livelihoods and lives of all depend upon it. Any person who hopes to sell his services ought to see that his prospects depend upon property owners. Their right to own and use property, coupled with their ability to manage it well, create job opportunities for others. If a person is not satisfied to be an employee of a property owner, he may turn to self-employment. In that case, he will need to save for tools—become a property owner himself—if he is to succeed.

So, in any case, whether a person be relatively wealthy or relatively poor, it is to his own best interest to respect and uphold the private ownership of property. When a government seizes private property, or otherwise clouds an owner's title in the name of war on poverty, it is the poor of that society who can least afford the costs of such warfare. They will be the first to starve.

Riots in History

Whenever a government exploits taxpayers to the point of serious inflation, which amounts to a heavy tax burden on the poor, riots and insurrection are to be expected.

What is happening in the urban centers of the United States today has happened before, and in strikingly similar fashion, among over-governed and over-taxed people throughout history. Official court historians always have ascribed the inevitable rioting to such handy scapegoats as gouging merchants, greedy landlords, brutal local policemen, slave-owning ancestors, and every other reason except the real one: too much government intervention and too little personal freedom.

This is not to defend the earlier practice of slavery in America and elsewhere or the mistaken and harmful practices of shortsighted marketeers or short-tempered lawmen. Human beings make mistakes; and each such mistake has consequences that ripple through society, often for years. But human progress is not a process of building molehill mistakes of the moment into permanent mountains of misery. Unless we can learn by our errors to do otherwise, we are condemned to keep on repeating them. And our most terrible mistake is to fall upon an earlier evil as the justification for a new one. The horrors of slavery can never be erased by a new reign of arson, looting, murder, and riotous brutality.

The French Revolution: from Inflation to Napoleon

A clearer view of current happenings in Newark, Detroit, and other trouble spots in the United States may be possible if we look back with that scholarly historian, Andrew Dickson White, at the sequence of events during the French Revolution when the United States was a mere babe in arms.[3]

Louis XVI had recklessly spent France to the verge of bankruptcy by 1789, and inflation was to be the "short road to prosperity." Despite abundant warnings from those who recalled the history and disaster of earlier inflationary practices, the members of the French National Assembly voted ever-larger and more frequent issues of irredeemable paper money. But the inflation, as always, aggravated the very evils it was proposed to cure.

What began as the confiscation of the property of the Church, the leading landlord of France at that time, became the excuse for more and more printing of worthless "assignats." This growing flood of "purchasing power" caused the skyrocketing of prices, prompting businessmen to expand operations but often in a wrong direction leading toward personal failure and bankruptcy and unemployed workers. And, as usual during inflation, wages failed to keep pace with rising costs of living. Workers' savings were exhausted, along with any reason that might have held for saving in the first place. Thus the relentless inflation took its toll from among the very poor it had promised so much to help. Meanwhile, the recklessly-spending and money-printing government had shifted the blame for rising prices onto merchants and landlords and other businessmen equally trapped by events; maximum price laws and other disrupting control measures were enacted with death penalties for violators. But the people rioted, regardless, and the guillotine eventually claimed the heads of those whose good intentions had brought on all the trouble.

And the only thing the people of France gained from that particular version of the Great Society was Napoleon!

The ways in which Louis XVI spent taxpayers' money in 1790 doubtless would seem foolish to heads of state in 1967. But there is no indication that Louis was giving the money to enemy nations, or waging war at the opposite side of the world on behalf of one unfriendly nation against other unfriendly nations, or planning to colonize the moon. It is true that modern rulers have found interesting new ways to bankrupt their country's treasury. And the resultant inflationary resort to the printing presses may be slightly more sophisticated today. But reckless spending of artificially created purchasing power still spells inflation, and today's riots by the tax-burdened and dispossessed poor of Detroit are very much the same as the riots of Paris in the 1790's.

Offering Explanations That Won't Stand Scrutiny

It is not that some of the looters are the great grandchildren of Negro slaves; doubtless among them also are to be found the great grandchildren of slave owners and of ardent Abolitionists of a century earlier.

It is not that the rioters are poor; the poor of the world have as good a record for peace and honesty and brotherly love and law-abiding citizenship as have those on any other rung of the economic ladder.

Nor is it that those who flout the laws of the land have been denied educational opportunity; many of their provocateurs and leaders in violence are holders of college degrees with campus training for insurrection.

Our riotous friends are the unhappy victims of the false promises and bulldozer practices of the welfare state.

These are individuals who have been dispossessed, driven from the modest homes they could afford in the name of slum clearance and urban renewal and public housing. They are urban dwellers obliged to pay in higher grocery bills for an annual $6 billion farm relief program. They are subject to draft for "somebody else's" war that seems far more likely to threaten than to strengthen American security. They are unemployed by reason of special privileges that have been extended to the leadership of organized labor unions. They are asked to pay for the protection granted industry in the form of tariffs, quotas, embargoes, and other price-hiking barriers to world commerce. They have been guaranteed subsistence, but with shackles attached. A slave to handouts and subsidies, for which he himself must pay in the end, is nonetheless a slave. Stripped of his self-responsibility and his self-respect, he may not be expected to understand or respect the lives or the properties of others who have earned their rights. The poor of our nation have been promised the moon—and presented the bill! And they riot against this evil they cannot understand.

Nor is it easy to understand. The aftermath of a Watts or a Newark or a Detroit riot must appear to the careful observer very much like the gaping wounds in "demonstration cities" when the Federal bulldozer of urban renewal has taken its toll of homes and businesses and displaced persons. It may be said for the rioting, looting, and burning that it is considerably faster and less costly than the legalized method of urban demolition. But that does not excuse the violence or the destruction involved in either procedure.

And what it will cost to rebuild the wrecked homes and businesses and lives all depends on whether it is attempted by the compulsory methods of government planning and taxation or by the voluntary cooperation of self-responsible and self-respecting individuals in the open competition of the market. What we can be certain of is that one method is warlike and the other is peaceful. And that should be sufficient reason for anyone to cast his vote for freedom.

Notes

[1] *U. S. News & World Report,* July 17, 1967, p. 44.

[2] Martin Anderson. *The Federal Bulldozer: A Critical Analysis of Urban Renewal, 1949-1962* (Cambridge, Massachusetts: The M.I.T. Press, 1964). 272 pp.

[3] Andrew Dickson White. *Fiat Money Inflation in France* (Irvington-on-Hudson, N. Y., Foundation for Economic Education, Inc.).

Social Cooperation and the Market

14. FREE WILL AND THE MARKET PLACE*

Frank Chodorov

Free will is the starting point of all ethical thinking and it plays an equally important part in the business of making a living. If man were not endowed with this capacity for making choices, he could not be held accountable for his behavior, any more than could a fish or a fowl—an amoral being, a thing without a sense of morals. So, if man were devoid of this capacity, his economics would be confined to grubbing along on whatever he found in nature. It is because man is capable of taking thought, of making evaluations and decisions in favor of this or that course, that we have a discipline called economics.

In making his ethical choices, man is guided by a code believed to have the sanction of God; and experience has shown that the good life to which his instinct impels him can be achieved only if he makes his decisions accordingly. The Ten Commandments have been called the Word of God; they can also be described as natural law, and natural law has been described as nature's way of applying means to ends. Thus, we say that nature in her inscrutable ways had determined that water shall always run down hill, never up; that is a natural law, we say, because it is without exception, inevitable, and self-enforcing. Therefore, when we decide to build ourselves a house, we set it at the bottom of the hill so as to avail ourselves of a supply of water. If we put the house at the top of the hill, nature will not cooperate in our obstinacy and we shall not have any water in the house; unless, of course, we discover and make use of some other natural law to overcome the force of gravity.

That is to say, nature is boss and we had better heed her teaching when we make decisions or we shall not achieve the ends we desire. But, her teaching is not freely given; we must apply ourselves diligently to a study of her ways to find out what they are. The prerequisite for a successful investigation is to admit that nature has the secret we are trying to uncover; if we begin by saying that in this or that field nature has no laws, that humans make their own way without reference to nature, we shall end up knowing nothing.

If, for instance, we discard the Ten Commandments, declaring them to be mere man-made conventions changeable at will, we end in chaos and disorder—evidence that we are on the wrong track. Likewise, if we declare that God in his infinite wisdom chose to disregard economics, that in ordering the world he overlooked the ways and means for man's making a living, that in this particular field man has to work out his own formulae, we will end up with a poor living.

"Economics" without Principles

And that is exactly what has happened in the study of economics; many experts in this field are of the opinion that nature can tell us nothing about the business of making a living; it's all a matter of human manipulation. That is why economics is so often a meaningless hodgepodge of expediencies, leading us to no understanding and no good end. I might add that the incongruities of ethical life,

*From *The Freeman*, January 1959. Adapted from an address before the American Farm Bureau's "Farm Family and Christian Resources" Conference at Madison, Wisconsin, October 30, 1958

such as divorce, juvenile delinquency, international friction, and so on, are largely the result of the current conceit that there is no warrant for ethics in nature, no positive laws for moral behavior; but that is another subject.

I shall try to present some evidence that nature has her own rules and regulations in the field of economics, indicating that we had better apply ourselves to learning about them if we would avoid the obviously unsatisfactory results from relying on man's ingenuity. Come with me into the laboratory of experience, which is the source of much understanding.

The First Pioneer

Let us cast our mind's eye back to the time when there was no Madison, Wisconsin, or any other city west of the Alleghenies, when only the seed of a later social integration was planted here—when a lone frontiersman decided to settle on this spot of earth. The primary consideration which influenced his decision was the possibility of making a living here. He selected what later became Madison because the land was fertile, water was plentiful, the forests abounded with wood for his comfort, meat for his sustenance, and hides for his raiment. This was the workshop from which he could expect good wages for his efforts. Without benefit of economic textbooks, he hit upon a couple of economic laws: (1) that production, or wealth, consists of useful things resulting from the application of human labor to natural resources; (2) that wages come from production.

These laws, these precepts of nature, are still in force and always will be despite the efforts of some "experts" to rescind them. Often the yearning for manna from heaven obscures the fact that only by the application of labor to raw materials can economic goods appear, but the yearning is so strong that men ask government to play God and reproduce the miracle of the wilderness.

Government, of course, can produce nothing, let alone a miracle; and when it presumes to drop manna on its chosen people, it simply takes what some produce and hands it over to others; its largess is never a free gift. And as for wages, they still come from production, even though there are sectarians who maintain that wages come from the safety vaults of a soulless boss. The consequences of disregarding these two dictates of nature are too well known to call for discussion.

Returning to our first pioneer, his initial wages are meager. That is because he is compelled by the condition of his existence to be a jack-of-all-trades, proficient in none. He produces little and therefore has little. But he is not satisfied with his lot for, unlike the beasts in the forest or the fish in the sea, man is not content merely to exist.

And here we hit upon a natural law which plays a prime role in man's economic life: He is the insatiable animal, always dreaming of ways and means for improving his circumstances and widening his horizon. The cabin built by the pioneer to protect himself from the elements was castle enough in the beginning; but soon he begins to think of a floor covering, of pictures on the wall, of a lean-to, of a clavichord to brighten his evenings at home and, at long last, of hot-and-cold running water to relieve him of the laborious pumping. Were it not for man's insatiability, there would be no such study as economics.

A Neighbor Arrives

But the things the pioneer dreams about are unattainable as long as he is compelled to go it alone. Along comes a second pioneer, and his choice of a place to work is based on the same consideration that influenced his predecessor. What wages can he get out of the land? However, as between this location and others of equal natural quality, this one is more desirable because of the presence of a neighbor. This fact alone assures a greater income, because there are jobs that two men can perform more easily than can one man alone, and some jobs that one man simply cannot do. Their wages are mutually improved by cooperation. Each has more satisfactions.

Others come, and every accretion to the population raises the wage level of the community. In the building of homes, in fighting fires and other hazards, in satisfying the need of entertainment or in the search for spiritual solace, a dozen people working together can accomplish more than twelve times what each one, working alone, can do. Still, the wage level of the community is rather low, for it is limited by the fact that all the workers are engaged in the primary business of existence on a self-sustaining, jack-of-all-trades basis.

At some point in the development of the community it occurs to one of the pioneers that he has an aptitude for blacksmithing; and if all the others would turn over to him their chores in this line, he could become very proficient at it, far better than any of his neighbors. In order for him to ply this trade the others must agree to supply him with his needs. Since their skill at blacksmithing is deficient, and since the time and effort they put into it is at the expense of something they can do better, an agreement is not hard to reach. Thus comes the tailor, the carpenter, the teacher, and a number of other specialists, each relieving the farmers of jobs that interfere with their farming. Specialization increases the productivity of each; and where there was scarcity, there is now abundance.

Specialists with Capital

The first condition necessary for specialization is population. The larger the population the greater the possibility of the specialization which makes for a rising wage level in the community. There is, however, another important condition necessary for this division of labor, and that is the presence of capital. The pioneers have in their barns and pantries more than they need for their immediate sustenance, and are quite willing to invest this superfluity in other satisfactions. Their savings enable them to employ the services of specialists; and the more they make use of these services the more they can produce and save, thus to employ more specialists.

This matter of savings, or capital, may be defined as that part of production not immediately consumed, which is employed in aiding further production, so that more consumable goods may become available. In man's search for a more abundant life he has learned that he can improve his circumstances by producing more than he can presently consume and putting this excess into the production of greater satisfactions.

Respect for Property

Man has always been a capitalist. In the beginning, he produced a wheel, something he could not eat or wear, but something that made his labors easier and more fruitful. His judgment told him what to do, and of his own free will he chose to do it. That makes him a capitalist, a maker and user of capital. The wheel, after many centuries, became a wagon, an automobile, a train, and an airplane—all aids in man's search for a better living. If man were not a capitalist, if he had chosen not to produce beyond requirements for immediate consumption—well, there would never have been what we call civilization.

However, a prerequisite for the appearance of capital is the assurance that the producer can retain for himself all he produces in the way of savings. If this excess of production over consumption is regularly taken from him, by robbers or tax-collectors or the elements, the tendency is to produce no more than can be consumed immediately. In that case, capital tends to disappear; and with the disappearance of capital, production declines, and so does man's standard of living.

From this fact we can deduce another law of nature: that security in the possession and enjoyment of the fruit of one's labor is a necessary condition for capital accumulation. Putting it another way, where private property is abolished, capital tends to disappear and production comes tumbling after. This law explains why slaves are poor producers and why a society in which slavery is practiced is a poor society. It also gives the lie to the promise of socialism in all its forms; where private property is denied, there you will find austerity rather than a functioning exchange economy.

The Trading Instinct

The possibility of specialization as population increases is enhanced by another peculiarly human characteristic—the trading instinct. A trade is the giving up of something one has in order to acquire something one wants. The trader puts less worth on what he possesses than on what he desires. This is what we call evaluation.

It is not necessary here to go into the theory, or theories, of value except to point out that evaluation is a psychological process. It springs from the human capacity to judge the intensity of various desires. The fisherman has more fish than he cares to eat but would like to add potatoes to his menu; he puts a lower value on fish than on potatoes. The farmer is in the opposite position, his barn being full of potatoes and his plate devoid of fish. If an exchange can be effected, both will profit, both will acquire an added satisfaction. In every trade—provided neither force nor fraud is involved—seller and buyer both profit.

Only man is a trader. No other creature is capable of estimating the intensity of its desires and of giving up what it has in order to get something it wants. Man alone has the gift of free will. To be sure, he may go wrong in his estimates and may make a trade that is to his disadvantage. In his moral life, too, he may err. But, when he makes the wrong moral choice, we hold that he should suffer the consequences, and hope that he will learn from the unpleasant experience.

So it must be in his search for a more abundant life. If in his search for a good life the human must be allowed to make use of his free will, why should he not be accorded the same right in the search for a more abundant life? Many of the persons who would abolish free choice in the market place logically conclude that man is not endowed with free will, that free will is a fiction, that man is merely a product of his environment. This premise ineluctably leads them to the denial of the soul and, of course, the denial of God.

Those who rail against the market place as if it were a den of iniquity, or against its techniques as being founded in man's inhumanity, overlook the function of the market place in bringing people into closer contact with one another. Remember, the market place makes specialization possible, but specialization makes men interdependent. The first pioneer somehow or other made his entire cabin; but his son, having accustomed himself to hiring a professional carpenter, can hardly put up a single shelf in a cabin. And today, if some catastrophe should cut off Madison from the surrounding farms, the citizens of the city would starve. If the market place were abolished, people would still pass the time of day or exchange recipes or bits of news; but they would no longer be dependent on one another, and their self-sufficiency would tend to break down their society. For that reason we can say that society and the market place are two sides of the same coin. If God intended man to be a social animal, he intended him to have a market place.

Traders Serve One Another

But, let us return to our imaginary experiment. We found that as the pioneer colony grew in numbers, a tendency toward specialization arose. It was found that by this division of labor more could be produced. But this profusion from specialization would serve no purpose unless some way were found to distribute it. The way is to trade. The shoemaker, for instance, makes a lot of shoes of various sizes, but he is not interested in shoes per se; after all, he can wear but one pair and of one particular size. He makes the other shoes because other people want them and will give him in exchange the things he wants: bread, raiment, books, what not—the things in which his interests naturally lie. He makes shoes in order to serve himself, but in order to serve himself he has to serve others. He has to render a social service in order to pursue his own search for a more abundant life.

In our lexicon we refer to a business undertaking by the government as a social service; but this is a misnomer, because we can never be certain that the service rendered by the government business is acceptable to society. Society is compelled to accept these services, or to pay for them even if unwanted. The element of force is never absent from a government-managed business. On the other hand, the private entrepreneur cannot exist unless society voluntarily accepts what he has to offer; he must render a social service or go out of business.

Profits Come from Patrons

Let us suppose that this shoemaker is especially efficient, that many people in the community like his service and therefore trade with him. He acquires what we call a profit. Has he done so at the expense of his customers? Do they lose because he has a profit? Or, do they not gain in proportion to the profit he makes? They patronize him because the shoes he offers are better than they could make themselves or could get elsewhere, and for that reason they are quite willing to trade with him. They want what they get more than they want what they give up and therefore profit even as he profits.

If he goes wrong in his estimate of their requirements, if he makes the wrong sizes, or styles that are not wanted, or uses inferior materials, people will not patronize him and he will suffer a loss. He will have no wage return for the labor he puts in and no return for the capital—the hides and machinery—which he uses in making his unwanted product. The best he can do under the circumstances, in order to recoup some of his investment, is to hold a bargain-basement sale. That is the correlative of profits—losses.

No entrepreneur is wise enough to predetermine the exact needs or desires of the community he hopes to serve and his errors of judgment always come home to plague him. But, the point to keep in mind is that when an entrepreneur profits, he does so because he has served his community well; and when he loses, the community does not gain. A business that fails does not prosper society.

The Distributive Function

The market place not only facilitates the distribution of abundances—including the abundances that nature has spread all over the globe, like the coal of Pennsylvania for the citrus fruit of Florida, or the oil of Iran for the coffee of Brazil—but it also directs the energies of all the specialists who make up society. This it does through the instrumentality of its price-indicator. On this instrument are recorded in unmistakable terms just what the various members of society want, and how much they want it. If the hand on this indicator goes up, if higher prices are bid for a certain commodity, the producers are advised that there is a demand for this commodity in excess of the supply, and they then know how best to invest their labors for their own profit and for the profit of society. A lower price, on the other hand, tells them that there is a superfluity of a certain commodity, and they know that to make more of it would entail a loss because society has a sufficiency.

The price-indicator is an automatic device for recording the freely expressed wishes of the community members, the tally of their dollar ballots for this or that satisfaction, the spontaneous and noncoercive regulator of productive effort. One who chooses to tamper with this delicate instrument does so at the risk of producing a scarcity of the things wanted or an overabundance of unwanted things; for he disturbs the natural order.

Beneficiaries of Competition

One more social function of the market place needs mentioning. It is the determinant of productive efficiency, provided, of course, it is permitted to operate according to the unimpeded motive power of free will. In the primitive economy we have been examining, one shoemaker can take care of the shoe needs of the community. Under those conditions, the efficiency of that server is determined by his skill, his industry, and his whim. He alone can fix the standard of the service he renders his customers, or the prices he charges. Assuming that they can go nowhere else for shoes, their only recourse if they do not like his services or his prices is either to go without or to make their own footwear.

As the community grows in size, another shoe specialist will show up to share the trade with the first one. With the appearance of a second shoemaker the standard of efficiency is no longer determined by one producer. It is determined by the rivalry between them for the trade of the community. One offers to fix shoes "while you wait," the other lowers his prices, and the first one comes back with a larger assortment of sizes or styles. This is competition.

Now the beneficiaries of the improved services resulting from competition are the members of society. The more competition and the keener the competition, the greater the fund of satisfactions in the market place. Oddly enough, the competitors do not suffer because the abundance resulting from their improved efficiency attracts more shoe customers; "competition," the old adage holds, "is good for business."

If, perchance, one of the competitors cannot keep up with the improving standard of performance, he may find himself out of business; but the increased productive activity resulting from the competition means that there are more productive jobs to be filled, and in all likelihood he can earn more as a foreman for one of the competitors than he could as an entrepreneur. Even those physically unable to care for themselves and dependent on others are benefited by competition; when there is an abundance in the market place, charity can be more liberal.

Immutable Laws Prevail

I am not attempting here a complete course in economics. What I have tried to show is that in economics, as in other disciplines, there are inflexible principles, inevitable consequences, immutable laws written into the nature of things. Exercising his free will, man can attempt to defy the law of gravitation by jumping off a high place; but the law operates without regard for his conceit, and he ends up with a broken neck.

So, if the first pioneer had set up with force of arms a claim to everything produced in the Madison area, other pioneers would not have come near, and the community known as Madison would never have been born. Or, if he could have collected tribute, also by force of arms, from every producer in the area, he would have driven prospective specialists to places where private property was respected. If the first shoemaker had established himself, with the help of law, as a monopolist, barring competition, the shoes that Madisonians wore would have been of poor quality, scarce, and costly; the same result would have followed any legal scheme to subsidize his inefficiency at the expense of taxpayers. If early Madisonians had decreed to abolish the market place with its price-indicator, specialization and exchange would have been thwarted and the economy of Madison would have been characterized by scarcity.

The laws of economics, like other natural laws, are self-enforcing and carry built-in sanctions. If these laws are either unknown or not heeded, the inevitable eventual penalty will be an economy of scarcity, a poor and uncoordinated society. Why? Because the laws of nature are expressions of the will of God. You cannot monkey with them without suffering the consequences.

15. I, PENCIL*
MY FAMILY TREE AS TOLD TO
Leonard E. Read

I am a lead pencil—the ordinary wooden pencil familiar to all boys and girls and adults who can read and write.[1]

Writing is both my vocation and my avocation; that's all I do.

You may wonder why I should write a genealogy. Well, to begin with, my story is interesting. And, next, I am a mystery—more so than a tree or a sunset or even a flash of lightning. But, sadly, I am taken for granted by those who use me, as if I were a mere incident and without background. This supercilious attitude relegates me to the level of the commonplace. This is a species of the grievous error in which mankind cannot too long persist without peril. For, as a wise man observed, "We are perishing for want of wonder, not for want of wonders."[2]

I, Pencil, simple though I appear to be, merit your wonder and awe, a claim I shall attempt to prove. In fact, if you can understand me—no, that's too much to ask of anyone—if you can become aware of the miraculousness which I symbolize, you can help save the freedom mankind is so unhappily losing. I have a profound lesson to teach. And I can teach this lesson better than can an automobile or an airplane or a mechanical dishwasher because—well, because I am seemingly so simple.

Simple? Yet, *not a single person on the face of this earth knows how to make me.* This sounds fantastic, doesn't it? Especially when it is realized that there are about one and one-half billion of my kind produced in the U.S.A. each year.

Pick me up and look me over. What do you see? Not much meets the eye—there's some wood, lacquer, the printed labeling, graphite lead, a bit of metal, and an eraser.

Just as you cannot trace your family tree back very far, so is it impossible for me to name and explain all my antecedents. But I would like to suggest enough of them to impress upon you the richness and complexity of my background.

My family tree begins with what in fact is a tree, a cedar of straight grain that grows in Northern California and Oregon. Now contemplate all the saws and trucks and rope and the countless other gear used in harvesting and carting the cedar logs to the railroad siding. Think of all the persons and the numberless skills that went into their fabrication: the mining of ore, the making of steel and its refinement into saws, axes, motors; the growing of hemp and bringing it through all the states to heavy and strong rope; the logging camps with their beds and mess halls, the cookery and the raising of all the foods. Why, untold thousands of persons had a hand in every cup of coffee the loggers drink!

The logs are shipped to a mill in San Leandro, California. Can you imagine the individuals who make flat cars and rails and railroad engines and who construct and install the communication systems incidental thereto? These legions are among my antecedents.

Consider the millwork in San Leandro. The cedar logs are cut into small, pencil-length slats less than one-fourth of an inch in thickness. These are kiln dried and then tinted for the same reason women put rouge on their faces. People prefer that I look pretty, not a pallid white. The slats are waxed and kiln dried again. How many skills went into the

*From *The Freeman*, December 1958

making of the tint and the kilns, into supplying the heat, the light and power, the belts, motors, and all the other things a mill requires? Sweepers in the mill among my ancestors? Yes, and included are the men who poured the concrete for the dam of a Pacific Gas & Electric Company hydroplant which supplies the mill's power!

Don't overlook the ancestors present and distant who have a hand in transporting sixty carloads of slats across the nation from California to Wilkes-Barre!

Complicated Machinery

Once in the pencil factory—$4,000,000 in machinery and building, all capital accumulated by thrifty and saving parents of mine—each slat is given eight grooves by a complex machine, after which another machine lays leads in every other slat, applies glue, and places another slat atop—a lead sandwich, so to speak. Seven brothers and I are mechanically carved from this "wood-clinched" sandwich.

My "lead" itself—it contains no lead at all—is complex. The graphite is mined in Ceylon. Consider these miners and those who make their many tools and the makers of the paper sacks in which the graphite is shipped and those who make the string that ties the sacks and those who put them aboard ships and those who make the ships. Even the lighthouse keepers along the way assisted in my birth—and the harbor pilots.

The graphite is mixed with clay from Mississippi in which ammonium hydroxide is used in the refining process. Then wetting agents are added such as sulfonated tallow—animal fats chemically reacted with sulfuric acid. After passing through numerous machines, the mixture finally appears as endless extrusions—as from a sausage grinder—cut to size, dried, and baked for several hours at 1,850 degrees Fahrenheit. To increase their strength and smoothness the leads are then treated with a hot mixture which includes candelilla wax from Mexico, paraffin wax, and hydrogenated natural fats.

My cedar receives six coats of lacquer. Do you know all of the ingredients of lacquer? Who would think that the growers of castor beans and the refiners of castor oil are a part of it? They are. Why, even the processes by which the lacquer is made a beautiful yellow involves the skills of more persons than one can enumerate!

Observe the labeling. That's a film formed by applying heat to carbon black mixed with resins. How do you make resins and what, pray, is carbon black?

My bit of metal—the ferrule—is brass. Think of all the persons who mine zinc and copper and those who have the skills to make shiny sheet brass from these products of nature. Those black rings on my ferrule are black nickel. What is black nickel and how is it applied? The complete story of why the center of my ferrule has no black nickel on it would take pages to explain.

Then there's my crowning glory, inelegantly referred to in the trade as "the plug," the part man uses to erase the errors he makes with me. An ingredient called "factice" is what does the erasing. It is a rubber-like product made by reacting rape seed oil from the Dutch East Indies with sulfur chloride. Rubber, contrary to the common notion, is only for binding purposes. Then, too, there are numerous vulcanizing and accelerating agents. The pumice comes from Italy; and the pigment which gives "the plug" its color is cadmium sulfide.

No One Knows

Does anyone wish to challenge my earlier assertion that no single person on the face of this earth knows how to make me?

Actually, millions of human beings have had a hand in my creation, no one of whom even knows more than a very few of the others. Now, you may say that I go too far in relating the picker of a coffee berry in far off Brazil and food growers elsewhere to my creation; that this is an extreme position. I shall stand by my claim. There isn't a single person in all these millions, including the president of the pencil company, who contributes more than a tiny, infinitesimal bit of know-how. From the standpoint of know-how the only difference between the miner of graphite in Ceylon and the logger in Oregon is in the *type* of know-how. Neither the miner nor the logger can be dispensed with, any more than can the chemist at the factory or the worker in the oil field—paraffin being a by-product of petroleum.

Here is an astounding fact: Neither the worker in the oil field nor the chemist nor the digger of graphite or clay nor any who mans or makes the ships or trains or trucks nor the one who runs the machine that does the knurling on my bit of metal nor the president of the company performs his singular task because he wants me. Each one wants me less, perhaps, than does a child in the first grade. Indeed, there are some among this vast multitude who never saw a pencil nor would they know how to use one. Their motivation is other than me. Perhaps it is something like this: Each of these millions sees that he can thus exchange his tiny know-how for the goods and services he needs or wants. I may or may not be among these items.

No Master Mind

There is a fact still more astounding: The absence of a master mind, of anyone dictating or forcibly directing these countless actions which bring me into being. No trace of such a person can be found. Instead, we find the Invisible Hand at work. This is the mystery to which I earlier referred.

It has been said that "only God can make a tree." Why do we agree with this? Isn't it because we realize that we ourselves could not make one? Indeed, can we even describe a tree? We cannot, except in superficial terms. We can say, for instance, that a certain molecular configuration manifests itself as a tree. But what mind is there among men that could even record, let alone direct, the constant changes in molecules that transpire in the life span of a tree? Such a feat is utterly unthinkable!

I, Pencil, am a complex combination of miracles: a tree, zinc, copper, graphite, and so on. But to these miracles which manifest themselves in Nature an even more extraordinary miracle has been added: the configuration of creative human energies—millions of tiny know-hows configurating naturally and spontaneously in response to human necessity and desire and *in the absence of any human master-minding!* Since only God can make a tree, I insist that only God could make me. Man can no more direct these millions of know-hows to bring me into being than he can put molecules together to create a tree.

The above is what I meant when writing, "If you can become aware of the miraculousness which I symbolize, you can help save the freedom mankind is so unhappily losing." For, if one is aware that these know-hows will naturally, yes, automatically, arrange themselves into creative and productive patterns in response to human necessity and demand—that is, in the absence of governmental or any other coercive master-minding—then one will possess an absolutely essential ingredient for freedom: *a faith in free men*. Freedom is impossible without this faith.

Once government has had a monopoly of a creative activity such, for instance, as the delivery of the mails, most individuals will believe that the mails could not be efficiently delivered by men acting freely. And here is the reason: Each one acknowledges that he himself doesn't know how to do all the things incident to mail delivery. He also recognizes that no other individual could do it. These assumptions are correct. No individual possesses enough know-how to perform a nation's mail delivery any more than any individual possesses enough know-how to make a pencil. Now, in the absence of a faith in free men—in the unawareness that millions of tiny know-hows would naturally and miraculously form and cooperate to satisfy this necessity—the individual cannot help but reach the erroneous conclusion that mail can be delivered only by governmental "master-minding."

If I, Pencil, were the only item that could offer testimony on what men can accomplish when free to try, then those with little faith would have a fair case. However, there is testimony galore; it's all about us and on every hand. Mail delivery is exceedingly simple when compared, for instance, to the making of an automobile or a calculating machine or a grain combine or a milling machine or to tens of thousands of other things. Delivery? Why, in this area where men have been left free to try, they deliver the human voice around the world in less than one second; they deliver an event visually and in motion to any person's home when it is happening; they deliver 150 passengers from Seattle to Baltimore in less than four hours; they deliver gas from Texas to one's range or furnace in New York at unbelievably low rates and without subsidy; they deliver each four pounds of oil from the Persian Gulf to our Eastern Seaboard—halfway around the world—for less money than the government charges for delivering a one-ounce letter across the street!

The lesson I have to teach is this: *Leave all creative energies uninhibited*. Merely organize society to act in harmony with this lesson. Let society's legal apparatus remove all obstacles the best it can. Permit these creative know-hows freely to flow. Have faith that free men will respond to the Invisible Hand. This faith will be confirmed. I, Pencil, seemingly simple though I am, offer the miracle of my creation as testimony that this is a practical faith, as practical as the sun, the rain, a cedar tree, the good earth.

Notes

[1]My official name is "Mongol 482." My many ingredients are assembled, fabricated, and finished by Eberhard Faber Pencil Company, Wilkes-Barre, Pennsylvania.

[2]G. K. Chesterton.

Prices, Pricing

16. COST-PLUS PRICING*

Paul L. Poirot

Every seller of a commodity or service wants to cover his costs of production and receive something over and above such costs if possible. He spends long hours keeping records and, with rare exception, believes that he actually sets the price of his goods and services by adding a margin above his expenditures.

The truth, however, is that all recorded costs of an item are washed out and rendered irrelevant by the actual market price at which that item is traded—a price determined by the competitive forces of supply and demand. That price becomes the new "cost" of consideration to the next user, regardless of how much labor he or any prior owner expended on that particular item. And if he sells it in turn to another willing buyer, the latter's demand will have as much to do with determining the price as do the supplier's recorded expenses. Cost, of course, influences the supply side of the market and thus the price; but costs incurred do not determine price.

To believe or to say that any item of commerce is but the sum of the costs incurred in producing it—a package of somebody's prior labor—is to introduce a confusing irrelevancy into the bargaining process that determines the price at which free trade takes place. The only relevant factors in a voluntary trade are that each party to the transaction, at the moment, values what he receives more than he values what he gives. Each thinks that he gains from the trade, no matter what costs were incurred to produce what he gives or gets in exchange.

That's all there is to the subjective theory of value. It takes into account the demand as well as the cost of production. And this determination of prices in the open competitive market affords the current running record of costs and returns that a businessman needs in order to calculate profit or loss and judge whether or not to continue a particular business activity.

His record of yesterday's costs and returns may afford him some clues as to the efficiency of his procedures. But today's prices are the nearest indication available to him as to what tomorrow's costs and returns may be. What are today's prices for the buildings and machinery in use as compared with other production facilities now on the market or waiting to be invented? What are today's prices for various raw materials as compared with available or potential substitutes? How do today's prices for hired help compare with prices for labor-saving machinery? And how do today's prices for his saleable commodity or service compare with prices for competing items?

The Labor Theory

Despite this marvelous facility of market pricing and economic calculation, a man as producer finds it almost impossible to view his product or service other than as the result of labor or work. If he's working for wages, he demands a wage rate high enough to keep pace with "the cost of living." If he's selling wheat or corn or beans, he wants prices high enough to cover his costs of production. If he's providing a postal service under an exclusive government monopoly, he wants postage rates to cover costs.

*From *The Freeman*, January 1971

In other words, the seller's inclination is to try to hedge against the forces of supply and demand so as to assure a price that would include a "fair" markup over costs. What he seeks, in effect, is a guaranteed customer. And the postal service monopoly is a good example of such a condition. If the customers do not cover the costs, other taxpayers are obliged to do so. Market prices, with competitive postal services, are forbidden. There is no way of knowing what might be the demand for or the supply of postal services if buyers and sellers were obliged to look to the market to tell them how much of which scarce resources to devote to such purposes. Resources are simply used in the postal monopoly, with no way to know whether the use represents conservation or waste. The force of government sees to it that the full costs are covered by taxpayers, regardless of the inefficiency and waste.

Outside the Market

Government pricing and government contracts, including the payment of subsidies of any kind, always are on a "cost-plus" basis because in those cases the efficient market method of pricing has been prohibited. Supply and demand are ruled out of the determination: the customer is led to believe the resources involved are not very scarce—relatively free; the supplier is guaranteed that taxpayers will cover his costs, whatever they may be. Such socialistic pricing affords no effective method of economic calculation by which to measure success or failure, profit or loss, conservation or waste. Thus, socialists are foredoomed to stumbling in the dark with their outmoded labor theory of value—the sum of costs.

As long as men continue to view goods and services as a package of labor or the sum of the costs of production, they will continue to turn to government for subsidies, handouts, privileges, guaranteed incomes, protectionism, and the like. The more this is done, the less chance there is to trade for gain in the open market—the only system of pricing that conserves rather than wastes scarce resources.[1] Chief and foremost among those scarce resources is man, not for his capacity to consume as the socialists imply, but for his productive power to serve himself by serving others.

Note

[1] It may be assumed that the most urgent purposes of consumers will be served in one way or another and that it is best to do it as efficiently as possible. A businessman's profit or loss is the measure of his efficiency—his capacity to minimize the cost of serving consumers. Profit denotes the conservation, and loss the waste, of scarce resources.

17. CHARGING "ALL THE TRAFFIC WILL BEAR!"*

Leonard E. Read

To be accused of charging "all the traffic will bear" for goods or services makes one a scalper, gouger, sharp practitioner or, at least, not graced with the milk of human kindness. Persons who think that charging all the traffic will bear is an antisocial practice will likely advocate such "corrective" socialistic steps as price or production or exchange controls.

Most of us shop around. We look for sellers who will offer us the best product at the lowest price, and for buyers of our own goods or services to whom we can make the most advantageous sale;

*Answer to Cliche of Socialism No. 45 (FEE, 1963)

to say that you and I act on the opposite principle would be arrant nonsense.

But let some good or service on which *we* have become dependent—a necessity, we call it—fall into "short supply," then let the fortunate few who possess the good or service charge all the traffic will bear, and watch the epithets fly. "The Shylock!" And for acting precisely as most all of us act when free to choose.

We would be less apt to destroy the free market, willing exchange, private property way of life were we to think less harshly of those who charge all the traffic will bear. On the contrary, we should shower them with our kindest sentiments when this so-called "short-supply-high-demand" situation most seriously threatens our economic welfare.[1] Actually, such pricing in response to the signals of a free and unfettered market can most quickly and justly bring supply and demand toward equilibrium. Charging all the traffic will bear is identical in principle to its economic opposite, the fire sale to dispose of burdensome stocks. Each is a rectifying, remedial action. To curse the former which tends to irritate us is as senseless as to condemn the latter which tends to please us. Each allocates available resources to the uses we prefer, as indicated by our buying or not buying.

The free market—freedom in exchange, with prices freely responsible to changing supply and demand—is, in fact, an enormous computer, far superior to any electronic computer man has ever devised, or ever will. Data from all over the world, of the most varied and complex nature—only fragments of which any one man or set of men can even be aware of, let alone assemble and feed into it—are automatically and quickly processed, answers coming out as prices. These prices are, in effect, stop and go signals which clearly say to all would-be enterprisers: "Get into this activity at once, the supply is comparatively short and the demand is comparatively heavy" or "Get out of this activity now, the supply is comparatively bountiful and the demand is comparatively negligible."[2]

It makes no difference what good or service is used to illustrate how this marvelous, impersonal computer works. Mowing lawns or operating a machine tool would do, as would a bag of wheat or a steel casting or a money loan or tomatoes.

Tomatoes, let us say, are suddenly in "short supply." Millions of people relish this fruit and, thus, the demand continues high. The few growers fortunate enough to have escaped the destructive blight discover that they can sell their small supply for two dollars per pound—and they do! Salad lovers who cannot afford to pay this "exorbitant" price are inclined to think unfavorably of these growers: "Why, they're highway robbers." Yet these fortunate few are only adhering closely to the computer's instructions; they are behaving precisely as you and I act when we accept an increase in our wages. This is splendid!

Assuming the market to be free, what would happen in this situation? Several corrective forces would automatically and immediately go to work. First, the high price, with promises of exceptional profit, would entice others to grow tomatoes; and even more important, it would miraculously lead to the development of blight-resistant strains. In the shortest possible time, there would be tomatoes galore, perhaps at a dollar per bushel—within the reach of all.

For contrast, imagine the other extreme: A law to keep the price at its old level. What would be the probable results? At that price (where competition had compressed profits to their lowest possible level) there would be little incentive for new tomato growers to enter the field. And, thus, favoritism instead of prices would necessarily determine the allocation of the reduced supply of tomatoes. It is conceivable that the hard feelings generated by such a system of allocation could even cause the remaining tomato growers to get into some less emotional business; tomatoes could even become extinct![3]

This fantastic computer—the free market and its pricing—presupposes freedom in exchange. Whenever price or wage or production controls are permitted, the data fed into the computer are made inaccurate; and when this happens, the signals it gives must to that extent be erroneous. This explains why we have huge quantities of wheat, butter, cotton, and other produce wasting in tax-paid storage—surpluses which frighten rather than please us.

The signals which emerge from the computer will be useful relative to how accurately the data fed into it reflect the supply-demand situations of all people on this earth. A socialistic sentiment, such as disapproval of those who charge all the traffic will bear, tends to set in motion distortions of the data. How? Economically unsound sentiments feed the fires of government controls. Instead of an automatic computer, the astounding services of which are "for free," we get a bureaucracy attempting an impossible task of data collection at a cost of many billions of dollars annually.

And, eventually, we'll get no tomatoes!

When all the ramifications are considered, the seller who refuses to charge "all the traffic will bear" is rendering us a positive disservice. He is failing to allocate scarce resources to the most desired uses, as you and I determine them by our buying or abstention.

Notes

[1]I say "so-called" shortage because, of course, any wanted product or service that commands any price at all is in short supply; for unlike air, no one can have all he wants of it free.

[2]As an aside: While the free market derives its title from freedom in exchange, there are two additional reasons why the title is justified—(1) its computing service is "for free," there are no rentals or taxes for the service, this computer is as gratuitous as the sun's energy and requires no more in the way of corporate structure or bureaucracy than does any other natural phenomenon; and (2) buyers and sellers are freed from the necessity of knowing all the trillions of whims, moods, needs, desires, dislikes, disasters, inventions, efficiencies, and whatever (data) that go into the making of the few signals (prices) they need for decision-making.

[3]Recall the rampant favoritism that went on during World War II whenever OPA pricing went below what the supply-demand price would have been. Countless grudges remain to this day!

18. HOW SHOULD PRICES BE DETERMINED?*

Henry Hazlitt

"How should prices be determined?" To this question we could make a short and simple answer: Prices should be determined by the market.

The answer is correct enough, but some elaboration is necessary to answer the practical problem concerning the wisdom of government price control.

Let us begin on the elementary level and say that prices are determined by the supply and demand. If the relative demand for a product increases, consumers will be willing to pay more for it. Their competitive bids will both oblige them individually to pay more for it and enable producers to get more for it. This will raise the profit margins of the producers of that product. This, in turn, will tend to attract more firms into the manufacture of that product, and induce existing firms to invest more capital into making it. The increased production will tend to reduce the price of the product again, and to reduce the profit margin in making it. The increased investment in new manufacturing equipment may lower the cost of production. Or—particularly if we are concerned with some extractive industry such as petroleum, gold, silver, or copper—the increased demand and output may raise the cost of production. In any case, the price will have a definite effect on demand, output, and cost of production just as these in turn will affect price. All four—demand, supply, cost, and price—are interrelated. A change in one will bring changes in the others.

Just as the demand, supply, cost, and price of any single commodity are all interrelated, so are the prices of all commodities related to each other. These relationships are both direct and indirect. Copper mines may yield silver as a by-product. This is connexity of production. If the price of copper goes too high, consumers may substitute aluminum for many uses. This is a connexity of substitution. Dacron and cotton are both used in drip-dry shirts; this is a connexity of consumption.

In addition to these relatively direct connections among prices, there is an inescapable interconnexity of all prices. One general factor of production,

*From *The Freeman*, February 1967. Reproduced from a paper presented before a special meeting of the Mont Pelerin Society in Tokyo, September, 1966

labor, can be diverted, in the short run or in the long run, directly or indirectly, from one line into any other line. If one commodity goes up in price, and consumers are unwilling or unable to substitute another, they will be forced to consume a little less of something else. All products are in competition for the consumer's dollar; and a change in any one price will affect an indefinite number of other prices.

No single price, therefore, can be considered an isolated object in itself. It is interrelated with all other prices. It is precisely through these interrelationships that society is able to solve the immensely difficult and always changing problem of how to allocate production among thousands of different commodities and services so that each may be supplied as nearly as possible in relation to the comparative urgency of the need or desire for it.

Because the desire and need for, and the supply and cost of, every individual commodity or service are constantly changing, prices and price relationships are constantly changing. They are changing yearly, monthly, weekly, daily, hourly. People who think that prices normally rest at some fixed point, or can be easily held to some "right" level, could profitably spend an hour watching the ticker tape of the stock market, or reading the daily report in the newspapers of what happened yesterday in the foreign exchange market, and in the markets for coffee, cocoa, sugar, wheat, corn, rice, and eggs; cotton, hides, wool, and rubber; copper, silver, lead, and zinc. They will find that none of these prices ever stands still. This is why the constant attempts of governments to lower, raise, or freeze a particular price, or to freeze the interrelationship of wages and prices just where it was on a given date ("holding the line") are bound to be disruptive wherever they are not futile.

Price Supports for Export Items

Let us begin by considering governmental efforts to keep prices up, or to raise them. Governments most frequently try to do this for commodities that constitute a principal item of export from their countries. Thus Japan once did it for silk and the British Empire for natural rubber; Brazil has done it and still periodically does it for coffee; and the United States has done it and still does it for cotton and wheat. The theory is that raising the price of these export commodities can only do good and no harm domestically because it will raise the incomes of domestic producers and do it almost wholly at the expense of the foreign consumers.

All of these schemes follow a typical course. It is soon discovered that the price of the commodity cannot be raised unless the supply is first reduced. This may lead in the beginning to the imposition of acreage restrictions. But the higher price gives an incentive to producers to increase their average yield per acre by planting the supported product only on their most productive acres, and by more intensive employment of fertilizers, irrigation, and labor. When the government discovers that this is happening, it turns to imposing absolute quantitative controls on each producer. This is usually based on each producer's previous production over a series of years. The result of this quota system is to keep out all new competition; to lock all existing producers into their previous relative position, and therefore to keep production costs high by removing the chief mechanisms and incentives for reducing such costs. The necessary readjustments are therefore prevented from taking place.

Meanwhile, however, market forces are still functioning in foreign countries. Foreigners object to paying the higher price. They cut down their purchases of the valorized commodity from the valorizing country, and search for other sources of supply. The higher price gives an incentive to other countries to start producing the valorized commodity. Thus, the British rubber scheme led Dutch producers to increase rubber production in Dutch dependencies. This not only lowered rubber prices, but caused the British to lose permanently their previous monopolistic position. In addition, the British scheme aroused resentment in the United States, the chief consumer, and stimulated the eventually successful development of synthetic rubber. In the same way, without going into detail, Brazil's coffee schemes and America's cotton schemes gave both a political and a price incentive to other countries to initiate or increase production of coffee and cotton, and both Brazil and the United States lost their previous monopolistic positions.

Meanwhile, at home, all these schemes require the setting up of an elaborate system of controls and an elaborate bureaucracy to formulate and enforce them. This has to be elaborate, because each individual producer must be controlled. An illustration of what happens may be found in the United States Department of Agriculture. In 1929, before most of the crop control schemes came into being, there were 24,000 persons employed in the

Department of Agriculture. Today there are 109,000. These enormous bureaucracies, of course, always have a vested interest in finding reasons why the controls they were hired to enforce should be continued and expanded. And of course these controls restrict the individual's liberty and set precedents for still further restrictions.

None of these consequences seem to discourage government efforts to boost prices of certain products above what would otherwise be their competitive market levels. We still have international coffee agreements and international wheat agreements. A particular irony is that the United States was among the sponsors in organizing the international coffee agreement, though its people are the chief consumers of coffee and therefore the most immediate victims of the agreement. Another irony is that the United States imposes *import* quotas on sugar, which necessarily discriminate in favor of some sugar exporting nations and therefore against others. These quotas force all American consumers to pay higher prices for sugar in order that a tiny minority of American sugar cane producers can get higher prices.

I need not point out that these attempts to "stabilize" or raise prices of primary agricultural products *politicalize* every price and production decision and create friction among nations.

Holding Prices Down

Now let us turn to governmental efforts to *lower* prices or at least to keep them from rising. These efforts occur repeatedly in most nations, not only in wartime, but in any time of inflation. The typical process is something like this. The government, for whatever reason, follows policies that increase the quantity of money and credit. This inevitably starts pushing up prices. But this is not popular with consumers. Therefore, the government promises that it will "hold the line" against further price increases.

Let us say it begins with bread and milk and other necessities. The first thing that happens, assuming that it can enforce its decrees, is that the profit margin in producing necessities falls, or is eliminated, for marginal producers, while the profit margin in producing luxuries is unchanged or goes higher. This reduces and discourages the production of the controlled necessities and relatively encourages the increased production of luxuries. But this is exactly the opposite result from what the price controllers had in mind. If the government then tries to prevent this discouragement to the production of the controlled commodities by keeping down the cost of the raw materials, labor and other factors of production that go into them, it must start controlling prices and wages in ever-widening circles until it is finally trying to control the price of everything.

But if it tries to do this thoroughly and consistently, it will find itself trying to control literally millions of prices and trillions of price cross-relationships. It will be fixing rigid allocations and quotas for each producer and for each consumer. Of course these controls will have to extend in detail to both importers and exporters.

If a government continues to create more currency on the one hand while rigidly holding down prices with the other, it will do immense harm. And let us note also that even if the government is not inflating the currency, but tries to hold either absolute or relative prices just where they were, or has instituted an "incomes policy" or "wage policy" drafted in accordance with some mechanical formula, it will do increasingly serious harm. For in a free market, even when the so-called price "level" is not changing, all prices are constantly changing in relation to each other. They are responding to changes in costs of production, of supply, and of demand for each commodity or service.

And these price changes, both absolute and relative, are in the overwhelming main both necessary and desirable. For they are drawing capital, labor, and other resources out of the production of goods and services that are less wanted and into the production of goods and services that are more wanted. They are adjusting the balance of production to the unceasing changes in demand. They are producing thousands of goods and services in the relative amounts in which they are socially wanted. These relative amounts are changing every day. Therefore the market adjustments and price and wage incentives that lead to these adjustments must be changing every day.

Price Control Distorts Production

Price control always reduces, unbalances, distorts, and discoordinates production. Price control becomes progressively harmful with the passage of time. Even a fixed price or price relationship that may be "right" or "reasonable" on the day it is set can become increasingly unreasonable or unworkable.

What governments never realize is that, so far

as any individual commodity is concerned, the cure for high prices is high prices. High prices lead to economy in consumption and stimulate and increase production. Both of these results increase supply and tend to bring prices down again.

Very well, someone may say; so government price control in many cases is harmful. But so far you have been talking as if the market were governed by perfect competition. But what of monopolistic markets? What of markets in which prices are controlled or fixed by huge corporations? Must not the government intervene here, if only to enforce competition or to bring about the price that real competition would bring if it existed?

The fears of most economists concerning the evils of "monopoly" have been unwarranted and certainly excessive. In the first place, it is very difficult to frame a satisfactory definition of economic monopoly. If there is only a single drug store, barber shop, or grocery in a small isolated town (and this is a typical situation), this store may be said to be enjoying a monopoly in that town. Again, everybody may be said to enjoy a monopoly of his own particular qualities or talents. Yehudi Menuhin has a monopoly of Menuhin's violin playing; Picasso of producing Picasso paintings; Elizabeth Taylor of her particular beauty and sex appeal; and so for lesser qualities and talents in every line.

On the other hand, nearly all economic monopolies are limited by the possibility of substitution. If copper piping is priced too high, consumers can substitute steel or plastic; if beef is too high, consumers can substitute lamb; if the original girl of your dreams rejects you, you can always marry somebody else. Thus, nearly every person, producer, or seller may enjoy a quasi monopoly within certain inner limits, but very few sellers are able to exploit that monopoly beyond certain outer limits. There has been a tremendous literature within recent years deploring the absence of perfect competition; there could have been equal emphasis on the absence of perfect monopoly. In real life competition is never perfect, but neither is monopoly.

Unable to find many examples of perfect monopoly, some economists have frightened themselves in recent years by conjuring up the specter of "oligopoly," the competition of the few. But they have come to their alarming conclusions only by inserting in their own *hypotheses* all sorts of imaginary secret agreements or tacit understandings between large producing units, and deducing what the results could be.

Now the mere *number* of competitors in a particular industry may have very little to do with the existence of effective competition. If General Electric and Westinghouse effectively compete, if General Motors and Ford and Chrysler effectively compete, if the Chase Manhattan and the First National City Bank effectively compete, and so on (and no person who has had direct experience with these great companies can doubt that they dominantly do), then the result for consumers, not only in price, but in quality of product or service, is not only as good as that which would be brought about by atomistic competition but much better, because consumers have the advantage of large-scale economies, and of large-scale research and development that small companies could not afford.

A Strange Numbers Game

The oligopoly theorists have had a baneful influence on the American antitrust division and on court decisions. The prosecutors and the courts have recently been playing a strange numbers game. In 1965, for example, a Federal district court held that a merger that had taken place between two New York City banks four years previously had been illegal, and must now be dissolved. The combined bank was not the largest in the city, but only the third largest; the merger had in fact enabled the bank to compete more effectively with its two larger competitors; its combined assets were still only one-eighth of those represented by all the banks of the city; and the merger itself had reduced the number of separate banks in New York from 71 to 70. (I should add that in the four years since the merger the number of *branch* bank offices in New York City had *increased* from 645 to 698.) The court agreed with the bank's lawyers that "the general public and small business have benefited" from bank mergers in the city. Nevertheless, the court continued, "practices harmless in themselves, or even those conferring benefits upon the community, cannot be tolerated when they tend to create a monopoly; those which restrict competition are unlawful no matter how beneficent they may be."

It is a strange thing, incidentally, that though politicians and the courts think it necessary to forbid an existing merger in order to increase the number of banks in a city from 70 to 71, they have no such insistence on big numbers in competition when it comes to political parties. The dominant American theory is that just two political parties are enough to give the American voter a real choice; that when there are more than this it merely causes confusion, and the people are not really served. There is this much truth in this political theory as applied in the economic realm. If they are really competing, only two firms in an industry are enough to create effective competition.

Monopolistic Pricing

The real problem is not whether or not there is "monopoly" in a market, but whether there is monopolistic pricing. A monopoly price can arise when the responsiveness of demand is such that the monopolist can obtain a higher net income by selling a smaller quantity of his product at a higher price than by selling a larger quantity at a lower price. It is assumed that in this way the monopolist can realize a higher price than would have prevailed under "pure competition."

The theory that there can be such a thing as a monopoly price, higher than a competitive price would have been, is certainly valid. The real question is, how *useful* is this theory either to the supposed monopolist in deciding his price policies or to the legislator, prosecutor, or court in framing antimonopoly policies? The monopolist, to be able to exploit his position, must know what the "demand curve" *is* for his product. He does not know; he can only guess; he must try to find out by trial and error. And it is not merely the unemotional price response of the consumers that the monopolist must keep in mind; it is what the effect of his pricing policies will probably be in gaining the goodwill or arousing the resentment of the consumer. More importantly, the monopolist must consider the effect of his pricing policies in either encouraging or discouraging the entrance of competitors into the field. He may actually decide that his wisest policy in the long run would be to fix a price no higher than he thinks pure competition would set, and perhaps even a little lower.

In any case, in the absence of competition, no one *knows* what the "competitive" price would be if it existed. Therefore, no one knows exactly how much higher an existing "monopoly" price is than a "competitive" price would be, and no one can be sure whether it is higher at all!

Yet antitrust policy, in the United States, at least, assumes that the courts can know how much an alleged monopoly or "conspiracy" price is above the competitive price that might-have-been. For when there is an alleged conspiracy to fix prices, purchasers are encouraged to sue to recover three times the amount they were allegedly forced to "overpay."

Our analysis leads us to the conclusion that governments should refrain, wherever possible, from trying to fix either maximum or minimum prices for anything. Where they have nationalized any service—the post office or the railroads, the telephone or electric power—they will of course have to establish pricing policies. And where they have granted monopolistic franchises—for subways, railroads, telephone or power companies—they will of course have to consider what price restrictions they will impose.

As to antimonopoly policy, whatever the present condition may be in other countries, I can testify that in the United States this policy shows hardly a trace of consistency. It is uncertain, discriminatory, retroactive, capricious, and shot through with contradictions. No company today, even a moderate sized company, can know when it will be held to have violated the antitrust laws, or why. It all depends on the economic bias of a particular court or judge.

There is immense hypocrisy about the subject. Politicians make eloquent speeches against "monopoly." Then they will impose tariffs and import quotas intended to protect monopoly and keep out competition; they will grant monopolistic franchises to bus companies or telephone companies; they will approve monopolistic patents and copyrights; they will try to control agricultural production to permit monopolistic farm prices. Above all, they will not only permit but impose labor monopolies on employers, and legally compel employers to "bargain" with these monopolies; and they will even allow these monopolies to impose their conditions by physical intimidation and coercion.

I suspect that the intellectual situation and the political climate in this respect is not much different in other countries. To work our way out of this existing legal chaos is, of course, a task for jurists as well as for economists. I have one modest suggestion: We can get a great deal of help from the old common law, which forbids fraud, misrepresentation, and all *physical* intimidation and coercion. "The end of the law," as John Locke reminded us in the seventeenth century, "is not to abolish or restrain, but to preserve and enlarge freedom." And so we can say today that in the economic realm, the aim of the law should not be to constrict, but to maximize price freedom and market freedom.

Savings, Tools and Production

19. LETTER TO HIS GRANDSON*

Fred I. Kent

Mr. Kent's grandson, then a schoolboy, was disturbed by the current fashion of disparaging the profit system. He had asked his grandfather to explain just how there can be a profit which is not taken from the work of someone else.

April 1942

My dear grandson:

I will answer your question as simply as I can. Profit is the result of enterprise which builds for others as well as for the enterpriser. Let us consider the operation of this fact in a primitive community, say of one hundred persons who are non-intelligent beyond the point of obtaining the mere necessities of living by working hard all day long.

Our primitive community, dwelling at the foot of a mountain, must have water. There is no water except at a spring near the top of the mountain: therefore, every day all the hundred persons climb to the top of the mountain. It takes them one hour to go up and back. They do this day in and day out, until at last one of them notices that the water from the spring runs down inside the mountain in the same direction that he goes when he comes down. He conceives the idea of digging a trough in the mountainside all the way down to the place where he has his habitation. He goes to work to build a trough. The other ninety-nine people are not even curious as to what he is doing.

*Reprinted from *Economic Council Letter*

Then one day this hundreth man turns a small part of the water from the spring into his trough and it runs down the mountain into a basin he has fashioned at the bottom. Whereupon he says to the ninety-nine others, who each spend an hour a day fetching their water, that if they will each give him the daily production of ten minutes of their time, he will give them water from his basin. He will then receive nine hundred and ninety minutes of the time of the other men each day, which will make it unnecessary for him to work sixteen hours a day in order to provide for his necessities. He is making a tremendous profit—but his enterprise has given each of the ninety-nine other people fifty additional minutes each day for himself.

The enterpriser, now having sixteen hours a day at his disposal and being naturally curious, spends part of his time watching the water run down the mountain. He sees that it pushes along stones and pieces of wood. So he develops a water wheel; then he notices that it has power and, finally, after many hours of contemplation and work, makes the water wheel run a mill to grind his corn.

This hundredth man then realizes that he has sufficient power to grind corn for the other ninety-nine. He says to them, "I will allow you to grind your corn in my mill if you will give me one tenth the time you save." They agree, and so the enterpriser now makes an additional profit. He uses the time paid him by the ninety-nine others to build a better house for himself, to increase his conveniences of living through new benches, openings in his house for light, and better protection from the cold. So it goes on, as this hundredth man constantly finds ways to save the ninety-nine the total expenditure of their time—one tenth of which he asks of them in payment for his enterprising.

This hundredth man's time finally becomes all his own to use as he sees fit. He does not have to work unless he chooses to. His food and shelter and clothing are provided by others. His mind, however, is ever working and the other ninety-nine are constantly having more time to themselves because of his thinking and planning.

For instance, he notices that one of the ninety-nine makes better shoes than the the others. He arranges for this man to spend all his time making shoes, because he can feed him and clothe him and arrange for his shelter from profits. The other ninety-eight do not now have to make their own shoes. They are charged one tenth the time they save. The ninety-ninth man is also able to work shorter hours because some of the time that is paid by each of the ninety-eight is allowed to him by the hundredth man.

As the days pass, another individual is seen by the hundredth man to be making better clothes than any of the others, and it is arranged that his time shall be given entirely to his specialty. And so on.

Due to the foresight of the hundredth man, a division of labor is created that results in more and more of those in the community doing the things for which they are best fitted. Everyone has a greater amount of time at his disposal. Each becomes interested, except the dullest, in what others are doing and wonders how he can better his own position. The final result is that each person begins to find his proper place in an intelligent community.

But suppose that, when the hundredth man had completed his trough down the mountain and said to the other ninety-nine, "If you will give me what it takes you ten minutes to produce, I will let you get water from my basin," they had turned on him and said, "We are ninety-nine and you are only one. We will take what water we want. You cannot prevent us and we will give you nothing." What would have happened then? The incentive of the most curious mind to build upon his enterprising thoughts would have been taken away. He would have seen that he could gain nothing by solving problems if he still had to use every waking hour to provide his living. There could have been no advancement in the community. The same stupidity that first existed would have remained. Life would have continued to be a drudge to everyone, with opportunity to do no more than work all day long just for a bare living.

But we will say the ninety-nine did not prevent the hundredth man from going on with his thinking, and the community prospered. And we will suppose that there were soon one hundred families. As the children grew up, it was realized that they should be taught the ways of life. There was now sufficient production so that it was possible to take others away from the work of providing for themselves, pay them, and set them to teaching the young.

Similarly, as intelligence grew the beauties of nature became apparent. Men tried to fix scenery and animals in drawings—and art was born. From the sounds heard in nature's studio and in the voices of the people, music was developed. And it became possible for those who were proficient in drawing and music to spend all their time at their art, giving of their creations to others in return for a portion of the community's production.

As these developments continued, each member of the community, while giving something from his own accomplishments, became more and more dependent upon the efforts of others. And, unless envy and jealousy and unfair laws intervened to restrict honest enterprisers who benefited all, progress promised to be constant.

Need we say more to prove that there can be profit from enterprise without taking anything from others, that such enterprise adds to the ease of living for everyone?

These principles are as active in a great nation such as the United States as in our imaginary community. Laws that kill incentive and cripple the honest enterpriser hold back progress. True profit is not something to be feared, because it works to the benefit of all.

We must endeavor to build, instead of tearing down what others have built. We must be fair to other men, or the world cannot be fair to us.

Sincerely,
Grandfather

20. TECHNOLOGICAL STATUS*

John W. Campbell

It has been said that "technology we can't understand appears to be magic." Actually, this applies only to technology more advanced than our own—for frequently we see some great technological device and, by familiarity, fail to recognize it for what it is.

Perhaps the Grade A No. 1 prime example is one which is now generally considered the perfect symbol of *non*-technology—the epitomization of the failure to develop technology.

The peasant-farmer, plodding along behind his horse-drawn plow as he sweats to till his fields, does seem, to us, about as untechnical as you can get. Yet in that pastoral scene is a technical breakthrough that properly ranks slightly behind harnessing fire, and perhaps a bit ahead of the wheel. (After all, all the native American civilizations got along without the wheel!)

It might be described in modern terms as "a solid-state power-handling device for coupling a heavy duty power source to heavy tractive loads." Or, more simply, as the device that freed human slaves from service as draft animals.

One of the reasons the Romans and Greeks needed so many slaves was that there was no known way of harnessing animals to heavy draft loads. Man, because of his bipedal posture and his hands, could have a harness slipped over his chest and shoulders, and by leaning into it, exert all his strength in pulling the load. It was literally true that a man could exert more pull than a 1,500-pound horse.

A horse's sloping chest, and lack of shoulders or grasping hands, made it impossible to tie him to a load except by putting a rope around his neck. Do that, and as soon as he pulls, he's choked by the rope at his throat; he can pull only lightly before his wind is cut off and he has to stop. True, some powerful horses can exert enough pull to move a relatively light chariot at a good speed that way—but as a coupling device it's exceedingly inefficient. The horse couldn't pull a plow, or a heavy dray.

Oxen, equipped by nature with some well-anchored horns, could do considerably better—but it was extremely tiring on even an ox's heavy neck muscles to hold his head down against the backward pull of the load.

Rapid, Heavy Transport

The horse collar, invented somewhere, sometime during the Middle Ages in Europe, was Man's first really successful device for harnessing powerful animal muscles to do the heavy hauling work that was needed. It made possible heavy transport—even on the horrible mud ruts they called roads. It vastly increased the amount of agricultural land that could be prepared and used during a single growing season; there was far more food available for men and motive power. Where before, horses and other animals had transported goods primarily as pack animals, transportation was expanded, quite suddenly, as greatly as it was a few centuries later with the invention of the steampowered railroad.

Naturally, with the potential of heavy, relatively rapid transportation available, the sedan chair went out of use as the coach came in, and pack-trains were replaced by loaded wagons. Inevitably the demand for more roads wide enough—and good enough!—for horse-drawn vehicles came, and the entire economy began speeding up.

The contact with the highly sophisticated and educated society of Islam was undoubtedly a tremendous factor in the development of the renaissance in the seacoast regions of the Mediterranean, where water transport made transportation reasonably effective. But it was the horse collar that

*From *The Freeman*, February 1969. Reprinted by permission from *Analog* Science Fiction-Science Fact. Copyright 1968 by the Condé Nast Publications, Inc.

brought an economic renaissance to most of Europe.

It's not at all easy to recognize technological importance—particularly when we're used to it. Certainly a horse collar seems a simple enough idea. . . .

Most moderns haven't actually seen and handled one, or studied one closely. Take a good look at the structure of a horse's chest and shoulders, and without studying a horse collar, try devising a form that will fit snugly onto those sloping curves and planes, allow the horse free movement of neck and forelegs, avoid concentrating the load on prominent bony areas, and so distribute it that the horse can exert his full strength without painful chafing. Then make it stay in place without aid of adhesive tapes, glue, or surgical implants!

The agricultural technicians of the Middle Ages who developed that gadget were not fools, even if they hadn't ever had a course in mechanical engineering, or force-analysis. And they did achieve something that the learned Greeks and the great Roman engineers did not; they harnessed the most effective power source in the world at the time.

And be it noted that that animal power source is still used as the basis for measuring our mechanical tractive engines—as Watt originally defined it in his sales-promotion literature for his new steam engines.

However, two horses can do a lot more plowing than a two-horsepower gasoline-engined tractor can; the gas job can't slow down in a tough spot, dig in its hooves, bellydown to the earth, and lunge with half a ton of hard-tensed muscle to drag the plow through.

Of course, the tractor is also not capable of self-repair, automatic routine maintenance, living off the fields it works, self-replication, or sense enough not to destroy itself by ramming itself over a cliff. In addition to operating on locally-available fuels, a horse is approximately twice as efficient as a tractor in conversion of chemical to mechanical energy.

Current Applications

The moral of this little story is not to be applied just to humans visiting alien planets; it applies very cruelly to situations right here on our own crazy, confused world. Backward nations—I will not be euphemistic and call them "underdeveloped" because they've had the same thousands of years to develop that Europe and America had, and simply didn't do so—do not recognize the importance of what could be called "the Horse Collar Revolution."

Those economically depressed nations want, most ardently, to join "the modern world"—i.e., to achieve the industrially-developed status of the high-level technological nations.

Now there are two kinds of "status"; one is what your neighbors think you are, and the other is what you actually have and can do. The first type of status is, of course, far and away the most popular, and the most eagerly sought.

One type of individual, if he happens to inherit a few thousand dollars, or hit it lucky in gambling, promptly puts it into fancy new clothes, a down payment on a fancy new car, and a fancy new woman or two, and has himself a whee of a time being admired and respected because man, he's got all the symbols of Status!

So in three months the fancy car is repossessed, the fancy woman moves off, and the fancy clothes prove to have poor durability.

Another approach is to spend the little inheritance on getting a small business started—maybe a neighborhood grocery, or a newsstand. Doesn't get you much Status, of course, and not much spectacular fun . . . but put to work that way a few thousand can support you for life.

It's just that it is *not* as much fun, and a few thousand won't do it unless you get in and work just as hard yourself, and that makes the whole idea much less popular.

Status Symbols

The national equivalent now showing up among the backward nations is that foreign aid—winning the numbers game, in the international lottery!—is spent on fancy Status projects. Hydroelectric plants are Status Symbols, man! That means you've *got* it!

Even if you don't have many electric lights or power machines in grass huts and fields plowed by men and women pulling wooden stick plows through the earth.

Steel mills are great international Status Symbols, too. Of course, what would *really* make one of those nations have Status with all its neighbors would be to have something really technical and ultra-fancy, like a few nuclear bombs.

Trouble is, nobody, except a few experts, in a few major Western nations, have the wisdom to see that the horse collar is one of the greatest technical developments of human history.

The basic plot in Christopher Anvil's "Royal Road" stemmed from an actual disaster of WW II; it didn't have the comfortable ending Anvil's story did. The lesson, bitterly learned then, is being re-learned most reluctantly by the backward countries today.

The Allies had a tremendous military need for roads and barracks and airfields in an area where there simply were none. It was a remote area; shipping simply wasn't to be had for sending in earth-moving machinery, bulldozers, power shovels, and so on. So local natives were hired, at high pay, to do the work.

The men who set up that operation didn't know what a subsistence-level economy was; they found out that fall and winter. The men they'd hired to work at such fine wages were, of course, the native farmers—who therefore didn't farm that year.

In Anvil's story, the thing was planned, and the aftermath was part of the plan; in the real event it wasn't planned that way—it just happened. There was no shipping to bring in food that winter, just as there had been no shipping to bring in earth-moving machinery. It was a horribly grim demonstration of the oft-repeated remark of philosophers that "you can't eat gold." There was a lot of money around—but no crops.

Repeating the Error

What's happening again and again in backward countries today is of the same order. The magnificent new dams and hydroelectric plants employ thousands of workers at good wages—and hire them away from food-production in a near-subsistence economy. The result is inadequate food production, incipient famine, and a desperate plea for help to feed the starving millions. But they sure have a great Status dam!

Oh, they get irrigation water, too—only sometimes the results haven't been any better thought out than the economic disaster of famine was. Many areas of the world have fairly fertile land lying on top of extremely saline under-soil—practically salt beds. When rain falls, the fresh water seeps downward, and keeps washing the salt back down to the under-soil where it is harmless. But run in irrigation water—the salt from below dissolves, and evaporation from the surface soil pulls the now-saline water up, where it in turn evaporates, and thus rapidly builds up a salt crust on the surface.

It takes several years of non-irrigation, and no crops, for natural rainfall to wash the salt back down so the land can be used again.

But don't you forget—that big irrigation dam and project is an international Status Symbol of high value!

If a nation has a primitive subsistence-level economy, this simply means that its food-and-goods production has economic value just barely sufficient to keep the population from starvation. And that in crop-failure years, there will be famine, and people will die of starvation.

In many, many such subsistence-level areas, if such famines occurred, there was literally nothing whatever anyone could do to help them. The thing happened repeatedly in India and in China; India, under the British, had railways and His Majesty's government did everything humanly possible to relieve the starvation. But the food needed to feed 300,000,000 starving people can't be gathered from the surrounding areas; they're subsistence-level economies, too. And the railroads weren't vast, heavy-traffic networks such as Europe and America had developed; they didn't have enough cars or engines. And shipping from half around the world took so long that even if the transport and grain were freely donated, it wouldn't get there in time to be very helpful.

In China, because of bad roads and no railroads at the time, there were huge areas where the *only* possible transport was by porters. (Mules can't climb ladders, and some of the routes required ladders to get up mountain "passes.") Since porters had to start in carrying their own food for the round trip, it was fairly easy to figure what distance of penetration was possible before the porter had consumed his total load in his own round-trip supply. No food whatever could be shipped into any more distant point. People in those inner areas simply starved to death because help was physically impossible.

Breaking the Habit

In subsistence-level economy areas today, what sort of help can the industrial nations give?

Well, first is the fact that Step no. 1 is to break down the cultural pattern of the people that holds them at the subsistence level. And at this step, naturally, the people will do all they can to destroy the vile invaders who are seeking to destroy their Way of Life, which is the Good, the True, and the Beautiful and Holy Way.

You can't do it by telling them that they *should* stop growing those inefficient crops, those crops that produce protein malnutrition, and learn how to raise these new and far more efficient nutritive crops.

There are problems involved that aren't economic or technical. The Israeli, for instance, have worked out techniques for growing watermelons, wheat, various fruits, and grains on sandy gravel irrigated with salt water. They can make the barren Negev Desert produce fine crops of excellent food—techniques that can be applied anywhere there are sand dunes, gravel, and sea water, or salt-water springs. It would work fine in huge areas of the Sahara. No vast irrigation dams needed for this project!

Unfortunately, the Arabs don't seem enthusiastic about accepting and applying this Jewish technique.

Even if it were an Arab development, the peoples of the area are tradition-oriented; it would take at least a generation to put over the idea of doing precisely those things which they *know* are wrong. For every farmer knows that salt water kills plants, and you can't grow plants in sand and stony gravel.

The odd thing is that the salt-water irrigation can *not* be used in "good soil"; it works only in the worst kind of gravel-sand soil.

Resistance to Change

The proper development of the backward areas requires recognition that *the people don't want to change.* They want their results to change—they want to *have* the fine things other nations have, but not to *build them.*

To pull up from a subsistence-level economy, the first step is building better roads, and a more efficient agriculture. *Not* irrigation projects, *not* tractor manufacturing plants and hydroelectric projects and establishing an internationally known air line, complete with twenty or so Boeing 707 jets. Man, those are real Status Symbols!

What's needed is the Horse Collar Revolution and its results. Draft animals can live off the local fields; they don't require exchanging scarce goods for foreign fuel supplies and replacement parts.

The road network has to be built up slowly; too many farmers diverted to vast construction projects and you have famine.

You need schools—schools that teach agriculture and medicine and veterinary medicine and simple local-irrigation techniques and public hygiene and basic nutrition. *Not* electronics, industrial chemistry, and jet-engine maintenance—not for a generation will that be valid. The few natives who are really cut out for that sort of work can be taught in other nations, where schools of that order are needed, and already exist. But don't expect them to come home—there will be nothing for them to come home to for a generation.

But no High Status schools?

Sorry—getting out of a subsistence system can't be achieved on Status—it has to be achieved by *Status,* the hard-work-and-practical-learning kind of real accomplishment.

The ancient truth prevails: God helps those who help themselves. Because even God can't help someone who won't help himself—that's what the ancient concept of Free Will implies!

The more developed nations can help effectively only where the national leaders have the wisdom to work for *real* accomplishment, not for high Status projects.

And be it noted—that "more developed nations" does *not* mean the U.S., the U.S.S.R., and other Western nations alone, by any means. One example has been cited; Israel has a technique that could immensely aid many backward nations right now.

The Philippines have developed a spectacularly productive new breed of rice by careful botanical research; they've done a bang-up job of it, and have a strain that yields three to four times as much food from a given area. It's a breed that could release two out of three rice-farmers in a subsistence-level nation to work on those needed roads and dams and other projects, without bringing starvation to the country.

The water buffalo is an extremely economic animal; it's one beastie that the Western world needs to accept and use as a domestic animal—and is needed far more widely in the world. The water buffalo yields high-quality milk, high-quality meat, and is an enormously powerful draft animal capable of working under muddy conditions which ruin the feet of most creatures. Moreover, the critter can yield meat, milk, and power when fed on an incredible diet consisting solely of rice stubble! The Thais have carried on a careful program of breeding for some decades, and now have breeds of water buffalo that run over a ton in weight.

Rather surprisingly, about the only area outside of the Southeast Asia region where water buffaloes are used in any numbers is in Italy, where some 40,000 of them are kept. The familiar Mozzarella Italian cheese—in its original, genuine form—is made from water-buffalo milk.

Only when many thousands, or millions, of agricultural workers can leave the farms for work without producing the inevitable famine—only when the agricultural economy gets above the subsistence level—can any nation become "advanced." Argentina isn't an industrial power—but has a highly developed agricultural economy. All of the highly industrialized nations *first* became highly successful agricultural nations.

Yet we—and unfortunately the backward nations!—see the horsedrawn plow and the farmer as symbols of low-status, nonindustrial economies.

The great trouble is that *people don't want to change*. It's not *just* the peoples in backward countries; the great economic advantages of the water buffalo have been around for centuries, yet only Italy among all the Western nations has accepted them. Why aren't they being raised in southern Louisiana, for instance, where there's plenty of land and climate of the type they particularly love?

In Africa, millions of children die of protein malnutrition because the natives raise traditional crops that do not provide the essential amino acids—and can't be induced to change their customs.

Indians in Central America suffered the same type of protein malnutrition; their one and only staple was corn—maize. And corn, like most grains, is deficient in lysine to an extent human beings can't live on it.

Anthropologists and nutritionists could get nowhere changing their dietary habits; finally, botanists succeeded in breeding a strain of corn that did contain adequate lysine, so the natives could go on doing as they'd always done—eating corn—and still get the food they needed to live.

That is not a solution to the problem.

Sure, it keeps the children alive—but it does not achieve the crucially important necessity. Those people will remain forever backward people unless *they* change.

A change in government does no good, for a government cannot remain in power if the people actively hate it. And so long as people insist on not changing their Good, Beautiful, Familiar, and Holy Traditional Way of Life—even if it's killing them!—the social system will not change. And they'll kill anyone, any government, that seeks to change them, if they possibly can. Only a powerfully entrenched and ruthlessly determined dictatorship can impose on them the basic changes they, the people, must make.

If, that is, you insist the change must be made in this generation.

Otherwise, you'll have to have patience, and wait while slow, steady, continuing pressures alter the Established Way of Things decade by decade.

Agriculture First

And the greatest, fastest progress will be made in the backward nations which gain least Technological Industrial Status Projects—and develop their agriculture most.

In a rice-eating nation, if one third of the rice-growers, raising high-production strains, using new and more efficient techniques, can sell twice as much rice for only seventy-five per cent of the cost—the rice farmer who would not change his traditional ways will be forced out of agriculture. His poor harvest won't be wanted. He'll lose his land, his home, all the things he has lived by and with.

Here, the ruthless dictator who forces him to change his way of life is not human—it's economic. It's even more ruthless and relentless. But it, too, has the same compelling message: "You *must* learn a new way of life—or die!"

At the same time, of course, the fine surplus of cheap rice means that industrial workers, road and dam builders, all sorts of people in all sorts of newly developing occupations, are living much better. The old near-starvation level of rice is gone—there's plenty to eat, at last.

Look, friends—industry didn't produce a high standard of living. A high standard of agriculture forced people to learn a new high standard of living and industry.

And that's the only way it will be—unless a completely ruthless, dedicated tyrant oppresses his helpless people into learning the new way of life *fast*.

21. WHERE KARL MARX WENT WRONG*

Samuel B. Pettengill

Now that the whole nation is talking about the communist threat to the country—at home and abroad—it seems a good time to ask what is really wrong with Marxism.

In 1848, Karl Marx and Friedrich Engels wrote *The Communist Manifesto,* which begins with these words: "A specter is haunting Europe—the specter of Communism." This reads like today's newspaper. Yet the words were written one year before gold was discovered in California, before the covered wagons began to roll across the plains. Please keep this date in mind. It is significant to what I shall say.

In London a few years later, Marx wrote *Das Kapital*—the "bible" of the Communists and Socialists. As a reporter, Marx was accurate. The conditions of the workers in England a century ago, as he pointed out, were very grim. Women with ropes over their shoulders pulled canal boats along the towpaths. Women were harnessed like beasts of burden to cars pulling coal out of British mines. Children went to work in the textile mills when they were nine or ten years old, and they worked 12 to 15 hours a day. It was said that the beds in which they slept never got cold as one shift took the place of the other. It was said that they were "machines by day and beasts by night." Tuberculosis and other diseases killed them off like flies.

Yes, conditions were terrible. Not only Marx, but other warm-hearted men—Charles Dickens, John Ruskin, Thomas Carlyle—poured out a literature of protest, which was read around the world.

On his facts, Marx can scarcely be challenged. But his diagnosis was wrong; and, therefore, the remedy he prescribed was wrong also.

Marx said that these terrible conditions were due to greed, exploitation, and the theft by the owners of the mines and mills of the "surplus value" produced by the workers. That was his diagnosis. And to some extent, it was partly correct. Man's inhumanity to man has always been a factor in human affairs. Greed can never be defended—whether in business or in government. Sympathy for the underdog will always have its work to do—always, certainly, in the communist nations with their forced labor camps and human slavery.

The remedy advanced by Marx was to preach the gospel of hate, of the class struggle, of the redistribution of wealth, of the confiscation of property and its ownership and management by the state—which always means the politicians. But greed and exploitation are not cured by socialism. Stalin and Molotov live like oriental potentates, giving state dinners that would make Nero and Caligula green with envy—all this in the name of the down-trodden proletariat!

Greed, however, was not the main reason for the conditions which Marx described. If all the wealth of the owners of the mines and mills had been redistributed to the workers, it would have relieved their condition but slightly, and for but a short time.

So, the class struggle, as the remedy for these conditions, was wrong. What then was the *real* trouble, and what is the *true* remedy?

Low Productivity at Fault

The real trouble was the low productivity of the workers. And, as workers can be paid only out of production—whether in England a century ago or in Russia today—wages must be low and hours of work long when production is low.

Production was low because tools and equipment were poor; because human backs had to do what slaves of iron and steel do today here in America; because capital had not been accumulated to buy better tools; because freedom had so recently

*Based on a radio address (ABC Network, April 6, 1947). Revised 1953 for publication by FEE

emerged from centuries of feudalism that the inventors and scientists and businessmen had not had a chance to dream and to plan. They have had that chance today here in America.

Listen. In 1940, before war increased our production, it was estimated that electric power alone in this country was performing work equal to the labor of 500,000,000 men, each working eight hours a day. This is equal to nearly ten times the total human labor force employed in America and 50 times the number employed in manufacturing—and that leaves out steam power and gasoline power and windmill power, with their tremendous contributions for increasing the productivity of workers and thereby lifting burdens from human backs.

No wonder America outproduced the world in this last war! No wonder wages are higher here than anywhere in the world! While Marx preached the gospel of hate and the class struggle, America gave the green light to the Edisons, the Whitneys, the Burbanks, and the Fords.

James Watt, the inventor of the steam engine which revolutionized the modern world, and those who followed him in the competitive struggle to make a better engine and sell it for less, did more to take women out of the coal mines and off the towpaths of the canal boats, more to take children out of the factories, than did all the Socialists and Communists and politicians of the world combined.

Yet Watt's name would be unknown today if one of these despised capitalists, a man named Matthew Boulton, had not risked $150,000 on Watt's invention. Would he, by the way, dare take that risk under today's taxation?

A Measure of Progress

One measure of the progress of civilization is the extent to which mechanical horsepower and tools supplement human labor. The steam engine did more to outlaw slavery, both in England and America, than did all the political humanitarians put together.

The laboratories do far more for mankind than do the legislatures. If modern Americans were to go back to the same tools and horsepower that were available when Benjamin Franklin was trying to capture lightning from the sky, our production of wealth would at once go down 90 per cent; wages would go down in proportion; hours of labor would increase to the limit of human endurance; the population would necessarily decrease drastically; and nothing that governments or humanitarians or labor unions or Communists could do would prevent it.

I mentioned the discovery of gold in California in connection with *The Communist Manifesto* of 1848. With pick and shovel and a pan in which to wash gravel from gold, didn't men work long hours for a meager return, or for none? Didn't they sleep in filthy cabins and live on jerked meat, and weren't they often covered with lice?

If you saw that great motion picture, *The Covered Wagon*, you will recall the scenes of terrible toil—of men and women and children pulling the wagons across rivers and the trackless desert and over the Continental Divide; of families, on foot, pushing handcarts from the Mississippi to Salt Lake.

Yet, were those conditions due to greed and exploitation? No, the people were working for themselves. What was wrong? The answer is *poor tools*. The plow of the pioneer was a wooden plow, constantly breaking, constantly needing repairs.

Poor Transportation

In Vermont where I was raised, a man back in my great-grandfather's time dug some iron ore out of a hill. He put 100 pounds in a bag on his back and walked 80 miles through the wilderness to sell it to an iron foundry in Troy, New York; and then he walked home—an infinite expenditure of human energy for an insignificant return.

What was wrong? Greed? Exploitation? The class struggle? No—he was working for himself. There was no relationship of employer and employee; no one was stealing the "surplus product" of his labor. He kept all of it—and it was little indeed.

What was wrong? Why did he have to work so hard for so little? The answer is *poor tools*. Today the steam engine, in the form of the modern locomotive, could move his 100 pounds of iron ore 80 miles for four cents—or a ton, one mile for one cent! Railroads, paved highways, motor trucks, and automobiles have solved his problem and will do it even better in the days to come, *if we stay American*.

Let us say that James Watt and the man who financed his project were not humanitarians. Let us say that they put their brains and money together in a common enterprise for the profit motive. What of it? Was the result good or bad? Did *they* take the women out of the coal mines or did

Karl Marx, with his gospel of hate and the class struggle?

What did the profit motive do? It made Watt and his partner, and all who followed them, work to make better engines and to offer them at a lower price to get the market from their competitors.

Was the result good or bad? The profit motive is just as honorable and useful to mankind as is the wage motive. Both do infinite good.

The wage motive prompts men to become skilled and efficient so they can produce more and earn higher wages; and because they do, all mankind benefits.

The profit motive prompts men to make better tools and to cut costs in order to sell cheaper; and again, all mankind benefits.

The radio which only 25 years ago sold for $300 now sells for $30 or less, and it is a better radio.

Has the result of the competitive struggle in the field of radio been good or bad? The result has been good—humanitarian, if you please. It brings the news of the world, good music, and discussions of public affairs to the remotest farmhouses and to people on their sickbeds.

Not many centuries ago, starvation was a common occurrence—even in England, where 90 per cent of the people lived on the land. Was the conquest of starvation a humanitarian thing? What conquered it? Who conquered it? Karl Marx? No!

In America, the time in the field required to raise an acre of wheat has gone down from 60 hours of human labor in 1830 to two hours or less in 1930. What caused this decrease? The steel plow, the tractor, the harvester, better seed, the conquest of insects and plant diseases, and cheap transportation were responsible. Today, American wheat feeds millions in a Europe that is adopting the philosophy of Karl Marx!

Aluminum was so expensive in 1870 that Napoleon III of France had an aluminum table set—more valuable than gold—for state dinners. Today, aluminum is commonplace in the American kitchen.

The Answer

No, my friends, Karl Marx did not have the answer—he lifted no burdens from human backs. The answer is not in the class struggle. The answer is in competitive free enterprise. The answer is in the cooperation of inventor and investor; in the cooperation of the manager and the worker with his know-how. The answer is to substitute slaves of iron and steel for the strength of human backs. The answer is constitutional liberty, which sets men free and says that what any man honestly makes is his "to have and to hold."

Wages can be paid only out of the product; and the larger the production, the higher the wage. The more money that is invested in horsepower and equipment—the more capital that is put to work—the less will children and women and men have to work at killing toil. The *true* remedy for our troubles is *more* capitalism, not *less*.

22. THE GREAT MISTAKE OF KARL MARX*

Benjamin F. Fairless

Karl Marx completely rejected the only economic system on earth under which it is possible for the workers themselves to own, to control, and to manage directly the facilities of production. And shocking as the news may be to the disciples of Marx, that system is capitalism!

*Address at 35th Annual Meeting of the Pennsylvania State Chamber of Commerce, October 22, 1952

Here in America, ownership of our biggest and most important industries is sold daily, in little pieces, on the stock market. It is constantly changing hands; and if the workers of this country truly wish to own the tools of production, they can do so very simply.

They do not have to seize the government by force of arms. They do not even have to win an election. All in the world they have to do is to buy, in the open market, the capital stock of the corporation they want to own—just as millions of other Americans have been doing for many decades.

Now I imagine that some persons may say: "Oh, that's all very good in theory; but, of course, it isn't possible in practice. No group of workers could ever purchase the great multibillion dollar corporations that we have today."

Well, the other day I did a little simple arithmetic. The results may be as amazing to you as they were to me. At today's market prices, the employees of U. S. Steel could buy every share of the outstanding common stock of the Corporation just as easily and just as cheaply as they can purchase one of the higher-priced automobiles.

We have approximately 300,000 employees. That is not just steelworkers, of course. It is all our workers—including me. And together, they could buy all the common stock of the Corporation by purchasing just 87 shares apiece. At today's prices, the total cost of 87 shares is less than $3,500. And at today's wages, the average steelworker earns that much in approximately ten months.

Ten Dollars

By investing $10 a week apiece—which is about what our steelworkers gained in the recent wage increase—the employees of U. S. Steel could buy all of the outstanding common stock in less than seven years; and—except for the relatively small fixed sum that is paid in dividends on the preferred stock—our employees would then be entitled to receive all of those so-called "bloated profits" they have heard so much about. But here, I'm afraid they would be in for a disappointing surprise. At current rates, the total dividend on 87 shares is only $261 a year.

But in order to control U. S. Steel, the employees would not even have to purchase 87 shares apiece; they would need only to purchase enough of the stock to give them a voting majority. Then they could elect their own Board of Directors, fire the present management, put their own president in my job, and run the business to suit themselves.

Before they become too overjoyed at this prospect, however, they should be warned that they still would not be their own bosses; for the true bosses of every American business are its customers. And unless those customers are satisfied as to the quality and price of the product, there will be no business and there will be no jobs. But as long as the new owners of the company could keep the customers happy, they could run the show exactly as they pleased.

If the workers of America ever did own the tools of production, all of us would quickly learn a few fundamental and simple economic truths that have somehow escaped a great many of our people. We would learn that this endless conflict between owner and worker over the division of income is the sheerest, unadulterated folly.

Of the total sum which the employees and the owners of U. S. Steel divided between them last year, more than 92 per cent went to the employees, while less than 8 per cent went to the owners. Yet that small share which went to the owners was the total "rent" we paid them for all of the billions of dollars worth of plants and furnaces and facilities we used in making steel. And without these facilities, of course, our men could not have made any steel at all.

A Startling Fact

Suppose the workers take everything the owners receive for the use of these tools—suppose they wipe out all of the dividends completely and forever—what would each get? Less than a dollar a day! And meanwhile this process would destroy the company, destroy our jobs, work infinite harm upon a vast segment of our national economy, and wipe out the savings which more than 275,000 of our fellow Americans have invested in our business. And for what? For the price of about three cartons of cigarettes a week, apiece!

American workers will never improve their standard of living by grabbing the meager share which the owners get. They will improve their position only by producing more; for if we produce more goods, we shall have more goods to divide among ourselves. If we produce fewer goods, we shall have less to divide and less to live on.

And there we have the simple, economic truth of the matter. To live better, we must produce more; but production is the result of teamwork, not of conflict. We cannot produce by fighting each other and hating each other; for by doing that, we destroy ourselves. And we shall only achieve our fullest measure of production when we begin to understand that the interests of worker and owner are *not* antagonistic, but identical—that under our American system of enterprise, it is impossible over a period of time for one to prosper while the other suffers.

23. THE ROLE OF SAVINGS*

Brian Summers

One of the least appreciated aspects of the private enterprise system is the role of savings in increasing the wealth of all the people. That the savings of *some* can increase the wealth of *all* may seem, at first glance, paradoxical, so let us consider for a moment just what happens when an individual —call him Joe—forgoes a little spending to put a sum in the bank.

Some people say: "The money that Joe has saved is money that won't be spent. The decrease in Joe's consumption can only mean a commensurate decrease in production and a resulting rise in unemployment. Saving should really be discouraged."

Saving is a form of spending! Joe's money doesn't just sit in the bank; the bank must lend it to someone in order to earn money to pay Joe interest. This lending is not only a form of spending, it is, in fact, the only kind of spending that actually increases wealth: *investment.*

What happens when money is invested? Say a corporation goes to Joe's bank and borrows money to build a factory. The corporation then spends Joe's money on building materials, machines, tools, and labor. The money that Joe has saved winds up being spent just the same as if he had spent it himself. There is no decrease in production and no rise in unemployment. In fact, as we shall see, there is an *increase* in production and a *decline* in unemployment!

Soon the factory is complete. The corporation then proceeds to hire workers. Joe's savings have increased employment!

How does the corporation hire workers? By offering better conditions of employment than their competitors. Perhaps the most important condition—as far as workers are concerned—is the level of wages. In all probability, the workers in the new factory have been lured by higher salaries. Joe's savings, whether he realizes it or not, have increased the wealth of workers in a factory he probably has never seen.

"You said that savings increase the wealth of *all* the people. What about the 210 million Americans who don't work in Joe's factory?"

Competitive Bidding

Consider first the workers in competing factories. If these factories don't want to lose their workers to new factories, they had better raise their wages. Joe's savings have increased salaries throughout an entire industry!

As for workers in other fields, we should remember that most of them are potential factory workers. If you want to keep your best farm hand from going off to work in Joe's industry or taking a job that has been vacated by someone else who went off to work in Joe's industry, you had better give him a raise. Competition among employers means that Joe's savings, and the savings of millions of other Americans, raise the wages of *all* workers.

"That is still not everybody! How about people who don't work?"

Every man, woman, and child—worker and nonworker—is a consumer. The end of economic activity—saving, factory building, working, and all the rest—is *consumption.* We should always keep this *end* in mind. The higher wages we have talked about would prove meaningless if they didn't result in increased consumption.

Joe's savings benefit *everyone* because the factory, machines, and tools they helped build are designed to produce goods that consumers will prefer to those already being offered on the market. The

*From *The Freeman*, May 1974

corporation that borrowed money from Joe's bank took a financial risk because they think that they can satisfy consumers better than their competitors. In other words, they hope to give the consumer more for his money. If they fail, then the loss is theirs. If they succeed, then consumers consume more of what *they* want and thus enjoy a higher standard of living. The consumer—each and every one of us—is the final judge and ultimate winner.

"Savings seem to be pretty good after all. What should be done to encourage more saving?"

Instead of doing things to encourage saving, we should undo things that discourage it. In particular, the law itself is probably the greatest hindrance potential savers face. Let us make a brief survey of some of the ways in which the law discourages saving.

To begin with, people can't save money they no longer have. Every dollar that goes in taxes is a dollar that won't be saved. Add up all the taxes that Joe pays, and he may find himself withdrawing from, rather than adding to, his bank account.

Tax Disincentives

In addition to the general level of taxation, several specific taxes are especially discouraging to savers. Corporate profits taxes, capital gains taxes, and taxes on dividends and bank account interest hit the saver particularly hard and must be taken into account by every potential saver.

High as taxes are, government spending is even higher. The difference, of course, is "made up" by running fiat money off the government printing presses—inflation. And inflation, combined with other ramifications of over-extended government, is enough to give even the most devoted saver cause to re-think his frugal habits.

The saver sees inflation galloping along faster than legal limits on interest rates. Even though he actually has lost money, in terms of purchasing power, he finds himself forced to pay taxes on his "earnings."

The saver sees inflation increasing the paper value of his capital holdings. When he sells his holdings he must pay capital gains taxes—even though his "capital gains," in terms of real wealth, actually may have been capital losses.

The saver sees inflation increasing the replacement costs of capital equipment—machines, spare parts, tools—while depreciation allowances are determined by original costs. He finds that depreciation allowances have become inadequate to pay for new equipment to replace the old.

The saver sees inflation increasing the paper profits of his corporation. In particular, inventory "profits"—the difference between the cost of producing an item and the cost of later replacing it in inventory after it has been sold—are a direct result of inflation. Were all these inventory "profits" available for investment in new inventory, the corporation could at least hold its own. However, almost half these "profits," on the average, wind up as corporate profits taxes. Thus, the saver may find his corporation losing money and paying profits taxes at the same time.

Inflation itself, even without being combined with various governmental controls and taxes, is discouraging to potential savers. With prices rising, people are encouraged to make purchases before prices go any higher, rather than to save for future purchases.

This brief survey of ways in which the law discourages saving is, of course, by no means complete. However, I would like to conclude with one factor that can never be measured, but which is nonetheless very real. This is the factor of uncertainty. In recent years, the United States government has grown so interventionistic that every few months the president is announcing "strong new" economic measures. Who knows what is next? Already we hear congressmen calling for a virtual nationalization of oil companies. Who is going to invest under such circumstances? To complete the destruction of the American economy, the government does not have to expropriate the means of production. It merely has to make conditions so onerous and so frightful that no one will dare invest in private enterprise.

A free market, and the belief that the market will continue to be free, is all the encouragement savers need.

24. TOOLS*

Jasper E. Crane

A prominent American industrialist made a trip through the Orient recently, and in every country he visited from Russia to Hong Kong and Japan he met and talked with the ruler of that country. In every one of these conversations he would ask what he called the "$64 question"—"You have heard of the high standard of living in the United States. What do you believe to be the cause of America's prosperity?" Most of those interviewed replied that it was our abundant natural resources with plentiful raw materials. The industrialist would then state that this was quite untrue, that some of these countries had more natural resources per capita than we did in America. The ruler of the country would then flounder about, but not one gave a reasonable reply. For instance, Nehru of India, a great man with complete authority over more than four hundred million people, thoughtfully considered the question and finally came out with the reply, "You're lucky."

Yet, the true answer to the $64 question is simple—the provision of tools in a free country.

That answer is clearly manifested in our own country's history as well as in other past and contemporary events. At the end of the eighteenth century, immediately after Independence, Americans turned to making things which the British, with their policy of mercantilism, had not permitted the colonials to do. There developed a great center of industry on the little Brandywine River, with 120 mills on the last twenty miles of that stream. Elsewhere, the growth of manufacturing industry throughout the country was prodigious. The tremendous release of energy among free men was the potent factor in manufacturing enterprises throughout the new nation. "Yankee ingenuity" was often spoken of, but the outburst of energy and the reasons for it have seldom been explained. It proceeded at an accelerating pace.

Throughout human history there have been occasional occurrences of increased freedom in various places, always accompanied by increased production and a better standard of living. The correct answer to the $64 question explains why this is always so.

We have recently witnessed the phenomenal progress of Western Germany. Prostrated by military defeat and in dire trouble in 1948, its situation seemed hopeless. Vice Chancellor Erhard consulted W. Ropke, the great economist at Geneva, and he advised, "Try freedom." Thereupon, despite the remonstrance of American officials in Germany, controls were taken off of wages and prices. In this climate of freer enterprise, the rebound of the German economy was theatrical. West Germany soon became the most prosperous country in Europe, with a much higher standard of living for themselves and for over six million refugees from communist countries. Moreover, they brought into their country great numbers of workers, particularly from Greece and Italy.

All goods and services are produced by changing the form, condition, and place of raw materials with the aid of human energy and tools. These are the three factors of production—human energy, raw materials, tools.

About 78 per cent of all private goods and services produced in the United States in 1965 came from firms using the corporate form of organization. The remaining 22 per cent of production covered the output of nonincorporated agriculture, shopkeepers, professions, personal and business service industries, and other unincorporated enterprises.

The relative importance of the three basic factors of production in noncorporate enterprises is difficult to judge, for lack of statistics, but some figures are available for corporate industry.

Tools are instruments of production (in addition to natural resources and human energy, mental

*From *The Freeman*, March 1968

and physical)—cultivated land, mechanical power, buildings, machinery, equipment, and apparatus of all sorts.

The use of tools by all animals other than man is practically nil. They use unchanged the raw materials presented by nature. Charles Kettering told the story of travelers in Africa who would sit around a bonfire to counteract the chill of the evening. When they retired to their tents, monkeys would come down from the trees to warm themselves by the fire. And, he added, no monkey was ever known to put a piece of wood on the fire!

One of Aesop's fables tells of the quarrel between the organs of digestion, each claiming that it did the major part of digestion and was not properly rewarded for its work. Their proper proportions of the digestive process can hardly be determined. However, the factors or elements of production of goods and services can be approximated by considering that a worker in the highly industrialized United States produces at least twenty times as much as a coolie laborer with only a tool such as a basket or other simple instrument. The toolless coolie is paid a few cents a day; the average American factory worker received $20.88 for an eight-hour day in 1965.

A prominent clergyman visiting Egypt found his sense of justice and decency offended by the fact that the "fellah" was paid only twelve cents a day. Yet, examination of the total income of Egypt showed that if it were divided equally to all the people, the daily wage would be thirteen cents a day. It wasn't a question of distribution of income to be corrected by a sense of charity; for that was all the "fellah" could earn in the Egyptian economy. What they needed was more tools.

In America, the corporate investment in tools averaged over $12,000 per worker last year, and in some industries, such as petroleum, it ran as high as $97,000 per worker.

Analysis of the facts of private production in the United States indicates that raw materials—the value of ore, oil, and minerals in the ground; uncultivated land; standing timber in the forests; naturally occurring raw foodstuffs; and the like—account for about 2 per cent of the final price paid for goods and services in a free market. In some products, such as textiles, raw materials may constitute as much as 6 per cent of this final value; but the average for all goods and services seems to be approximately 2 per cent. About 4 per cent of end values may be ascribed to unassisted human energy, physical and mental. About 94 per cent of the value of private goods and services produced in the United States, therefore, may be attributed to the use of tools. This high figure attributable to tools may surprise those who have not studied this matter; but it will be realized that production in other times and, sadly, even today in some places, depends on slave labor and crude tools.

Today in the United States, every worker has sixty "slaves" working for him in the form of mechanical power. Several times more power is released by the automobile than by all other mechanical energy and only a small portion of this motor car energy is used for production purposes. So we modify the statement above, the correct figure being close to twenty mechanical slaves for each worker, and that worker is paid seven to ten times as much as is paid out in dividends.

The truth of this is evident when we consider how much useful work a man can do on a farm or garden with only his bare hands as tools, and how dependent we are upon even the simple farm tools for winning livelihood from the land. It is clearly revealed when one sees in backward lands farmers plowing with a wooden plow or sharpened stick. One must realize that the amount of a farmer's production has been multiplied many times by the complicated and efficient farm machinery available today in the United States.

The proof of these assertions is clearly shown by the fact that when the white man came to America the estimated Indian population was two hundred thousand—all the country could support in their practically toolless economy. Today, there are two hundred million inhabitants (including almost four hundred thousand Indians) with a per capita income twenty-five times that of the Indian before the white man came.

The production of automobiles is truly marvelous. The assembly line was one of man's greatest inventions. A leading automobile manufacturer some years ago experimentally constructed an ordinary car by bringing simple tools to the point of manufacture, similar to the way in which a house is built. The result was a cost of $10,000 for that car, whereas his company was selling the model at the time for less than $2,000.

Another instance of the value of the best tools was given to me while visiting one of the largest motor car manufacturers in a foreign country a few years ago. The manager of the plant, and a great admirer of American methods, said that it cost them eighteen cents a pound to produce a car of the Chevrolet type; whereas, in Michigan the cost was ten cents a pound for the same type. Yet, the American worker received three times the daily wage of the worker in the plant abroad. They still had a long way to go in reducing manual operations and using better tools.

How Are Tools Supplied?

In a free country, investors in companies supply tools for use by the worker who has not sufficient capital to buy them himself. Such companies are in competition with other corporations in the same line of business. The payment investors receive for the use of tools they supply for manufacturing purposes averaged about 4.8 per cent of the market price of the goods produced over the past decade.

In a socialist country, government supplies the tools, but at a high cost. For instance, according to figures for Russia released some twenty years ago, the government in effect owned all tools and supplied them to the worker at markups averaging over 15 per cent of sales. Thus, the Russian worker at that time, although he did not realize it, was paying three times as much for his tools as did the American.

So-called "surplus income," both private and corporate, is not only a mighty force in helping to finance charitable, community, educational, and religious organizations, but is the principal source of the funds for providing tools.

Socialists claim that they will finance their services by appropriating "surplus income," by which they mean corporation profits and private income beyond the necessities of life. Every such effort has failed. Bismarck, taking over the Sozialpolitik from the socialists, thought to finance it by seizing the railroads and employing their income for the government's social services. Soon, railroad income turned into deficits. Heavier taxation followed and, finally, war and disaster.

Britain employed the Marxian formula of heavy and steeply graduated income taxes. This destroyed private fortunes. Clement Atlee boasted that while there once had been several thousand personal incomes of $16,000 or more per year after taxes, now there were only sixteen such fortunes left in the country. The deficits of British socialism have outrun the loans and gifts from America. Now the "luxuries" of the people—"beer, baccy, and bedding"—are taxed to fuel the socialist state. The resulting poverty, particularly in formerly thrifty Scotland, is appalling. But it is the consequence of government ownership and control of industry. And in Britain, as in other welfare states, what cannot be taxed directly is confiscated through inflation.

So-called "surplus income" is important in an economy, for out of corporate profits and the savings of the people comes the money needed to buy the tools. In fact, successful corporations and other cooperative enterprises retain much of their income for the renewal, improvement, and expansion of tools. This vital point is often ignored, people imagining that once an industry is fully operating, it needs no further supply of tools. The success of any industry depends on keeping its tools up-to-date by repairs, replacement, and improvement. This vital supply of equipment comes from adequate charges for depreciation and obsolescence, from income retained and invested in business, and from additional capital supplied by investors. Corporation dividends, along with personal savings such as are invested in savings banks and life insurance, are important phases in the process of providing tools.

The most valuable public-service income in any country is the part of savings used for buying tools. Capital formation in plant and properties is the life blood of a successful corporation, enabling it to continue and increase its services to customers. If earnings and savings are insufficient to meet the needs and growth of the business, the corporation goes downhill or succumbs. And a nation that thus cuts off the source of tools is destined to lose position in the world and dwell in poverty.

Those of socialistic philosophy object that the use of tools is at the expense of employment, that it throws people out of work. Historically, in England, the early use of labor-saving machinery was violently fought and the new equipment often destroyed on the ground that men were losing their jobs. The record shows, however, that labor-saving machinery not only lifted drudgery from men's backs but also greatly increased the production of goods and services, creating new jobs and greater income for all.

That the process of industrialization, the saving and investing in tools, is further advanced in the United States than elsewhere explains our high and rising wage rates and level of living. And of total corporate income in the country, 85 per cent goes to employees—the users of tools—and 15 per cent to the suppliers.

So, let us beware of foolish talk about the evils of this tool-using age! Let us not kill the goose that lays the golden eggs!

25. THE LIBERATION OF WOMEN*

Bettina Bien Greaves

"Vive la différence," say the French in referring to the difference between the sexes due to physical and physiological causes. This difference can be a source of delight to those free to enjoy it, but can generate ill-feeling and friction between the sexes if they are compelled by law to ignore it.[1] Our physical and physiological characteristics are bound to have economic consequences, which will persist so long as human life continues as we know it.

Legal and political rights, without distinction as to sex, have been recognized gradually by the governments of most civilized nations of the world. By legislation and common law decisions, women have acquired freedom on a par with men to act, own property, and make contracts in their own behalf. (This freedom is being eroded by the present trend toward socialism—to the disadvantage of both men and women. Special government privileges and subsidies, progressive taxation, legislation limiting the right of contract, hours of work, and so on, have already seriously interfered with the rights of property owners and the freedom of contract. But this is another story.) For all practical purposes, laws now deal with men and women pretty much the same.

Economic Opportunities

In recent decades, economic and professional opportunities have been opened to women. Step-by-step, insofar as social customs have permitted, and within the limitations imposed by the "différence" between the sexes which at least the French appreciate, women in this country are relatively free. They may now compete with men, each to the extent of her abilities, in seeking their chosen goals—economically and professionally.

The tremendous advances, which have made it possible for women to achieve recognition as persons—legally, politically, economically, and professionally—are undoubtedly due in large part to capitalistic contributions. Savers, inventors, and producers, operating in a relatively free market economy risking their own private property in the hope of profit, supplied the goods and services which have freed women from the daily drudgery and heavy manual labor expected of them for centuries simply to fulfill their roles as sexual companions, mothers to their children, and homemakers for their families. The improved production and preparation of food, more efficient transport, better retail outlets, and inventions of modern household appliances have given women more time to pursue interests outside the home.

In this day of push button kitchens, automatic timers, electric refrigeration, home freezers, mechanical beaters and choppers, prepared foods and instant mixes, a housewife cannot begin to conceive of the many strenuous chores her grandmothers and great-grandmothers coped with daily. Imagine a home without heat or electricity. Imagine a kitchen without a stove, refrigerator, or running water. Suppose there were no corner stores or supermarkets with milk, butter, bread, meat, vegetables, or soap. Think of a life when each family had to grow its own food, gather the fuel to cook it, tote all water, produce the textiles, and sew, patch, and mend the family clothing.

Early Household Hints

Early cookbooks offer helpful hints to save the housewife's time and energy, hints which no modern bride need consider. For instance, keep kettles of water, both hot and cold, handy always in the kitchen. Pine wood is an economical fuel for heating ovens but hard wood makes much hotter coals. Lamps will have a less disagreeable smell if you dip your wick-yarn in strong hot vinegar, and dry

*From *The Freeman*, February 1971

it. Teach children to prepare and braid straw for their own bonnets, and their brothers' hats. Fresh meat brought into the house should be carefully covered from the flies, put in the coldest place in the cellar, and then cooked promptly—especially in summer. Save all the nice pieces of fat to make lard, and put those that are not so nice into the soap grease.

The earliest cookbooks and housekeeping manuals appeared only about 200 years ago. Few women could read before then; and how-to-do-it information, so much of which was needed to run a household smoothly, was passed along by example and by word-of-mouth.

One early cookbook published in this country was *The American Frugal Housewife* by Mrs. Lydia Maria Childs (12th ed., 1832). The housewife of that day cooked over an open fire, roasted meat on a spit, or baked in a reflecting oven before the fire or in a brick oven built in the chimney. To fire up the oven was such a chore that one or two days a week were set aside just for baking. With good planning, five successive bakings could be done in the oven with one heating: "The bread first—then the puddings—afterward pastry—then cake and gingerbread—and lastly, custards." This last suggestion comes from Mrs. M. H. Cornelius, whose book, *The Young Housekeeper's Friend*, appeared in 1859. At the time she wrote, brick ovens were going out, cooking stoves and ranges coming in. Yet, boiled dinners, stews, soups, and steamed cakes and puddings prepared on top of the stove were still more popular with the cooks than cakes which called for firing up the oven.

In 1832, Mrs. Childs wrote for the rural housewife who had her own vegetable garden, a few fruit trees, and chickens. The whole family shared in the household chores, of course, and most housewives had extra help from a hired girl or a female relative living with the family. Yet, the responsibility for the work was the housewife's. She grew the herbs for flavoring, gathered the eggs, and ofttimes milked the cow. She baked with yeast of her own making, or used eggs or baking soda and cream of tartar for leavening—baking powder was not for sale until about 1850. She did the family's cooking, and did it all with crude utensils. She beat eggs with a fork or a wire whisk, and elbow grease—the rotary egg beater did not come into general use until the second half of the nineteenth century.

Housewives had to bake the family's bread regularly. This meant mixing the dough, usually in the evening, setting it to rise overnight, and kneading it "very thoroughly." Mrs. Cornelius wrote, "A half an hour is the least time to be given to kneading a baking of bread, unless you prefer, after having done this till it ceases to stick to your hands, to chop it with a chopping-knife four or five hundred strokes. An hour's kneading is not too much." Bread was the staff of life and good bread was a source of pride to the housewife.

Lack of refrigeration was a continual challenge. The housewife took care to use things before they spoiled or to find satisfactory ways to preserve them. Before the canning industry developed in the late 1800's, she had to preserve fruits and vegetables in season to be assured of provisions year round. In 1859, Mrs. Cornelius advised putting preserves in wide-necked bottles, pasting paper over the tops, and then brushing egg white over the paper with a feather to seal the bottles and discourage mold.

First, Get a Cow

The nineteenth century housewife had to be a Jill of all trades. The industrial revolution with its increased specialization and division of labor barely ruffled the surface of traditional housekeeping practices. The 1859 housewife purchased a few more household items than her grandmother could have in 1832. But she still had to kill her own fowl, cut up the family's meat, salt it, smoke it, or otherwise cure it and keep it safe from bugs and animals. To be sure of good dairy products, she was told: "The first requisite is to have a good cow." Keeping a cow added to the household chores. Someone had to feed the cow and milk her, day in and day out, set the milk for the cream to rise, and churn butter at least twice a week. Without refrigeration, keeping milk, cream, butter, and dairy utensils sweet was a continual worry. Now that dairy products are sold in stores, packaged and ready to use, men do most of this heavy manual labor on a mass production basis, using methods developed and equipment produced with the aid of increased savings and investments.

Doing the family wash was another backbreaking chore in the nineteenth century. First the soap had to be prepared from lye made out of wood ashes, and fat and grease saved from cooking. The water had to be toted and heated, heavy wash tubs filled, with countless trips back and forth to the stove. After the clothes were sorted, the finest and less soiled things were washed first, the coarser and dirtier items later in the same water. Most pieces were scrubbed by hand on a washboard. The white things were boiled. After washing, rinsing, boiling, wringing, bluing, and starching as necessary, the clothes were wrung and hung outdoors on a line. Doing the family wash took another full day of the housewife's time.

Ironing consumed most of a third day each week. The flat irons and special "polishing irons" for final touchups had to be heated on the stove and reheated again and again as they cooled.

Then Came Automation

The kitchen stove or range using wood or coal gradually came into use in the mid-nineteenth century. These had advantages over the open fireplace and the brick oven. With the use of gas and the construction of gas lines in the late 1800's, new cooking jets became available—gas ovens came considerably later—making meal preparations a little easier. The development of electricity, refrigeration, large scale specialized farming, improved transportation, professional bakeries, and the expansion of retail outlets have further liberated women from the grueling household labor which had been their lot in life. Automatic washing machines and dryers have taken the drudgery out of doing the family wash. Moth-proofed woolens and new miracle fibers have simplified the care of the family's clothing. Vacuum cleaners, floor polishers, and local dry cleaning establishments help to keep homes and their furnishings clean the year round, doing away with the need to scour the house and everything in it from top to bottom spring and fall. Refrigeration and other effective ways of preserving foods have freed the family menu from dependence on the season. When compared with her nineteenth century counterpart, the modern housewife is truly liberated from grinding household drudgery and endless kitchen chores.

When a housewife presses a button or turns a switch on a modern household appliance, she has at her command the labor of countless specialists —savers, investors, inventors, producers, and merchants—each of whom then helps with her daily chores. In effect, they help tote the wood when she turns up the thermostat. A twist of the faucet draws the water. Turning a dial will fire the oven. A push-button machine will wash, rinse, and wring the weekly wash. With a trip to a grocery store, the housewife can in effect grow the family's food, milk the cow, churn the butter, make the cheese, gather the eggs, knead and bake the bread, grind the spices, kill the poultry, cure the meat, preserve fruits and vegetables, and make the soap.

Capital, the Key

Each person in the world differs from every other person. Thanks to these differences, everyone benefits if each of us is free to concentrate in the field of his (or her) greatest aptitude and interest. There is some specialization and division of labor even in small groups and primitive communities. But under capitalism, with private property and the freedom to move, invest, and exchange goods and services throughout large areas and among increasingly large populations, it has been possible to develop and exploit our differences more fully than ever before, to everyone's advantage. It was this complex economic system, developed on the basis of highly specialized division of labor, which liberated women from their traditional household chores.

Women are different from men—and always will be. The woman of the 1970's has gained recognition as an individual under law. She may own property, make contracts and, thanks to the development of capitalism, now has time to pursue her special aptitudes and interests outside the home and thus compete with men economically and professionally. Rather than trying to compel denial by law of the physical and physiological differences between the sexes, let's acknowledge and accept them philosophically as the French do: "Vive la différence."

Note

[1] For a discussion of some effects of prohibiting discrimination on the basis of sex in economic dealings, see Gary North's "The Feminine Mistake: The Economics of Women's Liberation," *The Freeman*, January, 1971.

26. INDUSTRIALISM: FRIEND OR FOE?*

V. Orval Watts

Capitalistic industry today stands before Judge Public Opinion charged with various high crimes and misdemeanors.

Among the charges are (1) that it makes those who take part in it materialistic in tastes, interests, and ways of living; (2) that it standardizes people—turns them into robots, kills individualism; (3) that it concentrates "power" in the hands of a few who use this power with little regard for the welfare of others.

Those making the charges demand increasing government action to punish and prevent these alleged offenses against the common weal. Unfortunately, all too many Americans are ready to cast their ballots for the prosecution when they enter the polling booths on election days.

Yet, nearly all Americans show by their daily conduct that they really *like* what modern industry —big and little—does; and the vast majority of mankind look to the most industrialized, free-enterprise nation—the United States—as a Mecca which they would like most of all to visit and if possible make their permanent home.

Most people, worldwide, for example, like what modern industry produces. From chewing gum to cameras, from aspirin to automobiles, they buy machine-made goods. Moreover, they buy, often and abundantly, the products of the free-enterprise elite, that is, the products of the industrial giants; and they generally buy with confidence that they will get a fair deal. Similarly, where they can, millions of housewives go to the super-markets, chain stores, and big department stores for the necessaries of life, as well as for thousands of comforts, gadgets, and sundries from toothpaste to tissues, from soap to stockings, and from vitamins to vacuum cleaners. And when shoppers go to small stores, or dealers, they usually buy goods that big companies, in some way or other, have helped to make.

Millions of these customers also earn their wages and salaries in the employ of the biggest manufacturing, commercial, and financial firms where free-enterprise industrialism is supposedly doing most to turn them into dehumanized robots. Fully one-fourth of the working force of the United States prefer the wages, working conditions, and "fringe benefits" of the big employers; and I never met any of these who seemed ashamed of his employer. On the contrary, they generally appear proud to be associated with one of these outstanding enterprises.

More millions of Americans, including millions of employees and customers, also invest their savings in the stocks and bonds of these big companies. Or they put their money in banks, insurance companies, and other agencies which buy the securities of big companies in the belief that these are likely to be especially safe and profitable ways to invest the funds entrusted to them.

Big Businesses Foster Small Businesses

Millions of small businesses buy, sell, and service the products of the biggest industrial companies; and hundreds of thousands of small producers act as suppliers for the "big boys." For example, the United States Steel Co. buys from 50,000 small and medium-size concerns and sells to 100,000 more.

Thus, small and medium-size establishments do most of the business in the United States, the world's most industrialized country. A firm with less than 500 employees is a small or medium-size business by U.S. standards. Such firms, together with farmers and the self-employed, account for two-thirds or more of the total work force outside of government service.

*From *The Freeman*, April 1973

The fact is that big business gives rise to smaller businesses. So the "Big Four" in the automobile industry create opportunities for many thousands of dealers in cars and accessories, car "laundries," and garages, and the big oil producers and refineries create opportunities for more thousands of service stations. Furthermore, the growth of big business provides the jobs, income, and materials necessary for new enterprises to develop and market new products. Some of these may rise from a basement or garage to skyscraper status; but they all *start* small, and most of them *remain* small.

Without large-scale industrialism and big business, in fact, America would be still in the horse-and-buggy age, and so too would be the rest of the world. The industrial giants—railroad companies, producers of steel, aluminum and copper, auto manufacturers, producers of farm machinery and chemicals—these built the foundations of our modern economy, and they are still maintaining our unprecedented affluence.

We should remember, too, that mass merchandising is essential for large-scale industry. The great selling organizations—mail-order houses, department stores, chain stores, and supermarkets—have brought down the costs of trade as the great industrial organizations have reduced costs of extraction, transportation, and processing. *These "distributors" are as truly productive and as necessary for economic progress as the mines and factories.* The same may be said for finance. Without large-scale banking, investment, insurance, and brokerage there would be neither large-scale merchandising nor large-scale output of goods to market.

But is this affluence provided by modern industry too costly in terms of the human spirit and individual dignity? Does mass production turn human beings into materialistic, standardized robots?

Mass Production Means Mass Prosperity

True, "mass production" means standardization of products and methods, and this mass production implies a mass market. It is production for "the masses." At first thought—without looking at the facts—this seems to mean standardization of people—turning them into faceless non-persons. Yet, this mass production by way of standardization is precisely what the communist rulers of Russia and China want for their subjects because *it means mass prosperity*.

What big concerns arise in freedom to serve only a wealthy few? *In freedom,* big business must produce mainly for factory workers, farmers, stenographers, school teachers, bookkeepers, sales clerks, mechanics, waiters, government employees, carpenters, and plumbers, along with other modestly paid producers and their dependents. These buy most of the products of industry because they get most of the total income of this nation.

And let us not forget that the pensioners and "reliefers" also have radios, TV sets, and drip-dry shirts, along with the necessaries of life. If any American goes barefoot, it is from choice, not necessity, for our mass production has made shoes so abundant that Americans commonly give away or throw into the trash cans better shoes than the shoddy new footwear the victims of Communist "planning" can buy in their dingy shops.

But besides an abundance of the necessaries and comforts of life, and besides the great variety of recreations and entertainments, free-enterprise industry and business provide the high purchasing power and leisure necessary for cultivation of the arts and literature, for schooling and research, for books and free lectures on every conceivable subject. They provide these on a scale never known before the advent of modern industrialism, and have made them available even to the poorest of our population.

The victims of communist rule covet these fruits of free-enterprise capitalism; and their rulers try hard to establish the same great industries and marketing organizations that we have in the United States. And they do get a certain bigness and large-scale industry. But their industries, big and little, lack efficiency; and lacking efficiency, they progress only at a painfully slow rate—and I do mean *painfully*. Consequently, communist countries lag behind the U.S., economically, as far as they did 30 or 40 years ago.

But we come back to the question: does mass production and mass prosperity produce a mechanized, standardized, collectivized, materialistic people?

Industry Fosters Personality

In the answer to this question we find a strange paradox. *In freedom,* mass production actually personalizes—individualizes—both consumer goods and the uses we make of them. It continually creates a greater variety of occupations and greater opportunity for individuals to choose the kind of work and working conditions which best fit their particular interests and abilities. It provides increasing opportunities for intellectual and artistic pursuits, for extending each person's circle of friends, for increasing awareness and sensitivity, that is, for the development of personality. In short, modern free-enterprise industrialism *reduces* the amount of drudgery, the long hours of monotonous, mind-dulling toil, and the subsistence levels of poverty which held the vast majority of mankind at a near-animal level of mind and spirit for untold aeons of the past. It enables humans to become *persons.*

Furthermore, it is the opportunity for individuals to satisfy a vast variety of tastes and pursue countless individual interests—intellectual, artistic, literary and social, as well as recreational—that provides the drive and enterprise which in *freedom* gives rise to rapid economic progress, with its mass production and giant business organizations.

Look in on any typical American assemblage—a roomful of students, a concert audience, a crowd of diners—what do you see? Outside the ranks of the few militant revolutionaries, it is hard to find two persons dressed in any way alike. Similarly, if you ask Americans about their life experiences and expectations, their work and their leisure pursuits, you will find individual variations too numerous to list.

Where else but in highly industrialized America, the land where most of the giant businesses arose and flourish, will you find the *variety* of consumers' goods offered for sale, the *variety* of jobs, the *variety* of leisure pursuits, the proportion of the population in colleges and universities, the amount and *variety* of scientific research, the *wide circles of friends* possessed by everyone who wants them, the amount of *travel,* and the widespread *awareness* of human problems and opportunities? And, insofar as other nations permit freedom for private enterprise, they correspondingly provide opportunity for development of more humane and individualized personalities.

Communism Standardizes and Dehumanizes

This points to a seldom-noted paradox: When they gain power, as in Soviet Russia and Red China, socialist authorities impose on their people, by force, the very same mass production methods which they say make robots of workers in capitalistic countries. In fact, they often carry the standardization much further than in capitalistic countries and in more burdensome fashion, as, for example, in use of the manual labor of women street sweepers and construction workers. But despite thefts, loans and subsidies from capitalistic countries, and despite ruthless coercion to get labor and capital from their subjects, they fail to achieve the prosperity necessary for individualized living—except for a small minority of privileged bureaucrats and their favorites of the moment (ballet dancers, mistresses, champion athletes or chess players, and a few scientists).

The reason for the continued deprivations and standardized ways of living for the masses in communist countries should be obvious. Centralized planning, *imposed by legal force,* suppresses individual experimentation, reduces individual incentive, and denies individual responsibility. Indeed, suppressing individual freedom to experiment is precisely what socialists mean by "planned production."

Communists regard people as no more than complex machines to be manipulated by physical means as are inanimate tools. Or they look on the proletarian masses as rather dull-witted creatures to be fed, stalled and herded about as domesticated animals. Therefore, although communist governments impose on their subjects much standardization and some mechanization, they so dehumanize their people that they lose the individual enterprise necessary for mass prosperity and general economic progress. They have achieved a measure of *technical* ("material") progress; but they provide less opportunity for developing individual talent, personality, character, and intellect than prevailed three generations ago under czarist rule.

Despite the standardization of machines, materials, and gadgets, *free-enterprise* industrialism provides increasing opportunities for "the masses" to develop, individually, the highest human qualities. This freedom for individuation in these United States is precisely why we have so much big industry, big business, mass production, mass prosperity, and mass opportunity. It releases human energies and imagination which are the driving and directing factors in progress.

Why Communist Economies Are Backward

Under socialism and communism, on the other hand, the "planners" dictatorially restrict individuation of products and personal pursuits. As a result, they fail to develop the mass production and universal affluence which they so much covet and try to produce without regard for human life and human dignity. It is under socialism, or communism, therefore, that we find the actual concentration of power and rampant abuses of power. Only under socialism or communism can the few force the rise of great industries to serve their whims about what standardized goods their subjects should have, including the weapons for imperialism, war, and their own enslavement.

For these reasons, the victims of this concentrated power remain poor—drably dressed, badly housed, misinformed, restricted, standardized, materialistic and collectivized. As a consequence, their masters must maintain mine fields, great walls, and millions of armed guards to keep their people at home.

If we can understand these facts and the reasons for them, perhaps we can enlarge the freedom for enterprise which this and other "capitalistic" nations have so well demonstrated is necessary for all truly *human* ("humane") progress.

Freedom Depends on Understanding

I say we can "enlarge freedom" advisedly; and I mean that we can enlarge it everywhere that humans congregate.

Complete freedom is as unattainable as complete understanding. In fact, we gain in freedom—freedom from trespass, freedom from infringement of individual rights—*only* as we progress in understanding of human nature, human conduct, individual rights and responsibilities.

How many Americans, for example, understand that minimum-wage laws restrict the freedom of our young people and the less skilled adults? And how much thought do we give to the demoralizing effects of this tragic denial of opportunity to bear and discharge self-responsibility?

We know that "unemployment"—useless or destructive dissipation of human energies—demoralizes its victims. But how often do we hear or read of anyone relating the sudden rise in teen-age unemployment, especially among black teenagers, to the hikes in minimum-wage rates in the past 20 years in this country?

Yet, that relation is clear and obvious; and time and time again, research has verified it as well as any cause-and-effect relationship can be demonstrated in human affairs.

We hear and read that "welfare" is demoralizing millions of our fellow citizens. But how often do we stop to think that the confiscation of some two-thirds or more of business profits by taxes is restricting the freedom of every competent employer to offer jobs to unemployed job-seekers?

I repeat: *in freedom*, industrialism provides increasing opportunity for humans to develop morally, intellectually, physically, and esthetically; and this freedom is far from complete in these United States or anywhere else on earth.

But although it is an unattainable ideal, it is imperative that man pursue it. For that pursuit requires of us the pursuit of understanding that is the very wellspring of all human progress.

Wisdom is the principal thing; therefore get wisdom; and with all thy getting get understanding. And ye shall know the truth, and the truth shall make you free.

27. THE ECONOMIC ROLE OF SAVING AND CAPITAL GOODS*

Ludwig von Mises

As the popular philosophy of the common man sees it, human wealth and welfare are the products of the cooperation of two primordial factors: nature and human labor. All the things that enable man to live and to enjoy life are supplied either by nature or by work or by a combination of nature-given opportunities with human labor. As nature dispenses its gifts gratuitously, it follows that all the final fruits of production, the consumers' goods, ought to be allotted exclusively to the workers whose toil has created them. But unfortunately in this sinful world conditions are different. There the "predatory" classes of the "exploiters" want to reap although they have not sown. The landowners, the capitalists, and the entrepreneurs appropriate to themselves what by rights belongs to the workers who have produced it. All the evils of the world are the necessary effect of this originary wrong.

Such are the ideas that dominate the thinking of most of our contemporaries. The socialists and the syndicalists conclude that in order to render human affairs more satisfactory it is necessary to eliminate those whom their jargon calls the "robber barons," i.e., the entrepreneurs, the capitalists, and the landowners, entirely; the conduct of all production affairs ought to be entrusted either to the social apparatus of compulsion and coercion, the state (in the Marxian terminology called Society), or to the men employed in the individual plants or branches of production.

Other people are more considerate in their reformist zeal. They do not intend to expropriate those whom they call the "leisure class" entirely. They want only to take away from them as much as is needed to bring about "more equality" in the "distribution" of wealth and income.

But both groups, the party of the thoroughgoing socialists and that of the more cautious reformers, agree in the basic doctrine according to which profit and interest are "unearned" income, are therefore morally objectionable, are the cause of the misery of the great majority of all honest workingmen and their families, and ought to be sharply curbed, if not entirely abolished, in a decent and satisfactory organization of society.

Yet this whole interpretation of human conditions is fallacious. The policies engendered by it are pernicious from whatever point of view we may judge them. Western civilization is doomed if we do not succeed very soon in substituting reasonable methods of dealing with economic problems for the present disastrous methods.

Three Factors of Production

Mere work—that is, effort not guided by a rational plan and not aided by the employment of tools and intermediary products—brings about very little for the improvement of the worker's condition. Such work is not a specifically human device. It is what man has in common with all other animals. It is bestirring oneself instinctively and using one's bare hands to gather whatever is eatable and drinkable that can be found and appropriated.

Physical exertion turns into a factor of human production when it is directed by reason toward a definite end and employs tools and previously produced intermediary products. Mind—reason—is the most important equipment of man. In the human sphere, labor counts only as *one* item in a combination of natural resources, capital goods, and labor; all these three factors are employed, according to a definite plan devised by reason, for the attainment of an end chosen. Labor, in the sense in which this term is used in dealing with human affairs, is only one of several factors of production.

The establishment of this fact demolishes entire-

*From *The Freeman*, August 1963

ly all the theses and claims of the popular doctrine of exploitation. Those saving and thereby accumulating capital goods, and those abstaining from the consumption of previously accumulated capital goods, contribute their share to the outcome of the processes of production. Equally indispensable in the conduct of affairs is the role played by the human mind. Entrepreneurial judgment directs the toil of the workers and the employment of the capital goods toward the ultimate end of production, the best possible removal of what causes people to feel discontented and unhappy.

What distinguishes contemporary life in the countries of Western civilization from conditions as they prevailed in earlier ages—and still exist for the greater number of those living today—is not the changes in the supply of labor and the skill of the workers and not the familiarity with the exploits of pure science and their utilization by the applied sciences, by technology. It is the amount of capital accumulated. The issue has been intentionally obscured by the verbiage employed by the international and national government agencies dealing with what is called foreign aid for the underdeveloped countries. What these poor countries need in order to adopt the Western methods of mass production for the satisfaction of the wants of the masses is not information about a "know how." There is no secrecy about technological methods. They are taught at the technological schools and they are accurately described in textbooks, manuals, and periodical magazines. There are many experienced specialists available for the execution of every project that one may find practicable for these backward countries. What prevents a country like India from adopting the American methods of industry is the paucity of its supply of capital goods. As the Indian government's confiscatory policies are deterring foreign capitalists from investing in India and as its prosocialist bigotry sabotages domestic accumulation of capital, their country depends on the alms that Western nations are giving to it.

Consumers Direct the Use of Capital

Capital goods come into existence by saving. A part of the goods produced is withheld from immediate consumption and employed for processes the fruits of which will only mature at a later date. All material civilization is based upon this "capitalistic" approach to the problems of production. "Roundabout methods of production," as Boehm-Bawerk called them, are chosen because they generate a higher output per unit of input. Early man lived from hand to mouth. Civilized man produces tools and intermediary products in the pursuit of long-range designs that finally bring forth results which direct, less time-consuming methods could never have attained or only with an incomparably higher expenditure of labor and material factors.

Those saving—that is consuming less than their share of the goods produced—inaugurate progress toward general prosperity. For the seed they have sown enriches not only themselves but also all other strata of society.

It benefits the consumers. The capital goods are for the owner a dead fund, a liability rather than an asset, if not used in production for the best possible and cheapest provision of the people with the goods and services they are asking for most urgently. In the market economy the owners of capital goods are forced to employ their property as if it were entrusted to them by the consumers under the stipulation to invest it in those lines in which it best serves those consumers. Virtually, the capitalists are mandataries of the consumers, bound to comply with their wishes.

In order to attend to the orders received from the consumers, their real bosses, the capitalists must either themselves proceed to investment and the conduct of business or, if they are not prepared for such entrepreneurial activity or distrust their own abilities, hand over their funds to men whom they consider as better fitted for such a function. Whatever alternative they may choose, the supremacy of the consumers remains intact. No matter what the financial structure of the firm or company may be, the entrepreneur who operates with other peoples' money depends no less on the market, that is, the consumers, than the entrepreneur who fully owns his outfit.

There is no other method to make wage rates rise than by investing more capital per worker. More investment of capital means: to give to the laborer more efficient tools. With the aid of better tools and machines, the quantity of the products increases and their quality improves. As the employer consequently will be in a position to obtain from the consumers more for what the employee has produced in one hour of work, he is able—and, by the competition of other employers, forced—to pay a higher price for the man's work.

As the labor union doctrine sees it, the wage increases that they are obtaining by what is euphemistically called "collective bargaining" are not to burden the buyers of the products but should be absorbed by the employers. The latter should cut down what in the eyes of the communists is called "unearned income," that is, interest on the capital invested and the profits derived from success in filling wants of the consumers that until then had remained unsatisfied. Thus the unions hope to transfer step by step all this allegedly unearned income from the pockets of the capitalists and entrepreneurs into those of the employees.

What really happens on the market is, however, very different. At the market price *m* of the product *p*, all those who were prepared to spend *m* for a unit of *p* could buy as much as they wanted. The total quantity of *p* produced and offered for sale was *s*. It was not larger than *s* because with such a larger quantity the price, in order to clear the market, would have to drop below *m* to *m*-. But at this price of *m*- the producers with the highest costs would suffer losses and would thereby be forced to stop producing *p*. These marginal producers likewise incur losses and are forced to discontinue producing *p* if the wage increase enforced by the union (or by a governmental minimum wage decree) causes an increase of production costs not compensated by a rise in the price of *m* to *m*+. The resulting restriction of production necessitates a reduction of the labor force. The outcome of the union's "victory" is the unemployment of a number of workers.

The result is the same if the employers are in a position to shift the increase in production costs fully to the consumers, without a drop in the quantity of *p* produced and sold. If the consumers are spending more for the purchase of *p*, they must cut down their buying of some other commodity *q*. Then the demand for *q* drops and brings about unemployment of a part of the men who were previously engaged in turning out *q*.

The union doctrine qualifies interest received by the owners of the capital invested in the enterprise as "unearned" and concludes that it could be abolished entirely or considerably shortened without any harm to the employees and the consumers. The rise in production costs caused by wage increases could therefore be borne by shortening the company's net earnings and a corresponding reduction of the dividends paid to the shareholders. The same idea is at the bottom of the unions' claim that every increase in what they call productivity of labor (that is, in the sum of the prices received for the total output divided by the number of man hours spent in its production) should be added to the wage bill. Both methods mean confiscating for the benefit of the employees the whole or at least a considerable part of the returns on the capital provided by the saving of the capitalists. But what induces the capitalists to abstain from consuming their capital and to increase it by new saving is the fact that their forbearance is counterbalanced by the proceeds of their investments. If one deprives them of these proceeds, the only use they can make of the capital they own is to consume it and thus to inaugurate general progressive impoverishment.

The Only Sound Policy

What elevates the wage rates paid to the American workers above the rates paid in foreign countries is the fact that the investment of capital per worker is in this country higher than abroad. Saving, the accumulation of capital, has created and preserved up to now the high standard of living of the average American employee.

All the methods by which the federal government and the governments of the states, the political parties, and the unions are trying to improve the conditions of people anxious to earn wages and salaries are not only vain but directly pernicious. There is only one kind of policy that can effectively benefit the employees, namely, a policy that refrains from putting any obstacles in the way of further saving and accumulation of capital.

The Entrepreneur and the Profit and Loss System

28. IF MEN WERE FREE TO TRY*

John C. Sparks

Private ownership, private initiative, the hope of reward, and the expectation of achievement have always been primarily responsible for the advancement of mankind. Continued progress—be it spiritual, mental, or material—rests squarely upon a better understanding of the idea of individual freedom of choice and action, with personal responsibility for one's own decisions.

For the purpose of illustrating this idea, let us suppose you had lived in 1900 and somehow were confronted with the problem of seeking a solution within 54 years to any *one* of the following problems:

1. To build and maintain roads adequate for use of conveyances, their operators, and passengers.
2. To increase the average span of life by 30 years.
3. To convey instantly the sound of a voice speaking at one place to any other point or any number of points around the world.
4. To convey instantly the visual replica of an action, such as a presidential inauguration, to men and women in their living rooms all over America.
5. To develop a medical preventive against death from pneumonia.
6. To transport physically a person from Los Angeles to New York in less than four hours.
7. To build a horseless carriage of the qualities and capabilities described in the 1954 advertising folder of any automobile manufacturer.

Without much doubt you would have selected the first problem as the one easiest of solution. In fact, the other problems would have seemed fantastic and quite likely would have been rejected as the figments of someone's wild imagination.

Now, 54 years later, let us see which of these problems has been solved. Has the easiest problem been solved? No. Have the seemingly fantastic problems been solved? Yes, and we hardly give them a second thought.

It is not accidental that solutions have been found wherever the atmosphere of freedom and private ownership has prevailed wherein men could try out their ideas and succeed or fail on their own worthiness. Nor is it accidental that the coercive force of government—when hooked up to a creative field such as transportation—has been slow, plodding, and unimaginative in maintaining and replacing its facilities.

Does it not seem odd that a privately-owned automobile company found it expedient to sponsor a national contest with tremendous prizes and to conduct its own search in order to correct the faults of the publicly-owned and inadequate highway system? The highway dilemma has become more and more acute until someone other than the public owner seeks an answer. If the points of ownership had been reversed in 1900—that is, motorcar development in the hands of the government, and highways left to private individuals—we would today likely be participating in a contest sponsored by the privately-owned highway companies to suggest how to improve the government's horseless carriage so that it would keep pace with the fine and more-than-adequate highways.

How could roads be built and operated privately?

*Clipping of Note No. 63 (FEE, 1954)

I do not know. This is a subject to which none of us directs his creative attention. We never do think creatively on any activity pre-empted by government. It is not until an activity has been freed from monopoly that creative thought comes into play.

But go back to 1900. Could any of us then have told how to solve the six problems to which solutions have been found? Suppose, for instance, that someone could at that time have described the looks and performance of a 1954 automobile. Could any of us have told him how to make it? No, no more than we can describe how privately to build and operate highways today.

What accounts, then, for the 1954 automobile and other "fantastic" accomplishments? Government did not pre-empt these activities! Instead, these have been left to the area of free, uninhibited, creative thinking. Millions of man-hours of technically skilled, inventive thought have been at work. And the end is not yet. Nor will there be an end if the inhibitory influence of government is confined to its proper functions of protecting equally the life, liberty, and property of all citizens; if men are free to try their ideas in a competitive and voluntary market.

29. "FOR THE GOOD OF OTHERS"*

Leonard E. Read

A professor writes, "It seems to me that it is quite an unworthy goal for businessmen to go to work for the sake of bringing profit to the stockholders."

The head of a large corporation bemoans the bad image of business and contends that the first consideration of American business is, when rightly oriented, the well-being of employees and customers.

These positions typify a growing, collectivistic sentiment among corporate managers and academicians. Their view, in essence, is that one should go into business for the good of others; profit for the owners is an unworthy objective. A leading American socialist built his utopia around a similar notion: "Production for use and not for profit."

I suspect that there are no card-carrying altruists in this world, though there are those who *think of themselves* as such. "So many people who think they have a tender heart have only a soft mind."[1] Anyway, this is to say that there are no selfless persons; there are only those who get self-satisfaction out of the mistaken idea that they are selfless. Self-satisfaction motivates one as much as another. Some aim for this state of bliss by piling up money, others by minding your and my business, and still others by working "for the good of employees and customers." The individual who gives his worldly goods to others gets as much thrill from his action as did Midas in his penny pinching.

We differ from one another, of course, in how intelligently we interpret our self-interest. A Thomas Jefferson, for instance, is intelligent enough to see that his self-interest is best served when he attempts to perfect the society in which it is his lot to live. A pickpocket, on the other hand, thinks his self-interest is best served when he takes great risks for the sake of small gains. The difference between the two cannot be identified as selflessness and selfishness; it is simply a matter of intelligence.

Persons who get more thrills by "doing good" to others than by improving their own status—intellectual or spiritual or material—are drawn toward socialism which, theoretically, is consistent with and appealing to their manner of thinking.

Adam Smith, nearly two centuries ago (in *The Wealth of Nations),* stated what experience seems to confirm:

> I have never known much good done by those who affected to trade for the public good. . . .
>
> It is only for the sake of profit that any man em-

*From *The Freeman*, July 1963

ploys a capital in the support of industry; and he will always, therefore, endeavor to employ it in the support of that industry of which the produce is likely to be of the greatest value. . . .

He generally, indeed, neither intends to promote the public interest, nor knows how much he is promoting it. . . . By directing that industry in such a manner as its produce may be of the greatest value, he intends only his own gain, and he is in this, as in many other cases, *led by an invisible hand to promote an end which was no part of his intention*. Nor is it always the worse for the society that it was no part of it.

By pursuing his own interest he frequently promotes that of the society more effectually than when he really intends to promote it. (Italics supplied)

Let us reduce this debate to manageable proportions and reflect on what, for example, motivates a person to put his savings into a hamburger stand. The answer comes clear: to make as good a living as possible. We know from daily observations that it is the hope of profit, not humanitarian concern about the meatless diet of the population, which is responsible for the venture. Observe, however, that a large profit—the enterpriser's aim—signifies customer approval. By keeping his eye on his own gain, he assures that others are well served. Their repeated purchases, leading to the enterpriser's profit, prove this. Imagine how different this situation would be were the hamburger man to concentrate not on his own gain but only on the good of others!

Of course, to achieve a profit it is necessary that employees be given a wage and working conditions for which they will freely exchange their labor and that people be offered goods or services for which they will willingly exchange their dollars. This is the free market way!

Humanitarian? Yes, indeed: Assume that a surgeon has discovered how to do a brain surgery, that he can do only one a month that 1,000 persons a year need such an operation if they are to survive. How is the surgeon's scarce resource to be allocated? Charge whatever price is necessary to adjust supply to demand, say $50,000! "For shame," some will cry. "Your market system will save only wealthy people." For the moment, yes. But soon there will be hundreds of surgeons who will acquire the same skill; and, as in the case of the once scarce and expensive "miracle drugs," the price then will be within the reach of all.

Look to the improvement of your own position if you would be most considerate of others! And this is sound advice whether one's business consists of earning profit or doing basic research or practicing medicine or saving souls or whatever. The best charity is to set an example by which others may learn to help themselves.

Note

[1] Jacques Maritain: *Lettre à Jean Cocteau*.

30. FOOD FROM THOUGHT*

Charles W. Williams

Important events in the exciting history of food have interesting, divergent, and often accidental beginnings.

In 1856 a boy in Pittsburgh grew some extra horseradish in his mother's garden. He borrowed a wheelbarrow, which he filled with bottles of ground horseradish and sold to local grocers. The boy was Henry Heinz; and from this first bottle of horseradish sauce grew the intricate world-wide business of the H. J. Heinz Company. Before 1900 that one variety had grown to 57, which today numbers close to 570 in this far-flung food empire.

In 1904 Thomas Sullivan, a tea merchant, sent samples of his various blends of tea to a few of his customers packed in little, hand-sewn silk bags. To his amazement, orders began pouring in by the hundreds for his tea put up in bags. His customers

*From *The Freeman*, November 1968

had discovered that tea could be made quickly without muss or fuss by pouring boiling water over tea bags in cups. Thus, quite by accident, was the start of a million-dollar innovation in the sale of tea.

In 1890 a salesman living in Johnstown, New York, while watching the time it took his wife to make some calf's-foot jelly, decided that powdering gelatin would save a lot of time in the kitchen. Charles B. Knox put his idea into operation, hired salesmen to go into peoples' homes to show how easily his gelatin could be dissolved in water and used. His wife worked out recipes for aspics and desserts to be given away with each package. This was the beginning of Knox Gelatine known today by every American housewife.

Peter Cooper, the inventor of the "Tom Thumb" locomotives, also invented a process for mixing powdered gelatin, sugar, and fruit flavors. This was fifty years before it began to appear on grocers' shelves as Jell-O. He was too early; merchandising methods had not been developed to convince housewives of the need for ready prepared foods. Just before the beginning of this century spectacular advertising for its day pointed out how many desserts could be prepared from this inexpensive, neat, clean package of Jell-O. Recipe booklets were distributed by the millions, as many as 15 million in one year, unheard of in that day. Another billion-dollar food business was launched.

Count Rumford, born in Massachusetts, who later migrated to England, was a leading physicist of the nineteenth century. He built the first kitchen range designed for use in a prison in Munich. This proved so efficient and workable that many wealthy people commissioned Count Rumford to replace their open hearth type of cooking apparatus with these new contraptions in their manor kitchens. By 1850 many American manufacturers had adapted Rumford's invention and were producing cast iron ranges in many sizes and shapes, lavishly decorated. From an experimental prison range, the modern stove industry was born.

In 1914 a young scientist from Brooklyn, New York, named Clarence Birdseye joined a scientific expedition to Labrador. He was also an avid sportsman, so he lost no time. He cut a hole in the thick arctic ice to try his hand at fishing. The fish froze as soon as they were exposed to the subfreezing air, often before he had them off the hook. To his surprise, the fish could be kept frozen for weeks and then defrosted and cooked like a fresh fish without any loss of texture or flavor. After returning to the United States, Birdseye made the same discovery while hunting caribou. The steaks from the quick-frozen caribou could later be broiled to a juicy, flavorsome rareness. Because of World War I, he had to drop many additional experiments in quick-freezing all kinds of food. After the war he went into the fishery business in Gloucester, Massachusetts, and experimented with fast freezing on the side. With a tremendous amount of good salesmanship, he raised money for the first quick-frozen food company. The first Birdseye package went on sale to the public in 1930. It would have been difficult to believe, at that time, that within a relatively few years almost every segment of our giant American food industry would be in quick freezing.

In Boston in 1894 a boardinghouse keeper was criticized by a sailor in her rooming house because her puddings were lumpy. Insulted at first, she became interested when he explained that the South Sea island natives pounded tapioca to a smooth consistency and suggested that she experiment by running some through her coffee grinder. Sure enough from there on her puddings were as smooth as silk. Soon she was putting up her finely ground tapioca in bags and selling them to her neighbors. She chose a very magic name—"Minute Tapioca" —and soon found a big business on her hands. Many quickly prepared foods have since copied the word "minute," but today a minute does not seem fast enough and has been replaced by "instant."

Many people wonder how the Aunt Jemima trademark began. Chris L. Rutt, with a partner, had purchased a flour mill. After some experimenting they developed a packaged pancake mix to use the flours they produced. Then one evening in 1889, Rutt attended a vaudeville show. There he got the idea for a name that reflected the festive spirit long associated with pancakes. A tune called Aunt Jemima, which accompanied a New Orleans style cake walk, inspired the name of the first ready pancake mix.

Chiffon cake was billed in huge cake mix ads in the 1940's as the "first really new cake in a hundred years." Harry Baker was a professional baker and owned a pastry shop in Hollywood, California. For years celebrities had flocked to his store and raved about his cakes. Many cooks feel that their personal recipes should be very valuable to some big food manufacturer but are shocked to find that variations of nearly every recipe have already been tried in the research kitchens. Harry Baker was one of the lucky ones; he sold his recipes for many thousands of dollars to General Mills. The valuable secret of his chiffon cake was that instead of shortening he used salad oil.

Going back many years to 1520, Cortez, the Spanish conqueror of Mexico, observed native Mayan Indians treating tough meat with the juice of the papaya, a common fruit in most tropical lands. He noted this in his writings about his conquest. Strangely enough, this find lay dormant until recent years, when the tenderizing element in papayas was turned into a powder, put up in jars ready to sprinkle on the surface of meat to make chuck and round steaks as tender as sirloin and porterhouse. From this long-forgotten idea came Adolph's Meat Tenderizer, a necessity in many homes.

In 1824 a German doctor living in Venezuela had a Spanish wife who had been sickly for years. Determined to cure her, he worked for over a year on a formula of herbs and spices until he invented a tonic that he claimed brought her back to health. Sailors stopping at the little port of Angostura found that this blend of herbs, spices, and the blossoms of the blue Gentian plant would cure seasickness. They spread the fame of Angostura bitters around the world, the process being speeded when they learned to add it to their ration of rum. When it became an essential part of a Manhattan cocktail, its place in our lives was further assured. Later, it was found to be an excellent addition in many food recipes, and today Angostura Bitters is found on almost everyone's food shelf.

Early traveling merchants from the city of Hamburg, Germany, learned from the Tartars in the Baltic Sea area how to scrape raw meat, season it with salt, pepper, and onion juice to make what is still called tartar steak. The people of Hamburg soon adopted the tartar steak. After many years some unknown Hamburg cook made patties out of the raw meat and broiled them brown on the outside and still pretty raw on the inside—a true hamburger. Today in the butcher shops of America, ground hamburger meat accounts for 30 per cent of all the beef sold to consumers.

The Toll House was a country inn in Massachusetts noted for good food. In the early 1940's Ruth Wakefield, who was then mistress of the inn, started serving a crisp little cookie studded with bits of chocolate. Miss Wakefield readily gave her customers the recipe, and all of a sudden, bars of semi-sweet chocolate began vanishing from the shelves of the stores in the area. It didn't take long for the Nestle Company, and later Hershey, to smoke out the fact that everyone was making the cookie recipe from the Toll House; and soon they were selling millions of packages of chocolate bits specifically so people could make these wonderful cookies. Today it is America's most popular cookie, available frozen, in read-to-use cookie mixes, and already made in packages.

The early Chinese found that seaweed dried and ground into a powder and added like salt to food had a magical effect on meats and vegetables—all their natural flavor was enhanced. That's why Chinese food became so popular all over the world. Eventually our chemists discovered the flavor-enhancing element and called it glutamate. Today this product, monosodium glutamate, made from beet sugar waste, soy beans, or wheat, is a staple item in every market. It is known to American shoppers as Ac'cent.

Gail Borden, the son of a frontiersman, went to London in 1852 to sell a dehydrated meat biscuit at the International Exposition being held in England. He used all his money trying to put over his idea and had to travel steerage to get home. He was appalled at the crowded, miserable conditions imposed on the immigrant families coming to America. During the trip several infants died in their mothers' arms from milk from infected cows, which were carried on board most passenger vessels to furnish milk, cream, and butter for the passengers. Borden was sure there was a way to preserve milk for long voyages; but many before him had tried and failed, including Pasteur. After four years of intensive research, Borden perfected a process of condensing milk. In 1856 his patent was approved in Washington. After much work selling the idea to skeptics, the first canned milk was introduced to the American market and formed the cornerstone of the vast and diversified Borden Company.

In Battle Creek, Michigan, Ellen Gould White had a dream one night in which she was told by the

Lord that man should eat no meat, use no tobacco, tea, coffee, or alcoholic beverages. As a Seventh Day Adventist she established the "Health Reform Institute," a sort of sanitarium, where her guests ate nuts disguised as meat and drank a cereal beverage. This beverage was the creation of one of her guests named Charles William Post, who was suffering from ulcers. He named his beverage Postum. Post also invented the first dry breakfast cereal, which he called "Elijah's Manna." He decided to go into business producing his inventions; but the name Elijah's Manna ran into consumer resistance, so he changed it to "Grape Nuts."

In this same sanitarium was a surgeon named Dr. Harvey Kellogg, whose name along with Post's was destined to be on millions of cereal packages every year. One of Dr. Kellogg's patients had broken her false teeth on a piece of zwiebach, so he invented a paper-thin flake cereal from corn. Breakfast cereals immediately became a rage, and at one time there were as many as forty different companies in Battle Creek competing for this new health food business. So began the vast cereal business of today.

Margaret Rudkin was the wife of a stock broker and her son suffered from allergies. She made an old-fashioned loaf of bread from stone-milled whole wheat flour, hoping to build up her son's health. The bread helped her son; so her doctor persuaded her to bake the bread for some of his patients, and soon she was in business. When this bread was introduced in the thirties, it competed at 25¢ against the spongy white variety selling at 10¢. Within 10 years, Maggie Rudkin's Pepperidge Farm Bread was in demand all over the East Coast and other bakers were making similar loaves—another small beginning for a nationally-known company, Pepperidge Farms.

One night Teddy Roosevelt, who had been visiting the home of President Andrew Jackson, stopped for dinner at the Maxwell House, a famous eating place nearby. Roosevelt, a great extrovert, was so delighted with the coffee that when he finished he replaced the cup in the saucer with a formal gesture and cried out heartily, "that was good to the last drop," a phrase destined to make quite famous the coffee named after the Maxwell House.

St. Louis, Missouri, was the site of two important developments in the realm of food. In 1904 an Englishman was tending a booth at the St. Louis International Exposition demonstrating the virtues of a hot cup of tea. This was an insurmountable task during the hot July days in the Mid-West. Our Englishman, Richard Blechynden, disparagingly wiped the perspiration from his face as he watched the crowds pass him by. Finally, in desperation, he threw some ice into the hot tea urn and the crowds began to swarm around his booth. The drink was a sensation, and iced tea quickly became one of America's most popular thirst quenchers.

Still in St. Louis, but back in 1890, a physician ground and pounded peanuts to provide an easily-digested form of protein for his patients. The result was peanut butter, which was quickly and rightly adopted by food faddists all over the country. Today it is a staple found in almost every American kitchen. It's a rare mother who isn't thankful for healthful peanut butter when nothing else seems to tempt her children's appetites.

So, with these ancedotes, one can see that almost every great food company or food idea had a small but fascinating beginning. Some came quite by accident, others from diligent perseverance, reflecting the drive and ingenuity of the human race—free enterprise among free men.

31. WINDFALL PROFITS*

Robert G. Anderson

Of all aspects of the free market economic system, the role of profit-making by individuals is the one most subject to controversy. An air of apology seems to permeate any discussion of profit-making, even among those who generally commend the market society.

Companies seem duty-bound to defend their latest financial reports. Any increase in profits is contrasted with earlier periods of losses or "inadequate" profits. The relative smallness of profits is demonstrated in terms of capital invested, annual sales, or total wages. Public relations departments tremble over reported company success and gear themselves for the inevitable onslaught such favorable reports will bring.

Among the charges most feared is the accusation that the firm has reaped windfall profits. While "normal" profits might be tolerated, anything above so-called normalcy is invariably subject to public charges of exploitation. The implication subtly drawn is that windfall profits accrue as a result of someone else's losses. While the public might overlook small injustices, large profits are simply intolerable.

This massive assault on profit-making reflects a belief that profits are something extra, the elimination of which would result in a general improvement in human welfare, that profits are gained at the expense of others—"unearned" and "unjust."

This anti-profit mentality stems from a failure to understand the true nature and source of profits, the integral relationship existing between profits and losses, and their basic importance to the functioning of the market system. It is a failure to understand that an attack upon profits, even excess or windfall profits, is an attack upon the market system itself.

Within the framework of a free market price system, profits show which producers have best satisfied the wants of consumers. Profits appear as the result of actions taken earlier by those producers most successful in anticipating and serving the demands of the consumer. Profits demonstrate how well a producer has employed scarce resources in the past toward the satisfaction of consumer wants. Profits are a record of experience, a reward for satisfactory service rendered.

The process of profit-making, however, is not the same thing as the amount of profits recorded. Profits earned in the past serve as no specific guide for future productive activity, though the fact that they were earned may offer hope of future profits. Past profitable activity in a given form of production assures nothing about the future. Attempts to imitate activities that have been profitable have resulted in many business failures.

The opportunity for profit-making stems from the changing values of consumers over time, and the reflection of these changing values on prices. The individual who foresees correctly these developing changes in market prices, and acts upon his foresight, will be the profit-maker.

Adjusting to Change

If man were omniscient, or if his values were to remain static, the concept of profit and loss would not exist. But fallibility and change are part of the human condition and necessarily affect man's economic behavior.

Today's market prices are reflections of values previously held by consumers and of the production those values generated. The prices so established will be either too high or too low with respect to the market conditions of tomorrow, conditions which could only be known by knowing the future, which is impossible.

The profit-maker, however, must attempt the impossible. The uncertainty of the future overrides all human action. The fact that future prices are

*From *The Freeman*, May 1974

uncertain does not dissuade the potential profit-maker from acting.

It is this potential of profit-making that provides the entrepreneur's motivation and incentive for production. The entrepreneur identifies resources in today's market that he believes will possess a higher market value tomorrow. If his foresight about the future values of the consumers is correct, a profit can be realized. The magnitude of the profit will depend upon the degree of change in future market prices and the entrepreneurial decision to act on his foresight.

When the rise in prices is large, the entrepreneur holding the resources so affected will experience large profits. The identification of this development as excess or windfall profits has been grossly misleading. The fact that he did not anticipate the precise degree of change in prices is no basis for denying the owner of the resources his right to the gain.

The concept of windfall profit merely observes that large gains can be realized from drastic changes in consumer evaluations and their resultant impact on market prices. The owner of the affected resources experiences a dramatic and sudden increase in the value of his property. But, if consumer evaluations change in the other direction, market prices can just as suddenly and dramatically fall, causing windfall losses to the owners of resources so affected.

Windfall profits or losses simply emphasize the risk of productive activity resulting from the changing values of consumers. While the entrepreneur attempts to calculate future market conditions, he is not omniscient. An underestimate of future prices may yield him a higher profit than he had anticipated when he took productive action, but that same higher profit becomes the magnet for an influx of new competitive activity.

A Reliable Guide

With the profit and loss system as their guide, competing entrepreneurs decide how resources shall be directed for future consumption. Anticipated profitability attracts the productive capital of the entrepreneurs, but the ultimate profit is determined by the actions of the consumers. The entrepreneur's astuteness in judging the consumer's demands will decide whether profits or losses are to be realized by him in the future.

A significant contributor to a smoothly functioning market is the much maligned speculator. As an entrepreneur, the speculator acts in anticipation of the changing values of consumers. His buying and selling of resources creates a more orderly market, reducing erratic fluctuations in prices, and thus holds down the magnitude and severity of gains and losses. Accurate foresight by the speculator mitigates the errors of resource pricing and the consequent large profits or losses brought on by changing consumer tastes.

Once profits are understood to evolve from the actions of the consumers, it becomes pointless to speak of profits as being "fair," "normal," "excess," or whatever.

The decision on how to allocate existing resources into future use is made by entrepreneurs on the basis of their interpretation of the consumer's actions in the market place of the future. Through a subsequent return of profits and losses to the entrepreneur, the consumer is constantly signaling entrepreneurs, as to how to direct scarce resources toward best satisfying consumer wants.

This relationship between the entrepreneur and the consumer is much like that of a revocable trust. The trustee-entrepreneur allocates resources for the benefit of the trustor-consumer, a relationship perpetuated by profits and revoked by losses. Through the signal of these profits and losses the consumer steers the producer.

The allure of profit-making is the catalyst for productive activity. Sparked by an entrepreneurial decision on the future state of the market, resources are continually being directed into hopefully productive use. The soundness of the original decision is reflected by profits or losses generated by the venture. Without some prospect that profits will substantiate the original decision, no productive activity would be undertaken. The problem of determining how resources should be allocated could not be resolved. There would be no response to the will of the consumer in the market. The market would be in a state of chaos.

The Fundamental Issue Concerns Property Rights

The real controversy over the concept of excess or windfall profits evolves over who should be the beneficiary of these subsequent unanticipated changes in market prices. The fundamental issue in this controversy is one of property rights. In a free market system the entrepreneur subjects his property to risk in a productive activity in the hope of generating a profit. If his judgment of the future demand of the consumers proves correct, his property increases in value, and he profits. The extent of his gain is thus determined by the consumer. In a market system of private ownership the gains would therefore accrue to the owner of the property.

Similarly, the burden of windfall losses is borne by the entrepreneur. If he directs his property into productive activities later rejected by the consumer's changing values, he is responsible for his erroneous decision. The sudden abstention from buying on the part of the consumers causes a fall in the value of his property and a loss to the entrepreneur. Within such a market system, the entrepreneur subjects his property to risk—to the gain or loss that accrues from the changing tastes of the consumer.

The notion that windfall profits accrue at another's expense or loss is patently false. They result from the same forces that bring windfall losses: changes in the values of consumers. Such windfalls result from future uncertainty, and should accrue to the owners who expose their property to the risks of production.

Profits or Losses Stem from Changing Values of Consumers

Once it is understood that profits and losses evolve from the changing values of consumers, it becomes obvious that abolishing windfall profits or windfall losses is impossible. Fallibility and change are a part of our nature, and both large errors and great changes are inevitable. To deny to the entrepreneur the gains or losses resulting from such error or change does not eliminate gains or losses; it eliminates entrepreneurs, disrupts the market, and ultimately leaves everyone under the dead hand of government control.

As long as consumers continue to express their changing values in the market place, profits, anticipated or not, will continue to materialize. The only question is whether the gain in the value of the entrepreneur's property should accrue to the owner or to someone else.

When the government attempts to make itself the beneficiary of windfall profits, it can only disrupt the productive processes of the market. The natural adjustments in supply and demand that occur in the free market are hampered, and further disequilibrium develops. The consumer's urgent signal for increased production, which is the essence of windfall profits, cannot be heard or acted upon by producers to whom the market is closed. The ultimate consequence must inevitably be even higher prices for the resources involved. Thus, the expropriation of windfall profits is not only counterproductive, but also denies the sovereignty of the consumer in the structuring of society.

If the individual as consumer is to retain his personal liberty, if he is to remain the sovereign force in the structuring of society, he must be free to reflect fully his changing values in the market place. This requires that the profit and loss signal must remain unhampered. For that is the only signal to which entrepreneurs can reasonably respond.

32. THE ELITE UNDER CAPITALISM*

Ludwig von Mises

A long line of eminent authors, beginning with Adam Ferguson, tried to grasp the characteristic feature that distinguishes the modern capitalistic society, the market economy, from the older systems of the arrangement of social cooperation. They distinguished between warlike nations and commercial nations, between societies of a militant structure and those of individual freedom, between the society based on status and that based on contract. The appreciation of each of the two "ideal types" was, of course, different with the various authors. But they all agreed in establishing the contrast between the two types of social cooperation as well as in the cognition that no third prin-

*From *The Freeman*, January 1962

ciple of the arrangement of social affairs is thinkable and feasible.[1] One may disagree with some of the characteristics that they ascribed to each of the two types, but one must admit that the classification as such makes us comprehend essential facts of history as well as of contemporary social conflicts.

There are several reasons that prevent a full understanding of the significance of the distinction between these two types of society. There is in the first place the popular repugnance to assign to the inborn inequality of various individuals its due importance. There is furthermore the failure to realize the fundamental difference that exists between the meaning and the effects of private ownership of the means of production in the precapitalistic and in the capitalistic society. Finally, there is serious confusion brought about by the ambiguous employment of the term "economic power."

Inborn Inequality

The doctrine that ascribed all differences between individuals to postnatal influences is untenable. The fact that human beings are born unequal in regard to physical and mental capacities is not denied by any reasonable man, certainly also not by pediatrists. Some individuals surpass their fellow men in health and vigor, in brain power and aptitude for various performances, in energy and resolution. Some people are better fit for the pursuit of earthly affairs, some less. From this point of view we may—without indulging in any judgment of value—distinguish between superior and inferior men. Karl Marx referred to "the inequality of individual endowment and therefore productive capacity (Leistungsfähigkeit) as natural privileges" and was fully aware of the fact that men "would not be different individuals if they were not unequal."[2]

In the precapitalistic ages the better endowed, the "superior" people, took advantage of their superiority by seizing power and enthralling the masses of weaker, i.e., "inferior" men. Victorious warriors appropriated to themselves all the land available for hunting and fishing, cattle raising and tilling. Nothing was left to the rest of the people than to serve the princes and their retinue. They were serfs and slaves, landless and penniless underlings.

Such was by and large the state of affairs in most parts of the world in the ages in which the "heroes"[3] were supreme and "commercialism" was absent. But then, in a process that, although again and again frustrated by a renascence of the spirit of violence, went on for centuries and is still going on, the spirit of business, i.e., of peaceful cooperation under the principle of the division of labor, undermined the mentality of the "good old days." Capitalism—the market economy—radically transformed the economic and political organization of mankind.

In the precapitalistic society the superior men knew no other method of utilizing their own superiority than to subdue the masses of inferior people. But under capitalism the more able and more gifted men can profit from their superiority only by serving to the best of their abilities the wishes and wants of the majority of less gifted men. In the market economy the consumers are supreme. They determine, by their buying or abstention from buying, what should be produced, by whom and how, of what quality and in what quantity. The entrepreneurs, capitalists, and landowners who fail to satisfy in the best possible and cheapest way the most urgent of the not yet satisfied wishes of the consumers are forced to go out of business and forfeit their preferred position. In business offices and in laboratories the keenest minds are busy fructifying the most complex achievements of scientific research for the production of ever better implements and gadgets for people who have no inkling of the scientific theories that make the fabrication of such things possible. The bigger an enterprise is, the more it is forced to adjust its production activities to the changing whims and fancies of the masses, its masters. The fundamental principle of capitalism is mass production to supply the masses. It is the patronage of the masses that makes enterprises grow into bigness. The common man is supreme in the market economy. He is the customer "who is always right."

In the political sphere representative government is the corollary of the supremacy of the consumers in the market. The officeholders depend on the voters in a way similar to that in which the entrepreneurs and investors depend on the consumers. The same historical process that substituted the capitalistic mode of production for precapitalistic methods substituted popular government—democracy—for royal absolutism and other forms of government by the few. And wherever the market economy is superseded by socialism, autocracy makes a comeback. It does not matter whether the socialist or communist despotism is camouflaged by the use of aliases such as "dictatorship of the proletariat" or "people's democracy" or "Führer principle." It always amounts to a subjection of the many to the few.

It is hardly possible to misconstrue more improperly the state of affairs prevailing in the capitalistic society than by dubbing the capitalists and entrepreneurs a "ruling" class intent upon "exploiting" the masses of decent men. We do not have to raise the question how the men who under capitalism are businessmen would have tried to take advantage of their superior talents in any other thinkable organization of production activities. Under capitalism they are vying with one another in serving the masses of less gifted men. All their thoughts aim at perfecting the methods of supplying the consumers. Every year, every month, every week something unheard of before appears on the market and is very soon made accessible to the many. Precisely because they are producing for profit, the businessmen are producing for the use of the consumers.

Confusion Concerning Property

The second deficiency of the customary treatment of the problems of society's economic organization is the confusion produced by the indiscriminate employment of juridical concepts, first of all the concept of private property.

In the precapitalistic ages there prevailed by and large economic self-sufficiency, first of every household, later—with the gradual progress toward commercialism—of small regional units. The much greater part of all products did not reach the market. They were consumed without having been sold and bought. Under such conditions there was no essential difference between private ownership of producers' goods and that of consumers' goods. In each case property served the owner exclusively. To own something, whether a producers' good or a consumers' good, meant to have it for oneself alone and to deal with it for one's own satisfaction.

But it is different in the frame of a market economy. The owner of producer's goods, the capitalist, can derive advantage from his ownership only by employing them for the best possible satisfaction of the wants of the consumers. In the market economy property in the means of production is acquired and preserved by serving the public and is lost if the public becomes dissatisfied with the way in which it is served. Private property of the material factors of production is a public mandate, as it were, which is withdrawn as soon as the consumers think that other people would employ the capital goods more efficiently for their, viz., the consumers', benefit. By the instrumentality of the profit and loss system the capitalists are forced to deal with "their" property as if it were other peoples' property entrusted to them under the obligation to utilize it for the best possible provision of the virtual beneficiaries, the consumers. This real meaning of private ownership of the material factors of production under capitalism could be ignored and misinterpreted because all people—economists, lawyers, and laymen—had been led astray by the fact that the legal concept of property as developed by the juridical practices and doctrines of precapitalistic ages has been retained unchanged or only slightly altered while its effective meaning has been radically transformed.[4]

In the feudal society the economic situation of every individual was determined by the share allotted to him by the powers that be. The poor man was poor because little land or no land at all had been given to him. He could with good reason think —to say it openly would have been too dangerous—: I am poor because other people have more than a fair share. But in the frame of a capitalistic society the accumulation of additional capital by those who succeeded in utilizing their funds for the best possible provision of the consumers enriches not only the owners but all of the people, on the one hand by raising the marginal productivity of labor and thereby wages, and on the other hand by increasing the quantity of goods produced and brought to the market. The peoples of the economically backward countries are poorer than the Americans because their countries lack a sufficient number of successful capitalists and entrepreneurs.

A tendency toward an improvement of the standard of living of the masses can prevail only when and where the accumulation of new capital outruns the increase in population figures.

The formation of capital is a process performed with the cooperation of the consumers: only those entrepreneurs can earn surpluses whose activities satisfy best the public. And the utilization of the once accumulated capital is directed by the anticipation of the most urgent of the not yet fully satisfied wishes of the consumers. Thus capital comes into existence and is employed according to the wishes of the consumers.

When in dealing with market phenomena we apply the term "power," we must be fully aware of the fact that we are employing it with a connotation that is entirely different from the traditional connotation attached to it in dealing with issues of government and affairs of state.

Governmental power is the faculty to beat into submission all those who would dare to disobey the orders issued by the authorities. Nobody would call government an entity that lacks this faculty. Every governmental action is backed by constables, prison guards, and executioners. However beneficial a governmental action may appear, it is ultimately made possible only by the government's power to compel its subjects to do what many of them would not do if they were not threatened by the police and the penal courts. A government supported hospital serves charitable purposes. But the taxes collected that enable the authorities to spend money for the upkeep of the hospital are not paid voluntarily. The citizens pay taxes because not to pay them would bring them into prison and physical resistance to the revenue agents to the gallows.

It is true that the majority of the people willy-nilly acquiesce in this state of affairs and, as David Hume put it, "resign their own sentiments and passions to those of their rulers." They proceed in this way because they think that in the long run they serve better their own interests by being loyal to their government than by overturning it. But this does not alter the fact that governmental power means the exclusive faculty to frustrate any disobedience by the recourse to violence. As human nature is, the institution of government is an indispensable means to make civilized life possible. The alternative is anarchy and the law of the stronger. But the fact remains that government is the power to imprison and to kill.

The concept of economic power as applied by the socialist authors means something entirely different. The fact to which it refers is the capacity to influence other peoples' behavior by offering them something the acquisition of which they consider as more desirable than the avoidance of the sacrifice they have to make for it. In plain words: it means the invitation to enter into a bargain, an act of exchange. I will give you *a* if you give me *b*. There is no question of any compulsion nor of any threats. The buyer does not "rule" the seller and the seller does not "rule" the buyer.

Of course, in the market economy everybody's style of life is adjusted to the division of labor, and a return to self-sufficiency is out of the question. Everybody's bare survival would be jeopardized if suddenly he would be forced to experience the autarky of ages gone by. But in the regular course of market transactions there is no danger of such a relapse into the conditions of the primeval household economy. A faint image of the effects of any disturbance in the usual course of market exchanges is provided when labor union violence, benevolently tolerated or even openly encouraged and aided by the government, stops the activities of vital branches of business.

In the market economy every specialist—and there are no other people than specialists—depends on all other specialists. This mutuality is the characteristic feature of interpersonal relations under capitalism. The socialists ignore the fact of mutuality and speak of economic power. For example, as they see it, "the capacity to determine product" is one of the powers of the entrepreneur.[5] One can hardly misconstrue more radically the essential features of the market economy. It is not business, but the consumers who ultimately determine what should be produced. It is a silly fable that nations go to war because there is a munitions industry and that people are getting drunk because the distillers have "economic power." If one calls economic power the capacity to choose—or, as the socialists prefer to say, to "determine"—the product, one must establish the fact that this power is fully vested in the buyers and consumers.

"Modern civilization, nearly all civilization," said the great British economist, Edwin Cannan, "is based on the principle of making things pleasant for those who please the market and unpleasant for those who fail to do so."[6] The market, that means the buyers; the consumers, that means all of the people. To the contrary, under planning or socialism the goals of production are determined by the supreme planning authority; the individual gets what the authority thinks he ought to get. All this empty talk about the economic power of business aims at obliterating this fundamental distinction between freedom and bondage.

The "Power" of the Employer

People refer to economic power also in describing the internal conditions prevailing within the various enterprises. The owner of a private firm or the president of a corporation, it is said, enjoys within his outfit absolute power. He is free to indulge in his whims and fancies. All employees depend on his arbitrariness. They must stoop and obey or else face dismissal and starvation.

Such observations, too, ascribe to the employer powers that are vested in the consumers. The requirement to outstrip its competitors by serving the public in the cheapest and best possible way enjoins upon every enterprise the necessity to employ the personnel best fitted for the performance of the various functions entrusted to them. The individual enterprise must try to outdo its competitors not only by the employment of the most suitable methods of production and the purchase of the best fitted materials, but also by hiring the right type of workers. It is true that the head of an enterprise has the faculty to give vent to his sympathies or antipathies. He is free to prefer an inferior man to a better man; he may fire a valuable assistant and in his place employ an incompetent and inefficient substitute. But all the faults he commits in this regard affect the profitability of his enterprise. He has to pay for them in full. It is the very supremacy of the market that penalizes such capricious behavior. The market forces the entrepreneurs to deal with every employee exclusively from the point of view of the services he renders to the satisfaction of the consumers.

What curbs in all market transactions the temptation of indulging in malice and venom is precisely the costs involved in such behavior. The consumer is free to boycott for some reasons, popularly called noneconomic or irrational, the purveyor who would in the best and cheapest way satisfy his wants. But then he has to bear the consequences; he will either be less perfectly served or he will have to pay a higher price. Civil government enforces its commandments by recourse to violence or the threat of violence. The market does not need any recourse to violence because neglect of its rationality penalizes itself.

The critics of capitalism fully acknowledge this fact in pointing out that for private enterprise nothing counts but the striving after profit. Profit can be made only by satisfying the consumers better or cheaper or better and cheaper than others do. The consumer has in his capacity as customer the right to be full of whim and fancies. The businessman qua producer has only one aim: to provide for the consumer. If one deplores the businessman's unfeeling preoccupation with profit-seeking, one has to realize two things. First, that this attitude is prescribed to the entrepreneur by the consumers who are not prepared to accept any excuse for poor service. Secondly, that it is precisely this neglect of "the human angle" that prevents arbitrariness and partiality from affecting the employer-employee nexus.

To establish these facts does not amount either to a commendation or to a condemnation of the market economy or its political corollary, government by the people (representative government, democracy). Science is neutral with regard to any judgments of value. It neither approves nor condemns; it just describes and analyzes what is.

Stressing the fact that under unhampered capitalism the consumers are supreme in determining the goals of production does not imply any opinion about the moral and intellectual capacities of these individuals. The individuals qua consumers as well as qua voters are mortal men liable to error and may very often choose what in the long run will harm them. Philosophers may be right in severely criticizing the conduct of their fellow citizens. But there is, in a free society, no other means to avoid the evils resulting from one's fellows' bad judgment than to induce them to alter their ways of life voluntarily. Where there is freedom, this is the task incumbent upon the elite.

Men are unequal and the inherent inferiority of the many manifests itself also in the manner in which they enjoy the affluence capitalism bestows upon them. It would be a boon for mankind, say many authors, if the common man would spend less time and money for the satisfaction of vulgar appetites and more for higher and nobler gratifications. But should not the distinguished critics rather blame themselves than the masses? Why did they, whom fate and nature have blessed with moral and intellectual eminence, not better succeed in persuading the masses of inferior people to drop their vulgar tastes and habits? If something is wrong with the behavior of the many, the fault rests no more with the inferiority of the masses than with the inability or unwillingness of the elite to induce all other people to accept their own higher standards of value. The serious crisis of our civilization is caused not only by the shortcomings of the masses. It is no less the effect of a failure of the elite.

Notes

[1] See Ludwig von Mises, *Human Action* (New Haven, Conn.: Yale University Press, 1949), pp. 196-199.

[2] Critique of the Social-Democratic Program of Gotha (Letter to Bracke, May 5, 1875).

[3] Werner Sombart, *Händler und Helden* (Heroes and Hucksters) (Munich, 1915).

[4] It was the great Roman poet, Quintus Horatius Flaccus, who first alluded to this characteristic feature of property of producers' goods in a market economy. See Mises, *Socialism*, new edition, p. 42 n.

[5] Cf. for instance, A. A. Berle, Jr., *Power without Property* (New York: Harcourt, Brace, Inc.), 1959, p. 82.

[6] Edwin Cannan, *An Economist's Protest* (London: P. S. King & Son, Ltd., 1928), pp. VIf.

33. PROFITS*

Hans F. Sennholz

Although every businessman aims to earn a "profit," he usually knows very little about the economic nature of his objective. He may even succeed in earning a profit, and yet be unable to explain this excess of proceeds that accrues to him after all expenses are paid.

The same can be said about tax collectors who search for "profits" and aim to seize parts thereof for the state. And the accountants who reveal the "profits" by comparing the business revenue with the expenses. They all look at the totality of net income without any distinction of its various component parts.

The economist who analyzes the economic nature of "profits" actually perceives three entirely different sources of income.

Most proprietors and partners of small businesses who think they are reaping "profits" actually earn what economists call *managerial remuneration*. They are earning an income through their own managerial labor, supervising their employees, serving customers, working with salesmen, accountants, and auditors. Obviously, their services are very valuable in the labor market. They would earn a good salary if they were to work for the A & P or a 5 & 10¢ store. Therefore, that part of a businessman's income that is earned through his own labor exertion is a kind of wage or salary, and as such, totally unrelated to economic profits.

Most small businessmen with incomes up to $20,000 and $25,000 fall in this category. In the managerial labor market they would earn this income for services rendered to customers, for buying and selling, supervision of personnel, bookkeeping and accounting, and many other business activities.

But the majority of American enterprises earn an income in excess of managerial remuneration. The economist who dissects this residium finds yet two other heterogeneous parts. By far the largest part, which is earned by the majority of American enterprises, is *interest on the owner's or stockholder's invested capital.* It accrues to the owner on account of the time-consuming nature of the production process.

Interest

Whoever refrains from spending his income and wealth and, instead, invests them in time-consuming production can expect a return. For without it no one would relinquish his savings to provide capital for production. Interest ultimately flows from human nature. Men of all ages and races value their present cash more highly than a claim payable in the future. Therefore, in order to induce an investor to relinquish his cash for production, which will yield its fruits in the future, a premium, called originary interest, must be paid. In other words, the businessman who invests in his own enterprise should hope to earn on his investment the same kind of income as the lender who extends a loan to a borrower.

This basic interest return of some 4 per cent must accrue to business lest it withdraw its capital from production. As labor will leave an industry that pays low wages, so will capital shun an industry that does not yield a market return. If the government should tax it away or if labor unions should succeed in wresting this interest income from businessmen, production will necessarily contract and ultimately fall into deep depression. No additional capital will be placed at the disposal of an industry whose interest accrual is distributed to workers instead of owners. In fact, the liquid capital of that industry will even be withdrawn and turned to other employment where interest can still accrue. Capital consumption may even destroy

*From a speech to business executives, Dallas, Texas, April 23, 1965

what many generations before have built and accumulated.

It is difficult to ascertain the precise rate of originary interest which businessmen earn on account of the time-consuming nature of production. For reasons of comparison we cannot even use the market rate of interest applicable to loan funds because the market rate itself is a gross rate consisting of originary interest, an entrepreneurial profit component that flows from the risks of the individual loan, and finally, a risk premium that flows from the dangers of monetary depreciation wherever inflation is practiced. But for reasons of simple illustration of the originary interest rate, we may use the rate the U. S. government must pay for the use of funds. If we assume that the lender of funds to the U. S. government bears no debtor's risk and that inflation does not affect the loan value, we arrive at an interest rate that may constitute the originary rate, which is the rate businessmen should hope to earn as a basic interest return on their invested capital.

Suppose your net worth of business, stated in present value, amounts to $100,000. Originary interest on that amount would come to $4,000 a year, which you would earn even in such riskless investments as U. S. Treasury bonds or savings banks deposits. As a basis for this interest calculation you would take the estimated present market value of your net worth, for only the present value of your assets, and not the arbitrary book value reflecting past valuations or tax considerations, is meaningful for individual motivation and action.

A merchant with a business net worth of $100,000, spending long days in his shop serving customers, supervising his help, and otherwise managing the business may thus earn $4,000 interest and $20,000 managerial remuneration without actually reaping any profits.

Pure Profits—Temporary Response to Changing Market Conditions

Finally, there are enterprises that do earn *pure profits*. Through correct anticipation of future economic conditions, businessmen may earn what economists call *entrepreneurial profits*. For instance, through buying at a time when prices are low and selling when prices are higher, they may earn inventory profits. After interest allowance is made for the time of investment, stock market profits are pure profits. Of course, such profits are connected with risk on account of the uncertainty of the future. Instead of reaping profits, many businessmen suffer losses.

Contrary to popular belief, pure profits are only short-lived. Whenever a change in demand, supply, fashion, or technology opens up an opportunity for pure profits, the early producer reaps high returns. But immediately he will be imitated by competitors and newcomers. They will produce the same good, render identical services, apply similar methods of production, and thus depress prices until the pure profit disappears. The first hoola-hoop manufacturer undoubtedly reaped pure profits. But as soon as dozens of competitors had retooled their factories the market was flooded with hoola-hoops. Prices dropped rapidly until the pure profits had vanished. When the American people suddenly discovered their need for compact cars, American Motors, who was the early manufacturer, temporarily earned pure profits. After General Motors, Chrysler, and Ford invaded the field, American Motors profits returned to the market rate of interest or even changed to losses.

Pure profits are very elusive. But opportunities for profits will emerge as long as there are changes in demand, supply, fashion, population, technology, or even the weather. As all life is change, and economic adjustments need to be made continuously, opportunities for profits will arise again and again.

And yet, in spite of the competitive forces that work incessantly in a free economy to wipe out pure profits, we may observe numerous enterprises that succeed in earning them over lengthy periods of time. The reason must be sought not only in the superior management of some enterprises in which gifted entrepreneurs direct the speculative aspects of business, but also in the different degrees of risk connected with the various industries.

Industries that work with a minimum of risk in stable markets and with stagnant technology must expect to earn the lowest profits. When completely adjusted to consumer demand and without any anticipation of risk, pure profits would indeed be completely eliminated and only the originary interest return would remain. But as even a completely adjusted industry may face future risks, economic or political, and as the risk factor cannot be eliminated entirely from any productive investment, some remnant of pure profit is usually earned by the successful enterprises. This is the reason why even apparently riskless industries continue to earn a little more than the 4 per cent originary interest. The successful public utility, for instance, which may bear little investment risk, may earn 6 or 7 per cent, which consists of 4 per cent interest and 2 to 3 per cent pure profit. But the presence of risk also explains why some enterprises in the same industry only earn the interest return or even suffer loss.

On the other hand, the successful enterprises that continuously face high degrees of risk tend to earn higher profits. For several years during the cold-war rearmament, the manufacture of aircraft and parts was exceptionally profitable. According to some statistics, a few aircraft manufacturers earned more than 20 per cent of net worth. Even if we bear in mind that corporate net worth is usually understated when compared with present values, and earnings ratios therefore are considerably overstated, we must admit that exceptionally high profits were earned by the most successful enterprises. In short, economic activity that involves a great deal of risk must yield exceptionally high profits to the successful enterprise in order to attract the necessary capital. It is obvious that the aircraft industry that continuously faces a great many imponderables, and often has suffered heavy losses, could not attract the needed capital if no more could be expected than a one per cent profit above the originary interest. Or, oil exploration and drilling which entail great financial risks would not be carried on without high rewards for success.

Interference with Profits

Taxation of these high rewards, or their arbitrary distribution to workers, would eliminate the incentive for risk-taking. Why should a man risk his capital in production if he can only suffer losses? In that case he would shun every productive investment, and search for riskless employment of his funds. The economy thus becomes rigid and inflexible, and unable to adjust to changes in demand, supply, and technology. Expansion and modernization are severely hampered. A confiscatory taxation of pure profits, maliciously called "excess profits," destroys the vitality and dynamism of the market economy. (For an excellent discussion of profit and loss see Ludwig von Mises, *Planning for Freedom*, Libertarian Press, South Holland, Ill.)

And what are the effects of taxes levied on the 4 per cent basic interest return? As described above, interest is the payment for the use of capital over time. Without it capital cannot be invested and production must come to a standstill. When the government levies its confiscatory taxes on this basic income component, the market must fall into severe depression. In fact, the "multiplier" economists who usually apply their calculations to government spending would do much better calculating the depressive effects of this taxation. Let us assume, for instance, that the government imposes a tax of $1 billion on the interest return of business. At 4 per cent this interest constitutes the yield of $25 billion capital invested. And without this yield these $25 billion of business capital will be withdrawn from production, at least as far as it is liquid and can be withdrawn without heavy losses. For why should the owner keep his capital invested without a return?

The Great Depression gave dramatic proof of the depressive effects of confiscatory corporate taxation. And today, we can observe similar stagnating effects whenever the Federal or state governments raise their basic levies on business, such as the social security taxes and unemployment taxes which fall on every business regardless of its profitability.

And, finally, what are the economic effects of taxes that fall on the first-mentioned component, the managerial remuneration? Why should a merchant spend twelve to sixteen hours daily in his store if he cannot earn an income that is comparable with the salaries earned by other managers? If profit taxes encroach upon this income the independent businessman will be tempted to sell out to his big competitor and rather earn a salary as a branch manager than to face confiscatory profit taxes.

In economic life it is rather difficult to ascertain the impact of profit taxation. The same tax in some cases may fall on pure profits, in others on basic interest, and yet others on managerial remuneration. The effects, therefore, do vary. In some cases the tax merely prevents risky undertakings, in others it causes depressive restrictions of production, and in yet others it may cause the liquidation of small and medium-sized enterprises.

Addendum on Profit-Sharing

For many people, profit-sharing is thought to provide the solution to our labor problems. It is said to hold the key to industrial peace and represent the ideal of industrial democracy. According to a Senate Committee Report, profit-sharing is "essential to the ultimate maintenance of the capitalistic system." Even some businessmen praise it for giving employees a sense of partnership in the enterprise, raising worker morale, avoiding strikes, reducing turnover, increasing efficiency, and so on. In fact, profit-sharing is said to afford workers a stake in our capitalistic system.

These people do not seem to realize that the market economy *is* a sharing system. Although hampered and mutilated, American business continues to deliver ever more and better goods. Wages continue to rise on account of improved technology and increased capital investments, not because we work ever harder and longer hours. Competition forces investors and businessmen to share the fruits of their investments with their customers through lower prices and with their workers through higher wages.

But in popular terminology "profit-sharing" proposes to give the workers more than higher wages through competition in the labor market. It means an additional distribution of a businessman's earnings to his employees. Some proposals depend on government or union coercion, others aim at voluntary sharing. Most sharing firms are rather small in size and employment.

The economist who analyzes this supplementary sharing must ask a pointed question. Which part of the business surplus commonly called "profit" is to be divided between businessmen and workers? Is it the "managerial remuneration" which businessmen earn through their own managerial services? Why should independent businessmen yield their labor income while managers and supervisors in the service of large corporations continue to earn a market wage?

Is it the "pure profit" which businessmen are urged to share? Only a small percentage of American enterprises actually earn pure profits. Now, are the fortunate workers who found employment in profitable enterprises to earn more than their fellow workers in average firms? Should an accountant who serves a brilliant stockbroker earn $100,000 per year while his equally competent fellow accountants labor at $5,000 or $6,000? What is to determine his remuneration? But, whatever the sharing plan should provide, it introduces a dubious wage principle: a man's labor income is determined by the ability of his employer. I doubt that this is the matrix for human cooperation, the key to industrial peace. On the contrary, it would create new sources of conflict. Most workers who receive wages only would probably demand "equal pay" from their profitless employers, which would aggravate rather than alleviate the labor situation.

Many people fail to realize that industry doesn't have much profit to share. According to Claude Robinson's excellent analysis, 45 per cent of all companies, on the average, are reporting no profits. The average annual earnings for all manufacturing companies amount to eight and six-tenth cents per dollar of investment. "If we allow five cents as a form of interest," Robinson concludes, "the remaining three and six-tenths cents is left for entrepreneurial risk-taking. Should the three and six-tenths cents entrepreneurial fee be shared, it could at best mean an insignificant wage increase, and would surely decrease the willingness of owners to take the investment risks involved in providing better tools for workers. Sharing the entrepreneurial fee, therefore, would likely do the wage-earner more harm than good." (Claude Robinson, *Understanding Profits*. Princeton, N. J.: D. Van Nostrand, 1961, p. 315.)

Interest on Investment

And finally, there is the "interest" which capitalists usually earn on their invested funds. But, a forced reduction of this basic yield not only prevents capital formation but also causes its withdrawal and consumption. Such profit-sharing on a large scale causes stagnation and depression as the economic history of the past thirty-five years has repeatedly demonstrated.

Improvements in labor productivity and standards of living largely depend on the increased use of capital. Saving is a fundamental prerequisite of economic progress. It is hard to understand how anyone who has human betterment at heart can urge us to reduce the award of saving by sharing it with those who did not earn it but propose to consume it.

The friends of profit-sharing sometimes argue that if all companies would share their profits, labor productivity would rise greatly and everyone would benefit. But in this case, competition would again reduce prices and profits until there would be no excess profits to share. The benefits of rising productivity would thus accrue to consumers through lower prices and to workers through rising wages. Competition would not tolerate the existence of permanent profits to share. Therefore, profit-sharing can remain only a limited industrial practice.

In many cases even this limited sharing is sailing under false colors. Where labor actually becomes more productive through greater effort and application, its market value rises accordingly. Competition among businessmen will cause wages to rise. A businessman who then proposes to share his profits with his workers may merely be using this means to pay higher market wages. But instead of making payments every Friday, he may hold off paying for six months or a year, and call this profit-sharing. It is my opinion that most of the seemingly successful profit-sharing plans merely constitute plans for delayed payment of that part of wages that is earned through special effort and application.

In all such cases the workers would be well advised to insist on payment of higher wages rather than expose their earnings to the risks of business. Workers may even lose their delayed wages in case the business should lose money through poor management decisions.

34. WHY SPECULATORS?*

Percy L. Greaves, Jr.

Back in February, 1871, a group of free enterprisers found a way to help cotton growers adjust their production to market demand. They organized the New Orleans Cotton Exchange. There, for 93 years, cotton growers, wholesalers, manufacturers, and profit-seeking speculators could buy and sell cotton at free market prices for present and future delivery.

The prices paid and offered were published in the press. No cotton grower or user was long in doubt about the state of the cotton market, present or future. For there is no better indicator of the state of a commodity market than the prices at which that commodity is bought and sold for various dates of delivery.

The prices of the New Orleans Cotton Exchange were long a valuable guide for farmers and manufacturers alike. For farmers, they indicated how much land should be planted in cotton and how much in other crops. Through the growing season, future prices indicated how much time, care, and expense should be spent in tending crops. When future prices were high, no expense was spared to bring every possible ounce to market. When future prices were low, farmers were warned not to waste too much time and expense cultivating and picking that last possible ounce.

For manufacturers and other cotton buyers, the Cotton Exchange quotations provided a base for estimating or determining their future raw material costs. This in turn helped them calculate the prices on which they bid for future business. On orders accepted for delivery over long periods of time, they could always make sure of their raw material costs by immediately buying contracts for delivery of cotton on the dates they would need it.

Cotton Prices Controlled

On July 9, 1964, the New Orleans Cotton Exchange closed its doors to trading in "cotton futures," as contracts for future delivery are known. For years such sales have been fading away. With cotton prices more and more controlled by the government, neither farmers nor manufacturers need the information or insurance of a futures market.

When demand for cotton drops off, the government advances the subsidized price to farmers and stores all unsold cotton. When demand for cotton rises, cotton pours out of government subsidized warehouses and sells at the government set price. Either way, the taxpayers lose. Until present laws change or break down, cotton prices will be set by the government, cotton acreage will be guided by bureaucrats, and valuable men, materials, and tax money will continue to be wasted in nonproductive enterprise.

This situation reflects a complete lack of understanding of the rules of human behavior and the role of speculators in a free market society. It substitutes the wisdom of a few striving to stay in

*From *The Freeman*, November 1964

political power for the wisdom of those who spend their lives studying every facet of supply and demand before pledging their names and fortunes in support of their considered judgment.

It is human nature for men to try to improve their future conditions. That is the aim of every conscious human action. Men make mistakes, but they always aim at success in providing a better future for themselves or their loved ones. Free market transactions are merely the attempts of men to improve their own situations by social actions which also improve the situation of others. Barring force, fraud, or human error, all voluntary market transactions must improve the situations of all participants.

How Men Act

Actually, there are only three basic principles of human action. Men can act as gamblers, scientists, or speculators. Few acts fall entirely within any one classification. For every human action is confronted by elements of future uncertainty, such as those that exist in life itself.

Men act as gamblers when they know nothing in advance about the results except that some will win and others lose. There is nothing a man can know, study, learn, or experience that will help him to become a winner. When men gamble, the desired results depend upon pure chance. No skill whatsoever is involved.

Men act as scientists when they know in advance the results their actions will produce. Scientists deal only with solvable problems where conditions can be controlled and where identical actions in identical situations will always produce identical results. Automation is a modern example of scientifically directed action. In all scientific action, the repetition of prescribed procedure will always produce the same results. So, the more that scientists know about the laws of nature, the more they can undertake with prior certainty as to the actual results.

Men act as speculators when they have only partial knowledge and understanding of the results their actions are likely to produce. The more speculators know and understand, the better they can predict the future results of their actions. But they never can be certain of the actual results.

Most speculations involve people and how they will react to given situations. Since we can never know with certainty the future reactions of others, every action which involves others is a speculative action. Thus, all voluntary actions, including market actions, are speculative.

Why Men Specialize

The best way to increase the probability that speculative actions will produce the desired results is to increase our knowledge and understanding of all pertinent data, including the thoughts and ideas that motivate the actions and reactions of others. This takes time, study, experience, and economic analysis.

Men have found that the best way to gain more of the needed knowledge, experience, and understanding is for each one to select some limited area of human activity and then specialize in it. Out of this division-of-labor principle the whole market system has developed. In a market society, everyone specializes and then trades the products of his specialty for the products of other specialists, his partners in total social production.

This system permits scientists to specialize in the automatic mass production of inanimate objects of wealth with certainty as to the physical results. However, men cannot plan or plot the market value of their products with scientific certainty. All such values are relative and speculative. They depend on the ever-changing ideas of buying men as to which of the many things offered for sale will give them the most satisfaction for the sums they have to spend.

Specialization can and does help men engaged in marketing and other speculative social actions. It permits them to learn more about what they sell and also more about the needs and wants of those to whom they seek to sell. Thus they become wiser and more efficient speculators, wasting less time trying to sell the wrong things to the wrong people.

Perfect results depend on the perfect prediction of future conditions. Because of human fallibility, this is rarely possible. However, better predictions and thus better results are often achievable. Greater specialization tends to reduce errors and help men achieve better results.

Many men prefer the relative security of a reasonably assured steady income to the insecurity of a wholly speculative income—an income that may turn out to be very high, very low, or even a net loss. Such security-seeking people tend to become employees.

Others prefer the lure and excitement of speculation. Such people are the investors, employers, business promoters, and professional speculators.

They assume responsibility for the uncertainty of a business venture's future success or failure. Their likelihood of success depends largely on their ability to predict the future wants of buyers.

Better Foresight Pays

In a mass production market economy, the function of prediction and speculation falls primarily on investors, business promoters, and specialists rather than on consumers. When producers seek to act as scientists only, creating wealth by relying on the known laws of the physical sciences, they must find others to undertake the predictions and speculations as to the future conditions of the market.

Such specialists must estimate, at the time production starts, what consumer demand, competitive supplies, and other market conditions are likely to be at the time of sale. Such speculators then assume the responsibility that the planned production will meet the whims and wishes of consumers. Their income will depend on how correct their early predictions of future conditions prove to be.

As the division of labor has progressed, men and firms have tried to reduce their predictive and speculative functions to limited areas in which they become specialists with a better understanding than most other men. They concentrate on making or marketing certain goods and, in doing so, pay little attention to the market conditions of other goods, including their raw materials which may come from far-away sources with which they are unfamiliar.

Of course, the future prices they can get for their finished goods are in part dependent upon the ever-changing prices of the raw materials with which they are made. So, to protect themselves against future price fluctuations in their raw materials, businessmen sometimes engage in "hedging." By "hedging," they transfer the hazards resulting from the uncertainty of future prices to professional speculators in those products.

How Hedging Works

A good example of "hedging" is the case of the cotton shirt manufacturer. He is a specialist in making and selling shirts. He knows that the selling price of cotton shirts is largely dependent upon the price of raw cotton. He has little time to study the cotton-growing conditions around the world or the other prospective demands on the raw cotton supply. He is fully occupied with his own problems in the shirt business. However, he would like to avoid the consequences of unforeseen changes in the prices of raw cotton.

Under free market conditions, he can hedge by contracting to sell at current prices raw cotton which he need not buy or deliver until the date he expects to sell the shirts he is making. Then, if the price for shirts has fallen, due to a drop in raw cotton prices, he would buy raw cotton at the lower price to meet his hedging contract. The profit on his raw cotton transaction would offset his loss on the shirts.

On the other hand, if the prices of both raw cotton and cotton shirts have risen, the extra profits from his shirt sales will be offset by his losses on the hedging transaction in raw cotton. By hedging he can protect himself against all possible fluctuations in raw cotton prices which might affect the prices of the shirts he sells. He rids his mind of this worry so that he can concentrate on the details of the shirt business at which he is a specialist.

The man who takes his hedge is usually a professional cotton speculator. He is a specialist who studies and interprets all the available data and conditions that are likely to affect future raw cotton prices. He trades in cotton a thousand times for every once or twice by the average cotton manufacturer. He knows how much has been planted in the many cotton-growing countries. He studies the rainfall and other weather conditions which may affect the size of the various crops. He keeps up-to-date on laws and proposed laws that may affect raw cotton prices. He follows the ups and downs in foreign exchange and transportation costs.

He also keeps an eye open for changes in demand for each type of cotton. He has informed ideas about increased demands arising from new uses for cotton, as well as any decreases due to the substitution of synthetics. He watches developments in mass purchasing power, production, and consumption in faraway lands like India. In short, he learns all he can about anything that might affect the supply of, or demand for, cotton and thus bring about a change in future raw cotton prices.

As a well-informed specialist, the speculator is much better able to predict future cotton prices than is the man who specializes in growing cotton or manufacturing cotton shirts. Competition among speculators trading on a commodity exchange forces them to share the benefits of their knowledge with their customers.

Businessmen can protect themselves from some speculative losses by taking out insurance. However, customary insurance can only be bought for risks which are largely known or predictable. Losses from fire, death, theft, or transportation accidents are thus distributed over all those insured, instead of falling entirely on the ones who suffer a specific disaster. Future price changes do not fall in this category. They are the same for everyone. Only the well-informed specialist is equipped to speculate successfully and "insure" others against losses from price changes.

In popular thinking, the speculator is a bold, bad man who makes money at the expense of others. Many people believe he gains his livelihood by luck, gambling, or inside manipulation. There are, of course, a few dishonest speculators who lie and cheat, as do some in all occupations, but the honest speculator is a serious specialist who serves mankind. He constantly strives to obtain a better understanding of future market conditions. He then places this better understanding at the service of all interested parties. Whenever his predictions are wrong, it is he who loses. When he is right, he and everyone who trades with him benefit. For if they did not expect to benefit, they would not trade with him.

The service of a speculator is to smooth out some of the gaps between supply and demand and some of the extreme ups and downs in prices. He tries to buy when and where a commodity is plentiful and the price is low and to sell when and where the commodity is in short supply and the price is high. When he does this wisely and successfully, he tends to raise extremely low prices and reduce extremely high prices.

Frequently, the speculator is the first to foresee a future scarcity. When he does, he buys while prices are still low. His buying bids up prices, and consumption is thus more quickly adjusted to future conditions than if no one had foreseen the approaching scarcity. A larger quantity is then stored for future use and serves to reduce the hardships when the shortage becomes evident to all.

Since a price rise tends to encourage increased production, the sooner prices rise, the sooner new and additional production will be started and become available. So a successful speculator reduces both the time and the intensity of shortages as well as the hardships which always accompany shortages.

Likewise, speculators are often the first to foresee an increase in future supplies. When they do, they hasten to sell contracts for future delivery. This in turn drives down future prices earlier than would otherwise be the case. This tends to discourage new production that could only be sold at a loss. It also gives manufacturers a better idea of what future prices will actually be. So, here again the speculator tends to smooth out production and consumption to the benefit of all concerned.

A good example of how speculators serve society was provided in the coffee market a few years ago. A small newspaper item reported a sudden unexpected frost blight in Brazil. Speculators immediately realized that such a frost must have killed large numbers of coffee bushes. This meant much smaller future supplies for the United States. So the speculators promptly bought all the coffee they could below the price they thought would prevail when consumers became fully aware of the approaching shortage. This tended to raise coffee prices immediately.

The effect of this was to reduce consumption and stretch some of the existing supply into the shortage period. It likewise alerted coffee growers in other areas to be more careful in their picking and handling of coffee so that there was less waste. Higher prices encouraged them to get to market every last bean, which at lower prices would not have been worth the trouble. Higher prices also speeded up the planting of new bushes. Since it takes five years for a new coffee bush to bear berries, the sooner new planting was undertaken the shorter the period of shortage.

The speculators who first acted on this development served every coffee consumer. If these speculators had not driven up prices immediately, consumers would have continued drinking coffee at cheap prices for a time. Then, suddenly, they would have faced a still greater shortage and still higher prices than those that actually prevailed.

By buying when coffee supplies were still relatively plentiful and selling later when the shortage was known to all, speculators helped to level out the available supply and reduce the extreme height to which prices would otherwise have risen. Speculators make money only when they serve society by better distributing a limited supply over a period of time in such a manner that it gives greater satisfaction to consumers. They thus permit other businessmen and consumers to proceed with greater safety and less speculation in their own actions.

If a speculator buys a product thinking its price will rise and it later falls, he loses money for the simple reason that he has acted against the general welfare. He has sent out false indicators to producers and consumers alike. That happened just recently in the case of a large sugar importer. The firm bought large quantities of sugar when it was selling at 11¢ a pound. Its purchases were not hedged. In six months or so the price of sugar fell below 5¢ a pound and the importer was forced to file a petition under the National Bankruptcy Act.

Hedging with a professional speculator would have prevented that loss. Of course, if the speculator had made no better estimate about future sugar prices than the importer did, it might have been the speculator who filed under the bankruptcy law. But as a rule, speculators are the specialists who are best informed on what future prices are likely to be.

Fruits of Intervention

When governments set prices, quotas, acreage limits, or other hampering restrictions on the honorable activities of men, they countermand the checks and balances that the free market places on supply and demand. The result is always surpluses and shortages: the former, where producers' rewards are set too high; the latter, where they are set too low. Where there are surpluses of some things, there will always be shortages of others. For the men and materials subsidized to produce surpluses have been lured from producing those things which free market conditions would indicate that consumers prefer.

Political interference with free market processes can only burden the taxpayer and weaken the human impulses of free men which tend to bring demand and supply into balance at the point which provides the greatest consumer satisfaction. With the passage of time, each such intervention can only make matters worse. Then, if people still believe the remedy for every economic ill is more intervention, political interventions will increase further until the police state is reached.

In any such trend toward a police state, the speculators are among the first to be eliminated. They are the specialists who study world-wide markets in order to reduce the uncertainties that face all farmers and businessmen. Without the services of speculators, bottlenecks of production—a symptom of socialism—soon develop.

Men and materials are then wasted in the production of surpluses. As a result there are ever-increasing shortages in the things people want most but can't have because the means to produce them have been misdirected by government decree. The recent end to trading in cotton futures on the New Orleans Cotton Exchange is an omen that should make thoughtful men reflect on the road we are now traveling.

Labor, Wages and Employment

35. BARGAINING*

Paul L. Poirot

Bargaining means trying to negotiate a contract or to arrange a trade on terms satisfactory to both the buyer and the seller. That's why it takes two to make a bargain, and only two—a buyer and a seller, higgling over terms. If it's true bargaining, there is no interference by anyone else and no threat or suggestion of coercion or violence in any form.

Anyone who has been caught in a Christmas shopping rush or who has witnessed the operations in a public market on a busy day may question the idea that only two persons can take part in the bargaining procedure. At the time, it always seems as though several persons are involved. But this is merely an example of competition at work. The competing sellers offer their different lots of goods and services and the competing buyers bid for ownership of these various things. The presence of more than one potential buyer or seller widens the range for bargaining. But the actual bargaining is carried on between one buyer and one seller at a time, each of whom is free to accept or to reject the other fellow's best offer. The whole concept of bargaining presumes that there will be alternatives from which to choose—alternatives offered by competition as well as the alternative of rejecting all offers.

The satisfaction from bargaining, whether it leads to a trade or not, lies in the feeling of each party that he has obtained the best deal possible without resort to force or fraud. Competition helps each person decide what is best. Since competition and bargaining are so closely related, the two ideas may well be merged within the term "competitive bargaining"—competition between persons who recognize the rights of individuals to use what they have as a means of bargaining for what they want. Mankind has never discovered a basis for human relationships, other than competitive bargaining, which so encourages a person's own self-interest to operate to the benefit of others.

When a person voluntarily offers his goods or services for exchange, and when another person voluntarily agrees to the terms of the offer, exchange will take place. Both parties find satisfaction. It's not a question of one's gaining at the other's expense. The exchange works to their mutual benefit. Both gain. How much will each gain? Leave that to the judgment of those who practice competitive bargaining and who are directly involved in any specific transaction.

Trade occurs when both parties agree as to the price—when both see an advantage in trading. The terms of such trade are not anyone else's business—at least, not within the framework of truly competitive bargaining. There is no third party; even the government is supposed to keep its hands off except where someone tries to substitute violence for free choice in the market. Any other test of fairness for prices or wages is an abandonment of the private enterprise system.

The Right of Refusal

One of the important features of truly competitive bargaining is that a person has the right of refusal. He doesn't have to trade at another person's price. A man may keep what he has if he isn't satisfied with the other fellow's best offer. Such a re-

*FEE, September 1953

fusal to trade is quite a common thing in any market place. It is typical of the competitive system. It is a vital part of the bargaining procedure. It is as fair and just as the day is long. But a refusal to buy or to accept the terms offered certainly is no excuse for violent retaliation against the rightful owner or against any other person who might be willing to accept the owner's terms of trade.

A person may choose to quit a job if the wage or other conditions of employment are not satisfactory, just as a shopper returns a can of peaches to the shelf if the price is too high for her. Yet the housewife, by that act, does not pretend to have acquired a claim of ownership to the peaches. The next shopper who wants them may claim them at the price agreeable to the seller. An unhampered market will function in exactly that same fashion with respect to opportunities for employment.

Competitive bargaining has brought many benefits to the creative and highly productive men and women of America, just as all men and women can gain if they are willing to assume the responsibility of being free. But freedom to bargain is being forfeited by Americans who do not perceive that such freedom is based upon respect for the rights of others. The advantages of bargaining and trade are not to be found in the kind of collective action which calls for the suppression of individual freedom of choice. The only alternative to bargaining is compulsion. To exercise compulsion is to govern. In the final analysis, the alternative to competitive bargaining is government control—the government in command of all property and all lives—individuality surrendered to the state—compulsory collectivism.

Bargaining Representatives

Any employer or any employee who feels that he is personally unqualified to gauge the conditions of the market owes it to himself to seek the services of a qualified bargaining representative. And a qualified bargaining representative will be one who understands that his job is to find the right wages—those which just clear the market without bringing compulsion against a single person.

Bargaining has indeed helped to provide many of the material blessings available to American consumers today. And some of this bargaining has been of a "collective" nature in the sense that one party to the bargain has spoken in behalf of a number of cooperative individuals whose common and unanimous interest is in a specific action not designed to hurt someone else. However, much of what has passed for bargaining in America has not been bargaining at all, but a kind of compulsory collectivism which prefers coercion to voluntary agreement.

Bargaining is not facilitated by a powerful membership organization of competitors, whether they be competing for wages or for profits or for anything else which is scarce enough to have market value. It is a highly risky thing to delegate one's own right to bargain to any representative who pretends that such organizational control of competition is either necessary or desirable. A bargainer is one who cooperates with those who are willing; for that purpose, he needs no power of compulsion. He doesn't need coercive control of competitors. Such controls are the tools of persons who will use force if bargaining doesn't go to suit them. Those who are still free to bargain, and who like it that way, will think carefully before placing in the hands of others those personal rights and responsibilities which might be perverted into weapons of coercion.

The Value of a Service

Much of the dissension about wages arises from a failure to distinguish between the worth of an individual as such, and the value, for purposes of exchange, of the services offered by the individual. Among free men, the worth of an individual is not a matter to be determined in an economic sense. Certainly that problem is beyond the scope of this study, for we are not discussing the buying or selling of human beings. The purpose of bargaining, in this respect, is to arrive at the market value or exchange price of specific services voluntarily offered by individuals. A man offers to sell eight hours of his day in order that he may better utilize the balance of his day according to his own choice.

According to the expressions of preference in a free market, a higher exchange price may be offered for the services of one person than for another's services. There is great variation in the productive capacity of different individuals. This is as true among so-called hourly workers as it is among managerial workers. The efficiency of the capitalistic system stems from its tendency to concentrate the management of productive operations under the direction of the most capable managers. So it happens that a good manager may serve to coordinate the productive services of a large number of employees.

The control of capital also tends to be concentrated in the hands of the best managers. The owners of property—and to a large extent, they are simply those workers who have spent less than they earned—sometimes find it desirable to pool their property so as to attract the managerial services of an expert. Stockholders thus hire corporation management—agree to pay a manager for his services to them.

In order to best serve the interests of stockholders, the manager must be capable of coordinating the services of many individual employees in a way that is sufficiently satisfactory to each employee to attract that employee from alternative opportunities for the use of his services. So it is that a good manager serves a group of property owners as well as a group of employees, all in the interest of better service to customers. He serves to the extent that he is able to improve the productivity of all the property and all the labor which has voluntarily sought his management.

The Worker's Reserve

It is frequently argued that an employee is at a bargaining disadvantage when he seeks a favorable employment contract because he has less of a reserve to draw upon than does an employer. It is said that the employee needs bread for his family's supper, whereas the employer needs nothing more urgent than a new yacht. The effect of such dramatization is to draw attention from the subject of the employer-employee relationship. The employee wants the use of tools and managerial services, and the employer wants the workman's services so that together they may create something useful in exchange for bread, yachts, or whatever else either of them may choose to buy with his part of the product.

It is true that some employees have little except their weekly wages as a buffer against bill collectors. And if the loss of a week's wages is that serious to a man, it may be a sign that he isn't a good enough manager or, for some other reason, prefers not to try to make a living by working at a business of his own. Thus, he is in this sense dependent upon job opportunities created by others. But in a competitive society, a person is not bound to continue working for others, nor is he bound to depend upon any one employer for an opportunity to work. Some employees, of course, prefer not to change jobs; free men have that choice. Unless competition has been strangled by coercive intervention, employers will be competing against one another for the productive services of employees. This competition between employers for an employee's productive capacity is the thing that constitutes the employee's reserve, just as the reserve value of capital depends upon the competition for the use of that capital.

In this connection, it may be interesting to speculate for a moment as to just how an employee's reserve compares in dollar value with a reserve fund of capital. For instance, let us assume that a young employee might reasonably expect to find regular employment for a period of forty years at an average weekly wage of $100. For a nonworking person to draw a comparable income from a trust fund —assuming that it earns interest at the rate of three per cent and that the principal also is to be used up over the period of forty years—an original capital investment of $120,000 would be required. A person's capacity for productive work is truly a valuable reserve, equal in worth to the inheritance, from quite a "rich uncle." A young man has quite a stake in maintaining the kind of a competitive society in which such reserves are recognized as being private property.

The fact is that a man who is willing and able to work does have a kind of reserve—in a sense, a better reserve than is available to the man who has nothing except money or capital. Robinson Crusoe could have salvaged the ship's silver, but as a nonworking capitalist, he would have starved. According to the story, he saved his life by digging into his reserve capacity to work.

Employer and Employee

This same principle applies in our own kind of a complex society where each of us depends more or less upon exchange for his livelihood. If a man owns a million dollars, yet refuses to offer it in trade, he may go hungry, just as an employee may be faced with hunger if he refuses to turn his services to productive use. The market does not automatically guarantee subsistence to those who stop producing and trading while waiting for a better opportunity to present itself. An employee who chooses not to work may properly complain that he has no other means of support, but he ought to confine his complaint to the person who is solely responsible for his sad plight—himself. No one else has any right to make him work, nor any moral obligation to support him in his voluntary idleness.

The employee who wants to sit until an employer comes forth with a more attractive job offer may say that he doesn't have the reserve to enforce his demand, but what he means is that he doesn't have control over other employees who are willing to accept the jobs which are offered. To describe such circumstances as a lack of reserve is just another way of saying that competition exists.

Labor Government

. . . The compulsory industry-wide union can pretty well guarantee a manager that no competitor will be able to achieve superior labor efficiency. It is possible to believe that in some instances company management works closely with labor union management to tighten the grip of their joint industry-wide monopoly. The consequence is that whole industries—all competing employers and all competing employees—can be called out on strike by one man who has a closed-shop grip on all manpower authorized for employment in "his" industry. Consumers can thus be squeezed between the alternatives of paying more or of doing without the products of an entire industry. Competition gives way to compulsion. No employer is allowed to continue productive operations; the union won't let him hire employees. Nor can any employee stay on his job at the old wage, or bargain individually for a wage that might satisfy him; he, too, is compelled to strike until the demands of a single union official are met. That a union official may sometimes impose his will upon the consuming public without actually calling a strike does not modify the basic fact that such imposition constitutes monopoly power.

In one other manner, also, the power of the government has been granted to the officialdom of organized labor. Taxpayers are obliged to provide unemployment benefits for those who have been forced into idleness by the tactics of exclusion which labor unions practice. This is monopoly power in its most terrible form.

Perhaps the truth is that governmental planning and compulsion, as a substitute for the market, is in itself the evil which wrecks lives and makes for bad relationships within a society. If so, then it is wrong to give any person, or group, or so-called class, the right to plan and govern the social relationships of individuals.

To blame union organizers for usurping power and for exercising the authority which has been granted to them by law, is to miss the important point. The fact is that the power of compulsion cannot be thus exercised until it has first been delegated by our individual selves to the agency of government.

The self-interest of those who work and of those who have saved and accumulated capital is not detrimental to peaceful progress within society; rather, the thing to be feared and guarded against is the reckless abandonment of self-interest to a supposed class interest with the power to govern. And, if such power has developed and is being used to oppress other persons and groups within a society, the solution would seem to involve the displacement of such coercive power, not with a new "class" of governors, but with a new reliance upon freedom. The lifting of restraints and restrictions upon personal choice—the freeing of the market so that each may bargain with what is properly his own—is the only assurance of justice to every individual.

36. COLLECTIVE BARGAINING WRONG IN PRINCIPLE*

John W. Scoville

Although written before the passage of the Labor Management Relations Act of 1947 (Taft-Hartley) and of the Landrum-Griffin Act of 1959, the author's criticism of compulsory *collective bargaining still applies. On another occasion, he contrasted voluntary and coercive collective bargaining as follows:*

> If collective bargaining means that the workers in a plant form an organization and elect a spokesman (not necessarily an employee) to discuss wage rates, hours, working conditions, etc. with management, and if the employer agrees to the procedure, I can see no objection to such conduct. But this is not what labor men mean by collective bargaining. They consider that if the employer does not accept the demands of the union, the employees will go on strike and, by picket lines and violence, prevent other workers from taking their jobs. The strike will inflict such losses on the employer that he will capitulate and accept the terms of the union. I do not agree that strikes, picket lines, and violence against workers seeking the jobs of the strikers are "a necessary mechanism in modern, industrial society."

A great many people feel that collective bargaining is all right in principle and that what is needed is better men as labor leaders and union officials. Many industrialists will say, "Of course we believe in collective bargaining" or "We recognize that collective bargaining is here to stay" or "The employers in the past were not fair to labor," etc. These views are incorrect. Collective bargaining, like all other monopolistic practices, is wrong in principle.

About 1800, the English law condemned combinations, both of employers and employees. These combinations were rightly called conspiracies. But about 1824, the English law against the combination of laborers was repealed. I believe the English lived under the shadow of the French Revolution and were afraid of revolution breaking out in England. You will hear people say that the Wagner Act gave certain rights to labor. This is incorrect. I will read a letter I sent to *The Wall Street Journal* on this subject:

An agency for promoting private enterprise published a letter recently from which I quote:

> The National Labor Relations Act must be so rewritten that the rights and duties of employer and wage-earner in relation to each other and to the public are clearly defined. Individuals and minorities among wage-earners, whether union or non-union, must be protected against majorities. *The right of collective bargaining must at all times be maintained.* But every worker must have the right, free from coercion from any source, to join or refrain from joining a union.

Let us analyze this alleged *right of collective bargaining*.

Confining our discussion to civil rights, all rights are creations of the law.

All human acts fall in two categories:

1. Acts of which the law takes no notice;
2. Acts commanded or forbidden by law.

In the first category we are free to act; we have the right to act as we will. In the second category we have no right to disobey the command and no right to do what is forbidden.

A man has the right to marry. This *right* is in the first category, the law neither forbids nor commands. A young man asks ten maidens to marry him—and each maiden says no. So he goes to the legislature and says that women are denying him the right to marry. So the legislature passes a law which prohibits any woman from interfering with the right of a man to marry.

Armed with this law, the man goes to his favorite woman and demands that she marry him. If she refuses, the man goes to a National Marriage Relations Board which decides that the woman is engaged in an unfair marriage practice and that

*From an address to the Detroit (Michigan) Kiwanis Club, August 8, 1944

she cannot interfere with the man's right to marry. The Board draws up a marriage agreement or contract and compels the woman to sign it.

In this hypothetical case, we may observe:

1. The law took from the woman the right to decide whom she would marry or whether she should marry at all.

2. Before the law was passed, the right to marry meant that the man had a right to marry *if he could find a woman to marry him.*

3. After the law was passed, the right to marry meant something else—namely, the *right to compel a woman to marry him.*

4. The marriage contract signed by the woman was signed under duress, and was therefore not a contract at all, but a legal mandate.

The analogy between this case and the Wagner Act is clear. Employees always had the right to engage in collective bargaining, if they could find a willing employer; that is, the law did not interfere. The Wagner Act conferred no rights on employees. But it took away from the employer the right not to deal with a particular labor union or with any union. Under the Wagner Act, most labor agreements or contracts are signed by employers who are under duress—and hence are not really contracts.

The discussions between the employer and the labor union should not be called bargaining, for it is of the essence of bargaining that both parties are acting voluntarily. Would discussions between a highwayman and his victim be described as bargaining? In genuine bargaining each party makes offers. But labor unions, like bank robbers, make demands. Those who make demands have the power and the will to use force. The labor union threatens to strike if its demands are not met, thus inflicting a loss on the employer. The labor unions expect the higher wages in the future will exceed the present losses due to the strike. But the employer is faced with two losses—the loss due to the strike, or the loss which will come from meeting the demands.

The Wagner Act gives employees the power to inflict certain and indeterminate losses on employers, with the consent and assistance of the federal government. It substitutes *force* for *competition* as the mechanism for distributing the social product.

We should never refer to the Wagner Act as a law which confers upon workers the right of collective bargaining—but as a law which denies to employers the right to enter into voluntary agreements with their employees.

37. HOW WAGES ARE DETERMINED*

Percy L. Greaves, Jr.

Most people today seem to think that producers and sellers set prices. Likewise, they seem to think that employers set wage rates. They think businessmen get rich by setting low wages for their employees and high prices for their products.

This leads many to think that employers can be compelled by law or union pressure to raise workers' wages at the expense of the owners of a business. This has been done in an increasing number of cases for a short period of time, but such wage increases cannot be maintained in the long run. Actually, it is impossible to raise every worker's wages by law or union pressure. Every law or nonmarket pressure that raises wages for some, lowers them for others.

In analyzing every economic proposal, it is necessary to examine all of its effects, not only the short-run effects, but also the long-run effects, and not only the effects on those whom the advocates seek to benefit but also the effects on those who have to pay the costs. All of these inevitable effects should be weighed before passing judgment on any attempt to interfere with free market processes.

*Adapted from a June 13, 1969, lecture at Buenos Aires, Argentina, the full version of which forms a chapter of Mr. Greaves' *Understanding the Dollar Crisis* (Western Islands, 1973). From *The Freeman*, July 1970

In a free market you are free to take any of many jobs open to you. Each man takes that one which, from his point of view, he considers best. When everyone is free to do this and no one is permitted to trample on the equal freedom of others to do so, when no one or no group can prevent others from taking jobs for which they and the potential employers reach mutually satisfactory agreements, then the Golden Rule will prevail. More workers will be producing more goods for others and everyone will have more for himself. The result will be ever-increasing production and human satisfaction. Of course, in a free market society, men will still make mistakes. But free market practices tend to reduce such mistakes by penalizing most those who make them.

We may also have a few unfortunate people who need assistance from their fellow men. For such few cases, the free market not only encourages religious and other private charities but it also provides the means with which these charitable organizations can take care of the unfortunate. So these unfortunate few do not have to become a burden on the government. We are free to act voluntarily as good Christians and take care of our neighbors who are in trouble.

In any society, in any group of men, there will also be some who will try to help themselves at the expense of others. There will be some who wish to steal, or misrepresent, or resort to force. To protect peaceful productive citizens against those who resort to such antisocial actions, governments are necessary, and very necessary.

Consumers Determine Wage Rates

There is today a popular idea that employers exploit the workers. This fallacy has been growing ever more popular since the days of Karl Marx. It was Marx's idea that employers overworked employees, paying them much less than the money values of what they produced, while keeping the difference for themselves. According to this theory, rich employers get richer and richer while the poor workers get poorer and poorer. The time would come, Marx held, when the workers would break the chains which bound them to their employers and set up a socialist utopia. According to this idea, the poor worker is helpless in a market society. He has no choice. He must take the wage that is offered to him. There is no other employer who might bid for his services.

Actually, of course, that is not so. In the absence of any social interference, workers tend to get the full value that consumers will pay for their contribution. It is the interferences by governments and the interferences by labor unions supported by public opinion, even without the strength of laws, that prevent all potential workers from getting those market values they could contribute to society.

If the idea that unions help all workers is popular, then we are powerless to stop them from hampering the market competition. However, in an unhampered free market economy, competition tends to allocate to every factor of production, including workers, all that each contributes. It is the values that the ultimate consumers place on each particular contribution to total production that determine what businessmen can pay for that particular contribution.

The same principles apply to the wages paid for labor that apply to the sums paid for raw materials or any other factor of production.

In a free market, each employer seeks to hire as many workers as he profitably can. He hires employees up to the point at which it is no longer profitable for him to hire an additional worker because he cannot sell the product of that additional worker for the wage he must pay him. As he hires more workers, the wage rate tends to rise and as more units are produced, the market price he can get per unit tends to fall. This is the inevitable tendency of a free and unhampered market.

The more workers you hire, the higher wage rate you will have to pay. And you must pay the higher wage to all who do similar work. As you produce and offer more goods on the market, you can only sell them at lower prices. Eventually you reach the marginal point, where you make no profit on the last man you hire. Wage rates are ultimately set by the marginal productivity of labor, that is the market value added to the product produced by the marginal employee, the last man hired. This is the way the free market would work, if there were no interferences. Unfortunately, the free market is something that we have never had completely at any time and may never have. However, the nearer we get to it, the better off we shall all be.

Given the conditions which the employer faces, he must pay workers pretty much the values that consumers place on their contributions. If the employer pays a higher wage, he suffers a loss. If he does not then reduce his wage rate, his number of employees, and his production to what he can sell at a price that covers his costs, he will eventually be forced out of business. No businessman can long pay costs which he cannot get back from consumers.

In the long run it is the consumers who pay the wages. The businessman is merely a middleman. He tries to make a profit as a middleman, buying raw materials, hiring workers, and selling the products to consumers. He makes his profit, if any, by holding what he pays for the factors of production below what consumers will pay for the final product. However, once a profit appears, competitors continually bid up what must be paid for each factor of production, including labor. There is always a tendency in a free market for profits to be squeezed and disappear. This includes any profits obtained by paying workers wages lower than the market value of their contributions.

Free Competition Protects Workers

It cannot be denied that employers would always like to pay lower than the market wages. In *The Wealth of Nations,* published in 1776, Adam Smith mentioned that whenever businessmen get together they try to set wages and hold them down. However, in the free market, they are unable to do so. It is just not possible for all employers to get together and agree to hold wage rates down for any length of time. Once one employer finds he can profit by breaking such an agreement he will probably do so. If none breaks the agreement and if you have a free market society wherein anybody can become an employer, new employers will soon appear, to take advantage of the situation by offering workers more.

If the employer pays a wage lower than the market wage, that is less than the product of the worker can bring in the market, his profits will be such that he can expand his production and his number of employees. If he fails to do so and fails to raise his wage rates in doing so, he will invite new competition. In either case, market competition will raise the wage rates to the value produced by the marginal employee. And there is always a marginal employee.

In most industries there are also marginal companies. These are the companies that are just breaking even. If their costs go up a little bit, they will suffer a loss. Then they will soon be out of business because money losers cannot stay in business indefinitely.

No businessman in a free market society can long pay a worker a dollar an hour and sell his product for five dollars an hour. Why not? Because you and I and thousands of others like us would be very happy to go into that business, pay those men two dollars and sell their product for five dollars if we could. Others would soon offer to pay them three dollars, four dollars, or even four-fifty. In fact, large corporations would be very happy to make profits of just two cents an hour for every worker they employ. They are just not able to pay them much less than the market value of their product. The last one employed would not yield them any profit, particularly in a free society where anyone who thinks he sees a chance to make a profit can come in and bid away any employee who is paid less than the market value of his contribution.

The frequent refutation is, "Yes, but most people do not have the capital to start a business." Let's remember there are many savers eager to invest their money where they can earn more. If they can be shown a situation where they can earn more, they will be happy to make the needed capital available. All you need to do is to show them where a profit higher than current interest rates can be made.

Whenever there is a profit in a free market society, it attracts competition, and competition always reduces prices. This is how the market constantly allocates consumers a share of every increase or improvement in production.

Savings Raise Wages

The real secret of higher wages is increased savings per capita. Increased savings are a result of producing more than is consumed. If more goods and services are produced than consumed, then these unconsumed goods and services are available for making tools, factories and other things needed to help increase production. American living standards have gone up over the years because generation after generation our parents have provided their children with a better start in life than their parents had. The history of our country has largely been that the first generation of immigrants provided their children with an elementary school education, the next generation saved enough to provide their children with a high school education, and the third generation sent their children through college. Now, many are going on to graduate work. In this way, each generation provided the next generation with a higher standard of living. In each case, this higher education was the result of increased savings. The earlier generations just could not afford to provide their children with what most American children now have.

When there are savings in a capitalistic system, people do not put them under a mattress. They do not dig a hole and hide them as people do in India or China where savers are afraid that if they put up a factory, the property would be seized. No, in a capitalistic society people invest their savings where they hope they will earn a return. In a capitalistic society, savings are not accumulated by the rich only. One of the great advantages of a capitalistic society is that low-income people can also invest their savings and earn a return on them. They can buy savings bonds. They can put their money in the savings banks. They can buy life insurance. Then, the banks and the life insurance companies make their savings available to businessmen and large corporations.

As a matter of fact, it is the low-income people who are the great creditors of our day. They are the ones who are hurt the most by low interest rates. It is largely the higher-income people who are debtors and who benefit from low interest rates. They are stockholders and their corporations borrow the money saved by low-income people. One of the great advantages of the free market system is that it provides a way for low-income people to participate in the earnings that savings provide.

Effect of New Savings

Savings are, of course, the only real source of old age security and higher living standards. When new savings are invested, the very first thing they do, whether they are invested in a new company or in an expansion of an old company, is to bid up wages and the prices of raw materials. They bid up everything that is needed to expand production, including labor, and you cannot make anything without labor.

Labor is one of the scarcest things in this world. There are many mines that are not mined because the available supplies of labor are worth more in other occupations. The same is true of farm lands. The same is true of every occupation. Every economic endeavor is limited by the high costs of labor. Labor is always scarce. The market allocates the scarce supplies of labor to the production of those goods and services for which consumers are expected to pay the highest prices. Other goods and services are not available because of this very shortage of labor.

With new savings, there are employers or "entrepreneurs" who are constantly trying to employ more workers. They have to bid up wage rates for the limited quantities of labor available in the market place. The factor which helps labor most is the increased savings which permit employers to bid them away from their previously lower-paying jobs. After these savings are turned into new or larger factories, they must produce goods and services previously not available.

The managers of these new expansions must determine what to produce. They try to find out what is not available that is next in importance on the value scales of consumers. They then expand the production of those things not sufficiently available that they think customers want most. They bring more production to the market. Each worker, working with more or better tools, produces more. If there has been no increase in the money supply, as more goods reach the market, the result must be lower prices. With lower prices for consumers' goods, everyone can buy more with his limited money supply. The only way that a society can raise the real wages of all its workers is to increase the amount of savings available per worker.

For example, American steel companies need an investment of some $20,000 per worker, for workers to get the high wages they are paid. In a market economy these high wages are shared by all. The barber, who has not changed his methods very much in the last century or two, competes in the labor market with steel workers, each of whom uses about $20,000 of equipment. Wage rates of all workers are thus set by the average savings available to help workers increase their production. These higher wages and lower prices must appear before the savers can get any of their money back, much less any interest or profit on their speculative investment.

Profits may come, but they can only come later if buyers, of their own free will, decide that the new market offerings are better bargains than all other available goods and services. This is the secret of progressively higher living standards in a free market society. The secret of higher wages is more savings per available worker. A man with a modern expensive earth-moving machine can move far more earth than the strongest man using his hands or even a shovel. As more and better tools become available and as more goods are produced, there will be a higher standard of living for everyone who participates in the market economy.

Effect of Present Union Policies

Consider now the effect of present-day union policies upon our economy. The essence of labor union policies today is (1) to restrict production and (2) to prevent the unemployed, or those employed at lower wages, from improving their economic situation by underbidding union-imposed wage rates. We cannot improve the general welfare by following union policies that restrict production by making high wages higher for some workers, with the result that low wages are kept low or nonexistent for other workers.

Whenever union workers get a raise above free market wage rates, this increase raises production costs, and as a result prices must be raised to consumers. With higher prices, fewer goods are sold. When fewer goods are sold, some of the workers are laid off and the laid-off workers must then compete for the lower-paying jobs. Their competition in these next lower-paying jobs drives some previously employed workers out of jobs. This forces their wage opportunities still lower. Such policies restrict production and keep men from working where they can produce the goods most wanted by society.

Much of this is, of course, due to the popular fallacy that only an equal exchange is a fair exchange and that if one person, the employer, for example, gains, he must have done so at the expense of the worker. This is responsible for so much of the antagonism against the capitalist, against the investor, against the saver—the belief that his gain is unearned and that the capitalist or saver is getting something at the expense of the worker. This is Karl Marx's exploitation theory. It is the theory of class warfare as opposed to the market theory of voluntary social cooperation.

Marx put great stress on this. He believed that under the natural law of wages, employers worked the workers too long. Workers produced enough to support and reproduce themselves in, let us say, ten hours. Employers worked them eleven or twelve hours. According to this idea, what workers produced in the extra hour or two was taken and kept by the capitalists. So one of the chief policies of labor unions has been to demand shorter hours for the same pay. If you shorten hours for the same pay, you have less production. Less production does not provide a higher standard of living. If widely practiced, it must mean higher prices and a lower standard of living. Of course, when this happens as a result of free market processes, it means that market participants prefer to take some of their potential increased production in the form of more leisure.

Another fallacy in this area is the argument that money wages must be raised in order to provide workers with the purchasing power to buy their production. Actually, higher living standards require more production, not more money. Workers can only buy what is produced. If production is reduced because fewer workers are hired, increasing money wages does not provide any more goods. This is an old fallacy. There is no way to increase the purchasing power of one worker by increasing his wages without at the same time decreasing the purchasing power of other workers.

The employer has no power to set wages. He cannot in the long run pay more than the consumer will repay him. Nor can he long pay less than the market value of labor's contribution. This Marxian idea simply does not stand up. Yet, today many people honestly and sincerely subscribe to this idea that employers have too much power. Their failure to understand free market economics permits them to believe that in a modern industrial society employers have great power while the poor workers are helpless. Actually, in a free market society it is ultimately the consumers who set prices and thus the wages that employers can and must pay.

How Labor Unions Affect Wages

Questioning the virtues of organized labor today is like questioning or attacking religion, monogamy, motherhood, or the home. In public opinion, the test of whether one is for or against labor or the workers or the poor in general is your attitude toward labor unions. One simply cannot argue that certain union policies hurt labor and expect to be taken seriously. The fact is, of course, that union policies *have* hurt workers in general and particularly those at the lower end of the income scale.

The essence of present-day union wage policies is to reduce production and to keep the unemployed from finding work and the low-paid from competing for higher-paying jobs. Such policies are not going to raise the nation's standard of living. We can never improve the general welfare by policies which reduce production. Unions make high wages higher for some, but they make costs higher for other people and thus reduce the goods and services that consumers, including workers, can buy in the market place.

The unemployed, those at the bottom of the economic ladder, have no voice in union affairs or in setting wage rates. They are completely shut out. Union officers care very little about nonmembers or beginners trying to get started. There are cases in New York where a man cannot get into a union unless his father was in it before him. Since, under the law, only union members can work in certain trades, this has hurt Negroes trying to enter trades white unions have monopolized. If one's father had to be in the union, how can a Negro ever get into that union? This has applied to other low-income minorities in times past. The unions do not help the relatively poor. They help the aristocrats of labor at the expense of low-income workers. They get privileges for their members at the expense of other workers or would-be workers and they raise prices for all consumers.

Combinations of workers can only raise wages if they can raise the value or the quantity of the product that they produce. Now, of course, if the quantity produced is smaller, other things remaining the same, the value per unit is greater. However, the available quantity will satisfy fewer consumers and thus provide less human satisfaction. So, if the unions do not increase production, the only way they can raise the relative value of a unit of labor is to reduce the units of labor employed and the quantity of goods produced in that industry. Without the power to keep out other workers, unions can do little to raise the market value of what their members produce. This does not help either the workers excluded or consumers in general.

We live in an age of mass production for mass consumption. If we do not have mass production, we cannot have mass consumption. So by reducing the amount of production, unions are not helping workers in general. By setting wages at higher than free market wage rates, unions reduce the amount that can be sold. They throw people out of the jobs where they could be most productive. What the unions gain for their own members results in a loss to those who are excluded from cooperating in the task, and it results in a loss to all consumers as they will have to pay higher prices per unit for a smaller quantity of goods and services. Every consumer who does not share the union's gains will have to go without something he could have bought if the union gain had not raised prices.

The control of wage rates is also the control of entry into a trade or industry. Such control also determines rates at which a company or industry expands or contracts. In a free society, if the wages in an industry were lower than those forced by unions, that industry would expand. When unions raise the wages of an industry, that industry either has to contract, or, if it stays the same size, it is prevented from expanding as it would if it could pay free market wages.

Expanding means paying higher wages to attract the more workers needed. It also means producing more goods that consumers want most and lowering prices so the same wages will buy more. Of course, there is also a tendency toward the elimination of profits. Unions can protect their members from the competition of other workers merely by raising union wage rates, because then the employer cannot afford to employ any more. This is one of the inevitable results of the union seniority principle. Those with high seniority are not worried about those who lose jobs because of higher union wages.

Effect of Union Policies on Savings

One of the most important factors in the labor situation is the effect of union policies on employers, savers, and investors. Many think that wages can be raised at the expense of the employer or the investing owners, and thus higher wages need not hurt the consumer. They think you can just reduce profits a little bit more and that will take care of the higher wage costs. As we have tried to make clear, the way to raise the wages of workers is to increase the savings invested in tools that workers can use to increase their production.

The accompanying table may help to give us a better understanding of some of the problems faced by workers and by those who try to make a living by employing people. Assume a steamship which cost $2 million to build and which is expected to last 20 years. The yearly depreciation and interest charge would then be $150,000. The owners assume an expected market revenue of $14,100 per week. It is expected to operate 50 weeks of the year. The people who are investing this $2 million considered it carefully in advance. If their forecast is correct, they expect their weekly costs will be:

Depreciation and interest	$3,000
Labor wages	8,000
Other operating costs	2,100

and they hope for profits of $1,000 over and above the interest which they could get by lending the

Steamship Costs $2 Million and Lasts 20 Years
Yearly Depreciation and Interest Charge—$150,000
Market Revenue $14,100 per Week (50 weeks)

Weekly Cost	Free Market Wage Rates	Union Forces Wages Up 10%	25%	50%
Labor Wages	$ 8,000	$ 8,800	$10,000	$12,000
Other Operating Costs	2,100	2,100	2,100	2,100
Depreciation and Interest	3,000	3,000	2,000*	none*
Profit	1,000	200	none	none
Totals	$14,100	$14,100	$14,100	$14,100

*Amount available toward $3,000 expense.

money out. The total of the items mentioned comes to $14,100.

Of course, if they foresee future developments incorrectly, they will suffer a loss. But if they have foreseen future operations correctly, if they have calculated their labor and other costs correctly, and if they have estimated correctly what the public will pay for the service, then and then only will they earn the estimated profits. Then only will they earn the estimated profit and be able to replace the ship and continue to employ the workers after 20 years.

In order to make this problem easy to understand, we shall assume that this ship is on a lake and cannot be moved to be used any place else. So once this investment is made, those who have turned their savings into a steamship cannot withdraw them. If a labor union has the power, either through public opinion or through the laws of the land, to raise wages above those prevailing in the market at the time, the investors will then be at the mercy of the unions.

Now, we shall assume in the second column of figures that the union is able to threaten a strike or otherwise use its power to raise wages 10 per cent. This increases the cost of labor to $8,800 and reduces the profit, beyond the charge for interest, to $200. Under such a situation, the owners will continue operating. They will still get a small profit, smaller than they had calculated, yet more than they would have gotten if they had lent their money out at market rates of interest. They are still —you might say—ahead of the game.

The union members, having found it easy to use their power to get this 10 per cent increase, are still not satisfied. They try it again. Let us assume that this time they increase wages to 25 per cent above free market wages. You see the results in the next column—a situation in which the workers are then getting a weekly total of $10,000 in wages. There are no longer any profits after interest. In fact, the employers are not covering their depreciation and interest. They are only getting two-thirds of this expense, or $2,000. Under such circumstances, they will still operate the steamship. If they stopped operating, they would get nothing for depreciation and interest. $2,000 is better than nothing. Everyone prefers a little something to nothing. We even prefer a small loss to a larger loss. At this rate, when the ship is worn out, the owners will not be able to replace it. They will not have depreciated enough. So, of course, when the ship is worn out, this business will be ended and the men will lose their jobs.

But assume the union workers do not see this. Suppose they go on and ask for a further increase. This time we assume they seek a total increase of 50 per cent. Then you find the situation in the last column where you have arrived at the margin. The owners receive nothing for their capital, no allowance at all for depreciation or interest on their capital. The operating income would just cover the wages of the workers and other operating costs. Then, it no longer pays the investors to operate their steamship. They have reached the point where they would be operating the ship for nothing. This they do not care to do. So the operation comes to an end and the men lose their jobs. They have killed a good thing.

Savers Can Be Scared Away

All this is not very far from reality. For many years, from 1837 to 1947, we had in the United States the old Fall River Line. It was a steamship line that provided overnight boat service between the beautiful harbor of New York and Fall River, Massachusetts, a short train ride from Boston. It was a trip that many people enjoyed and a cheap way to ship freight. The unions kept raising the wages of their members until the steamship line was forced out of business.

There are lessons to be learned from this illustration. Businessmen can get caught. Investors can get caught. Savers can get caught. Once they put their money into particular forms of capital they are caught. When unions can raise wages to the point that business income covers only part of the depreciation and interest expenses, the investors will still operate their business, because any income is better than writing off the investment as a complete loss. But what is the effect of this on potential investors? Would you, if you had any savings and saw this happening, try to go into competition or start a similar service elsewhere?

This is the problem that workers face. Yes, unions can temporarily raise some workers' incomes. But they also reduce the competition for workers and in the long run they reduce the number of high-paying jobs available. In real life, tools, machines, and other capital goods wear out or become obsolete one by one. They do not all go to pieces at one time. A typewriter wears out and it is replaced. Some small machinery wears out from time to time, but whole factories seldom wear out all at once. Unions can push wages up so long as it still pays to replace the worn-out parts and continue operations. This permits businesses already established to stay in operation, but it greatly discourages the starting of new businesses.

These union policies thus tend to stifle the very thing that encourages competition for workers and raises wages. If we are to have higher real wages, higher real income, that is, more goods and services, we must have more savings and more businesses competing for the workers. This union policy, of forcing wage rates above those that would prevail in a free competitive market, reduces the savings and the number of employers who compete for workers. Under such policies, people with savings will tend to put them under the mattress or send them out of the country.

There are many people in many parts of the world who are sending their savings outside of their country, just because of such conditions. They no longer feel that it is safe to invest savings in their own country. Other people stop saving. Why save, if your savings are going to be confiscated? Why not spend, live high, and have a good time while you are here? Still others will put their savings in government bonds in the belief that they will be safer there than invested in private enterprises. But the money will then be spent to buy votes and the interest on the government's debt will become an added burden on the taxpayers and on the workers too. So we see that if union wages are forced up above free market wage rates, they end by killing the goose that lays the golden eggs of higher wages for all, that is, the increased invested savings that provide higher and higher standards of living for all.

Only Savings Can Reduce Economic Hardships

The reason why we have so much starvation in so many countries, in India for instance, is because private property is not protected. Investments are not protected. After India became independent of England, Nehru said that India needed and wanted foreign capital. It is true, he admitted, that India was going to be socialist but he added, if you will put your capital in India, we will promise not to confiscate it "for at least ten years." How much money would you or any sane person invest in India under such conditions?

If workers want to raise their wages, they must adopt policies which will encourage savings. We have had this problem in the Western world for a good many years now, for most of this century. However, as union wages have gone up in the more productive industries, which unions can most easily organize, and in what we call bottleneck industries, like transportation, the unions can shut down other industries. They raise the wages of some, but raising wages raises the prices, and with higher prices fewer articles are sold, which means fewer men are employed in the organized industries. The workers kept from jobs in these industries must then compete in some other lower-paying industry. This drives those wages down unless those workers too are organized into politically privileged unions. Then more workers are thrown into competition with still lower-paid workers, until some of them are, by these very "pro labor" policies, forced to work for wages on which they cannot keep body and soul together. Then we feel sorry for them.

The popular remedy today for such very low wages is a minimum wage law. The minimum wage law says that you cannot employ a man unless you pay him a specified minimum wage. In the United States, this is now $1.60 an hour. We still do not have a dictatorship. Until we do, employers will only employ people if they can hope to get the $1.60 back from consumers. If the consumer says a man's contribution is only worth $1.50, the employer is not going to pay him $1.60.

The employer is only an agent of the consumer. So the man becomes legally unemployable. It is now illegal for anyone to hire him. He cannot legally earn what he could in a free market, which is to say, the highest amount any consumer will pay for his contribution. So unemployment insurance was invented to take care of these people. When unemployment insurance payments expire, the popular remedy is relief or welfare payments, which become a burden on taxpayers who are, of course, in the long run, the workers. The only possible outcome of such policies is higher prices, higher taxes, less production, and more poverty.

People with the best of intentions and the least economic understanding constantly try to help the people on the bottom of the economic ladder by governmental intervention. We have had the National Recovery Act, which was supposed to help both business and labor by letting them organize with government help to set high prices and high wages. We had the Agriculture Adjustment Act. We had the Securities and Exchange Act. We had many such acts with nice sounding names and preambles expressing the best intentions.

The real question always is: Are such laws a sound means for obtaining the desired or specified ends?

The National Recovery Act did not produce national recovery. The Agriculture Adjustment Act did not adjust agriculture to consumers' wishes. We have had surplus after surplus. We have given billions of taxpayers' dollars to the farmers and after thirty-five years still do. The so-called farm problem is still with us. Only one such law has lived up to its name. The Unemployment Insurance Act has guaranteed that we will have unemployment.

These interventions did not increase production. In a free market society everybody can get a job at the highest wage the consumers will pay for his contribution. He cannot long get any higher wage; and nothing that government can do will change this situation or improve it. But many workers and voters believe unions can raise the wages of all workers.

Governments, of course, have to do what is popular; they cannot do what is unpopular. Today it is popular to think that no worker's wages should ever be allowed to fluctuate downwards. Wage rates, it is thought, should only move upward. So our laws and labor unions attempt to prevent any reductions in money wages.

The market system permits consumers to change their wishes and wants. When these shift, employers have to change the things they produce to satisfy the customers. The way this happens in a free market is that the prices of things no longer wanted in such large quantities go down, while the prices of things for which demand has increased go up. Businessmen switch from producing losing lines of goods to producing goods on which they hope to make a profit. They stop producing goods that can only be sold at a loss. When the demand changes, they make fewer candles, for instance, and switch to producing electric bulbs and lamps. And so it is that workers must switch to different industries.

Nowadays, we no longer permit any wages to fall. So if employers can no longer pay the union-demanded wages, they must cease operations altogether and fire everybody, including those who might be satisfied with slightly lower wages until they can find better-paying jobs.

Employers and Employees Not Enemies

In real life, workers and investors in the same company are not competitors. Production and marketing are not class warfare. Savers, employers, and employees of the same company are team workers. A demand for a Ford automobile is a demand for a Ford factory and for Ford workers. All those needed to produce the factory and the autos are a team. Anything which helps an automobile company helps all those who are on the team, either as investors or workers. The ultimate demand of consumers is for a team combination and it is this free combination that is going to help all of us have more of the things we want most.

The demand for workers at higher wages should come from those putting increased investments to work. New investments always seek new workers. Then all other employers have to pay the new higher wages, because no employer can keep workers if a competitor is offering higher wages. Present union policies cannot raise the wages of all workers. They lead only to higher prices and lower production.

If we are going to stop the ever upward wage-price spiral before there is a complete collapse in the value of the monetary unit, we must create a climate that will lead to the repeal of all laws which permit unions to exclude qualified workers from competing for jobs in union-organized industries. We must stop subsidizing unemployment and permit wages to be set by free market competition in the service of consumers.

This is not the policy in most countries of the world. Under present policies, workers are getting higher money wages which are lower real wages because the value of the monetary unit is constantly being diluted. We are going into progressive inflation. Savers are being liquidated. Their property is being confiscated. New savers are scared away.

Politicians are constantly afraid, and rightly so, of doing things which are unpopular. They endorse popular spending measures, but they shun the resulting costs; and to stay popular they have resorted to inflation. This is the so-called Keynesian policy. It is set forth in John Maynard Keynes' book, *The General Theory of Employment, Interest and Money*. The key sentence is: "A movement by employers to revise money wage bargains downwards will be more strongly resisted than a gradual and automatic lowering of real wages as a result of rising prices."

This was the policy endorsed by Keynes. It is the policy of most governments in the Western world today. Keynes knew, as every economist does, that the only way that you can employ more people is to lower the wage rate. But ever since World War I this had become politically difficult in Great Britain. Powerful British labor unions, with the help of the Fabian Socialists, had built up public pressures which opposed any lowering of any money wages. British politicians of all parties were afraid to resist this popular union policy. So in 1931, when the number of unemployed became unbearable, the politicians in office preferred to lower wages by devaluing the British pound. The workers kept their puffed-up pound wages but their pounds bought less.

In 1936, Keynes gave this political policy academic sanction in the book and sentence just quoted. Since then, most Western nations have adopted this "Full Employment" policy. In essence, when unemployment is considered too high, wages are lowered by lowering the value of the monetary unit. This is done by increasing the quantity of the monetary units. We have gotten into a situation of ever-rising wages and prices with more and more workers paid less than they would earn in a free market.

Neither union leaders nor union workers are stupid people. Keynes and the British politicians were able to fool the employees in England when they first tried this scheme in 1931. They changed all the index numbers, making it difficult to document the price rises reflecting the lower purchasing power of the pound. But now every union has a statistician, who can see from the official cost of living indices that prices are going up. And when they go up, the unions demand still higher wages. This system of Keynes' has just about reached the end of the road. You can no longer fool the workers by lowering the value of the monetary unit. They are now wise to what is happening and they are not going to take it much longer.

The only final answer to this problem is more economic education showing that the only way to keep raising wages permanently is to increase production and the way to do this is to encourage savings. For it is only increased savings that can provide workers with more and better education and more and better tools with which they can produce and buy more and better products that they want most.

38. JOBS FOR ALL*

Percy L. Greaves, Jr.

Life is an unfinished series of wanting things. From the day we are born to the day we die, we want things we don't have. If we didn't, we wouldn't be normal human beings. We would have no reason to eat, work, or get married. All life is a struggle to satisfy more of our wants.

As our society is organized, the normal way to get more of what we want is to take a job. Then we can use the dollars we earn to buy more of the things we want for ourselves and our loved ones. Without a job, or a business of our own, we would all have to grow our own food and make our own clothes as well as anything else we wanted. Taking a job where we can use tools supplied by savers is the easiest way for most of us to satisfy more of our wants.

So most men want a job. To be without a job is most depressing. Continued unemployment, through no fault of one's own, is probably the darkest future any man can face. Such longtime mass unemployment is one of the great curses of our age.

The human misery, degradation, and moral temptation are not all. Besides these setbacks to the human spirit, there is the great unseen loss of the wealth the idle might have produced if they had been employed. This loss is shared by all. In a market economy every dollar holder can buy a share of the total wealth offered for sale. The greater the wealth produced and offered for sale, the more anyone can buy with each of his dollars. So we all have a stake in reducing unemployment and encouraging the production of more of the things men want most.

Yet millions of able and willing men have recently remained unemployed for months on end. What is the answer?

Let's use our heads. When we want to sell something, we sell it to the highest bidder. He buys it for the lowest price he can. That is what happens at auctions every day. It happens at the corn and cotton markets as well as the stock exchanges. Even the grocer with perishable fruits and vegetables reduces his prices until a highest bidder buys them.

That way, the seller gets the highest anyone is willing to pay, while the buyer pays the lowest price any seller will freely accept. Both buyer and seller get the highest possible satisfaction from every transaction. That is the way of the free market.

There is no reason why these same free market principles can't be applied to the services of working men. It would be very simple, requiring only two things. First, let every job seeker choose that job which offers him what he considers the best returns he can get for the services he has to sell. Second, let every prospective employer choose those job seekers who offer what he considers the best services he can get for the wages he can pay. Competition would soon see to it that no one was paid too much or too little.

Of course, such a simple solution would put an end to all privileges for those now overpaid. No union would then be able to hold up employers and consumers for more than they need pay in a free and competitive market. By forcing some wages above free market rates, some unions now get higher wages for their members than such workers would receive in a free society. But these forced higher wages for some mean that others must accept lower wages or unemployment (unless the government resorts to inflation). These lower wages and unemployment (as well as this pressure for inflation) would disappear if every man, including the unemployed, were free to compete for every

*From *The Freeman*, February 1959

job. As long as some of men's wants remain unsatisfied, there will be enough jobs to go around.

A free job market would provide "full employment" and greater production of the things men want most. Competition might drive down some dollar wage rates, but living standards would have to be higher. With more goods and services competing for every dollar, prices would be lower and everyone with a dollar would be entitled to a share of the increased production. Those now overpaid might temporarily suffer, but in the long run we would all be able to satisfy more of our wants.

With a free market in jobs, every man would be free to take the best offer available. Every employer would also be free to hire the applicants that pleased him most. No one would remain long unemployed. There would be jobs for all, more wealth produced, and a greater satisfaction of everyone's wants. What is more, the economic loss and dread of unemployment would evaporate.

39. WAGES AND PRODUCTIVITY*

W. M. Curtiss

In discussions of wage rates, whether for individuals, firms, or for the entire economy, we hear a lot about the increasing productivity of the worker, and that wages must rise to reflect such increases. A large steel company recently has negotiated a contract with its workers which says, in effect, "If your productivity increases, your wages will keep pace." Is this the way wages are or should be determined in an open society? Just what are the implications, if all wages were determined by this method?

How come that a boy today gets $3.00 or $4.00 for mowing the same lawn you did as a lad for 25 or 50 cents? Has the productivity of boys increased that much? True, a boy with a power mower can do the job faster; but when he's finished, the total accomplishment is no greater than when done a generation ago. In fact, the job may have been done better then, if you consider the trimming which boys with power mowers tend to neglect.

Or, take a haircut—$2.00 now compared to the quarter you paid for your first one! Electric clippers, to be sure; but again, you are interested in the finished job rather than the barber's speed.

So it goes, for one service after another—a cleaning woman, window washing and hanging screens, car waxing, house painting—whatever the service, you find it costs a lot more to get the job done than when you were a boy.

When you think about it, you realize that inflation is a factor—a dollar doesn't go as far as it once did. That might account for perhaps a doubling of the price, but what about the rest of the increase?

Supply and Demand

In a free market, wages are determined by competitive forces of supply and demand. A manufacturer, after very careful planning, concludes that he can make and sell so many of a particular item at a given price. He must assemble his resources, including his plant, his equipment, his managerial talent, and workers, and hope to recover the cost of these things from the price buyers will pay for the finished product.

So, the manufacturer goes into the labor market to hire men to work for him. If his offered wage isn't high enough to get the workers he needs, then he must either give up the project or figure how to recombine his resources in such a way that he can pay higher wages and still come out ahead. He may do this by simplifying his manufacturing processes, by introducing more or better machinery, or by innovations of some sort.

The worker, on the other hand, will look after his interest, too, and will consider moving to a new job if it seems more attractive to him for reasons of higher pay, better working conditions, shorter days, more vacation, or whatever.

But, suppose some manufacturer comes along with an item he can make and sell very profitably. It may be because of patents he holds, or special

*From *The Freeman*, November 1963

skills or processes that only he knows about. He may be able to afford to pay wages half again as high as the going wage in the area and still come out ahead. Shouldn't he do this?

In a free market, he is at liberty to pay the higher wage if he wishes. But if he has had some experience in manufacturing, he knows that competition is behind every tree and someone will figure out a way to put a competing product on the market that will undersell his, with his high labor costs, in which case he may find himself without his expected buyers. So, he probably will decide he should pay the going wage for his workers, or just enough more to fill his needs, and use most of his technological advantages to reduce prices to the buyer and build his market. If, in the early stages, he is able to gain a handsome profit for himself and his stockholders, he will have a cushion with which to meet the competition certain to come.

All this has nothing to do with a particular businessman offering his workers production incentives. He may believe that his workers will produce more for him if he gives them every Wednesday afternoon off, or he may give them a share in the profits of the firm, or he may pay them on a piecework basis. That must be each employer's decision; but most will offer a base wage rate not greatly different from the going wage in the area.

Competition the Key

But, what has all this to do with the cost of getting my lawn mowed, or a haircut, or hiring a woman to clean my house? Why have wages in the services increased over the years about as much as those in highly automated industries? In one instance, efficiency of doing the job may not have increased at all, while in the other, it may have increased tenfold.

Competition is the answer. If you want a man to cut your hair, you must pay enough to keep him from going to work in a factory or at some other occupation. As a result, we have what may be referred to as a wage level for the entire economy. This is a somewhat mythical figure, not too meaningful because of the variability of individual skills. For example, consumers will pay a great deal more for the services of a skilled brain surgeon than for the services of a messenger.

The calculation of a wage level for a country is a tremendously complicated procedure and not too satisfactory at best. Nevertheless, it is a useful if not precise tool in comparing the economy of one country with another. We know, for example, that the general level of wages is much higher in the United States than in India, which leads to certain conclusions about how wages may be improved in any economy.

With a free market, in an advanced economy, most of the returns from production go to the workers—roughly 85 to 90 per cent. Competition *forces* this. If workers are supplied with good tools and equipment, they are more productive and their wage level is higher than it would be otherwise. This is a generalization regarding all workers. The general wage level is higher in a country where there is a relatively high investment in tools and equipment per worker. It is just that simple! In the United States, the investment per worker in tools may be $20,000, and it is not unheard of to find a particular business with an investment of $100,000 in tools and equipment per worker.

The road, then, to a higher wage level is through savings and investment in the tools of production. There is no other.

A high investment in tools and equipment benefits the barber, the cleaning woman, and all service employees, even though the investment is not directly for their work. Competition sees to this.

A Negative Bonus

However enlightened it may appear on the surface, the wages of an individual worker or for a group of workers cannot be tied to the productivity of their job or to the profitability of a particular firm. If this were the case, a highly skilled worker might find himself working for a negative "bonus" in a firm which, for some reason, happens to be operating at a loss.

The same may be said for tying wages to a cost-of-living index. A fair wage, both to the worker and the employer, can only be established by bargaining between the two interested parties—the worker taking what appears to him to be the best he can get and the employer, all things considered, getting the best deal for himself.

The lesson here is that while productivity of workers is highly important when considering a general wage level, productivity does not determine what the wage rate ought to be for any given firm or industry within the economy. The effect of general productivity on wages is automatic in a free market with competition. And all workers stand to gain when tools and capital are made available to some of them.

40. COMPETITION, MONOPOLY AND THE ROLE OF GOVERNMENT*

Sylvester Petro

The great monopoly problem mankind has to face today is not an outgrowth of the operation of the market economy. It is a product of purposive action on the part of governments. It is not one of the evils inherent in capitalism as the demagogues trumpet. It is, on the contrary, the fruit of policies hostile to capitalism and intent upon sabotaging and destroying its operation.

—LUDWIG VON MISES, *Human Action*

In the free society government keeps the peace, protects private property, and enforces contracts. Government must do these things effectively, and it must do nothing else; otherwise, the conditions indispensable to personal freedom in society are absent. Whether or not a free society is attainable no mortal man can know; the limits of our knowledge are too narrow. But one thing we do know: that until at least the advocates of the free society are fully aware of the conditions necessary to its existence, it can never come about. For they must ever be on guard against new movements, ideas, and principles which would endanger its realization. And on the other hand, they must be sharply aware of existing impediments so that they may direct their energies intelligently to the removal of the causes of current imperfections.

I take up with considerable trepidation the task of arguing that government should quit trying to promote competition by means of the antitrust laws, especially since some proponents of the free society believe that vigorous enforcement of those laws is absolutely indispensable. Yet, antitrust laws are inconsistent with the basic principles of the free society, private property, and freedom of contract; they deprive persons of private property in some cases and outlaw certain contracts which would otherwise be valid. Moreover, they expand the role of government far beyond that envisaged by the theory of the free society and thus amount to an unconscious admission that the fundamental theory itself is incoherent; for antitrust policy implicitly accepts the Marxian premise that a laissez faire economy will result in the decay of competition and in the emergence of abusive monopoly. Finally, and this may be the most pressing reason for the present article, in their attempt to promote competition the antitrust laws may in fact be inhibiting it.

Vague and Uncertain Laws

One of the basic evils in the antitrust laws is the vagueness and uncertainty of their application. They have produced mainly confusion. Seventy some years ago the antitrust laws prevented the Great Northern Railway and the Northern Pacific from merging, although but a minor fragment of their respective lines overlapped in competition. But a few years later United States Steel was permitted to consolidate a vast preponderance of the steel production of the country under one management. Since then we have been off on another antimerger binge, and so Bethlehem and Youngstown have been enjoined from doing on a smaller scale what U.S. Steel did on a grand scale. Socony and other integrated oil companies were told that they might not buy up distress oil at prices set in competitive markets. But only a few years earlier the Appalachian Coals Association had been permitted to act as exclusive marketing agent for most of the coal production of an entire region. Forty years after its foresight, courage, and capital had been instrumental in developing the great General Motors productive complex, the du Pont Company was ordered to give up control of its G.M. stock be-

*From *The Freeman*, February 1974

cause of a relatively picayune buyer-seller relationship between them. Only space limitations preclude an almost endless listing of equally contradictory and inequitable results of the unpredictable eruptions from the antitrust volcano. At present, the allegedly competitive policies of the Sherman Act are mocked by those patently anticompetitive components of the antitrust laws, the Robinson-Patman Act and the fair-trade laws.

Thus, to the careful and honest observer the antitrust laws appear to be a charter of confusion, rather than the "charter of economic liberty" which oratory calls them. They have been transmogrified by the political vagaries to which their vagueness makes them susceptible into an insult to the idea that laws should apply equally to all. Some may regard these consequences as merely unfortunate incidents of a generally praiseworthy program. Yet we need continually to remind ourselves that law is for the benefit of the citizenry, rather than for the sport of government and of the legal profession. The main function of law is to provide people with clear and sound rules of the game, so that they may pursue their affairs with a minimum of doubt and uncertainty.

While aggravating the existing uncertainties of life, the antitrust laws can make no demonstrable claim to improving competition, despite the contentions of enthusiastic trustbusters. I have heard it said that the result of breaking up large firms is to create competition among its fragments, and thus to contribute to social well-being. But a moment's reflection will expose this as a bare and unsupportable assertion. Even though additional firms may be created by breaking up large businesses, the result is not necessarily in the social interest, nor does it necessarily create or improve competition. The social interest and competition are not automatically served by an increase in the number of firms. It is a commonplace that competition may be more vigorous and the service to society greater when an industry has few firms than when it has many. The question from the point of view of society is not how many firms there are, but how efficiently and progressively the firms—no matter how few or how numerous—utilize scarce resources in the service of the public. Maybe production will improve after a single large producer is split into fragments; but it is equally possible that it will not. No one can tell in advance, and it is also impossible to do so after the fact. The only thing that can be said with certainty about the breaking up of businesses is that government's power has been used to deny property rights rather than to protect them. If we really believe that private property is the most valuable institution of the free society, and that in it lies the strength of the free society, then it is wrong to abrogate that institution on the basis of pure guesswork.

Monopoly Unionism

The antitrust approach to improving competition loses even more of its glamor when one understands that the most abusive and socially dangerous monopoly which exists today in this country is the direct product of special governmental privileges. Labor unions are today the most destructive monopolies in our system, and they are also the greatest beneficiaries of governmental special privileges.

First and foremost, there is the virtual privilege of violence, which trade unions alone enjoy. Neither individuals nor other organizations are so privileged. Memory is strangely short as regards union violence, and yet every big union in America has used it habitually, in both organizing and "collective bargaining."

Of the men who resist union membership, many are beaten and some are killed. They have much more to fear than do persons who reject the blandishments of sellers of other goods or services. And this is true despite the fact that the right *not* to join a union is as firmly entrenched in legal theory and the theory of the free society as is the right to buy as one wishes or to refuse to buy when one so wishes.

In 1959, the United Mine Workers engaged in one of its periodic purges of the nonunion mines which spring up continually owing to the uneconomic wage forced upon the organized mines by the UMW. An Associated Press dispatch, dated April 10, 1959, reported that "one nonunion operator has been killed, five union members charged in the fatal shooting, and three ramps damaged by dynamite since the strike began March 9. It has made idle more than 7,000 men over the union's demands for a $34.25 a day wage, a $2.00 increase." The grimmest aspect of the dispatch lay in the news that Governor A. B. Chandler of Kentucky was *threatening*—after a full month of terror and pillage by the union—to order National Guardsmen into the coal fields.

This is no isolated case. On the contrary, violence and physical obstruction are standard features of most strikes, except where the struck employers "voluntarily" shut down their businesses, in accordance with the Reuther theory of enlightened management which I have described in *Power Unlimited: The Corruption of Union Leadership* (Ronald Press, 1959). A special dispatch to *The New York Times*, dated August 5, 1959, reported that "a siege was lifted today for 267 supervisory employees at the United States Steel Company's Fairless Works here. . . . From now on the supervisory personnel will be allowed to enter and leave the plant at will for maintenance." The dispatch is silent concerning the probable consequence of any attempt by the steel companies to maintain production. But the fact that supervisors were besieged because of maintenance operations suggests that rank-and-file workers who attempted to engage in production would be mauled. It is not out of order to infer that the siege of the supervisors, otherwise a pretty silly act, was intended to get across that message.

The careful student of industrial warfare will discern a pattern of violence which reveals an institutionalized, professional touch. Mass picketing, goon squads (or "flying squadrons" as they are known in the Auto Workers union), home demonstrations, paint bombs, and perhaps most egregious of all, the "passes" which striking unions issue to management personnel for limited purposes—these are the carefully tooled components of the ultimate monopoly power of unions.

As a matter of fact, we have become so befuddled by, and so weary of, the terror, destruction, and waste of the unions' organizing wars that we view with relief and contentment one of the most prodigious contracts in restraint of trade ever executed—the celebrated "no-raiding pact" of the AFL-CIO. No division of markets by any industrial firm has ever achieved such proportions. The "no-raiding pact" divides the whole organizable working force in accordance with the ideas of the union leaders who swing the most weight in the AFL-CIO. It determines which unions are "entitled" to which employees. The theory of modern labor relations law is that employees have a right to unions of their own choosing. Reversing that principle, the "no-raiding pact" asserts that the choice belongs to the union leadership. If any business group were so openly to dictate the choices of consumers, it would be prosecuted by sundry federal agencies and hailed before one or another, or perhaps many Congressional committees. It would not receive congratulatory telegrams from the chief politicians of the nation.

Government Intervention

The more one examines American labor law the more one becomes convinced of the validity of Professor Mises' theory that no abusive monopoly is possible in a market economy without the help of government in one form or another. If employers were permitted to band together peacefully in order to *resist* unionization, as unions are permitted to engage in coercive concerted activities in order to *compel* unionization, it is probable that the purely economic (nonviolent) pressures of unions would not be as effective as they have been in increasing the size and power of the big unions. But the government has taken from employers *all* power to resist unionization, by peaceful as well as by violent means. At the same time it has permitted unions to retain the most effective methods of economic coercion. And so picketing, boycotts, and other more subtle modes of compulsory unionism are in many instances as effective in compelling unwilling membership—in the absence of countervailing economic pressures from employers—as sheer physical violence.

Monopoly unionism owes much, too, to direct and positive help from government. Consider the vigorous prohibition of company-assisted independent unions which has prevailed for over twenty years. Although such small unions might at times best serve the interests of employees, the early National Labor Relations Board practically outlawed all independent unions, and more recent decisions continue to favor the big affiliated unions.

The Majority-Rule Principle

But perhaps the most significant contribution of government to monopoly unionism is the majority-rule principle which makes any union selected by a majority of votes in an "appropriate bargaining unit" the exclusive representative of all employees in that unit, including those who have not voted at all, as well as those who have expressly rejected the union as bargaining representative. Majority rule is a monopolistic principle; it is always to be contrasted with individual freedom of action. But it is particularly prone to monopolistic abuse in labor relations. Determination of the "appropriate bargaining unit" is left to the virtually unreviewable discretion of the National Labor Relations Board. And that agency has in numerous instances felt duty-bound to carve out the bargaining unit most favorable to the election of unions. Indeed, politicians might learn something about gerrymandering from studying the unit determinations of the Labor Board.

Even if the gerrymandering could be eliminated, the majority-rule principle would remain a source of monopolistic abuse, based on monopoly power granted and enforced by government. A union may be certified exclusive representative in a 1,000-man bargaining unit on the basis of as few as 301 affirmative votes, for an election will be considered valid in such a unit when 600 employees participate. If a bare majority then votes in favor of the union, the remaining 699 are saddled with the union as their *exclusive* bargaining representative, whether or not they want it.

Competitive Safeguards

Society has nothing to fear from unions which without privileged compulsion negotiate labor contracts and perform other lawful and useful jobs for workers who have voluntarily engaged their services. For they are then but another of the consensual service associations or agencies which a free society breeds so prolifically. Moreover, the free society has demonstrated that its fundamental mechanism, free competition in open markets, is tough and resilient enough to defend against exploitation by any genuinely voluntary association. The critical problem arises when a man or an association destroys society's chief defense mechanism by violent and coercive conduct, or when that mechanism is blacked out by special privilege from government. For then, without the checks and balances of free men vying against free men in civilized competition, society lies as prone to exploitation by the unscrupulous as a rich store would be without guards and burglar alarms.

When the sources and components of union monopoly are understood, it becomes clear that the antitrust laws cannot cure the problem. The fundamental source is to be found in failures and errors of government which the most elaborately conceived antitrust laws could not cure. The basic job of government is to keep the peace. It has not kept the peace in labor relations. Local, state, and federal governments have all failed to prevent labor goons and massed picket lines from interfering with the freedom of action of nonunion employees and of employers in bargaining disputes. (See my book, *The Kingsport Strike*, Arlington House, 1967.) A similar failure in organizing campaigns has permitted unions which would be pygmies, if they represented only workers who wanted them, to become giants. The antitrust laws would equally clearly do nothing to remedy the monopolistic consequences of the positive aids granted by government to the big unions, such as the majority-rule principle and the virtual outlawry of small independent unions.

I am convinced that the socially dangerous aspects of big unionism have been brought about by the errors and failures of government which we have been considering. Government has on the one hand been tolerating the violence and economic coercion by means of which the big unions have attained their present power, and it has, on the other hand, positively intervened in their support. Moreover for the last forty years or more, officers of the national administration have played a critical role in the key industrial disputes which have set the pattern of the so-called inflationary wage-cost push.

The latter is a much more important fact than it may seem at first view. It suggests that the checks and balances of free enterprise are adequate to protect the public even from the artificially constructed compulsory labor monopolies which we now know. Moreover, it is not unreasonable to infer that those checks will work even more effectively if politicians not only stay out of negotiations but also enforce the laws against compulsory organization. These considerations suggest that the logical first step for those concerned about union power is to insist that government remove the present special privileges which unions enjoy and then wait patiently, to see if the program will work itself out without further government intervention.

Government's Limited Role, As Outlined by Mark Twain

I believe that the same approach should be taken in respect to *businesses* suspected of monopolistic abuses. Rather than following the hit-or-miss political vagaries of the antitrust approach, it would be better to make sure that all special privileges, such as tariffs, exclusive franchises, and other governmental devices for blocking access to markets are withdrawn. Repeal of the tax laws which unfairly prevent high earners from amassing the capital necessary to compete with existing firms would also help much more than antitrust prosecutions do in promoting competition. In short, if government would confine itself to protecting property and contract rights, and if it would desist from impairing those rights, it would be doing all that government can do to promote competition. And we should not need to be greatly concerned about monopolies and contracts in restraint of trade. For, as Mark Twain's account of the career of the riverboat pilots' monopoly in the nineteenth century demonstrates, the free enterprise system is in itself fully capable of destroying all abusive restraints upon competition which are not supported and protected by government.

In the years before the Civil War, Twain writes in *Life on the Mississippi,* the river steamboat pilots formed an association which was to become, as Twain put it, "the tightest monopoly in the world." Having gone through many trials in building up its membership, a sudden increase in the demand for pilots gave the association its first break. It held members to their oath against working with any nonmember, and soon nonmembers began having difficulty getting berths. This difficulty was increased by the association pilots' safety record, which grew out of an ingenious method evolved by the association for current reports on the ever-changing Mississippi channel. Since the information in these reports was confined to members of the association, and since nonmembers had no comparable navigation guide, the number of boats lost or damaged by the latter soon became obviously disproportionate. "One black day," Twain writes, "every captain was formally ordered (by the underwriters) to immediately discharge his outsiders and take association pilots in their stead."

The association was then in the driver's seat. It forbade all apprentices for five years and strictly controlled their number thereafter. It went into the insurance business, insuring not only the lives of members but steamboat losses as well. By United States law the signature of two licensed pilots was necessary before any new pilot could be made. "Now there was nobody outside of the association competent to sign," says Twain and "consequently the making of pilots was at an end." The association proceeded to force wages up to five hundred dollars per month on the Mississippi and to seven hundred dollars on some of its tributaries. Captains' wages naturally had to climb to at least the level of the pilots', and soon the increased costs had to be reflected in increased rates. Then society's checks and balances went to work. This is Twain's summation:

"As I have remarked, the pilots' association was now the compactest monopoly in the world, perhaps, and seemed simply indestructible. And yet the days of its glory were numbered. First, the new railroad . . . began to divert the passenger travel from the steamers; next the war came and almost entirely annihilated the steamboating industry during several years . . . then the treasurer of the St. Louis association put his hand into the till and walked off with every dollar of the ample fund; and finally, the railroads intruding everywhere, there was little for steamers to do but carry freights; so straightway some genius from the Atlantic coast introduced the plan of towing a dozen steamer cargoes down to New Orleans at the tail of a vulgar little tugboat; and behold, in the twinkling of an eye, as it were, the association and the noble science of piloting were things of the dead and pathetic past!"

The moral: government's job is done when it defends the right of competitive businessmen or workers to take over functions which are being abused by monopolistic groups. The deeper moral is that monopolistic abuses rarely survive without a basis in one form or another of special privilege granted by government. The long steel, auto, and other big strikes we have suffered would not have lasted nearly so long if government had effectively protected the right of the companies to keep their plants operating and the right of employees to continue working during the strike.

41. THE ECONOMICS AND POLITICS OF MY JOB*

Ludwig von Mises

Our economic system—the market economy or capitalism—is a system of consumers' supremacy. The customer is sovereign; he is, says a popular slogan, "always right." Businessmen are under the necessity of turning out what the consumers ask for and they must sell their wares at prices which the consumers can afford and are prepared to pay. A business operation is a manifest failure if the proceeds from the sales do not reimburse the businessman for all he has expended in producing the article. Thus the consumers in buying at a definite price determine also the height of the wages that are paid to all those engaged in the industries.

It follows that an employer cannot pay more to an employee than the equivalent of the value the latter's work, *according to the judgment of the buying public*, adds to the merchandise. (This is the reason why the movie star gets much more than the charwoman.) If he were to pay more, he would not recover his outlays from the purchasers; he would suffer losses and would finally go bankrupt. In paying wages, the employer acts as a mandatory of the consumers, as it were. It is upon the consumers that the incidence of the wage payments falls. As the immense majority of the goods produced are bought and consumed by people who are themselves receiving wages and salaries, it is obvious that in spending their earnings the wage earners and employees themselves are foremost in determining the height of the compensation they will get.

What Makes Wages Rise?

The buyers do not pay for the toil and trouble the worker took nor for the length of time he spent in working. They pay for the products. The better the tools are which the worker uses in his job, the more he can perform in an hour, the higher is, consequently, his remuneration. What makes wages rise and renders the material conditions of the wage earners more satisfactory is improvement in the technological equipment.

American wages are higher than wages in other countries because the capital invested per head of the worker is greater and the plants are thereby in the position to use the most efficient tools and machines. What is called the American way of life is the result of the fact that the United States has put fewer obstacles in the way of saving and capital accumulation than other nations.

The economic backwardness of such countries as India consists precisely in the fact that their policies hinder both the accumulation of domestic capital and the investment of foreign capital. As the capital required is lacking, the Indian enterprises are prevented from employing sufficient quantities of modern equipment, are therefore producing much less per man-hour, and can only afford to pay wage rates which, compared with American wage rates, appear as shockingly low.

There is only one way that leads to an improvement of the standard of living for the wage-earning masses—the increase in the amount of capital invested. All other methods, however popular they may be, are not only futile, but are actually detrimental to the well-being of those they allegedly want to benefit.

The fundamental question is: Is it possible to raise wage rates *for all those eager to find jobs* above the height they would have attained on an unhampered labor market?

Public opinion believes that the improvement in the conditions of the wage earners is an achievement of the unions and of various legislative measures. It gives to unionism and to legislation credit for the rise in wage rates, the shortening of hours of work, the disappearance of child labor, and many other changes. The prevalence of this belief made unionism popular and is responsible for the

*From *The Freeman*, May 1958

trend in labor legislation of the last decades. As people think that they owe to unionism their high standard of living, they condone violence, coercion, and intimidation on the part of unionized labor and are indifferent to the curtailment of personal freedom inherent in the union-shop and closed-shop clauses. As long as these fallacies prevail upon the minds of the voters, it is vain to expect a resolute departure from the policies mistakenly called progressive.

What Causes Unemployment?

Yet this popular doctrine misconstrues every aspect of economic reality. The height of wage rates at which all those eager to get jobs can be employed depends on the marginal productivity of labor, or, in other words, on the worker's contribution to the usefulness of the product.

The more capital—other things being equal—is invested, the higher wages climb on the free labor market, i.e., on the labor market not manipulated by the government and the unions. At these market wage rates all those eager to employ workers can hire as many as they want. At these market wage rates all those who want to be employed can get a job. There prevails on a free labor market a tendency toward full employment. In fact, the policy of letting the free market determine the height of wage rates is the only reasonable and successful full-employment policy. If wage rates, either by union pressure and compulsion or by government decree, are raised above this height, lasting unemployment of a part of the potential labor force develops.

These opinions are passionately rejected by the union bosses and their followers among politicians and the self-styled intellectuals. The panacea they recommend to fight unemployment is credit expansion and inflation, euphemistically called "an easy money policy."

As has been pointed out above, an addition to the available stock of capital previously accumulated makes a further improvement of the industries' technological equipment possible, thus raises the marginal productivity of labor and consequently also wage rates. But credit expansion, whether it is effected by issuing additional banknotes or by granting additional credits on bank accounts subject to check, does not add anything to the nation's wealth of capital goods. It merely creates the illusion of an increase in the amount of funds available for an expansion of production. Because they can obtain cheaper credit, people erroneously believe that the country's wealth has thereby been increased and that therefore certain projects that could not be executed before are now feasible. The inauguration of these projects enhances the demand for labor and for raw materials and makes wage rates and commodity prices rise. An artificial boom is kindled.

Inflation and Unemployment

Under the conditions of this boom, nominal wage rates which before the credit expansion were too high for the state of the market and therefore created unemployment of a part of the potential labor force are no longer too high and the unemployed can get jobs again. However, this happens only because under the changed monetary and credit conditions prices are rising or, what is the same expressed in other words, the purchasing power of the monetary unit drops. Then the same amount of nominal wages—wage rates expressed in terms of money—means less in real wages—in terms of commodities that can be bought by the monetary unit. Inflation can cure unemployment only by curtailing the wage earner's *real* wages. But then the unions ask for a new increase in wages in order to keep pace with the rising cost of living and we are back where we were before, in a situation in which large scale unemployment can only be prevented by a further expansion of credit.

This is what happened in this country as well as in many other countries in the last years. The unions, supported by the government, forced the enterprises to agree to wage rates that went beyond the potential market rates, that is, the rates which the public was prepared to refund to the employers in purchasing their products. This would have inevitably resulted in rising unemployment figures. But the government policies tried to prevent the emergence of serious unemployment by credit expansion—inflation. The outcome was rising prices, renewed demands for higher wages and reiterated credit expansion; in short, protracted inflation.

Inflation Can't Go On Endlessly

But finally the authorities became frightened. They know that inflation cannot go on endlessly. If one does not stop in time the pernicious policy of increasing the quantity of money and fiduciary media, the nation's currency system collapses entirely. The monetary unit's purchasing power sinks to a point which for all practical purposes is not better than zero. This happened again and again, in this country with the Continental Currency in 1781, in France in 1796, in Germany in 1923. It is never too early for a nation to realize that inflation cannot be considered as a way of life and that it is imperative to return to sound monetary policies.

What Causes the Slump?

It is not the task of this article to deal with all the consequences which the termination of inflationary measures brings about. We have only to establish the fact that the return to monetary stability does not *generate* a crisis. It only brings to light the malinvestments and other mistakes that were made under the hallucination of the illusory prosperity created by the easy money. People become aware of the faults committed and, no longer blinded by the phantom of cheap credit, begin to readjust their activities to the real state of the supply of material factors of production. It is this—certainly painful, but unavoidable—readjustment that constitutes the depression.

One of the unpleasant features of this process of discarding chimeras and returning to a sober estimate of reality concerns the height of wage rates. Under the impact of the progressing inflationary policy the union bureaucracy acquired the habit of asking at regular intervals for wage raises, and business, after some sham resistance, yielded. As a result these rates were at the moment too high for the state of the market and would have brought about a conspicuous amount of unemployment. But the ceaselessly progressing inflation very soon caught up with them. Then the unions asked again for new raises and so on.

The Purchasing Power Argument

It does not matter what kind of justification the unions and their henchmen advance in favor of their claims. The unavoidable effects of forcing the employers to remunerate work done at higher rates than those the consumers are willing to restore to them in buying the products are always the same: rising unemployment figures.

At the present juncture the unions try to rake up the old hundred-times-refuted purchasing power fable. They declare that putting more money into the hands of the wage earners—by raising wage rates, increasing the benefits to the unemployed, and embarking upon new public works—would enable the workers to spend more and thereby stimulate business and lead the economy out of the recession into prosperity. This is the spurious pro-inflation argument to make all people happy through printing paper bills.

Of course, if the quantity of the circulating media is increased, those into whose pockets the new fictitious wealth comes—whether they are workers or farmers or any other kind of people—will increase their spending. But it is precisely this increase in spending that inevitably brings about a general tendency of all prices to rise. Thus the help that an inflationary action could give to the wage earners is only of a short duration. To perpetuate it, one would have to resort again and again to new inflationary measures. It is clear that this leads to disaster.

There is a lot of nonsense said about these things. Some people assert that wage raises are "inflationary." But they are not in themselves inflationary. Nothing is inflationary except inflation, i. e., an increase in the quantity of money in circulation and credit subject to check (checkbook money). And under present conditions nobody but the government can bring an inflation into being. What the unions can generate by forcing the employers to accept wage rates higher than the potential market rates is not inflation and not higher commodity prices, but unemployment of a part of the people anxious to get a job. Inflation is a policy to which the government resorts in order to prevent the large scale unemployment the unions' wage raising would otherwise bring about.

The Dilemma of Present-Day Policies

The dilemma which this country and many others have to face is very serious. The extremely popular method of raising wage rates above the height the unhampered labor market would have established would produce catastrophic mass unemployment if inflationary credit expansion were not to rescue it. But inflation has not only very pernicious social effects. It cannot go on endlessly without resulting in the complete breakdown of the whole monetary system.

Public opinion, entirely under the sway of the fallacious labor union doctrines, sympathizes more or less with the union bosses' demand for a considerable rise in wage rates. As conditions are today, the unions have the power to make the employers submit to their dictates. They can call strikes and, without being restrained by the authorities, resort with impunity to violence against those willing to work. They are aware of the fact that the enhancement of wage rates will increase the number of jobless. The only remedy they suggest is more ample funds for unemployment compensation and a more ample supply of credit, i. e., inflation. The government, meekly yielding to a misguided public opinion and worried about the outcome of the impending election campaign, has unfortunately already begun to reverse its attempts to return to a sound monetary policy. Thus we are again committed to the pernicious methods of meddling with the supply of money. We are going on with the inflation that with accelerated speed makes the purchasing power of the dollar shrink. Where will it end? This is the question which Mr. Reuther and all the rest never ask.

The Wage Earner's Stake

Only stupendous ignorance can call the policies adopted by the self-styled progressives "pro-labor" policies. The wage earner like every other citizen is firmly interested in the preservation of the dollar's purchasing power. If, thanks to his union, his weekly earnings are raised above the market rate, he must very soon discover that the upward movement in prices not only deprives him of the advantages he expected, but besides makes the value of his savings, of his insurance policy, and of his pension rights dwindle. And, still worse, he may lose his job and will not find another.

All political parties and pressure groups protest that they are opposed to inflation. But what they really mean is that they do not like the unavoidable consequences of inflation, namely, the rise in living costs. Actually they favor all policies that necessarily bring about an increase in the quantity of the circulating media. They ask not only for an easy money policy to make the unions' endless wage boosting possible but also for more government spending and—at the same time—for tax abatement through raising the exemptions.

Duped by the spurious Marxian concept of irreconcilable conflicts between the interests of the social classes, people assume that the interests of the propertied classes alone are opposed to the unions' demand for higher wage rates. In fact, the wage earners are no less interested than any other groups or classes in a return to sound money. A lot has been said in the last months about the harm fraudulent officers have inflicted upon the union membership. But the havoc done to the workers by the union's excessive wage boosting is much more detrimental.

It would be an exaggeration to contend that the tactics of the unions are the sole threat to monetary stability and to a reasonable economic policy. Organized wage earners are not the only pressure group whose claims menace today the stability of our monetary system. But they are the most powerful and most influential of these groups and the primary responsibility rests with them.

Capitalism and the Common Man

Capitalism has improved the standard of living of the wage earners to an unprecedented extent. The average American family enjoys today amenities of which, only a hundred years ago, not even the richest nabobs dreamed. All this well-being is conditioned by the increase in savings and capital accumulated; without these funds that enable business to make practical use of scientific and technological progress the American worker would not produce more and better things per hour of work than the Asiatic coolies, would not earn more, and would, like them, wretchedly live on the verge of starvation. All measures which—like our income and corporation tax system—aim at preventing further capital accumulation or even at capital decumulation are therefore virtually antilabor and antisocial.

One further observation must still be made about this matter of saving and capital formation. The improvement of well-being brought about by capitalism made it possible for the common man to save and thus to become a capitalist himself in a modest way. A considerable part of the capital working in American business is the counterpart of the savings of the masses. Millions of wage earners own saving deposits, bonds, and insurance policies. All these claims are payable in dollars and their worth depends on the soundness of the nation's money. To preserve the dollar's purchasing power is also from this point of view of vital interest to the masses. In order to attain this end, it is not enough to print upon the banknotes the noble maxim, *In God we trust.* One must adopt an appropriate policy.

Money, Credit and Banking

42. MILLION DOLLAR DREAM*

I dreamed I had a million dollars and need never work again.

I thought of all the things I could now do because I had a million bucks. I would have the fanciest food money could buy. I would buy a fine house. Only the sportiest and most expensive automobile would suit me from now on. Clothing? Only the richest and finest would ever cover me again. Oh, I was in clover all right. My fondest wishes had come true.

In my dream I dressed and, being hungry, went to breakfast. There wasn't any. My wife was in tears. The food she had ordered the day before hadn't been delivered. Not even a bottle of milk or the morning newspaper greeted me when I opened the door. I tried to telephone the grocery but the line was dead. I said, "Oh, well, I'll take a walk and bring back something for breakfast."

The street was deserted. Not a bus, street car, or cab was in sight. I walked on and on. Nothing in sight. Thinking something had happened only to my neighborhood. I went to another. Not even a train was moving. Then people began to appear on the street—first, only a few, then many, then hundreds. I joined them and began asking questions: "What has happened? Where can I buy food?" Then I got the jolt. Somebody said, "Don't you know? Everybody has a million dollars and nobody has to work any more."

*From *The Freeman*, March 1957. Reproduced by permission of The Employers' Association of Chicago

At first I was stunned. I thought that somehow a mistake, a ghastly mistake had been made—but there was no mistake. It was really true. Everybody had a million dollars and thought that work was over for him.

Then it dawned on me as never before that all of us are dependent upon all of the rest of us; that to a small extent at least my labor had a place, a part, in the total welfare of mankind. With an angry shout I tossed to the winds even the thought of a million dollars.

Then I woke up. My dream was over. The sun was shining, the birds singing, my wife rattling the breakfast things. I looked out the window and saw a world of people moving about their tasks, each contributing a little to my life and living, just as I contribute to theirs. I called to my wife, "Hurry up with that breakfast, sweetheart, I want to get to work."

EDITOR'S NOTE: *This fable, reproduced by permission of The Employers' Association of Chicago, illustrates that money is not wealth. Nor has it exchange value except as the owners and producers of goods and services find that it facilitates their trading with one another.*

A society of nothing but consumers is indeed a dream that no amount of money can bring to realization. Anyone who attempts to issue money with no provision for its redemption in goods or services is due the same rude awakening that is in store for every dreamer of something for nothing.

43. NOT WORTH A CONTINENTAL*

Pelatiah Webster

EDITOR'S NOTE:
"Not worth a continental" is a descriptive phrase born of an early American experiment in deficit financing. If its lessons are ignored or forgotten, that experience will have been as worthless as the Continental currency itself.

Pelatiah Webster, "an able though not conspicuous citizen" of Philadelphia (1726-1795), is credited by James Madison and others as having been the first advocate of a constitutional convention. Though he was not a delegate, many points in the Constitution conform to an outline he had proposed several years prior to the Convention.

The "fatal mistakes" of deficit financing, inflation, and price control were understood by men like Webster. Lessons learned the hard way during the period of revolutionary America had a determining influence on those who founded the republic.

The Continental Congress authorized the printing of paper money but depended upon enabling legislation by the respective states under the Tender Acts to give negotiability to the irredeemable paper and to keep it in circulation on a par with the "hard money" of those days. Webster considered it his duty as a citizen to criticize monetary enforcement legislation then being proposed by the Assembly of Pennsylvania. The proposal was offered by the Assembly for public consideration on November 29, and was enacted into law, despite Webster's protest, on December 19, 1780.

It is too soon to tell the full impact of Webster's observations, for they were written with the hope "that our fatal mistakes may be a caution and a warning to future financiers who may live and act in any country which may happen to be in circumstances similar to ours at that time." Yet the circumstances in which we find ourselves today, the penalties of deficit financing and other uneconomic practices are the same as they were in 1780.

The text has been stripped of some archaisms of grammar and expression, but Webster's ideas and lucid style are intact.

•

The fatal error—that the credit and currency of the Continental money could be kept up and supported by acts of compulsion—entered so deep into the minds of Congress and of all departments of administration through the states that no considerations of justice, religion, or policy, or even experience of its utter inefficacy, could eradicate it. It seemed to be a kind of obstinate delirium, totally deaf to every argument drawn from justice and right, from its natural tendency and mischief, from common sense, and even common safety.

Congress began, as early as January 11, 1776, to hold up and recommend this *maxim of maniasm*, when Continental money was but five months old. Congress then resolved that "whoever should refuse to receive in payment Continental bills, etc., should be deemed and treated as an enemy of his country, and be precluded from all trade and intercourse with the inhabitants . . ."—that is, should be outlawed, which is the severest penalty, except of life and limb, known in our laws.

These Fatal Measures

This ruinous principle was continued in practice for five successive years, and appeared in all shapes and forms—in tender acts, in limitations of prices, in awful and threatening declarations, in penal laws with dreadful and ruinous punishments, and in every other way that could be devised. And all were executed with a relentless severity by the highest authorities then in being, namely, by Congress, assemblies and conventions of the states, by committees of inspection (whose

*First published December 13, 1780 in Philadelphia under the title "Strictures On Tender Acts"

powers in those days were nearly sovereign) and even by military force. Men of all descriptions stood trembling before this monster of force without daring to lift a hand against it during all this period. Its unrestrained energy ever proved ineffectual to its purposes, but in every instance increased the evils it was designed to remedy, and destroyed the benefits it was intended to promote. At best its utmost effect was like that of water sprinkled on a blacksmith's forge, which indeed deadens the flame for a moment, but never fails to increase the heat and force of the internal fire. Many thousand families of full and comfortable fortune were ruined by these fatal measures, and lie in ruins to this day, without the least benefit to the country or to the great and noble cause in which we were then engaged.

I do not mention these things from any pleasure I have in opening the wounds of my country or exposing its errors, but with a hope that our fatal mistakes may be a caution and warning to future financiers who may live and act in any country which may happen to be in circumstances similar to ours at that time.

A Standard of Value

The nature of a Tender-Act is no more or less than establishing by law the standard value of money, and has the same use with respect to the currency that the legal standard pound, bushel, yard, or gallon has to those goods, the quantities of which are usually ascertained by those weights and measures. Therefore, to call anything a pound or shilling, which really is not so, and make it a legal standard, is an error of the same nature as diminishing the standard bushel, yard, or gallon, or making a law that a foot shall be the legal yard, an ounce the legal pound, a peck the legal bushel, or a quart the legal gallon, and compelling everybody to receive all goods due to them by such deficient measures.

Further, to make anything the legal standard, which is not of fixed but variable nature, is an error of the same kind and mischief as the others—for example, to make a turnip the standard pound weight, which may dry up in the course of a year to a pith of not more than two or three ounces, or to make a flannel string the standard yard, which will shrink in using to half its length. The absurdity of this is too glaring to need anything further said on it.

But to come to the matter now in question. The first observation which occurs to me is that the bills, which are made a tender, contain a public promise of money to be paid in six years. On which I beg leave to remark that the best and most indubitable security of money to be paid in six years, or any future time, is not so good or valuable as ready cash.

Therefore, the law which obliges a man to accept these bills instead of ready cash obliges him to receive a less valuable thing in full payment of a more valuable one, and injures him to the amount of the difference. This is a direct violation of the laws of commutative justice—laws grounded in the nature of human rights, supported by the most necessary natural principles, and enjoined by the most express authority of God Almighty. No legislature on earth should have right to infringe or abrogate this freedom of choice in the exchange of goods for goods.

Again, the security arising from the public promise is not generally deemed certain. The public faith has been so often violated, and the sufferings of individuals thence arising have been so multiplied and extensive, that the general confidence of our people in that security is much lessened. Since a chance or uncertainty can never be so valuable as a certainty, those bills must and will be considered as less valuable than they would be if the security on which they depended were free of all doubt or uncertainty; and consequently, the discount of their value will always be estimated by, and of course be equal to, this difference. Therefore, the injustice of forcing them on the subject at full value of present cash is greatly increased.

These positions and reasonings are grounded on such notoriety of fact that any explanation or proof is needless; and I hope an objection against a law, drawn from the most manifest and acknowledged injustice of its operation and effect, will not be deemed trivial or be easily set aside or got over.

An Honest Man

Suppose a man of grave countenance and character should, in distress, apply to his neighbor for the loan of 1000 silver dollars, with solemn promise on his honor and truth to repay them in a month, and in the meantime the Tender-Act under consideration should pass into a law, and the borrower, at the month's end, should tender 1000 of the new paper dollars in payment.

I beg leave here to ask of every member of the Assembly who voted for that law, and every other man who is a member of this state, what their sentiments of that action would be, and in what light they would view the borrower who tendered the paper dollars—that is, two-fifths of the debt[1]—in payment of the silver ones he had received: Would they consider him as an upright, honest man, or a shameless rascal?

In whichever of the two characters they may choose to consider such a man, it may be proper to note that the act in question, if passed into a law, would protect him, and not only so, but would subject the lender to the loss of the whole money if he refused to receive it. This is a somewhat delicate matter which it is painful to dwell long upon. I will therefore close what I have to say on it with a few very serious remarks, the truth, justice, and propriety of which I humbly submit to the reader:

1. The worst kind of evil, and that which corrupts and endangers any community most, is that iniquity which is framed by a law; for this places the mischief in the very spot—on the very seat—to which every one ought to look and apply for a remedy.

2. It cannot be consistent with the honor, the policy, the interest, or character of an Assembly of Pennsylvania to make a law which, by its natural operation, shall afford protection to manifest injustice, deliberate knavery, and known wrong.

3. No cause or end can be so good—so heavenly in its origin, so excellent in its nature, so perfect in its principles, and so useful in its operation—as to require or justify infernal means to promote it. By infernal means I mean such as are most opposed to Heaven and its laws, most repugnant to natural principles of equity which are all derived from Heaven, and most destructive of the rights of human nature which are essential to the happiness of society. Such laws are engraven by Heaven on the heart of every man. Some wicked men have formerly said, "Let us do evil, that good may come," whose damnation is just.

But perhaps this sort of argument may not have all the effect I could wish on the mind of every reader. I therefore proceed to another argument, which goes to the nature and principle of the act itself: The credit or value of money cannot, in the very nature of the thing, be supplied, preserved, or restored by penal laws or any coercive methods. The subject is incompatible to force; it is out of its reach, and never can be made susceptible of it or controllable by it.

The thing which makes money an object of desire—which gives it strength of motive on the hearts of all men—is the general confidence, the opinion which it gains as a sovereign means of obtaining everything needful. This confidence, this opinion, exists in the mind only, and is not compellable or assailable by force, but must be grounded on that evidence and reason which the mind can see and believe. And it is no more subject to the action of force than any other passion, sentiment, or affection of the mind; any more than faith, love, or esteem.

It is not more absurd to attempt to impel faith into the heart of an unbeliever by fire and faggot, or to whip love into your mistress with a cowskin, then to force value or credit into your money by penal laws.

Trial and Error

You may, indeed, by force compel a man to deliver his goods for money which he does not esteem, and the same force may compel him to deliver his goods without any money at all. But the credit or value of the money cannot be helped by all this, as appears by countless examples. Plain facts are stubborn and undeniable proof of this. Indeed, this has been tried among ourselves in such extent of places and variety of shapes—and in every instance been found ineffectual—that I am amazed to see any attempt to revive it under any devisable form whatsoever. Countless are the instances of flagrant oppression and wrong, and even ruin, which have been the sad effects of these dreadful experiments, with infinite detriment to the community in general, without effecting in any one instance the ends intended. The facts on which this argument depends are fresh in everyone's memory.

I could wish, for the honor of my country, to draw a veil over what is past, and that wisdom might be derived from past errors sufficient to induce everyone to avoid them in the future. In conclusion, from the contemplation of the nature of the thing, and of the facts and experiments which have been made in every variety of mode and supported by every degree of power and exertion, it appears as plain and undeniable as intuitive proof that the credit or value of money is not in its nature controllable by force. Therefore, any attempt to reach it in that way must end in disappointment. The greater the efforts—and the higher the authority which may be exerted in that way—the greater must be the chagrin, shame, and mortification when the baseless fabric shall vanish into smoke.

Natural Value

The only possible method then of giving value or credit to money is to give it such qualities, and clothe it with such circumstances, as shall make it a sure means of procuring every needful thing; for money that will not answer all things is defective, and has not in it the full nature and qualities of money. In this way only it will grow fast enough into esteem, and become a sufficient object of desire, to answer every end and use of money. Therefore, when the question is proposed: "How shall we give credit or value to our money?" the answer, the only true answer, is: "Bring it into demand, make it necessary to everyone, make it a high means of happiness and a sure remedy of misery." To attempt this in any other way is to go against nature, and of course into difficulty, only to obtain shameful disappointment in the end.

There is nothing better than to take things in their natural way. A great and difficult work may be accomplished by easy diligence if a good method and a wise choice of means are adopted; but a small work may be made difficult, very soon, if taken at the wrong end and pursued by unnatural means. There is a right and a wrong method of doing everything. You may lead with a thread what you cannot drive with whips and scorpions. The Britons have found this to their cost in the unnatural means they have pursued to preserve and recover their dominions in America. I wish we might be made wise by their errors. *Happy is he who is made cautious by observing the dangers of others.*

I would be willing to learn wisdom from Great Britain. *It is right to be taught even by an enemy.* Amidst all their madness, and in all their distresses for money, they never once thought of making their bank or exchequer bills a tender, or supporting their currency by penal laws. But these considerations may have little effect on some minds who are not very delicate in their choice of means, but seem resolved to carry their point, God willing or not.

I therefore hasten to another topic of argument. It appears to me the act is founded in mistaken and very bad policy, and by its natural operation must produce many effects extremely prejudicial to our great and most important interests.

It seems plain to me that the act has a fatal tendency to destroy the great motives of industry, and to dishearten and discourage men of every profession and occupation from pursuing their business on any large scale or to any great effect. Therefore, it will prevent the production of those supplies derived from husbandry and manufactures, which are essential to our safety, support, and comfort. Few men will bestow their labor, attention, and good money, with zeal, to procure goods and commodities for sale, which they know they must sell for money which they esteem bad, or at best doubtful.

The extent and dreadful effects of this are unavoidable and immense. If the industry of the farmer and tradesman is discouraged, and they cease to strive for large crops and fabrics, the consequence must be a universal diminution and scarcity of the produce of the country and of the most important articles of living, as well as commerce. The general industry of the country is of such vast importance—is an object of such magnitude—that to check it is to bring on ruin, poverty, famine, and distress, with idleness, vice, corruption of morals, and every species of evil. As money is the sinews of every business, the introducing of a doubtful medium—and forcing it into currency by penal laws—must weaken and lessen every branch of business in proportion to the diminution of inducement found in the money.

The same thing will render the procurement of supplies for the army difficult, if not utterly impracticable. Most men will hold back their goods from the market rather than sell them for money of a doubtful credit. There will be no possible way of collecting them but to send a superior force into the country and there take them by violence from the owner, which will occasion such an expense as will double the cost of the supplies by the time they get to the army, and be subject to a thousand frauds. This is the most obvious and natural operation of the act if we consider its own nature only, and it is confirmed by such ample experience, recent in the memory of every man, that it can leave no doubt but all this mischief must follow the act from its first operation.

Bad Money Corrupts Men

I apprehend the act will, by its natural operation, tend to corrupt the morality of the people, sap the support, if not the very foundation, of our independence, lessen the respect due to our legislature, and destroy that reverence for our laws which is absolutely necessary to their proper operation and the peace and protection of society. Many people will be so terrified with the apprehension of seeing their real substance—the fruit of their labor and anxious attention—converted into a bundle of paper bills of uncertain value, that to avoid this evil they will have strong inducements to rack their invention for all devisable ways and methods of avoiding it. This will give rise to countless frauds, ambiguities, lies, quibbles, and shams. It will introduce the habit and give a kind of facility to the practice of such guile and feats of art as will endanger the uprightness, plain honesty, and noble sincerity which ever mark the character of a happy and virtuous people.

Many, who wish well to our independence and have many necessaries for our army which they would wish to supply, yet will be held back from offering their goods because of the doubtful value of the bills in which those supplies must be paid for. Instances of this sort I conceive will be so numerous as greatly to affect the supplies of our army and, of course, the support of our independence. The injuries and sufferings of people who are compelled to take said bills in satisfaction of contracts for real money will induce them in their rage to use the legislature, who formed the act, with great liberty and, perhaps, gross disrespect. The habit of reproaching the legislature and eluding the injurious act will become general, and pave the way to an habitual and universal abhorrence of our legislature and contempt of our laws, with a kind of facility and artful dexterity in eluding the force of the whole code.

I freely submit it to my readers as to whether these consequences are at all unnatural or ill-drawn, if the surmises are at all groundless, or the painting a whit too strong. No art of government is more necessary than that of keeping up the dignity and respectability of the legislatures and all courts and officers of government, and exciting and preserving in the hearts of the people a high reverence for the laws. And anything which endangers these great supports of the state ought to be avoided as a deadly evil.

Bad Money Destroys Foreign Respect

The act, I apprehend, will give a bad appearance to our credit, honor, and respectability in the eyes of our neighbors on this continent, and the nations of Europe, and other more distant parts of the world. For when they learn that our own people must be compelled by the loss of half their estates and imprisonment of their persons to trust the public faith, they will at once conclude there must be some great danger, some shocking mischief dormant there, which the people nearest to and best acquainted with it abhor so much. And of course, as they are out of the reach of our confiscations and imprisonments, they will have little inducement to trust or esteem us.

Finally, the act will give great exultation and encouragement to our enemies, and induce them to prolong the war, and thereby increase the horrid penalty of imprisonment which is to last during the war. When they see that our money has become so detestable that it requires such an act as this to compel our own people to take it, they must at least be convinced that its nature is greatly corrupted and its efficacy and use nearly at an end. When we see the passionate admirers of a great beauty forced by lashes and tortures into her embraces, we at once conclude that she has lost her charms and has become dangerous and loathsome.

It cannot be fairly objected to these strictures that they suppose the bills funded by this act are of less value than hard money. The act itself implies this. The Assembly never thought of wasting time in framing an act to compel people to take English guineas, Portuguese joes, and Spanish dollars under penalty of confiscation and imprisonment.

I dare think that there is not a man to be found, either in the Assembly or out of it, that would esteem himself so rich and safe in the possession of 1000 of these dollars as of 1000 Spanish ones. The most effectual way to impress a sense of the deficiency of the act on the minds of all men, and even discover the idea which the Assembly themselves have of it, is to enforce it by penalties of extreme severity. For if there were no deficiency in the act it could not possibly require such penalties to give it all necessary effect, nor is it likely that the Assembly would add the sanction of horrid penalties to any of their acts unless they thought there was need of them.

The enormity of the penalty deserves remark. The penalty for refusing a dollar of these bills is greater than for stealing ten times the sum.

Destroys Contracts and Credit

Further, the act alters, and of course destroys, the nature and value of public and private contracts, and this strikes at the root of all public and private credit. Who can lend money with any security, and of course, who can borrow, let his necessity and distress be ever so great? Who can purchase on credit or make any contract for future payment? Indeed, all confidence of our fellow-citizens in one another is hereby destroyed, as well as all faith of individuals in the public credit.

Upon the whole matter, the bills must rest on the credit of their funds, their quantity, and other circumstances. If these are sufficient to give them a currency at full value, they will pass readily enough without the help of penal laws. If these are not sufficient, they must and will depreciate and thereby destroy the end of their own creation. This will proceed from such strong natural principles, such physical causes, as cannot, in the nature of the thing, be checked or controlled by penal laws or any other application of force.

These strictures are humbly offered to public consideration. The facts alleged are all open to view and well understood. If the remarks and reasonings are just, they will carry conviction; if they are not so, they are liable to anyone's correction.

Note

[1]On March 18, 1780, the Continental Congress officially had recognized the debauchery of its currency, allowing it to exchange for specie at the rate of 40:1. By the time this piece was written, the unofficial exchange rate had further widened to 100:1. This probably explains Webster's illustration—"two-fifths of the debt."

44. THE VALUE OF MONEY*

Hans F. Sennholz

Most economists are in agreement that the inflation in the United States during the past three years has been the worst since the early 1940's, taking account of both severity and duration. But they cannot agree on the nature of the inflation that is engulfing the American economy. To some, inflation denotes a spectacular rise in consumer prices; to others, an excessive aggregate demand; and to at least one economist, it is the creation of new money by our monetary authorities.

This disagreement among economists is more than an academic difference on the meaning of a popular term. It reflects professional confusion as to the cause of the inflation problem and the policies that might help to correct it.

A review of some basic principles of economics that are applicable to money may shed light on the problem.

Two basic questions need to be answered: (1) What are the factors that originally afforded value to money, and (2) What are the factors that effect changes in the "objective exchange value of money" or its purchasing power?

Money is a medium of exchange that facilitates trade in goods and services. Wherever people progressed beyond simple barter, they began to use their most marketable goods as media of exchange. In primitive societies they used cattle, or measures of grain, salt, or fish. In early civilizations where the division of labor extended to larger areas, gold or silver emerged as the most marketable good and finally as the only medium of exchange, called money. It is obvious that the chieftains, kings, and heads of state did not invent the use of money. But they frequently usurped control over it whenever they suffered budget deficits and could gain revenue from currency debasement.

When an economic good is sought and wanted, not only for its use in consumption or production but also for purposes of exchange, to be held in reserve for later exchanges, the demand for it obviously increases. We may then speak of two partial demands which combine to raise its value in exchange—its purchasing power.

The Origin of Money Value

People seek money because it has purchasing power; and part of this purchasing power is generated by the people's demand for money. But is this not reasoning in a vicious circle?

It is not! According to Ludwig von Mises' "re-

*From *The Freeman*, November 1969

gression theory," we must be mindful of the time factor. Our quest for cash holdings is conditioned by money purchasing power in the immediate past, which in turn was affected by earlier purchasing power, and so on until we arrive at the very inception of the monetary demand. At that particular moment, the purchasing power of a certain quantity of gold or silver was determined by its nonmonetary uses only.

This leads to the interesting conclusion that the universal use of paper monies today would be inconceivable without their prior use as "substitutes" for real money, such as gold and silver, for which there was a nonmonetary demand. Only when man grew accustomed to these substitutes, and governments deprived him of his freedom to employ gold and silver as media of exchange, did government tender paper emerge as the legal or "fiat money." It has value and purchasing power, although it lacks any nonmonetary demand, because the people now direct their monetary demand toward government tender paper. If for any reason this public demand should cease or be redirected toward real goods as media of exchange, the fiat money would lose its entire value. The Continental Dollar and various foreign currencies over the years illustrate the point.

On Demand and Supply

The purchasing power of money is determined by the demand for and supply of money, like the prices of all other economic goods and services. The particular relation between this demand and supply determines its particular purchasing power. So, let us first look at those factors that exert an influence on individual demand for money.

As money is a medium of exchange, our demand for it may be influenced by considerations of facts and circumstances either on the goods side of the exchange or on the money side. Therefore, we may speak of goods-induced factors and money-induced factors.

A simple example may illustrate the former. Let us assume we live in a medieval town that is cut off from all fresh supplies by an enemy army. There is great want and starvation. Although the quantity of money did not change—no gold or silver has left our beleaguered town—its purchasing power must decline. For everyone seeks to reduce his cash holdings in exchange for some scarce food in order to assure survival.

The situation is similar in all cases where the supply of available goods is decreased although the quantity of money in the people's cash holdings remains unchanged. In a war, when the channels of supply are cut off by the enemy or economic output is reduced for lack of labor power, the value of money tends to decline and goods prices rise even though the quantity of money may remain unchanged. A bad harvest in an agricultural economy may visibly weaken the currency. Similarly, a general strike that paralyzes an economy and greatly reduces the supply of goods and services raises goods prices and simultaneously lowers the purchasing power of money. In fact, every strike or sabotage of economic production tends to affect prices and money value even though this may not be visible to many observers.

Some economists also cite the level of taxation as an important factor in the determination of the exchange value of money. According to Colin Clark, whenever governments consume more than 25 per cent of national product, the reduction in productive capacity as a result of such an oppressive tax burden causes goods prices to rise and the purchasing power of money to fall. According to that view, with which one may disagree, high rates of taxation are the main cause of "inflation." At any rate, there can be no doubt that the American dollar has suffered severely from the burdens of Federal, state, and local government spending and taxing that exceed 35 per cent of American national product.

Yet, this purchasing power loss of the dollar would have been greater by far if a remarkable rise in industrial productivity had not worked in the opposite direction. In spite of the ever-growing burden of government and despite the phenomenal increase in the supply of money (to be further discussed below), both of which would reduce the value of the dollar, American commerce and industry managed to increase the supply of marketable goods, thus bolstering the dollar's purchasing power. Under most difficult circumstances, businessmen managed to form more capital and improve production technology, and thus made available more and better economic goods which in turn helped to stabilize the dollar. Without this remarkable achievement by American entrepreneurs and capitalists, the U.S. dollar surely would have followed the way of many other national currencies to radical depreciation and devaluation.

There also are a number of factors that affect the demand for money on the money side of an exchange. A growing population, for instance, with millions of maturing individuals eager to establish cash holdings, generates new demand, which in turn tends to raise the purchasing power of money and to reduce goods prices. On the other hand, a declining population would generate the opposite effect.

Changes in the division of labor bring about changes in the exchange value of money. Increased specialization and trade raises the demand and exchange value of money. The nineteenth century frontier farmer who tamed the West with plow and gun was largely self-sufficient. His demand for money was small when compared with that of his great grandson who raises only corn and buys all his foodstuff in the supermarket. Under a modern and a highly advanced division of labor, one needs money for the satisfaction of all his wants through exchange. It is obvious that such demand tends to raise the exchange value of money. On the other hand, deterioration of this division of labor and return to self-sufficient production, which we can observe in many parts of Asia, Africa, and South America, generates the opposite effect.

Development and improvement of a monetary clearing system also exert an influence toward lower money value. Clearing means offsetting payments by banks or brokers. It reduces the demand for money, as only net balances are settled by cash payments.

The American clearing system which gradually developed over more than 130 years from local to regional and national clearing, slowly reduced the need and demand for cash and thus its purchasing power. Of course, this reduction of the dollar's exchange value was negligible when compared with that caused by other factors, especially the huge increase in money supply.

Business practices, too, may influence the demand for money and therefore its value. It is customary for business to settle its obligations on the first of the month. Tax payments are due on certain dates. The growing popularity of credit cards reduces the need for money holdings throughout the month, but concentrates it at the beginning of the month when payments fall due. All such variations in demand affect the objective exchange value of money.

The Desires of Individuals for Larger or Smaller Holdings

The most important determinant of purchasing power of money under this heading of "money-induced factors" is the very attitude of the people toward money and their possession of certain cash holdings. They may decide for one reason or another to increase or reduce their holdings. An increase of cash holdings by many individuals tends to raise the exchange value of money, reduction of cash holdings tends to lower it.

This is so well understood that even the mathematical economists emphasize the money "velocity" in their equations and calculations of money value. Velocity of circulation is defined as the average number of times in a year which a dollar serves as income (the income velocity) or as an expenditure (the transaction's velocity). Of course, this economic use of a term borrowed from physics ignores acting man who increases or reduces his cash holdings. Even when it is in transport, money is under the control of its owners who choose to spend it or hold it, make or delay payment, lend or borrow. The mathematical economist who weighs and measures, and thereby ignores the choices and preferences of acting individuals, is tempted to control and manipulate this "velocity" in order to influence the value of money. He may even blame individuals (who refuse to act in accordance with his model) for monetary depreciation or appreciation. And governments are only too eager to echo this blame; while they are creating ever new quantities of printing press money, they will restrain individuals in order to control money velocity.

It is true, the propensity to increase or reduce cash holdings by many people exerts an important influence on the purchasing power of money. But in order to radically change their holdings, individuals must have cogent reasons. They endeavor to raise their holdings whenever they foresee depressions ahead. And they usually lower their holdings whenever they anticipate more inflation and declining money value. In short, they tend to react rationally and naturally to certain trends and policies. Government cannot change or prevent this reaction; it can merely change its own policies that brought forth the reaction.

The Supply of Money

No determinant of demand, whether it affects the goods side of an exchange or the money side, is subject to such wide variations as is the supply of money. During the age of the gold coin standard when gold coins were circulating freely, the supply of money was narrowly circumscribed by the supply of gold. But today when governments have complete control over money and banking, when central banks can create or withdraw money at will, the quantity of money changes significantly from year to year, even from week to week. The student of money and banking now must carefully watch the official statistics of money supply in order to understand current economic trends.

Of course, the ever-changing supply of money must not be viewed as a factor that evenly and uniformly changes the level of goods prices. The total supply of money in a given economy does not confront the total supply of goods. Changes in money supply always act through the cash holdings of individuals, who react to changes in their personal incomes and to changing interest rates in the loan market. It is through acting individuals that supply changes exert their influences on various goods prices.

In the United States, we have two monetary authorities that continually change the money supply: the U.S. Treasury and the Federal Reserve System. As of February 28, 1969, the U.S. Treasury had issued some $6.7 billion of money, of which $5.1 billion were fractional coins. The Federal Reserve System had issued $46.3 billion in notes and, in addition, was holding some $22 billion of bank reserves. Commercial banks were holding approximately $150 billion in demand deposits and some $201 billion in time deposits, all of which are payable on demand in "legal money," which is Federal Reserve and Treasury money.

How Government Creates Money

The vast power of money creation held by the Federal Reserve System, which is our central bank and monetary arm of the U.S. Government, becomes visible only when we compare today's supply of money with that in the past. Let us, therefore, look at the volume of Federal Reserve Bank credit on various dates since 1929:

Date	*Total in Billions*
1929 June	$ 1.3
1939 Dec.	2.6
1949 Dec.	22.5
1959 Dec.	29.4
1969 Aug. 20	58.2

SOURCE: *Federal Reserve Bulletins.*

These figures clearly reveal the nature and extent of the inflation that has engulfed us since the early 1930's. The 1940's and again the 1960's stand out as the periods of most rapid inflation and credit expansion.

Why and how do our "monetary authorities" create such massive quantities of money that inevitably lead to lower money value? During the 1940's, the emergency argument was cited to justify the printing of any quantity the government wanted for the war effort. During the 1960's, the Federal government through its Federal Reserve System was printing feverishly in order to achieve full employment and a more desirable rate of economic growth. Furthermore, the ever-growing public demand for economic redistribution inflicted budgetary deficits, the financing of which was facilitated by money creation.

How was it done? The Federal Reserve has at its disposal three different instruments of control which can be used singly or jointly to change the money supply. It may conduct "open-market purchases," i.e., it buys U.S. Treasury obligations in the capital market and pays for them with newly-created cash or credit. Nearly all the money issued since 1929 was created by this method. Or, the Federal Reserve may lower its discount rate, which is the rate it charges commercial banks for accommodation. If it lowers its rate below that of the market, demand will exceed supply, which the Federal Reserve then stands ready to provide. Or finally, the Federal Reserve may reduce the reserve requirements of commercial banks. Such a reduction will set Federal Reserve money free for loans or investments by commercial banks.

It does not matter how the new money supply is created. The essential fact is the creation by the monetary authorities. You and I cannot print money, for this would be counterfeiting and punishable by law. But our monetary authorities are creating new quantities every day of the week at the discretion of our government leaders. This fact alone explains why ours is an age of inflation and monetary destruction.

Variable Responses

The Quantity Theory, which offers one of the oldest explanations in economic literature, demonstrates the connection between variations in the value of money and the supply of money. Of course, it is erroneous to assume, as some earlier economists have done, that changes in the value of money must be proportionate to changes in the quantity of money, so that doubling the money supply would double goods prices and reduce by one-half the value of money.

As was pointed out above, changes in supply always work through the cash holdings of the people. When the government resorts to a policy of inflation, some people may react by delaying their purchases of certain goods and services in the hope that prices will soon decline again. In other words, they may increase their cash holdings and thereby counteract the price-raising effect of the government policy. From the inflators' point of view, this reaction is ideal, for they may continue to inflate while these people through their reaction may prevent the worst effects of inflation. This is probably the reason why the U.S. Government, through post office posters, billboards, and other propaganda, endeavors to persuade the American people to save more money whenever the government itself resorts to inflation.

When more and more individuals begin to realize that the inflation is a willful policy and that it will not end very soon, they may react by reducing their cash holdings. Why should they hold cash that depreciates, and why should they not purchase more goods and services right now before prices rise again? This reaction intensifies the price-raising effects of the inflation. While government inflates and people reduce their money demand, goods prices will rise rapidly and the purchasing power of money decline accordingly.

It may happen that the government may temporarily halt its inflation, and yet the people continue to reduce their cash demand. The central bank inflators may then point to the stability of the money supply, and blame the people for "irrational" behavior and reaction. The government thus exculpates itself and condemns the spending habits of the people for the inflation. But in reality, the people merely react to past experiences and therefore anticipate an early return of inflationary policies. The monetary development during most of 1969 reflected this situation.

Finally, the people may totally and irrevocably distrust the official fiat money. When in desperation they finally conclude that the inflation will not end before their money is essentially destroyed, they may rush to liquidate their remaining cash holdings. When any purchase of goods and services is more advantageous than holding rapidly depreciating cash, the value of money approaches zero. The money then ceases to be money, the sole medium of exchange.

When government takes control over money, it not only takes possession of an important command post over the economic lives of the people but also acquires a lucrative source of revenue. Under the ever-growing pressures for government services and functions, this source of revenue—which can be made to flow quietly without much notice by the public—constitutes a great temptation for weak administrators who like to spend money without raising it through unpopular taxation. The supply of money not only is the best indicator as to the value of money, but reflects the state of the nation and the thinking of the people.

45. THE GOLD PROBLEM*

Ludwig von Mises

Why gold?

Because, as conditions are today and for the time that can be foreseen today, the gold standard alone makes the determination of money's purchasing power independent of the ambitions and machinations of dictators, political parties, and pressure groups. The gold standard alone is what the nineteenth century liberals, the champions of representative government, civil liberties, and prosperity for all, called sound money.

The eminence and usefulness of the gold standard consists in the fact that it makes the supply of money depend on the profitability of mining gold, and thus checks large-scale inflationary ventures on the part of governments. The gold standard did not fail. The governments sabotaged it and still go on sabotaging it. But no government is powerful enough to destroy the gold standard as

*From *The Freeman*, June 1965

long as the market economy is not entirely suppressed by the establishment of socialism in every part of the world.

Governments believe that it is the gold standard's fault alone that their inflationary schemes not only fail to produce the expected benefits but unavoidably bring about conditions that also in the eyes of the rulers themselves and of all of the people are considered as much worse than the alleged or real evils they were designed to eliminate. But for the gold standard, they are told by hosts of pseudo-economists, they could make everybody perfectly prosperous.

Let us test the three doctrines advanced for the support of this fable of government omnipotence.

The Santa Claus Power of the State

The state is God, said Ferdinand Lassalle, the founder of the German socialist movement. As such the state has the power to "create" unlimited quantities of money and thus to make everybody happy. Irreverent people branded such a policy of "creating" money as inflation. The official terminology calls it nowadays "deficit spending."

But whatever the name used in dealing with this phenomenon may be, its meaning is obvious. The government increases the quantity of money in circulation. Then a greater quantity of money "chases," as a rather silly but popular way of talking about these problems says, a quantity of goods and services that has not increased. The government's action did not add anything to the available amount of useful things and services. It merely makes the prices paid for them soar.

If the government wants to raise the income of some people—e.g., government employees—it has to confiscate by taxation a part of some other people's incomes and to distribute the amount collected among its employees. Then the taxpayers are forced to restrict their spending, while the recipients of the higher salaries are increasing their spending to the same amount. There does not result a conspicuous change in the purchasing power of the monetary unit.

But if the government provides the money it wants for the payment of higher salaries by printing it, the new money in the hands of the beneficiaries of the higher salaries constitutes on the market an additional demand for the not increased quantity of goods and services offered for sale. The unavoidable result is a general tendency of prices to rise.

Any attempts the governments and their propaganda offices make to conceal this concatenation of events are vain. Deficit spending means increasing the quantity of money in circulation. That the official terminology avoids calling it inflation, is of no avail whatever.

The government and its chiefs do not have the powers of the mythical Santa Claus. They cannot spend but by taking out of the pockets of some people.

The "Cheap Money" Fallacy

Interest is the difference in the valuation of present goods and future goods. It is the discount in the valuation of future goods as against that of present goods. It cannot be "abolished" as long as people prefer an apple available today to an apple available only in a year, in ten years, or in a hundred years. The height of the originary rate of interest, which is the main component of the market rate of interest as determined on the loan market, reflects the difference in people's valuation of present and future satisfaction of needs. The disappearance of interest, that is an interest rate of zero, would mean that people do not care a whit about satisfying any of their present wants and are *exclusively* intent upon satisfying their future wants, their wants of the later years, decades, and centuries to come. People would only save and invest and never consume. On the other hand, if people were to stop making any provision for the future, be it even the future of the tomorrow, would not save at all and consume all capital goods accumulated by previous generations, the rate of interest would rise beyond any limits.

It is thus obvious that the height of the market rate of interest ultimately does not depend on the whims, fancies, and the pecuniary interests of the personnel operating the government apparatus of coercion and compulsion, the much referred to "public sector" of the economy. But the government has the power to push the Federal Reserve System and the banks subject to it into a policy of cheap money. Then the banks are expanding credit. Underbidding the rate of interest as established on the not-manipulated loan market, they offer additional credit created out of nothing. Thus they are intentionally falsifying the businessmen's estimation of market conditions. Although the supply of capital goods (that can only be increased by additional saving) remained unchanged, the illusion of a richer supply of capital is conjured up.

Business is induced to embark upon projects which a sober calculation, not misled by the cheap-money ventures, would have disclosed as malinvestments. The additional quantities of credit inundating the market make prices and wages soar. An artificial boom, a boom built entirely upon the illusions of easy money, develops. But such a boom cannot last. Sooner or later it must become clear that, under the illusions created by the credit expansion, business has embarked upon projects for the execution of which it is not rich enough. When this malinvestment becomes visible, the boom collapses. The depression that follows is the process of liquidating the errors committed in the ecstasies of the artificial boom, is the return to calm reasoning and a reasonable conduct of affairs within the limits of the available supply of capital goods. It is a painful process, but it is a process of recovery.

Credit expansion is not a nostrum to make people happy. The boom it engenders must inevitably lead to a debacle.

If it were possible to substitute credit expansion (cheap money) for the accumulation of capital goods by saving, there would not be any poverty in the world. The economically backward nations would not have to complain about the insufficiency of their capital equipment. All they would have to do for the improvement of their conditions would be to expand credit more and more. No "foreign aid" schemes would have emerged. In granting foreign aid to the backward nations, the American government implicitly acknowledges that credit expansion is no substitute for capital accumulation through saving.

The Failure of Minimum Wage Legislation and of Labor Unionism

The height of wage rates is determined by the consumers' appraisal of the value the worker's labor adds to the value of the article available for sale. As the immense majority of the consumers are themselves earners of wages and salaries, this means that the determination of the compensation for work and services rendered is made by the same kind of people who are receiving these wages and salaries. The fat earnings of the movie star and the boxing champion are provided by the welders, street sweepers, and charwomen who attend the performances and matches.

An entrepreneur who would try to pay a hired man less than the amount this man's work adds to the value of the product would be priced out of the labor market by the competition of other entrepreneurs eager to earn money. On the other hand, no entrepreneur can pay more to his helpers than the amount the consumers are prepared to refund to him in buying the product. If he were to pay higher wages, he would suffer losses and would be ejected from the ranks of the businessmen.

Governments decreeing minimum wage laws above the level of the market wage rates restrict the number of hands that can find jobs. They are producing unemployment of a part of the labor force. The same is true for what is euphemistically called "collective bargaining." The only difference between the two methods concerns the apparatus enforcing the minimum wage. The government enforces its orders in resorting to policemen and prison guards. The unions "picket." They and their members and officials have acquired the power and the right to commit wrongs to person and property, to deprive individuals of the means of earning a livelihood, and to commit many other acts which no one can do with impunity.[1] Nobody is today in a position to disobey an order issued by a union. To the employers no other choice is left than either to surrender to the dictates of the unions or to go out of business.

But governments and unions are impotent against economic law. Violence can prevent the employers from hiring help at potential market rates, but it cannot force them to employ all those who are anxious to get jobs. The result of the governments' and the unions' meddling with the height of wage rates cannot be anything else than an incessant increase in the number of unemployed.

To prevent this outcome the government-manipulated banking systems of all Western nations are resorting to inflation. Increasing the quantity of money in circulation and thereby lowering the purchasing power of the monetary unit, they are cutting down the oversized payrolls to a height consonant with the state of the market. This is today called Keynesian full-employment policy. It is in fact a method to perpetuate by continued inflation the futile attempts of governments and labor unions to meddle with the conditions of the labor market. As soon as the progress of inflation has adjusted wage rates so far as to avoid a spread of unemployment, government and unions resume with renewed zeal their ventures to raise wage rates above the level at which every job-seeker can find a job.

The experience of this age of the New Deal, the Fair Deal, the New Frontier, and the Great Society confirms the fundamental thesis of British nineteenth-century liberalism: there is but one means to improve the material conditions of all of the wage earners, viz., to increase the per-head quota of capital invested. This result can only be brought about by additional saving and capital accumulation, never by government decrees, labor union violence and intimidation, and inflation. The foes of the gold standard are wrong also in this regard.

U. S. Gold Holdings Shrinking

In many parts of the earth an increasing number of people realize that the U. S. and most of the other nations are firmly committed to a policy of progressing inflation. They have learned enough from the experience of the last decades to conclude that on account of these inflationary policies the ounce of gold will one day become more expensive in terms both of the currency of the U. S. and of their own country. They are alarmed and would like to avoid being victimized by this outcome.

Americans are forbidden to own gold coins and gold ingots. Their attempts to protect their financial assets consist in the methods that the Germans in the most spectacular inflation that history knows called *"Flucht in die Sachwerte."* They are investing in common stock and real estate and prefer to have debts payable in legal tender money to having claims payable in it.

Even in the countries in which people are free to buy gold there are up to now no conspicuous purchases of gold on the part of financially potent individuals and institutions. Up to the moment at which French agencies began to buy gold, the buyers of gold were mostly people with modest incomes anxious to keep a few gold coins as a reserve for rainy days. It was the purchases on the part of such people that via the London gold market reduced the gold holdings of the United States.

There is only one method available to prevent a farther reduction of the American gold reserve: radical abandonment of deficit spending as well as of any kind of "easy money" policy.

Note

[1] Cf. Roscoe Pound, *Legal Immunities of Labor Unions*, Washington, D. C., 1957, p. 21.

46. HOW MUCH MONEY?*

Percy L. Greaves, Jr.

Most people want more money. So do I. But I wouldn't keep it long. I would soon spend it for the things I need or want. So would most people. In other words, for most of us, more money is merely a means for buying what we really want. Only misers want more money for the sake of holding onto it permanently.

However, if more money is to be given out, most of us would like to get some of it. If we can't get any for ourselves, the next best thing, from our viewpoint, would be for it to be given to those who might buy our goods or services. For then it is likely their increased spending would make us richer.

*From *The Freeman*, May 1965

From such reasoning, many have come to believe that spreading more money around is a good thing—not only for their personal needs, but also for solving most all of the nation's problems. For them, more money becomes the source of prosperity. So they approve all sorts of government programs for pumping more money into the economy.

If such programs are helpful, why not have more money for everyone? Why not have the government create and give everyone $100 or $200 or, better yet, $1,000? Why not have the government do it every year or every month or, better yet, every week?

Of course, such a system would not work. But why not? When we understand why not, we will know why every attempt to create prosperity by creating more money will not work. When we have learned the answer, we shall have taken a long step toward eliminating the greatest cause of both human misery and the decay of great civilizations.

One way to find the answer is to analyze the logic which seemingly supports the idea that more money in a nation's economy means more prosperity for all. If we can spot an error in the chain of reasoning, we should be able to make it clear to others. Once such an error is generally recognized, the popularity of government money-creation programs will soon disappear. Neither moral leaders nor voting majorities will long endorse ideas they know to be false.

Perhaps the basic thought that supports an ever-increasing money supply is the popular idea that more business requires more money: if we produce more goods and services, customers must have more money with which to buy the additional goods and services. From this, it is assumed that the need for prosperity and "economic growth" makes it the government's duty to pump out more purchasing power to the politically worthy in the form of more money or subsidies paid for by the creation of more money.

Support for such reasoning is found in an idea that goes back at least to medieval days. In the thirteenth and fourteenth centuries some of the world's best minds believed there was a "just price" for everything. The "just price" was then thought to be determined by a fixed cost of production. Actual prices might fluctuate slightly from day to day or season to season, but they were always expected to return to the basic "just price," reflecting the supposedly never-changing number of man-hours required for production.

From such thinking, it naturally follows that increased production can only be sold when consumers have more money. More goods might be needed for any of several reasons, let us say for an increased population. However, no matter how much they were needed, they would remain unsold and unused unless buyers were supplied additional funds with which to buy them at, or near, the "just price."

What is the situation in real life? What do businessmen do when they have more goods to sell than customers will buy at their asking price?

They reduce prices. They advertise sales at mark-down prices. If that doesn't work, they reduce their prices again and again until all their surplus goods are sold. *Any economic good can always be sold, if the price is right.*

The way to move increased production into consumption is to adjust prices downward. Businessmen, who have made mistakes in judging consumer wants, will suffer losses. Those who provide what consumers prefer will earn profits. Lower prices will benefit all consumers and mean lower costs for future business operations. Under such a flexible price system, there is no need for more money. Businessmen soon learn to convert available supplies of labor and raw materials into those goods for which consumers will willingly pay the highest prices.

What Are Prices?

Prices are quantities of money. They reflect a complex of interrelated market conditions and individual value judgments at any one time and place. Each price reflects not only the available supply of that good in relation to the supply of all other available goods and services, but also the demand of individuals for that good in relation to their demand for all other available goods and services.

But even this is only one side of price-determining factors. The money side must also be taken into consideration. Every price also reflects not only the supply of money held by each market participant, but also—since very few people ever spend their last cent—how much money each participant decides to keep for his future needs and unknown contingencies.

Prices thus depend on many things besides the cost of production. They depend primarily on the relative values that consumers place on the satisfactions they expect to get from owning the particular mixture of goods and services that they select. However, prices also depend on the amount of money available both to each individual and to all individuals. In a free market economy, unhampered prices easily adjust to reflect consumer demand no matter what the total supply of money or who owns how much of it.

What is This Thing Called Money?

Money is a commodity that is used for facilitating indirect exchange. Money first appeared when individuals recognized the advantages of the division of labor and saw that indirect exchange was easier and more efficient than the clumsy, time-consuming direct exchange of barter.

In the earliest days of specialized production,

those who made shoes or caught fish soon found that if they wanted to buy a house, it was easier to buy it with a quantity of a universally desired commodity than with quantities of shoes or fresh fish.

So, they first exchanged their shoes or fish for a quantity of that commodity which they knew was most in demand. Such a commodity would keep and not spoil. It could be divided without loss. And most important, all people would value it no matter what the size of their feet or their desire for fish. The commodity which best meets these qualifications soon becomes a community's medium of exchange, or money.

Many things have been used as money. In this country we once used the wampum beads of Indians and the shells found on our shores. As time passed, reason and experience indicated that the commodities best suited for use as money were the precious metals, silver and gold. By the beginning of this century, the prime money of the world had become gold. And so it is today. Gold is the commodity most in demand in world markets.

Money is always that commodity which all sellers are most happy to accept for their goods or services, if the quantity or price offered is considered sufficient. Money is thus the most marketable commodity of a market society. It is also the most important single commodity of a market society. This is so because it forms a part of every market transaction and whatever affects its value affects every transaction and every contemplated transaction.

Kinds of Goods

There are three types of economic goods:

1. Consumers' goods.
2. Producers' goods.
3. Money.

Consumers' goods are those goods which are valued because they supply satisfaction to those who use or consume them. Producers' goods are goods which are valued because they can be used to make or produce consumers' goods. They include raw materials, tools, machines, factories, railroads, and the like. Money is that good which is valued because it can be used as a medium of exchange. It is the only type of economic good that is not consumed by its normal usage.

In the case of consumers' goods and producers' goods, every additional unit that is produced and offered for sale increases the wealth not only of the owner but of everyone else. Every additional automobile that is produced not only makes the manufacturer richer but it also makes every member of the market society richer.

How?

The more useful things there are in this world, the larger the numbers of human needs or wants that can be satisfied. The market system is a process for distributing a part of every increase in production to every participant in that market economy. When there is no increase in the money supply, the more goods that are offered for sale, the lower prices will be—and, consequently, the more each person can buy with the limited amount of money he has to spend. So every increase in production for a market economy normally means more for every member of that economy.

On the other hand, when any consumers' goods or producers' goods are lost or destroyed, not only the owner but all members of the market community suffer losses. With fewer goods available in the market place, and assuming no increase in the money supply, prices must tend to rise. Everybody's limited supply of money will thus buy less.

Recently, a Montreal apartment house was destroyed by an explosion. The loss to the occupants and the owners or insurance companies is obvious. The loss to all of us may be less obvious, but nevertheless it is a fact.

The market society has lost forever the services and contributions of all those who were killed. It has also lost for a time the contributions of all those whose injuries temporarily incapacitated them. There is also a loss for all of us in the fact that human services and producers' goods must be used to clear away the wreckage and rebuild what was destroyed. This diversion of labor and producers' goods means the market will never be able to offer the things that such labor and producers' goods could otherwise have been used to produce. With fewer things available in the market, prices will tend to be higher. Such higher prices will force each one of us to get along with a little less than would have been the case if there had been no explosion.

Thus, we are all sufferers from every catastrophe. Be it an airplane crash, a tornado, or a fire in some distant community, we all lose a little bit. And all these little bits often add up to a significant sum.

This is particularly true of war losses. Every American killed in Vietnam hurts every one of us not only in the heart but also in the pocketbook. Our government must supply some monetary compensation to his family and an income, however little, to his dependents. In such cases, the loss may continue for years. The killed man's services are lost for his normal life span and his dependents become a long-term burden on the nation's taxpayers and consumers. Such losses can never be measured or calculated, but they are real nonetheless.

So, in a market society every increase in consumers' goods or producers' goods permits us to buy more with whatever money we have, and every decrease in consumers' goods or producers' goods means ultimately higher prices and less for our money. Increased supplies of such economic goods help both the producers and everyone else who owns one or more units of money.

Limited Goods Available

With money, the situation is quite different. Any increase in the supply of money helps those who receive some of the new supply, but it hurts all those who do not. Those who receive some of the new supply can rush out and buy a larger share of the goods and services in the market place. Those who receive none of the new money supply will then find less available for them to buy. Prices will rise and they will get less for their money.

Pumping more money into a nation's economy merely helps some people at the expense of others. It must, by its very nature, send prices up higher than they would have been, if the money supply had not been increased. Those with no part of the new money supply must be satisfied with less. It does not and cannot increase the quantity of goods and services available.

There are some who claim that increasing the money supply puts more men to work. This can only be so when there is unemployment resulting from pushing wage rates above those of a free market by such political measures as minimum wage laws and legally sanctioned labor union pressures. Under such conditions, increasing the money supply reduces the value of each monetary unit and thus reduces the real value of all wages. By doing this, it brings the higher-than-free-market wage rates nearer to what they would be in a free market. This in turn brings employment nearer to what it would be in a free market, where there is a job for all who want to work.[1]

Those who create and slip new supplies of money into the economy are silently transferring wealth which rightfully belongs to savers and producers to those who, without contributing to society, are the first to spend the new money in the market place. When this is done by private persons, they are called counterfeiters. Their attempts to help themselves at the expense of others are easily recognized. When caught, they are soon placed where they can add no more to the money supply.

In recent generations our major problem has not been private counterfeiters. It has been governments. Over the years, governments have found ways to increase the money supply that not more than one or two persons in a million can detect. This is particularly true when production is increasing and when more and more of the monetary units are held off the market. Nonetheless, whether prices go up or not, every time a government increases the money supply, it is taking wealth from some and giving it to others.

This semi-hidden increase in the money supply occurs in two ways:

One, by the creation and issuance of money against government securities. This is a favorite way to finance government deficits. Government securities that private investors will not buy, because they pay lower-than-free-market interest rates, are sold to commercial banks. The banks pay for such securities by merely adding the price of the securities to government bank accounts. The government can then draw checks to pay suppliers, employees, and subsidy recipients. (This process is encouraged and increased by technical actions and direct purchases of the nation's central bank. In the United States, these powers reside in the Federal Reserve Board, which has not been hesitant about using them.)

The government thus receives purchasing power without contributing anything to the goods and services offered in the market place. It thus gets something for nothing. As a result, there is less available for those spending and investing dollars they have received for their contributions to society. The consequence of such government spending is that prices are higher than they would otherwise have been.

Two, the other major semi-hidden means of increasing the money supply is for banks to lend money to private individuals or organizations by merely creating or adding a credit to the borrowers' checking accounts. In such cases, they are not lending the savings of depositors. They are merely creating dollars, in the form of bank accounts, by simple bookkeeping entries. The borrowers are thereby enabled to draw checks or ask for newly created money with which to buy a part of the goods and services available in the market place. This means that those responsible for the production of these goods and services must be satisfied with less than the share they would have received if the money supply had not been so increased.

By such systems of money creation, our government and our government-controlled banking system have, from the end of 1945, increased the nation's money supply from $132.5 billion to an estimated $289.9 billion by the end of 1964. This is an increase of $157.4 billion. During the same period, the gold stock, held as a reserve against this money and valued at $35 an ounce, fell from $20.1 billion to $15.4 billion. The increase in the money supply for 1964 amounted to $21.0 billion.[2]

All these new dollars provided the first recipients with wealth which, had there been no artificial additions to the money supply, would have gone to those spenders and investors who received their dollars in return for contributions to society. Last year alone, political favorites were helped to the tune of $21 billion, at the expense of all the nation's producers and savers of real wealth.

These money-increasing policies remain hidden from most people, particularly when prices do not rise rapidly. It is now popular to say there is no inflation unless official price indexes rise appreciably. This popular corruption of the term inflation, originally defined as an increase in the money supply, makes it seem safe for the government to increase the money supply so long as the government's own price indexes do not rise noticeably. So, if these price indexes can somehow be kept down, the government can continue buying or allocating wealth which has been created by private individuals who must be satisfied with less than the free market value of their contributions.

Price Rise Kept Down

Since World War II, there have been two continuing situations which have helped to keep official price indexes from reflecting the full effect of this huge increase in the money supply. The first such situation is that throughout this period American production of wealth has continued to increase. The second is that during these years foreigners and their banks and governments have taken and held off the market increasing supplies of dollars.

If there had been no upward manipulation of the money supply, the increased production of wealth would have resulted in lower prices. This would have provided more for everyone who earned or saved a dollar. It would also have reduced costs and increased the amount of goods and services that would have been sold at home and abroad.

As it was, with prices rising slowly over the 1945-64 period, the Federal government and our government-controlled banking system have been able to allocate the benefits of increased production, and a little bit more, to favored bank borrowers who pay lower than free market interest rates and those who received Federal funds over and above the sums collected in taxes or borrowed from private individuals or corporations.

Untold billions of dollars have also gone into the hands or bank accounts of international organizations, foreigners, their banks, and governments. Many of these dollar holders consider $35 to be worth more than an ounce of gold. Such dollar holders have felt they could always get the gold and, meanwhile, they can get interest by leaving their dollars on deposit with American banks. Foreign governments could even count such deposits as part of their reserves against their own currencies. For example, the more dollars held by the Bank of France, the more it can expand the supply of French francs. So the inflations of many European governments are built on top of the great increase in their holdings of dollars.

Short term liabilities of American banks to foreigners at the end of 1945 were only $6.9 billion.[3] By the end of last year, they had risen to an estimated $28.8 billion, an increase of $20.9 billion.[4] How many more dollars rest in foreign billfolds or under foreign mattresses cannot even be guessed. Should such foreign dollar holders lose confidence in the ability of their central banks to get an ounce of gold for every $35 presented to our government, more and more of these dollars will return to our shores where their presence will bid up American prices.

This whole process of increasing the money supply by semi-hidden manipulations is not only highly questionable from the viewpoint of morality and economic incentives, but it also has a highly disorganizing effect on the production pattern of our economy. Over the years, as these newly created dollars have found their way into the market, they have forced profit-seeking enterprises to allocate a growing part of production to the spenders of the newly created dollars, leaving less production available for the spenders of dollars which represent contributions to society. Once this artificial creation of dollars comes to an end, as it must eventually, those businesses whose sales have become dependent upon the spending of the newly created dollars will lose their customers.

This will call for a reorganization of the nation's production facilities. Such reorganizations of business have become known as depressions. The depression can be short, with a minimum of human misery, if prices, wage rates, and interest rates are left free to reflect a true picture of the ever-changing demands of consumers and supplies of labor, raw materials, and savings. Private business will then move promptly and efficiently to employ what is available to produce the highest valued mixture of goods and services. Any interference with the free market indicators will not only slow down recovery but also misdirect some efforts and reduce the ability of business to satisfy as much human need as a completely free economy would.

The day of reckoning can only be put off so long. Once the nation's workers and savers realize that such semi-hidden increases in the money supply are appropriating a part of their purchasing power, they may take their dollars out of government bonds, savings banks, life insurance policies, and the like in order to buy goods or invest in real estate or common stocks, and even borrow at the banks to do so. If this trend should develop, the government would soon be forced to adopt sound fiscal and monetary policies.

The same effect might be produced by a rush of foreign dollar holders to spend the dollars they now consider as good as one thirty-fifth of an ounce of gold. In any case, an ever-increasing supply of dollars and ever-increasing prices will eventually bring on a "runaway inflation," unless the government stops its present practices before the situation gets completely out of hand.

The important thing to remember is that increases in the nation's money supply can never benefit the nation's economy. Such increases in the money supply do not and cannot increase the supply of goods and services that a free economy would produce. Such inflations of the money supply can only help some at the expense of others. Even such help for the politically favored is at best only temporary. As prices rise, it takes ever bigger doses of new money to have the same effect, and this in turn means still higher prices.

The fact is that no matter what the volume of business may be, any given supply of money is sufficient to perform all the services money can perform for an economy. All that is needed for continued prosperity is for the government to let prices, wage rates, and interest rates fluctuate so that they reveal rather than hide the true state of market conditions.

Under the paper money standard, politicians are easily tempted to keep voting for just a little more spending than last year, and just a little less taxing than last year. The gap can be covered by a semi-hidden increase in the money supply—just a little more than last year. Then, too, the illusions of prosperity are often helped along by an easy money policy—holding interest rates below those of a free market. This tends to increase the demand for loans above the amount of real savings available for lending. The banks then meet the demand for more credit by the bookkeeping device of increasing the bank accounts of borrowers.

Clever financial officials must then find ways to put off the day of reckoning. If gold continues to flow out, private travel, imports, and investments can be blamed and controls instituted. When the first controls do not succeed, more and more controls can be added.

When these fail, public attention can always be diverted by a war. War is now generally considered a sufficient excuse for more inflation and a completely controlled economy of the type Hitler established in Germany.

No man or government should ever be trusted with the legal power to increase a nation's money supply at will.

The great advantage of the gold standard is that gold cannot be created by printing presses or by bookkeeping entries. When a country is on the gold standard, politicians who want to vote for spending measures must also vote for increased taxes or sanction the issuance of government securities paying free market interest rates that will attract the funds of private savers and investors. Under a true gold standard, men remain free, the quantity of money is determined by market forces, and both the manipulated inflations and the resulting depressions are eliminated, along with all the poverty and human misery that they cause.

Notes

[1]See "Jobs for All" by Percy L. Greaves, Jr., (Reading No. 38)

[2]Figures from the *Federal Reserve Bulletin*, February 1965. Figures for the money supply include those for currency outside of banks, demand deposits, and time deposits of commercial banks which in practice may be withdrawn on demand.

[3]Federal Reserve Board "Supplement" to *Banking and Monetary Statistics*, Sec. 15. International Finance.

[4]*Federal Reserve Bulletin*, February, 1965.

47. BACK TO GOLD?*

Henry Hazlitt

In February of this year President de Gaulle of France startled the financial world by calling for a return to an international gold standard. American and British monetary managers replied that he was asking for the restoration of a world lost forever. But some eminent economists strongly endorsed his proposal. They argued that only a return to national currencies directly convertible into gold could bring an end to the chronic monetary inflation of the last twenty years in nearly every country in the world.

What is the gold standard? How did it come about? When and why was it abandoned? And why is there now in many quarters a strong demand for its restoration?

We can best understand the answers to these questions by a glance into history. In primitive societies exchange was conducted by barter. But as labor and production became more divided and specialized, a man found it hard to find someone who happened to have just what he wanted and happened to want just what he had. So people tried to exchange their goods first for some article that nearly everybody wanted so that they could exchange this article in turn for the exact things they happened to want.

This common commodity became a medium of exchange—money.

All sorts of things have been used in human history as such a common medium of exchange—cattle, tobacco, precious stones, the precious metals, particularly silver and gold. Finally gold became dominant, the "standard" money.

Gold had tremendous advantages. It could be fashioned into beautiful ornaments and jewelry. Because it was both beautiful and scarce, gold combined very high value with comparatively little weight and bulk; it could therefore be easily held and stored. Gold "kept" indefinitely; it did not spoil or rust; it was not only durable but practically indestructible. Gold could be hammered or stamped into almost any shape or precisely divided into any desired size or unit of weight. There were chemical and other tests that could establish whether it was genuine. And as it could be stamped into coins of a precise weight, the values of all other goods could be exactly expressed in units of gold. It therefore became not only the medium of exchange but the "standard of value." Records show that gold was being used as a form of money as long ago as 3,000 B.C. Gold coins were struck as early as 800 or 700 B.C.

One of gold's very advantages, however, also presented a problem. Its high value compared with its weight and bulk increased the risks of its being stolen. In the sixteenth and even into the nineteenth centuries (as one will find from the plays of Ben Jonson and Molière and the novels of George Eliot and Balzac) some people kept almost their entire fortunes in gold in their own houses. But most people came more and more into the habit of leaving their gold for safekeeping in the vaults of goldsmiths. The goldsmiths gave them a receipt for it.

The Origin of Banks

Then came a development that probably no one had originally foreseen. The people who had left their gold in a goldsmith's vault found, when they wanted to make a purchase or pay a debt, that they did not have to go to the vaults themselves for their gold. They could simply issue an order to the goldsmith to pay over the gold to the person from whom they had purchased something. This second man might find in turn that he did not want the actual gold; he was content to leave it for safekeeping at the goldsmith's, and in turn issue orders to the goldsmith to pay specified amounts of gold to still a third person. And so on.

This was the origin of banks, and of both bank

*From *The Freeman*, October 1965

notes and checks. If the receipts were made out by the goldsmith or banker himself, for round sums payable to bearer, they were bank notes. If they were orders to pay made out by the legal owners of the gold themselves, for varying specified amounts to be paid to particular persons, they were checks. In either case, though the ownership of the gold constantly changed and the bank notes circulated, the gold itself almost never left the vault!

When the goldsmiths and banks made the discovery that their customers rarely demanded the actual gold, they came to feel that it was safe to issue more notes promising to pay gold than the actual amount of gold they had on hand. They counted on the high unlikelihood that everybody would demand his gold at once.

This practice seemed safe and even prudent for another reason. An honest bank did not simply issue more notes, more IOU's, than the amount of actual gold it had in its vaults. It would make loans to borrowers secured by salable assets of the borrowers. The bank notes issued in excess of the gold held by the bank were also secured by these assets. An honest bank's assets therefore continued to remain at least equal to its liabilities.

There was one catch. The bank's liabilities, which were in gold, were all payable *on demand*, without prior notice. But its assets, consisting mainly of its loans to customers, were most of them payable only on some date in the future. The bank might be "solvent" (in the sense that the value of its assets equaled the value of its liabilities) but it would be at least partly "illiquid." If all its depositors demanded their gold at once, it could not possibly pay them all.

Yet such a situation might not develop in a lifetime. So in nearly every country the banks went on expanding their credit until the amount of bank-note and demand-deposit liabilities (that is, the amount of "money") was several times the amount of gold held in the banks' vaults.

The Fractional Reserve

In the United States today there are $11 of Federal Reserve notes and demand-deposit liabilities—i.e., $11 of money—for every $1 of gold.

Up until 1929, this situation—a gold standard with only a "fractional" gold reserve—was accepted as sound by the great body of monetary economists, and even as the best system attainable. There were two things about it, however, that were commonly overlooked. First, if there was, say, four, five, or ten times as much note and deposit "money" in circulation as the amount of gold against which this money had been issued, it meant that prices were far higher as a result of this more abundant money, perhaps four, five, or ten times higher, then if there had been no more money than the amount of gold. And business was built upon, and had become dependent upon, this amount of money and this level of wages and prices.

Now if, in this situation, some big bank or company failed, or the prices of stocks tumbled, or some other event precipitated a collapse of confidence, prices of commodities might begin to fall; more failures would be touched off; banks would refuse to renew loans; they would start calling old loans; goods would be dumped on the market. As the amount of loans was contracted, the amount of bank notes and deposits against them would also shrink. In short, the supply of money itself would begin to fall. This would touch off a still further decline of prices and buying and a further decline of confidence.

That is the story of every major depression. It is the story of the Great Depression from 1929 to 1933.

From Boom to Slump

What happened in 1929 and after, some economists argue, is that the gold standard "collapsed." They say we should never go back to it or depend upon it again. But other economists argue that it was not the gold standard that "collapsed" but unsound political and economic policies that destroyed it. Excessive expansion of credit, they say, is bound to lead in the end to a violent contraction of credit. A boom stimulated by easy credit and cheap money must be followed by a crisis and a slump.

In 1944, however, at a conference in Bretton Woods, New Hampshire, the official representatives of 44 nations decided—mainly under the influence of John Maynard Keynes of Great Britain and Harry Dexter White of the United States—to set up a new international currency system in which the central banks of the leading countries would cooperate with each other and coordinate their currency systems through an International Monetary Fund. They would all deposit "quotas" in the Fund, only one-quarter of which need be in gold, and the rest in their own currencies. They would all be entitled to draw on this Fund quickly for credits and other currencies.

The United States alone explicitly undertook to keep its currency convertible at all times into gold. This privilege of converting their dollars was not given to its own citizens, who were forbidden to hold gold (except in the form of jewelry or teeth fillings); the privilege was given only to foreign central banks and official international institutions. Our government pledged itself to convert these foreign holdings of dollars into gold on demand at the fixed rate of $35 an ounce. Two-way convertibility at this rate meant that a dollar was the equivalent of one-thirty-fifth of an ounce of gold.

The other currencies were not tied to gold in this direct way. They were simply tied to the dollar by the commitment of the various countries not to let their currencies fluctuate (in terms of the dollar) by more than 1 per cent either way from their adopted par values. The other countries could hold and count dollars as part of their reserves on the same basis as if dollars were gold.

International Monetary Fund Promotes Inflation

The system has not worked well. There is no evidence that it has "shortened the duration and lessened the degree of disequilibrium in the international balances of payments of members," which was one of its six principal declared purposes. It has not maintained a stable value and purchasing power of the currencies of individual members. This vital need was not even a declared purpose.

In fact, under it inflation and depreciation of currencies have been rampant. Of the 48 or so national members of the Fund in 1949, practically all except the United States devalued their currencies (i.e., reduced their value) that year following devaluation of the British pound from $4.03 to $2.80. Of the 102 present members of the Fund, the great majority have either formally devalued since they joined, or allowed their currencies to fall in value since then as compared with the dollar.

The dollar itself, since 1945, has lost 43 per cent of its purchasing power. In the last ten years alone the German mark has lost 19 per cent of its purchasing power, the British pound 26 per cent, the Italian lira 27 per cent, the French franc 36 per cent, and leading South American currencies from 92 to 95 per cent.

In addition, the two "key" currencies, the currencies that can be used as reserves by other countries—the British pound sterling and the U. S. dollar—have been plagued by special problems. In the last twelve months the pound has had to be repeatedly rescued by huge loans, totaling more than $4 billion, from the Fund and from a group of other countries.

Balance of Payments

The United States has been harassed since the end of 1957 by a serious and apparently chronic "deficit in the balance of payments." This is the name given to the excess in the amount of dollars going abroad (for foreign aid, for investments, for tourist expenditures, for imports, and for other payments) over the amount of dollars coming in (in payment for our exports to foreign countries, etc.). This deficit in the balance of payments has been running since the end of 1957 at a rate of more than $3 billion a year. In the seven-year period to the end of 1964, the total deficit in our balance of payments came to $24.6 billion.

This had led, among other things, to a fall in the amount of gold holdings of the United States from $22.9 billion at the end of 1957 to $13.9 billion now—a loss of $9 billion gold to foreign countries.

Other changes have taken place. As a result of the chronic deficit in the balance of payments, foreigners have short-term claims on the United States of $27.8 billion. And $19 billion of these are held by foreign central banks and international organizations that have a legal right to demand gold for them. This is $5 billion more gold than we hold altogether. Even of the $13.9 billion gold that we do hold, the Treasury is still legally obliged to keep some $8.8 billion against outstanding Federal Reserve notes.

This is why officials and economists not only in the United States but all over the Western world are now discussing a world monetary reform. Most of them are putting forward proposals to increase "reserves" and to increase "liquidity." They argue that there isn't enough "liquidity"—that is, that there isn't enough money and credit, or soon won't be—to conduct the constantly growing volume of world trade. Most of them tell us that the gold standard is outmoded. In any case, they say, there isn't enough gold in the world to serve as the basis for national currencies and international settlements.

But the advocates of a return to a full gold standard, who though now in a minority include some of the world's most distinguished economists, are not impressed by these arguments for still further monetary expansion. They say these are merely arguments for still further inflation. And they contend that this further monetary expansion or inflation, apart from its positive dangers, would be a futile means even of achieving the ends that the expansionists themselves have in mind.

Suppose, say the gold-standard advocates, we were to double the amount of money now in the world. We could not, in the long run, conduct any greater volume of business and trade than we could before. For the result of increasing the amount of money would be merely to increase correspondingly the wages and prices at which business and trade were conducted. In other words, the result of doubling the supply of money, other things remaining unchanged, would be roughly to cut in half the purchasing power of the currency unit. The process would be as ridiculous as it would be futile. This is the sad lesson that inflating countries soon or late learn to their sorrow.

The Great Merit of Gold

The detractors of gold complain that it is difficult and costly to increase the supply of the metal, and that this depends upon the "accidents" of discovery of new mines or the invention of better processes of extraction. But the advocates of a gold standard argue that this is precisely gold's great merit. The supply of gold is governed by nature; it is not, like the supply of paper money, subject merely to the schemes of demagogues or the whims of politicians. Nobody ever thinks he has quite enough money. Once the idea is accepted that money is something whose supply is determined simply by the printing press, it becomes impossible for the politicians in power to resist the constant demands for further inflation. Gold may not be a theoretically perfect basis for money; but it has the merit of making the money supply, and therefore the value of the monetary unit, independent of governmental manipulation and political pressure.

And this is a tremendous merit. When a country is not on a gold standard, when its citizens are not even permitted to own gold, when they are told that irredeemable paper money is just as good, when they are compelled to accept payment in such paper of debts or pensions that are owed to them, when what they have put aside, for retirement or old-age, in savings banks or insurance policies, consists of this irredeemable paper money, then they are left without protection as the issue of this paper money is increased and the purchasing power of each unit falls; then they can be completely impoverished by the political decisions of the "monetary managers."

I have just said that the dollar itself, "the best currency in the world," has lost 43 per cent of its purchasing power of twenty years ago. This means that a man who retired with $10,000 of savings in 1945 now finds that that capital will buy less than three-fifths as much as it did then.

But Americans, so far, have been the very lucky ones. The situation is much worse in England, and still worse in France. In some South American countries practically the whole value of people's savings—92 to 95 cents in every dollar—has been wiped out in the last ten years.

Not a Managed Money

The tremendous merit of gold is, if we want to put it that way, a negative one: It is *not* a managed paper money that can ruin everyone who is legally forced to accept it or who puts his confidence in it. The technical criticisms of the gold standard become utterly trivial when compared with this single merit. The experience of the last twenty years in practically every country proves that the monetary managers are the pawns of the politicians, and cannot be trusted.

Many people, including economists who ought to know better, talk as if the world had already abandoned the gold standard. They are mistaken. The world's currencies are still tied to gold, though in a loose, indirect, and precarious way. Other currencies are tied to the American dollar, and convertible into it, at definite "official" rates (unfortunately subject to sudden change) through the International Monetary Fund. And the dollar is still, though in an increasingly restricted way, convertible into gold at $35 an ounce.

Indeed, the American problem today, and the world problem today, is precisely how to maintain this limited convertibility of the dollar (and hence indirectly of other currencies) into a fixed quantity of gold. This is why the American loss of gold, and the growing claims against our gold supply, are being viewed with such concern.

The crucial question that the world has now to answer is this: As the present system and present policies are rapidly becoming untenable, shall the world's currencies abandon all links to gold, and leave the supply of each nation's money to be determined by political management, or shall the world's leading currencies return to a gold standard—that is, shall each leading currency be made once again fully convertible into gold on demand at a fixed rate?

Whatever may have been the shortcomings of the old gold standard, as it operated in the nineteenth and the early twentieth century, it gave the world, in fact, an international money. When all leading currencies were directly convertible into a fixed amount of gold on demand, they were of course at all times convertible into each other at the equivalent fixed cross rates. Businessmen in every country could have confidence in the currencies of other countries. In final settlement, gold was the one universally acceptable currency everywhere. It is still the one universally acceptable commodity to those who are still legally allowed to get it.

Instead of ignoring or deploring or combating this fact, the world's governments might start building on it once more.

48. ETERNAL LOVE*

Lawrence Noonan

You are a member of the jury in this fictional court case

The courtroom was hushed as the judge entered the chamber. It was crowded and many people could find standing room only. The trial, of course, had attracted nationwide interest and you could almost reach out and feel the expectancy.

The defendant, Charles Akins, was a rather small and timid looking man. Perhaps the timidity was a matter of fear—surely the somber courtroom and the overpowering majesty of the law were enough to inspire fear in a defendant. Mr. Akins certainly did not look like a criminal. As a matter of fact, he really looked quite respectable. But he did look frightened. And yet, there was determination there. And just a gleam of courage shining through, too.

Perhaps we should tell you now that the year was 1984. Not that there was anything so special about '84. Children went to school, grew up, worked, got married, and reared their own children. People went to church, voted, talked politics, argued, and endeavored to understand the subtleties of economics. But, all of it was just a little bit different. Especially in the way that people looked at things.

The Judge, the Honorable Warren Faber, having completed the preliminary ceremonies, was looking rather curiously, we thought, at the defendant.

"Mr. Akins," he said, "it is my understanding that you have retained no counsel and that you wish to defend yourself. Considering the gravity of the charge against you, I feel that you might like to reconsider."

"No, your honor," Akins replied, "I am going to defend myself."

"Mr. Akins, you are charged with a federal offense and are being tried in a federal court. You are charged with usurping the function of the government, of undermining and attempting to replace the monetary system of this country. With serious charges of this nature why will you not avail yourself of counsel?"

Mr. Akins seemed to be shivering slightly.

"Your honor, the facts have already been more or less determined. This is a matter of right or wrong. There isn't any legal thing involved here. I'm not guilty of anything. I simply want to tell what happened. I want to tell my story. I don't need any lawyer to do that."

The Prosecuting Attorney, Arnold Spear, leaped to his feet.

"Your honor, I object. The defendant is attempting to tell the court what is right and wrong. Further, I object to the statement that all of the facts are known."

"Objection overruled. This court will make its findings when the time comes. The defendant does

*From *The Freeman*, May 1960

have the right to represent himself. Mr. Akins, you have been sworn in. Now tell us what you consider to be your story."

"Well, this is the way it was. Back in 1957 my company, Trans-World Mining, became interested in increasing the market for our principal product —platinum. We had expanded our mining considerably and we needed more in the way of sales. We believed that platinum could be used far more extensively in jewelry and we bought a well-known jewelry manufacturing firm. We experimented with combining platinum with another metal, and we came up with something very beautiful and practical."

Judge Faber interrupted. "Mr. Akins, let me interrupt a minute. Up to this point you have simply told us that you were a mining company and had turned to the manufacture of jewelry from platinum?"

"Yes sir, that is correct. We had considerable success with the manufacture of jewelry, but as the years went by we began to notice a very unusual thing."

The Judge leaned forward intently. There was absolute quiet in the courtroom.

"We had manufactured small disk-like pieces of jewelry with some fine detail work on each side. Each piece had a small hole near one edge and we had intended them as pieces suitable for pendants. They sold for fifty, a hundred, and two hundred dollars apiece. Frankly, we had not expected to sell too many of them. But as time passed, we began to experience something unusual. As I said, in the beginning, we didn't know how much to expect in the way of sales from a simple little piece like this. But as the years went by, the sales on this one small piece of adornment jewelry exceeded the sale of everything else the company was making! We couldn't understand it. These small pieces—originally priced at $50 to $200, and later at higher figures as the dollar price of platinum rose along with prices of everything else—were going like hot cakes. This went on and on. Finally, I had a market research outfit do a survey to find out why we were selling so many of these."

Charles Akins paused and licked his lips. The audience in the room was quiet but tense. Although they didn't have a doubt about the outcome of the trial, it was fascinating to hear this story from the man himself. After all, you didn't defy the government these days and get away with it!

Akins went on. "We discovered that people were buying these as an investment. People had become terribly afraid of the government's solvency. The government had issued barrels full of paper money. It wasn't even backed by gold any more. You couldn't even get gold."

Arnold Spear had jumped to his feet again. There was contempt in his eyes as he looked toward the defendant.

"Your honor, the defendant is beating about the bush. These things about paper money and gold are ridiculous! He's completely dodging the main issue—what was written on those coins?"

Little Mr. Akins was growing bolder.

"Your honor, it is my turn now to object. This was not a coin. We did not make these as coins. We did put an inscription on this piece of jewelry which conveyed—in a foreign tongue—Eternal Love. We had expected that this piece would be used for gift purposes. However, many people also interpreted this quotation to mean Eternal Value. Later on, this piece of jewelry began to be used by people in trade. They recognized and trusted the purity of its alloy. It had real value to them not only as an ornament but also as a medium of exchange. And as it came more and more into use in trade, this new use gave it still added value. People began saving them, hoarding them. We increased our production many times. We almost eliminated the manufacture of all other platinum items. The people wanted these. They were demanding them."

Akins paused again. He seemed to be either waiting to be challenged by the Prosecuting Attorney or for a request for clarification from the Judge. Nothing happened. Both the Judge and Arnold Spear had become absorbed in the story.

Akins proceeded now with growing confidence. He was on familiar ground. Regardless of the outcome, he had only one course and he followed it.

"Naturally, we were in business to make a profit. However, we, too, had become very apprehensive about the monetary situation and the government's policy. We finally decided that in addition to selling the platinum pieces, we would also make them the basis of our accounting and billing system—our private monetary unit. Thus, we began to use them as a medium of exchange. Of course, we were soon threatened by the Treasury Department. But they couldn't really do anything about it. Anyway, they didn't try. But later the value of the paper money in the country became almost worthless and they tried to blame Trans-World Mining for it. There was wild inflation. But the platinum pieces kept their value. People kept these whereas they would have kept gold if they could have gotten it. The government's paper money became almost worthless."

There was now both triumph and despair in Akins' voice.

"Well, it was almost incredible what had happened. The chaos became almost indescribable. People became frantic to get more of these platinum pieces. Where the value of paper money was going down and down, the value of the platinum piece was going up. It became the only sound means of exchange in the country."

Sadly he continued. "People came to realize that sound money was just as important as liberty itself. They found that there wasn't any honest freedom without honest money."

Another pause. "But now the government needs a scapegoat and they've got me. They want to put their own blame on someone else."

We won't bore you with the cross examination by Arnold Spear, the Prosecuting Attorney. He was eager for a conviction and the rhetoric thundered in the court. He likened Akins to one guilty of treason, of plotting the downfall of his own country. Akins was morally a leach and legally far worse. The thunder rolled on and on.

We don't know yet what the verdict is. The jury is still out.

Competition, "Big Business," and Monopoly

49. THE COW IN THE APARTMENT*

Burton Rascoe

Haven't you at one time or another remarked, or heard, without protest, a friend remark: "Radio and TV would be all right if it weren't for the commercials," or "He used to be a pretty good writer, but he is turning out nothing but commercial stuff nowadays," or "Commerce and religion don't mix well," or "It's the commercial angle that is tied in with the project that I object to"?

If so, have you ever realized that every one of those expressions and others like them are nothing whatever but displays and airings of baseless and rather vulgar snobbery?

We are all—every single one of us—engaged in trade. Trade is our way of helping ourselves and others.

The man who deposits a bottle full of milk before my apartment door every morning is in trade, even though he belongs to a driver's union; and his being in trade is a way of helping me and others. Since I live in an apartment in the city, I can't keep a cow handy, even if I knew how to milk her. Even if it were possible for me to keep a cow in the apartment, the cow would produce more milk than I can use. I couldn't stop milking her; for if I did, she would go dry. I would have an unproductive cow on my hands in an apartment, and the cost of feeding and cleaning up after her would be great. If I tried to get back some of the cost by selling the surplus, I would have to go into business, buy bottles and sterilizing and pasteurizing chemicals and equipment, solicit customers, keep books, keep publicly displayed the O.P.A.[1] milk prices, file and pay quarterly income taxes, get, display, and keep paid up on, the necessary licenses, submit to regular federal, state, and municipal food and hygiene inspection, promptly report all symptoms of hoof-and-mouth disease, ticks or other cow afflictions, dun my delinquent customers, and Lord knows what all—and the surplus milk from one cow would cost me X-dollars for every 28¢ bottle of milk I sold.

So my milkman, in trade, helps me in more ways than he probably realizes; and he also helps so many other people. By helping the milk company to keep together, he even helps me to enjoy certain dramas on my TV. From the aggregate of profits in fractions of mills on the 28¢ bottle of milk, the company seeks to increase the number of persons it helps in the same way it does me.

One of the ways the company can increase its number of milk customers is by advertising; and one of these ways of advertising is by helping the television companies to keep in business by buying time from the companies for the televising of dramas for which writers, directors, producers, camera operators, electricians, costumers, make-up artists, script girls, announcers, and actors must be hired.

Every aspect of all this is commercial, from the creative talent of the writer of the drama, who trades the product of his brains for cash to the rest of the studio, to the work of the scrub woman who cleans up the studio. But the only thing that is labeled "commercial" is the selling-talk for the milk company, which appears at the beginning, in the middle, and at the end of the TV drama, and which consumes not more than three minutes of the TV audience's time.

*From *Ideas on Liberty,* September 1955

Yet those three minutes are entirely devoted by the company to the helping of others—commercial script-writers, actors, scenic artists, cameramen, electricians, and others—all of whom are provided with a means of livelihood by the indispensable and economically justifiable "commercial" which makes it possible to see a good drama, well acted, without cost in my living room.

It is impossible honestly to make a great deal of money without doing a great deal of good.

Note

[1]The O.P.A. (established 1941) had its counterpart in the Price Commission, set up under the President's Wage-Price Freeze, August 15, 1971, and new control boards will undoubtedly be created if new controls are enacted.

50. FREEDOM TO SHOP AROUND*

Hart Buck

Because we are human beings and not animals, we have at our command two principles whose realization secures us an immensely better living than animals can ever get for themselves.

In the first place, two people can work to produce more than twice as many valuable things as one can. In the second place, two people, simply by exchanging things they have, can each end up with more of the things they want.

Through these two principles, we can produce and enjoy immeasurably more as members of an economy than we could as so many Robinson Crusoes or even Swiss Families Robinson. Through a third principle—freedom to shop—we can make the most of the economy we live in, and produce for our enjoyment more than ever.

This embraces not only the housewife's freedom to shop for her detergent where she need pay least for it but also the producer's freedom to shop for his materials where he can get them cheapest; the investor's freedom to shop for the biggest return for his money; the employer's freedom to shop for the kind of help that will give him the biggest production for what he pays; and the worker's freedom to shop for the job that pays him best.

Competition is nothing but freedom looked at upside down. In a market where buyers are free to shop around, sellers must outdo each other to get and keep customers. Through competition there is produced the maximum of goods and services that the public wants most. Competition does not mean "dog eat dog." Instead, it is the necessary preface to cooperation. Competition helps us to decide with whom we can best cooperate in production.

The driving force behind the free market is the enterprise of the businessman. He is the man who sees a chance to turn unused resources to account, and produce something out of them which the public will want. He buys materials, secures tools, hires helpers, and sells his product in the hope of recovering all his costs; including the cost of his own time and the cost of any tools that may be his. Perhaps he does not recover his costs, which means that some better use could have been made of all the resources involved, so that everybody loses all round. Or else he may be lucky, and recover all his costs plus something extra. The extra is profit, and nothing else is.

On the free market, his costs will tend up, and his prices will tend down, through the pressure of competition. They will so adjust themselves in time that the businessman will earn no more than he could get by renting his tools to some other businessman and going to work for him. When that happens, he has no profit any more. Profits are the businessman's return for trying something new and desirable. When it is no longer new, profits stop. Profits are temporary only, but the gain to consumers, investors, and workers is permanent.

Most of us think of the businessman as distinct from the investor or the worker; we think of him instead as the operator of a going business. So typically he is; nevertheless, every investor is a businessman when he invests his money in hopes of a

*From an address delivered before the Queensway Lions Club (Toronto, Canada) February 10, 1954

bigger return some day than his investment brings him now; and, most important, every worker takes on the character of a businessman when he fits himself for one line of work rather than another, in hopes of turning his own capacities to the best account possible in the end. You might say, therefore, that all of them are speculators, and so they are. Enterprise is speculation, and speculation is enterprise. Both of them mean anticipating in advance what other people will want, and facing the possibility that they won't want it. Under the free market everyone is free to anticipate and speculate.

As businessmen and speculators—even if we are investors or workers—we may feel handicapped, not by our own freedom to shop around, but by other people's; and so we may try to stop them, or to get the government to do it for us. We may succeed; this involves controlling the supply of some factor of production, and turning out at our own price a smaller product than the customers would take if we didn't control the supply. But if we do, we may find that the pressure of competition makes us pay extra for the factors of production whose supply we don't control. As monopolists, therefore, we may find ourselves no better off than if we had no monopoly. The public, on the other hand, loses the goods that the monopoly keeps them from getting.

Under the free market, therefore, some people may get special benefits temporarily, but everybody benefits permanently. Under a market that is not free, some people may get special benefits for a time, but everybody loses permanently. It is never under the free market that some people benefit at other people's expense. This results, instead, from interference with the free market.

51. SIX MISCONCEPTIONS ABOUT CONSUMER WELFARE*

Joel Dean

The American consumer is, in the Great Society, the forgotten man. Antipoverty programs, the closed shop, foreign aid, minimum wage hikes benefit him little and are ultimately at his expense.

The consumer cannot count on the unselfish munificence of the government to look after his interests. Instead, he had best place himself in the hands of the self-serving competitor. The forces of competition alone can be counted on to compel suppliers, in an enterprise system geared to self-interest, to achieve results which will advance the welfare of the consumer.

The vigor of the competitive process is, therefore, our main assurance of social benefit and consumer welfare. Protecting and strengthening the competitive process (which is quite different from protecting the individual competitor) is the white hope of the consumer.

The main peril to competition is not bigness, not concentration, not conglomerates (variegated product lines), not mergers, not even price conspiracies. Instead, the main peril is prejudice: distrust of the competitive system in its modern guise. The roots of this prejudice are basic misunderstandings concerning the economics of consumer welfare. Six economic fallacies are particularly important:

1. That competition is declining and is now an untrustworthy control device.
2. That competition becomes "cut-throat" unless curbed by government.
3. That profits are at the expense of the consumer.
4. That advertising makes consumers captive and is economic waste.
5. That the best way to take care of the incompetent is to make competition soft.
6. That job security is best attained by slowing down economic progress.

*From *The Freeman*, January 1966

Let's look briefly at each of these misconceptions. Although unobtrusive and eminently respectable, these economic misunderstandings are pervasive and perilous. They are working to undermine the protection that the consumer gets from vigorous competition.

1. Competition Is Declining and Is Now an Untrustworthy Control Device

Looking back nostalgically at the Tom Sawyer economy, we get a glowing glimpse of a structure of competition quite different from today's. We see small, independent, local business firms by the thousands: the local grist mill, lumber mill, brewery, and carriage shop. What we forget is that each of these glorified competitors had a tight little locational monopoly sheltered by miserable transportation. What we often fail to see in our modern economy is the competition that counts. This competition is outside the purview of the conventional antitrust case. It creeps in on little cat feet, unobtrusively at first. It is not quite respectable at the start (for example, the discount houses and early supermarkets). It often works its beneficial miracles below the surface of consumer consciousness through the vehicle of "value-analysis" by industrial purchasers (such as the revolution in welding, die casting, and oxygen furnaces). Its fiercest fighting front is often the research laboratory. This is the competition that counts because it produces decisive cost savings, usually as a result of revolutionary new technology or spectacular rearrangement of functions, or dramatic displacement by substitutes. Generally speaking, it is outside the purview of the conventional antitrust case and the stereotyped concentration indices.

It is frequently an invader from outer space, that is, from a different industry or a foreign nation.

This is the competition that keeps the American economy among the most competitive in the world and that assures the American consumer a high and rising standard of living.

2. Competition Becomes "Cut-Throat" Unless Curbed by Government

One heritage of the great depression is a generalized fear of excessive competition. This fear leads on to the belief that the government must restrain these excesses by legislating minimum profit margins, for example, state "fair trade" statutes and laws against "selling below cost." This misconception has had an important role in shaping public policy, which is opposed to competition in several sectors of our economy, notably agriculture and transportation. Thus, despite formal professions of faith, the evidence is that we really don't believe in an enterprise economy—at least in these sectors. The precedent and the preconception that lie behind it are perilous for other sectors of our economy.

"Cut-throat" competition is a bogeyman whose influence is powerful but unwarranted. It is unwarranted because the degenerative tendency is a myth, probably. Even if true, it's hard to see how competition can really be excessively vigorous from the viewpoint of the national interest. The misconception arises partly from confusing injury to an individual competitor with injury to the competitive process. Competition, if it is effectively to serve the consumer, must injure individual rivals and even annihilate some. And the notion that this elimination of the unfit will inevitably reduce surviving competitors to a sole monopolist is a theoretical extrapolation, unsupported by experience and applicable in only a few industries where scale economies are overwhelming relative to the small size of the market.

3. Profits Are at the Expense of the Consumer

It is almost standard operating practice for people who profess concern for consumer welfare to view corporate profits as being at the expense of the consumer and opposed to his welfare. This antiprofit bias infuses the viewpoints of many officials in big government and particularly of those in regulatory commissions.

We should all recognize that profits are usually an index of success in serving the public. In a competitive industry, most of the profits go to the more efficient suppliers, not to the marginal supplier whose costly output is nonetheless required to satisfy the full demand at the prevailing market price. The consumer gets a bargain in the few profit pennies per dollar he appears to pay. He pays less than appears for two reasons. First, because losses that are not formally book-kept are not offset against reported corporate profits. Second, because equity capital, which is costly, is treated in accounting as a free good. The consumer gets a bargain, not only because corporate profits are partly illusory, but because the hope of profits and fear of losses (what makes the mare go) is the cheapest known form of incentive and remuneration.

4. Advertising Makes Consumers Captive and Is Economic Waste

Appalled by the huge sums spent on the advertising and annoyed by being a part of a captive audience, grieved by the gullibility of all consumers except themselves, and aroused by exposures of the hidden persuaders, many well-meaning reformers believe that advertising disfranchises the consumer and wastefully cancels claim against outrageous counterclaim.

Looking at the matter from the standpoint of the national interest in consumer welfare, we should recognize that advertising economizes leisure and is a cheap way for consumers to pre-shop. The most that advertising can do is to get a person to try the product; and his own experience with it, plus reports from his acquaintances and the synthetic experience of consumer research services, develops immunizing skepticism.

We should also recognize that advertising opens many more doors to new and beneficial competition than it closes. The best weapon against the hidden persuader of one manufacturer's advertising is that of his competitor, particularly the countervailing power of distributor brands which erode the consumer franchise of a manufacturer's brand.

5. The Best Way to Take Care of the Incompetent Is To Make Competition Soft

Much anticompetitive legislation and administrative and judicial case law is rooted in the thoroughly American and highly laudable desire to take care of the incompetent. The question is not whether society will look after the unfortunate. In this our society is doing a good job. The danger, instead, is that we will take care of them in the wrong way, that is, in a way that will deter incentives for self-improvement and will block the automatic adjustments of a competitive economy and prevent its serving consumers best. Charitable treatment of the less fortunate will be more efficient and less damaging to the growth and strength of our economy if it is entirely divorced from trying to protect the individual competitor against the consequences of his own non-competitiveness.

6. Job Security Is Best Attained by Slowing Down Economic Progress

The quest for job security is universal. Each of us is very much alive to any peril to our job. Most of us would like to feel that a beneficent government will look after this vital matter and make sure that economic change will not imperil our job.

Unfortunately, the competitive process has few champions and no lobby. The job security of the individual citizen can best be achieved, not by placing roadblocks in the path of technological progress, but instead by removing them. Society is better off to help the individual solve his problem of adapting to economic progress by supplying information, incentives, and opportunities for re-education, rather than by trying to slow down economic progress.

•

Economic misunderstandings like these six are causing a widespread, almost unconscious prejudice against competition. There is disconcerting reluctance to rely upon competition for the impersonal force which compels individual competitors, each geared to self-interest and trying to increase his own market power, to unconsciously serve society.

52. IS ECONOMIC FREEDOM POSSIBLE?*

Benjamin A. Rogge

The real debate on domestic policy in the United States at mid-century concerns the proper role of government—and those who wish for less government in economic affairs are obviously losing. The judges, in this case the voters of the United States, have been giving verdict after verdict to those who argue for more government intervention.

Those of us who are losing the debate often ascribe our losses to the work of men in academic life and elsewhere who are preaching socialism and trying to subvert the traditional American system of free enterprise. This easy and tempting explanation implies that our un-American opponents should be silent, and thus permit true American principles to prevail.

This explanation is both untrue and dangerous. It is dangerous because it could lead us to impose restraints on freedom of speech and of press that would indeed be un-American. It is dangerous because it leads us to relax our efforts to prepare and present our own case as powerfully and persuasively as possible. It is untrue, because not one in five hundred of those who favor more government intervention is a committed socialist or even basically opposed to free private enterprise. On the contrary, most of them are committed to the free market arrangement and believe that their proposals are designed to strengthen rather than to weaken it. Specifically, they argue that the market arrangement can survive only if certain of its weaknesses and failures are offset by appropriate government action.

For example, it is alleged that the free market economy tends to be unstable, alternating between boom and bust, and that this instability will destroy the economy unless corrected by appropriate government action. Though this is a serious charge, I believe both the analysis and the call for government action are mistaken.

*From *The Freeman*, April 1963

What I prefer to discuss here is an equally serious charge made against the free market by its friends.

Their charge is that economic freedom, though desirable, is not strictly possible—that in an unhampered market the individual would not be truly free but would be imposed upon by monopolies of various kinds and degrees. This charge appears in the preamble to one piece of interventionist legislation after another. Thus, the worker is said to need special protection because of the monopoly power of the employer. The farmer must be protected against monopolies on both sides of his market. Certain kinds of business firms must be protected against certain other kinds. Certain price decisions must be influenced by government because of the monopoly power of the firms involved. And on and on it goes. Clearly, if private monopoly is indeed this ubiquitous, a presumption is established in favor of a substantial role for government.

In my opinion, however, and this is to be the central thesis of my argument, the unhampered market tends to be a competitive market. In fact, strong action by government is all that can prevent its being a competitive market.

Phrased another way, my thesis is that positions of monopoly power tend to be short-lived and relatively ineffective, except as they receive the positive assistance and protection of government. Or phrased still another way, government in the United States has done far more to promote monopoly than to promote and permit competition.

Good for Others, Not for Me!

In developing the argument, I admit that there are certain very human attitudes which tend to work against competition. Although each of us may approve of competition as a general principle, we are less than anxious to face competition in our own personal activities. Competition is good in principle, we say, but not in our particular industry or occupation, or not when it comes from overseas, or not when it comes from people improperly trained in this occupation.

A natural outcome of this attitude is the attempt to reduce competition by cooperative action among would-be competitors. This tendency was clearly recognized by Adam Smith, the father of free market economics. In *The Wealth of Nations* published in 1776, he wrote as follows: "People of the same trade rarely meet together even for merriment and diversion except that it end in some contrivance to raise prices."

A second reason for questioning the possibility of a truly free economy is the influence of advancing technology on the size of the firm. The continuing technological revolution has produced a situation in one industry after another where, to be efficient, a firm must represent a large accumulation of capital, translated into buildings, machinery, and distribution organizations of great size and complexity. This growth in the size of the efficient firm is another challenge to the maintenance of the competitive economy.

A third reason often advanced for skepticism about competition is the difficulty of keeping oneself informed on the alternatives facing him in the multiple markets in which he operates, and the associated difficulty of retaining the mobility to shift his course of action in response to changes in those market alternatives.

A Temptation To Connive

The modern economic world is indeed a complex and confusing world, and these charges deserve serious attention. Let us take the charge that collusion rather than competition tends to be the distinguishing characteristic of the unregulated market economy. It is true that men are always tempted to practice collusion. However, it is equally true that the same forces which lead to the formation of cartel agreements tend to destroy those agreements.

The principal force involved here is simply the desire to make money. For example, suppose that a number of farmers agree to hold livestock off the market in a local area. The effect of this, of course, is to cause livestock prices to rise in that area. But with each increase in price, the individual farmer is under greater temptation to break the rules of the cartel and sell his hogs or beef cattle. At the same time, each increase in price attracts more livestock to that local market from farms outside the agreement area. The members of the cartel must then battle both their own members and outsiders to maintain the effectiveness of their operation.

In the same way, if a number of business firms agree to divide the total market into exclusive territories, the resulting price increase tempts each firm to try to increase its sales so as to increase its profits. However, each firm's own territory provides only limited opportunities for increased sales, and the temptation is enormous to expand sales by poaching on the neighboring, forbidden markets.

Cartels in America

The history of cartels in America is a history of brief initial successes followed by increased cheating on the agreement, then serious internal conflict, and eventual breakdown and dissolution of the cartel. This was the history of cartels long before the government made such agreements illegal per se, when the only restraining influence was the time-honored common law practice of court refusal to enforce cartel contracts. I could provide one case history after another to support my thesis. At the same time, I know of no cartel agreement in the history of this country that has been both effective and long-lived except those that have had the explicit support of government.

The farm program in this country in the last 35 years has been nothing more nor less than a government sponsored and operated cartel arrangement among otherwise competing producers. The nonfarm citizens have had to pay both the higher food and fiber prices and the cost of operating the cartel producing those higher prices.

In the same way, the trade union, a cartel arrangement among otherwise competing sellers of the services of labor, has been given the explicit support of government. In addition, trade unions have been permitted methods of enforcing their cartel rules that have made a mockery of the legal prohibition against assault.

In the same way, certain business and professional groups have been given legal protection in their cartel arrangements through licensing and franchise protection and through so-called fair trade laws.

The seriousness of these actions by government lies not only in the economic consequences but also in the violation of an important cornerstone of the free society—equality before the law. The union member, the farmer, and certain businessmen have been encouraged and assisted in doing precisely that for which other businessmen are sent to jail. The blindfolded goddess of justice has been encouraged to peek, and she now says with the jurists of the ancient regime, "First, tell me who you are, and then I will tell you what your rights are."

To summarize the point: although there is a natural tendency toward collusion among those who otherwise would be competing, there is an equally natural and ultimately stronger tendency for such collusive agreements to break down. The greatest contribution the government can make in this regard is to stop assisting and encouraging cartel groups.

Adam Smith followed the words I quoted above on "people of the same trade," and so forth, by saying, "There is no law that would be consistent with either liberty or justice that could prevent such meetings, but surely the government should do nothing to encourage such meetings, or to make such meetings necessary."

We have in the traditions of our common law refusal to enforce cartel agreements all that is really needed to prevent such agreements from destroying the basic competitiveness of the American economy.

Growth in Size of Firm

I turn now to the second argument: the threat to competition that is said to be posed by the growth in the size of the firm. Here again, there is no disputing the fact that advancing technology has led to larger and larger firms in many industries. However, in some industries advancing technology has made it possible for small, even household units to compete successfully with the giant firms. The development of efficient and relatively inexpensive tools, for example, has made it possible for many a husband to run a basement factory for producing furniture, at least for use in his own home.

But rather than rest the case on this possibility, I would further point out that the growth in the size of the firm often has been matched, or more than matched, by the growth in the size of the market. It is the size of the firm relative to the market that is important, and not the absolute size of the firm. Advancing technology also has been at work in transportation and communication, and this has had the effect of widening all markets.

For example, as a result of the automobile, no giant supermarket today has as much control over its market as did one small store in the small Midwestern town where I was raised. The United States Steel Corporation has less control of its market than did many a small backyard iron foundry in the last century. Transportation costs shielded the backyard operation from competition located no more than a few miles away. U. S. Steel, on the other hand, faces competition from firms in every steel producing country in the world.

In the same way, the worker living in a small town with only one major employer usually has the real alternative today of driving no more than 25 miles to dozens of other employment opportunities. Thus, in many cases, improved transport and communication facilities have widened markets more rapidly than firms have grown in size, and competition has increased rather than diminished.

A second way in which markets have been widened by advancing technology is through the development of substitute products and materials. Thus, the major steel companies, in almost every use for steel, face tremendous competition from substitute materials—aluminum, wood, concrete, plastics—even glass. In fact, it is quite unrealistic to speak of this arrangement as the steel industry. There really exists an entire complex of firms and industries, and no one firm—no one industry even—approaches monopoly power when so used. The typical textbook, man-on-the-street way of defining industry—and hence, of evaluating monopoly power—is both unrealistic and dangerous. It leads to a gross exaggeration of the market power actually possessed by the firms involved.

But again, let us not rest the case on these possibilities of widening markets. In spite of these powerful influences, there still can exist situations in which a given firm, or small group of firms, dominate a given market—no matter how wide that market has become. Do these not constitute hard core cases of monopoly, calling for government action to break them up or offset their consequences by creating counter monopolies of labor or agriculture or other business firms? My answer is no!

Success Through Service

To begin with, it is extremely unlikely that a firm can acquire market power except by laudable efficiency in serving the wishes of consumers. Is this firm to be rewarded for its efficiency by government antitrust action? And, if so, what of the consumer and the service he has been receiving?

Furthermore, if this firm uses its market power to raise prices above the competitive level, other firms will be tempted to enter the industry. These other firms can include large, diversified companies with adequate capital to invade any market. In this country in recent years we have seen many cases of large firms in a given industry suddenly finding themselves facing the competition of other large firms, already established in other fields, but coming into this market to reap the rewards of diversification and higher profit margins. The result is that even the powerful firm in a dominant position in its own market must behave as if it faced immediate important competition, because a failure to do so would soon attract that competition.

Beyond this, the very process of technological progress which may have created this dominant firm tends, over time, to weaken its position. Other firms with newer, better ideas will come into the field, and the original firm will find its share of the market shrinking. Thus, in spite of the fact that the Supreme Court decided long ago against breaking up the United States Steel Company, that company's percentage share of steel sold by American producers has declined steadily from over 75 per cent to around 35 per cent.

It is the little foxes, indeed, who nibble away at the market, who improvise and experiment, whose administrative simplicity permits daring moves, who reduce the stature of the giant to one quite consistent with almost any meaningful definition of competition. This process of short-run market power being replaced by someone else's short-run reign, in turn supplanted by a third, and so on, was eloquently described by the late great Austrian and Harvard University economist, Joseph Schumpeter. He argued, not only that the dominance attained through technological advance is short-lived, but also that it is this possibility of at least short-run market power and security that induces firms to undertake the technological explorations which are revolutionizing the modern world.

In summary, then, although the process is not perfect nor instantaneous, there are powerful forces always at work in the modern world to create a dynamic and effective competitive process, protecting each element in the economy from each other.

Turn now to the third charge, to the claim that individuals in the modern complex economy do not possess the necessary knowledge and mobility to force competitive practices on those with whom they deal.

I would first say that the modern economy, with its advanced techniques of communication and transportation, provides the individual with more information and better and cheaper means of transport than ever before in the history of the world. But beyond that, it is not necessary that all individuals in a given market be completely informed and completely mobile for adequate competitive pressures to exist.

For example, I know almost nothing about the workings of a television set. What protects me then, when I buy a television set or have one repaired? It is the fact that there are a substantial number of men who do have the required technical knowledge. The television dealer who expects to prosper and survive must meet the demands of all with whom he deals, or quickly lose out to other more reputable and reliable dealers. On the other hand, in certain areas I am the better informed buyer, and in these areas I protect the less well-informed.

In the same way, I have a personal commitment to the college where I work and the community where I live which seriously reduces my mobility. Here, I am protected in part by the good will of those who employ me, but I am protected as well by the fact that the college must offer a general program of working conditions and salaries that will retain the uncommitted and that will attract the appropriate staff replacements and additions.

Not All Must Move at Once

This same process works to effect the many adjustments that must continually be made in a dynamic economy. Usually, in a dying industry or area, not all workers must leave at once. The process customarily takes years. The adjustments are made by the sizable mobile element in every work force, thus protecting the less mobile from loss of employment or exploitation. The adjustment process can be left to each individual and does not require that everyone have complete knowledge and complete mobility.

Another variant of this argument is the charge that the consumer is deliberately misled and confused by advertising, and hence falls easy prey to noncompetitive sellers. I have heard this argument presented by many people from all income levels and all walks of life. But I have yet to find one of them who would admit that he himself was the helpless victim of Madison Avenue. It is always "they"—a vague and never identified "they"—who are thus bamboozled. The fact is that advertising itself is competitive, an expression of the basic competitiveness of the American economy, a process through which all of us receive the necessary information for the making of decisions.

In summarizing my answers to the charges that have been made against the possibility of a truly competitive free market, let me repeat, I do not insist that the processes at work produce instant pure competition, in every market in the country, at every moment of time. I say only that the forces are sufficiently strong, and work in good enough time, to give us a workably competitive economy, an economy that does not need government action to offset the noncompetitive elements.

More Harm than Good

When I have admitted that the system is not perfect, does this not leave a case at least for government antitrust legislation to handle the imperfections that remain? In theory, a case might be made for this; but in practice, I see no evidence that antitrust legislation and action ever can be devised to correct the few imperfections without the greater possibility of destroying dynamic competitive firms.

How is one to distinguish between the firm that has acquired temporary market power through greater efficiency and the one that has acquired power without being efficient? To break up the firm that is efficient is to work against true competition rather than to promote it. Nor can we seek to maintain competition by maintaining competitors. This has been a common thrust of our antitrust action. Yet, in fact, it thwarts competition rather than promotes it. Under true competition, the resources come under the control of those firms which have proved themselves the most efficient in serving the interests of consumers. The weeding-out process is severe and effective. To stop that process, to try to maintain a given number of competitors, is to promote inefficiency, not competition.

Another direction taken by our antitrust laws has been that of prohibiting unfair competition. Unfair competition has been defined as selling below cost in order to drive out rivals and thus gain a dominant position in the market. In practice, though, it is virtually impossible to distinguish between low prices that are a natural part of competitive maneuvering and those that are designed to establish market dominance. In practice, then, this legislation has done much more to reduce the competitiveness of the economy than to enhance it. In addition, it has contributed to a general climate for business decision-making characterized by uncertainty and confusion. Thus, one major electrical manufacturing firm recently was under indictment for charging prices that were thought to be too high and at the same time for charging prices that were thought to be too low.

Antitrust legislation generally has been subjected to such varied interpretations that the most experienced legal staff in the country cannot, with any certainty, advise a company on what practices will be illegal under the legislation. Surely, this reflects the basic philosophical and practical weakness of the antitrust approach itself.

In conclusion, then, I would offer as the only meaningful definition of monopoly the following one used by Adam Smith: "Monopoly is a government grant of exclusive trading privileges." If this definition be accepted, it follows that what the government must do, and all that it must do, to promote competition is to stop fostering and protecting monopoly, whether it be in business, or in the professions, or in agriculture, or in labor. In the words of the great Belgian historian, Henri Pirenne, in his study of the emergence of competitive capitalism from the blight of the government-protected guild economy: "Capitalism is not in itself opposed to the tendencies of human nature, but its restriction is. Economic liberty is spontaneous."

53. THE PHANTOM CALLED "MONOPOLY"*

Hans F. Sennholz

In their denunciation of capitalism the socialists use some frightful phantoms. The oldest and perhaps the most effective one is the notion that monopolistic concentration of business inheres permanently and inseparably in capitalism. They depict in vivid colors the horrors of monopolistic capitalism and then conclude that a free enterprise economy obviously requires governmental restraint lest it deteriorate to a chaotic system of business monopolies and public oppression.

Recalling the era of "trusts" and "tycoons" around the turn of this century, these socialists valiantly defend the Sherman Antitrust Act of 1890, the Federal Trade Commission Act, and the Clayton Antitrust Act of 1914 which aim at the suppression of business monopoly. And they will be shocked if anyone casts doubt on the wisdom of the antitrust legislation.

Unfortunately, even free enterprisers are divided on this point. Some defend our antitrust legislation and the governmental supervision of big business which it entails, while others summarily reject the prevailing notions on monopoly and the antitrust activity of the government.

An unbiased investigation of the monopoly problem might well begin with the question: Are monopolies inherently bad? Are they identical with destruction of competition, with enormous monopolistic gains, and with gouging of workers and consumers? Under what conditions, if any, are monopolies really the evil organizations which they are assumed to be?

In an unhampered market economy a monopoly affords no cause for alarm. A company that has exclusive control of a commodity or service in a particular market is prevented from exploiting the situation by the following competitive factors: potential competition, competition of substitutes, and the elasticity of demand.

*From *The Freeman*, March 1960

In the United States thousands of different commodities are each produced by a single producer, i.e., by a monopolist, and no one seems to care about it. The 5 and 10 cent stores are full of items produced by monopolists. And yet, all these items are sold at competitive prices. Why? Because of potential competition. As long as there is potential competition, a monopolist cannot charge monopolistic prices.

Potential Competition

Potential competition exists in all fields of production and commerce which anyone is free to enter. In other words, wherever government does not prevent free entry through licenses, franchises, and other controls, potential competition exists. Most corporations are searching continuously for new lines and items of production. They are eager to invade any field in which business earnings are unusually high.

The invasion of another field by a corporation may involve no more than a simple retooling or reorganization that is achieved in a few weeks or months. Or, brand new facilities may be employed for an invasion. Thus one producer, whether he is a monopolist, duopolist, or a competitor among many, always faces the potential competition of all other producers.

Even if a corporation the size of General Motors were a monopolist with regard to certain commodities, it would have to act as if it were a single producer among many. For it continuously faces potential competition from the Fords, Chryslers, General Electrics, and others. These potential competitors undoubtedly have the resources, technical know-how, and marketing organizations to compete with General Motors.

But even if competitors of similar size and structure should be absent, the monopolist must be mindful of the potential competition that can arise overnight. Numerous financiers, promoters, and speculators continuously search for opportunities to establish new enterprises. They have formed new giant companies in the past. And they are willing to risk their capital again if they see an opportunity for profits.

Dreading the promoter who may invade his field, the monopolist therefore must act as if he were surrounded by numerous competitors. He must be alert and always "competitive." He must continuously improve his product and reduce its price. For if he should relax, another company will soon invade his field. The newcomer is likely to be a formidable competitor for he has new machinery and equipment. He has new ideas and applies new methods of production. And he enjoys the good will of all customers. Indeed, a monopolist who relaxes invites disaster.

If an enterprise nevertheless enjoys a monopolistic position, it must by necessity be the most efficient producer in the field. In other words, *in an industry endowed with freedom of entrance, a monopoly is an efficiency monopoly.* For the government to impose restrictions on it or even dissolve it by force would be to destroy the most efficient producer and invite the less efficient to enter the field. In this case, the economy suffers a net loss in output and efficiency.

In my hometown a small manufacturer succeeded in gaining a monopolistic position in the production of creep testers, which are machines that test the behavior of materials at elevated temperatures. When I inquired into the reasons for his astonishing position, he explained with a smile: "I completely routed my two competitors, both billion-dollar corporations, by continuously improving the quality of my product and reducing its price. They finally abandoned the field." Obviously, he would immediately invite his formidable competitors to re-enter the field if he failed to improve his product in the future, or charged monopolistic prices.

That government has not investigated or prosecuted this monopolist probably is due to the smallness of his operations. Experience, however, suggests that such large corporations as General Motors, du Pont, or U.S. Steel would face governmental investigation and prosecution if they were the monopolist. If this is true—and unfortunately there is no reason to doubt it—governmental prosecution aims at big business rather than at monopolies.

But even if American enterprises failed to compete with each other and potential competition failed to exert a restraining influence on monopolists—which is a most unrealistic assumption—the people would escape monopolistic pricing through recourse to substitutes. In many fields the competition of substitutes is more important than that of competing producers.

People's wants may be satisfied by a variety of products and materials. In the manufacture of clothing, for instance, a dozen different materials vie with each other for the consumer's dollar. The monopolist of any one material is powerless because monopolistic pricing would induce consumers to switch immediately to other materials. The producers of suspenders compete not only with each other and with potential competitors, but also with the producers of belts. In the transportation industry the railroads compete with trucks, cars, airplanes, pipelines, and ships. In the building industry lumber competes with aluminum, steel, bricks, and stones. And Bayer's aspirin competes with Anacin and Bufferin.

In some cases, the adoption of substitutes requires large capital outlays which producers are not willing to make immediately. Complete substitution then will take time, although it will ultimately be as effective as immediate substitution. A railroad that wants to substitute oil for coal needs large capital for the purchase of diesel engines. Therefore, it may switch from coal to oil only when it needs to replace worn-out coal locomotives. A house owner may switch from coal to oil or natural gas when his old coal furnace must be replaced. Thus, within a period of several years, substitution will have its restraining effect on a monopolist.

Demand Elasticity

The existence of substitutes makes for demand elasticity which, in turn, makes monopolistic pricing unprofitable; for higher product prices would greatly curtail product demand, and thus sales and income, of the monopolist. Therefore, he again must act as if he were a competitor among many.

The same is true in all cases of demand elasticity, whether or not there are substitutes. For instance, electricity for heating must compete with such substitutes as oil, gas, and coal. However, as a source of light and of energy for power tools, it probably faces no substitutes. An electricity monopolist, nevertheless, would be greatly restrained by potential competition and demand elasticity.

If electricity prices would rise considerably, the most important consumers, such as industrial plants and other business organizations, would soon produce their own electricity. With the proper equipment anyone can produce his own. Of course, the monopolist may counteract this danger by charging different rates to his different classes of customers: low rates to all industrial users who are apt to produce their own electricity, and higher rates to all others. Assuming that residential users do not readily resort to independent power production, are they not liable to fall in the grip of a monopolist? No! Demand elasticity would prevent this. Many people undoubtedly could reduce their consumption of electricity without suffering mentionable discomfort. A house owner who may enjoy the light of a hundred bulbs on a winter evening might easily curtail his consumption if electricity charges should increase greatly. But this curtailment of demand would reduce the sales and income of the monopolist.

All producers in fact compete with all other producers for the consumer's dollars. The manufacturer of television sets competes with the manufacturer of freezers and refrigerators. If the monopolist of one commodity—say, television sets—should raise his price, the consumer may forego the purchase of a new set and buy instead a new refrigerator. We consumers do not allocate our income to the satisfaction of categories of wants but to that of specific wants yielding the greatest net addition to our well-being. This addition, in turn, is determined by the urgency of our wants and by the cost of acquisition. Rising costs obviously affect us adversely, which may induce us to purchase an entirely different product that now contributes most to our well-being.

Consumer resistance to monopolistic pricing finds expression in yet another form. People who suspect monopolistic practice by a producer tend to favor any newcomer who would compete with him. Any enterprise striving to invade the field is assured the patronage and good will of all dissatisfied consumers. In our example of the electricity monopolist, the industrial user producing electricity for his own consumption may decide to supply power also to his workers and neighbors who, at lower rates, would gladly transfer their patronage. Thus, in a free economy, even the electricity monopolist is greatly limited in his pricing policies.

The same limitations apply in all other industries, including the public utilities. A mail monopoly would face not only the people's demand elasticity for mailing services but also the potential competition by the numerous intercompany mailing systems. At the present time hundreds of companies have intercompany mail delivery systems that could expand their services to include their workers, customers, and other people in their communities if the law allowed. The case is the same with other "public utilities" supplying goods and services such as water, telephone, and telegraph.

On Optimum Growth

In a system of unhampered economic freedom, a monopolistic market position could be attained only through efficiency. Without government intervention, an efficient enterprise tends to grow until it reaches its optimum size at which the unit costs of production are lowest. This optimum depends on the nature of the industry, the state of the product and capital markets, the rate of taxation, and the caliber of management. Obviously, a steel company requires a much larger capital outlay and work force than does a dentist's office or a barber shop. Also, the enterprise managed by a brilliant businessman has a higher point of optimum than one managed by his mediocre successors. A monopolistic position can be attained only if the optimum size suffices to supply completely a given market.

The territorial expanse of the market which a monopoly is capable of supplying depends on two factors: the difference between the unit costs of production of the monopolist and those of his potential competitors, which determines the margin of superiority of the monopolist, and the unit costs of transportation, which are determined by the nature of the product and by the distances involved. A bulky commodity such as cement, for instance, is burdened with high costs of transportation. Consequently, the market of the cement monopolist will be relatively small, for an increase in distance from plant to consumer rapidly increases his unit costs. On the other hand, commodities with relatively low transportation costs such as watches or diamonds can be distributed over vast market areas.

This analysis of the territorial range of markets also reveals that bulky item monopolies are in a relatively favorable position to conduct monopolistic policies. While an American producer of watches must cope with foreign competitors all over the globe, a cement producer may be little concerned about the competition of another producer some 100 miles away. He may indeed be tempted to restrict output and raise prices in order to maximize his income. But, of course, such action would invite other producers to invade the territory of the monopolist. Another corporation soon would build a modern plant in that territory. With a new plant and the good will of all consumers, it undoubtedly would rout the monopolist.

It is apparent that a change in transportation costs, production technology, management, or any other cost factor can upset a monopolistic position. Also, a concentration beyond the optimum point is an invitation to failure, for the unit costs of production tend to increase again. The monopolist who disregards this fact invites potential competitors to invade his field and reduce him to his optimum size. There is no need for government to break up a giant enterprise; if it were too large, the competitors would reduce it.

This is not to deny that even in a capitalist economy a monopoly may temporarily reduce output and charge monopolistic prices. Having reached a monopolistic position through efficiency, a businessman may attempt henceforth to follow monopolistic policies. But the foregoing analysis clearly indicates that his attempts are bound to be short-lived. Soon, he will face a crucial struggle with powerful invaders producing with new equipment and enjoying the good will of the public. Of course, it is most unnatural and unlikely for a businessman to rise to eminence through product improvements and lower prices, and then suddenly to turn toward output curtailment and price increases. But if he should act in such a manner, which is conceivable, he practices self-destruction.

It cannot be denied that in our interventionist world many monopolies actually have the power to restrict output and charge monopolistic prices. But the reason for this unfortunate state of affairs is to be found in the multiplicity of government restrictions of competition. If the government prevents competitors from entering the field, the people lose their protection by potential competition. The public utility that enjoys an exclusive franchise is a local monopoly. In this case, the people's only line of resistance is their demand elasticity and perhaps, also, their recourse to independent production. Meanwhile, the planners resort to political controls.

Through franchises, licenses, patents, tariffs, and other restrictions, modern government has in fact created thousands of monopolies. Having thus crippled and hampered competition, it then proceeds to control the monopolies. Political bodies now decide vital economic questions in many important industries. They regulate our railroads, airlines, and other means of transportation. They grant exclusive franchises in radio, television, telephone, and telegraph. They monopolize the production and marketing of electricity, water, and gas. They issue patents that assure their recipients monopolistic positions. And, finally, they own and operate the whole postal industry and prevent competition through fines and imprisonments. In all these cases, the government effectively restricts competition and thus creates local or national monopolies.

Labor legislation has granted monopolistic powers to labor unions, which control whole industries employing hundreds of thousands of workers. They close down vital industries and cripple the entire economy. Through the union shop arrangement, or directly through brute force, they dictate employment conditions in thousands of enterprises. All this is done in perfectly legal sanctity without interference by the government. On the contrary, the legal framework for this union power is provided by the very government that professes to oppose monopolistic practices and positions in the economy.

This frightful union power, in turn, forces enterprises to unite. A small businessman cannot possibly meet the challenge of a powerful industry union. He therefore is tempted to sell out to a giant corporation with greater power of resistance. Of course, even the giant corporation will be closed by unions. But it cannot be destroyed as easily as can a smaller company.

Effects of Tax Policy

The confiscatory taxation imposed by the interventionist state causes the same industrial concentration. The middle-aged founder and owner of a million-dollar enterprise is forced to sell out to a large corporation for fear of confiscatory estate taxation. In case of his sudden demise his widow and heirs, who may not be qualified to carry on his business, will face confiscatory inheritance taxes. They would have to liquidate the business in a very short time to meet the tax liabilities. As the sale of a specialized business requires great skill and good timing, the sale by the widow probably would entail large losses. Therefore, a responsible businessman will arrange the liquidation of his own enterprise in good time. He himself will sell out to his corporate competitors and invest the proceeds in marketable securities. Government bonds, for instance, can be readily sold for estate tax purposes. Thus, hundreds of small companies disappear every year.

Especially the most efficient small enterprises tend to be liquidated on account of tax considerations. A going concern that generates profits is taxed at a rate of 52 per cent after which the corporate owner may be taxed at rates up to 91 per cent. If the owner should decide to liquidate his enterprise during the year, his profits are subject to a capital gains tax amounting to 25 per cent. It is obvious that a businessman is tempted to generate a maximum amount of profits in a given year and then quickly sell or liquidate his enterprise. Thus, hundreds of efficient "collapsible" companies disappear every year.

Governments Create Cartels

Since the rise of political intervention in economic affairs, governments have frequently organized or fostered the organization of cartels. These are combinations of enterprises for the purpose of controlling the output or marketing of a commodity or trade through regulation of production, allocation of markets, price fixing, or other means. This regulation always aims at assuring the cartel members a "fair" income, which means a higher income than they otherwise would have.

The German government led the way toward cartelization of key industries. From about 1880 to 1930 it organized more than 2,100 cartels. It was prompted to this disastrous policy by yet another intervention: its labor legislation. Since the 1880's, the German government had imposed tremendous "social" costs on its industry through social security legislation and other measures that increased labor costs and reduced labor efficiency. Without further government intervention, this social legislation would have put German producers at a competitive disadvantage against foreign producers. Under the new burden of social costs, they would have lost not only many foreign markets but probably some domestic markets as well. Then there would have been depression and unemployment until German wages declined sufficiently to offset the social security costs.

Instead of facing depression and unemployment, the German government decided to form cartels. It imposed high tariffs on foreign goods, which protected the German industries laboring under the heavy burden of labor legislation. Businessmen were thus enabled to raise prices, which meant that workers were obliged to pay for their social benefits through higher product prices instead of lower wages. In order to prevent unemployment in the export industries, the government encouraged them to sell their products at world market prices. Such sales involved losses, due to the burden of social costs, so the cartels adopted profit-sharing schemes by which the producers supplying the domestic market at higher prices were forced to subsidize exporters. Thus, the cartels commenced dumping, which tended to destroy the world market and the world division of labor.

In the United States the formation of trusts proceeded along similar lines. However, the motivating force was different. There was no social legislation depressing the American economy. Yet, the McKinley administration, by imposing high import restrictions, quite unintentionally achieved the same sort of trustification as was done intentionally by the Bismarck administration in Germany.

The Dingley Tariff of 1897, which became known as "the mother of trusts," granted tariff protection to basic industries. With industrial imports from Europe greatly reduced, the American producers enjoyed monopolistic positions. Consolidations took place on a large scale. During the "Golden Age of Trusts" between 1897 and 1904, 425 trusts were organized with a total capital of more than $20 billion.

This trustification of American industry was promoted by yet another factor for which the government was solely responsible. This was the rapid credit expansion that culminated in the panic of 1907 and the ensuing depression. "Easy money" permitted the organization of new corporations. It made the promotion of combinations most profitable, as new securities could be sold at premium prices. Consequently, Wall Street financiers eagerly promoted mergers and reorganizations on a vast scale. When, in 1903, investors began to question the overcapitalization of the industrial combines, a trust-share panic developed which signaled the temporary end of trustification.

Two decades later, when the Federal Reserve System was flooding the capital market with huge quantities of new credit, gigantic trusts again made their appearance. Easy financing permitted the organization of powerful holding companies that controlled production through several layers of subsidiaries. They reigned supreme in all industries that were sheltered from healthy competition through government franchises, charters, tariffs, and other restrictions. In the field of public utilities, nine holding company systems—among which the Insull group was outstanding—controlled about three-quarters of the power resources in the United States. Holding companies dominated one-fifth of the railroad mileage. As was to be expected, this period of industrial combination came to an end with the stock market crash in 1929.

A few years later, the Roosevelt administration resorted to extensive industry combinations in order to control the American economy. Under the National Industrial Recovery Act, the industries were organized along the lines of a cartel with codes that regulated most phases of production. The objective was shorter work hours, reduced production, higher prices. Under the Agricultural Adjustment Act, American agriculture was organized to reduce production by plowing under crops and thus raise agricultural prices artificially. It is a record of history that all these measures failed dismally. Instead of reviving the economy, they kept it in the grip of deep and lengthy depression. But it was the American government that enacted and enforced these policies which the enemies of capitalism ascribe to private corporations.

Antitrust Legislation

The failure to distinguish between the monopolistic tendencies of government and the propensity of private corporations to grow to optimum size probably underlies the American antitrust movement. Our Founding Fathers were fully aware of this difference. They were so hostile to monopoly power granted by government that Thomas Jefferson wanted to include an antimonopoly provision in the articles of the Constitution. But their hostility was aimed at monopolistic policies as they were conducted by the colonial powers of Europe before the age of capitalism. They condemned "mercantilism" which was an economic system similar to modern socialism. As Adam Smith had pointed out, monopoly was "the chief engine of mercantilism."

It was entirely natural that the nineteenth century disciples of capitalism should continue to oppose monopolistic endeavors. The common law as it developed in the United States reflected their attitude. But during the 1880's, the prevailing ideology began to change. Under the influence of new schools of thought that were hostile to various aspects of capitalism, the American public began to view with alarm the growth of industrial enterprise. Advancing technology, especially in the manufacturing and transportation fields, and the rapid accumulation of capital, made private enterprises grow by leaps and bounds. But such growth in most cases merely moved toward optimum size. Of course, in some cases a very successful entrepreneur may have overexpanded his organization, which sooner or later resulted in losses and failure. In other cases, government franchises, patents, tariffs, and other trade restrictions actually promoted the growth of monopolies. But public opinion, which was molded by numerous "antimonopoly parties," by the Populist and Grange movements, laid the blame solely on private enterprise. Thus, while the Founding Fathers had clearly recognized the role of government in every monopoly, their descendants from the 1880's on saw only the "monopolizing businessman."

Kansas was the first state to enact an antitrust law in 1889. It was quickly followed by other states. In 1890, in performance of campaign commitments and in response to widespread public demand, the federal government passed the Sherman Antitrust Act. The act set forth as a national policy the proposition that restraint of trade and monopolistic market positions of private corporations are contrary to the public interest. Later legislation included the Clayton Antitrust Act and the Federal Trade Commission Act, the Robinson-Patman Act, certain provisions of the Wilson Tariff Act, the Webb-Pomerene Act, and the miscellaneous provisions of other acts.

Responsibility for the enforcement of the antitrust laws was placed with the Antitrust Division of the Department of Justice. From a modest beginning, this division has grown today into a large bureaucracy with swarms of lawyers and investigators. During President Harrison's administration only seven cases were instituted against large corporations. President T. R. Roosevelt initiated 44 cases. Taft began 80, and Wilson 90. Coolidge's administration instituted 83 prosecutions, Roosevelt's 332, and Truman's 169. It is significant that the Roosevelt administration filed its 332 formal charges although its National Industrial Recovery Administration had suspended the Sherman Act and was occupied with organizing the American economy along the lines of a cartel. Under President Eisenhower's administration, the number of prosecutions per year promises to be even higher than under any preceding administration.

These figures suggest that the antitrust prosecution of American corporations shows a marked tendency toward acceleration. Two reasons may account for this ominous development. First, the growing antitrust bureaucracy feels compelled to bring proof for the justification of its existence and growth. An antitrust lawyer knows of no better evidence of his worth than the number of his prosecutions. Consequently, he will file more and more charges against businessmen. Then, these charges, being made in the limelight of nationwide publicity, poison the political atmosphere and create further business hostility that demands more charges. In fact, the antitrust charges of the U.S. Justice Department have created a badly distorted picture of our enterprise economy, which has contributed to the rise of a political ideology that is opposed to capitalism. Today, the Antitrust Division is an efficient arm of government omnipotence. It has prosecuted virtually every large corporation in the country and continues to embarrass and harass thousands of businessmen, especially the most eminent.

The New Ideology

Of course, the government lawyers and eager politicians offer a different explanation for the acceleration of their antitrust activity. According to them, the mature capitalist economy, such as the American, tends to deteriorate into a monopolistic economy that deprives small enterprises of fair and equal chances; increased monopolization requires increasing antitrust prosecution; the restraint of trade by big business is the cause, and the government actions are its effect, not vice versa.

No matter how plausible, this is a vicious line of thought taken from the armory of Marxism. According to Karl Marx, the proclaimed father of modern socialism and communism, the exploitation of the workers by the capitalists leads to industrial concentration and monopolization. A declining number of industrialists grow richer and richer while the masses of the people form an ever-growing army of paupers and unemployed. Finally, this process of concentration will come to a head when the people expropriate the expropriators. Thus, socialism is born.

Our statist politicians and antitrust bureaucrats embrace the first half of this Marxian explanation. They subscribe to the theory that our capitalist system breeds monopolies. But then they part with Marx by proclaiming their desire to save this monopoly-breeding system from its own destruction. They propose to destroy the monopolies through government action.

We need not here refute this argumentation. Our foregoing discussion of potential competition, competition of substitutes, and the optimum size of capitalist enterprises contains a cogent refutation. But we wonder about the sincerity of the government intention to preserve our capitalist system. How can it seriously oppose monopolies if the government itself continuously is creating them?

A modern offshoot of the Marxian concentration theory is the "monopolistic competition theory" which is propagated at hundreds of our colleges and universities. It was first stated by Edward H. Chamberlin of Harvard University and Mrs. Joan Robinson of Cambridge University. Both believe that the old idea of alternative—either monopoly or competition—is fallacious, and that both situations are combined in our economic system. The monopoly of each producer in his own brand is the starting point that gives producers the power to "administer prices," gouge consumers, and exploit workers. Pure or perfect competition, they believe, can only exist if the number of competing producers is large and if they deal in perfectly standardized products.

The foregoing discussion of potential competition clearly denies the requirement of numerous competitors. Competition is at work, even if there be only one producer. For, in an industry without government franchises or other entrance restrictions, the monopolist must act as if he were surrounded by hundreds of competitors. If he were to attempt to restrict output in order to raise prices, he would invite immediate invasion by other producers.

The requirement of a perfectly standardized product is based on the assumption that consumers can be pulled into a monopolistic grip by trade names, minor product variations, by advertisement, and other producer devices. Once you drive a Ford car, you will always be sold on Ford products. This consumer habit will give Ford a monopolistic position which entails the power to charge monopolistic prices.

We reject this assumption of a dull and gullible public. We believe that people continuously shop around, comparing the quality of products with different trade names and labels. Many consumers switch brands and suppliers, always seeking the better product for their money. Consequently, the

Ford manufacturers compete not only with General Motors cars, Chrysler cars, American Motors cars, all foreign cars, but also with the manufacturers of houses, freezers, washers, dryers, and so on. For the high price of one product may induce us to buy an entirely different product.

The monopolistic competition theory offers as frail a foundation for government antitrust activity as the Marxian concentration theory itself. Both fail to describe and explain capitalism. But they are succeeding in destroying American big business which is the mainstay of our high standard of living. In fact, they are destroying competition and individual enterprise.

54. ADVERTISING*

Israel M. Kirzner

Advertising has been badly treated by many scholars who should know better. Not only Marxists and liberals, but even conservatives have given advertising a bad press. Let us examine some of the criticisms.

- First, many advertising messages are said to be offensive—by esthetic or ethical and moral standards. Unfettered, unhampered, laissez-faire capitalism, it is contended, would propagate such messages in a way that could very well demoralize and offend the tastes and morals of members of society.
- Second, advertising, it is argued, is deceitful, fraudulent, full of lies. Misinformation is spread by advertising, in print, on the airwaves, and this does harm to the members of society; for that reason advertising should be controlled, limited, taxed away.
- Third, it is argued that where advertising is not deceitful, it is at best persuasive. That is, it attempts to change people's tastes. It attempts not to fulfill the desires of man but to change his desires to fit that which has been produced. The claim of the market economist has always been that the free market generates the flow of production along the lines that satisfy consumer tastes; their tastes determine what shall be produced—briefly, consumer sovereignty. On the contrary, the critics of advertising argue, capitalism has developed into a system where producers produce and then mold men's minds to buy that which has been produced. Rather than production being governed by consumer sovereignty, quite the reverse: the consumer is governed by producer sovereignty.
- A fourth criticism has been that advertising propagates monopoly and is antithetical to competition. In a competitive economy, it is pointed out, there would be no advertising; each seller would sell as much as he would like to sell without having to convince consumers to buy that which they would not otherwise have bought. So, advertising is made possible by imperfections in the market. More seriously, it is contended, advertising leads toward monopoly by building up a wall of good will, a protective wall of loyalty among consumers which renders a particular product immune to outside competition. Competing products, which do not share in the fruits of the advertising campaign, find themselves on the outside. This barrier to entry may gradually lead a particular producer to control a share of the market which is rendered invulnerable to the winds of outside competition.
- Finally—and this in a way sums up all of these criticisms—advertising is condemned as wasteful. The consumer pays a price for a product which covers a very large sum of money spent on advertising. Advertising does not change the commodity that has been purchased; it could have been produced and sold at a much lower price without the advertising. In other words, resources are being used and paid for by the consumer without his receiving anything that he could not have received in their absence.

These are serious criticisms. We have learned to expect them to be emphasized by contemporary liberal economists. To Marxist thinkers, again, advertising is essential for capitalism; it is seen as a socially useless device necessary in order to get excess production sold. They see no positive elements in advertising at all. But even conservative thinkers and economists have pointed out some apparent limitations, weaknesses, criticisms of advertising.

*From *The Freeman*, September 1972

The Free Economy and How It Functions

It is not my purpose here to defend each and every advertising message. I would rather discuss a free economy, a laissez-faire economy, pure capitalism. I would like to show that in such a world, advertising would emerge with a positive role to play; that it would add to the efficiency with which consumer wants are satisfied; and that, while the real world is far from perfect, a large volume of the criticism would fade away were it understood what role advertising, in fact, has to play in a pure market economy.

Let me imagine a world, a free market, in which there are no deceitful men at all. All the messages beamed to consumers and prospective consumers would be, as far as the advertisers themselves believe, the strict truth. We will consider later the implications of the fact that men are imperfect and that men succumb to the temptation in selling something to say a little bit less, a little bit more, than the exact truth. In the meantime, let us talk about a world of honest men, men who do not try to deceive.

Further, let us imagine a pure market economy with government intervention kept to the absolute minimum—the night watchman role. The government stands to the sidelines and ensures the protection of private property rights, the enforcement of contracts freely entered into. Everyone then proceeds to play the game of the free market economy with producers producing that which they believe can be sold to the consumers at the highest possible money price. Entrepreneur producers, who detect where resources are currently being used in less than optimum fashion, take these resources and transfer them to other uses in the economy where they will serve consumer wants which the entrepreneurs believe are more urgently desired, as measured by the amounts of money consumers are willing to pay for various products.

We will assume that there is freedom of entry into all industries. No entrepreneur has sole control over any resource that is uniquely necessary for the production of a given product. No government licenses are required in order to enter into the practice of a given profession or to introduce a particular product. All entrepreneurs are free to produce what they believe to be profitable. All resource owners are free to sell their resources, whether labor, natural resources, capital goods. They are free to sell or rent these resources to the highest bidder. In this way the agitation of the market gradually shuffles resources around until they begin to be used to produce those products which consumers value most highly. Consumers arrange their spending to buy the commodities they believe to be most urgently needed by themselves. And the market flows on in the way that we understand it.

Open Competition

We say this is a free market, a laissez-faire, competitive system. But we do not mean a *perfectly* competitive market, as this notion has been developed by the neo-classical economists. In a perfectly competitive market, each seller faces a demand curve which is perfectly horizontal. That is to say, each seller believes that he can sell as much as he would like to sell without having to lower the price. Each buyer faces a perfectly horizontal supply curve and each buyer believes that he can buy as much as he would like to buy of anything without having to offer a higher price. In such a world of "perfect competition," we have what we call an "equilibrium" situation, that is a situation where all things have already been fully adjusted to one another. All activities, all decisions have been fully coordinated by the market so that there are no disappointments. No participant in the economy discovers that he could have done something better. No participant in the economy discovers that he has made plans to do something which it turns out he cannot do.

In this model of the perfectly competitive economy, there would in fact be *no* competition in the sense in which the layman, or the businessman, understands the term. The term "competition" to the businessman, the layman, means an activity designed to outstrip one's competitors, a rivalrous activity designed to get ahead of one's colleagues, or those with whom one is competing. In a world of equilibrium, a world of "perfect competition," there would be no room for further rivalry. There would be no reason to attempt to do something better than is currently being done. There would, in fact, be no competition in the everyday sense of the term.

When we describe the laissez-faire economy as competitive, we mean something quite different. We mean an economy in which there is complete freedom of entry; if anyone believes that he can produce something that can serve consumers' wants more faithfully, he can try to do it. If anyone believes that the current producers are producing at a price which is too high, then he is free to try to produce and sell at a lower price. This is what competition means. It does not mean that the market has already attained the "equilibrium" situation, which goes under the very embarrassing technical name of "perfectly competitive economy."

Now, economists and others understand generally that competition means price competition: offering to sell at a lower price than your competitors are asking, or offering to buy at a higher price than your competitors are bidding. Entrepreneurs will offer higher prices than others are offering for scarce labor. They will offer to sell a product at lower prices than the competing store is asking. This is what price competition means. This is the most obvious form in which competition manifests itself.

However, we must remember that there is another kind of competition, sometimes called "non-price competition," sometimes called "quality competition." Competition takes the form not only of producing the identical product which your competitors are producing and selling it at a lower price, not only in buying the identical resource which your competitors are buying and offering a higher price. Competition means sometimes offering a better product, or perhaps an inferior product, a product which is more in line with what the entrepreneur believes consumers are in fact desirous of purchasing. It means producing a different model of a product, a different quality, putting it in a different package, selling it in a store with a different kind of lighting, selling it along with an offer of free parking, selling through salesmen who smile more genuinely, more sincerely. It means competing in many, many ways besides the pure price which is asked of the consumer in monetary terms.

With freedom of entry, every entrepreneur is free to choose the exact package, the exact opportunity which he will lay before the public. Each opportunity, each package has many dimensions. He can choose the specifications for his package by changing many, many of these variables. The precise opportunity that he will lay before the public will be that which, in his opinion, is more urgently desired by the consumer as compared with that which happens to be produced by others. So long as there's freedom of entry, the fact that my product is different from his does not mean that I am a monopolist.

The late Professor Edward H. Chamberlin of Harvard did economics a great disservice in arguing that because a producer is producing a unique product, slightly different from what the fellow across the street is producing, in some sense he is a monopolist. So long as there's freedom of entry, so long as the man across the road *can* do exactly what I'm doing, the fact that he is *not* doing exactly what I'm doing is simply the result of his different entrepreneurial judgment. He believes that he can do better with *his* model. I believe I can do better with *mine*. I believe that free parking is more important to consumers than fancy lighting in the store. He gives a different package than I do. Not because he couldn't do what I'm doing, not because I couldn't do what he's doing, but because each believes that he knows better what the consumer is most anxious to acquire. This is what we mean by competition in the broadest sense, not merely price competition, but quality competition in its manifold possible manifestations.

Professor Chamberlin popularized a distinction which was not original with him but which owes its present widely circulated popularity primarily to his work. That is a distinction between "production costs" and "selling costs." In his book of almost forty years ago, *The Theory of Monopolistic Competition*, Chamberlin argued that there are two kinds of costs which manufacturers, producers, sellers, suppliers incur. First, they incur the fabrication costs, the costs of producing what it is they want to sell. Second, they incur additional expenditures that do not produce the product or change it or improve it, but merely get it sold. Advertising, of course, is the most obvious example which Chamberlin cited. But "selling costs" of all kinds were considered by him to be sharply different from "production costs." In his original formulation, Chamberlin argued that "production costs" are costs incurred to produce the product for a given Demand Curve while "selling costs" simply shift the Demand Curve over to the right. That is to say, the same product is now purchased in greater quantities at a given price but the product is the same.

A False Distinction

The fallacy in the distinction between production costs and selling costs is fairly easy to notice. In fact, it is impossible for the outside observer—except as he resorts to arbitrary judgments of value—to distinguish between expenditures which do, and expenditures which do not, alter the product. We know as economists that a product is not an objective quantity of steel or paper. A product is that which is perceived, understood, desired by a consumer. If there are two products otherwise similar to the outside eye which happen to be considered to be different products by the consumer, then to the economist these *are* different products.

Ludwig von Mises gives the example, which cannot be improved upon, of eating in a restaurant. A man has a choice of two restaurants, serving identical meals, identical food. But in one restaurant they haven't swept the floor for six weeks. The meals are the same. The food is the same. How shall we describe the money spent by the other restaurant in sweeping the floor? "Production costs" or "selling costs?" Does sweeping change the food? No. Surely, then, it could be argued that this is strictly a "selling cost." It is like advertising. The food remains the same; but, because you have a man sweeping out the floor, more people come to this restaurant than to that. But this is nonsense. What you buy when you enter a restaurant is not the food alone. What you buy is a meal, served in certain surroundings. If the surroundings are more desirable, it's a different meal, it's a different package. That which has been spent to change the package is as much production cost as the salary paid to the cook; no difference.

Another example that I recall was the case of the coal being run out of Newcastle and traveling along the railroad toward London. Every mile that coal travels nearer the London drawing room, the Demand Curve shifts over to the right. How shall we describe that transportation cost? "Production cost" or "selling cost?" Of course, it's "production cost." In fact, it's "selling cost" too. All "production costs" are "selling costs." All costs of production are incurred in order to produce something which will be more desirable than the raw materials.

You take raw meat and turn it into cooked steak. The act of changing the raw meat into cooked steak is to make the consumer desire it more eagerly. Does this simply shift the Demand Curve over to the right? Of course, it does that. It does it by changing the product.

Another example supposes there are two identical pieces of steel, except that one piece has been blessed, while the other piece is subject to a spiritual taint, which to the scientist is not there but which is very vivid and vital to the consumer. How shall we describe the expenditure on the commodities? Shall we describe the difference between them as nonexistent? Or should we not recognize that, if something is spiritually tainted to the consumer—in his view, not necessarily in mine or yours or the economist's or other than in the mind of the consumer—then he will not buy the tainted item, even though to the objective laboratory scientist there's no difference between the items? The economist has recognized these as two different commodities. There'll be two Demand Curves. The fact that the scientist doesn't see any difference—they look the same, they smell the same, if you touch them they feel the same—is irrelevant. We know, as economists, that what we find in a commodity is not the objective matter that is inside it, but how it is received by the consumer.

Clearly then, the distinction between a so-called "selling cost" and "production cost" is quite arbitrary. It depends entirely on the value judgments of the outside observer. The outside observer can say that this particular selling effort does not change the product, but in that situation he is arrogating to himself the prerogative of pronouncing what is and what is not a product. That is something which violates our fundamental notions of individual consumer freedom: that a consumer's needs are defined by no one else other than himself. This may seem quite a detour from advertising and yet it is all relevant to the question of what role advertising has to play.

The Provision of Information

Let us consider how some of these notions apply to the matter of information. One of the standard defenses for advertising is that it provides a service which consumers value: the provision of knowledge, the provision of information. People buy books. People go to college. People enroll in all kinds of courses. Advertising is simply another way of providing information. To be sure, it would seem that the information provided by suppliers comes from a tainted source, but don't forget that we are imagining for the meantime a world without deceitful people.

We can even relax that assumption for a moment. It may be cheaper for the consumer to get his information from the supplier or the producer than from an outside source. In other words, if you, a consumer, have the choice of acquiring information about a particular product—either more cheaply from the producer or more expensively from an outside, "objective" source—you may decide that, on balance, you're likely to get a better deal, penny-for-penny, information-wise, by reading the information of the producer, scanning it perhaps with some skepticism, but nonetheless relying on that rather than buying it from an outside source. Technically, this involves what is known as the problem of transactions costs. It may be more economical for the information to be packaged together with the product, or at least to be produced jointly with the product, than to have the information produced and communicated by an outside source. This is a possibility not to be ignored.

Advertising provides information, and this goes a long way to explain the role which advertising and other kinds of selling efforts must play. Does this not seem to contradict the point just made, that there is no distinction between "production costs" and "selling costs"? Surely information about a product is distinct from the product. Surely the costs incurred to provide information are a different kind of costs than the costs incurred to produce the product. The answer is clearly, no. Information is produced; it is desired; it is a product; it is purchased jointly with the product itself; it is a part of the package; and it is something which consumers value. Its provision is not something performed on the outside that makes people consume something which they would not have consumed before. It is something for which people are willing to pay; it is a service.

You can distinguish different parts of a service You can distinguish between four wheels and a car. But the four wheels are complementary commodities. That is to say, the usefulness of the one is virtually nil without the availability of the other. The car and gasoline are two separate products, to be sure, and yet they are purchased jointly, perhaps from different producers, different suppliers, but they are nonetheless parts of a total package, a total product. If it happens that the information is produced and sold jointly with the product itself, then we have no reason to question the characteristics of the costs of providing information as true "production costs," not producing necessarily the physical commodity about which information is produced, but producing information which is independently desired by consumers, independently but jointly demanded, complementarily used together with the "product" itself. In other words, the service of providing information is the service of providing something which is needed just as importantly as the "product" itself.

There is another aspect of advertising which is often overlooked. Information is exceedingly important. But, surely, it is argued, information can be provided without the characteristics of advertising that we know, without the color, without the emotion, without the offensive aspects of advertising. Surely information can be provided in simple straightforward terms. The address of this and this store is this and this place. These and these qualities of commodities are available at these and these prices. Why do illustrated advertising messages have to be projected? Why do all kinds of obviously uninformative matter have to be introduced into advertising messages? This is what renders the information aspects of advertising so suspect. The Marxists simply laugh it away. They say it is ridiculous to contend that advertising provides any kind of genuine information. If one rests the defense of advertising on its informative role, then one has a lot of explaining to do. One has to explain why information that could be provided in clear cut, straightforward terms is provided in such garish and loud forms, in the way that we know it.

The answer, I think, is that advertising does much more than provide information which the consumer wishes to have. This is something which is often overlooked, even by economists. Supposing I set up a gas station. I buy gasoline and I have it poured into my cellar, my tanks. I have a pump carefully hidden behind some bushes, and cars that come down the road can buy gas if they know that I'm here. But I don't go to the effort to let them know I'm here. I don't put out a sign. Well, gas without information is like a car without gas. Information is a service required complementarily with the gas.

Supposing, then, I take a piece of paper, type very neatly in capital letters, "GAS," and stick it on my door. Cars speed down the road in need of gas, but they don't stop to read my sign. What is missing here? Information is missing. Don't people want information? Yes. They would like to know where the gas station is, but it's a well kept secret. Now, people *are* looking for that information. It's my task as an entrepreneur not only to have gas available but to have it in a form which is known to consumers. It is my task to supply gas-which-is-known-about, not to provide gas *and* information.

I have not only to produce opportunities which are available to consumers; I have to make consumers aware of these opportunities. This is a point which is often overlooked. An opportunity which is not known, an opportunity to which a consumer is not fully awakened, is simply not an opportunity. I am not fulfilling my entrepreneurial task unless

I project to the consumer the awareness of the opportunity. How do I do that? I do that, not with a little sign on my door, but with a big neon sign, saying GAS; and better than that I chalk up the price; and better than that I make sure that the price is lower than the price at nearby stations; and I do all the other things that are necessary to *make* the consumer *fully* aware of the opportunity that I am in fact prepared to put before him. In other words, the final package consists not only of abstract academic information but in having the final product placed in front of the consumer in such a form that he cannot miss it.

Free $10 Bills!

The strange thing about the world in which we live is that it is a world in which $10 bills are floating around, free $10 bills! The problem is that very few of us notice these $10 bills. It is the role of the entrepreneur to notice the existence of $10 bills. An entrepreneur buys resources for $10 and he sells the product for $20. He is aware that resources available for $10 are currently being used in less than optimum fashion, that commodities for which consumers are willing to pay $20 are not being produced, and he puts these things together. He sees the $10 bill and makes the combination which other people do not see. Anybody might do it—freedom of entry. The entrepreneur notices the $10 bill, gets it for himself by placing in front of the consumer something which he had not noticed. If the consumer knew where he could buy resources for $10 and get the product that is worth $20, he wouldn't buy from the entrepreneur. He would do it himself. Since he doesn't know, I, as entrepreneur, have to create this opportunity and make the consumer aware.

It is not enough to buy gas and put it in the ground. The entrepreneur puts it in the ground in a form that the consumer recognizes. To do this requires much more than fabrication. It requires communication. It requires more than simple information. It requires more than writing a book, publishing it, and having it on a library shelf. It requires more than putting something in a newspaper in a classified ad and expecting the consumer to see it. You have to put it in front of the consumer in a form that he *will* see. Otherwise, you're not performing your entrepreneurial task.

Advertising has grown. Compare the volume of advertising today with the volume of 100 years ago and it has grown tremendously. More! Consider the price of a commodity that you buy in a drug store or in a supermarket. Find out what portion of that price can be attributed to advertising costs and it turns out that a much larger percentage of the final cost to the consumer can be attributed to advertising today than could have been attributed 50 years ago, 70 years ago, 100 years ago. Why is this? Why has advertising expenditure grown in proportion to total value of output? Why has advertising expenditure grown in proportion to the price of a finished commodity? Why has advertising apparently grown more offensive, more loud, more shrill? It's fairly easy to understand.

I give, as example, the lobby walls of a college building that I know very well. At one time this was a handsome lobby with walls of thick marble; you could walk from one end of the building to the other and the walls would be clear. Some years ago an enterprising entrepreneur decided to use some free advertising space. He pasted up a sign. It was the only sign on the wall; everybody looked at it, saw the message. I don't remember what the message was or whether it was torn down, but I do remember that soon afterward those walls were full of signs. As you walked down the passage, you could read all kinds of messages, all kinds of student activities, non-student activities, student non-activities. It was fairly easy to learn about what was going on simply by reading the signs.

At first, the signs did not have to be big. But as advertisers saw the opportunity, the free space gradually filled up. The Ricardian rent theory came into play; all the free land was in use. And as the free land or space was taken, of course, it became more and more important to get up early to paste up your sign. That was the "rent," the high price, getting up early. But more than that, it became necessary now to arouse all kinds of interest in me in order to get me to read these signs. In other words, the variety and multiplicity of messages make it harder and harder to get a hearing.

The Price of Affluence

We live in a world which is often described as an "affluent society." An affluent society is one in which there are many, many opportunities placed before consumers. The consumer enters a supermarket and if he is to make a sensible, intelligent decision he is going to have to spend several hours calculating very carefully, reading, rereading everything that's on the packages and doing a complete research job before feeding all the information into the computer and waiting for the optimum package to be read off. It's a tough job to be a consumer. And the multiplicity of opportunities makes it necessary for advertisers, for producers, to project more and more provocative messages if they want to be heard. This is a cost of affluence. It is a cost, certainly; something that we'd much rather do without, if we could; but we can't.

The number of commodities that have been produced is so great that in order for any one particular product to be brought to the attention of the consumer a large volume of advertising is necessary. And we can expect to get more and more. Is it part of production costs? Very definitely, yes. It is completely arbitrary for anyone to argue that, whether or not the consumer knows it, the commodity is there anyway, so that when he pays the price which includes the advertising communication he is paying *more* than is necessary for the opportunity made available. For an opportunity to be made available, it must be in a form which it is impossible to miss. And this is what advertising is all about.

One more word about the offensiveness of advertising. Ultimately in a free market, consumers tend to get what they want. The kinds of products produced will reflect the desires of the consumer. A society which wants moral objects will get moral objects. A society which wants immoral objects will tend to get immoral objects. Advertised communication is part of the total package produced and made available to consumers. The kind of advertising we get, sad to say, is what we deserve. The kind of advertising we get reflects the kind of people that we are. No doubt, a different kind of advertising would be better, more moral, more ethical in many respects; but I'm afraid we have no one to blame but ourselves, as in all cases where one deplores that which is produced by a market society.

A final word about deceit. Of course, deceitful advertising is to be condemned on both moral and economic grounds. But we have to put it in perspective. Let me read from one very eminent economist who writes as follows:

"The formation of wants is a complex process. No doubt wants are modified by Madison Avenue. They are modified by Washington, by the university faculties and by churches. And it is not at all clear that Madison Avenue has the advantage when it comes to false claims and exaggerations."[1]

Take with a Grain of Salt

In other words, we live in a world where you have to be careful what you read, to whom you listen, whom to believe. And it's true of everything, every aspect of life. If one were to believe everything projected at him, he would be in a sorry state.

It is very easy to pick out the wrong messages to believe. Now, this doesn't in any way condone or justify deceitful messages of any kind. We have to recognize, however, while particular producers may have a short-run interest in projecting a message to consumers of doubtful veracity, that so long as there's freedom of competition the consumer has his choice not only of which product to buy but whom to believe. And notice what is the alternative in this world of imperfect human beings. The alternative, of course, is government control—still by imperfect human beings. So there is no way to render oneself invulnerable to the possibility of false, fraudulent, deceitful messages.

It would be nice to live in a world where no deceitful men were present. It would be cheaper. You could believe any message received. You wouldn't have to check out the credentials of every advertiser. But that is not the world in which we live. You check out the credit standing of individuals, the character of people with whom you deal; and this is an unavoidable, necessary cost. To blame advertising for the imperfections and weaknesses of mankind is unfair. Advertising would exist under any type of free market system. Advertising would be less deceitful if men were less deceitful. It would be more ethical, less offensive, if men were less offensive and more ethical. But advertising itself is an integral, inescapable aspect of the market economy.

Note

[1] H. Demsetz, "The Technostructure, Forty-Six Years Later," (*Yale Law Journal*, 1968), p. 810.

Interregional Trade

55. THE CANDLEMAKERS' PETITION*

Frederic Bastiat

EDITOR'S NOTE: *The author did most of his writing during the years before—and immediately following—the Revolution of February 1848. This was a period when France was adopting many socialistic policies. As a Deputy to the Legislative Assembly, Mr. Bastiat studied each interventionist measure and explained how it must inevitably hurt the people. Protective tariffs were his special target. He pointed out that "protection" gives a special privilege to certain producers. He showed how tariffs add to the cost of imports, and reduce competition from abroad, benefiting certain producers at the expense of other producers and of consumers who must pay the higher prices or go without.*

We candlemakers are suffering from the unfair competition of a foreign rival. This foreign manufacturer of light has such an advantage over us that he floods our domestic markets with his product. And he offers it at a fantastically low price. The moment this foreigner appears in our country, all our customers desert us and turn to him. As a result, an entire domestic industry is rendered completely stagnant. And even more, since the lighting industry has countless ramifications with other native industries, they, too, are injured. This foreign manufacturer who competes against us without mercy is none other than the sun itself!

Here is our petition: Please pass a law ordering the closing of all windows, skylights, shutters, curtains, and blinds—that is, all openings, holes, and cracks through which the light of the sun is able to enter houses. This free sunlight is hurting the business of us deserving manufacturers of candles. Since we have always served our country well, gratitude demands that our country ought not to abandon us now to this unequal competition.

We hope that you gentlemen will not regard our petition as mere satire, or refuse it without at least hearing our reasons in support of it.

First, if you make it as difficult as possible for the people to have access to natural light, and thus create an increased demand for artificial light, will not all domestic manufacturers be stimulated thereby?

For example, if more tallow is consumed, naturally there must be more cattle and sheep. As a result, there will also be more meat, wool, and hides. There will even be more manure, which is the basis of agriculture.

Next, if more oil is consumed for lighting, we shall have extensive olive groves and rape [variety of mustard] fields.

Also, our wastelands will be covered with pines and other resinous trees and plants. As a result of this, there will be numerous swarms of bees to increase the production of honey. In fact, all branches of agriculture will show an increased development.

The same applies to the shipping industry. The increased demand for whale oil will then require thousands of ships for whale fishing. In a short time, this will result in a navy capable of upholding the honor of our country and gratifying the patriotic sentiments of the candlemakers and other persons in related industries.

The manufacturers of lighting fixtures—candle-

*Translated and slightly condensed by Dean Russell from *Selected Works of Frederic Bastiat*, Volume 1, Paris: Guillaumin, 1863, pp. 58-59

sticks, lamps, candelabra, chandeliers, crystals, bronzes, and so on—will be especially stimulated. The resulting warehouses and display rooms will make our present-day shops look poor indeed.

The resin collectors on the heights along the seacoast, as well as the coal miners in the depths of the earth, will rejoice at their higher wages and increased prosperity. In fact, gentlemen, the condition of every citizen of our country—from the wealthiest owner of coal mines to the poorest seller of matches—will be improved by the success of our petition.

To this Petition of the Candlemakers, Bastiat in effect replied:

You neglect the consumer in your plea. Whenever the consumer's interest is opposed to that of the producer you sacrifice the consumer's—for the sake of increased work and employment. The consumer wants goods as cheaply as possible, even imports, if they are inexpensive. "But," you reply, "producers are interested in excluding cheap imports. Similarly, consumers may welcome free natural light, but producers of artificial light are interested in excluding it."

Nature and human labor cooperate in the production of commodities in various proportions, depending on the country and the climate. Nature's part is always "free." If a Lisbon orange sells in Paris for half the price of a Paris orange, it is because nature and, thus, free heat does for it what artificial and, therefore, expensive heat must do for the other. A part of the Portuguese orange is furnished free.

When we can acquire goods from abroad for less labor than if we make them ourselves, the difference is a gift. When the donor, like the sun in furnishing light, asks for nothing, the gift is complete. The question we would ask—and we pose it formally—is this: "Do you prefer that our people have the benefit of consuming free and inexpensive commodities? Or would you impose on them the supposed advantages of hard work and expensive production?"

(Paraphrased from the original)

56. FREE TRADE: DOMESTIC/FOREIGN*

Dean Russell

The most persuasive argument I ever heard for protective tariffs was offered by an Egyptian student. He pointed out correctly that the low production of the Egyptian workers is due primarily to their primitive tools. He informed me that (contrary to general belief) the low production standards in Egypt actually result in high labor costs when measured on a realistic *per unit produced* basis. He then argued that the workers in the underdeveloped nations just couldn't possibly compete against industrial workers with their efficient machines and the resulting high production and *low labor cost per unit.* And he concluded that if the government didn't protect the low-paid Egyptian workers against competition from the more advanced industrial nations, most of them would soon lose their jobs to the high-paid men with the machines.

Actually, my Egyptian friend's argument for protection against so-called *expensive* foreign labor is not any more valid than are the arguments by my own countrymen for protection against so-called *cheap* foreign labor. In reality, the *trade itself* necessarily causes real wages to rise in all nations that participate. In order to understand this better, let us start with a statement that is not subject to argument: No person in Egypt or Guatemala or the United States will voluntarily trade with a person in another country (or even next door) unless he puts a higher value on what he gets than on what he gives up. And thus both parties to *any* trade (domestic or foreign) necessarily benefit (or at least expect to benefit) from the trade.

*This article is one of a series of lectures delivered at the Centro de Estudios Económico Sociales, Guatemala City, April 6-10, 1964. Reprinted from *The Freeman*, July 1964

Actually, there is no exclusively economic or theoretical justification for discussing domestic and foreign trade separately; they are identical in all respects—except for the purely arbitrary and artificial interventions of government. For example, in the United States, a manufacturer in southern California has no particular difficulties in trading with a company in northern Maine, some 4,000 miles away. But when the same manufacturer tries to trade with a company in Tijuana, Mexico—perhaps 4 miles away—he encounters all sorts of frustrating and noneconomic prohibitions and compulsions that have been devised by the two governments.

The problems of transportation and distance (as such) are not something peculiar to international trade. Nor do differences of language and religion constitute special problems in trading across national boundaries.

For example, a Catholic manufacturer who speaks only Italian in Lugano, Switzerland, has no problem at all in trading with a Protestant retailer who speaks only German in Zurich. But when he attempts to trade with his Italian cousin just across the border (both speaking the same language and belonging to the same church), he encounters problems that are often insurmountable. All of these problems are, without exception, created by government and are thus completely artificial and unnecessary.

Canada offers an example of how vast distances, different wage scales, different languages, different religions, and different racial and cultural backgrounds present no real trade problems at all. But let a Canadian try to buy an automobile from Detroit, just across the border!

Even different moneys (lira, peso, dollar, or whatever) present no real problem to any trader—if the various moneys can be freely bought and sold. But when this is forbidden, problems do appear; again, however, they are artificial problems and are due entirely to governmental rules and regulations.

At Home and Abroad

Any argument for free trade and the division of labor within a nation is automatically and necessarily an argument for free trade and the division of labor internationally. If a person advocates free trade domestically, he cannot logically advocate protective tariffs and other similar measures that prevent goods and services from moving freely across national boundaries. It is simply not true that a nation and a people are made more prosperous by compelling themselves to pay two and three times as much as they need to pay for the goods and services they want. It just does not make sense to improve the means of moving goods from one nation to another, and then to cancel out the savings in transportation costs by passing laws to hamper the resulting trade. I am convinced that such contradictions arise more from lack of understanding than from evil intentions.

For example, the idea of creating and protecting domestic industries and jobs by restricting foreign imports is still generally found at the bottom of most arguments for protective tariffs. This objective is at least understandable. And it *is* unquestionably true that if it were not for government protection against foreign competition, many persons in Guatemala and the United States would lose their jobs. Further, a considerable number of companies in both nations would be forced out of business and would suffer heavy losses of capital. But the persons who are quick to point out these economic realities seem unaware of the multitude of jobs and industries in Guatemala and the United States that actually depend on foreign trade.

For example, the advocates of protective tariffs in my own country dramatize the story of the jobs and industries that are destroyed or threatened by the $16 billion of yearly imports into the United States. But they just ignore the far larger number of jobs and industries that are involved in our $20 billion of exports—automotive and electrical equipment, steel mill products, machine tools, coal and cotton, petroleum products, and many others. In a manner of speaking, prohibitive tariffs could destroy 20 United States jobs and companies for every 16 saved or created. And worse still, the companies most likely to be injured by restrictive trade policies are our most efficient ones that tend to pay the highest wages. The advocates of protective tariffs completely ignore the obvious fact that foreigners cannot continue to buy from us unless they are permitted to sell to us.

A Huge Market

In reality, the absence of tariffs and similar trade restrictions among the 50 states in my country goes a long way to explain why our level of living is so high. This absence of internal trade restrictions permits and encourages competition, natural specialization and division of labor, survival of the most efficient managers and companies, and especially the free movement of labor and capital from one industry and one section of the nation to other industries and sections. The final result of all this is better jobs at higher pay for all employees, lower prices for all consumers, and perhaps even higher profits for those owners and managers of capital who are capable of operating in a free and competitive economy.

Just as free trade among the states of the United States has brought this result, just so would free trade among the nations of the world bring similar results to all of them. To help us understand why this is so and how it would work, let us refer briefly to the concept of trade according to the principle of "comparative advantage" as developed by David Ricardo.

This *comparative* advantage idea is often confused with an *absolute* advantage, such as coffee produced in Guatemala but not in the United States. But according to the Ricardian example, two nations must produce the same two (or more) products before this principle applies. And still following Ricardo, the comparison is always first made *within one of the nations alone*. The comparison concerns the "substitution ratio" or "alternate opportunity cost" of producing *domestically* one of the two products instead of the other. Then exactly the same comparison is made *domestically within the other nation*. Whenever the physical cost or substitution ratio for the two products in one country differs from the same cost or substitution ratio for *the same two products* in the other country, a "comparative advantage situation" exists. Each nation can then profit by concentrating on producing one of the products at home and trading a part of it abroad for the other.

Delivering the Paper

Now I am well aware that the above explanation of Ricardo's comparative advantage principle of trade is too condensed and complicated for general lecture purposes. So I will merely refer you to any textbook on international trade for the full development of it. I will here confine myself to applying *the same idea* in more familiar situations and in less technical terms. But even so, the reality behind my examples and conclusions are still Ricardian.

Here is my first example of Ricardo and his comparative advantage idea in modern dress: As I write these words, I can see my "newspaper delivery boy" plodding slowly toward my door. He is late as usual. And perhaps the reason I am watching him is to see if he will again step on another one of my prized flowers planted along the sidewalk. Now if you will look upon him and me as representing two nations—and let lecturing and delivering newspapers represent the two products produced in both countries—I can illustrate quite simply the essential idea behind Ricardo's law of comparative advantage.

Positively and beyond any shadow of a doubt, I can deliver newspapers more efficiently than my paper boy can. Since I can deliver more of them in a given period of time, I can earn more money than he can. And since I would be much neater and much more pleasant while doing the job, doubtless the traditional "tips" would be larger for me than they are for him. In short, the market would pay me more to do that delivery job than it now pays him.

I'll also hazard the guess that I can make better speeches than my paper boy can. I know, however, that he *can* make speeches; in fact, he made a couple of them to me when I recently suggested that he should not leave my paper on the open porch during a rain storm. Thus, I will here maintain that I can do both of these jobs better than he can; I have an *absolute* advantage over him in delivering lectures *and* in delivering newspapers. Even so (and to get at Ricardo's point), he has a *comparative* advantage over me in delivering newspapers. And based on what the market will pay me to deliver newspapers and to make lectures, I have a comparative advantage over him in the speech-making business. Here is how it works.

The Scope of the Handicap

Let's say the market pays my paper boy 50 cents an hour to deliver papers. My guess is that he would earn almost nothing as a speech-maker, but let's be generous and allow 5 cents an hour. To follow Ricardo, his substitution ration is 50 to 5 or 10 to 1. That is, in the same amount of time, he can earn 10 times as much delivering newspapers as he can earn by making speeches.

I am confident that the market will pay me better for both jobs. Let's say I could earn $1 per hour delivering newspapers, and $20 an hour as a lecturer. Thus, for every hour that I spend delivering newspapers for $1, the alternate opportunity cost to me is the $20 I could earn as a lecturer and teacher. Thus, it clearly pays me to devote my full working time to lecturing, teaching, and writing instead of delivering papers. Even though I can do a better job than my "competitor" in delivering newspapers, he still has a comparative advantage over me; or, technically, his comparative *disadvantage* is less in delivering papers than in delivering lectures. The fact that I have an *absolute* advantage in both categories is of no consequence. As the Ricardian principle illustrates, I will continue to pay my so-so paper boy to deliver my newspaper because (comparatively) my advantage over him is far greater in lecturing than in delivering papers.

It Still Pays To Trade

And so it is with trade between nations. As Ricardo pointed out, one nation can be more efficient in *every* category than another nation—and yet because of a comparative advantage, it is still profitable for the more efficient nation to trade with the less efficient nation. But how does one discover these comparative advantages among the various nations in today's world?

Well, first, it is necessary that you and I and everyone else can freely buy and sell and exchange the moneys of the two nations being compared. For when free exchange is permitted, then prices and wage rates in the two nations will tend to be based on reality instead of wishful thinking. And when trade is based on reality, *comparative* advantages are not hard to find. Select two jobs or two products that exist in both nations. Now examine the wage rates and prices paid in one of the nations for the jobs or products. Now compare the wages and prices for the *same* jobs and products in the other nation.

Unless the comparative substitution ratios are identical (highly unlikely), trade will occur between the two nations. Each nation will concentrate on the production of the item in which it has the greatest comparative advantage (or the least comparative disadvantage). Both nations will profit from this trade, even when one of them has an absolute advantage in producing both products.

Comparative advantages can be found in general categories as well as in specific products and services. For example, I am confident that, *compared to the United States,* the cost of capital is higher than the cost of labor here in Guatemala. If so, the United States enjoys a comparative advantage over Guatemala in capital costs, and Guatemala enjoys a comparative advantage over the United States in labor costs.

Given this situation, one would logically expect "labor intensive" products to go from Guatemala to the United States, and "capital intensive" products to flow from the United States to Guatemala. And I am confident that such would be the case, if our two governments would abolish the trade restrictions that each has placed against the other. If this were done, both nations would necessarily profit thereby.

Again, this comparative advantage *principle* works the same between persons within a nation as it does between nations. For example, the famous showman, Billy Rose, was also a champion typist. But he operated on the principle of comparative advantage when he hired a typist and devoted his own time to producing shows and writing newspaper columns. The fact that he could type faster and better than his secretary is beside the point. Both he and she enjoyed a higher level of living because of that division of labor, just as the level of living in any and all nations rises when trade is permitted to operate according to this principle.

Likewise, a surgeon may know how to wash his surgical instruments better than does the person he actually hires to wash them. But obviously, *everyone* profits by his decision to devote his full time to the job (surgery) at which he enjoys the greatest *comparative* advantage, as measured by the price the market will pay him for performing the two tasks.

As another familiar example of how Ricardo's comparative advantage idea works in everyday life, take the insurance salesman who pays a man $1.50 an hour to work for him in his yard during the day. Let's assume that the caliber of the work done by the yardman is not as good as the owner himself could do—or, at any rate, *thinks* he could do. So why doesn't he do the work himself and save $1.50 an hour? The answer is that he would not necessarily save $1.50 an hour but might actually lose $3.50 an hour by working in his own yard. That development is due to the fact that his average hourly earnings as an insurance salesman are $5. He has a *comparative* advantage selling insurance instead of raking leaves. The pricing mechanism of the free market shows this beyond any shadow of a doubt.

And so it is with trade among nations. Every nation enjoys a comparative advantage in some product or service, even though it may be due only to some institutional or historical reason. That nation (and the people in general in that nation) would enjoy a higher level of living if it specialized in those goods and services in which it enjoys such an advantage.

Let the Market Decide

How can we citizens of Guatemala and the United States discover which are the products and services in which each enjoys a comparative advantage? Easy! Just remove all artificial restrictions against trade, including monetary exchange. Then observe what the importers and exporters in Guatemala do. I doubt that many of them can explain to you Ricardo's comparative advantage principle, but every one of them will search the world's markets to see what and where he can buy most advantageously. Nor do any of them need to hear this lecture in order to know where in the world the most profitable demand exists for Guatemalan products and services. While the producers and buyers in Guatemala and the United States may not be able to explain the Ricardian theory on which they operate, they will still quickly indicate to us which products and services enjoy a comparative advantage in which nation. You and I need only follow the free market price signals in our buying and selling.

We are foolish indeed to continue to impose tariffs and other restrictions against trade between our nations; the only result of such misguided and uneconomic governmental interventions is that we pay more and get less.

57. ON FOREIGN TRADE*

David Ricardo

Under a system of perfectly free commerce, each country naturally devotes its capital and labour to such employments as are most beneficial to each. This pursuit of individual advantage is admirably connected with the universal good of the whole. By stimulating industry, by rewarding ingenuity, and by using most efficaciously the peculiar powers bestowed by nature, it distributes labour most effectively and most economically: while, by increasing the general mass of productions, it diffuses general benefit, and binds together, by one common tie of interest and intercourse, the universal society of nations throughout the civilised world. It is this principle which determines that wine shall be made in France and Portugal, that corn shall be grown in America and Poland, and that hardware and other goods shall be manufactured in England.

*Excerpted from Chapter VII of *Principles of Political Economy and Taxation* (1817). Ricardo, an economist of the "Classical School," deserves credit for having been among the first to point out the advantages of specialization and trade, even if one party to the transaction could produce everything better and cheaper than the other.

In one and the same country, profits are, generally speaking, always on the same level; or differ only as the employment of capital may be more or less secure and agreeable. It is not so between different countries. If the profits of capital employed in Yorkshire should exceed those of capital employed in London, capital would speedily move from London to Yorkshire, and an equality of profits would be effected; but if in consequence of the diminished rate of production in the lands of England, from the increase of capital and population, wages should rise and profits fall, it would not follow that capital and population would necessarily move from England to Holland, or Spain, or Russia, where profits might be higher.

If Portugal had no commercial connection with other countries, instead of employing a great part of her capital and industry in the production of wines, with which she purchases for her own use the cloth and hardware of other countries, she would be obliged to devote a part of that capital to the manufacture of those commodities, which she would thus obtain probably inferior in quality as well as quantity.

The quantity of wine which she shall give in exchange for the cloth of England is not determined by the respective quantities of labour devoted to the production of each, as it would be if both commodities were manufactured in England, or both in Portugal.

England may be so circumstanced that to produce the cloth may require the labour of 100 men for one year; and if she attempted to make the wine, it might require the labour of 120 men for the same time. England would therefore find it her interest to import wine, and to purchase it by the exportation of cloth.

To produce the wine in Portugal might require only the labour of 80 men for one year, and to produce the cloth in the same country might require the labour of 90 men for the same time. It would therefore be advantageous for her to export wine in exchange for cloth. This exchange might even take place notwithstanding that the commodity imported by Portugal could be produced there with less labour than in England. Though she could make the cloth with the labour of 90 men, she would import it from a country where it required the labour of 100 men to produce it, because it would be advantageous to her rather to employ her capital in the production of wine, for which she would obtain more cloth from England, than she could produce by diverting a portion of her capital from the cultivation of vines to the manufacture of cloth.

Thus England would give the produce of the labour of 100 men for the produce of the labour of 80. Such an exchange could not take place between the individuals of the same country. The labour of 100 Englishmen cannot be given for that of 80 Englishmen, but the produce of the labour of 100 Englishmen may be given for the produce of the labour of 80 Portuguese, 60 Russians, or 120 East Indians. The difference in this respect, between a single country and many, is easily accounted for, by considering the difficulty with which capital moves from one country to another, to seek a more profitable employment, and the activity with which it invariably passes from one province to another in the same country.[1]

It would undoubtedly be advantageous to the capitalists of England, and to the consumers in both countries, that under such circumstances the wine and the cloth should both be made in Portugal, and therefore that the capital and labour of England employed in making cloth should be removed to Portugal for that purpose. In that case, the relative value of these commodities would be regulated by the same principle as if one were the produce of Yorkshire and the other of London: and in every other case, if capital freely flowed towards those countries where it could be most profitably employed, there could be no difference in the rate of profit, and no other difference in the real or labour price of commodities than the additional quantity of labour required to convey them to the various markets where they were to be sold.

Experience, however, shows that the fancied or real insecurity of capital, when not under the immediate control of its owner, together with the natural disinclination which every man has to quit the country of his birth and connections, and intrust himself, with all his habits fixed, to a strange government and new laws, check the emigration of capital. . . .

Note

[1] It will appear, then, that a country possessing very considerable advantages in machinery and skill, and which may therefore be enabled to manufacture commodities with much less labour than her neighbours, may, in return for such commodities, import a portion of the corn required for its consumption, even if its land were more fertile and corn could be grown with less labour than in the country from which it was imported. Two men can both make shoes and hats, and one is superior to the other in both employments; but in making hats he can only exceed his competitor by one-fifth or 20 per cent, and in making shoes he can excel him by one-third or 33 per cent—will it not be for the interest of both that the superior man should employ himself exclusively in making shoes, and the inferior man in making hats?

58. FOREIGN INVESTMENT VS. FOREIGN AID*

Henry Hazlitt

At the beginning of Chapter III of his *History of England,* Thomas Babington Macaulay wrote:

"In every experimental science there is a tendency toward perfection. In every human being there is a wish to ameliorate his own condition. These two principles have often sufficed, even when counteracted by great public calamities and by bad institutions, to carry civilization rapidly forward. No ordinary misfortune, no ordinary misgovernment, will do so much to make a nation wretched as the constant effort of every man to better himself will do to make a nation prosperous. It has often been found that profuse expenditures, heavy taxation, absurd commercial restrictions, corrupt tribunals, disastrous wars, seditions, persecutions, conflagrations, inundations, have not been able to destroy capital so fast as the exertions of private citizens have been able to create it. It can easily be proved that, in our own land, the national wealth has, during at least six centuries, been almost uninterruptedly increasing. . . . This progress, having continued during many ages, became at length, about the middle of the eighteenth century, portentously rapid, and has proceeded, during the nineteenth, with accelerated velocity."

We too often forget this basic truth. Would-be humanitarians speak constantly today of "the vicious circle of poverty." Poverty, they tell us, produces malnutrition and disease, which produce apathy and idleness, which perpetuate poverty; and no progress is possible without help from outside. This theory is today propounded unceasingly, as if it were axiomatic. Yet the history of nations and individuals shows it to be false.

It is not only "the natural effort which every man is continually making to better his own condition" (as Adam Smith put it even before Macaulay) that we need to consider, but the constant effort of most families to give their children a "better start" than they enjoyed themselves. The poorest people under the most primitive conditions work first of all for food, then for clothing and shelter. Once they have provided a rudimentary shelter, more of their energies are released for increasing the quantity or improving the quality of their food and clothing and shelter. And for providing tools. Once they have acquired a few tools, part of their time and energies can be released for making more and better tools. And so, as Macaulay emphasized, economic progress can become accelerative.

One reason it took so many centuries before this acceleration actually began, is that as men increased their production of the means of subsistence, more of their children survived. This meant that their increased production was in fact mainly used to support an increasing population. Aggregate production, population, and consumption all increased; but per capita production and consumption barely increased at all. Not until the Industrial Revolution began in the late eighteenth century did the rate of production begin to increase by so much that, in spite of leading to an unprecedented increase in population, it led also to an increase in per capita production. In the Western world this increase has continued ever since.

So a country can, in fact, starting from the most primitive conditions, lift itself from poverty to abundance. If this were not so, the world could never have arrived at its present state of wealth. Every country started poor. As a matter of historic fact, most nations raised themselves from "hopeless" poverty to at least a less wretched poverty purely by their own efforts.

Specialization and Trade

One of the ways by which each nation or region did this was by division of labor within its own territory and by the mutual exchange of services and products. Each man enormously increased his out-

*From *The Freeman*, October 1970

put by eventually specializing in a single activity—by becoming a farmer, butcher, baker, mason, bricklayer, or tailor—and exchanging his product with his neighbors. In time this process extended beyond national boundaries, enabling each nation to specialize more than before in the products or services that it was able to supply more plentifully or cheaply than others, and by exchange and trade to supply itself with goods and services from others more plentifully or cheaply than it could supply them for itself.

But this was only one way in which foreign trade accelerated the mutual enrichment of nations. In addition to being able to supply itself with more goods and cheaper goods as a result of foreign trade, each nation supplied itself with goods and services that it could otherwise not produce at all, and of which it would perhaps not even have known the existence.

Thus foreign trade *educates* each nation that participates in it, and not only through such obvious means as the exchange of books and periodicals. This educational effect is particularly important when hitherto backward countries open their doors to industrially advanced countries. One of the most dramatic examples of this occurred in 1854, when Commodore Perry at the head of a U.S. naval force "persuaded" the Japanese, after 250 years of isolation, to open their doors to trade and communication with the U.S. and the rest of the world. Part of Perry's success, significantly, was the result of bringing and showing the Japanese such things as a modern telescope, a model telegraph, and a model railway, which delighted and amazed them.

Some Steps May Be Skipped

Western reformers today, praising some hitherto backward country, in Africa or Asia, will explain how much smarter its natives are than we of the West because they have "leaped in a single decade from the seventeenth into the twentieth century." But the leap, while praiseworthy, is not so surprising when one recalls that what the natives mainly did was to import the machines, instruments, technology, and know-how that had been developed during those three centuries by the scientists and technicians of the West. The backward countries were able to bypass home coal furnaces, gaslight, the street car, and even, in most cases, the railroad, and to import Western automobiles, Western knowledge of road-building, Western airplanes and airliners, telephones, central oil heaters, electric light, radio and television, refrigerators and airconditioning, electric heaters, stoves, dishwashers and clothes washers, machine tools, factories, plants, and Western technicians, and then to send some of their youth to Western colleges and universities to become technicians, engineers, and scientists. The backward countries imported, in brief, their "great leap forward."

In fact, not merely the recently backward countries of Asia and Africa, but every great industrialized Western nation, not excluding the United States, owes a very great part—indeed, the major part—of its present technological knowledge and productivity to discoveries, inventions, and improvements imported from other nations. Notwithstanding the elegant elucidations by the classical economists, very few of us today appreciate all that the world and each nation owes to foreign trade, not only in services and products, but even more in knowledge, ideas, and ideals.

International Investment

Historically, international trade gradually led to international investment. Among independent nations, international investment developed inevitably when the exporters of one nation, in order to increase their sales, sold on short-term credit, and later on longer-term credit, to the importers of another. It developed also because capital was scarcer in the less developed nation, and interest rates were higher. It developed on a larger scale when men emigrated from one country to another, starting businesses in the new country, taking their capital as well as their skills with them.

In fact, what is now known as "portfolio" investment—the purchase by the nationals of one country of the stocks or bonds of the companies of another—has usually been less important quantitatively than this "direct" investment. In 1967 U.S. private investments abroad were estimated to total $93 billion, of which $12 billion were short-term assets and claims, and $81 billion long-term. Of American long-term private investments abroad, $22 billion were portfolio investments and $59 billion direct investments.

The export of private capital for private investment has on the whole been extremely profitable for the capital-exporting countries. In every one of the twenty years from 1945 to 1964 inclusive, for example, the income from old direct foreign investments by U.S. companies exceeded the outflow of new direct investments. In that twenty-year period new outflows of direct investments totaled $22.8 billion, but income from old direct investments came to $37.1 billion, plus $4.6 billion from royalties and fees, leaving an excess inflow of $18.9 billion. In fact, with the exception of 1928, 1929, and 1931, U.S. income from direct foreign investments exceeded new capital outlays in every year since 1919.[1]

Our direct foreign investments also greatly stimulated our merchandise exports. The U.S. Department of Commerce found that in 1964, for example, $6.3 billion, or 25 per cent of our total exports in that year, went to affiliates of American companies overseas.

It is one of the ironies of our time, however, that the U.S. government decided to put the entire blame for the recent "balance-of-payments deficit" on American investments abroad; and beginning in mid-1963, started to penalize and restrict such investment.

The advantages of international investment to the capital importing country should be even more obvious. In any backward country there are almost unlimited potential ventures, or "investment opportunities," that are not undertaken chiefly because the capital to start them does not exist. It is the domestic lack of capital that makes it so difficult for the "underdeveloped" country to climb out of its wretched condition. Outside capital can enormously accelerate its rate of improvement.

Investment from abroad, like domestic investment, can be of two kinds: the first is in the form of fixed interest-bearing loans, the second in the form of direct equity investment in which the foreign investor takes both the risks and the profits. The politicians of the capital-importing country usually prefer the first. They see their nationals, say, making 15 or 30 per cent annual gross profit on a venture, paying off the foreign lender at a rate of only 6 per cent, and keeping the difference as net profit. If the foreign investor makes a similar assessment of the situation, however, he naturally prefers to make the direct equity investment himself.

But the foreigner's preference in this regard does not necessarily mean that the capital-importing country is injured. It is to its own advantage if its government puts no vexatious restrictions on the form or conditions of the private foreign investment. For if the foreign investor imports, in addition to his capital, his own (usually) superior management, experience, and technical know-how, his enterprise may be more likely to succeed. He cannot help but give employment to labor in the capital-importing country, even if he is allowed to bring in labor freely from his own. Self-interest and wage-rate differentials will probably soon lead him to displace most of whatever common or even skilled labor he originally brings in from his own country with the labor of the host country. He will usually supply the capital-importing country itself with some article or amenity it did not have before. He will raise the average marginal productivity of labor in the country in which he has built his plant or made his investment, and his enterprise will tend to raise wages there. And if his investment proves particularly profitable, he will probably keep reinvesting most of his profits in it as long as the market seems to justify the reinvestment.

There is still another benefit to the capital-importing country from private foreign investment. The foreign investors will naturally seek out first the most profitable investment opportunities. If they choose wisely, these will also be the investments that produce the greatest surplus of market value over costs and are therefore economically most productive. When the originally most productive investment opportunities have been exploited to a point where the comparative rate of return begins to diminish, the foreign investors will look for the next most productive investment opportunities, originally passed over. And so on. Private foreign investment will therefore tend to promote the most rapid rate of economic improvements.

Foreigners Are Suspect

It is unfortunate, however, that just as the government of the private-capital-exporting country today tends to regard its capital exports with alarm as a threat to its "balance of payments," the government of the private-capital-importing country today tends to regard its capital imports at least with suspicion if not with even greater alarm. Doesn't the private-capital-exporting country make a profit on this capital? And if so, mustn't this profit necessarily be at the expense of the capital-importing country? Mustn't the latter country somehow be giving away its patrimony? It seems impossible for the anticapitalist mentality (which prevails among the politicians of the world, particularly in the underdeveloped countries) to recognize that both sides normally benefit from any voluntary economic transaction, whether a purchase-sale or a loan-investment, domestic or international.

Chief among the many fears of the politicians of the capital-importing country is that foreign investors "take the money out of the country." To the extent that this is true, it is true also of domestic investment. If a home owner in Philadelphia gets a mortgage from an investor in New York, he may point out that his interest and amortization payments are going out of Philadelphia and even out of Pennsylvania. But he can do this with a straight face only by forgetting that he originally borrowed the money from the New York lender either because he could not raise it at all in his home city or because he got better terms than he could get in his home city. If the New Yorker makes an equity investment in Pennsylvania, he may take out all the net profits; but he probably employs Pennsylvania labor to build his factory and operate it. And he probably pays out $85 to $90 annually for labor, supplies, rent, etc., mainly in Pennsylvania, for every $10 he takes back to New York. (In 1969, American manufacturing corporations showed a net profit after taxes of only 5.4 per cent on total value of sales.) "They take the money out of the country" is an objection against foreign investors resulting even more from xenophobia than from anticapitalism.

Fear of Foreign Control

Another objection to foreign investment by politicians of the capital-importing country is that the foreign investors may "dominate" the borrowing country's economy. The implication (made in 1965 by the de Gaulle government of France, for example) is that American-owned companies might come to have too much to say about the economic decisions of the government of the countries in which they are located. The real danger, however, is the other way round. The foreign-owned company puts itself at the mercy of the government of the host country. Its capital in the form of buildings, equipment, drilled wells and refineries, developed mines, and even bank deposits, may be trapped. In the last twenty-five years, particularly in Latin America and the Middle East, as American oil companies and others have found to their sorrow, the dangers of discriminatory labor legislation, onerous taxation, harassment, or even expropriation, are very real.

Yet the anticapitalistic, xenophobic, and other prejudices against private foreign investment have been so widespread, in both the countries that would gain from importing capital and the countries that would profit from exporting it, that the governments in both sets of countries have imposed taxes, laws and regulations, red tape, and other obstacles to discourage it.

At the same time, paradoxically, there has grown up in the last quarter-century powerful political pressures in both sets of countries in favor of the richer countries *giving capital away* to the poorer in the form of government-to-government "aid."

The Marshall Plan

This present curious giveaway mania (it can only be called that on the part of the countries making the grants) got started as the result of an historical accident. During World War II, the United States had been pouring supplies—munitions, industrial equipment, foodstuffs—into the countries of its allies and cobelligerents. These were all nominally "loans." American Lend-Lease to Great Britain, for example, came to some $30 billion and to Soviet Russia to $11 billion.

But when the war ended, Americans were informed not only that the Lend-Lease recipients could not repay and had no intention of repaying, but that the countries receiving these loans in wartime had become dependent upon them and were still in desperate straits, and that further credits were necessary to stave off disaster.

This was the origin of the Marshall Plan.

On June 5, 1947, General George C. Marshall, then American Secretary of State, made at Harvard the world's most expensive commencement address, in which he said:

"The truth of the matter is that Europe's requirements, for the next three or four years, of foreign food and other essential products—principally from America—are so much greater than her present ability to pay that she must have substantial additional help, or face economic, social, and political deterioration of a very grave character."

Whereupon Congress authorized the spending in the following three-and-a-half years of some $12 billion in aid.

This aid was widely credited with restoring economic health to "free" Europe and halting the march of communism in the recipient countries. It is true that Europe did finally recover from the ravages of World War II—as it had recovered from the ravages of World War I. And it is true that, apart from Yugoslavia, the countries not occupied by Soviet Russia did not go communist. But whether the Marshall Plan accelerated or retarded this recovery, or substantially affected the extent of communist penetration in Europe, can never be proved. What can be said is that the plight of Europe in 1947 was at least as much the result of misguided European governmental economic policies as of physical devastation caused by the war. Europe's recovery was far slower than it could have been, with or without the Marshall Plan.

This was dramatically demonstrated in West Germany in 1948, when the actions between June 20 and July 8 of Economic Minister Ludwig Erhard in simultaneously halting inflation, introducing a thoroughgoing currency reform, and removing the strangling network of price controls, brought the German "miracle" of recovery.

As Dr. Erhard himself described his action: "We decided upon and re-introduced the old rules of a free economy, the rules of *laissez-faire*. We abolished practically all controls over allocation, prices, and wages, and replaced them with a price mechanism controlled predominantly by money."

The result was that German industrial production in the second half of 1948 rose from 45 per cent to nearly 75 per cent of the 1936 level, while steel production doubled that year.

It is sometimes claimed that it was Germany's share of Marshall aid that brought on the recovery. But nothing similar occurred in Great Britain, for example, which received more than twice as much Marshall aid. The German per capita gross national product, measured in constant prices, increased 64 per cent between 1950 and 1958, whereas the per capita increase in Great Britain, similarly measured, rose only 15 per cent.

Once American politicians got the idea that the American taxpayer owed other countries a living, it followed logically that his duty could not be limited to just a few. Surely that duty was to see that poverty was abolished everywhere in the world. And so in his inaugural address of January 20, 1949, President Truman called for "a bold new program" to make "the benefits of our scientific advances and industrial progress available for the improvement and growth of underdeveloped areas. . . . This program can greatly increase the industrial activity in other nations and can raise substantially their standards of living."

Because it was so labeled in the Truman address, this program became known as "Point Four." Under it the "emergency" foreign aid of the Marshall Plan, which was originally to run for three or four years at most, was universalized, and has now been running for more than twenty years. So far as its advocates and built-in bureaucracy are concerned, it is to last until foreign poverty has been abolished from the face of the earth, or until the per capita "gap" between incomes in the backward countries and the advanced countries has been closed—even if that takes forever.

The cost of the program already is appalling. Total disbursements to foreign nations, in the fiscal years 1946 through 1970, came to $131 billion. The total net interest paid on what the U.S. borrowed to give away these funds amounted in the same period to $68 billion, bringing the grand total through the 25-year period to $199 billion.[2]

This money went altogether to some 130 nations. Even in the fiscal year 1970, the aid program was still operating in 99 nations and five territories of the world, with 51,000 persons on the payroll, including U.S. and foreign personnel. Congressman Otto E. Passman, chairman of the Foreign Operations Subcommittee on Appropriations, declared on July 1, 1969: "Of the three-and-a-half billion people of the world, all but 36 million have received aid from the U.S."

Domestic Repercussions

Even the colossal totals just cited do not measure the total loss that the foreign giveaway program has imposed on the American economy. Foreign aid has had the most serious economic side-effects. It has led to grave distortions in our economy. It has undermined our currency, and contributed toward driving us off the gold standard. It has accelerated our inflation. It was sufficient in itself to account for the total of our Federal deficits in the 1946-70 period. The $199 billion foreign aid total exceeds by $116 billion even the $83 billion increase in our gross national debt during the same years. Foreign aid has also been sufficient in itself to account for all our balance-of-payments deficits (which our government's policies blame on private foreign investment).

The advocates of foreign aid may choose to argue that though our chronic Federal budget deficits in the last 25 years *could* be imputed to foreign aid, we could alternatively impute those deficits to other expenditures, and assume that the foreign aid was paid for entirely by raising additional taxes. But such an assumption would hardly improve the case for foreign aid. It would mean that taxes during this quarter-century averaged at least $5 billion higher each year than they would have otherwise. It would be difficult to exaggerate the setbacks to personal working incentives, to new ventures, to profits, to capital investment, to employment, to wages, to living standards, that an annual burden of $5 billion in additional taxation can cause.

If, finally, we make the "neutral" assumption that our $131 or $199 billion in foreign aid (whichever way we choose to calculate the sum) was financed in exact proportion to our actual deficit and tax totals in the 25-year period, we merely make it responsible for part of both sets of evils.

In sum, the foreign aid program has immensely set back our own potential capital development. It ought to be obvious that a foreign giveaway program can raise the standards of living of the so-called "underdeveloped areas" of the world only by lowering our own living standards compared with what they could otherwise be. If our taxpayers are forced to contribute millions of dollars for hydroelectric plants in Africa or Asia, they obviously have that much less for productive investment in the U.S. If they contribute $10 million for a housing project in Uruguay, they have just that much less for their own housing, or any other cost equivalent, at home. Even our own socialist and statist do-gooders would be shaken if it occurred to them to consider how much might have been done with that $131 or $199 billion of foreign aid to mitigate pollution at home, build subsidized housing, and relieve "the plight of our cities." Free enterprisers, of course, will lament the foreign giveaway on the far more realistic calculation of how enormously the production, and the wealth and welfare of every class of our population, could have been increased by $131 to $199 billion in more private investment in new and better tools and cost-reducing equipment, and in higher living standards, and in more and better homes, hospitals, schools, and universities.

The Political Arguments

What have been the economic or political compensations to the United States for the staggering cost of its foreign aid program? Most of them have been illusory.

When our successive Presidents and foreign aid officials make inspirational speeches in favor of foreign aid, they dwell chiefly on its alleged humanitarian virtues, on the need for American generosity and compassion, on our duty to relieve the suffering and share the burdens of all mankind. But when they are trying to get the necessary appropriations out of Congress, they recognize the advisability of additional arguments. So they appeal to the American taxpayer's material self-interest. It will redound to his benefit, they argue, in three ways: 1. It will increase our foreign trade, and consequently the profits from it. 2. It will keep the underdeveloped countries from going communist. 3. It will turn the recipients of our grants into our eternally grateful friends.

The answers to these arguments are clear:

1. Particular exporters may profit on net balance from the foreign aid program, but they necessarily do so at the expense of the American taxpayer. It makes little difference in the end whether we give other countries the dollars to pay for our goods, or whether we directly give them the goods. We cannot grow rich by giving our goods or our dollars away. We can only grow poorer. (I would be ashamed of stating this truism if our foreign aid advocates did not so systematically ignore it.)

2. There is no convincing evidence that our foreign aid played any role whatever in reversing, halting, or even slowing down any drift toward communism. Our aid to Cuba in the early years of the program, and even our special favoritism toward it in assigning sugar quotas and the like, did not prevent it from going communist in 1958. Our $769 million of aid to the United Arab Republic did not prevent it from coming under Russian domination. Our $460 million aid to Peru did not prevent it from seizing American private properties there. Neither our $7,715 million aid to India, nor our $3,637 million aid to Pakistan, prevented either country from moving deeper and deeper into socialism and despotic economic controls. Our aid, in fact, subsidized these very programs, or made them possible. And so it goes, country after country.

3. Instead of turning the recipients into grateful friends, there is ever-fresh evidence that our foreign aid program has had precisely the opposite effect. It is pre-eminently the American embassies and the official American libraries that are mobbed and stoned, the American flag that is burned, the Yanks that are told to go home. And the head of almost every government that accepts American aid finds it necessary to denounce and insult the United States at regular intervals in order to prove to his own people that he is not subservient and no puppet.

So foreign aid hurts both the economic and political interest of the country that extends it.

But all this might be overlooked, in a broad humanitarian view, if foreign aid accomplished its main ostensible purpose of raising the living levels of the countries that received it. Yet both reason and experience make it clear that in the long run it has precisely the opposite effect.

Of course, a country cannot give away $131 billion without its doing *something* abroad (though we must always keep in mind the reservation—instead of something *else* at home). If the money is spent on a public housing project, on a hydroelectric dam, on a steel mill (no matter how uneconomic or ill-advised), the housing or the dam or the mill is brought into existence. It is visible and undeniable. But to point to that is to point only to the visible gross gain while ignoring the costs and the offsets. In all sorts of ways—economic, political, spiritual—the aid in the long run hurts the recipient country. It becomes dependent on the aid. It loses self-respect and self-reliance. The poor country becomes a pauperized country, a beggar country.

There is a profound contrast between the effects of foreign aid and of voluntary private investment. Foreign aid goes from government to government. It is therefore almost inevitably statist and socialistic. A good part of it goes into providing more goods for immediate consumption, which may do nothing to increase the country's productive capacity. The rest goes into government projects, government five-year plans, government airlines, government hydroelectric plants and dams, or government steel mills, erected principally for prestige reasons, and for looking impressive in colored photographs, and regardless of whether the projects are economically justified or self-supporting. As a result, real economic improvement is retarded.

The Insoluble Dilemma

From the very beginning, foreign aid has faced an insoluble dilemma. I called attention to this in a book published in 1947, *Will Dollars Save the World?*, when the Marshall Plan was proposed but not yet enacted:

"Intergovernmental loans [they have since become mainly gifts, which only intensifies the problem] are on the horns of this dilemma. If on the one hand they are made without conditions, the funds are squandered and dissipated and fail to accomplish their purpose. They may even be used for the precise opposite of the purpose that the lender had in mind. But if the lending government attempts to impose conditions, its attempt causes immediate resentment. It is called 'dollar diplomacy'; or 'American imperialism'; or 'interfering in the internal affairs' of the borrowing nation. The resentment is quickly exploited by the Communists in that nation."

In the 23 years since the foreign-aid program was launched, the administrators have not only failed to find their way out of this dilemma; they have refused even to acknowledge its existence. They have zigzagged from one course to the other, and ended by following the worst course of all: they have insisted that the recipient governments adopt "growth policies"—which mean, in practice, government "planning," controls, inflation, ambitious nationalized projects—in brief, socialism.

If the foreign aid were not offered in the first place, the recipient government would find it advisable to try to attract foreign private investment. To do this it would have to abandon its socialistic and inflationary policies, its exchange controls, its laws against taking money out of the country. It would have to abandon harassment of private business, restrictive labor laws, and discriminatory taxation. It would have to give assurances against nationalization, expropriation, and seizure.

Specifically, if the nationals of a poor country wanted to borrow foreign capital for a private project, and had to pay a going rate of, say, 7 per cent interest for the loan, their project would have to be one that promised to yield at least 7 per cent before the foreign investors would be interested. If the government of the poor country, on the other hand, can get the money from a foreign government without having to pay interest at all, it need not trouble to ask itself whether the proposed project is likely to prove economic and self-liquidating or not. The essential market guide to comparative need and utility is then completely removed. What decides priorities is the grandiose dreams of the government planners, unembarrassed by bothersome calculations of comparative costs and usefulness.

The Conditions for Progress

Where foreign government aid is not freely offered, however, a poor country, to attract private foreign investment, must establish an actual record of respecting private property and maintaining free markets. Such a free-enterprise policy by itself, even if it did not at first attract a single dollar of foreign investment, would give enormous stimulus to the economy of the country that adopted it. It would first of all stop the flight of capital on the part of its own nationals and stimulate *domestic* investment. It is constantly forgotten that both domestic and foreign capital investment are encouraged (or discouraged) by the same means.

It is not true, to repeat, that the poor countries are necessarily caught in a "vicious circle of poverty," from which they cannot escape without massive handouts from abroad. It is not true that "the rich countries are getting richer while the poor countries are getting poorer." It is not true that the "gap" between the living standards of the poor countries and the rich countries is growing ever wider. Certainly that is not true in any *proportionate* sense. From 1945 to 1955, for example, the average rate of growth of Latin American countries in national income was 4.5 per cent per annum, and in output per head 2.4 per cent—both rates appreciably higher than the corresponding figure for the United States.[3]

Intervention Breeds Waste

The foreign aid ideology is merely the relief ideology, the guaranteed-income ideology, applied on an international scale. Its remedy, like the domestic relief remedy, is to "abolish poverty" by seizing from the rich to give to the poor. Both proposals systematically ignore the reasons for the poverty they seek to cure. Neither draws any distinction between the poverty caused by misfortune and the poverty brought on by shiftlessness and folly. The advocates of both proposals forget that their chief attention should be directed to restoring the incentives, self-reliance, and *production* of the poor family or the poor country, and that the principal means of doing this is through the free market.

In sum, government-to-government foreign aid promotes statism, centralized planning, socialism, dependence, pauperization, inefficiency, and waste. It prolongs the poverty it is designed to cure. Voluntary private investment in private enterprise, on the other hand, promotes capitalism, production, independence, and self-reliance. It is by attracting foreign private investment that the great industrial nations of the world were once helped. It is so that America itself was helped by British capital, in the nineteenth century, in building its railroads and exploiting its great national resources. It is so that the still "underdeveloped areas" of the world can most effectively be helped today to develop their own great potentialities and to raise the living standards of their masses.

Notes:

[1] See *The United States Balance of Payments* (Washington: International Economic Policy Association, 1966), pp. 21 and 22.

[2] Source: Foreign Operations Subcommittee on Appropriations, House of Representatives, July 1, 1970.

[3] Cf. "Some Observations on 'Gapology,' " by P. T. Bauer and John B. Wood in *Economic Age* (London), November-December 1969. Professor Bauer is one of the few academic economists who have seriously analyzed the fallacies of foreign aid. See also his Yale lecture on foreign aid published by The Institute of Economic Affairs (London), 1966, and his article on "Development Economics" in *Roads to Freedom: Essays in Honour of Friedrich A. von Hayek* (London: Routledge & Kegan Paul, 1969). I may also refer the reader to my own book, *Will Dollars Save the World?* (Appleton, 1947), to my pamphlet, *Illusions of Point Four* (Irvington-on-Hudson, New York: Foundation for Economic Education, 1950), and to my chapter on "The Fallacy of Foreign Aid" in my *Man Vs. the Welfare State* (Arlington House, 1969).

59. RESTRICTIONS ON INTERNATIONAL TRADE*

W. Marshall Curtiss

A businessman is always under the necessity of adjusting the conduct of his business to the institutional conditions of his country. In the long run he is, in his capacity as entrepreneur and capitalist, neither favored nor injured by tariffs or the absence of tariffs.

LUDWIG VON MISES, *Human Action*

If there is one point of fairly general agreement among economists throughout the world and throughout time, it is that trade should remain free from all sorts of governmental restrictions and interventions. It would seem unnecessary to repeat over and over why the material welfare of individuals is enhanced through the division of labor and freedom to trade.

But restrictions still exist! Tariffs and other barriers to trade seem to move through cycles, relaxed at times, and then reapplied. Why, in the face of reasoned arguments by leading intellectuals, do restrictions to trade have such an appeal to lawmakers? In other words, who is it and what is it that moves the lawmakers to take such action?

The cry for protection comes in many voices. A glove manufacturer resents finding imported gloves in the market. It is natural for any firm to take any legal steps available to sustain profits and remain in business. If a way can be found to eliminate this foreign competition, perhaps convince the government to raise some sort of barrier to the foreign gloves—a tariff, or a quota, or an embargo—then the glovemaker might be able to continue in business, competing with domestic firms as always, but avoiding the foreign competitor.

The glove industry may maintain a lobby in Washington to try to convince the lawmakers that unless protection is provided, thousands of jobs will be lost, unemployment will rise, and companies will go bankrupt. And it may all be true! At least it often is convincing enough to the lawmakers.

What happened to the logical argument of the economists who said protection hurts the consumer? Well, the argument stands, but the consumer's voice is faint. What if it does cost a few pennies more to buy a pair of gloves? Compared with the loss of a job or a failing company, this is nothing! Or so it seems to those seeking protection.

We Accept Domestic Competition

Now, suppose a domestic firm is in financial trouble, in no way caused by imports. Does it send a lobby to Washington and ask for help? Not ordinarily. In domestic trade, we accept the idea that a firm must compete without special favors. True enough, companies do fail; men do lose their jobs; but the consumer is not penalized by interventions that reduce production and make things cost more.

If the failure of the *Edsel* automobile had been because of foreign competition, it might have been argued that a tariff on imports would have saved the car and preserved thousands of jobs. Had the maker been a one-product firm, it might have been saved from bankruptcy. But, no; it was a domestic firm that misjudged consumer acceptance of a product; and that was that! The *Edsel* is reported to have cost the Ford Motor Company $250 million.

A more recent example is that of *Corfam* which the du Pont Company developed to compete with natural leather for footwear. After seven years and a reported $100 million, du Pont discontinued production of *Corfam*.

Only the size of these write-offs makes these two items newsworthy. Thousands of new products

*From *Toward Liberty*, the Ludwig von Mises 90th Birthday Collection, copyright 1971 by The Institute for Humane Studies (Menlo Park, California).

are tried each year, and there are many failures. Unless a company has other profitable items which will carry such losses, the company may fail, as many do.

The testing of consumer preferences goes on constantly. Ordinarily, we wouldn't think of asking the government to prevent the failure of a given product. We accept such failure as one of the regulatory aspects of competition and the market. But let the competition be from a foreign country, even though it benefit consumers the same as domestic competition, and there arises a clamor to erect some sort of barrier to save jobs, or to save firms, or to build a fence around our high standard of living, or whatever.

Politics of International Trade

The justifications for tariffs and other forms of protection include the arguments that they keep our wages high, prevent unemployment, protect infant industries, help with national defense, prohibit trade with the enemy, discourage dumping, and so on.

Trade barriers or threats of trade barriers are often used in the formulation of foreign policy. "We will reduce our restrictions if you will do likewise." Or: "Let us reduce our restrictions against underdeveloped countries so that they can benefit from sales to us." Or: "Let us stop buying chrome from an African nation whose internal policies we do not approve." Among the reasons for trade restrictions must be included foreign policy. Or, as one author recently stated, "trade policy in the United States is a political matter."

But of all the pressures upon the members of Congress and the Executive to enact trade restrictions, few are greater than those exerted by business firms or associations representing business firms. Individual consumers who have the most to gain through the reduction or elimination of trade barriers, and who have voting power enough to elect or defeat any candidate for office, are practically powerless in comparison with business lobbies.

As an illustration, note the results of recent attempts to cut back certain phases of defense spending. Now, the production of something to be destroyed in combat obviously is worthless so far as contributing to the level of living of a people is concerned. If those workers and resources were used to produce housing, build highways, provide medical care, teaching, plumbing, auto repairs, and the like, then consumers would be that much better off.

But let it be suggested that we shut down our war machine and the protests are deafening. Workers will lose their jobs; companies will fail; the entire economy will suffer.

Granted, there are difficult adjustments to be made. But the fact that a worker is not needed in an airplane factory shouldn't preclude his finding a productive job elsewhere. One sympathizes with a worker in an industry that is being "wound down," especially in a one-industry community. In the recent discussion of continuing research and development of the SST, many in Congress, and many members of the press based their argument chiefly on the fact that thousands of workers would be disemployed and business firms would fail. The same arguments have been used in trying to maintain our outer space program. Such arguments have a strong emotional appeal and carry considerable persuasive force.

Many of the same arguments are used to establish trade restrictions, and with equally disastrous economic consequences.

Five Basic Principles

In discussing foreign trade, it is well to keep in mind certain basic principles:

(1) *Trade between two individuals, entered into freely, always results in benefits to both parties.* Otherwise, why should they trade? What anyone else may think of their judgment is beside the point.

(2) *There always is a comparative advantage in producing some products and importing others.* Production costs in one nation may be lower than in another nation for every item produced in either nation. But the people of these respective nations may still find it profitable to trade with one another.

It is often thought that only nations like Great Britain or other maritime nations benefit by trade, simply because there are so many things they do not produce domestically. True, the United States could close its borders to all imports and exports and still there might be a relatively high level of living for its citizens; but not as high as would be possible through trade with foreigners.

(3) *Consumption is the sole purpose of production.* Adam Smith explained this nearly 200 years ago. Production is to supply consumers' wants. It is not to make jobs, or to keep a business solvent, or to make one nation dependent on another. Naturally,

some of these things happen as a by-product of production and trade, but that should not be the objective.

(4) *Trade ordinarily will be most satisfactory to all concerned when individuals or their agents who have something to trade deal with other individuals or their agents who want the other side of that trade.* Governments should be involved as little as possible; first, because they are not concerned, and secondly, because there is always the temptation to use the trade for purposes other than satisfying consumers.

If an individual in this country wanted to trade some of his own property for something offered by a Russian citizen, we would think little about it, knowing that each party to the trade considered he was better off than before. But if government enters one or both sides of such a trade, there is often the suspicion, sometimes justified, that one party is seeking a military or political advantage.

(5) *Imports require exports.* Foreign trade appears complicated because it often takes an indirect or roundabout route through several nations. In addition, monies of several nations with complex exchange rates are usually involved. But it finally boils down to the fact that a nation which imports must export something in exchange.

Many people appear to believe that we might eventually be inundated with imports to the extent that practically all production in this country, all jobs, all business firms, might be wiped out. They fail to see that foreign goods cannot continue to come into this country unless something goes out to pay for them.

The Reciprocity Argument

A popular argument in support of tariffs is that we will reduce our obstacles to trade if other nations will reduce theirs. In other words, we must do it together.

The lack of understanding of international trade and the effect of restrictions is reflected in this press release in *The New York Times* for March 31, 1971. "The European Economic Community decided today to give generalized trade preferences to developing countries beginning July 1." The implication is: "If you are poor, we will let you sell to us." The truth, of course, is that voluntary exchange, whether the participants be rich or poor, benefits the buyer as well as the seller. Had the "developing country" previously been subject to trade restrictions, then, of course, it would gain from the relaxation of those restrictions. But the increased trade also would be of benefit to the "affluent" buying nation.

When diplomats from different countries discuss the reduction of trade barriers, it almost always has the appearance of a high-level bargaining session. How little can we give up in reducing our restrictions on imports in order to gain some reduction in their restrictions against our exports? It never seems to occur to them that we stand to gain by opening our gates entirely, whatever the other nation does. Certainly our consumers would stand to benefit. But, always of diplomatic concern is the effect on firms and on jobs.

A great deal of consideration is given to "most favored nation" reductions. If we give one nation the "benefit" of our reduction, then all nations are entitled to this great benefaction. Actually, unilateral action in reducing our restrictions against imports would benefit our consumers, and might end most of the seemingly endless bargaining over reduction by other countries in return.

Who knows? It might soon be discovered that trade policy should not be a political issue but that free trade between citizens of all nations, rich and poor alike, benefits all consumers.

How Can Free Trade Be Achieved?

Politicians, in the legislative as well as the executive branches of government, respond to pressures of various kinds from their constituents. So long as the pressure for trade restrictions exceeds that for free trade, we can expect restrictions to continue.

Considerable attention just now is directed at textiles, especially the textile trade with Japan. Had such trade been strictly between individuals without the intrusion of governments, many of our present problems would have been avoided. Following World War II, our government made concessions to help rebuild the Japanese economy. It delivered cotton for less than our own textile manufacturers had to pay for it; it practically gave new textile mills to the Japanese. Little wonder that American textile manufacturers resented this unfair competition and sought to restrict imports from Japan. Now, a quarter of a century after the war, while the effects of that kind of "foreign policy" may have worn off, the arguments against Japanese textiles persist and carry weight with legislators.

Over the years, many economic injustices, including misuse of capital and labor, have resulted from trade restrictions. To remove them all at once and go back to free trade is bound to require difficult adjustments on the part of business firms. No wonder they try, in any legal way they can, to protect any remaining shelters or even increase their protection.

Who Speaks for the Consumer?

From the standpoint of a manufacturer, the so-called benefits of protection and disadvantages of free trade are short-run and disappear once adjustments to the changed situation are made. The firm still must compete with other domestic firms as well as with imports, even if over a tariff wall. But it is these short-run adjustments that the legislators hear about—the layoff of workers, the reduced profits, and even business failures. The longer-run genuine benefits of free trade to consumers arouse little excitement. This is especially true in a country like the United States where imports are a relatively small part of all trade. Who is there to speak for the consumers? The professional protectors seem so interested in auto seat belts, unit pricing, packaging, advertising, truth-in-lending, and ecology that they aren't likely to get to the matter of free trade for some time.

Most families present a combination of consumer and producer interests, interests which may seem to be in conflict with regard to trade restrictions. For example, suppose two members of the family work in the local textile mill. The most important day-to-day problem to the family is making certain that these two mill workers are employed and bring home their weekly pay checks. So, if they are convinced that imported textiles may eliminate their jobs, then they are apt to be protectionists. Attesting to this is a story in a recent Sunday supplement headlined "Twilight of a Textile Town." In this article, it was reported that a mill which had been the town's leading industry for 70 years went bankrupt and put 844 textile workers out of work. Furthermore, "50 textile plants in the South have shut down since 1969. The Department of Labor has estimated that 27,200 Southern textile workers lost their jobs in 1970 alone."

This is a serious situation, apparently calling for a political solution. What is not so obvious is that even if all imports of textiles were stopped, after a short period of adjustment, domestic firms would find strong competition with each other and marginal firms would continue to face failure.

An illustration of how adjustments can be made to a declining industry is related in the *New England Letter* for April, 1971, published by The First National Bank of Boston. The study shows how, in the early 1950's, many textile mills were liquidated and a basic weakness was shown in the leather and shoe industries. Some of the textile mills are now among those in trouble in the South. Had the problem been handled with political solutions, no doubt New England textiles could have been "protected" in a way that would have kept the mills going with employment and jobs as usual.

But, instead, New England industry changed, in part, to the maufacture of transportation equipment, electrical equipment, and instruments, to name only three. This new type of manufacturing is more export-oriented and enjoys a better international competitive position. It has the greater "comparative advantage" that economists have been talking about. It uses higher skills from its workers, and the "value added in manufacturing" is relatively high. Thus, in the long run, the return to labor stands to exceed what it was and what it might have been in the production of textiles, shoes, and leather goods. True, some of the newer types of industry have been closely tied to government defense contracts, and with a recent cutback, unemployment increased. However, a basis for export and for increased production for consumers is there.

Adjustments to changes like these are often difficult and must not be passed off lightly. But such changes in an expanding and progressive economy are always going on. Attempts to stop them with artificial restraints are certain to be more painful than is the process of adjusting.

Man Must Choose Between Freedom and Protectionism

As observed earlier, most economists agree that protectionism is unsound. The consumer is served best by allowing people to trade freely with each other, not only domestically but world wide. But restrictions continue to persist, placed there for political reasons. The incentive to erect barriers to trade is a political response to pressure from individuals, groups of workers, industrial groups, and others who think they will gain from protective measures such as tariffs, quotas, and the like.

Because the consumer is the disadvantaged party, it may be argued that the solution lies in his education. But as previously shown, the consumer's stake as consumer of a protected product often is much less important to him than his job as a producer of a potentially protected product. Therefore, it seems doubtful that consumers, as a group, can be effective in bringing political pressure on lawmakers to offset the pressure for protection exerted by other groups.

After two centuries and more of expounding the advantages of free trade, it must seem trite to say that education must be relied upon to bring about a correction of the wrongs caused by protectionism. Nevertheless, there seems to be no short cut. While the consumer, qua consumer, must be included among those educated, it would seem that emphasis should be placed on convincing lawmakers of the advantages of free trade so that they can better withstand the pressures put upon them by their constituents who think they need and deserve protection from competitors.

60. THE FAILURE OF INTERNATIONAL COMMODITY AGREEMENTS*

Karl Brandt

It is, if I am not mistaken, the goal of all free countries with government by law to diminish poverty, squalor, and drudgery for the greatest number of their citizens, and to expand opportunities to all self-respecting, responsible citizens to develop their personal potential. This goal includes the obligation of the nation to respect the dignity and integrity of all men of good will.

If this national goal is accepted, the economy must have the institutional framework to promote the gradual improvement of the real income of the people by improving the productivity of human, natural, and man-made resources. This requires, in the production of goods and services, more division of labor, specialization, and increased efficiency from research, innovation, and better management. But in order to have some orientation for such endeavor it is essential to give the consumer the sovereign power to allocate resources to the satisfaction of his needs and of his more and more refined wants. This provides the powerful incentive to all people to make the effort to earn the money to get the goods and services they want. Such an arrangement is ideally guaranteed in the market with freely moving prices by the daily plebiscite in which housewives and the consumer in general express their preference in francs and centimes, or dollars and cents.

In the modern economy, in which this allocation of resources applies to all goods, durable and nondurable, to houses and motor vehicles, and to all services—educational, medical, culinary, artistic, and to entertainment, travel, insurance, recreation, and multitudes of others—economic growth is bound to accelerate and to become all-pervasive. Such dynamic growth, to be stable and continuous, requires a high degree of mobility of human resources, such as shifts from the production of goods to the performance of services.

Such economic growth or development, which requires above all stability of the national currency and the discipline of monetary and fiscal policies to keep inflation in check, calls also for an optimum of foreign trade. It is generally agreed that the promotion of peaceful relations in this turbulent and dynamic world requires economic development in all countries, particularly those with still predominantly rural living conditions. This development in formerly colonial and other industrially retarded countries is definitely needed for

*Slightly condensed from the English version of his first address as a foreign member of the Académie d'Agriculture of France, delivered in Paris in French, May 27, 1964. Reprinted from *The Freeman*, March 1965

the healthy development of the advanced nations, because industrial economies maintain growth and stability by a reliable flow of essential raw materials.

The Need for Leadership

Of all the conditions for increasing the income of the people in the world's rural countries, by far the most strategic are continued healthy and stable growth of the leading industrial countries and their avoidance of prolonged economic stagnation or contraction. Any idea of accelerating growth in underdeveloped countries by sapping the strength of industrial nations belongs in the moth-eaten fabric of ideas of Marxian determinism and the fata morgana of the dictatorially-ruled "paradise for all proletarians." Since these grand ideas have been tried for close to 40 years in a laboratory experiment with several hundred million people, they have lost their luster and gaudy colors.

Today, the economies of industrial and developing countries are mutually interdependent, as is the guardianship of peaceful cohabitation of nations. Hence, while the industrial countries need an adequate and growing flow of primary material from developing countries, they will pay for these, as well as for manufactured goods from light industries, by exporting to those countries an increasing volume of manufactured producer and consumer goods, and will also help them to industrialize gradually.

If this mutually beneficial exchange is to flourish, all nations must act in accordance with their optimal comparative advantage, i.e., the opportunity to produce and sell at lower unit costs. To let this principle work requires optimal diminution or removal of hindrances to trade expansion, not only import quotas and customs duties but the whole arsenal of nontariff trade impediments in lieu of duties.

All the proposed solutions have one common denominator. They suggest that, by setting up international and regional world-wide administrative machinery to control and regulate prices for optimal financial liquidity of developing countries, the pace of raising the income of the poorest people in the most agrarian countries can be accelerated at will, and that more perfect equity and justice in distribution among independent nations can be attained.

Perhaps the most persuasive and yet the most dubious proposal to remedy the instability of foreign exchange earnings of developing countries is the device of international commodity agreements, abbreviated in the literature as ICA. This form of intervention in the international market for primary commodities is an excellent example that makes clear where the generating power originates that drives a national economy, and how complex and delicate a self-adjusting system the market economy actually is. When I speak of the market economy, I do not mean a laissez-faire system with no rules, but a competitive private enterprise economy with effective enforcement by the government of regulations, quality standards, and rules for competition.

International commodity agreements are arrangements between contracting governments, aimed at preventing precipitous price declines of a primary commodity on the world market, in order to avoid serious balance of payment and illiquidity problems for the governments of the exporting countries. But the attempt to forestall disastrous price declines also demands that brakes be put on too steeply rising prices, because such increases may unduly stimulate expansion of production, with resulting sharp price declines later.

This remedy for price instability consists basically of a type of market intervention that was adopted in the late twenties and early thirties on the European continent, in the United States, and in other parts of the world: farm income support through guaranteed minimum prices for specified agricultural commodities. These price support policies amount to a compulsory government-controlled cartel, with innumerable variations in detail. Since more than 30 years of experience with this policy have accrued in the industrially advanced countries and in the world market, it is relevant for our discussion to summarize the *modus operandi* and the economic results of this remedial counteraction to price instability.

Once the government supports the price of a commodity, the price can theoretically still move, but only above the so-called "floor" or guaranteed minimum. By political compromise this level is deliberately set above equilibrium, which by definition is the price that would clear the market. The politically set level is meant to be remunerative to the high cost or marginal producers, the low income farmers on whose behalf price stabilization is mainly established. It is therefore unavoidable that the price, and the elimination of any risk of its change by government guarantee, will act as a forceful incentive, especially to efficient producers, to expand the area for the specific crop. To counteract this the government imposes an area limit, the so-called "acreage allotment." Some sort of base is needed for its determination; usually a historical base is chosen, such as each farmer's actual average acreage of the crop cultivated in several base years. However, the common experience in all countries is that the combination of a profitable guaranteed price with the acreage allotment acts as a still more effective incentive for increasing output per unit of land on limited acreage by more intensive farming. More fertilizer, better seed, more irrigation, better pest and weed control, more cultivation, and various other methods are used. Hence, the government has to buy and store more grain to keep the price at the support level.

The Sorry Results

Up to this point the results of this intervention are already remarkable:

1. There is no longer any mobility of the geographical location of production. It is frozen from the moment the allotments are established.

2. The unintentionally subsidized intensification of production has created surpluses that exceed effective demand.

3. Therefore, the government has to finance and operate storage of commodity stockpiles.

4. Hence, the government at taxpayers' expense has entered the commodity business.

5. The price can no longer move upward but is tightly pinned to the "floor." Instead of a price support or the guarantee of a minimum price, one has a fixed, totally inflexible price.

6. This fixed price still governs producers, processors, everybody in the trade chain, and consumers. The price signals are set in false position for all of them. Although an excess supply exists, everybody can act only according to the price which indicates shortage, namely by consuming less, by substituting other commodities. The processors and the speculative trade reduce stock carrying because the government keeps the excess stocks at public expense.

7. In other words: without any intent to do so, the government has socialized stock carrying.

8. As a further result, the most effective commodity price and supply stabilizing institution, the commodity exchange with its trading in future delivery contracts, is made idle.

However, even those are by no means all the side effects. The Treasury has to pay for moving the commodity into and out of storage and for storing it, as well as for losses when the surplus is disposed of. Thus, there are innumerable secondary beneficiaries of stockpiling excess output, such as railroads, truckers, labor union members, and many others. All these receivers of windfalls acquire a vested interest in maintaining farm price supports. Much worse is the fact that the market in farm real estate discounts the subsidy-earning value of the acreage allotment. Hence, price stabilization of farm products boosts the value of farm land; in due time higher land prices and rents on leased land increase the costs of farming and force more intensive use. This is another unintentional side effect.

Marketing Quotas Assigned

When the excess production begins to bleed the Treasury too badly, the next step is to tighten the cartel by efforts to control the supply in the market. In addition to the acreage allotment the government imposes on all farms a marketing quota, which is established by subdividing a national quota prorated in accordance with individual acreage allotments. This national quota is fixed by a precarious government estimate of how large the domestic consumption and the net export may be one year later. Since the marketing quota tends to be smaller than the output, it immediately poses the problem of a black market and the necessity of suppressing it by heavy penalties. Output that exceeds the marketing quota can be stored, converted, or consumed by the farmer, but it cannot be marketed legally. Even in countries with a customarily law-abiding farm population, the temptation to profit by disposing of such illegal supply by barter or other black deals is strong, and actual enforcement is difficult.

The cartel price-fixing for agricultural commodities also unintentionally subsidizes increased production of the same commodity in other countries. Price-fixing thus creates effective competition abroad. Since it is politically unpopular and difficult to lower the guaranteed price level even when costs of production are declining, stabilization by political decision is practically identical with "stabilizing upward."

Finally, the greatest ordeal for the government agency responsible for operating the cartel is the obligation to dispose of the accumulated excess stocks so as not to undermine the fixed price. Such disposal would be simple if it were done by destroying the supply. Grain could be burned or dumped in the ocean, although even this costs money. But powerful social, moral, and political taboos prevent this solution for any major nonperishable food commodity. Only in the case of coffee in Brazil was destruction used as a market-corrective action. Therefore, the government must seek to release the excess of staple food commodities in foreign countries as gifts, on credit, or with lowered prices. Except for the gifts, this amounts to dumping, and has a deleterious impact upon producers in the recipient country, and secondarily on the exporting country's foreign markets and on its foreign economic relations.

A Commodity in Quarantine Still Affects the Market

It is a psychological fact that a commodity kept off the market by a government, in quarantine, so to say, is still a powerful factor influencing both the price and the actions of all parties in the market. Grain "in jail" is still grain, because if it is not destroyed it will in due time appear as market supply.

National commodity markets are a remarkably effective system of communicating vessels in which millions of interested consumers, retailers, wholesalers, speculators, and farmers keep the flow going. The idea of inserting into the market, via detours, major quantities of supply, under perfect quarantine or segregated from the ordinary supply, belongs in the realm of fiction. Only private charity distribution can minimize the impact on the market. Even the ably administrated food stamp plan of the late thirties in the United States proved that free food did not cause additional consumption of food, but actually subsidized consumption of other goods and services. To change the determined consumer's preference in his family budget decisions takes far more than free distribution of goods, the more so the poorer and prouder he is.

The cartel operation produces still other undesirable side effects. In many instances, particularly for industrial raw material products in agriculture such as cotton, jute, hemp, and sisal, the raised fixed price gives the greatest incentive to producers of substitutes. This exerts pressure on consumption of the original product, say cotton, at the expense of the farmer, whose marketing quota will be cut if national consumption shrinks.

The industrial temperate zone countries, which make a virtue out of the backwash of domestic political necessity and subsidize exports of agricultural raw materials such as cotton, thereby slide to the next necessity of granting more subsidies. Manufacturers of cotton textiles, who have to compete in the foreign market as well as in the domestic one, now need a subsidy to restore equal raw material costs. And so there are three recipients of subsidies: the farmer; the exporter of the farm product; and the manufacturer who uses the raw material.

However, I have not nearly exhausted the appalling record of unforeseen and unwanted distortions of economic processes caused by government intervention that attempts to remedy instability of commodity prices. Subsidized surplus disposal by gifts diverted to other countries can assist private charity that reaches the destitute, the sick, and helpless widows and orphans. But it cannot cure the causes of poverty. Only increased productivity on farms, in craftshops, in factories, and in the wholesale and retail trade can do that. It is here that the disposal of surpluses from abroad does its greatest harm. The majority of people in underdeveloped countries are small farmers who earn their cash income by selling farm commodities. Dumping such commodities in their market may be a boon to some of their customers in the cities, but the farmers resent it, and it diminishes the incentive for them to produce more.

One Control Leads to Others

I have yet to give the reasons why I believe that, whatever action may be taken to mitigate the impact of unstable commodity prices on the balance of payments of developing countries, the International Commodity Agreement method is not only inadequate and dubious but outright harmful to the best interests of the developing countries and to world trade in general. Basically, the sobering experience of sovereign governments of advanced nations with this enigmatic cartel policy in their national markets applies also to the immeasurably more difficult situation in the international commodity market.

The worst feature of all market intervention with price fixing is that, while dealing with one commodity or a few closely related commodities, this inevitably changes the relations between the price of the regulated commodity and the prices of all other commodities and services. The insertion of one rigid price into a range of flexibile prices for some 160 or 170 agricultural products is like a boy who knows nothing about the meaning or the effects of the different positions turning switches at the control board of an automated factory. The far-reaching adjustments that farmers and all other affected parties must make to the accidental price relationships caused by fixing the price of one commodity are unpredictable. Therefore, such isolated treatment of the price mechanism for one country contributes more uncertainty tomorrow than there was instability prior to price fixing. The case for all such trouble-multiplying cures rests on the assertion that the adjustment of supply and demand under the rule of flexible prices does not function—an assertion that contradicts all evidence and economic experience.

The intent of stabilization is realized so long as the stabilization is upward. When, however, larger stocks have been accumulated and their disposal is unavoidable, the same consequences arise as in the case of price supports in domestic markets. Necessity commands that besides regular commercial sales, concessional sales be undertaken, or part of the supply be given away. This procedure leads to serious disorganization and corrosion of markets. The United States, with $6 billion worth of agricultural exports, disposes of over 30 per cent in the form of concessional deals. This is not done on principle. Far from it. It is simply the accumulated backwash of an ill-chosen method of social income support.

Enforcement of ICA regulations is even more difficult than is enforcement in single countries. When one begins to speak of "policing the markets of coffee beans," I wonder how one dares suggest the feasibility of such control in vast areas where the United Nations is faced with the problem of preventing the murder of rural people by armed bands.

Problems of the Board

Aside from the dubious state of effective government administration, a serious question is whether competing countries can possibly agree on export or production quotas and thus freeze the geographical location of production, or administer shifts in location. The board of an ICA must try to achieve principles of equity and justice for all signatory parties to the multigovernment cartel. Originally, commodity agreements included exporting countries only and thus represented producer interests exclusively. They led to defensive policies by importing countries and their effect was nullified. Naturally, the enthusiasm of producers diminished as consumers won equal representation on ICA boards. Yet, without importing governments, such cartels are doomed.

Today, all such agreements include major importing as well as exporting countries. This demands far more wisdom than the fairest and ablest board possesses. Suppose one exporter earns 80 per cent of foreign exchange from the commodity, another 20 per cent. When quota restrictions are necessary to raise the price, will the exports from both countries be cut by the same percentage? If not, what principle shall determine the degree of discrimination and the number of years it shall last? If drastic changes in costs of production or handling or transportation of the regulated commodity occur, which apply to one or more countries but not to all, shall all nevertheless receive the same price? If the commodity comprises a range of qualities, with lower grades produced at disproportionately lower costs, shall quotas treat all the same? Such questions indicate that ICA's are bound to end up with all kinds of soft political compromises on the main points of control over supply and even of price arrangements.

As soon as there is a serious contingency of substitution for the commodity by other natural, processed, or synthetic products, ICA price stabilization begins to sound the death knell for the original commodity. I indicated earlier that in many cases price supports operate, via detours of economic processes, to the long-run detriment of the cartelized producers. To prove my point that ICA's may become deadly poison I have only to mention the cases of rubber, wool, linseed oil, or tungnut oil.

Natural rubber was one of the commodities on which price stabilization ideas were tested in a world-wide experiment under Dutch and British management. The attempted producer-exporter cartel was mainly instrumental in pushing rubber plantations into other tropical areas, in stimulating experiments with other latex-yielding crops, and in boosting synthetic production of plastomers with large government subsidies in industrial countries. To kill the remaining industrial use of linseed oil, tungnut oil, or soybean oil, one need only fix the prices internationally.

Five ICA's are at present in existence: on wheat, sugar, coffee, olive oil, and tin. Only four, excluding olive oil, are important. The one for wheat is proclaimed by its supporters the outstanding success. It can be proved beyond discussion that the ICA's for wheat, sugar, and coffee amount to no more than sanctimonious declarations of good intentions. They have neither stabilized the incomes of the exporting countries nor avoided the whole range of unintentional distortions of world trade that do far more harm than good. Insofar as the wheat agreement has given some semblance of stabilizing price—though not income—it was due to the fact that the governments of the United States and Canada shouldered the burden of carrying the gigantic excess stocks. But both governments have had to enter into a multitude of noncommercial disposal arrangements that violate the principles of truly competitive international trade.

There is one little defect in all plans for administering economic progress at specified growth rates, which the econometricians usually fail to mention: no genius, no power in this world, has the ability to forecast the future supply, the demand, or the price for any commodity, or to predict the performance of one or of many national economies one, three, or five years from now. The most fabulous computers have not changed this situation one bit. We now know much faster and more accurately what has happened up to today. But as to the future, we get the wrong guesstimates also much faster, and with more scientistic trimming.

Restrictive compulsory cartel policies that raise prices to benefit high cost producers and artificially throttle output and supply to maintain such arbitrarily fixed prices, belong in the tool chest of the static society and its dirigism. Such policies are technically possible, but they are the antithesis of what the dynamic economy of an open and free humane society requires.

I expect much sound development in those primary material exporting countries that succeed in taming the monster inflation and, relying on their producers' ability to compete, pave the way for sound private investment of foreign capital, as the transfer of funds from government to government diminishes.

History of Economic Thought

61. THE FORMATION AND FUNCTION OF PRICES*

Hans F. Sennholz

For almost two thousand years economic investigation was handicapped by the common notion that economic exchange is fair only as long as each party gets exactly as much as he gives the other. This notion of equality in exchange even permeated the writings of the classical economists.

Back in the 1870's the Englishman Jevons, the Swiss Walras, and the Austrian Menger irrefutably exploded this philosophical foundation. The Austrian School, especially, built a new foundation on the cognition that economic exchange results from a *difference in individual valuations*, not from an equality of costs. According to Menger, "the principle that leads men to exchange is the same principle that guides them in their economic activity as a whole; it is the endeavor to insure the greatest possible satisfaction of their wants." Exchange comes to an end as soon as one party to the exchange should judge both goods of equal value.

In the terminology of the economists, the value of a good is determined by its marginal utility. This means that the value of a good is determined by the importance of the least important want that can be satisfied by the available supply of goods. A simple example first used by Boehm-Bawerk, the eminent Austrian economist, may illustrate this principle.

A pioneer farmer in the jungle of Brazil has just harvested five sacks of grain. They are his only means of subsistence until the next harvest. One sack is absolutely essential as the food supply which is to keep him alive. A second sack is to assure his full strength and complete health until the next harvest. The third sack is to be used for the raising of poultry which provides nutriment in the form of meat. The fourth sack is devoted to the distilling of brandy. And finally, after his modest personal wants are thus provided for, he can think of no better use for his fifth sack than to feed it to a number of parrots whose antics give him some entertainment.

It is obvious that the various uses to which the grain is put do not rank equally in importance to him. His life and health depend on the first two sacks, while the fifth and last sack "at the margin" has the least importance or "utility." If he were to lose this last sack, our frontier farmer would suffer a loss of well-being no greater than the pleasure of parrot entertainment. Or, if he should have an opportunity to trade with another frontiersman who happens to pass his solitary log cabin, he will be willing to exchange one sack for any other good that in his judgment exceeds the pleasure of parrot entertainment.

But now let us assume that our frontier farmer has a total supply of only three sacks. His valuation of any one sack will be the utility provided by the third and last sack, which affords him the meat. Loss of any one of three sacks would be much more serious, its value and price therefore much higher. Our farmer could be induced to exchange this sack only if the usefulness of the good he is offered would exceed the utility derived from the consumption of meat.

And finally, let us assume that he possesses only a single sack of grain. It is obvious that any ex-

*From a lecture given in Guatemala and Costa Rica, November 1964. Reprinted from *The Freeman*, February 1965

change is out of the question as his life depends on it. He would rather fight than risk loss of this sack.

The Law of Supply and Demand

This discussion of the principles of valuation is not merely academic. In a highly developed exchange economy these principles explain the familiar observation that the value and price of goods vary inversely to their quantity. The larger the supply of goods the lower will be the value of the individual good, and vice versa. This elementary principle is the basis of the price doctrine known as the *law of supply and demand*. Stated in a more detailed manner, the following factors determine market prices: the value of the desired good according to the subjective judgment of the buyer and his subjective value of the medium of exchange; the subjective value of the good for the seller and his subjective value of the medium of exchange.

In a given market there can be only *one* price. Whenever businessmen discover discrepancies in prices of goods at different locations, they will endeavor to buy in the lower-price markets and sell in the higher-price markets. But these operations tend to equalize all prices. Or, if they discover discrepancies between producers' goods prices and the anticipated prices of consumers' goods, they may embark upon production in order to take advantage of the price differences.

Value and price constitute the very foundation of the economics of the market society, for it is through value and price that the people give purpose and aim to the production process. No matter what their ultimate motivation may be, whether material or ideal, noble or base, the people judge goods and services according to their suitability for the attainment of their desired objectives. They ascribe value to consumers' goods and determine their prices. And according to Boehm-Bawerk's irrefutable "imputation theory," they even determine indirectly the prices of all factors of production and the income of every member of the market economy.

The prices of the consumers' goods condition and determine the prices of the factors of production: land, labor, and capital. Businessmen appraise the production factors in accordance with the anticipated prices of the products. On the market, the price and remuneration of each factor then emerges from the bids of the competing highest bidders. The businessmen, in order to acquire the necessary production factors, outbid each other by bidding higher prices than their competitors. Their bids are limited by their anticipation of the prices of the products.

The pricing process thus reveals itself as a social process in which all members of society participate. Through buying or abstaining from buying through cooperation and competition, the millions of consumers ultimately determine the price structure of the market and the allocation of the income of each individual.

Prices Are Production Signals

Market prices direct economic production. They determine the selection of the factors of production, particularly the land and resources that are employed—or left unused. Market prices are the essential signals that provide meaning and direction to the market economy. The entrepreneurs and capitalists are merely the consumers' agents, and must cater to their wishes and preferences. Through their judgments of value and expressions of price, the consumers decide what is to be produced and in what quantity and quality; where it is to be produced and by whom; what method of production is to be employed; what material is to be used; and they make numerous other decisions. Indeed, the baton of price makes every member of the market economy a conductor of the production process.

Prices also direct investments. True, it may appear that the businessman determines the investment of savings and the direction of production. But he does not exercise this control arbitrarily, as his own desires dictate. On the contrary, he is guided by the prices of products. Where lively demand assures or promises profitable prices, he expands his production. Where prices decline, he restricts production. Expansion and contraction of production tend to alternate until an equilibrium has been established between supply and demand. In final analysis, then, it is the consumer—not the businessman—who determines the direction of production through his buying or abstention from buying.

If, for instance, every individual member of the market society were to consume all his income, then the demand for consumers' goods would determine prices in such a way that businessmen would be induced to produce consumers' goods only. The stock of capital goods will stay the same, provided people do not consume more than their income. If they consume more, the stock of capital goods is necessarily diminished.

If, on the other hand, people save part of their incomes and reduce consumption expenditures, the prices of consumption goods decline. Businessmen thus are forced to adjust their production to the changes demanded. Let us assume that people, on the average, save 25 per cent of their incomes. Then, businessmen, through the agency of prices, would assign only 75 per cent of production to immediate consumption and the rest to increasing capital.

Our knowledge of prices also discloses the most crucial shortcoming of socialism and the immense superiority of the market order. Without the yardstick of prices, economic calculation is impossible. Without prices, how is the economic planner to calculate the results of production? He cannot compare the vast number of different materials, kinds of labor, capital goods, land, and methods of production with the yields of production. Without the price yardstick, he cannot ascertain whether certain procedures actually increase the productivity and output of his system. It is true, he may calculate in kind. But such a calculation permits no value comparison between the costs of production and its yield. Other socialist substitutes for the price denominator, such as the calculation of labor time, are equally spurious.

Government Interference with Prices

Economic theory reveals irrefutably that government intervention causes effects that tend to be undesirable, even from the point of view of those who design that intervention. To interfere with prices, wages, and the rates of interest through government orders and prohibitions is to deprive the people of their central position as sovereigns of the market process. It compels entrepreneurs to obey government orders rather than the value judgments and price signals of consumers. In short, government intervention curtails the economic freedom of the people and enhances the power of politicians and government officials.

The price theory also explains the various other economic problems of socialism and the interventionist state. It explains, for instance, the unemployment suffered in the industrial areas, the agricultural surpluses accumulated in government bins and warehouses; it even explains the gold and dollar shortages suffered by many central banks all over the world.

The market price equates the demand for and the supply of goods and services. It is the very function of price to establish this equilibrium. At the free market price, anyone willing to sell can sell, and anyone willing to buy can buy. Surpluses or shortages are inconceivable where market prices continuously adjust supply and production to the demand exerted by the consumers.

But whenever government by law or decree endeavors to raise a price, a surplus inevitably results. The motivation for such a policy may indeed be laudable: to raise the farmers' income and improve their living conditions. But the artificially high price causes the supply to increase and the demand to decline. A surplus is thus created, which finds some producers unable to sell their goods at the official price. This very effect explains the $8 billion agricultural surplus now held by the U.S. Government.

It also explains the chronic unemployment of some 5 million people in the United States. For political and social reasons and in attempted defiance of the law of supply and demand, the U.S. Government has enacted minimum wage legislation that is pricing millions of workers right out of the market. The minimum wage is set at $1.25 per hour—to which must be added approximately 30¢ in fringe costs such as social security, vacations and paid holidays, health, and other benefits—so that the minimum employment costs of an American worker exceed $1.55 an hour. But in the world of economic reality, there are millions of unskilled workers, teenagers, and elderly workers whose productivity rates are lower than this minimum. Consequently, no businessman will employ them unless he is able to sustain continuous losses on their employment. In fact, these unfortunate people are unemployable as long as the official minimum wage exceeds their individual productivity in the market. This kind of labor legislation, even when conceived in good intentions, has bred a great variety of problems which give rise and impetus to more radical government intervention.

Money Problems Explained

The price theory also explains most money problems in the world. For several years after World War II, many underdeveloped countries suffered a chronic gold and dollar shortage. And in recent years, the United States itself has had serious balance-of-payments problems, which are reflected in European countries as a dollar flood.

No matter what the official explanations may be, our knowledge of prices provides us with an understanding of these international money problems. Price theory reveals the operation of "Gresham's Law," according to which an inflated depreciated currency causes gold to leave the country. Gresham's Law merely constitutes the monetary case of the general price theory, which teaches that a shortage inevitably results whenever the government fixes an official price that is below the market price. When the official exchange ratio between gold and paper money understates the value of gold, or overstates the paper, a shortage of gold must inevitably emerge.

And finally, our knowledge of the nature of prices and of the consequences of government interference with prices also explains the "shortages" of goods and services suffered in many countries. Whether the interference is in the form of emergency or wartime controls, international commodity agreements, price stops, wage stops, rent stops, or "usury laws" that artificially limit the yield of capital—and whether they are imposed on the people of America, Africa, Asia, or Europe—government controls over prices control and impoverish the people. And yet, omnipotent governments all over the world are bent on substituting threats and coercion for the laws of the market.

62. THE CONSUMER THEORY OF PROSPERITY*

John Stuart Mill

Among the mistakes [of the preclassical writers] which were most pernicious in their direct consequences . . . was the immense importance attached to consumption. The great end of legislation in matters of national wealth . . . was to create consumers. . . . This object, under the varying names of an extensive demand, a brisk circulation, a great expenditure of money, and sometimes *totidem verbis* a large consumption, was conceived to be the great condition of prosperity.

It is not necessary, in the present state of the science, to contest this doctrine in the most flagrantly absurd of its forms or of its applications. The utility of a large government expenditure for the purpose of encouraging industry is no longer maintained. . . .

In opposition to these palpable absurdities, it was triumphantly established by political economists that consumption never needs encouragement. . . . The person who saves his income is no less a consumer than he who spends it: he consumes it in a different way; it supplies food and clothing to be consumed, tools and materials to be used, by productive laborers. Consumption, therefore, already takes place to the greatest extent which the amount of production admits of; but, of the two kinds of consumption, reproductive and unproductive, the former alone adds to the national wealth, the latter impairs it. What is consumed for mere enjoyment is gone; what is consumed for reproduction leaves commodities of equal value, commonly with the addition of a profit. The usual effect of the attempts of government to encourage consumption is merely to prevent saving; that is, to promote unproductive consumption at the expense of reproductive, and diminish the national wealth by the very means which were intended to increase it.

What a country wants to make it richer is never consumption, but production. Where there is the latter, we may be sure that there is no want of the former. To produce, implies that the producer desires to consume; why else should he give himself useless labor? He may not wish to consume what he himself produces, but his motive for producing and selling is the desire to buy. Therefore, if the

*Excerpts selected by Henry Hazlitt for quotation in *The Failure of the "New Economics"* (Princeton: D. Van Nostrand, 1959) from Mill's *Essays on Some Unsettled Questions of Political Economy* (1830)

producers generally produce and sell more and more, they certainly also buy more and more.

From what has been already said, it is obvious that periods of "brisk demand" are also the periods of greatest production: the national capital is never called into full employment but at those periods. This, however, is no reason for desiring such times; it is not desirable that the whole capital of the country should be in full employment. For, the calculations of producers and traders being of necessity imperfect, there are always some commodities which are more or less in excess, as there are always some which are in deficiency. If, therefore, the whole truth were known, there would always be some classes of producers contracting, not extending, their operations. If *all* are endeavoring to extend them, it is a certain proof that some general delusion is afloat.

The commonest cause of such delusion is some general, or very extensive, rise of prices (whether caused by speculation or by the currency) which persuades all dealers that they are growing rich. And hence, an increase of production really takes place during the progress of depreciation, as long as the existence of depreciation is not suspected. . . . But when the delusion vanishes and the truth is disclosed, those whose commodities are relatively in excess must diminish their production or be ruined: and if during the high prices they have built mills and erected machinery, they will be likely to repent at leisure.

Unreasonable hopes and unreasonable fears alternately rule with tyrannical sway over the minds of a majority of the mercantile public; general eagerness to buy and general reluctance to buy, succeed one another in a manner more or less marked, at brief intervals. Except during short periods of transition, there is almost always either great briskness of business or great stagnation; either the principal producers of almost all the leading articles of industry have as many orders as they can possible execute, or the dealers in almost all commodities have their warehouses full of unsold goods.

General Superabundance

In this last case, it is commonly said that there is a general superabundance; and as those economists who have contested the possibility of general superabundance would none of them deny the possibility or even the frequent occurrence of the phenomenon which we have just noticed, it would seem incumbent on them to show that the expression to which they object is not applicable to a state of things in which all or most commodities remain unsold, in the same sense in which there is said to be a superabundance of any one commodity when it remains in the warehouses of dealers for want of a market.

Whoever offers a commodity for sale desires to obtain a commodity in exchange for it, and is therefore a buyer by the mere fact of his being a seller. The sellers and the buyers, for all commodities taken together, must, by the metaphysical necessity of the case, be an exact equipoise to each other; and if there be more sellers than buyers of one thing, there must be more buyers than sellers for another.

This argument is evidently founded on the supposition of a state of barter; and, on that supposition, it is perfectly incontestable. When two persons perform an act of barter, each of them is at once a seller and a buyer. He cannot sell without buying. Unless he chooses to buy some other person's commodity, he does not sell his own.

If, however, we suppose that money is used, these propositions cease to be exactly true. . . . Interchange by means of money is therefore, as has been often observed, ultimately nothing but barter. But there is this difference—that in the case of barter, the selling and the buying are simultaneously confounded in one operation; you sell what you have, and buy what you want, by one indivisible act, and you cannot do the one without doing the other.

Now the effect of the employment of money, and even the utility of it, is that it enables this one act of interchange to be divided into two separate acts or operations; one of which may be performed now, and the other a year hence, or whenever it shall be most convenient. Although he who sells, really sells only to buy, he need not buy at the same moment when he sells; and he does not therefore necessarily add to the *immediate* demand for one commodity when he adds to the supply of another. The buying and selling being now separated, it may very well occur that there may be, at some given time, a very general inclination to sell with as little delay as possible, accompanied with an equally general inclination to defer all purchases as long as possible.

This is always actually the case, in those periods which are described as periods of general excess. And no one, after sufficient explanation, will contest the possibility of general excess, in this sense of the word. The state of things which we have just described, and which is of no uncommon occurrence, amounts to it.

For when there is a general anxiety to sell, and a general disinclination to buy, commodities of all kinds remain for a long time unsold, and those which find an immediate market do so at a very low price. . . . There is stagnation to those who are not obliged to sell, and distress to those who are. . . .

In order to render the argument for the impossibility of an excess of all commodities applicable to the case in which a circulating medium is employed, money must itself be considered as a commodity. It must, undoubtedly, be admitted that there cannot be an excess of all other commodities, and an excess of money at the same time.

But those who have, at periods such as we have described, affirmed that there was an excess of all commodities, never pretended that money was one of these commodities; they held that there was not an excess, but a deficiency of the circulating medium. What they called a general superabundance, was not a superabundance of commodities relatively to commodities, but a superabundance of all commodities relatively to money.

What it amounted to was, that persons in general, at that particular time, from a general expectation of being called upon to meet sudden demands, liked better to possess money than any other commodity. Money, consequently, was in request, and all other commodities were in comparative disrepute. In extreme cases, money is collected in masses, and hoarded; in the milder cases, people merely defer parting with their money, or coming under any new engagements to part with it. But the result is, that all commodities fall in price, or become unsalable. . . .

It is, however, of the utmost importance to observe that excess of all commodities, in the only sense in which it is possible, means only a temporary fall in their value relatively to money. To suppose that the markets for all commodities could, in any other sense than this, be overstocked, involves the absurdity that commodities may fall in value relatively to themselves.

The argument against the possibility of general overproduction is quite conclusive, so far as it applies to the doctrine that a country may accumulate capital too fast; that produce in general may, by increasing faster than the demand for it, reduce all producers to distress. This proposition, strange to say, was almost a received doctrine as lately as thirty years ago; and the merit of those who have exploded it is much greater than might be inferred from the extreme obviousness of its absurdity when it is stated in its native simplicity.

It is true that if all the wants of all the inhabitants of a country were fully satisfied, no further capital could find useful employment; but, in that case, none would be accumulated. So long as there remain any persons not possessed, we do not say of subsistence, but of the most refined luxuries, and who would work to possess them, there is employment for capital. . . . Nothing can be more chimerical than the fear that the accumulation of capital should produce poverty and not wealth, or that it will ever take place too fast for its own end. Nothing is more true than that it is produce which constitutes the market for produce, and that every increase of production, if distributed without miscalculation among all kinds of produce in the proportion which private interest would dictate, creates, or rather constitutes its own demand.

This is the truth which the deniers of general overproduction have seized and enforced. . . .

The essentials of the doctrine are preserved when it is allowed that there cannot be permanent excess of production, or of accumulation; though it be at the same time admitted, that as there may be a temporary excess of any one article considered separately, so may there of commodities generally, not in consequence of overproduction, but of a want of commercial confidence.

63. OF THE DEMAND OR MARKET FOR PRODUCTS*

Jean Baptiste Say

It is common to hear adventurers in the different channels of industry assert, that their difficulty lies not in the production, but in the disposal of commodities; that products would always be abundant, if there were but a ready demand, or market for them. When the demand for their commodities is slow, difficult, and productive of little advantage, they pronounce money to be scarce; the grand object of their desire is, a consumption brisk enough to quicken sales and keep up prices. But ask them what peculiar causes and circumstances facilitate the demand for their products, and you will soon perceive that most of them have extremely vague notions of these matters; that their observation of facts is imperfect, and their explanation still more so; that they treat doubtful points as matter of certainty, often pray for what is directly opposite to their interests, and importunately solicit from authority a protection of the most mischievous tendency.

To enable us to form clear and correct practical notions in regard to markets for the products of industry, we must carefully analyse the best established and most certain facts, and apply to them the inferences we have already deduced from a similar way of proceeding; and thus perhaps we may arrive at new and important truths, that may serve to enlighten the views of the agents of industry, and to give confidence to the measures of governments anxious to afford them encouragement.

A man who applies his labour to the investing of objects with value by the creation of utility of some sort, cannot expect such a value to be appreciated and paid for, unless where other men have the means of purchasing it. Now, of what do these means consist? Of other values of other products, likewise the fruits of industry, capital, and land. Which leads us to a conclusion that may at first sight appear paradoxical, namely, that it is production which opens a demand for products.

Should a tradesman say, "I do not want other products for my woollens, I want money," there could be little difficulty in convincing him that his customers could not pay him in money, without having first procured it by the sale of some other commodities of their own. "Yonder farmer," he may be told, "will buy your woollens, if his crops be good, and will buy more or less according to their abundance or scantiness; he can buy none at all, if his crops fail altogether. Neither can you buy his wool nor his corn yourself, unless you contrive to get woollens or some other article to buy withal. You say, you only want money; I say, you want other commodities, and not money. For what, in point of fact, do you want the money? Is it not for the purchase of raw materials or stock for your trade, or victuals for your support?[1] Wherefore, it is products that you want, and not money. The silver coin you will have received on the sale of your own products, and given in the purchase of those of other people, will the next moment execute the same office between other contracting parties, and so from one to another to infinity; just as a public vehicle successively transports objects one after another. If you can not find a ready sale for your commodity, will you say, it is merely for want of a vehicle to transport it? For, after all, money is but the agent of the transfer of values. Its whole utility has consisted in conveying to your hands the value of the commodities, which your customer has sold, for the purpose of buying again from you; and the very next purchase you make, it will again convey to a third person the value of the products you may have sold

*In this chapter from Say's principal work, first published 1803 in French, *A Treatise on Political Economy* (the 5th American edition, 1832) he presents his "Law of the Markets." He explains here that supply creates its own demand, that every good or service provides its producer with some purchasing power. Thus widespread economic depression cannot be due to a general scarcity of money nor to general over-production.

to others. So that you will have bought, and every body must buy, the objects of want or desire, each with the value of his respective products transformed into money for the moment only. Otherwise, how could it be possible that there should now be bought and sold in France five or six times as many commodities, as in the miserable reign of Charles VI? Is it not obvious, that five or six times as many commodities must have been produced, and that they must have served to purchase one or the other?"

Slow Sales Not Due to Scarcity of Money

Thus, to say that sales are dull, owing to the scarcity of money, is to mistake the means for the cause; an error that proceeds from the circumstance, that almost all produce is in the first instance exchanged for money, before it is ultimately converted into other produce: and the commodity, which recurs so repeatedly in use, appears to vulgar apprehensions the most important of commodities, and the end and object of all transactions, whereas it is only the medium. Sales cannot be said to be dull because money is scarce, but because other products are so. There is always money enough to conduct the circulation and mutual interchange of other values, when those values really exist. Should the increase of traffic require more money to facilitate it, the want is easily supplied, and is a strong indication of prosperity —a proof that a great abundance of values has been created, which it is wished to exchange for other values. In such cases, merchants know well enough how to find substitutes for the product serving as the medium of exchange or money:[2] and money itself soon pours in, for this reason, that all produce naturally gravitates to that place where it is most in demand. It is a good sign when the business is too great for the money; just in the same way as it is a good sign when the goods are too plentiful for the warehouses.

When a superabundant article can find no vent [cannot be sold], the scarcity of money has so little to do with the obstruction of its sale, that the sellers would gladly receive its value in goods for their own consumption at the current price of the day: they would not ask for money, or have any occasion for that product, since the only use they could make of it would be to convert it forthwith into articles of their own consumption.[3]

This observation is applicable to all cases, where there is a supply of commodities or of services in the market. They will universally find the most extensive demand in those places, where the most of values are produced; because in no other places are the sole means of purchase created, that is, values. Money performs but a momentary function in this double exchange; and when the transaction is finally closed, it will always be found, that one kind of commodity has been exchanged for another.

Production Creates Purchasing Power

It is worth while to remark, that a product is no sooner created, than it, from that instant, affords a market for other products to the full extent of its own value. When the producer has put the finishing hand to his product, he is most anxious to sell it immediately, lest its value should diminish in his hands. Nor is he less anxious to dispose of the money he may get for it; for the value of money is also perishable. But the only way of getting rid of money is in the purchase of some product or other. Thus, the mere circumstance of the creation of one product immediately opens a vent for other products.

For this reason, a good harvest is favourable, not only to the agriculturist, but likewise to the dealers in all commodities generally. The greater the crop, the larger are the purchases of the growers. A bad harvest, on the contrary, hurts the sale of commodities at large. And so it is also with the products of manufacture and commerce. The success of one branch of commerce supplies more ample means of purchase, and consequently opens a market for the products of all the other branches; on the other hand, the stagnation of one channel of manufacture, or of commerce, is felt in all the rest.

But it may be asked, if this be so, how does it happen, that there is at times so great a glut of commodities in the market, and so much difficulty in finding a vent for them? Why cannot one of these superabundant commodities be exchanged for another? I answer that the glut of a particular commodity arises from its having outrun the total demand for it in one or two ways; either because it has been produced in excessive abundance, or because the production of other commodities has fallen short.

It is because the production of some commodities has declined, that other commodities are superabundant. To use a more hackneyed phrase, people have bought less, because they have made less profit;[4] and they have made less profit for one or two causes; either they have found difficulties in the employment of their productive means, or these means have themselves been deficient.

It is observable, moreover, that precisely at the same time that one commodity makes a loss, another commodity is making excessive profit.[5] And, since such profits must operate as a powerful stimulus to the cultivation of that particular kind of products, there must needs be some violent means, or some extraordinary cause, a political or natural convulsion, or the avarice or ignorance of authority, to perpetuate this scarcity on the one hand, and consequent glut on the other. No sooner is the cause of this political disease removed, than the means of production feel a natural impulse towards the vacant channels, the replenishment of which restores activity to all the others. One kind of production would seldom outstrip every other, and its products be disproportionately cheapened, were production left entirely free.[6]

Should a producer imagine, that many other classes, yielding no material products, are his customers and consumers equally with the classes that raise themselves a product of their own; as, for example, public functionaries, physicians, lawyers, churchmen, &c., and thence infer, that there is a class of demand other than that of the actual producers, he would but expose the shallowness and superficiality of his ideas. A priest [priests then were supported at least in part by taxes] goes to a shop to buy a gown or a surplice; he takes the value, that is to make the purchase, in the form of money. Whence had he that money? From some tax-gatherer who has taken it from a taxpayer. But whence did this latter derive it? From the value he has himself produced. This value, first produced by the taxpayer, and afterwards turned into money, and given to the priest for his salary, has enabled him to make the purchase. The priest stands in the place of the producer, who might himself have laid the value of his product on his own account, in the purchase, perhaps, not of a gown or surplice, but of some other more serviceable product. The consumption of the particular product, the gown or surplice, has but supplanted that of some other product. It is quite impossible that the purchase of one product can be affected, otherwise than by the value of another.[7]

From this important truth may be deduced the following important conclusions:

1. *That, in every community the more numerous are the producers, and the more various their productions, the more prompt, numerous, and extensive are the markets for those productions;* and by a natural consequence, the more profitable are they to the producers; for price rises with the demand. But this advantage is to be derived from real production alone, and not from a forced circulation of products; for a value once created is not augmented in its passage from one hand to another, nor by being seized and expended by the government, instead of by an individual. The man, that lives upon the productions of other people, originates no demand for those productions; he merely puts himself in the place of the producer, to the great injury of production, as we shall presently see.

2. *That each individual is interested in the general prosperity of all, and that the success of one branch of industry promotes that of all the others.* In fact, whatever profession or line of business a man may devote himself to, he is the better paid and the more readily finds employment, in proportion as he sees others thriving equally around him. A man of talent, that scarcely vegetates in a retrograde state of society, would find a thousand ways of turning his faculties to account in a thriving community that could afford to employ and reward his ability. A merchant established in a rich and populous town, sells to a much larger amount than one who sets up in a poor district, with a population sunk in indolence and apathy. What could an active maufacturer, or an intelligent merchant, do in a small deserted and semi-barbarous town in a remote corner of Poland or Westphalia? Though in no fear of a competitor, he could sell but little, because little was produced; whilst at Paris, Amsterdam, or London, in spite of the competition of a hundred dealers in his own line, he might do business on the largest scale. The reason is obvious: he is surrounded with people who produce largely in an infinity of ways, and who make purchases, each with his respective products, that is to say, with the money arising from the sale of what he may have produced.

This is the true source of the gains made by the town's people out of the country people, and again by the latter out of the former; both of them have wherewith to buy more largely, the more amply they themselves produce. A city, standing in the centre of a rich surrounding country, feels no want of rich and numerous customers; and, on the other hand, the vicinity of an opulent city gives additional value to the produce of the country. The division of nations into agricultural, manufacturing, and commercial, is idle enough. For the success of a people in agriculture is a stimulus to its manufacturing and commercial prosperity; and the flourishing condition of its manufacture and commerce reflects a benefit upon its agriculture also.[8]

The position of a nation, in respect of its neighbours, is analogous to the relation of one of its provinces to the others, or of the country to the town; it has an interest in their prosperity, being sure to profit by their opulence. The government of the United States, therefore, acted most wisely, in their attempt, about the year 1802, to civilize their savage neighbours, the Creek Indians. The design was to introduce habits of industry amongst them, and make them producers capable of carrying on a barter trade with the States of the Union; for there is nothing to be got by dealing with a people that have nothing to pay. It is useful and honourable to mankind, that one nation among so many should conduct itself uniformly upon liberal principles. The brilliant results of this enlightened policy will demonstrate, that the systems and theories really destructive and fallacious, are the exclusive and jealous maxims acted upon by the old European governments, and by them most impudently styled *practical truths,* for no other reason, as it would seem, than because they have the misfortune to put them in practice. The United States will have the honour of proving experimentally, that true policy goes hand-in-hand with moderation and humanity.[9]

3. *From this fruitful principle, we may draw this further conclusion, that it is no injury to the internal or national industry and production to buy and import commodities from abroad;* for nothing can be bought from strangers, except with native products, which find a vent in this external traffic. Should it be objected, that this foreign produce may have been bought with specie, I answer, specie is not always a native product, but must have been bought itself with the products of native industry; so that, whether the foreign articles be paid for in specie or in home products, the vent for national industry is the same in both cases.[10]

4. *The same principle leads to the conclusion, that the encouragement of mere consumption is no benefit to commerce;* for the difficulty lies in supplying the means, not in stimulating the desire of consumption; and we have seen that production alone, furnishes those means. Thus, it is the aim of good government to stimulate production, of bad government to encourage consumption.

The Law of Markets

For the same reason that the creation of a new product is the opening of a new market for other products, the consumption or destruction of a product is the stoppage of a vent for them. This is no evil where the end of the product has been answered by its destruction, which end is the satisfying of some human want, or the creation of some new product designed for such a satisfaction. Indeed, if the nation be in a thriving condition, the gross national re-production exceeds the gross consumption. The consumed products have fulfilled their office, as it is natural and fitting they should; the consumption, however, has opened no new market, but just the reverse.[11]

Having once arrived at the clear conviction, that the general demand for products is brisk in proportion to the activity of production, we need not trouble ourselves much to inquire towards what channel of industry production may be most advantageously directed. The products created give rise to various degrees of demand, according to the wants, the manners, the comparative capital, industry, and natural resources of each country; the article most in request owing to the competition of buyers, yields the best interest of money to the capitalist, the largest profits to the adventurer, and the best wages to the labourer; and the agency of their respective services is naturally attracted by these advantages towards those particular channels.

In a community, city, province, or nation, that produces abundantly, and adds every moment to the sum of its products, almost all the branches of commerce, manufacture, and generally of industry, yield handsome profits, because the demand is great, and because there is always a large quantity of products in the market, ready to bid for new productive services. And, *vice versa,* wherever, by reason of the blunders of the nation or its government, production is stationary, or does not keep pace with consumption, the demand gradually declines, the value of the product is less than the charges of its production; no productive exertion is properly rewarded; profits and wages decrease; the employment of capital becomes less advantageous and more hazardous; it is consumed piecemeal, not through extravagance, but through necessity, and because the sources of profit are dried up.[12] The labouring classes experience a want of work; families before in tolerable circumstances, are more cramped and confined; and those before in difficulties are left altogether destitute. Depopulation, misery, and returning barbarism, occupy the place of abundance and happiness.

Such are the concomitants of declining production, which are only to be remedied by frugality, intelligence, activity, and freedom.

Notes

[1]Even when money is obtained with a view to hoard or bury it, the ultimate object is always to employ it in a purchase of some kind. The heir of the lucky finder uses it in that way, if the miser does not; for money, as money, has no other use than to buy with.

[2]By bills at sight, or after date, bank-notes, running-credits, write-offs, &c. as at London and Amsterdam.

[3]I speak here of their aggregate consumption, whether unproductive and designed to satisfy the personal wants of themselves and their families, or expended in the sustenance of reproductive industry. The woollen or cotton manufacturer operates a two-fold consumption of wool and cotton: (1) for his personal wear; (2) for the supply of his manufacture; but, be the purpose of his consumption what it may, whether personal gratification or reproduction, he must needs buy what he consumes with what he produces.

[4]Individual profits must, in every description of production, from the general merchant to the common artisan, be derived from the participation in the values produced.

[5]The reader may easily apply these maxims to any time or country he is acquainted with. We have had a striking instance in France during the years 1811, 1812, and 1813; when the high prices of colonial produce of wheat, and other articles, went hand-in-hand with the low price of many others that could find no advantageous market.

[6]These considerations have hitherto been almost wholly overlooked, though forming the basis of correct conclusions in matters of commerce, and of its regulation by the national authority. The right course where it has, by good luck, been pursued, appears to have been selected by accident or, at most, by a confused idea of its propriety, without either self-conviction or the ability to convince other people.

Sismondi [the Swiss historian] seems not to have very well understood the principles laid down in this work. He cites the immense quantity of manufactured products with which England has of late inundated the markets of other nations as a proof that it is possible for industry to be too productive. But the glut thus occasioned proves nothing more than the feebleness of production in those countries that have been thus glutted with English manufactures. If Brazil produced wherewithal to purchase the English goods exported thither, those goods would not glut her market. Were England to admit the import of the products of the United States, she would find a better market for her own in those States. The English government, by the exorbitance of its taxation upon import and consumption, virtually interdicts to its subjects many kinds of importation, thus obligating the merchant to offer to foreign countries a higher price for those articles, whose import is practicable, as sugar, coffee, gold, silver, &c. for the price of the precious metals to them is enhanced by the low price of their commodities, which accounts for the ruinous returns of their commerce.

I would not be understood to maintain in this chapter, that one product can not be raised in too great abundance, in relation to all others; but merely that nothing is more favourable to the demand of one product, than the supply of another; that the import of English manufactures into Brazil would cease to be excessive and be rapidly absorbed, if Brazil produce on her side returns sufficiently ample; to which end it would be necessary that the legislative bodies of either country should consent, the one to free production, the other to free importation. In Brazil every thing is grasped by monopoly, and property is not exempt from the invasion of the government. In England, the heavy duties are a serious obstruction to the foreign commerce of the nation, inasmuch as they circumscribe the choice of returns. I happen myself to know of a most valuable and scientific collection of natural history, which could not be imported from Brazil into England by reason of the exorbitant duties.

[The views of *Sismondi*, in this particular, have been since adopted by our own Thomas Malthus, and those of our author by David Ricardo. This difference of opinion had given rise to an interesting discussion between our author and Malthus, to whom he has recently addressed a correspondence on this and other parts of the science. . . . Translator]

[7]The capitalist, in spending the interest of his capital, spends his portion of the products raised by the employment of that capital. Should he ever spend the principal, still he consumes products only; for capital consists of products, devoted indeed to reproductive, but susceptible of unproductive consumption; to which it is in fact consigned whenever it is wasted or dilapidated.

[8]A productive establishment on a large scale is sure to animate the industry of the whole neighbourhood. "In Mexico," says Alexander Humboldt [German scientist and explorer], "the best cultivated tract, and that which brings to the recollection of the traveller the most beautiful part of French scenery, is the level country extending from Salamanca as far as Silao, Guanaxuato, and Villa de Leon, and encircling the richest mines of the known world. Wherever the veins of precious metal have been discovered and worked, even in the most desert part of the Cordilleras, and in the most barren and insulated spots, the working of the mines, instead of interrupting the business of superficial cultivation, has given it more than usual activity. The opening of a considerable vein is sure to be followed by the immediate erection of a town; farming concerns are established in the vicinity; and the spot so lately insulated in the midst of wild and desert mountains, is soon brought into contact with the tracts before in tillage."

[9]It is only by the recent advances of political economy, that these most important truths have been made manifest, not to vulgar apprehension alone, but even to the most distinguished and enlightened observers. We read in Voltaire that "such is the lot of humanity, that the patriotic desire for one's country's grandeur, is but a wish for the humiliation of one's neighbours;—that it is clearly impossible for one country to gain, except by the loss of another." *Dictionnaire Philosophique*. By a continuation of the same false reasoning, he goes on to declare, that a thorough citizen of the world cannot wish his country to be greater or less, richer or poorer. It is true, that he would not desire her to extend the limits of her dominion, because, in so doing, she might endanger her own well-being; but he will desire her to progress in wealth, for her progressive prosperity promotes that of all other nations.

[10]This effect has been sensibly experienced in Brazil of late years. The large imports of European commodities, which the freedom of navigation directed to the markets of Brazil, has been so favourable to its native productions and commerce, that Brazilian products never found so good a sale. So there is an instance of a national benefit arising from importation. By the way, it might have perhaps been better for Brazil if the prices of her products and the profits of her producers had risen more slowly and gradually; for exorbitant prices never lead to the establishment of a permanent commercial intercourse; it is better to gain by the multiplication of one's own products than by their increased price.

[11]If the barren consumption of a product be of itself adverse to re-production, and a diminution *pro tanto* of the existing de-

mand or vent for produce, how shall we designate that degree of insanity, which would induce a government deliberately to burn and destroy the imports of foreign products, and thus to annihilate the sole advantage accruing from unproductive consumption, that is to say, the gratification of the wants of the consumer?

[12]Consumption of this kind gives no encouragement to future production, but devours products already in existence. No additional demand can be created, until there be new products raised; there is only an exchange of one product for another. Neither can one branch of industry suffer without affecting the rest.

64. MARX'S VIEW OF THE DIVISION OF LABOR*

Gary North

The division of labor is a subject which has fascinated social scientists for millennia. Before the advent of modern times, philosophers and theologians concerned themselves with the implications of the idea. Plato saw as the ultimate form of society a community in which social functions would be rigidly separated and maintained; society would be divided into definite functional groups: warriors, artisans, unskilled laborers, rulers. St. Paul, in his first letter to the church at Corinth, went so far as to describe the universal Church in terms of a body: there are hands, feet, eyes, and all are under the head, Christ. Anyone who intends to deal seriously with the study of society must grapple with the question of the division of labor. Karl Marx was no exception.

Marx was more than a mere economist. He was a social scientist in the full meaning of the phrase. The heart of his system was based on the idea of human *production*. Mankind, Marx asserted, is a totally autonomous species-being, and as such man is the sole creator of the world in which he finds himself. A man cannot be defined apart from his labor: "As individuals express their life, so they are. What they are, therefore, coincides with their production, both with *what* they produce and with *how* they produce."[1] The very fact that man rationally organizes production is what distinguishes him from the animal kingdom, according to Marx. The concept of production was a kind of intellectual "Archimedean point" for Marx. Every sphere of human life must be interpreted in terms of this single idea: "Religion, family, state, law, science, art, etc., are only *particular* modes of production, and fall under its general law."[2] Given this total reliance on the concept of human labor, it is quite understandable why the division of labor played such an important role in the overall Marxian framework.

Property vs. Labor

Marx had a vision of a perfect human society. In this sense, Martin Buber was absolutely correct in including a chapter on Marx in his *Paths in Utopia*. Marx believed in the existence of a society which preceded recorded human history. In this world, men experienced no sense of alienation because there was no alienated production. Somehow (and here Marx was never very clear) men fell into patterns of alienated production, and from this, private property arose.[3] Men began to appropriate the products of other men's labor for their own purposes. In this way, the very products of a man's hands came to be used as a means of enslaving him to another. This theme, which Marx announced as early as 1844, is basic to all of Marx's later economic writings.

Under this system of alienated labor, Marx argued, man's very life forces are stolen from him. The source of man's immediate difficulty is, in this view, the division of labor. The division of labor was, for Marx, the very essence of all that is wrong with the world. It is contrary to man's real essence. The division of labor pits man against his fellow man; it creates class differences; it destroys the unity of the human race. Marx had an almost theological concern with the unity of mankind, and

*Adapted from *Marx's Religion of Revolution* (Nutley, New Jersey: Craig Press, 1968). Reprinted from *The Freeman*, January 1969

his hostility to the division of labor was therefore total (even totalitarian).

Class Warfare

Marx's analysis of the division of labor is remarkably similar to Rousseau's.[4] Both argued that the desire for private property led to the division of labor, and this in turn gave rise to the existence of separate social classes based on economic differences. The Marxist analysis of politics relies completely upon the validity of this assumption. Without economic classes, there would be no need for a State, since a State is, by definition, nothing more than an instrument of social control used by the members of one class to suppress the members of another.[5] Thus, when the proletarian revolution comes, the proletarian class must use the State to destroy the remnants of bourgeois capitalism and the ideology of capitalism. The opposition must be stamped out; here is the meaning of the famous "ten steps" outlined in the *Communist Manifesto*. Once the opposition is totally eradicated, there will be no more need for a State, since only one class, the proletariat, will be in existence. "In place of the old bourgeois society, with its classes and class antagonisms, we shall have an association in which the free development of each is the condition for the development of all."[6]

Marx actually believed that in the communist society beyond the Revolution, the division of labor would be utterly destroyed. All specialization would disappear. This implies that for the purposes of economic production and rational economic planning, all men (and all geographical areas) are created equal. It is precisely this that Christians, conservatives, and libertarians have always denied. Marx wrote in *The German Ideology* (1845-46):

> . . . in communist society, where nobody has one exclusive sphere of activity but each can become accomplished in any branch he wishes, society regulates the general production and thus makes it possible for me to do one thing today and another tomorrow, to hunt in the morning, fish in the afternoon, rear cattle in the evening, criticize after dinner, just as I have a mind, without ever becoming hunter, fisherman, shepherd or critic.[7]

A Utopian Ideal

A more utopian ideal cannot be encountered in serious economic literature. While some commentators think that Marx later abandoned this radical view, the evidence supporting such a conclusion is meager. Marx never explicitly repudiated it (although the more outspoken Engels did, for all intents and purposes). Even if Marx had abandoned the view, the basic problems would still remain. How could a communist society abandon the specialization of labor that has made possible the wealth of modern industrialized society and at the same time retain modern mass production methods? How could the communist paradise keep mankind from sliding back into the primitive, highly unproductive, unskilled, low capital intensity production techniques that have kept the majority of men in near starvation conditions throughout most of human history?

The whole question of economic production "beyond the Revolution" was a serious stumbling stone for Marx. He admitted that there would be many problems of production and especially distribution during the period of the so-called "dictatorship of the proletariat." This period is merely the "first phase of communist society as it is when it has just emerged after prolonged birth pangs from capitalist society."[8] Marx never expected great things from this society. However, in the "higher phase of communist society," the rule of economic justice shall become a reality: "From each according to his ability, to each according to his needs!"[9] This will be easy to accomplish, since the vast quantities of wealth which are waiting to be released will be freed from the fetters and restraints of capitalist productive techniques. As Mises has pointed out, "Tacitly underlying Marxian theory is the nebulous idea that natural factors of production are such that they need not be economized."[10] Maurice Cornforth, the Marxist philosopher, confirms Mises' suspicion that Marxists see all scarcity as a product of institutional defects rather than as a basic fact of the order of the world in which we live:

> The eventual and final abolition of shortages constitutes the economic condition for entering upon a communist society. When there is socialized production the products of which are socially appropriated, when science and scientific planning have resulted in the production of absolute abundance, and when labour has been so enlightened and organized that all can without sacrifice of personal inclinations contribute their working abilities to the common fund, everyone will receive a share according to his needs.[11]

Who Shall Plan?

A critical problem for the Marxist is the whole question of communist planning: How is production to be directed? By what standards should the society allocate scarce resources? Whatever Marx's personal dreams were concerning the abolition of scarcity, resources are not in infinite supply. It is because of this very fact that society must *plan* production. Marx saw this activity as basic to the definition of man, yet this very activity implies the existence of scarcity, a peculiar paradox for Marxism. The fact remains that automobiles do not grow on trees. Someone must decide how many automobiles should be produced in comparison with the number of refrigerators. Planning is inherent in all economic production, and Marx recognized this: "Modern universal intercourse can be controlled by individuals, therefore, only when controlled by all."[12] But how can they "all" register their preferences? If there is no private property (and, therefore, no free market economy), and if there is no State planning—no political planning—then who decides which goods are to be produced and which goods are not? Murray Rothbard has stated this dilemma quite accurately:

> Rejecting private property, especially capital, the Left Socialists were then trapped in an inner contradiction: if the State is to disappear after the Revolution (immediately for Bakunin, gradually "withering" for Marx), then how is the "collective" to run its property without becoming an enormous State itself, in fact even if not in name? This was the contradiction which neither the Marxists nor the Bakunists were ever able to resolve.[13]

The Problem of Scarcity

The need to coordinate production implies the existence of scarcities which the production is designed to alleviate. If everyone had all he desired at the moment of wanting it, production would be unnecessary. Raw materials must be fashioned into goods or indirectly into services, and these goods shipped from place to place. Such actions require *time* (interest on the investment of capital goods), *planning* (profit for success and loss for *failure*), and *labor* (wages). In short, *production* demands *planning*. No society is ever faced with the problem "to plan or not to plan." The issue which confronts society is the question of *whose* plan to use. Karl Marx denied the validity of the free market's planning, since the free market is based upon the private ownership of the means of production, including the use of money. Money, for Marx, is the crystallized essence of alienated production; it is the heart of capitalism's dynamism. It was his fervent hope to abolish the use of money forever.[14] At the same time, he denied the validity of centralized planning by the State. How could he keep his "association" from becoming a State? The Fabian writer, G. D. H. Cole, has seen clearly what the demand for a classless society necessitates: "But a classless society means, in the modern world, a society in which the distribution of incomes is collectively controlled, as a political function of society itself. It means further that this controlled distribution of incomes must be made on such a basis as to allow no room for the growth of class differences."[15] In other words, given the necessity of a political function in a supposedly stateless world, how can the Marxists escape the warning once offered by Leon Trotsky: "In a country where the sole employer is the State, opposition means death by slow starvation. The old principle: who does not work shall not eat, has been replaced by a new one: who does not obey shall not eat."[16]

Ultimately, the acceptance of the existence of scarcity must be a part of any sane social analysis. In contrast to this Rousseauian-Marxian view of the division of labor stands both the traditional Christian view and the libertarian view of Professor Mises. Men have a natural propensity to consume. If unrestrained, this tendency might result in looting, destruction, and even murder.

The Need to Produce

The desire to consume must be tempered by a willingness to produce, and to exchange the fruits of production on a value for value received basis. Each person then consumes only what he has earned, while extending the same right to others. One of the chief checks on men's actions is the fact of economic scarcity. In order to extract from a resisting earth the wealth that men desire, they are forced to cooperate. Their cooperation can be voluntary, on a free market, or it can be enforced from above by some political entity.

Scarcity makes necessary an economic division of labor. Those with certain talents can best serve their own interests and society's interests by concentrating their activities in the areas of production in which they are most efficient. Such specialization is required if productivity is to be increased. If men wish to have more material goods and greater personal services, they must choose occupations in which they can become effective producers. Those who favor a free market arrangement argue that each man is better equipped than some remote board of supervisors to arrange his own affairs and choose his own calling according to his desires, talents, and dreams. But whether the State directs production or the demand of a free market, the specialization of labor is mandatory. This specialization promotes social harmony; the division of labor forces men to restrain their hostile actions against each other if they wish to have effective, productive economic cooperation.

In this perspective, the division of labor promotes social unity without requiring collective uniformity. It acknowledges the existence of human differences, geographical differences, and scarcity; in doing so, it faces the world in a realistic fashion, trying to work out the best possible solution in the face of a fundamental, inescapable condition of man. In short, the cause of economic scarcity is not the "deformed social institutions" as the socialists and Marxists assert; it is basic to the human condition. While this does not sanction total specialization, since man is not a machine, it does demand that men acknowledge the existence of reality. It does demand that the division of labor be accepted by social theorists as a positive social benefit.[17]

A Faulty Premise

Anyone who wishes to understand why the Marxian system was so totally at odds with the nineteenth century world, and why it is so completely unworkable in practice, can do no better than examine Marx's attitude toward the division of labor. It becomes obvious why he always shied away from constructing "blueprints for the communist paradise" and concentrated on lashing the capitalist framework: his view of the future was utopian. He expected man to be regenerated by the violence of the Revolution. The world beyond would be fundamentally different: there would be no scarcity, no fighting, and ultimately, no evil. The laws of that commonwealth would not be comformable with the laws that operate under bourgeois capitalism. Thus, for the most part, Marx remained silent about the paradise to come. He had to. There was no possible way to reconcile his hopes for the future with the reality of the world. Marx was an escapist; he wanted to flee from time, scarcity, and earthly limitations. His economic analysis was directed at this world, and therefore totally critical; his hopes for the future were utopian, unrealistic, and in the last analysis, *religious*. His scheme was a religion—a religion of revolution.

Notes

[1] *The German Ideology* (London: Lawrence & Wishart, 1965), p. 32.

[2] "Private Property and Communism," *The Economic and Philosophic Manuscripts of 1844*, edited by Dirk J. Struik (New York: International Publishers, 1964), p. 136.

[3] "Estranged Labor," *ibid.*, pp. 116-17.

[4] J. J. Rousseau, *Discourse on the Origin of Inequality*, in G. D. H. Cole (ed.), *The Social Contract and Discourses* (London: Dent, 1966), esp. pp. 195-208. Cf. Robert A. Nisbet, "Rousseau and Totalitarianism," *Journal of Politics*, V (1943), pp. 93-114.

[5] *German Ideology*, pp. 44-45.

[6] *The Communist Manifesto* (1848), in *Marx-Engels Selected Works* (Moscow: Foreign Languages Publishing House, 1962), I, p. 54. For a critique of this view of the State, see my study, *Marx's Religion of Revolution* (Nutley, New Jersey: Craig Press, 1968), p. 112.

[7] *German Ideology*, pp. 44-45.

[8] *Critique of the Gotha Program* (1875), in *Marx-Engels Selected Works*, II, p. 24. This is one of the few places in which Marx presented some picture of the post-Revolutionary world.

[9] *Ibid.*

[10] Ludwig von Mises, *Socialism* (New Haven: Yale, [1922] 1951; London: Jonathan Cape, 1969), p. 164.

[11] Maurice Cornforth, *Marxism and the Linguistic Philosophy* (New York: International Publishers, 1965), p. 327.

[12] *German Ideology*, p. 84.

[13] Murray N. Rothbard, "Left and Right: The Prospects for Liberty," *Left and Right*, I (1965), p. 8.

[14] "On the Jewish Question," (1843-44), in T. B. Bottomore, *Karl Marx: Early Writings* (New York: McGraw-Hill, 1964), pp. 34-40.

[15] G. D. H. Cole, *The Meaning of Marxism* (Ann Arbor: University of Michigan Press, [1948] 1964), p. 249.

[16] Leon Trotsky, *The Revolution Betrayed* (1936), quoted by F. A. Hayek, *The Road to Serfdom* (University of Chicago Press, 1944), p. 119.

[17] Mises, *Socialism*, pp. 60-62.

65. THE FALLACY OF "INTRINSIC VALUE"*

Gary North

If people value something, it has value; if people do not value something, it does not have value; and there is no intrinsic about it.

RT. HON. J. ENOCH POWELL, M.P.

"Ideas die hard," says an old proverb. Even in an age of rapid change such as our own, the slogans, clichés, and errors of earlier times seem to persist, it often seems that the truths that once brought peace, stability, and steady progress are the first things to be abandoned, while the errors persist undaunted. Henry Hazlitt once wrote of John Maynard Keynes that the true things he said were not new, and the new things he said were not true. Yet it is the new aspect of Keynes' "New Economics" that has fascinated today's guild of economists.

The triumph of the slogan is understandable. We are limited creatures. We cannot attain exhaustive knowledge of anything, and certainly not of everything. As a result, we find ourselves at the mercy of the expert; simultaneously, we live our day-to-day lives in terms of ideas that we cannot be continually re-examining. Some things must be accepted on faith or by experience; we have neither the time nor capacity to rethink everything we know. Still, no intelligent person dares to neglect the possibility that his opinion in some area or other may be open to question. At times it is vital that we reconsider a subject, especially if it is a barrier to clear thinking or effective action. If our error is in a realm of life in which we claim to be experts, or at least skilled amateurs, then the necessity of careful reasoning is exceptionally important. The persistence of some erroneous line of reasoning here, simply because this unexamined train of thought is familiar to us, can be disastrous.

Take, for example, the labor theory of value. Classical economics—by which we mean that body of economic thought which was in vogue from the time of Adam Smith (1770's) until the marginalist-subjective schools arose (1870's)—was confounded by the problem of value. It proposed a cause-and-effect relationship between human labor and value: abstract human labor (which itself was an abstract concept derived more from mechanics than human experience) was produced by laborers on their jobs; this abstract human labor was in some way embodied in the products of that labor, and this is the source of all value. Certain inescapable problems arose under this presupposition. Why did selling prices fail to correspond to the total payments made to labor? How did the phenomenon of profit appear? What was the origin of interest? On a more concrete level, why did an uncut diamond bring a higher price on the market than an intricate mechanism like a clock? They could explain the disparity of selling prices of jewels and selling prices of clocks in terms of supply and demand, but their labor theory of value never fitted into this explanation. It was an extraneous issue.

Contradictions of Marx

Karl Marx was the last major economist to hold to the labor theory. In this sense, he was the last of the great classical economists. He wanted to demonstrate that capitalism, by its own internal contradictions, was doomed to a final destruction. Unfortunately for Marx's predictions, what he regarded as a basic set of contradictions of capitalism was merely a set of contradictions in the reasoning of the classical economists. He confused a faulty explanation of the capitalist process with the actual operation of the capitalist system. Ironically, Marx fell into a pit which he always reserved for his enemies: he looked not at the empirical data as such, but at an interpretation of the data—not at the "substructure" of the society, but the

*From *The Freeman*, June 1969

ideological "superstructure." *Das Kapital* was published in 1867; by 1871, the marginalist assault had been launched by Carl Menger of Austria and W. S. Jevons of England. The labor theory of value which had undergirded Marx's whole analysis of capitalism was destroyed. When Boehm-Bawerk, the Austrian economist who was to gain fame as Menger's most rigorous disciple, offered his criticisms of Marx in 1884 (and again in 1896), it was clear (to non-Marxists, anyway) that the Marxian framework had gone down with the classical ship.[1]

What the new theory did was to reverse the cause-and-effect relationship of the classical school. The *value of labor* is derivative: it stems from the *value of labor's product*. This, in turn, is the outcome of supply and demand. People desire certain products; these products are not in unlimited supply in relation to the demand. Or, to put it another way, at zero price, some of the demand is left unsatiated. The value of the product is not derived from labor; the reverse is true. Thus, value is not something intrinsic to either the labor or the product; value is *imputed* by acting men. Value is not a metaphysically existing substance; an object is simply valued (passive) by someone who actively values it. Marx always chided capitalist thinkers for making a "fetishism of commodities," i.e., ascribing to economic goods a life of their own apart from the human and social relations that make possible the creation of the goods. But this is precisely his labor theory of value. It hypothesized the existence of "congealed labor time" which supposedly gives value to commodities. Had he turned to the individuals who actively participate in all economic action he would have been led to abandon his own brand of "commodity fetishism." Marx, the self-proclaimed empiricist, was befuddled by his own *a priori* theory.

Contemporary Errors

Yet we should not be too hasty in ridiculing Marx for his insistence on viewing value as something intrinsic in an economic good. People are so used to thinking in these terms that few of us are free from some variety of this basic error. Homes are seen as containing something called "equity"; factories "possess" investments, almost as if these investments were held in some kind of suspension within the factory walls.[2] The Marxist, of course, has a vested interest in this line of reasoning: the master taught it. Why others continue to indulge in such speculation is a perplexing problem. It is a case where the "common sense" economics of the man in the street is in error.

Conservatives do not like communism. As a result, they are willing to reject the familiar tenets of Marx's economics. Those who have read at least excerpts from *Capital* and who are aware of the labor theory of value are usually willing to abandon the idea. Unfortunately, it would seem that they abandon it in name only, simply because Marx happened to believe it. They have not abandoned the fundamental approach to economics which Marx employed, namely, the fallacy of intrinsic value. The most common application of this erroneous concept, at least in conservative circles, is the idea that gold and silver possess intrinsic value, while paper money does not. This error deserves special attention.

There are a number of reasons why conservatives make this mistake. They are guided by the best of intentions. They see that paper money and bank credit have led in the past and are leading today to virulent inflations. They fear the economic and social dislocations associated with inflation. They may also see that the modern socialist and interventionist states have used inflationary deficit spending policies to increase their power at the expense of private, voluntary associations. Some of the more sophisticated observers may even have understood the link between inflationary policies and depressions—booms and busts—and they may have concluded, quite correctly, that these trade cycles are not endemic to capitalism as such, but only to economic systems that permit policies of inflation.[3] They associate inflation with policies of the state or the state-licensed monopolies, fractional reserve banks, rather than the voluntary market economy. Nevertheless, they persist in defending the use of specie metals as the only currency (along with fully redeemable paper IOU's to specie metals) in terms of the intrinsic value of the metals.

Value: Historic vs. Intrinsic

There is a basic confusion here. The confusion rests on a mixing up of two very different propositions: (1) gold and silver are *historically* valuable; and (2) gold and silver have *intrinsic* value. The first proposition is indisputably correct; in fact there are few economic or historical statements that could be said to be more absolute. Professor Mises has built his whole theory of money on the fact that gold and silver (especially gold) were first valued because of properties other than their monetary function: brilliance, malleability, social prestige, and so forth. It was precisely *because* people valued these metals so highly that they were to become instruments of trade, i.e., money.[4] Since they are so readily marketable, more so than other goods, they can become money.

Today we value silver and gold for many reasons, and on first glance, monetary purposes are not the main ones for most people. That is because so few populations are legally permitted to use gold in trade, and the statist policies of inflation have brought Gresham's famous law into operation: silver coins have gone into hoards, since the value of their silver content is greater than their face value as coins. But on the international markets, gold has not yet been dethroned; governments and central banks do not always trust each other, but they do trust the historic value of gold.

Why this historic value? I do not want to involve myself in a rarefied philosophical debate concerning metaphysics, but I think it is safe to say that gold does have certain intrinsic qualities. It is highly durable, easily divisible, transportable, and most of all, it is *scarce*. Money must be all of these, to one degree or another, if it is to function as a means of exchange. It is vital that we get our categories straight in our minds: *it is not value that is intrinsic to gold, but only the physical properties that are valued by acting men*. Gold's physical properties are the product of nature; its value is the product of acting men.

It would be a terrible mistake, however, to de-emphasize the historic value of gold and silver merely because they possess no intrinsic value. That mistake is the one which the opponents of gold would have us make. They are equally guilty of mixing up the categories of intrinsic value and historic value, only they argue from the other direction. Conservatives appreciate the fact of gold's historic value, but they mistakenly argue their case in terms of gold's intrinsic value. Their opponents do not appreciate the argument from history, but they spend their time refuting the conservatives' erroneous presentation. They assume that because gold has no intrinsic value (true), gold's historic value as a means of exchange is somehow invalidated. The two positions are diametrically opposed, yet they focus on a common ground which is irrelevant to both positions; the conservatives do not help their case for gold by an appeal to intrinsic value, and gold's opponents do not refute the case for gold by demonstrating the error of that appeal.

Gold's overwhelming acceptance historically by most men in most societies is a lasting testimony to its value as a means of exchange. It should not be referred to as "a storehouse of value," as it is in so many textbooks. What we should say is that gold is readily marketable and for that reason a valuable thing to store. This position of gold in history is a self-perpetuating phenomenon: people tend to accept gold because they and others have in the past; they assume that others will be willing to accept gold in exchange for goods in the future. This assumption of *continuity* is basic to all goods that function as money. Continuity is therefore a function of both the physical properties of gold and of men's estimations concerning other men's future valuations. In short, it involves nature, man, and time. In estimating the importance of gold for an economic system's proper functioning, we must take into consideration all three factors, keeping each clear in our minds. This is why we need economic analysis; without it, we wander blindly.

Ignorance in the short run is seldom profitable; in the long run, it is invariably disastrous. Fallacious argumentation can too easily be turned against one by his enemies. Just as Marx used the fallacious labor theory of value against those classical economists who tried to defend the free market in terms of that theory, so the opponents of gold can use the intrinsic value theory against those who try to defend the gold standard with it. This is not to say that logic alone will convince men of the validity of a full gold coin standard; logic is always a tool used by men of varying presuppositions, and these are in turn the product of pre-theoretical valuations. We should not trust in logic to save the world. But ignorance is far worse: it knows neither its presuppositions nor the probable results of its arguments. It lacks consistency, it lacks clarity, and it can be turned against its user by the enemy. Therefore, let the defenders of the gold standard acknowledge the advent of modern, subjectivist economic reasoning. Let us face the fact that if Boehm-Bawerk's refutation of Marx's labor theory of value is valid, then all other applications of the fallacy of intrinsic value are equally invalid.

If we cannot learn to think consistently on this point, then we will be grist for the inflationists' mill. The inflationistic Juggernaut may resemble a charging elephant in our era. It may be too late to stop it with a small caliber rifle, but we know it cannot be stopped with a pop-gun.

Notes

[1] Cf. Gary North, *Marx's Religion of Revolution* (Nutley, New Jersey: Craig Press, 1968), ch. 5, especially pp. 155-70. See also Dean Lipton, "The Man Who Answered Marx" (Reading no. 66).

[2] Cf. Gary North, "Urban Renewal and the Doctrine of Sunk Costs," *The Freeman* (May, 1969).

[3] I have summarized this neo-Austrian theory of the trade cycle in my essay, "Repressed Depression," *The Freeman* (April, 1969).

[4] Ludwig von Mises, *The Theory of Money and Credit* (New Haven, Conn.: Yale University Press, [1912] 1953; FEE, 1971), pp. 109 ff.

66. THE MAN WHO ANSWERED MARX*

Dean Lipton

It is a safe bet that for every million persons who have heard of Karl Marx not more than one or two can recall the name of Eugen von Boehm-Bawerk. In a major sense, this is unfortunate, for Boehm-Bawerk was the man who answered Marx.

Nevertheless, it is quite understandable. Marx was primarily a propagandist, a polemicist, a gifted sloganizer. His life story from the time he was the editor of a radical newspaper in Germany to the years he struggled for control of the First International was the deliberate attempt to sway the minds of men. He was a politician in the guise of journalist, philosopher, and economic thinker. About all this, Boehm-Bawerk could not have cared less. He was the dedicated scientist searching for truth. He refined economic ideas and concepts in a way that few others ever had or could. Where Marx borrowed heavily—and uncritically—from any past economist whose ideas could help him prove a point, Boehm-Bawerk would cut away at their falsity, never concerned with anything except arriving at the core of essential truth.

It was, of course, only natural that he would eventually clash with the ideas promoted by Karl Marx. They were starting their ascendant curve during the time Boehm-Bawerk was growing into manhood and beginning to think about the shape of the world, and the principles upon which human freedom and prosperity were based.

Eugen von Boehm-Bawerk was born in 1851. Three years earlier Marx (and his collaborator, Friedrich Engels) had published *The Communist Manifesto* containing the ringing declaration: "WORKERS OF THE WORLD UNITE! YOU HAVE NOTHING TO LOSE BUT YOUR CHAINS." In 1867, when Boehm-Bawerk was just sixteen, there appeared the first volume of *Das Kapital,* the book which was to become the bible of so-called scientific or modern socialism.

Many of the young European intellectuals were swayed by Marxist ideas, but there is no record that Boehm-Bawerk ever was. In part, this was probably due to his teacher and mentor, the famous Carl Menger, who among other things formulated the important theory of marginal utility. At first, Boehm-Bawerk was only one of a group of brilliant, young economists gathered loosely around Menger, originating the renowned "Austrian" school of economics. But, in time, he surpassed them all, becoming the master, the man whose work left the greatest impact. Historically, he and the other "Austrian" economists performed two important and vital functions. First, they made corrections in the inaccuracies they saw in the work of the "Classical" economists, even daring to take on such masters of the past as Adam Smith and David Ricardo. Secondly, they were the main economic critics of Marx and his followers in the closing years of the nineteenth century and the opening years of this one.

There was another curious paradox between Karl Marx and Eugen von Boehm-Bawerk which should be mentioned. The politically-minded Marx never held public office. He was unable even to hold all of his followers, all the men who thought in a general way like him, together in the one enclave he knew was necessary for the quick seizure of power. Proudhon quarreled with the Marxists

*From *The Freeman*, October 1967

during the volatile days of the Paris Commune. The Marxists expelled Bakunin from the International. Lassalle broke with Marx to form his own Socialist party.

The nonpolitical Boehm-Bawerk was appointed Minister of Finance in three different Austrian cabinets (1895, 1897-98, and 1900-04.) But in each instance it was the office seeking the man. Boehm-Bawerk had no political ambitions, but the political leaders of the Austria of his time knew that he had no peers in the fields of economics and finance. The post he enjoyed most was the one he held for a long time as Honorary Professor of Political Economy at the University of Vienna.

Capital and Interest

Even if Boehm-Bawerk had not exposed the Marxist fallacies, his work would have had lasting significance. He was among the first to explore the complicated labyrinth of price fluctuations. Although many have tried, no one has successfully supplanted his two theories of interest. Here, it is only fair to point out that both were hinted at by Nassau William Senior, an English economist, in 1836. However, Senior had left them in an unfinished state, and it was Boehm-Bawerk's work which pointed up their importance.

In the abstinence theory, he demonstrated that interest was compensation for the postponement or waiting for the satisfaction of a person's wants. While this idea may seem commonplace today, it wasn't in Boehm-Bawerk's time. His second theory dealt with the importance of interest to the productive process. He insisted that it was the most efficient way to secure capital investments, stating that even a socialist state would have to make use of it, or some equivalent, if it were to survive economically. The experiences of Soviet Russia in the years immediately following the Russian Revolution proved him right.

In 1894, the final two volumes of Marx's *Das Kapital* were published posthumously. They had been edited from Marx's notes by his long-time associate, Friedrich Engels, and we, of course, have no way of knowing how different they might have been if Marx had lived to do his own editing. However, the chances are reasonably good that the two versions would not have differed in any significant respect. Marx and Engels were intellectual twins. A common thread running through all of their ideas was the "exploitation of labor." According to them, every economic process of a free society was designed to exploit the workingman.

With his usual logical thoroughness, Boehm-Bawerk disposed of this argument in whatever Marxist theory it occurred. Marx argued that interest was derived only by exploiting labor. Boehm-Bawerk answered this contention by pointing out that if interest were the just compensation for saving as he conclusively proved in his abstinence theory, and absolutely essential to the productive processes of a modern industrial nation, it could not be exploitative in the Marxist sense.

Another sample of Marxist reasoning was that all the profits of the entrepreneur and the capitalist were "surplus value" created by labor. If labor had not been exploited, there would be no profit. The corollary to this, of course, was that all so-called "surplus value" should be returned to the worker.

Boehm-Bawerk pointed out that as long as a major part of "surplus value" was re-invested in a nation's industrial capacity—and not used to satisfy the capitalist's or entrepreneur's personal wants—it went back to the people in an ever-rising standard of living. In another one of his uncanny predictions, he foretold that under socialism "surplus value" would not be returned to labor, any more than it was under capitalism. If it were, the socialist nation would lack the means to build or maintain an industrial economy. Again the experiences of both Soviet Russia and Communist China proved him right. In fact, both Russia and China expropriated so much of the worker's product that millions of people were deliberately starved, so that rapid industrialization could be achieved.

Labor Theory of Value Exposed

But it was on the Marxist Labor Theory of Value that Boehm-Bawerk turned the full force of his powerful mind. The idea that labor "created" value did not originate with Marx. Sir William Petty developed something like it two centuries earlier, and Ricardo devised a similar theory. Marx borrowed the Ricardian concept, and added a few sophisticated touches to it. He himself admitted that his whole theoretical structure rested upon the Labor Theory of Value, and that if it could be disproved, "scientific" socialism would be rendered invalid.

After Boehm-Bawerk finished demolishing it, there was not a single major economist who would accept the Labor Theory of Value as anything other than an interesting historical oddity. Even many branches of World Socialism, such as the Fabian Socialists in England, discarded it as untenable.

The "ambiguities and contradictions" in Marx's language offended good sense, Boehm-Bawerk pointed out. Marx claimed that the value of a product was determined by the "socially useful" labor involved in its production. Boehm-Bawerk found the phraseology meaningless, and pointed out that it differed little from Adam Smith's distinction between productive and unproductive labor. Smith had used the artisan as an example of productive labor and the menial servant to illustrate unproductive labor. Boehm-Bawerk stated that if the servant's efforts released his master to perform productive work, then his labor was also productive.

The universal application of Boehm-Bawerk's analysis can be seen by taking the case of a widow with young children who re-enters the labor force as a stenographer. Without someone to care for the children, she would be unable to work, and so the girl she hires as a baby sitter certainly performs productive or essential work.

Utility, Scarcity, and Choice

To demonstrate the validity of the Labor Theory of Value, Marx used the diamond, insisting that it was valuable because of the amount of labor expended to mine it. In other words, a diamond at the bottom of a deep mine shaft requiring the work of many men to dig would be worth more than a diamond found accidentally on the surface of the ground. Quite obviously, any diamond merchant who estimated the worth of a stone on this basis instead of the usual reasons such as the number of carats or its crystalline flawlessness would go out of business in short order.

To Marx, value was a concrete condition created in much the same manner that an article might be manufactured. To Boehm-Bawerk, it was a relative system of measurement depending at any time on external factors. He demonstrated that the Marxist concept failed to take two important elements into consideration: utility (or usefulness) and the nearly-equally important subjective quality of want or desire. Despite the appearing solidity of the Labor Theory of Value, it was nebulous, vague, and unpredictable. It lacked every characteristic that a science was supposed to have. Conversely, the Boehm-Bawerkian law worked with mathematical precision.

It could be summarized into the following formula:

1. Utility is the basis of value.
2. Scarcity is the measure of value.
3. Price is the evidence of value.

Nothing is valuable unless it is in some way or degree useful. The decrease or increase of its value is dependent on the rise or decline of its supply. Valuable goods are costly either in terms of other goods or money. To this he added another factor for the determination of price: the subjective quality of want. If no one wanted an article—no matter how scarce it was—its price could hardly be very great.

The importance of want or desire is self-evident. The more the seller values an article, the higher his asking price will be. The more the buyer wants the article, the more he is willing to pay for it. This, of course, works in reverse. The lower the buyer's personal evaluation of an article, the less he will be willing to pay for it. If a seller places little value on an article, he will be willing to sell it for a low price.

Subjective Value Judgments

Boehm-Bawerk covered all possible criticism before it could be leveled. He did it so well that the Marxists ever since have found themselves in the position of having to answer the unanswerable. Take the way he disposed of any future objection to the utilitarian basis for value in his monumental work, *The Positive Theory of Capital*,[1] for instance. After noting that such infinitely more useful items as bread and water ordinarily are far less valuable than diamonds or pearls, he points out that they only appear to be because under normal circumstances they are in such abundant supply while pearls and diamonds are relatively rare. But when food becomes scarce, the value of a sandwich to a starving man is far greater than that of a large and flawless diamond. A man dying of thirst in the desert will run first to a canteen of water before he even considers the bag of pearls lying a few feet away.

Boehm-Bawerk finally concluded: "Thus those very facts which, at first sight, seemed to contradict our theory that the amount of value is dependent on the amount of utility condition, on closer examination afford a striking confirmation of it."

Note

[1] *The Positive Theory of Capital* is Part II in the 3-part translation of Boehm-Bawerk's *Capital and Interest* (South Holland, Illinois: Libertarian Press, 1959).

Capitalism/The Hampered Market/Socialism

67. A KING OF LONG AGO*

Lewis Love

There once lived a king in a distant land—a just and wise old king, for he had observed and learned much about his people and about himself and his power. His people were free to go their way, and were fearful of the king and his soldiers, for his rule granted no privilege to one that was not a privilege to all equally. And they were free to petition their king and seek his wisdom in their affairs.

Thus there came one day to the royal court an artisan, a mason, and a beggar who was lame.

"O great and wise king," they cried, "we are sorely troubled with our plight." "I," said the artisan, "make many useful goods. I use great skill and labor long, and yet when I am finished, the people will not pay my price."

"And I," said the mason, "am a layer of stone for houses and fine walls, yet I am idle, for no one gives me work."

"I am a poor lame beggar," said the third man, "who seeks alms from those who pass, as they find it in their hearts to do so, but alms are so few as to be of great concern lest I perish."

*From *Rotagraph,* March 16, 1962 (Fort Worth, Texas, Rotary Club). Reprinted from *The Freeman*, July 1962

"I can see that your trouble is great," consoled the king, "and what would you ask of me?"

Then, they spoke as a group, the artisan, the mason, and the beggar who was lame: "Your power is very great, our king, and you can make the people see the folly of their ways and aid us in our troubles."

"Perhaps," said the king, "perhaps my power is great, but I must use it wisely or it shall be lost." And he called to the captain of his guard.

"Bring forth three swords," he commanded, "one for each of these men, and instruct them in their use. These three shall go forth in the land and compel those who will not voluntarily deal with them to obey their command."

"No! no!" the three men called out, "this we did not ask. We are men of honor and could not set upon our fellow man to compel him to our will. This we cannot do. It is you, O king, who must use the power."

"You ask me to do that which you would not do because of honor?" questioned the king. "Is honor one thing to a beggar and another to a king? I, too, am an honorable man, and that which is dishonorable for you will never be less dishonorable for your king."

68. THE COMMUNIST IDEA (PART I)*

Karl Marx and Friedrich Engels

EDITOR'S NOTE: We were warned of the general procedure and the specific measures for a successful communist or socialist revolution by Karl Marx, the "father" of communism, in 1848:

We have seen . . . that the first step in the revolution by the working class is to raise the proletariat to the position of the ruling class; to win the battle of democracy. The proletariat will use its political supremacy to wrest, by degrees, all capital from the bourgeoisie; to centralize all instruments of production in the hands of the State . . .

These measures will, of course, be different in different countries. Nevertheless in the most advanced countries the following will be pretty generally applicable:

1. Abolition of property in land and application of all rents of land to public purposes.
2. A heavy progressive or graduated income tax.
3. Abolition of all right of inheritance.
4. Confiscation of the property of all emigrants and rebels.
5. Centralization of credit in the hands of the State, by means of a national bank with State capital and an exclusive monopoly.
6. Centralization of the means of communication and transport in the hands of the State.
7. Extension of factories and instruments of production owned by the State; the bringing into cultivation of waste lands, and the improvement of the soil generally in accordance with a common plan.
8. Equal liability of all to labor. Establishment of industrial armies, especially for agriculture.
9. Combination of agriculture with manufacturing industries: gradual abolition of the distinction between town and country, by a more equable distribution of the population over the country.
10. Free education for all children in public schools. Abolition of children's factory labor in its present form. Combination of education with industrial production, etc., etc.

*Clipping of Note No. 25 (FEE, 1950). Reprinted from *The Communist Manifesto*

69. THE COMMUNIST IDEA (PART II)*

Earl Browder

State capitalism leaped forward to a new high point in America in the decade 1939-1949. . . . State capitalism, in substance if not in formal aspects, has progressed farther in America than in Great Britain under the Labor Government, despite its nationalization of certain industries, which is a formal stage not yet reached in America; the actual, substantial concentration of the guiding reins of national economy in governmental hands

*Clipping of Note No. 28 (FEE, 1950). Reprinted from *Keynes, Foster and Marx: State Capitalism and Progress* (1950)

is probably on a higher level in the U.S.A.

[*In appraising a list of 22 specific items of American governmental policy, Mr. Browder states:*]

They have the single feature in common that . . . they express *the growth of state capitalism*. . . . [This is] an essential feature of the confirmation of the Marxist theory. . . . It represents the maturing of the objective (material) prerequisites for socialism, the basic factor which makes socialism inevitable. . . .

1. Government deficit financing.
2. Manipulation of bank reserves requirements.
3. Insurance of bank deposits.
4. Guarantee of mortgages.
5. Control of bank credits.
6. Tinkering with the currency system.
7. Regulation of installment buying.
8. Price controls.
9. Price support for farm products.
10. Agricultural credits.
11. R.F.C. loans to business corporations.
12. Social security systems for workers.
13. Various benefits for veterans.
14. Government housing.
15. Public works to provide employment.
16. Many projects for the conservation of natural resources.
17. Juggling of the tax structure.
18. New tariff regulations.
19. Government-organized foreign loans.
20. The Employment Act.
21. The President's economic committee.
22. Last but by no means least, stimulated war armaments production on a large scale.

70. A LESSON IN SOCIALISM*

Thomas J. Shelly

As a teacher in the public schools, I find that the socialist-communist idea of taking "from each according to his ability," and giving "to each according to his need" is now generally accepted without question by most of our pupils. In an effort to explain the fallacy in this theory, I sometimes try this approach with my pupils:

When one of the brighter or harder-working pupils makes a grade of 95 on a test, I suggest that I take away 20 points and give them to a student who has made only 55 points on his test. Thus each would contribute according to his ability and—since both would have a passing mark—each would receive according to his need. After I have juggled the grades of all the other pupils in this fashion, the result is usually a "common ownership" grade of between 75 and 80—the minimum needed for passing, or for survival. Then I speculate with the pupils as to the probable results if I actually used the socialistic theory for grading papers.

First, the highly productive pupils—and they are always a minority in school as well as in life—would soon lose all incentive for producing. Why strive to make a high grade if part of it is taken from you by "authority" and given to someone else?

Second, the less productive pupils—a majority in school as elsewhere—would, for a time, be relieved of the necessity to study or to produce. This socialist-communist system would continue until the high producers had sunk—or had been driven down—to the level of the low producers. At that point, in order for anyone to survive, the "authority" would have no alternative but to begin a system of compulsory labor and punishments against even the low producers. They, of course, would then complain bitterly, but without understanding.

Finally I return the discussion to the ideas of freedom and enterprise—the market economy—where each person has freedom of choice and is responsible for his own decisions and welfare.

Gratifyingly enough, most of my pupils then understand what I mean when I explain that socialism—even in a democracy—will eventually result in a living-death for all except the "authorities" and a few of their favorite lackeys.

*Clipping of Note No. 36 (FEE, 1951)

71. THE TALE OF THE LITTLE RED HEN*

W. A. Paton

(Adapted from earlier versions)

Early one morning the Little Red Hen was out looking for something to eat, and in the course of her search she came upon several plump, fresh kernels of wheat, spilled by somebody in the road. She was just about to swallow them when the thought occurred to her that perhaps she might instead get into the wheat business in a small way by planting the kernels. So she called to some of her farm friends: "Look, I've found some wheat. Who will help me dig up some ground so that we can plant this wheat and raise a crop?"

The "friends" didn't take kindly to the idea. "Not I," quacked the duck. "Not I," honked the goose. "Not I," grunted the pig.

"Well, I will then," said the Little Red Hen. She picked out a nice piece of ground near the fence and worked hard scratching it up into good loose soil. Then she made some holes, well spaced, dropped a kernel in each hole, and filled them carefully with dirt.

The Little Red Hen visited her bit of wheat field every day, pulled out the weeds that came up, used her sprinkling can to water the soil when there wasn't enough rain. Soon the green wheat sprouts broke through the ground and grew into sturdy plants, and finally the stalks and wheat heads appeared and ripened. When the wheat was ready to cut, the Little Red Hen appealed to her "friends" again: "Who will help me cut the wheat and take it to the mill?"

"Not I," said the duck. "Not I," said the goose. "Not I," said the pig.

"Well, I will then," said the Little Red Hen. She cut the wheat stalk by stalk with her shears, bound it into several bundles and carried each bundle on her back over the hill and down by the river to the mill. The miller spread the wheat out on his threshing floor and pounded the heads with his flail until the kernels were all separated from the husks. Then he blew away the straw and chaff and ground the beautiful red wheat into flour. He put the flour in a sack (after taking out his toll for the work he'd done), tied up the sack, and gave it to the Little Red Hen. She carried it on her back all the way home—a long, hard trip. When she had the sack of flour safely in her house, she went out and called to her "friends" once more. "Who will help me make my flour into dough and bake it into bread?"

"Not I," said the duck. "Not I," said the goose. "Not I," said the pig.

"Well, I will then," said the Little Red Hen. She bustled about making the flour into dough, and putting it in her round baking pan. After the dough had risen, she put it in the oven and late in the afternoon she took it out (being careful not to burn herself), and there on the table was a round loaf of the loveliest brown bread anyone ever saw or smelled!

The Little Red Hen then went to the door and—with a bit of a glint in her eye—called out: "Who will help me eat this lovely loaf of bread that I have baked?"

"*I* will," quacked the duck, very loudly, "*I* will," promptly honked the goose. "*I* will," squealed the pig. And all three rushed to the door of the Little Red Hen's house.

But they didn't get any encouragement from that point on. "No," said the Little Red Hen. "I found the wheat; I prepared the soil and planted it; I pulled the weeds and watered the ground when it got too dry; I cut the wheat and carried it all the way to the mill; I carried the flour home myself; I made the flour into dough and baked it. None of you would help until it came time to eat. And I'm going to eat *my own bread* all by myself." She shut the door with a bang, and sat down to a good meal of hot bread, with plenty of butter on it! And it didn't bother her a bit that she was not

*From *The Freeman*, November 1961

sharing the results of her foresight, initiative, and labor with those unwilling to contribute to production but very eager to consume what someone else had produced.

Unfortunately, the fable's ending doesn't square with the facts of life in 1961 America. The duck, the goose, and the pig, constituting a democratic majority, have authorized their income tax collector to take from the very productive little hen up to nine-tenths of the bread she has earned. Added to this ruinous levy there may be a sizable fine to which she is subject for having grown wheat in excess of the quota allowed her under the farm price-support program. Far from enjoying the whole loaf she produced by her own efforts, she'll be lucky in 1961 if her "needy" neighbors leave her as much as a crumb.

72. THE BEETLE AND THE CENTIPEDE*

W. A. Paton

In the cool of the evening, so the story goes, Mr. Beetle and Miss Centipede came out from under the rocks and started to do a bit of gossiping as was the practice among such creatures in the old days.

"Good evening, my dear Miss Centipede," said Mr. Beetle, in his best voice, and "Good evening to you, Mr. Beetle," the lady replied in sprightly fashion.

After some discussion of the weather, the food supply, and the hazards recently encountered, the conversation slowed down and in an effort to keep the visit going Mr. Beetle hit upon a new topic.

"Miss Centipede," he said, "the part of your anatomy that has intrigued me most for a long time—although I don't think I've mentioned it before—is your beautiful array of legs, and I'm also greatly impressed by the marvelous skill you display in manipulating them as you scurry about. I have only six legs to keep track of, but I don't move very briskly and am regarded as rather awkward by all my friends. You, on the other hand, with fifty legs on the right side and fifty more on the left, handle all this equipment with no apparent difficulty, and travel with speed, and most gracefully, in any direction you choose to go, and change your course as you wish without the slightest hesitation. Tell me, my dear Miss Centipede, how in the world do you do it?"

On hearing this little speech Miss Centipede tossed her head and rolled her eyes coquettishly (the reader may need to use a little imagination here), and replied:

"Good Mr. Beetle, you make far too much of something that is really quite simple. I get about smoothly and gracefully—I admit it, you see—because it is actually very easy for me to keep my legs in order and have them respond to my wishes."

Mr. Beetle was not satisfied. "It may seem easy to you," he said, "but your pedal apparatus looks very complicated to me, and I don't see how you can keep from getting tangled up—getting your wires crossed, so to speak—at least occasionally. I wish you'd tell me how you really go about it. Suppose, for example, that you want to move the sixteenth leg on your left side, just how do you issue the proper instructions to accomplish this?"

"There's nothing to it," she said jauntily; "I'll show you." Miss Centipede then tackled the prescribed chore. She twisted and squirmed, went through all sorts of contortions, got up quite a sweat in fact, and all without achieving the desired result. Finally, instead of moving the sixteenth leg on the left she managed a pitiful little twitch of the eleventh leg (counting from the front) on the right.

Mr. Beetle now realized that he had started something that should have been left alone, and as Miss Centipede continued her struggle he became genuinely alarmed.

"Please, Miss Centipede," he begged, "don't

*From *The Freeman*, September 1963

bother your pretty head any longer with my silly inquiry. The matter is of no consequence and I'm afraid you are making yourself ill. We can discuss this some other time."

But Miss Centipede had her back up and according to all the accounts of the episode she kept on trying desperately for an hour or so until she was completely exhausted. But this wasn't the worst of it. When she finally gave up she had become so confused that she couldn't move at all! One writer introduces a dab of verse in telling about this unhappy outcome, somewhat as follows according to my hazy recollection:

She wrought herself to such a pitch
She stretched out, helpless, in the ditch.

And the poor creature was permanently paralyzed thereafter, from all fifty waists down, and finally died of starvation.

This tale has a moral for these days—one that is fairly evident to anyone familiar with and concerned about the impact of the tide of government intervention upon the intricate mechanism of the free market. Among the wonders of human society—perhaps the greatest of them all—is our network of exchange activities and the accompanying mosaic of prices. It is this instrument which has fostered and implemented a truly astonishing degree of specialization in production, and has made available an almost countless array of consumer goods and services. Operating through the price structure, the market acknowledges and integrates the inclinations and choices of millions of individuals, and the system promptly reflects the constantly changing attitudes and circumstances of the host of participants. It is in this connection that the term "miracle" has often been applied to describe the functioning of the free competitive market. Without directives, without government intervention, without central planning, the impersonal forces of the market, acting *automatically*, direct the allocation of resources, appraise the contributions of the productive factors, and distribute the product. But this marvelous mechanism, not anyone's invention but the very essence of economic development and activity, can undoubtedly be crippled and finally wrecked altogether by conscious interference and tinkering. Left alone, with the power of the state confined to checking predatory actions, the market performs wonders in guiding economic conduct; loaded with price fixing, government regulation, bureaucratic intervention and planning, the market apparatus falters and eventually becomes ineffective. In his classes years ago Fred M. Taylor laid great stress on the need for a hands-off policy if the price system were to be effective in directing economic activity, and his favorite admonition in this connection was: "Don't monkey with the thermostat."

The bad results of present-day interference with the market are everywhere apparent, but there are few signs of any abatement of the socialist trend. The planners are twisting and squirming, like Miss Centipede, and each additional effort to control the economy sets up a chain of new contortions and dislocations. But the dedicated interventionists who are now in the saddle don't seem to be afraid of the stagnation and paralysis awaiting them—and the rest of us, unfortunately—at the end of the road.

73. NOT YOURS TO GIVE*

David Crockett

One day in the House of Representatives, a bill was taken up appropriating money for the benefit of a widow of a distinguished naval officer. Several beautiful speeches had been made in its support. The Speaker was just about to put the question when Crockett arose:

"Mr. Speaker—I have as much respect for the memory of the deceased, and as much sympathy for the sufferings of the living, if suffering there

*From *The Life of Colonel David Crockett*, compiled by Edward S. Ellis (Philadelphia: Porter & Coates, 1884)

be, as any man in this House, but we must not permit our respect for the dead or our sympathy for a part of the living to lead us into an act of injustice to the balance of the living. I will not go into an argument to prove that Congress has no power to appropriate this money as an act of charity. Every member upon this floor knows it. We have the right, as individuals, to give away as much of our own money as we please in charity; but as members of Congress we have no right so to appropriate a dollar of the public money. Some eloquent appeals have been made to us upon the ground that it is a debt due the deceased. Mr. Speaker, the deceased lived long after the close of the war; he was in office to the day of his death, and I have never heard that the government was in arrears to him.

"Every man in this House knows it is not a debt. We cannot, without the grossest corruption, appropriate this money as the payment of a debt. We have not the semblance of authority to appropriate it as charity. Mr. Speaker, I have said we have the right to give as much money of our own as we please. I am the poorest man on this floor. I cannot vote for this bill, but I will give one week's pay to the object, and if every member of Congress will do the same, it will amount to more than the bill asks."

He took his seat. Nobody replied. The bill was put upon its passage, and, instead of passing unanimously, as was generally supposed, and as, no doubt, it would, but for that speech, it received but few votes, and, of course, was lost.

Later, when asked by a friend why he had opposed the appropriation, Crockett gave this explanation:

"Several years ago I was one evening standing on the steps of the Capitol with some other members of Congress, when our attention was attracted by a great light over in Georgetown. It was evidently a large fire. We jumped into a hack and drove over as fast as we could. In spite of all that could be done, many houses were burned and many families made houseless, and, besides, some of them had lost all but the clothes they had on. The weather was very cold, and when I saw so many women and children suffering, I felt that something ought to be done for them. The next morning a bill was introduced appropriating $20,000 for their relief. We put aside all other business and rushed it through as soon as it could be done.

"The next summer, when it began to be time to think about the election, I concluded I would take a scout around among the boys of my district. I had no opposition there, but, as the election was some time off, I did not know what might turn up. When riding one day in a part of my district in which I was more of a stranger than any other, I saw a man in a field plowing and coming toward the road. I gauged my gait so that we should meet as he came to the fence. As he came up, I spoke to the man. He replied politely, but, as I thought, rather coldly.

"I began: 'Well, friend, I am one of those unfortunate beings called candidates, and—'

" 'Yes, I know you; you are Colonel Crockett. I have seen you once before, and voted for you the last time you were elected. I suppose you are out electioneering now, but you had better not waste your time or mine. I shall not vote for you again.'

"This was a sockdolager . . . I begged him to tell me what was the matter.

" 'Well, Colonel, it is hardly worth-while to waste time or words upon it. I do not see how it can be mended, but you gave a vote last winter which shows that either you have not capacity to understand the Constitution, or that you are wanting in the honesty and firmness to be guided by it. In either case you are not the man to represent me. But I beg your pardon for expressing it in that way. I did not intend to avail myself of the privilege of the constituent to speak plainly to a candidate for the purpose of insulting or wounding you. I intend by it only to say that your understanding of the Constitution is very different from mine; and I will say to you what, but for my rudeness, I should not have said, that I believe you to be honest. . . . But an understanding of the Constitution different from mine I cannot overlook, because the Constitution, to be worth anything, must be held sacred, and rigidly observed in all its provisions. The man who wields power and misinterprets it is the more dangerous the more honest he is.'

"'I admit the truth of all you say, but there must be some mistake about it, for I do not remember that I gave any vote last winter upon any constitutional question.'

" 'No, Colonel, there's no mistake. Though I live here in the backwoods and seldom go from home, I take the papers from Washington and read very carefully all the proceedings of Congress. My papers say that last winter you voted for a bill to appropriate $20,000 to some sufferers by a fire in Georgetown. Is that true?'

"'Well, my friend; I may as well own up. You

have got me there. But certainly nobody will complain that a great and rich country like ours should give the insignificant sum of $20,000 to relieve its suffering women and children, particularly with a full and overflowing Treasury, and I am sure, if you had been there, you would have done just as I did.'

"'It is not the amount, Colonel, that I complain of; it is the principle. In the first place, the government ought to have in the Treasury no more than enough for its legitimate purposes. But that has nothing to do with the question. The power of collecting and disbursing money at pleasure is the most dangerous power that can be intrusted to man, particularly under our system of collecting revenue by a tariff, which reaches every man in the country, no matter how poor he may be, and the poorer he is the more he pays in proportion to his means. What is worse, it presses upon him without his knowledge where the weight centers, for there is not a man in the United States who can ever guess how much he pays to the government. So you see, that while you are contributing to relieve one, you are drawing it from thousands who are even worse off than he. If you had the right to give anything, the amount was simply a matter of discretion with you, and you had as much right to give $20,000,000 as $20,000. If you have the right to give to one, you have the right to give to all; and, as the Constitution neither defines charity nor stipulates the amount, you are at liberty to give to any and everything which you may believe, or profess to believe, is a charity, and to any amount you may think proper. You will very easily perceive what a wide door this would open for fraud and corruption and favoritism, on the one hand, and for robbing the people on the other. No, Colonel, Congress has no right to give charity. Individual members may give as much of their own money as they please, but they have no right to touch a dollar of the public money for that purpose. If twice as many houses had been burned in this county as in Georgetown, neither you nor any other member of Congress would have thought of appropriating a dollar for our relief. There are about two hundred and forty members of Congress. If they had shown their sympathy for the sufferers by contributing each one week's pay, it would have made over $13,000. There are plenty of wealthy men in and around Washington who could have given $20,000 without depriving themselves of even a luxury of life. The congressmen chose to keep their own money, which, if reports be true, some of them spend not very creditably; and the people about Washington, no doubt, applauded you for relieving them from the necessity of giving by giving what was not yours to give. The people have delegated to Congress, by the Constitution, the power to do certain things. To do these, it is authorized to collect and pay moneys, and for nothing else. Everything beyond this is usurpation, and a violation of the Constitution.

"'So you see, Colonel, you have violated the Constitution in what I consider a vital point. It is a precedent fraught with danger to the country, for when Congress once begins to stretch its power beyond the limits of the Constitution, there is no limit to it, and no security for the people. I have no doubt you acted honestly, but that does not make it any better, except as far as you are personally concerned, and you see that I cannot vote for you.'

"I tell you I felt streaked. I saw if I should have opposition, and this man should go to talking, he would set others to talking, and in that district I was a gone fawn-skin. I could not answer him, and the fact is, I was so fully convinced that he was right, I did not want to. But I must satisfy him, and I said to him:

"'Well, my friend, you hit the nail upon the head when you said I had not sense enough to understand the Constitution. I intended to be guided by it, and thought I had studied it fully. I have heard many speeches in Congress about the powers of Congress, but what you have said here at your plow has got more hard, sound sense in it than all the fine speeches I ever heard. If I had ever taken the view of it that you have, I would have put my head into the fire before I would have given that vote; and if you will forgive me and vote for me again, if I ever vote for another unconstitutional law I wish I may be shot.'

"He laughingly replied: 'Yes, Colonel, you have sworn to that once before, but I will trust you again upon one condition. You say that you are convinced that your vote was wrong. Your acknowledgment of it will do more good than beating you for it. If, as you go around the district, you will tell people about this vote, and that you are satisfied it was wrong, I will not only vote for you, but will do what I can to keep down opposition, and, perhaps, I may exert some little influence in that way.'

"'If I don't,' said I, 'I wish I may be shot; and to convince you that I am in earnest in what I say I will come back this way in a week or ten days, and if you will get up a gathering of the people, I will make a speech to them. Get up a barbecue, and I will pay for it.'

"'No, Colonel, we are not rich people in this section, but we have plenty of provisions to contribute for a barbecue, and some to spare for those who have none. The push of crops will be over in a few days, and we can then afford a day for a barbecue. This is Thursday; I will see to getting it up on Saturday week. Come to my house on Friday, and we will go together, and I promise you a very respectable crowd to see and hear you.'

"'Well, I will be here. But one thing more before I say good-by. I must know your name.'

"'My name is Bunce.'

"'Not Horatio Bunce?'

"'Yes.'

"'Well, Mr. Bunce, I never saw you before, though you say you have seen me, but I know you very well. I am glad I have met you, and very proud that I may hope to have you for my friend.'

"It was one of the luckiest hits of my life that I met him. He mingled but little with the public, but was widely known for his remarkable intelligence and incorruptible integrity, and for a heart brimful and running over with kindness and benevolence, which showed themselves not only in words but in acts. He was the oracle of the whole country around him, and his fame had extended far beyond the circle of his immediate acquaintance. Though I had never met him before, I had heard much of him, and but for this meeting it is very likely I should have had opposition, and had been beaten. One thing is very certain, no man could now stand up in that district under such a vote.

"At the appointed time I was at his house, having told our conversation to every crowd I had met, and to every man I stayed all night with, and I found that it gave the people an interest and a confidence in me stronger than I had ever seen manifested before.

"Though I was considerably fatigued when I reached his house, and, under ordinary circumstances, should have gone early to bed, I kept him up until midnight, talking about the principles and affairs of government, and got more real, true knowledge of them than I had got all my life before.

"I have known and seen much of him since, for I respect him—no, that is not the word—I reverence and love him more than any living man, and I go to see him two or three times every year; and I will tell you, sir, if every one who professes to be a Christian lived and acted and enjoyed it as he does, the religion of Christ would take the world by storm.

"But to return to my story. The next morning we went to the barbecue, and, to my surprise, found about a thousand men there. I met a good many whom I had not known before, and they and my friend introduced me around until I had got pretty well acquainted—at least, they all knew me.

"In due time notice was given that I would speak to them. They gathered up around a stand that had been erected. I opened my speech by saying:

"'Fellow-citizens—I present myself before you today feeling like a new man. My eyes have lately been opened to truths which ignorance or prejudice, or both, had heretofore hidden from my view. I feel that I can today offer you the ability to render you more valuable service than I have ever been able to render before. I am here today more for the purpose of acknowledging my error than to seek your votes. That I should make this acknowledgment is due to myself as well as to you. Whether you will vote for me is a matter for your consideration only.'

"I went on to tell them about the fire and my vote for the appropriation and then told them why I was satisfied it was wrong. I closed by saying:

"'And now, fellow-citizens, it remains only for me to tell you that the most of the speech you have listened to with so much interest was simply a repetition of the arguments by which your neighbor, Mr. Bunce, convinced me of my error.

"'It is the best speech I ever made in my life, but he is entitled to the credit for it. And now I hope he is satisfied with his convert and that he will get up here and tell you so.'

"He came upon the stand and said:

"'Fellow-citizens—It affords me great pleasure to comply with the request of Colonel Crockett. I have always considered him a thoroughly honest man, and I am satisfied that he will faithfully perform all that he has promised you today.'

"He went down, and there went up from that crowd such a shout for Davy Crockett as his name never called forth before.

"I am not much given to tears, but I was taken with a choking then and felt some big drops rolling down my cheeks. And I tell you now that the remembrance of those few words spoken by such a man, and the honest, hearty shout they produced, is worth more to me than all the honors I have received and all the reputation I have ever made, or ever shall make, as a member of Congress.

"Now, sir," concluded Crockett, "you know why I made that speech yesterday.

"There is one thing now to which I will call your attention. You remember that I proposed to give a week's pay. There are in that House many very wealthy men—men who think nothing of spending a week's pay, or a dozen of them, for a dinner or a wine party when they have something to accomplish by it. Some of those same men made beautiful speeches upon the great debt of gratitude which the country owed the deceased—a debt which could not be paid by money—and the insignificance and worthlessness of money, particularly so insignificant a sum as $10,000, when weighed against the honor of the nation. Yet not one of them responded to my proposition. Money with them is nothing but trash when it is to come out of the people. But it is the one great thing for which most of them are striving, and many of them sacrifice honor, integrity, and justice to obtain it."

74. INTERVENTION LEADS TO TOTAL CONTROL*

Gustavo R. Velasco

The central problem of our time is the economic organization of society. It is not necessary to adhere to historical materialism in order to recognize this or to realize, as well, that upon the manner in which society solves this problem depends the resolution of many others which today appear to be insoluble, such as the discovery of a way to overcome and transcend present nationalisms, the establishment of peaceful conditions in the world, and the utilization for constructive ends of the latest wonderful discoveries of science. Throughout the course of history we find various types of economic structures; however, humanity cannot, at a given moment, choose an economic system in the same way as a man with unlimited time or money might pick one of the trips offered by a tourist agency. The only alternative that exists for a serious thinker today is that between a free economy and a controlled economy.[1]

But is there no third road? Is it not intolerable to attempt to push us into one or the other pigeonhole, that of supporters of economic freedom or of believers in state control? The purpose of the present work is to submit this widely-held belief in a "middle way" to a critical examination.

The name of the third road is interventionism. Its practical importance derives from the fact that in Mexico as in the United States and in those European countries where debate is still possible, there are many people who reject communism, sometimes even with horror because of its excesses and persecutions, but who at the same time, deluded by a persistent and insidious propaganda, are unwilling to declare themselves in favor of capitalism, which they believe to be the cause of poverty, or of crises, or of social injustice, or an order inferior from an ethical point of view. Whatever truth there may be in these strictures, and notwithstanding the fact that I believe each one of them to be the result of misinterpretation or of stark ignorance both of the facts and of economic theory, this is clearly not the occasion to expose and refute them. I would rather inquire into what lies behind such broad but vague labels as "capitalism" or "socialism" and examine and evaluate the essential characteristics of each system.

Characteristics of Capitalism

It will be found, for example, that capitalism is characterized by the existence of the following institutions:

1. freedom of enterprise, that is, freedom to engage in the work, activity, or business desired, to develop it and to reap the benefits which may re-

*From *The Freeman*, January 1970

sult therefrom, as well as to suffer the losses which it may produce;

2. private ownership, not only of consumer goods, but also of natural resources, capital, and productive goods;

3. competition;

4. a free market, with freedom of choice by the consumers, freedom to make any deal, and a price system.

On the other hand, what distinguishes socialism and communism is centralized control of the means of production in the hands of the state. The essential thing is that, ultimately, under socialism only one will decides. This demonstrates its ineradicably dictatorial character, the inanity of attempts to combine socialism with free competition and the price system, and the confusion of those people who imagine that a planned economy is compatible with liberty and democracy.[2] As a result, every one of the institutions listed above will vanish under socialism, leaving us instead with bureaucrats and policemen behind each street corner, if not inside our very homes, as in George Orwell's novel, *1984*.

Once the discussion is undertaken on this more concrete ground, it will gain in clarity and objectivity. When it is realized that planned economy implies that we may be directed to do any work, if necessary as forced labor; that we can be deprived of all right to property; that all of us will become public employees; and that we may even be forbidden to decide what we shall eat, I am sure that believers in this system will be much fewer and that there will be a large number of men resolved to defend the system of economic freedom which has lifted great parts of humanity out of the misery in which they lived until the eighteenth century. Even so, the complexity of modern life, the difficulty presented by economic problems—especially those provoked by a third of a century of mistaken policies (since the First World War and especially since the Great Depression)—the fact that not everyone can analyze them and apply or follow the reasoning of economic theory, and other circumstances to which I shall refer later, leave more than one opportunity for the appearance and espousal of interventionist theories. In fact, in the dispute between the two opposing systems of liberty and regimentation, it is interventionism that has gained ground.

Unlike capitalism and communism, which are well-defined forms of organization readily distinguishable from each other, interventionism does not constitute a third structure different from these two. Interventionism does not seek to destroy the fundamental institutions of a free economy or to displace it. Neither does it have as a declared purpose the establishment of centralized direction of the means of production. Its object is a combination, a solution intermediate between capitalism and communism, in which the disadvantages and abuses of the former would be eliminated without falling into the evils and pernicious consequences of the latter. For this purpose, liberty is restricted and all the resources of the state are put into play, with the threat or the ultimate application of that power which it alone can wield, that is, coercion and violence. Since interventionism and socialism are in agreement insofar as both criticize a free economy, what characterizes and identifies the former is the feature which I have just noted and from which it derives its name: the intervention by the state, the utilization of its apparatus and power in all cases where the functioning of the system of freedom produces a result different from that which the proponents of interventionism consider ethical or desirable.

What a noble purpose! What a neat solution! To preserve the advantages of individual initiative without falling into any of the dangers of collectivism. To couple the energies of society and the unity of the state, and in one single harmonious effort, to attain justice, social peace, and prosperity. It should not be surprising that this beautiful utopia has seduced generous and enlightened minds from the remotest times. In fact, although there are some who present it as the latest novelty, interventionism is as old as history. In the first written legislative compilation which has been preserved, the Code of Hammurabi, we find laws which fix prices; and this form of intervention, together with innumerable others, persisted in Egypt, China, Greece, Rome, the Middle Ages, the Renaissance, the Mercantile Age, and the French Revolution, and emerges in our day with greater pretensions than ever.

The Market in Operation

A complete examination of interventionism, which does not claim to be a substitute for the market system but simply a corrective measure, should start with a study of the operation of the free market. In this way it would be possible to determine the accuracy of the two central arguments of the critics of the free market: the assertion, on the one hand, that even if the system of economic freedom does tend toward the optimum application of productive resources, and therefore toward the largest possible output, conditions never really correspond to the basic assumptions of laissez-faire theory, and so the latter is, to that extent, limited and deficient; and the emphasis, on the other hand, upon those results of the free play of individual interests which are deemed undesirable. But let us grant those points to the opposing side, despite the fact that some are inaccurate and others are greatly exaggerated. In any case, the conclusion which rightly follows when one finds an imperfection in the working of the free market is the need of improving it and of achieving its efficient operation, not of disorganizing and destroying it. Since interventionism bases all its claims on its alleged ability to accomplish better results than a free economy, let us investigate how it operates in its turn and, more concretely, whether it can attain the aims which the governments and the persons who resort to it declare that they pursue.

In the economic field, these aims cannot but be greater abundance for the greatest possible number of the inhabitants of a country. In other words, the primary aim of interventionism is not different from that of capitalism or even of communism.[3]

In case there is any doubt about this, it is sufficient to call attention to the name with which the partisans of the latest brand of interventionism have baptized their creation: they call it the "welfare state," that is, a political body which has as its objective the welfare of the masses. And the welfare which is promised is, in the first place, economic welfare.

Classes of Intervention

Although official intervention takes extremely varied forms, analysis permits us to classify them into three groups: (1) measures whose principal object is to divert the factors of production from the channels which they would have entered in a free market, toward others preferred by their authors; (2) measures whose object is to modify the data which are a result of the market; (3) measures whose object is to change the distribution of production and, in general, of wealth.

Intervention of the first class can be either direct (prohibition of certain industries, decrees to the effect that enough factories or firms exist in certain lines, production quotas) or indirect (protective tariffs, subsidies). In order to modify the indications of the market, recourse is had to price-fixing (only for the sake of brevity do I use this word, since the figures selected as a result of the decision of an entity with compulsory force cannot be considered as prices, which, by definition, are the result of the interaction of individuals in the market). In practice we find both maximum prices (rents, consumer goods) and minimum prices (parity prices for certain agricultural products, salaries), and we observe that sometimes the government decrees them and imposes them directly, while on other occasions it permits this to be done by private groups (legalized monopolies, labor unions), to which it lends the support of its authority, or permits them the use of physical force and violence (strikes, shutdowns of plants and offices). In the three types of measures which I have mentioned, recourse is had to the fiscal powers of the government; nevertheless, it is in the case of the third group of measures that this kind of official activity (provision of free services, progressive income and inheritance taxes) is resorted to most frequently.

Restriction Invariably Diminishes Production of Goods and Services

Based on this outline of the most frequent forms of interference, let us examine the results to be expected from each one. As I pointed out above, its operation, its yield, are the only criteria with which to judge the so-called third road in the economic field, for it is in precisely this respect that it presents itself as superior to the capitalistic system which it criticizes. In other words, what interventionism has to prove is that it can increase production, raise the general standard of living, and consequently assure greater welfare to all the population.

The deflection of production into channels different from those which it would enter in an unhampered market is so obviously restrictive that it is no exaggeration to speak of restrictionism when designating the totality of measures which the state employs for this purpose. In every case it prohibits a certain kind of production (in the broadest sense of the word and including, therefore, commerce, personal services, banking and transportation), or certain procedures are forbidden, or are made more difficult or more expensive. It could be stated *a priori* that, given the tendency of the free market to the optimum use of the factors of production and to the maximum satisfaction of the most urgent human needs, these shackles can result only in a deterioration of the productive process and in impoverishment of the community. A detailed examination of any one of the restrictive devices will fully corroborate this.

Let us suppose a restriction of the number of factories dedicated to a certain branch of production or of the quantity of articles which they can manufacture. Let us suppose also that this restriction is complied with or is enforced. Naturally, the price of the product concerned will go up; the profits derived from the industry in question will increase. Those who participate in it, salaried workers, investors, entrepreneurs, will be better off from receiving their respective incomes more surely or even in greater proportion than before. It would seem, therefore, that the measure is beneficial in general and that it should be approved.

Gains Offset by Losses

Whoever believes this suffers from evident myopia. When the consumers find themselves obligated to pay more for the restricted item, they will automatically have less to spend for other articles. Consequently, what the interested parties in industry A gain, those who depend on industries B, C, and D will lose. No net advantage whatsoever exists for society. On the contrary, and since wealth is created through expending a certain quantity of the factors of production and since restriction of that quantity cannot increase but only diminish the amount of goods produced, from the general viewpoint the result is a net loss, equal in amount to that of the production which was prevented. One group gained, but at the expense of the community. Taken as a whole, the latter is poorer and not richer. Interventionism not only did not attain its objective, but produced a result exactly opposite to the one it sought.

Even easier is the demonstration in the case of price fixing, a demonstration which has been given so many times that one feels reluctant to take up the reader's time with it. The function of prices is to achieve a balance between supply and demand. When the government immobilizes them at a level lower than the one determined by the market, demand increases, since buyers will feel more inclined to acquire goods and since there will also be a great increase in the number of those who could not do so at the previous price, but who find it possible at the fixed price. If instead, prices are set at levels higher than those established on the market, it will be the sellers who will flock to it, and supply will exceed demand. In either instance, the market fails to fulfill its functions; a new principle for the distribution of available goods becomes indispensable, and queues, rationing, and the black market appear in the one case, and overproduction and chronic unemployment in the other. This is due to the fact that in addition to allocating the articles already produced, prices fill a mediate but even more important function, that of guiding and directing production.

Prices are signals, indications, to producers, of the fields in which there exists an unsatisfied demand and in which production should therefore be intensified; and of those others where supply cannot be wholly absorbed and in which future production should consequently be curtailed. Producers respond to these stimuli to the fullest extent possible in each set of circumstances, because of their desire to obtain profits and to avoid losses. And the result for society is the employment of the factors of production in those directions which will satisfy the most important and urgent needs of the consumers.[4]

Changing the Signals

Let us consider now what happens in a system in which the signals have ceased to function truthfully, that is to say, in which the government orders buyers and sellers to abide by certain amounts whose only likeness to prices lies in the fact that they are expressed in legal tender currency. If the official figure is lower than the market price, marginal producers—those whose costs are highest—will lose money and will be eliminated. The other producers will continue their activities but will not increase their investments; on the contrary, they will divert to other ends the nonspecific factors at their disposal and will even retire completely as soon as they can do so, in order to engage in the production of goods which offer greater profits. As a result, the supply of the controlled commodity, the more important since it is generally a staple of life, will diminish instead of increasing as the government desired.

Exactly the same thing will happen, except in the opposite direction, in the case of minimum prices or salaries. When the authorities discover that not all the farmers who cultivate a certain crop can earn sufficient money to continue producing it, they set a parity price below which it may not descend. Now, the unsatisfactory former price was not capricious; there was a reason for it and this could only be an excess of supply or a lack of demand. The imposition of minimum prices perpetuates these conditions and prevents production from adjusting itself to consumption, by keeping marginal producers in business and by even attracting new producers who, if they had been confronted with a lower price, would have applied their resources to the production of different goods.

And so, with controlled prices, as with restrictive measures, the real result that is attained is exactly the opposite of the one sought by their proponents. The conditions that are created are not better, but worse, than those which existed prior to their establishment. Some groups may be benefited and enriched, but society as a whole loses and is impoverished.

Not Income, but Expense

I shall not attempt here to discuss the method of redistributing wealth represented by the inflationary and credit expansion policies followed by most contemporary governments. As for the other measures aimed at achieving a distribution different from that determined by the capitalistic order—for example, by organizing gratuitous or semi-gratuitous services (low-cost housing programs, socialized medical services—it is so obvious that they entail an expenditure rather than an income that when attempts are made in their defense the arguments revolve exclusively around the justice of providing them. In other words, the proponents of these measures avoid justifying them in the economic field, in which interventionism boasts of its power to win the argument and in which it is the purpose of this document to examine them. If we do so, it will be easy to verify that, since the state cannot provide anybody with anything which it has not previously, and more or less surreptitiously, taken away from him or which it does not take away from other producers, the net effect of its absorption of all kinds of activities is to transfer from the interested parties to the administration the power to decide and to spend.

On the whole, this must have less efficient results and yield a smaller return for the community, because to the less perfect satisfaction (always from the point of view of the consumer) of the needs which one wants to fill must be added the disturbances originated by politics and the complications, mistakes and immoralities of bureaucracy. Above all, the social resources available for these purposes do not increase just because the heavy body of the state is interposed between them and their use, but rather diminish through having to bear the high and ever-increasing cost of the services so deceptively called free.

Saving Discouraged

In general and independently, therefore, of the use to which the government puts the funds which it collects, there is no doubt but that taxation beyond certain limits discourages the accumulation of capital, as in the United States, or even has the opposite result of encouraging the dissipation and consumption of existing capital, as in England. Matters are, of course, much worse in the case of expropriations and confiscations, especially when they are not isolated and extraordinary acts, since they can only be compared in their effects to those cataclysms which paralyze even the will to reconstruct and after which recovery is as slow as it is painful.

Again, the failure of the ambitious interventionist program is confirmed; no country can make itself rich by taking away from some people in order to give to others and by terrorizing and demoralizing all of them. It is true that whoever cuts the cake—in this case, the state and, more concretely, professional politicians, their friends, and the groups which support them or which they favor—gets the best share; yet neither does the total distributed become greater nor is the general mass of the population benefited, but rather it becomes more impoverished by such distribution.

As a result of the foregoing, it can be stated with certainty that isolated interventionist measures do not produce wealth, but scarcity—not abundance, but poverty. This is not a value judgment; neither is it a case of condemning these measures because they limit freedom and lead to totalitarianism. In the field which belongs to economic science, that of showing us the consequence of our actions and of enabling us to behave consistently, it can be demonstrated that the results of state interventionism are contrary to the aims that it seeks and that from the point of view of those who want intervention—not from my point of view or in the opinion of the friends of capitalism—it ends in a situation which is worse than the one it set out to improve. Interventionist policies must, therefore, result in failure and frustration, or else go on extending both horizontally and vertically until they end in complete economic control and in socialism of the Nazi type.

This course must offer great temptation to those who have embarked upon interventionist adventures and represents one of the greatest threats of such a policy. Upon observing that the maximum price fixed for milk, for example, causes this product to disappear from the market, let us fix the prices of other activities and commodities, such as pasteurization, milk containers, transportation. If production has been diverted to butter and cheese, let us fix their prices and limit the amount which can be made of them. If this does not produce the desired result either, let us freeze the salaries of such persons as may be engaged in the milk industry or even of those connected with it, and go a step further and prevent the producers by force from abandoning this field. If the supply of milk grows less every day, let us follow the internal logic of interventionism and take the ultimate step: let us control everything, without exception. Then we shall have eliminated the market completely, we shall find ourselves at the opposite extreme from where we started, and we shall have established a system which is indistinguishable from the communism which we began by repudiating.

There is no doubt, therefore, that interventionism constitutes an extremely efficacious instrument in the struggle begun some time ago for the purpose of destroying the liberal society in which, in spite of everything, we still live. In the first place, it lends invaluable support to those who are working to establish communism but who realize that they would meet very strong opposition if they openly advocate that form of economic organization. Perhaps even more serious is the fact that interventionism complicates and aggravates economic problems to such a degree that the majority of people, among them the majority of the classes which previously performed the most important of directive functions, that of supplying the ideas which guide society, are bewildered and perplexed and even come to believe that these problems admit of no perfect solution. But does not this situation cause surprise?

If, in the field of ideas, the failures of interventionism are indisputable, if not only the bankruptcy of this policy but also its catastrophic effects and the danger which it presents are visible on all sides, especially in those countries which have carried it the furthest, why does it not pass forever into oblivion, ashamed of the confusion which it has wrought and of the countless ills which it has brought upon humanity? The explanation is complicated, but in my opinion it should be attempted because it will help to dissipate the mental fog which has descended upon a great number of our fellow men and left them irresolute and deprived of the will to respond to the challenge of our times.

Reasons for Confusion

Let me list briefly some of the reasons for this:

(a) Man is by temperament a compromiser, especially when confronted with matters which he does not understand and which he thinks do not affect him directly. The majority believes that the debate concerns only a mythical class, "the capitalist" or "the bankers," and the government. What is more natural than to think that each one must be partly right and that as between the freedom demanded by the former and the complete control which everyone instinctively fears, the solution must lie in the golden mean of interventionism?

(b) Both in economic matters and in general, without the aid of science our perception and interpretation of phenomena are rough and misleading. Scientific knowledge aims precisely at broadening our field of vision and our understanding and making them more accurate. But just as an ignorant person does not observe that the world is round, so also in economic matters he sees no further than the near and immediate effects of an act or a policy. The masses are incapable of understanding the secondary consequences which those acts or policies generate in time or space; nor will they follow the long and rather complicated reasoning necessary to explain them. Since interventionist measures seem at first to be successful and may benefit special groups, a man without economic knowledge needs no further proof to be convinced of their efficacy.

(c) In the economic process we all have a dual personality: on the one hand, we are producers; on the other, consumers. Although frequently and with a notorious lack of logic, government intervention is asked against consumers when prices decrease, and protests are made and official aid invoked against producers when prices increase, the predominant interest of the majority of people is their interest as producers. This is more direct and specialized, since the interests that consumers have in common are diffuse and lend themselves but little to the organization of groups which would further them. And thus we see that in the democratic countries the voters cast their ballots in favor of their interests as producers and against the general welfare, which would usually coincide with their interest as consumers.

Whether the explanations which I put forward are accepted or whether other causes are found for the regrettable blindness of our contemporaries in face of the disaster of interventionism, I repeat that this system has won ground since the First World War opened the door to it. Is it to be anticipated that it will continue, as it has up to now, to extend and intensify itself more all the time?

It is not to be believed. Interventionism has lived off the reserves accumulated under capitalism and thus has succeeded in hiding to some extent its excesses; but these reserves have already been dissipated in some countries, while in others their exhaustion is only a question of time. Interventionism is essentially unstable as I believe I have demonstrated, because it is not a real third system but a makeshift which fluctuates between the capitalism from which it starts and the communism which it does not wish to reach. Consequently, either humanity has a lucid moment and holds back at the edge of the abyss, or else it plunges into it and into the new dark age of which a terrifying prelude has been furnished us by Hitler's Germany and Stalin's Russia.

What cannot be doubted is the danger in which we live. Let us not forget that interventionism constitutes a seeming, but in fact self-defeating and suicidal solution which does not raise the standard of living but lowers it, which does not create wealth but consumes it. Its basic philosophy is mistaken and pernicious. Like the collectivism to which it believes it is raising an obstacle, it mistrusts the individual and his innate capabilities, and seeks salvation in an entity supposedly free from his limitations and weaknesses, which would be outside of society and superior to it. In practice, interventionism is nothing but statism. Moreover, by attributing to the state an omniscience and an omnipotence which nothing justifies—neither theoretical reasoning nor historical experience—interventionism professes a true idolatry of the state and is even inferior in this aspect to communism, which at least in theory does not exalt the state and even speaks, deludedly, of its fading away.

In the same way, interventionism is inimical to individual liberty. It is not a question simply of the fact that its specific means of action are orders and prohibitions and that it necessarily implies a reduction of liberty and an increase in compulsion. The evil stems from a much deeper source, from the fact that contrarily to the naive thesis that it is possible to separate what is economic from what is not, liberty is indivisible. Since there exist no purely economic motivations which can be separated from the other objectives which we seek in life, any diminution in the sphere of economic liberty results in a loss of freedom in other fields. In other words, there is no economic sector of life inferior to others and clearly marked off from them, in which it would be possible for the state to project itself without resultant ill effects upon personal liberty. All intervention in the means implies an intervention in the ends. Automatically, the decision as to what objectives we must fulfill and as to the relative rank of the values which they tend to realize, is shifted to a great extent from the individual to the state, until it is completely absorbed by the latter in communism, which for this reason, is inescapably totalitarian.

The Greatest Danger: The Statification of Life

What can be surprising, after the foregoing, about the necessary results, observable everywhere, of statism and of the abandonment of liberty? The state grows and hypertrophies until it assumes the proportions of a Leviathan or a Behemoth. Instead of being a center of union and a representative of the general interest, it becomes a cause of conflict and an instrument of private appetites upon which each group brings pressure or which it is anxious to dominate in order to apply governmental compulsion and strength for its own benefit. Political institutions become deformed and corrupt, because, having been conceived for other purposes and in a different atmosphere, they prove inadequate in a state which is impatient of restrictions and hampered by law. Not only in public life and in the administration does immorality increase as a result of the power which the organs of the state acquire over economic matters, but the people as a whole become accustomed to the phenomena which accompany interventionism: smuggling, bribery, black market, governmental favors; they cease to believe in self-reliance and lose their sense of responsibility, seeking prosperity at the expense of others and changing from citizens to subjects and from free men to wards of the government.

The problem of interventionism is not, as may be seen, purely economic, but much more general. Although its political and social repercussions are undeniably of the utmost importance, I continue to believe that it is only after subjecting it to economic analysis that one can pass a decisive judgment on it. And I would conclude, with Ortega y Gasset: "This is the greatest danger which threatens civilization today: the statification of life, state interventionism, the absorption of all social spontaneity which, in the final instance, sustains, nurtures, and impels human destinies."[5]

Notes

[1]Syndicalism, with its variant, corporativism, cannot be taken seriously nor has either passed beyond mere words. Whoever believes that I reject them peremptorily may consult, among others, the confutation of the eminent German economist, Wilhelm Röpke, in his book, *The Social Crisis of Our Time*.

[2]Socialism has attracted so many well-intentioned souls who sincerely abhor the fatal consequences which I point out, that my use of the two terms "socialism" and "communism" as interchangeable cannot help provoking an indignant protest. I admit that there exist differences between the two systems, the principal ones being (a) one of scope: socialism would nationalize only basic industries; for communism, in principle, there are no limits to nationalization; (b) another of method: socialism trusts to a gradual and peaceful process; communism believes in revolutionary and violent action; (c) finally, socialism would like to proceed in accordance with accepted standards of morality and preserve freedom, especially civil and political freedom, and democracy; communism rejects traditional morality, and although it speaks, for tactical reasons, of "true liberty" and "popular democracy," it is fundamentally antiliberal and antidemocratic.

These differences are secondary and are not sufficient to obscure the main question, which is that of the location of control over economic life. Moreover, the last difference, the most important, is no more than a pious hope. The road followed by England, despite the extremely strong liberal tradition of its people and the fact that it has not passed beyond the initial stages of socialization proves this quite conclusively.

[3]In all systems, in addition to economic objectives, other ends are sought of a varied nature, moral humanitarian, nationalistic, and so forth. Nobody doubts that many can be attained by means of official action. But it is equally clear that from the economic viewpoint these measures represent an expenditure, not an income. Economic science neither approves nor disapproves of them. It confines itself to throwing light upon their true nature.

[4]Obviously, in accordance with the scale of values of the consumers themselves. To this it is objected that the market directs production toward the fields which bring highest profits and not toward those most necessary to society or which are "truly useful." The fault does not lie with the market system, but with the desires of men. What is needed, therefore, is to instruct and convince the latter so that they will not want things of scant "social utility" (such as chewing gum or bullfights) or which are even harmful or immoral (such as alcoholic beverages or the services of cabaret girls and prostitutes). But whoever criticizes a free economy on this account and shields himself behind supposedly economic arguments in order to impose his personal preferences, reveals very little democratic spirit and a great deal of superiority and paternalism.

[5]*The Revolt of the Masses.* Complete Works (in Spanish). Book IV, page 225.

Economic History

75. FOOD CONTROL DURING FORTY-SIX CENTURIES: A CONTRIBUTION TO THE HISTORY OF PRICE FIXING*

Mary G. Lacy

The man, or class of men, who controls the supply of essential foods is in possession of the supreme power. The safeguarding of the food supply has therefore been the concern of governments since they have been in existence. They had to exercise this control in order to hold the supreme power, because all the people need food and it is the only commodity of which this is true.

In connection with this control it would seem that every possible expedient and experiment had been tried. One of the most frequent methods of control used has been the limitation of prices by legal enactment. The results have been astonishingly uniform considering the variety of conditions and circumstances under which the experiments have taken place. They make an interesting record and one which contains food for thought, for the problem of the people's welfare has been much the same in all ages and it is not yet solved.[1]

Egypt, 2830 B.C.

As far back as the fifth dynasty in Egypt, which historians place at 2830 B.C. at the latest, there was inscribed on the tomb of the Monarch Henku: "I was lord and overseer of southern grain in this nome."

In the book of Genesis (12)† there are various references dating back to the time of Abraham to the fact that Egypt was a granary where all the people were sure of finding a plenteous store of corn.

The well-known story of Joseph shows how the control of the food supply by the government reduced a people to slavery. Joseph gathered and stored for Pharaoh in years of abundance one-fifth of all the harvests. The improvident Egyptians lived well and laid by no stores. When famine came they and the people in the nearby countries went to Joseph and bought food from him until all their money was gone; then they gave him their cattle for food. After they had bartered away all their cattle they offered their land and themselves in exchange for subsistence. Having thus reduced them to slavery as the price of life, Joseph about 1700 B.C.[2] gave them seed and put them on the land again. Flavius Josephus tells the story as follows:

"When famine came, the multitude, sorely oppressed, repaired in crowds to the stores and magazines of the king. The situation of the poorer and common sort was piteous beyond description; for having laid in but a very scanty store, and not being able to obtain a supply without ready money, when that was exhausted, they were reduced to the necessity of exchanging their cattle, slaves, lands, nay their last little all, to procure grain from the king's granaries to protract a needy miserable life. When by these means they became totally destitute, they were abandoned to a desolate world, that the king might secure their bartered possessions . . . But when at length the

*An address before the Agricultural History Society, Washington, D. C., March 16, 1922

†Numbers in parentheses refer to "List of References" at conclusion of article.

river overflowed, watered the earth, revived dropping nature, and produced a fertile aspect, Joseph made the tour of the kingdom, and summoning his respective landholders, restored to them such parts as they had sold to the king, on condition of their paying a fifth, as tribute to him by virtue of his prerogative, and then enjoined them to the same diligence in their improvements, as if they were to derive the emoluments resulting from the whole. Transported at the returning prospect of plenty, and the restitution of their landed property, the people applied themselves to agriculture with unremitting assiduity; so that by this well-timed act of policy, Joseph established his own authority in Egypt, and increased the standing revenue of all its succeeding monarchs."

The great Egyptologist Erman (9) corroborates the testimony of Josephus by giving an account of the government control over grain, and descriptions of the granaries[3] which were surprisingly like our elevators—the grain being poured in at the top and taken out at the bottom by means of a sliding door. The outstanding result of the Egyptian control of the grain crop was a system of land tenure by which the land became the property of the monarch, and was rented from him by the agricultural class.

China, 424-387 B.C.

In his study entitled, "The Economic Principles of Confucius and His School," Dr. Chen tells us that in China (6) it was recognized from very early times that—

" . . . there are two sets of interests, those of producers and those of consumers. But nothing more markedly affects the interests of both sides at once than prices. Therefore, price is the great problem for society as a whole. According to the Confucian theory, the government should level prices by the adjustment of demand and supply, in order to guarantee the cost of the producer and satisfy the wants of the consumer.

"Its chief aim is to destroy all monopoly so that the independent or small producer can be protected on the one side, and the consumer on the other. It prevents the middleman from making large profits, and gives the seller and buyer full gain." "It is the task of the superior man to adjust demand and supply so as to keep prices on a level."

The means used by the Chinese government to this end are of the greatest interest, because of the economic principles involved and also because of their antiquity.

We are told that, "According to the official system of Chou (about 1122 B.C.), the superintendent of grain[4] looked around the fields and determined the amount of grain to be collected or issued, in accordance with the condition of the crop; fulfilling the deficit of their demand and adjusting their supply." (6)

"When Li K'o became the minister of Wei he said that if the price of grain were too high, it would hurt the consumers, and that if it were too low, it would hurt the farmers. If the consumers were hurt, the people would emigrate, and if the farmers were hurt, the state would be poor. The bad results of a high price and a low price are the same. Therefore, a good statesman would keep the people from injury and give more encouragement to the farmers."

After describing the bad condition of the farmers, he gives the following for equalizing the price of grain:

"Those who want to equalize the price of grain must be careful to look at the crop. There are three grades of good crops: The first, the second, and the lowest. In an ordinary year one hundred acres of land yield one hundred fifty bushels of grain." In the first grade of good crop the amount is fourfold—that is, one hundred acres yield six hundred bushels. Throughout one year, a family of five persons needs two hundred bushels for their living, so that they have a surplus of four hundred bushels. The government should buy three hundred bushels from them, leaving them a surplus of one hundred bushels. In the second grade of good crop, the amount of grain is threefold—that is, one hundred acres yield four hundred fifty bushels. The family would then have a surplus of three hundred bushels. The government should buy two hundred bushels, leaving them one hundred bushels. In the lowest grade of good crop, the amount is twofold—that is, three hundred bushels. The family would then have a surplus of one hundred bushels. The government should buy fifty bushels and leave them the other half. The purchase of the government is for the purpose of limiting the supply according to the amount demanded by the people, and it should be stopped when the price is normal. This policy will prevent the price of grain from falling below the normal and keep the farmers from injury.

"There are also three grades of famine: the great famine, the middle famine, and the small famine. During the small famine one hundred acres yield two-thirds as much grain as in the ordinary year—that is, one hundred bushels. The government should then sell at the normal price what it has bought in the lowest grade of good crop. During the middle famine, the hundred acres yield one-half as much grain as in an ordinary year—that is seventy bushels. The government should now sell what it has bought in the second grade of good crop. During the great famine the amount of grain is only one-fifth of what it is in an ordinary year—that is thirty bushels. The government should sell what it has bought in the first grade of good crop. Therefore, even if famine, flood, and drought should occur, the price of grain would not be high, and the people would not be obliged to emigrate. This would come about because the government takes the surplus of good crops to fill the insufficiency of bad years. In other words, the government controls the excess of supply in a good year in order to meet the demand in a bad year.

"The Policy of Li K'o is for the benefit of both society as a whole and the agricultural class . . . when his scheme was carried out in Wei, he not only made the people rich, but also made the state strong."

The principle of adjusting the supply and demand of grain is found also in the writing of Mencius, who lived 372-289 B.C. Dr. Chen quotes him as saying to King Hui of Laing:

"When the grain is so abundant that the dogs and swine eat the food of man, you do not make any collection for storage. When there are people dying from famine on the roads, you do not issue the stores of your granaries for them. When people thus die, and you say, 'It is not owing to me; it is owing to the year,' in what does this differ from stabbing a man and killing him, and then saying, 'It was not I; it was the weapon'?"

The starving millions of China during 1921 might well have wished for so statesmanlike an advocate in the councils of their government as this fearless economist three hundred years before the Christian era. Dr. Chen proceeds to say:

"The principle of equalizing the price of grain advocated by Li K'o and Mencius was adopted into the system of 'constantly normal granary.' During the reign of Han Hsuan Ti, when there were good crops for many years, the price of one bushel of grain was as low as five pennies. Then the farmers suffered greatly. In 498 (54 B.C.) Keng Shou-ch'ang proposed that the government should buy grain from places near the capital instead of transporting it from the eastern provinces. According to the old custom of the Han dynasty, the government transported annually from the eastern provinces four million bushels of grain to supply the capital, which was in the province of Shensi, in northwestern China. As this transportation was by means of the waterway, the number of laborers amounted to sixty thousand. By the plan of Keng Shou-ch'ang, which was approved and carried out by the emperor, the government saved more than half the expenses of transportation, and the farmers got more profit. Then Keng Shou-ch'ang proposed that all the provinces along the boundary of the empire should establish granaries. When the price of grain was low, they should buy it at the normal price, higher than the market price, in order to profit the farmers."

Dr. Chen points out that equalization of the price of grain is a very beneficial and practical scheme. It benefits the people without cost to the state. When the price is too low, though the government buys the grain at a price higher than the market rate, this does not mean a waste to the government. When the price is too high, though the government sells the grain at a price lower than the market rate, it does not mean a loss to the government. Even if it should be an expense to the government, the social benefit is much greater than the public expense. On the contrary, as a matter of fact, the system has been more than once administered so as to make money for the government.

The few criticisms which have been made of it are shown by Dr. Chen ". . . To be the results not of the original law itself, but of the administration of man. The chief difficulty in administering it is that it is not easy for officials to undertake commercial functions along with political duties."

Athens, 404-337 B.C.

Xenophen (2) tells us that in Athens a knowledge of the grain business was considered one of the qualities of a statesman. This was probably because Attica needed a considerable importation of grain, as the country did not produce a sufficient amount for its needs. It was brought to market in the Piraeus from all quarters, from Pontus, Thrace,

Syria, Egypt, Lybia, and Sicily. A great quantity was imported, but not all for domestic use—some of it was to be sold in the Piraeus to foreigners. It has been estimated by Boeckh (2) that Attica needed annually 3,400,000 medimni[5] of grain, about half of which it could produce in a good season. This left, as the lowest of needed importations, 1,700,000 medimni or 1,133,333 1/3 bushels. In an unpropitious season, when the domestic crop was scanty, this amount of importation was far from sufficient, so that one of the first objects of an Athenian statesman was to provide for an adequate supply of imported grain, and the regulations in regard to the grain trade were very important. Boeckh in his "Public Economy of the Athenians" says:

"The exportation of grain was absolutely prohibited. It was required by law that two-thirds of the grain which came from a foreign country to the Attic emporium should be brought into the city; that is, only a third of the grain brought into the emporium in the Piraeus could be exported from it to other lands. The execution of this law was committed to the overseers of the emporium.

"In order to prevent as much as possible the accumulation of grain and the withholding it from sale, forestalling it was confined within very narrow bounds. It was not allowed to buy at one time more than fifty backloads. (About 75 bushels.) The transgression of this law was punished with death. The grain dealers were also not permitted to sell the medimnus of grain at a higher price than one obulus (three cents) more than they had paid for it. These dealers, who were commonly aliens under the protection of the state, enhanced the price, notwithstanding by overbidding others in the purchase of grain in time of scarcity, and they often sold it the same day on which they purchased it at an advance of a drachma (17.1 cents) on the medimnus. Lysias cannot relate particulars enough respecting the profligacy of these extortioners. They were hated full as much as the same class in modern times . . . 'Were they not menaced with the punishment of death,' said he, 'they would hardly be endurable.' While the Ageranomi (market masters) had the superintendence of the sale of all other commodities, the state, in order to prevent the extortion of the grain dealers, appointed a particular body of officers called the Sitephylaces (grain inspectors) to have the oversight of this single business . . . They kept accounts of the grain imported, and besides the oversight of grain, they had also the inspection of meal and bread, that they might be sold according to legal weight and price."

The Oration against the grain dealers delivered by Lysias (19) about 387 B.C., is of the greatest interest because of the light it throws on the speculative practices of the grain dealers in Athens, the great wheat market of the eastern Mediterranean, and the attempts of an harrassed government to control them. From it we glean that in spite of the rigorous laws which were in force regulating the traffic in grain, that "corners" were not uncommon. He wrote:

"For when you happen to be most in want of grain, they grab it and are unwilling to sell, and you may be well satisfied to buy from them at any price whatever and take your leave of them so that sometimes when there is peace we are reduced to a state of siege by them."

We learn also that the "market masters," who as we have said before had the superintendence of the sale of all other commodities, were not considered sufficient to handle the grain trade also but that "grain inspectors" were appointed for this duty alone and it required fifteen of them to take care of the trade in the city and port of Athens.[6] Being a grain inspector at that time was no sinecure, for Lysias says:

"Ofttimes you imposed upon them, citizens though they were, the most severe penalties, because they were unable to master the scoundrelism of these dealers. What then should the malefactors themselves suffer at your hands, when you even put to death those who are not able to maintain a watch over them?"

We learn further that there were "combinations in restraint of trade" at this early date nearly four centuries before the Christian era, for Lysias says:

"For if you shall find them guiltless when they themselves admit that they made a combination against the importers, you will seem to plot against the skippers who came here."

We also learn that the results of even the most severe punishments, unaccompanied by any constructive substitute for the forbidden practices, were highly unsatisfactory, for Lysias says:

"But it is necessary, gentlemen of the jury, to chastise them not only for the sake of the past, but also as an example for the future; for as things now are they will be hardly endurable. And consider that in consequence of this vocation very many already have stood trial for their life; and so great are the emoluments which they derive from it that they prefer to risk their life every day rather than to cease to draw from you unjust profits. And indeed not even if they entreat you and supplicate, would you justly pity them, but much more rather the citizens who perished on account of their wickedness, and the importers against whom they made a combination . . . If then you shall condemn them, you shall act justly and you will buy grain cheaper; otherwise, dearer."

Rome, 301-361 A.D.

Rome, not having had the foresight to prevent it, found herself confronted at the close of the third century of the Christian era with a condition of high prices which was very menacing. Diocletian, with characteristic vigor, proceeded to correct this condition by law and issued his famous Edict (20) in 301 A.D., Abbott (1) tells us:

"In his effort to bring prices down to what he considered a normal level, Diocletian did not content himself with such half measures as we are trying in our attempts to suppress combinations in restraint of trade, but he boldly fixed the maximum prices at which beef, grain, eggs, clothing, and other articles should be sold and prescribed the penalty of death for anyone who disposed of his wares at a higher figure."

Prices are specified for between seven and eight hundred different items—practically all the articles which his subjects would have occasion to buy. Wages also are fixed—teachers, advocates, bricklayers, tailors, weavers, physicians—all are included. "The carpenter and joiner are paid by the day, the teacher by the month, the knife grinder, the tailor, the barber by the piece, and the coppersmith according to the amount of metal which he uses." Abbott calls attention to the fact that the prices given in the Edict are not normal but maximum. As the prevailing prices were so high, however, it is not probable that the maximum prices differed very greatly from them. The net result was failure and the law had to be repealed because of its impotence in correcting the condition of affairs. Lactantius (17) in 314 A.D. writes as follows of Diocletian and his Edict:

"After that the many oppressions which he put in practice had brought a general dearth upon the empire, then he set himself to regulate the prices of all vendible things. There was also much blood shed upon very slight and trifling accounts; and the people brought provisions no more to markets, since they could not get a reasonable price for them and this increased the dearth so much, that at last after many had died by it, the law itself was laid aside."

The historian Gibbon (13) tells us that sixty years after Diocletian's effort to control the cost of living by fixing prices, the Emperor Julian made a similar attempt, with no greater success. He writes:

"The inclemency of the season had affected the harvests of Syria; and the price of bread in the markets of Antioch had naturally risen in proportion to the scarcity of corn. But the fair and reasonable proportion was soon violated by the rapacious arts of monopoly. In this unequal contest, in which the produce of the land is claimed by one party as his exclusive property; is used by another as a lucrative object of trade; and is required by a third for the daily and necessary support of life; all the profits of the intermediate agents are accumulated on the head of the defenseless consumers . . . When the luxurious citizens of Antioch complained of the high price of poultry and fish, Julian publicly declared that a frugal city ought to be satisfied with a regular supply of wine, oil, and bread; but he acknowledged that it was the duty of a sovereign to provide for the subsistence of his people. With this salutary view, the emperor ventured on a very dangerous and doubtful step, of fixing, by legal authority, the value of corn. He enacted that, in a time of scarcity it should be sold at a price which had seldom been known in the most plentiful years; and that his own example might strengthen his laws, he sent into the market four hundred and twenty-two moddi, or measures, which were drawn by his order from the granaries of Hierapolis, of Chalcis, and even of Egypt. The consequences might have been foreseen and were soon felt. The imperial wheat was purchased by the rich merchants, the proprietors of land, or of corn, withheld from that city the accustomed supply, and the small quantities that appeared in the market were secretly sold at an advanced and illegal price."

Thus ended Julian's attempt to fix prices arbitrarily. It should be noted that both in the case of Diocletian and Julian the effect of the price fixing was the withholding from the market of the needed food, making necessary the abrogation of the laws by which the prices were fixed.

Great Britain, 1199-1815[7]

Litman (18) in his "Prices and Price Control in Great Britain and the U.S. During the World War" tells us that:

"An attempt to control both the wholesale and the retail price of wine by fixing a maximum was made by the British Government in 1199. The measure failed and in 1330, after a long period of ineffectiveness, a new law was passed which required the merchants to sell at a 'reasonable' price, the latter to be based on import price, plus expenses. This new measure of control proved as futile as the old one.

"The first attempt to regulate the price of wheat and bread was made in 1202. The most important ordinance on the matter was by Henry III. This ordinance fixed changing weights for the farthing loaf to correspond to six penny varieties in the price of the quarter of wheat from 12 pence to 12 shillings. The law was enforced locally on sundry occasions, but fell gradually into disuse."

Not until 1815, however, were the last laws fixing the prices of bread repealed, after a continuous existence of five and a half centuries. The official document (14) recommending their repeal enumerates the ways in which these laws have worked out to show that their repeal is in the interest of the public welfare.

Belgium, 1584-85

John Fiske (11) in one of his essays ascribes the downfall of the city of Antwerp in 1585 to the bungling price-fixing legislation of the Government. He says:

"The turning point of the great Dutch revolution, so far as it concerned the provinces which now constitute Belgium, was the famous siege and capture of Antwerp. The siege was long and the resistance obstinate and the city would probably not have been captured if famine had not come to the assistance of the besiegers. It is interesting to inquire what steps the civic authorities had taken to prevent such a calamity. Finding that speculators were accumulating and hoarding up provisions in anticipation of a season of high prices, they affixed a very low maximum price to everything which could be eaten, and prescribed severe penalties for all who should attempt to take more than the sum by law decreed. The consequences of this policy were twofold. It was a long time before the Duke of Parma, who was besieging the city, succeeded in so blockading the Scheldt as to prevent ships laden with eatables from coming in below. Corn and preserved meats might have been hurried into the beleagured city by thousands of tons. But no merchant would run the risk of having his ships sunk by the Duke's batteries merely for the sake of finding a market no better than many others which could be reached with no risk at all. The business of Government is to legislate for men as they are, not as it is supposed they ought to be. If provisions had brought a high price in Antwerp, they would have been carried thither. As it was the city by its own stupidity blockaded itself far more effectually than the Duke of Parma could have done.

"In the second place the enforced lowness of prices prevented any general retrenchment on the part of the citizens. Nobody felt it necessary to economize. So the city lived in high spirits until all at once provisions gave out and the Government had to step in again to palliate the distress which it had wrought.

"In this way a bungling act of legislation helped to decide for the worse a campaign which involved the territorial integrity and future welfare of what might have become a great nation performing a valuable function in the system of European communities."

India, 1770 and 1866

The famines of India are prominent features in her history. William Hunter (15) in his remarkable book entitled, "Annals of Rural Bengal," writes:

"Lower Bengal gathers in three harvests each year; in the spring, in the early autumn, and in December, the last being the great rice crop, the harvest on which the sustenance of the people depends. The December crop failed utterly in 1770 and fully a third of the population died. This disaster stands out in the contemporary records in appalling proportions. It forms, indeed, the key to the history of Bengal during the succeeding forty years.

"In 1770 the Government by interdicting what it was pleased to term the monopoly of grain, prevented prices from rising at once to their natural rates. The province had a certain amount of food in it and this food had to last nine months. Private enterprise if left to itself would have stored up the general supply at the harvest with a view to realizing a larger profit at a later period in the scarcity.

"Prices would in consequence have immediately risen, compelling the population to reduce their consumption from the very beginning of the dearth. The general stock would thus have been husbanded and the pressure equally spread over the whole nine months instead of being concentrated upon the last six. Instead of this the Government in 1770 prohibited under penalties all speculation in rice. A government which, in a season of high prices, does anything to check speculation acts about as sagely as the skipper of a wrecked vessel who should refuse to put his crew upon half rations.

"Very different was the procedure of the Government at the time of the famine of 1866. Far from trying to check speculation, as in 1770, the Government did all in its power to stimulate it. In the earlier famine one could hardly engage in the grain trade without becoming amenable to the law. In 1866 respectable men in vast numbers went into the trade; for the Government, by publishing weekly returns of the rates in every district, rendered the traffic both easy and safe. Everyone knew where to buy grain cheapest and where to sell it dearest and food was accordingly bought from the districts which could best spare it and carried to those which most urgently needed it.

"In 1770 the price of grain, in place of promptly rising to three half-pence a pound, as in 1865-66, continued at three farthings during the earlier months of the famine. During the latter months it advanced to two pence, and in certain localities reached four pence."

Colonial U.S., 1633-1779

Passing now to the eighteenth century some observations will not be amiss on the price-fixing measures resorted to in our country during Colonial days and the early years of the Republic, and also in France during the tragic period of the French Revolution.

Both of these periods have been so ably described that little seems necessary except to give the reference to the literature. Winthrop (24) tells us, in 1633:

"The scarcity of workmen has caused them to raise their wages to an excessive rate, so as a carpenter would have three shillings the day, a laborer two shillings and six pence, etc.; and, accordingly those who had commodities to sell, advanced their prices sometimes double to that they cost in England, so as it grew to a general complaint, which the court, taking knowledge of, as also of some further evils, which were sprung out of the excessive rates of wages, they made an order that carpenters, masons, etc., should take but two shillings the day, and laborers but eighteen pence, and that no commodity should be sold at above four pence in the shilling more than it cost for ready money in England; oil, wine, etc., and cheese, in regard to the hazard of bringing, etc. (excepted)."

Bolles (3) gives an excellent account of the experiment of price fixing in the early years of the United States in the attempt to stop the rise in price of the necessities of life, caused by the declining value of the continental paper currency.

Pelatiah Webster (21) discusses the legal limitation of prices with vigor and lucidity and shows by resistless logic that such legislation defeats its own end in several ways, the most important of which is the withholding of commodities from the market which it inevitably produces.

On December 20, 1777, Sir Henry Clinton, in charge of the British forces occupying New York, made a proclamation (7) as follows:

"Whereas it is consonant not only to the common principles of humanity but to the wisdom and policy of all well regulated states, in certain exigencies, to guard against the extortion of individuals, who raise the necessaries of life, without which other parts of the community can not subsist; and whereas the farmers in Long Island and Staten Island, are possessed of great quantities of wheat, rye, and Indian corn for sale beyond what they want for their own consumption; and it is highly unreasonable that those who may stand in need of those articles, should be left at the mercy of the farmer; and whereas it is equally just and reasonable that every encouragement should be given to the industry of the husbandman, and that in all public regulations respecting the price of the produce of his lands, regard should be had to that of the conveniences which he is obliged to purchase, and whereas the present rates at which wheat, flour, rye meal, and Indian meal are sold, do vastly exceed in proportion the advance price of those articles which the farmer stands in need of purchasing, and I being well satisfied, from the best information, and most accurate estimates, that the following prices upon the articles above mentioned will be liberal and generous, have thought it fit to issue this Proclamation, and do hereby order and direct, that the prices to be hereafter demanded for the said articles shall not exceed the following rates, viz.:

"A bushel of wheat, weighing fifty-eight pounds, twelve shillings, with an allowance or deduction in proportion for a greater or lesser weight. A bushel of rye or Indian corn, seven shillings," etc.

The proclamation proceeds to state that the farmer shall declare how much grain he has and if he presumes to sell for a higher price than the one stipulated or "refuse to sell the same at those prices, shall be subject to have his whole crop of grain, or quantity of flour or meal, concerning which such offence shall happen, seized and confiscated, and himself liable to imprisonment for such offense."

Davis (8) in his able and comprehensive treatment of limitation of prices in Massachusetts, gives much information relating to this subject in the other states also. Felt (10) gives extracts from the text of the "Act to prevent monopoly and oppression." He also gives the actual prices set for the various commodities, and in appendix 2 gives "Prices of grain, etc., appointed by the general court and taken as currency." These prices are of much interest as they go back to 1642 and were legal tender at that time.

Weeden (22) writes in his "Economic and Social History of New England, 1620-1789":

"The colonial history of the United States affords many instances of the failure of fixed prices to remedy the evils they were designed to cure. The governor and council of New England fixed the price of beaver at 6s in fair exchange for English goods at 30 per cent profit, with the freight added. The scarcity of corn which was selling at 10s 'the strike' led to the prohibition of its sale to the Indians. Under the pressure of this prohibition the price of beaver advanced to 10s and 20s per pound, the natives having refused to part with beaver unless given corn. The court was obliged to remove the fixed rate and the price which ruled was 20s. An equally fruitless attempt was made to regulate the price of labor. These regulations were inforced for about six months and then were repealed."

France, 1789-1793

As regards the limitation of prices in France during the Revolution, there seems nothing to add to Bourne's (4) discussion of this subject in the "Journal of Political Economy" for February and March, 1919. We cannot fail to note, however, that the system failed signally in France as elsewhere because supplies were withheld from the markets. The producers could not be forced to declare what they had and without this knowledge the Government could not prosecute for withholding them. Bourne writes:

"The arguments in the convention relative to the matter ran the whole gamut from the principles of economic liberty advocated by the economists of the day to the radical abstractions of Robespierre and his followers, who swept commerce aside by maintaining that 'the food necessary to man is sacred as life itself,' and 'The fruits of the earth like the atmosphere belong to all men.'

"One of the most interesting of the many suggestions made in the convention was that of Barbaroux who advocated 'a plan to form local associations to collect and circulate information about the crops. In other words, for coercion he would substitute cooperation, believing that the French citizens, farmers and merchants included, would not turn a deaf ear to an appeal for common action against the oncoming peril' (famine). Price fixing finally became one of the characteristic features of the Reign of Terror, and when Robespierre and his councilors passed through the streets of Paris in the carts of the executioners the mob jeered saying, 'There goes the dirty maximum.'"

Summary

The history of government limitation of price seems to teach one clear lesson: That in attempting to ease the burdens of the people in a time of high prices by artificially setting a limit to them, the people are not relieved but only exchange one set of ills for another which is greater. Among these ills are (1) the withholding of goods from the market, because consumers being in the majority, price fixing is usually in their interest; (2) the dividing of the community into two hostile camps, one only of which considers that the government acts in its interest; (3) the practical difficulties of enforcing such limitation in prices which in the very nature of the case requires the cooperation of both producer and consumer to make it effective.

Egypt took entire control of the grain trade and saved the people from starvation, but took over the land in return.

China worked out a system of control of supply and demand which kept prices normal. She seems to have been the only country which recognized the whole price question as being a symptom and not the disease itself, and because she recognized this fact seems to have come nearer than any other country to solving the problem of supplying the people with the food they needed at a price they could pay.

Athens regulated the grain trade and set prices by legal enactment but found herself unable to enforce them.

Rome made a colossal experiment in controlling prices by legal enactment, but it utterly failed.

Great Britain had on her statute books laws fixing the price of bread continuously for more than 500 years. The price of wheat, fish, and wine was also regulated, but all such laws were abrogated in 1815, because of their failure to accomplish the purpose for which they were designed.

Antwerp was overthrown in 1585, and at least one historian of note declares that price-fixing legislation was largely responsible for its downfall.

India has learned in the hard school of experience that even in times of famine, price fixing is a very dangerous expedient because it removes one of the most powerful checks on consumption; namely, high prices.

The Colonial United States tried the same experiment at various places and times but failed utterly to secure satisfactory results.

Revolutionary France tried the same measures, but the protagonists of the movement perished on the guillotine. The dreary story of France's efforts to limit prices is distinguished from that of the other countries we have noted because of the proposal of Barbaroux to enlist the aid of both producer and consumer in the effort of the Government to control the food supply in the interest of the people's welfare. This proposition was not carried out but it furnished the first indication of the goal of cooperation towards which we are still pressing.

Notes

[1]No attempt has been made in this paper to cover the history of price fixing since 1800 government monopolies such as the Brazilian valorization of coffee, the tobacco monopoly in France, and that of sugar in Germany, as well as others which might be mentioned, have been fully reported by others. The history of price fixing in the U.S. during the War of 1914-18 has also been written in the Bulletins of the War Industries Board, on the history of prices during the war. Litman gives a good account for Great Britain and the U.S. in his "Prices and Price Control in Great Britain and the U.S. During the War."

[2]Some scholars place the date at 2082 B.C. and still others at 1500 B.C. It was probably in the reign of Aphobis, at the end of the 17th dynasty, according to Dr. Henry Brugsch, in his history of Egypt under the Pharaohs. Trans. by Philip Smith. (London, John Murray, v. 1, p. 300-306.)

[3]Original sources:

Lepsius, Richard. Denkmaler aus Aegypten und Aethiopien. Berlin. 1849-59 v. 3, p. 76, 77.

Papyrus Abbott, published in the "Select Papyri in the Hieratic Character" from the Collections of the British Museum, London, 1844-60.

[4]It is evident from the context that "grain" as used in these translations means *rice*.

[5]A medimnus was equal to 2/3 of a bushel or 8 gallons.

[6]The population of the whole of Attica at this time was about 500,000, of which Athens comprised about 180,000.

[7]The English corn laws from 1804 to 1846 furnish probably the best known instance of governmental attempts to stabilize prices in more modern times. The corn statutes of these years are simply a record of the impotence of legislation to maintain the price of a commodity at a high point when all the natural economic causes in operation are opposed to it. Encyclopedia Brit. 11th ed., v. 7, p. 177.

List of References

1. Abbott, Frank Frost.
   The Common People of Ancient Rome. New York, Scribner, 1911 p. 150-151.
2. Boeckh, August.
   The Public Economy of the Athenians . . . Tr. by Anthony Lamb, Boston, Little Brown & Company, 1857. Book 1, chap. 15.
3. Bolles, Albert S.
   The Financial History of the United States from 1774-1789. Fourth ed. New York, D. Appleton, 1896, p. 158-173.
4. Bourne, Henry E.
   Food Control and Price Fixing in Revolutionary France. (Journal of Political Economy. V. 27, p. 73-94, 108-209. Feb. and March 1919.)
5. Breasted, James Henry.
   Ancient Records of Egypt. Chicago, Univ. of Chicago Press, 1906-07, v. 1, p. 126.
6. Chen, Huan-Chang.
   The Economic Principles of Confucius and His School, N.Y., Longmans, Green and Co., 1911. (In Columbia Univ. Studies in history, economics, and public law. V. 44 and 45.)
7. Clinton, Sir Henry.
   Proclamation Dec. 20, 1777. (In the Remembrancer; or impartial repository of public events. Ed. by John Almon. London [v. 6.] 1778. p. 57-58.)
8. Davis, Andrew McFarland.
   The Limitation of Prices in Massachusetts, 1776-1779. (In Colonial society of Massachusetts. Publications v. 10, Boston, 1907. p. 119-134)
9. Erman, Adolph.
   Life in Ancient Egypt . . . Tr. by H. M. Tirard. London and N.Y. Macmillan & Co., 1894, p. 107-108, 433-434.
10. Felt, Joseph B.
   An Historical Account of Massachusetts Currency. Boston, Perkins, and Marvin, 1839, p. 170-173, 184-185, 242-245.
11. Fiske, John.
   The Unseen World and Other Essays. Boston, 1904, p. 20.
12. Genesis XII, 1-10; XLI, 54; XLII, 2.
13. Gibbon, Edward.
   The History of the Decline and Fall of the Roman Empire. N.Y. Fred de Fau, 1906, v. 4, p. 111-112.
14. Great Britain, Parliament. House of Commons.
   Report from the Committee of the House of Commons on Laws Relating to the Manufacture, Sale, and Assize of Bread. 6 June, 1815.

15. Hunter, William W.
Annals of Rural Bengal. Ed. 7, London, Smith, Elder & Co., 1897.
16. Josephus, Flavius.
History of the Antiquities of the Jews. Ed. by George Henry Mayard, London, C. Cooke, 1789. Bk. 11, Chap. VI & VIII.
17. Lactantius, L.C.F.
A Relation of the Death of the Primitive Persecutors. Written originally in Latin . . . Englished by Gilbert Burnet, D.D. Amsterdam, 1687, p. 67-68.
18. Litman, Simon.
Prices and Price Control in Great Britain and the United States During the World War. N.Y., Oxford Univ. Press, 1920.
19. Lysias.
Against the Grain Dealers. (In eight orations of Lysias. Ed. by Morris H. Morgan. Boston, Ginn & Co., 1895, p. 89-103.) For translation see Botsford, G. W., and E. G. Sihler, Hellenic civilization. N.Y. Columbia Univ. Press, 1915, p. 426-430.
20. Mommsen, Theodor.
Corpus in Scriptionum Latinarum. Berloni apud Georgium Reinerum, 1889, v. 3 (Suppl. pt. 1) p. 1926-1953.
21. Webster, Pelatiah.
Political Essays. Philadelphia. Joseph Cruikshank, 1791, p. 11-18.
22. Weeden, William B.
Economic and Social History of New England, 1620-1789. Houghton, Boston, 1890.
23. Wilkinson, J. Gardner.
The Manners and Customs of the Ancient Egyptians. London. John Murray, 1878, v. 2, p. 378.
24. Winthrop, John.
The History of New England from 1630-1649. Boston Phelps and Farnham, 1825, v. 1, p. 116.

76. HOW TO END POVERTY*

Dean Russell

Our political leaders have recently declared war against poverty in the United States. And they are now in the process of mobilizing the nation's manpower and resources for the coming battle.

The general philosophy behind these recurring governmental campaigns to stop poverty is familiar indeed to students of economic history. As merely one of countless possible examples on the same general theme, let us first look briefly at the so-called Industrial Revolution in the England of 150 years or so ago.

Perhaps the two most famous of the reformers of that era were the classical economist, Karl Marx, and the successful businessman who became his collaborator, Friedrich Engels. Those two men were the intellectual leaders of the war against poverty in their time. And as is still the case with most of our own intellectual and political leaders today, the only solution that Marx and Engels ever offered to end poverty was to have the government increase its compulsions and prohibitions over the people in their economic activities.

It is not necessary here to question the accuracy of those reports by Karl Marx in which he described the degrading living conditions of the people who worked in those early factory towns of industrial Britain. While his research was confined to extensive reading in the British Museum, I will here assume that his statements on the harsh working conditions of that time were essentially true in a reportorial sense. But most unfortunately for poor people everywhere, Marx completely missed both the reality and the portent behind what he was reporting. And thus he offered a totally erroneous solution to the problems of poverty and how to raise the level of living of the general population.

The Socialist Theory

The famous theory endorsed by Karl Marx to improve the well-being of mankind was based firmly on governmental ownership and operation of the means of producing and distributing all goods and services; later on, he appears to have agreed that heavy governmental controls, without total state ownership, might also effectively accomplish the task. That ancient but ever-new theory has been increasing in popularity all over the world, ever since Marx refurbished it again in his program to end poverty by positive governmental action. Under a different name (and with a few changes in nonessentials), that same socialist theory of economics is

*From *The Freeman*, August 1964

the inspiration behind the current governmental plans to end poverty in the United States.

Perhaps the best source for a summary of the philosophy and program of Karl Marx is his major book, *Das Kapital.* As I here list the main points of his theory, I am confident that you will find most of them as familiar as today's newspaper or political speech or sermon or textbook on economics.

Departure from Classical School

Since Karl Marx was trained in the "classical school" of economics of Adam Smith and David Ricardo, he was well aware that increasing capital accumulation is necessary for increasing industrial growth. And he readily agreed with the classical economists that as capital (machinery) increases, the result will be more and more production of more and more products. So far, so good.

But at this point, Marx deviated from the prevailing economic thought of his time and claimed that the unplanned and uncontrolled production of a free market will result in general surpluses that can't be sold; that is, the workers won't have enough purchasing power to buy the products they produce. This development will cause factories to shut down until the surpluses can be disposed of in some manner. Thus, booms will be followed at regular intervals by busts. Throughout the economic ups and downs of these business cycles, however, the rich will get richer and the poor will get poorer, according to Marx. This will continue as long as there is uncontrolled private ownership and production in a market economy that (according to Marx) is necessarily based on increasing monopolies, jungle competition, and anarchic production. The unorganized, oppressed, and politically helpless workers will be exploited mercilessly. Many (perhaps most) of them will lose their jobs to the ever-increasing and more efficient machines. And while the workers who are fortunate enough to have jobs will increase their production, they will be paid lower wages than before.

Marx predicted categorically that widespread poverty, mass starvation, and death among the working classes are the inevitable results of capital formation and industrialization in a market (non-socialist) economy of private ownership. His financial backer and literary collaborator, Friedrich Engels, said much the same thing in his book, *The Condition of the Working Classes in England in 1844.* For example, he claimed that the peasants and their children in agrarian England were far healthier, happier, and more prosperous than the workers of industrial England after 1700 and the advent of machinery for mass production.

Trimming the Facts To Fit the Theory

One of the most astounding facts of economic history is this: At the time that Marx and Engels formulated and published their theory, the statistical proof of its falseness was publicly available. Further, both Marx and Engels were aware of this evidence; one can only assume that they simply ignored it because it did not fit into their theory.

Here are the statistics referred to—the population figures for England and Wales from 1600 through 1831, figures that Karl Marx could not possibly have missed during his years of extensive research in this general area.

Year	*Population*
1600	around 5 million*
1700	more than 5 million*
1750	more than 6 million*
1801	9 million (census)
1820	12 million (census)
1831	16 million (census)

*Rough estimate

Among the voluminous statistics of this same type that were available to Marx and Engels, one also finds this: In London in 1750, about 70 per cent of all children died before age five; by 1830, the figure had fallen below 30 per cent.

If the theories of economics and history advanced by Karl Marx were valid, these population figures would have to be the reverse of what they are. If there were any merit at all to the theory of socialism, children would have died earlier (and the population would have diminished) as the number of machines increased in Great Britain from 1700 to 1900 in an increasingly free market.

But the truth of the matter is, of course, the reverse. As industrialization in the competitive market economy grew, the life expectancy of children (and also of adults) grew right along with it. The population had been barely moving forward for two or three hundred years in an agrarian economy with few machines. But with increasing machinery —and especially the invention of the steam engine and the rapid industrialization that followed it—the population soon doubled, and then trebled.

One should also remember that it was during this period that hundreds-of-thousands of British subjects were migrating to all parts of the world.

Thus, the statistics on population growth given above are really understated.

The reason that the evidence is contrary to socialist theory is simply because (basically) socialist theories of economics and history were (and still are) totally false. But before we examine the validity of that sweeping condemnation, let us mention two possibilities other than machines in a market economy that might explain this increase in life expectancy.

Was it due to new medical knowledge and practices? No, for the most part, those improvements came *after* the machines, not before.

Was it due to more governmental controls and welfare schemes? No, governmental interferences in the economy were *decreasing* during this period. Percentagewise, there was less government welfare instead of more. The economy was becoming increasingly free.

A False Theory

At this point, however, I would like to agree with Marx on one of his ideas—that is, before one can understand history, he must first have some understanding of economic theory. Economics is certainly not the sole determinant of history, as Marx claimed it to be. But at least it is important enough to explain the nonsense that is so often encountered in the deductions of historians who have no real understanding of economic theory. The misinterpretation of history by the socialist philosophers, however, was, of course, not due to the *absence* of economic theory but rather to the endorsement of *false* theory.

A Better Theory Proposed

Since it is obvious that the socialist theories of history and economics do not fit the facts of the Industrial Revolution, and are thus false, then what theory does explain this period of fantastic economic growth? Well, here is my own theory, in four simple parts. Let us see if it helps in any way to explain the facts:

1. Persons who have enough to eat will live longer than persons who don't have enough to eat. That statement is not intended to be humorous; actually, it is an oft-ignored fact that is fundamental to any economic theory that explains why human beings act as they do. And I am reasonably confident that Karl Marx would have agreed with it.

2. Other things being equal, a man with a wheelbarrow and shovel can move more dirt from "hither to yon" than can a man using only his hands. That is, a man with a machine can produce more than a man without a machine; or, capital formation increases production. Again, Marx would surely have agreed with me. But on the heart of my theory—the next two points—he would have been in total disagreement.

3. The employee who is working in a factory for wages in a free economy will be paid more if he produces more. I could here use marginal analysis to support the theory. But for my present purpose of simplified explanation, I need only point out this fact: Competition among employers in a *free* economy will guarantee that result; for since each employer is in business to earn profits, each will try to secure the services of the workers who produce the most in the shortest period of time. The only way this can be done in a *free* market is to offer higher real wages. If that is not so, then we are faced with the absurd theory that the policy of employers in an economy of choice is to voluntarily pay most to the employees who produce the least.

4. Persons who are producing, selling, and buying what *they* choose to produce, sell, and buy will have more of what *they* want than will persons who are compelled to produce, sell, and buy what they don't want. If that sounds like a mere play on words, it isn't. For what I have said is that the market economy of free choice (with the government restricted to preserving the peace and suppressing fraud) provides more people with the things *they* want than does any other economic arrangement. Or expressed in other words: If the objective of an economic system is to provide the maximum amount of goods and services that peaceful persons want, obviously there must be freedom of choice and exchange. This essential requirement for maximum material well-being exists in a free market economy, and *only* in a free market economy. The socialist theory of a controlled economy (that is, a controlled people) is necessarily based on the idea that when peaceful persons are compelled to produce, sell, and buy what they would not voluntarily produce, sell, and buy, they really have more of what they want than is the case when they are free to choose.

A Priori Reasoning

Well, there you have the nonsocialist theory of economics as best I can state it in brief form. It is, essentially, the exact opposite of the socialist theory. And thus you can now better understand my sweeping statement that the socialist theory of government ownership or control of production and distribution is totally false and must always finally produce the reverse of what its advocates say they wish to accomplish. That is as true in the United States as elsewhere, currently or at any other time.

Now I wish to say two things about this theory. First, of course, I didn't invent it; I suspect, however, that I have simplified it considerably. Second, the inventors did not first look at the facts and then work out a theory to fit them. That isn't how theory is developed. For example, the first "sputnik" that circled the earth did not generate a theory; instead, the prior theory generated the first man-made orbit around the earth.

You and I know *a priori* that a man with a wheelbarrow and shovel can move more earth in a given period of time than can a man without a wheelbarrow and shovel. We don't need any facts to prove it. The theory is self-evident. The man who invented the wheelbarrow did it because he knew in advance that he could thereby "produce more" with that tool than he could without it. And so it is with the three other *a priori* theories I have cited above. Since they are unquestionably true, I know that certain results must necessarily follow their application.

I know that as more machines appeared *in an increasingly free market* in Great Britain after 1700, there would be more food and other goods and services. The people would live longer. And under the conditions of that particular time, the population could be expected to increase rapidly. That economic theory doesn't really need "statistical proof" since it is self-evident and is based on the fact that every person is well aware that he will live longer with food than without food. The opposing socialist theory is not false merely because the statistics disprove it; the theory is false on a self-evident basis. Since socialist economic theory is false *a priori,* naturally the results in practice must finally be disastrous. That is why millions of Russians starved to death under the communist economic system after 1918; persons were literally prevented from producing food. It was not due so much to lack of political freedom as it was to the utter nonsense of socialist economic theory; the results could not be otherwise.

And even today, the only reason that the Russian people manage to stay alive at all is because they cheat against their socialist theory. This cheating is on a mammoth scale and, fortunately for the Russian people, it appears to be increasing. The officials permit a tremendous amount of "free enterprise" food growing; they use unrestricted market prices to distribute vast quantities of food and considerable amounts of consumer goods; the managers of factories can now fire inefficient workers and hire ones who produce more; the government planners have rejected the Marxian idea of government unemployment compensation that pays a person not to work; further, make-work schemes that are now protected by law in the United States would result in long prison sentences for persons who openly practiced them in the Soviet Union; the free market prices of the world are used by the socialist planners in Russia to guide their production procedures and goals; the "profit motive" rather than the "firing squad" is now increasingly used as the incentive to get better management and more production; and so on through thousands of free market violations of socialism.

The truth is simple and harsh: If the Russians didn't cheat against the economic theory on which their system is based, they would all literally starve to death. And even at best, they must still depend on other nations to send them food. It is to be hoped that future leaders in Russia will finally accept fully the fact that persons who have enough to eat will live longer than persons who don't have enough to eat, and that they will then adopt the policy of leaving persons free to produce the food they want instead of compelling them to produce "moon shots" that they would never produce voluntarily.

The adoption and practice of false economic theory explains why millions of men, women, and children are literally starving and dying in China today. The total economic collapse in Cuba today is not due primarily to the fact that Cuba has a dictator; it is because that dictator operates on socialist economic theory. The present socialist economic system in Cuba can't possibly work in practice because it is false in theory. It is totally contrary to how all human beings choose to act when they are free to do so.

Some Things Explained

With my own theory cited above, I know in advance that (other things being somewhat equal) the people in a comparatively free economy will have a higher level of living than will the people in a less free economy.

I know that West Germany has to be more prosperous than East Germany. My *a priori* theory says that it cannot be otherwise. And since the economy in Poland is a little bit more free than the economy in Russia, my theory says that the Poles should be expected to have a slightly higher level of living than the Russians. They do, even though the still-heavy controls over the economy in Poland still mean a distressingly low level of living for the unfortunate Polish people.

My economic theory says that the Japanese in their comparatively free market should have a higher level of living than had the Japanese under the former controlled economy. They do. Further, my theory implies that the economic "growth rate" in Japan should be high. It is; in fact, the rate there appears to be the highest in the world.

With my theory, I can now make some sense out of history, a thing that Karl Marx was never able to do. I now better understand why ancient Athens enjoyed its phenomenal growth rate for 150 years or so. I can now better understand why it declined and collapsed. In each case, the key I search for is the *comparative* freedom enjoyed by the citizens in the economic areas—that is, the extent of private ownership and of the freedom of persons to exchange goods and services voluntarily.

I now know why a much higher level of living developed in Venezuela than in Brazil in our own era. And I also now understand why the level of living in Venezuela has (percentagewise) not increased as fast during the past few years as it did formerly. I can now also understand the situations in Argentina and India. Finally, I can now understand why the real level of living per capita in my own country is not increasing (percentagewise and on the average) as fast as it used to before 1930 and the general acceptance of the philosophy of the welfare state and the controlled economy. Further, my theory says that the battle plans of the current war against poverty in the United States (more socialism) must eventually bring the reverse of the announced aims.

Well, you pick your own time and place, and examine it from the viewpoints of the two theories here advanced—Marx's socialist theory of economics and my own free market theory. If other things are reasonably equal, you will always find that (over a significant period of time) the people in the "more free" economy will be more prosperous than the people in the "less free" economy. This is self-evident because free people will always produce more of what *they* want than will people in a controlled economy who are prevented from choosing what they will produce. It cannot be otherwise.

The size of the country and the extent of its natural resources are not as vital for a high level of living in today's world as is the economic philosophy endorsed by the nation's leaders; for example, small and resource-poor Switzerland has a comparatively high level of living. When one considers the amount of foreign capital that goes there —and *why* it goes there—no one should be surprised at this result. And no one who understands economic theory is in the least surprised at the fantastic "growth rate" of tiny Hong Kong with essentially *no* natural resources.

Now I would like to end where I started—with the Industrial Revolution. Please note that I have not denied the horrors of that period. I am aware that there were cases of six-year-old children who worked ten hours a day—and that they lived in filth and often suffered injury from those primitive machines. All I have said is that life expectancy for children working in those factories was higher than was the life expectancy of children in the preindustrial society. The children of the Industrial Revolution era had more to eat, even though they still didn't have enough. They had more to eat because they could produce more with machines than without machines, and could trade their industrial products for more and better food. They still didn't have all they wanted to eat because they still couldn't produce enough with the still-primitive machines they had. But as capital accumulated and more and better machines came into existence, they produced more. And thus they had more to eat. And thus they lived longer.

I maintain that living to age nine is better than dying at age five. As more capital was accumulated in an increasingly free market economy, the children lived even longer. Finally there was enough capital available to permit a man to produce enough to put his children into schools, and for his wife to change her factory job for the job of homekeeping. It was machines under private ownership, not child labor laws, that finally took the children permanently out of the factories and put them into schools. If you doubt this, think of what would necessarily happen to children today if there were no machines.

The private accumulation of capital in a free market economy has always meant an increasingly higher level of living. This is what it always will mean. Thus the most practical thing that you and I can do to end poverty in the United States or elsewhere is to insist that the market shall be free. Nothing else is required; anything else will fail.

77. AMERICAN COMMUNISM*

Percy L. Greaves, Jr.

PART I. Jamestown

Jamestown, the first English settlement in America, was founded on Christianity and communism. The original settlers were forced to use the forms of the State religion in their worship of God. They were lured to the Virginia shores with promises of social security and the abundant life. They were all to be fed and clothed out of a common store.

Fortunately for us, they survived a succession of famines and tyrannies to provide us with a heritage of liberty—liberty to worship God and produce wealth as each of us sees fit without injury to our fellowmen.

In 1606, his Divine Majesty, James I of England, granted the London Company the first Charter rights to settle "alongst the coasts of Virginia." The "sundry Knights, Gentlemen, Merchants and other Adventurers" were commended to propagate the "Christian religion to such People, as yet live in Darkness and miserable Ignorance of the true Knowledge and Worship of God."

The original band of 105 men landed in May, 1607, with their "religious and courageous divine," the Reverend Robert Hunt. One of their first tasks in Jamestown was to arrange a place of worship. This was done by stretching sails between tree trunks for a covering. A board was then nailed between two trees to form a pulpit and reading desk. Captain John Smith later wrote that "our walls were rails of wood, our seats unhewn trees." This crude affair was soon replaced by a log church. There Mr. Hunt read Church of England services every morning and every evening. He preached twice on Sundays, and held communion at regular intervals. He was always sure of a large congregation.

As commanded in their Charter, the settlers tried to convert the "Infidels and Savages, living in those Parts" to Christianity. They were not very successful in this matter. Pocahontas, the first Indian maiden to marry an Englishman, became a Christian, and the colonists strove to convert others "from the worship of the devils to the service of God." A 1610 report told those in England to "Doubt not God will raise our State and build his church in this excellent clime."

Despite this religious background the Colony almost foundered several times due to famine and disease. In the first six months more than 60 of the original 105 died. Out of every shipload that arrived, less than half would survive their first 12 months in the new land. The winter of 1609-10 was known as "The Starving Time." The population dwindled from about 500 souls to 60. The Colony was saved time and time again by the happy arrival of new ships with food and supplies. Captain John Smith saved many by his ability to obtain food from the Indians. He did this largely through trickery and their fear of gunpowder.

Some of the early Jamestown history reads a bit like that of our own day. Those who had been guaranteed an easy living with social security did not feel that they had to work. There was much stealing, and selling of public property to the Indians for private profit. Within six or seven weeks after the arrival of one ship, more than 200 much-needed hatchets, chisels, mattocks and pickaxes disappeared. Undoubtedly they had been black-marketed to the Indians.

All the real work of the Colony was done by one-fifth of the men. Four-fifths were pure parasites. Finally, in exasperation, Captain John Smith proclaimed, "But I protest by that God that made me, since necessity hath not power to force you to gather for yourselves those fruits the earth doth yield, you shall not only gather them for yourselves, but for those that are sick . . . and he that gathereth not every day as much as I do, the next day shall be set beyond the river, and be banished from the Fort as a drone, till he amend his condition or starve." There were many charges of laziness, and much

*From *Christian Economics* January 29 and March 25, 1952

misery. Finally, Captain Smith decreed "You must obey this now for the law, that he who will not work shall not eat."

Captain Smith was deposed in the fall of 1609. "The Starving Time" followed and all was despair. The following spring the few survivors boarded their ships and set sail for England. At the mouth of the James River they met 500 new colonists. They turned about and started over under a new Charter and a new Governor, Lord De La Warr. The men were ordered to work from six to ten in the morning, and from two to four in the afternoon. After his first year as Governor, Lord De La Warr left the Colony in charge of an easy-going deputy.

The Colony fared very poorly until Sir Thomas Dale was placed in charge in 1611. He took drastic measures. Many thought him a tyrant. He was merciless to the law-breakers of that era, but friendly and helpful to the upright who would work. Anyone who demeaned a clergyman was soundly whipped in public. He made it a capital crime to stay away from church services, or to conduct unlicensed trading with the Indians.

Private Plots Allotted

The Secretary of the Colony, Ralph Hamor, best described Dale's success in his 1614 report. He stated that when he arrived, four years earlier, there were less than 60 persons scarcely able "to go alone," and now, in 1614, there were many times that number and "there is that plenty of food, which every man by his own industry may easily and doth procure that the poorest there and most in want, hath not been so much pinched with hunger this four years that if he would take any pains, he knew not where to fetch a good meal's meat . . . they have more plenty than other, the reason hereof is at hand, for formerly, when our people were fed out of the common store and labored jointly in the manuring of the ground, and planting corn, glad was the man that could slip from his labor, nay the most honest of them in a general business, would not take so much faithful and true pains in a week, as now he will do in a day, neither cared they for the increase, presuming that howsoever their harvest prospered, the general store must maintain them, by which means we reaped not so much corn from the labors of 30 men, as three men have done for themselves: to prevent which mischief hereafter Sir Thomas Dale hath taken a new course, throughout the whole Colony, by which means, the general store (apparel only excepted) shall not be charged with anything: and this it is, he hath allotted to every man in the Colony, three English acres of clear Corn ground, which every man is to mature and tend, being in the nature of Farmers, and they are not called unto any service or labor belonging to the Colony, more than one month in the year, which shall neither be in seed time, or in Harvest, for which, doing no other duty to the Colony, they are yearly to pay into the store two barrels and a half of corn: there to be reserved to keep new men, which shall be sent over, the first year after their arrival."

And so it was that putting an end to communism put an end to famine. Serious crimes and internal disorders abated. But the trials of the Colony were not over. Sir Thomas Dale was succeeded by Samuel Argall who ruled as a tyrant from 1617 to 1619. As Henry Cabot Lodge in his "History of the English Colonies in America" reports, "He (Argall) oppressed the colonists and robbed them of their property. . . . They had no protection against the tyrant. . . . Complaints soon found their way to England."

Argall was finally replaced by Sir George Yeardley. This great Governor arrived in 1619 and established the first representative government here in America. The Colony soon had a written Constitution providing for a legislature of two houses. Members of the upper house were called Councillors, and those of the lower house, Burgesses. The new Assembly opened with a prayer for "the equality of all men before the law." This meant that "persons of quality" were to be subject to the same punishments as others.

Yeardley confirmed the titles of all estates in those who held them before Argall's disastrous reign. The rights of property were maintained against all arbitrary taxes. Every man was encouraged to "sell as dear as he could." A free economy was established. The colonists were no longer forced to trade at the common store, but could buy and sell where they pleased. Within a year after this "veritable revolution" the population increased from 600 to more than 4,000. Although the Colony had many other trials its days of famine were over forever.

The Virginia colonists were then able "to live together, in the Fear and True Worship of Almighty God, Christian Peace, and civil Quietness, each with other, whereby every one may, with more Safety, Pleasure, and Profit, enjoy that, whereunto they shall attain with great Pain and Peril."

PART II. Plymouth

Plymouth, the second English speaking colony in America, was founded on communism and the freedom of religion. The Pilgrims came to the stern New England coast in quest of an "asylum where conscience, property and person might be secure." As a later colonist phrased it, they came in search of "soul freedom." They thought communism could help them.

We in America owe much to these early Puritans. Their pilgrimage and principles have been a basic part of this country's spiritual and material success. Their devotion to God and freedom surpasses the understanding of most modern men. They would brook no interference with their freedom to worship God according to their own fashion.

The Puritans were an early product of the Reformation. They had no faith in the forms and rituals of most churches. They rebelled not only against the rites of the Roman Catholic Church, which they called the "gross darkness of popery," but also against the rules of worship laid down by Queen Elizabeth and King James. They believed "that not even a ceremony should be tolerated, unless it was enjoined by the word of God." The Bible was their religious authority. They would yield to no earthly sovereign in their worship of God.

The Puritans were not appeasers, pussyfooters or Milquetoasts. As the great historian George Bancroft reports, "the Puritan martyrs never sought, by concessions to escape the flames. For them, compromise was itself apostasy." When they were ordered to attend Church of England services or face exile or death, they remained loyal to their own simple services.

They believed that God had given them the right to choose their pastors and worship the Lord as they saw fit. Accordingly, they resolved to leave their mother land and seek asylum in freedom-loving Holland. Their religious persecutors did everything possible to keep them in England. In 1608, after many trials and much loss of property, they finally managed their escape to Holland.

In his "History of Plymouth Plantation," Governor William Bradford describes the life of the Puritans in Holland in these words, "such was the true piety, the humble zeal, & fervent love of this people towards God and His ways, and the single heartedness & sincere affection one towards another, that they came as near the primitive pattern of the first churches, as any other church of these later times have done."

After a decade in this foreign land, they became restless. They wanted a place of their own. The twelve-year truce between Spain and Holland was drawing to a close. They feared a new European war. So, after much prayer and consultation, they decided to move on to the New World where they could shake the "yoke of antichristian bondage, and as the Lord's free people, join themselves into a church estate, in the fellowship of the gospel, to walk in all His ways, made known, or to be made known unto them, according to their best endeavors, whatsoever it should cost them, the Lord assisting them."

Once they made the decision, "those that were to go, prepared themselves with all speed, and sold of their estates and put in their moneys into the common stock, which was disposed by those appointed, for the making of general provisions." Agreements were made with English adventurers who helped finance the enterprise in the hope of future profits. The good Puritans, however, were not thinking of material things. They were thinking of a refuge where no one could tell them how to worship God.

Based on Communism

The original agreement provided "that all such persons as are of this colony, are to have their meat, drink, apparel, and all provisions out of the common stock & goods of the said colony." Today we might call that "social security." It was further provided that during the first seven years, "all profits & benefits that are got by trade, traffic, trucking, working, fishing, or any other means of any person or persons, remained still in the common stock." Many of the colonists had hoped that they would be allowed to own their own homes and improved lands. They even hoped that they might be allowed to work two days a week for their own "private employment" but this was denied them.

After several false starts, they were forced to leave their second ship behind. The jam-packed Mayflower finally reached the shores of Cape Cod on November 11, 1620. It took another month to find a suitable place to land and build new homes in the deep snows of that New England winter. Before they landed, they drew up the famous Mayflower Compact in which they agreed "in the presence of God, and of one another," to obey "such just & equal Laws, Ordinances, Acts, Constitutions,

& Offices, from time to time, as shall be thought meet & convenient for the general Good of the colony; unto which we promise all due Submission and Obedience."

Early Famines

The hard New England winter of 1620-21 took a severe toll. As Bradford reported it, "of 100 & odd persons, scarce 50 remained." This first, tough winter was followed by two years of famine and starvation. The clumsy colonists working together for their "common wealth" were scarcely able to find or produce enough to keep themselves alive. Their woes increased with the arrival of new colonists. Hungry mouths multiplied while their "common wealth" melted.

When the crops of 1622 were harvested, "all had their hungry bellies filled," but they added little to the common store which had to last another twelve months. Governor Bradford attributed their poor harvest chiefly to "their weakness for want of food, to tend it as they should have done. Also much was stolen both by night and day, before it became scarce eatable, & much more afterward. And though many were well whipped (when they were taken) for a few ears of corn, yet hunger made others (whom conscience did not restrain) to venture. So as it well appeared the famine must still ensue the next year also."

These good Christian men, with little thought of material comforts, were unable to make collectivism work. Communism failed to provide them with the strength they needed to live and worship God as was their simple wont.

Private Enterprise Proclaimed

"So they began to think how they might raise as much corn as they could, and obtain a better crop than they had done, that they might not still thus languish in misery. At length, after much debate of things, the Governor (with the advice of the chief amongst them) gave way that they should set corn every man for his own particular, and in that regard trust to themselves in all other things to go on in the general way as before. And so assigned to every family a parcel of land, according to the proportion of their number for that end, only for present use (but made no division for inheritance), and ranged all boys & youth under some family. This had very good success; for it made all hands very industrious, so as much more corn was planted than otherwise would have been by any means the Governor or any other could use, and saved him a great deal of trouble, and gave far better content. The women now went willingly into the field, and took their little ones with them to set corn, which before would allege weakness, and inability; whom to have compelled would have been thought great tyranny and oppression.

"The experience that was had in this common course and condition, tried sundry years, and that amongst godly and sober men, may well evince the vanity of that conceit of Plato and other ancients, applauded by some of later times;—that the taking away of property, and bringing in community into a common wealth, would make them happy and flourishing: as if they were wiser than God.

"For this community was found to breed much confusion and discontent, and retard much employment that would have been to their benefit and comfort. For the young men that were most able and fit for labor & service did repine that they should spend their time & strength to work for other men's wives and children, without any recompense. The strong, or man of parts, had no more in division of victuals & clothes, than he that was weak and not able to do a quarter the other could; this was thought injustice. The aged and graver men to be ranked and equalized in labors and victuals, clothes, etc., with the meaner & younger sort, thought it some indignity & disrespect unto them. And for mens wives to be commanded to do service for other men, as dressing their meat, washing their clothes, etc., they deemed it a kind of slavery, neither could many husbands well brook it.

Crops a Plenty

"Upon the point all being to have alike, and all to do alike, they thought themselves in the like condition, and one as good as another; and so, if it did not cut of those relations that God hath set amongst men, yet it did at least much diminish and take of the mutual respects that should be preserved amongst them. And would have been worse if they had been men of another condition. Let none object this is men's corruption, and nothing to the course itself. I answer, seeing all men have this corruption in them, God in his wisdom saw another course fitter for them."

The following summer they had a great drouth. So, they set aside a day for prayer and communion with God. Their prayers were answered. The gentle patter of rain came and continued at frequent intervals for a fortnight. Years later Governor Bradford wrote in his 1623 report, "By this time harvest was come, and instead of famine, now God gave them plenty, and the face of things was changed, to the rejoicing of the hearts of many, for which they blessed God. And the effect of their particular planting was well seen, for all had, one way & other, pretty well to bring the year about, and some of the abler sort and more industrious had to spare, and sell to others, so as any general want or famine hath not been amongst them since to this day."

By the end of another year the colony was able to export "a boats load of corn." Though the colony's problems were many, the primitive problem of starvation had been licked. The Plymouth experience was similar to that at Jamestown. When free enterprise replaced communism, abundance replaced scarcity. It was only with the help of free enterprise that freedom of religion was maintained. The two go hand in hand.

As Bradford reported, "*out of small beginnings, great things have been produced; and as one small candle may light a thousand, so the light here kindled hath shown to many, yea, in some sort to our whole nation.*"

78. FACTS ABOUT THE "INDUSTRIAL REVOLUTION"*

Ludwig von Mises

An examination of the so-called horrors of the "Industrial Revolution" and the persistent myth that industrial progress is a plot against employees.

Socialist and interventionist authors assert that the history of modern industrialism and especially the history of the British "Industrial Revolution" provide an empirical verification of the "realistic" or "institutional" doctrine and utterly explode the "abstract" dogmatism of the economists.[1]

The economists flatly deny that labor unions and government prolabor legislation can and did lastingly benefit the whole class of wage earners and raise their standard of living. But the facts, say the anti-economists, have refuted these fallacies. As they see it, the statesmen and legislators who enacted the factory acts displayed a better insight into reality than the economists; while laissez-faire philosophy allegedly taught that the sufferings of the toiling masses are unavoidable, the common sense of laymen succeeded in quelling the worst excesses of profit-seeking business. The improvement in the conditions of the workers, they say, is entirely an achievement of governments and labor unions.

Such are the ideas permeating most of the historical studies dealing with the evolution of modern industrialism. The authors begin by sketching an idyllic image of conditions as they prevailed on the eve of the "Industrial Revolution." At that time, they tell us, things were, by and large, satisfactory. The peasants were happy. So also were the industrial workers under the domestic system. They worked in their own cottages and enjoyed a certain economic independence since they owned a garden plot and their tools. But then "the Industrial Revolution fell like a war or a plague" on these people.[2] The factory system reduced the free worker to virtual slavery; it lowered his standard of living to the level of bare subsistence; in cramming women and children into the mills it destroyed family life and sapped the very foundations of society, morality, and public health. A small minority of ruthless exploiters had cleverly succeeded in imposing their yoke upon the immense majority.

The truth is that economic conditions were highly unsatisfactory on the eve of the Industrial Rev-

*Extracted from *Human Action* (Yale, 1949, 1963; Regnery, 1966), Chapter XXI, latter part of Section 7. Reprinted from *The Freeman*, February 1956

olution. The traditional social system was not elastic enough to provide for the needs of a rapidly increasing population. Neither farming nor the guilds had any use for the additional hands. Business was imbued with the inherited spirit of privilege and exclusive monopoly; its institutional foundations were licenses and the grant of a patent of monopoly; its philosophy was restriction and the prohibition of competition both domestic and foreign. The number of people for whom there was no room left in the rigid system of paternalism and government tutelage of business grew rapidly. They were virtually outcasts. The apathetic majority of these wretched people lived from the crumbs that fell from the tables of the established castes. In the harvest season they earned a trifle by occasional help on farms, for the rest they depended upon private charity and communal poor relief. Thousands of the most vigorous youths of these strata were pressed into the service of the Royal Army and Navy; many of them were killed or maimed in action; many more perished ingloriously from the hardships of the barbarous discipline, from tropical diseases, or from syphillis.[3] Other thousands, the boldest and most ruthless of their class, infested the country as vagabonds, beggars, tramps, robbers, and prostitutes. The authorities did not know of any means to cope with these individuals other than the poorhouse and the workhouse. The support the government gave to the popular resentment against the introduction of new inventions and labor-saving devices made things quite hopeless.

The factory system developed in a continuous struggle against innumerable obstacles. It had to fight popular prejudice, old established customs, legally binding rules and regulations, the animosity of the authorities, the vested interests of privileged groups, the envy of the guilds. The capital equipment of the individual firms was insufficient, the provision of credit extremely difficult and costly. Technological and commercial experience was lacking. Most factory owners failed; comparatively few succeeded. Profits were sometimes considerable, but so were losses. It took many decades until the common practice of reinvesting the greater part of profits earned accumulated adequate capital for the conduct of affairs on a broader scale.

That the factories could thrive in spite of all these hindrances was due to two reasons. First there were the teachings of the new social philosophy expounded by economists, who demolished the prestige of mercantilism, paternalism, and restrictionism. They exploded the superstitious belief that labor-saving devices and processes cause unemployment and reduce all people to poverty and decay. The laissez-faire economists were the pioneers of the unprecedented technological achievements of the last two hundred years.

Then there was another factor that weakened the opposition to innovations. The factories freed the authorities and the ruling landed aristocracy from an embarrassing problem that had grown too large for them. They provided sustenance for the masses of paupers. They emptied the poor houses, the workhouses, and the prisons. They converted starving beggars into self-supporting breadwinners.

The factory owners did not have the power to compel anybody to take a factory job. They could only hire people who were ready to work for the wages offered to them. Low as these wage rates were, they were nonetheless much more than these paupers could earn in any other field open to them. It is a distortion of facts to say that the factories carried off the housewives from the nurseries and the kitchens and the children from their play. These women had nothing to cook with and to feed their children. These children were destitute and starving. Their only refuge was the factory. It saved them, in the strict sense of the term, from death by starvation.

It is deplorable that such conditions existed. But if one wants to blame those responsible, one must not blame the factory owners who—driven by selfishness, of course, and not by "altruism"—did all they could to eradicate the evils. What had caused these evils was the economic order of the precapitalistic era, the order of the "good old days."

In the first decades of the Industrial Revolution the standard of living of the factory workers was shockingly bad when compared with contemporary conditions of the upper classes and with the present conditions of the industrial masses. Hours of work were long, the sanitary conditions in the workshops deplorable. The individual's capacity to work was used up rapidly. But the fact remains that for the surplus population which the enclosure movement had reduced to dire wretchedness and for which there was literally no room left in the frame of the prevailing system of production, work in the factories was salvation. These people thronged into the plants for no reason other than the urge to improve their standard of living.

The laissez-faire ideology and its offshoot, the

"Industrial Revolution," blasted the ideological and institutional barriers to progress and welfare. They demolished the social order in which a constantly increasing number of people were doomed to abject need and destitution. The processing trades of earlier ages had almost exclusively catered to the wants of the well-to-do. Their expansion was limited by the amount of luxuries the wealthier strata of the population could afford. Those not engaged in the production of primary commodities could earn a living only as far as the upper classes were disposed to utilize their skill and services. But now a different principle came into operation. The factory system inaugurated a new mode of marketing as well as of production. Its characteristic feature was that the manufactures were not designed for the consumption of a few well-to-do only, but for the consumption of those who had hitherto played but a negligible role as consumers. Cheap things for the many, was the objective of the factory system. The classical factory of the early days of the Industrial Revolution was the cotton mill. Now, the cotton goods it turned out were not something the rich were asking for. These wealthy people clung to silk, linen, and cambric.

Whenever the factory with its methods of mass production by means of power-driven machines invaded a new branch of production, it started with the production of cheap goods for the broad masses. The factories turned to the production of more refined and therefore more expensive goods only at a later stage, when the unprecedented improvement in the masses' standard of living which they caused made it profitable to apply the methods of mass production also to these better articles. Thus, for instance, the factory-made shoe was for many years bought only by the "proletarians" while the wealthier consumers continued to patronize the custom shoemakers. The much talked about sweatshops did not produce clothes for the rich, but for people in modest circumstances. The fashionable ladies and gentlemen preferred and still do prefer custom-made frocks and suits.

The outstanding fact about the Industrial Revolution is that it opened an age of mass production for the needs of the masses. The wage earners are no longer people toiling merely for other people's well-being. They themselves are the main consumers of the products the factories turn out. Big business depends upon mass consumption. There is, in present-day America, not a single branch of big business that would not cater to the needs of the masses. The very principle of capitalist entrepreneurship is to provide for the common man. In his capacity as consumer the common man is the sovereign whose buying or abstention from buying decides the fate of entrepreneurial activities. There is in the market economy no other means of acquiring and preserving wealth than by supplying the masses in the best and cheapest way with all the goods they ask for.

Blinded by their prejudices, many historians and writers have entirely failed to recognize this fundamental fact. As they see it, wage earners toil for the benefit of other people. They never raise the question who these "other" people are.

Mr. and Mrs. Hammond tell us that the workers were happier in 1760 than they were in 1830.[4] This is an arbitrary value judgment. There is no means of comparing and measuring the happiness of different people and of the same people at different times. We may agree for the sake of argument that an individual who was born in 1740 was happier in 1760 than in 1830. But let us not forget that in 1770 (according to the estimate of Arthur Young) England had 8.5 million inhabitants, while in 1831 (according to the census) the figure was 16 million.[5] This conspicuous increase was mainly conditioned by the Industrial Revolution. With regard to these additional Englishmen the assertion of the eminent historians can only be approved by those who endorse the melancholy verses of Sophocles: "Not to be born is, beyond all question, the best; but when a man has once seen the light of day, this is next best, that speedily he should return to that place whence he came."

The early industrialists were for the most part men who had their origin in the same social strata from which their workers came. They lived very modestly, spent only a fraction of their earnings for their households, and put the rest back into the business. But as the entrepreneurs grew richer, the sons of successful businessmen began to intrude into the circles of the ruling class. The highborn gentlemen envied the wealth of the parvenus and resented their sympathies with the reform movement. They hit back by investigating the material and moral conditions of the factory hands and enacting factory legislation.

The history of capitalism in Great Britain as well as in all other capitalist countries is a record of an unceasing tendency toward the improvement in the wage earners' standard of living. This evolution coincided with the development of prolabor legislation and the spread of labor unionism on the one hand and with the increase in the marginal productivity of labor on the other hand. The economists assert that the improvement in the workers' material conditions is due to the increase in the per capita quota of capital invested and the technological achievements which the employment of this additional capital brought about. As far as labor legislation and union pressure did not exceed the limits of what the workers would have got without them as a necessary consequence of the acceleration of capital accumulation as compared with population, they were superfluous. As far as they exceeded these limits, they were harmful to the interests of the masses. They delayed the accumulation of capital, thus slowing down the tendency toward a rise in the marginal productivity of labor and in wage rates. They conferred privileges on some groups of wage earners at the expense of other groups. They created mass unemployment and decreased the amount of products available for the workers in their capacity as consumers.

The apologists of government interference with business and of labor unionism ascribe all the improvements in the conditions of the workers to the actions of governments and unions. Except for them, they contend, the workers' standard of living would be no higher today than it was in the early years of the factory system.

It is obvious that this controversy cannot be settled by appeal to historical experience. With regard to the establishment of the facts there is no disagreement between the two groups. Their antagonism concerns the interpretation of events, and this interpretation must be guided by the theory chosen. The epistemological and logical considerations which determine the correctness or incorrectness of a theory are logically and temporarily antecedent to the elucidation of the historical problem involved. The historical facts as such neither prove nor disprove any theory. They need to be interpreted in the light of theoretical insight.

Most of the authors who wrote the history of the conditions of labor under capitalism were ignorant of economics and boasted of this ignorance. However, this contempt for sound economic reasoning did not mean that they approached the topic of their studies without prepossession and without bias in favor of any theory. They were guided by the popular fallacies concerning governmental omnipotence and the alleged blessings of labor unionism. It is beyond question that the Webbs as well as Lujo Brentano and a host of minor authors were at the very start of their studies imbued with a fanatical dislike of the market economy and an enthusiastic endorsement of the doctrines of socialism and interventionism. They were certainly honest and sincere in their convictions and tried to do their best. Their candor and probity exonerates them as individuals; it does not exonerate them as historians. However pure the intentions of a historian may be, there is no excuse for his recourse to fallacious doctrines. The first duty of a historian is to examine with the utmost care all the doctrines to which he resorts in dealing with the subject matter of his work. If he neglects to do this and naively espouses the garbled and confused ideas of popular opinion, he is not a historian but an apologist and propagandist.

The antagonism between the two opposite points of view is not merely a historical problem. It refers no less to the most burning problems of the present day. It is the matter of controversy in what is called in present-day America the problem of industrial relations.

Let us stress one aspect of the matter only. Vast areas—Eastern Asia, the East Indies, Southern and Southeastern Europe, Latin America—are only superficially affected by modern capitalism. Conditions in these countries by and large do not differ from those of England on the eve of the "Industrial Revolution." There are millions and millions of people for whom there is no secure place left in the traditional economic setting. The fate of these wretched masses can be improved only by industrialization. What they need most is entrepreneurs and capitalists. As their own foolish policies have deprived these nations of the further enjoyment of the assistance imported foreign capital hitherto gave them, they must embark upon domestic capital accumulation. They must go through all the stages through which the evolution of Western industrialism had to pass. They must start with comparatively low wage rates and long hours of work. But, deluded by the doctrines prevailing in present-day Western Europe and North America, their statesmen think that they can proceed in a different way. They encourage labor-union pressure and alleged prolabor legislation. Their interventionist radicalism nips in the bud all attempts to create domestic industries. These men do not comprehend that industrialization cannot begin with the adoption of the precepts of the International Labor Office and the principles of the American Congress of Industrial Organizations. Their stubborn dogmatism spells the doom of the Indian and

Chinese coolies, the Mexican peons, and millions of other peoples, desperately struggling on the verge of starvation.

Notes

[1]The attribution of the phrase "the Industrial Revolution" to the reigns of the two last Hanoverian Georges was the outcome of deliberate attempts to melodramatize economic history in order to fit it into the Procrustean Marxian schemes. The transition from medieval methods of production to those of the free enterprise system was a long process that started centuries before 1760 and, even in England, was not finished in 1830. Yet, it is true that England's industrial development was considerably accelerated in the second half of the eighteenth century. It is therefore permissible to use the term "Industrial Revolution" in the examination of the emotional connotations with which Fabianism, Marxism, the Historical School, and Institutionalism have loaded it.

[2]J. L. Hammond and Barbara Hammond, *The Skilled Labourer* 1760-1832 (2d ed. London, 1920). p. 4.

[3]In the Seven Years' War 1,512 British seamen were killed in battle while 133,708 died of disease or were missing. Cf. W. L. Dorn, *Competition for Empire* 1740-1763 (New York, 1940). p. 114.

[4]J. L. Hammond and Barbara Hammond, *loc. cit.*

[5]F. C. Dietz, *An Economic History of England* (New York, 1942). pp. 279 and 392.

79. PROGRESS OR REGRESS?*

Hans F. Sennholz

Not long ago, a small Pennsylvania corporation received the Presidential "E" award for its contribution to export trade and the nation's balance of payments. In its fiscal year, 1965, the company sold more than $16 million of its products to foreign customers. Since 1960, its sales abroad returned $55 million to the United States.

It seems that some American policies are reverting to the principles and doctrines of the seventeenth century. Others are repeating the errors and follies of the dark Middle Ages. In 1628 the best known mercantilist writer, Thomas Mun, urged his countrymen always "to sell more to strangers yearly than we consume of theirs in value." In 1667 the most famous of German mercantilist writers, Becher, advocated as a most important economic rule and axiom "that it is always better to sell goods to others than to buy goods from others, for the former brings a certain advantage and the latter inevitable damage." In 1712, Charles King in *The British Merchant* declared the export of finished products "in the highest degree beneficial," the export of natural products "so much clear gain," and the corresponding import "so much real loss."

Napoleon Bonaparte applied this idea on a huge scale in his Continental System. He gave public recognition, bestowed medals, and issued citations to Frenchmen who exported manufactured goods to England.

In recent years our *foreign trade policies* gradually have fallen under the sway of seventeenth century economic thought. Our "unfavorable" balance of payments caused the Eisenhower Administration to prohibit American ownership of gold in foreign countries. Since then, the United States government added a "voluntary" program that restricts bank and business investments abroad in order to keep money and gold in the United States. Furthermore, a punitive tax on American purchases of foreign securities aims to curb our heavy losses of gold. Those are some of the steps already taken toward comprehensive government control over all our foreign trade and transactions.

In England, comprehensive foreign exchange control dates back to the darkness of the Middle Ages. Until the reign of Charles I (1628) the office of Royal Exchanger handled all exchange operations and all trade in precious metals.[1] Exportation of bullion and coin was summarily outlawed until 1663 when the prohibition was narrowed to English coins only.

In France exportation of gold and silver was outlawed from the Middle Ages until the eighteenth century. The usual penalty for taking coins out of the realm was death. In Spain and Portugal the

*From *The Freeman*, April 1966

export of bullion and coins went on undisturbed for more than 200 years as if no prohibitions existed, even though the penalty was death.

The "Spending" Multiplier

In recent months we have witnessed a marked increase in government and private *spending* and a strong rise in economic activity. The demand for goods and services has been stimulated by expansionary government and Federal Reserve actions. Spending, whether by governments or citizens is considered the powerful engine of economic progress and prosperity.

Spendthrifts of all ages have advanced similar economic doctrines. In 1686, for instance, the Austrian writer, Wilhelm Schroetter, Thomas Mun's pupil, wrote: "The more a manufacturer causes money to pass from one hand to another, the more useful it is to the country, for so many people does it maintain." And at another place: "Through the exchange of money the sustenance of so many people is multiplied."

Thrift was regarded as the cause of unemployment, for real income was thought to diminish if money were withdrawn from circulation. For this reason Schroetter wrote a long discussion on "How a Prince Should Limit his Thrift." In 1695 the English writer, Cary, advocated the same principle with even greater clarity. He stated that everybody's spending causes income to rise. If everybody increases his spending, according to Cary, everybody "might then live more plentifully."[2]

Export Embargoes

On Jan. 21, 1966, the United States and British governments placed *curbs on exportation* of copper in order to protect their shares of dwindling world supplies of the metal. The United States Commerce Department sharply expanded its controls over exports of copper from the United States and clamped tight limits on a broad range of categories, including shipments overseas of copper ores and refined copper.

In England, this policy of "provision" dated back to the twelfth century and lasted until the nineteenth. Export prohibitions on iron, copper and bell metal were repealed in 1694. Other restrictions that were imposed by Henry II, in 1176 and 1177, lasted until 1822. The high-water mark was reached under Edward III about the middle of the fourteenth century.

In France, export restrictions were first imposed during the thirteenth and fourteenth centuries. They aimed at keeping essential materials, particularly foodstuffs, within the country. At the beginning of the nineteenth century, Napoleon still conducted a "policy of provision" with regard to foodstuffs. The first French law that permitted their exportation was enacted in 1819.[3]

Early "Poor Laws"

Even our *war on poverty* declared by the present administration is not new at all. During the period of the Stuarts and of the Tudors, the English government endeavored to aid the low income classes of society. The avowed aim of an act of Parliament in 1603 was to raise the wages of textile workers. Minimum wage rates were fixed, and manufacturers were fined one shilling for every penny of wages paid below the prescribed rates. Especially in the years 1629 to 1640, a wide "policy of welfare" was pursued.

In order to prevent unemployment, businessmen were compelled to continue their operations even when suffering losses. They had to keep wages high, and were imprisoned in case of disobedience. For the benefit of the poor, food prices were intensively controlled. Grain was to be sold under cost price.

Already in 1563, the Elizabethan Statute of Artificers tried to regulate labor conditions in all details, and it remained on the books until 1814. In order to assure "just" wages to the working population, wage rates were fixed anew each year by the Justices of the Peacc according "to the plenty or scarcity of the time." The Justices in turn had to consider the cost of living by referring to "the prices of all kind of victuals, fuel, raiment and apparel, both linen and woolen, and also house rent." Wage fixing in sixteenth-century London was similar in many respects to wage fixing in London today.

Regulation of Business

If you believe that government *regulations of commerce and industry* are new and progressive, you should study the twelfth century English industrial regulations. At least since 1197, the English state had tried to regulate the technique of manufacture. For the cloth industry, for instance, the English government prescribed the various dimensions of cloth, technique of production, dyeing, stretching, finishing, the tools of trade, the packaging and labeling, and so on. Similar regulations, more or less complete, were imposed on all other industries.

In France, Louis XIV, the Sun King, appointed *intendants* and inspectors who were charged with the regulation of industry. From the handling of raw materials to all subsequent stages of production, these servants of the king controlled the production process.

The system of control obviously necessitated a variety of penalties. Frequently, "defective" goods were confiscated or cut to pieces, money fines were imposed, or the right to practice the craft or conduct the business was withdrawn. According to a decree of 1670, the name of the offending merchant was to be posted, and the offender himself could be placed in a pillory for public derision.

In spite of countless regulations and limitations that aimed to achieve uniform standards, corruption and personal favoritism blunted the controls. The government could make individual exceptions to any prescription. Personal influence was as important as it is today.

Mercantilism Persists

For instance, the medical profession today labors under the professional discipline of several regulatory agencies. Under the *ancien régime,* training and examination of physicians also was a serious government matter. Under the watchful eyes of the government, ancient quackery was to be perpetuated. In some cases, persons with no training whatsoever were practicing the business of healing and offering salves and medicaments because they curried favor with the inspectors, or succeeded in winning over the lackeys, valets, mistresses, and adventuresses of the Court. Royal charters, permits from princes, and acquired titles of physicians of the king or queen, of surgeons of the navy, and the like, sanctioned all kinds of quackery.

The methods of favoritism, currying favors, obtaining franchises, licenses, or government orders have not changed materially since the seventeenth century. Diamonds and minks, personal connections and right contacts, government positions and offices, seem to retain their significance for professional success and financial reward.

How modern and progressive are our prevailing doctrines and official policies? A historian who attempts to dissect the so-called modern version of political economy may be surprised to discover its true age. Despite claims of originality, many of the modern are of ancient origin. Some stem from the armory of Marxism and Fabian socialism as they were developed during the nineteenth century. Others date back to the age of Mercantilism that prevailed in Western Europe from the sixteenth to the eighteenth century. And still others have survived from the darkness of the Middle Ages. Much that passes for progress today is but a regression into the follies of the past.

Notes

[1] Cf. Eli F. Heckscher, *Mercantilism,* Vol. II, p. 246.

[2] *An Essay on the State of England, in relation to its Trade,* London, 1695, p. 148 ff; cited in Heckscher. Vol II, p. 209.

[3] *Ibid,* p. 92.

Summary

80. HELLO!*

Joan Wilke

If you're familiar with English detective stories, you know that "hello" is much more than a salutation. It's a surprise!

It's what every good English detective says when he stumbles upon a previously overlooked, wonderful, important, delightful little clue that is sure to unravel the whole mystery.

That's why "hello" is such a fine greeting—whether to a stranger or an old friend. It's the expectation of discovery. The anticipation of some new and wonderful revelation . . . or some new meaning in something long familiar.

Freedom is the only philosophy that treats life realistically—as a mystery that will unravel surprise by surprise.

Only freedom can accommodate the day-to-day surprises that arise from truth and error, wisdom and folly, the simple and complex, the limited and limitless.

It allows for disappointments and failures as well as success.

Everyone benefits freely (and willingly!) from success when it happens, but no one is forced to share another's failure unless all futures are bound up through a collective. So freedom magnifies and spreads success and minimizes and confines failure. Collectivism does just the opposite.

Freedom offers no pat answers to pat problems because it always anticipates some new discovery or variation.

Collectivism proudly asserts it has the answers, and concretizes them into laws, thereby perpetuating the old and obstructing the new.

Freedom treats life as a process, not a thing. A continuous happening, not something that happened. So it is an invitation to life, not an encroachment on it. It is a beckoning, not a coercive force. It recognizes life as a series of beginnings.

All forms of materialistic collectivism treat life as though it's over, in the sense that it is predictable. It is so preoccupied with the present that it rejects the past and considers the future a projection of the present.

It worships "change" but, being oriented to the current situation, considers change simply a rearrangement of existing conditions, intellectually contrived and politically manipulated. It never anticipates real change . . . only repetition of existing conditions.

In limiting life to its own predictions, it necessarily brings about the conditions it predicted, since life only repeats itself when restricted.

Freedom recognizes that life's secrets already exist and lie undiscovered, waiting to be stumbled upon in a series of delighted "hellos." Collectivism drearily limits itself to the idea that what is discovered is what exists, so it mechanically distributes the accumulated surprises of the past without allowing for the continuing surprise of new discovery.

Freedom is nourished by expectation.

Collectivism cannot survive without fears . . . real or imaginary . . . grouped together and therefore exchanged and exaggerated in such handholding gatherings as unions and pressure groups or any combination formed for the force that will allay its fears.

The future is determined largely by the choice in-

*From *The Freeman*, January 1968

dividuals make between expecting the best or the worst.

Whereas fear paralyzes, expectation energizes.

The most remarkable person I know . . . and the freest . . . always seems to have this air of anticipation about him. When he comes through a door or around a corner, he has the manner of one who has heard a firecracker go off and has come to see what the celebration is all about. He's in a state of perpetual "hello!" With his attitude, I doubt that he's ever disappointed, because he would see the most ordinary thing with extraordinary delight.

His attitude strikes me as that which is most appropriate for a free man.

81. FREE MARKET DISCIPLINES*

Leonard E. Read

Contrary to socialistic tenets, the free market is the only mechanism that can sensibly, logically, intelligently discipline production and consumption. For it is only when the market is free that economic calculation is possible.[1] Free pricing is the key. When prices are high, production is encouraged and consumption is discouraged; when prices fall, the reverse holds true. Thus, production and consumption are always moving toward equilibrium. Shortages and surpluses are not in the lexicon of free market economics.

Conceded, the above is no news to those who apprehend free market economics; they well know of its disciplinary influence as regards production and consumption. This alone warrants our support of the free market. However, the free market has two other quite remarkable disciplinary possibilities which have seldom been explored.

Before making that exploration, it is necessary to recognize the limitations of the free market. The market is a mechanism, and thus it is wholly lacking in moral and spiritual suasion; further, it embodies no coercive force whatsoever. In these respects, the market is without disciplinary possibilities.

"Like all mechanisms, the market, with its function for the economizing of time and effort, is servant alike to the good, the compassionate, and the perceptive as well as to the evil, the inconsiderate, and the oblivious."[2] Scrupulosity is not among its characteristics.

The free market is a name we give to the economic activities—a short-hand term, we might say—of a people acting freely, voluntarily, privately, cooperatively, competitively. It is distinguished by universal freedom of choice and the absence of coercive force. Ideally, only defensive force—government—is employed to put down fraud, violence, predation, and other aggressions.

Given a society of freely choosing individuals, the market is that which exists as a consequence—it is a mechanism that is otherwise nondefinitive. It is the procession of economic events that occur when authoritarianism—political or otherwise—is absent.

While private enterprise is often practiced in a manner consonant with free market principles, the two terms are not synonymous. Piracy is an enterprise and also private. Many businesses when in league with unions, for instance—willingly or not—feature elements of coercion and thus are not examples of the free market at work.

The free market has only been approximated, never fully attained, and, doubtless, never will be realized. It is an out-of-reach ideal; we can only move toward or away from it. Yet, in the U.S.A., even in these days of a rapidly growing interventionism, the free market flourishes to a remarkable extent. To appreciate this, merely envision the countless willing exchanges—hundreds of millions daily—such as Mrs. Jones swapping a shawl she has made for a goose Mrs. Smith has raised, or the money you pay for a phone call or a quart of milk. In these instances, each party gains, for each desires what he gets more than what he surrenders. In a word, the free market is individual desire

*From *The Freeman*, November 1969

speaking in exchange terms. When the desire for Bibles is accommodated in noncoerced exchange, we can conclude, quite accurately, that we are witnessing a market for Bibles. Or when the desire for pornography is being thus accommodated, we can conclude that there is a market for trash. I repeat, scrupulosity is not a feature of the market.

When the desires of people are depraved, a free market will accommodate the depravity. And it will accommodate excellence with equal alacrity. It is "servant alike to good . . . and evil."

It is because the free market serves evil as well as good that many people think they can rid society of evil by slaying this faithful, *amoral* servant. This is comparable to destroying the sun because we don't like the shadows we cast or breaking the mirror so that we won't have to see the reflection of what we really are.

When I sit in front of a TV and view trash, I tend to rant and rave at what I'm seeing. Wake up: What I hear and see is a reflection of what's in me! Thus, my only corrective is to read a good book or otherwise cease to patronize such low-grade performances.

The market is but a response to—a mirror of—our desires. Once this harsh reality is grasped, the market becomes a disciplinary force. To elaborate: Say that a person desires, buys, and reads a filthy book. Were he to realize that what he's reading is a picture of what's in his own make-up, such a realization, by itself, would tend to change him for the better. The market would then reflect the improvement. But note that the market has no such effect on those who are oblivious to this fact. *It's the knowledge of this character-revealing fact that makes of the market a disciplinary force.* I am only trying to point out the market's potentiality in this respect.

Instead of cursing evil, stay out of the market for it; the evil will cease to the extent we cease patronizing it. Trying to rid ourselves of trash by running to government for morality laws is like trying to minimize the effects of inflation by wage, price, and other controls. Both destroy the market, that is, the reflection of ourselves. Such tactics are at the intellectual level of mirror-smashing, attempts not to see ourselves as we are. The market's potentiality as a disciplinary force is thereby removed. To slay this faithful, amoral servant is to blindfold, deceive, and hoodwink ourselves. Next to forswearing a faith in an Infinite Intelligence over and beyond our own minds, denying the market is to erase the best point of reference man can have. So much for the first somewhat unexplored possibility of the market as a disciplinary force.

Imperfect Man

Now to the second. This cannot be explained unless we are aware of our numerous shortcomings, of how narrow our virtues and talents really are—everyone's, no exceptions.

Let's take, for example, the greatest mathematical genius who ever lived. He's a giant in his field. Yet, without any question, he's a know-nothing in countless other ways. This goes for outstanding generals, chemists, physicists, scientists of whatever brand. No one ever gets more than an infinitesimal peek at the Cosmic Scheme, at the over-all luminosity, even at himself. We must see that the biggest among us is tiny. And one who denies this about himself is displaying the greatest ignorance of all: he doesn't even know how little he knows! "If we wish to know anything, we must resign ourselves to being ignorant of much."[3]

Reflect on this human reality, on imperfect man, particularly on the more imaginative and brilliant individuals among us. While they possess an outstanding and remarkable aptitude or two, they too are day dreamers. "If only I had a million dollars," is a dream that flashes across countless minds. Many of these specialists want above all else to pursue their own peculiar bent whether it be going to the moon, genetic alteration of other human beings, releasing the atom's energy, or whatever.

Knowing so much about one thing and so little about everything else, they are unable to know what effect their ambitions, if achieved, might have on the human situation. Just as a baby with a stick of dynamite and a match is unaware of what the consequences might be!

The lamentable fact is that scientists, pseudo scientists, and other technologists have been given a wishing well: the Federal grab bag. They, thus, are encouraged to carry out any experiment their hearts desire, without let or hindrance. Leaving aside the destruction of our economy by inflation—featured in the grab bag's financing—they are alarmingly endangering all the people on this earth, even the earth itself. And primarily because they suffer no restraining and disciplinary forces; their passions and ambitions are on the loose!

The remedy? Let these ambitions be submitted to the discipline of the market precisely as are most other commodities and services. Go to the moon?

Of course; that is, when the market permits the venture, if enough people voluntarily subscribe the cash. Release the atom's energy? By all means; that is, when the market is ready for it.

Am I saying that the market has a wisdom superior to the President of the United States, or the Congress, or a bureaucracy? I am not. The market is a mechanism and is neither wise nor moral. I am only claiming that it has disciplinary qualities. To understand why requires no more than a knowledge of what the components of this mechanism are: millions upon millions of individual preferences, choices, desires. *The market is an obstacle course;* before I can pursue my bent or aptitude or obsession, I must gain an adequate, voluntary approval or assent! No wishing well, this! My own aspirations, regardless of how determined, or lofty, or depraved, do not control the verdict. What these others—impersonal as a computer—will put up in willing exchange for my offering spells my success or failure, allows me to pursue my bent or not.

There are exceptions to this rule, of course. For instance, some of us who may be unable to win in the market will, like Van Gogh, face starvation in order to pursue our passions. The threat of starvation, however, is quite a discipline in itself; at least, not much is likely to be uncovered in these circumstances that will destroy life on earth. It takes big financing to do unearthly things.

The market very often returns fortunes for comparative junk and, on occasion, returns nothing at all for great and beneficial achievements—temporarily, that is. Eventually, in a free society, the junk goes to the junk heap and achievements are rewarded.

I believe that anyone should follow his star; but let him do so with his own resources or with such resources as others will voluntarily supply. This is to say that I believe in the market, a tough disciplinary mechanism. I do not believe in cars without brakes, impulses without repulses, ambitions without check points, wishes run riot. Societal schemes that are all sail and no ballast head society for disaster!

The rebuttal to this line of reasoning is heard over and over again: "But we voted for it," meaning that the Federal grab bag—open sesame with other people's income—has been democratically approved. Granted! But this is nonsense: The fruits of the labor of one man are not up for grabs by others, that is, not rationally.[4] This is not a votable matter, except if one's premise be a socialistic society. What's right and what's wrong are not to be determined at the shallow level of nosecounting or opinion polls. To argue otherwise is to place the same value on the views of morons as you do on your own.

As a disciplinary force over wild aspirations, the President of the United States, a member of Congress, a bureaucrat is not only less effective than the market but less effective than any single buyer or seller in the market. An individual, when a government official, considers only how much of other people's money should be spent. The motivation in this instance favors spending over economizing. The same individual, in the free market, considers how much of his *own* property he is willing to put on the line. The motivation in this instance is self-interest. And this is tough! Ambitions as silly as tracking the meanderings of polar bears by a Nimbus satellite stand a chance for satisfaction when a grab bag made up of other people's money is readily at hand;[5] whereas, the free market gives short shrift to projects that are at or near the bottom of individual preferences.

True, were personal ambitions subjected to the disciplines of the market, trips to the moon would have to be postponed. Atomic energy might be a phenomenon of the future. Many other scientific explorations—some secret—taking place today in our universities and Federally financed would, under the discipline of the market, still be safely stored in imaginative minds.

This is no argument against technological breakthroughs. It is merely to suggest that these illuminations be financially encouraged only as the free market permits. The resulting steadiness in progress might then be harmonious with an expanded understanding of what it is we really want and can live with.

I repeat, societal schemes that are all sail and no ballast head society for disaster. The free market is ballast—a stabilizer—we might well put to use if we would avoid wreckage in the stormy seas of political chaos.

Notes

[1] Professor Ludwig von Mises establishes this point, irrefutably, in his book, *Socialism* (New Haven: Yale [1922] 1951; London: Jonathan Cape, Ltd., 1969).

[2] See "Value—The Soul of Economics," by W. H. Pitt. *The Freeman*, September, 1969.

[3] John Henry Newman.

[4] For what I consider to be a rationally constructed explanation of this point, see "The American System and Majority Rule" by Edmund A. Opitz, *The Freeman*, November, 1962.

[5] See "The Migration of Polar Bears," *Scientific American*, February, 1968.

Glossary

These definitions are offered in the attempt to explain some of the more significant economic terms in the light of the subjective value, marginal utility, theory of economics, on which the defense of a free and unhampered market must rest. Anyone interested in more detailed explanations of the meaning of these and other economic terms should find it helpful to refer to *Mises Made Easier: A Glossary for Ludwig von Mises' HUMAN ACTION* by Percy L. Greaves, Jr. (Dobbs Ferry, N.Y. 10522: Free Market Books, P. O. 298, 1974).

BBG

A

Action—the purposive attempt on the part of an individual to relieve a "felt uneasiness" or dissatisfaction, to attain a goal or end, to acquire economic goods, to satisfy economic wants or needs. Three conditions necessarily precede action: (a) some "felt uneasiness," (b) an idea concerning a preferred situation, and (c) the hope or expectation that purposive action will have some chance of success. Three essentials must be present to carry out an action: (a) a plan, (b) time and (c) resources. Several factors may interfere to obstruct or hamper an individual's action from having the results intended: (a) accidents, (b) natural phenomena, (c) the actions of other persons, (d) changes due to the passage of time and (e) mistakes.

"Administered price"—a term which carries the implication that a large-scale producer can fix almost any high price per unit he chooses for his output and maintain it in spite of the wishes of consumers. The fact is, however, that no seller can "administer" prices on a free market. He can only ask and *hope* consumers will pay. If consumers refuse to pay what he asks, he must either come down in his price per unit or make fewer, if any, sales.

Advertising—the act or process of publicizing or furnishing information about a good or service with a view to persuading potential customers to buy. Advertising is often criticized for being unnecessary, wasteful, misleading, in bad taste and unconcerned with the interests of consumers. Criticism may be justified in some cases. However, advertising a product is really a necessary step in the process of its production, i.e., in transforming raw materials into a completely finished product in the hands of its final consumer.

Aggregate—the sum, total, or composite of many parts; thus the term "aggregate economics" is used to describe the field of study which deals with statistics based on the activities of large numbers of persons, groups, collectives, etc. See "Macro-economics."

Agricultural economy—a society in which most of the people are farmers, relying primarily on agricultural production to obtain the things they want and need to consume or to trade.

Ancient civilizations—the early cultural and economic societies based on considerably more specialization and division of labor than the much earlier primitive societies (see below). In this SYLLABUS we shall refer primarily to the civilizations centered around the Mediterranean, from which Western culture arose—the Egyptian, Babylonian, Assyrian, Phoenician, Cretan, Greek and Roman. These ancient civilizations were "Status societies" (see below).

Antitrust legislation—laws intended to inhibit corporations and persons engaged in interstate commerce from taking actions which the Federal Trade Commission or the courts may interpret as "tending to create a monopoly," "lessen competition" or lead to "restraint of trade."

A Posteriori **knowledge**—something *learned;* information or data acquired from experience, experiment, observation and/or historical study.

A Priori **knowledge**—something we know "instinctively," inherently, innately, without consciously having to learn it. The ***a priori*** categories of knowledge are:

1. Regularity
2. Logic
3. Causality
4. Time
5. Change
6. Value

Assets—objects (material or immaterial) which have value to someone. In business parlance, the word assets normally refers to objects that have a ***market value*** which may be calculated in terms of money.

Austrian School of Economics—the set of economic theories which explain economic phenomena logically as the outcome of purposive actions by individuals. The method of "Austrian" economists is to use logic to reason from basic *a priori* assumptions. Their subject matter is purposive human action; they explain every economic phenomenon as the outcome of the actions and ideas of individuals. The Austrian School of Economics, so-called because its founders and, until very recently, its leading spokesmen were born in the old Austro-Hungarian Empire, is the marginal utility, subjective value "school" of economics.

Autarky—an economically, self-sufficient economy. In an autarky, the inhabitants produce within their own geographical borders essentially all the goods and services they consume.

Automation—a fairly new term for mechanization, i.e., the automatic performance of an operation using machines or tools created by men but which, once produced by human beings, need only be set in operation by them to function mechanically—unless and until they break down. The development and application of tools, technology and other labor-saving devices made possible by savings and investment, arising out of specialization and the division of labor. The use of technically-sophisticated equipment that operates almost automatically.

B

Balance of payments—a statement of accounts, balance sheet, listing in monetary terms, an individual's, firm's, social unit's, legal entity's or nation's total debts and total credits, for a certain period of time. Accounting procedures are such that a balance sheet always balances—total debits and total credits are always equal. A nation's balance of payments is the composite of the individual balances of payments of all its inhabitants. Because every individual sees to his own personal receipts and expenditures, there is no need to fear a one-way flow in, or out of, the country of either cash or goods—unless some outside forces interfere to prevent individuals from acting on their own best judgment and personal preferences.

Balance of trade—a statement giving the estimated monetary value of an individual's, firm's, social unit's, legal entity's or nation's total exports and imports of goods, services and/or money for a certain period of time. A nation's balance of trade is the composite of the individual balances of trade of all its inhabitants. The balance of trade, unlike the balance of payments, need not balance at all times. When money savings are being accumulated, cash income will exceed outgo; when they are spent, cash outgo will exceed income. Mercantilists (see below) consider a nation's balance of trade favorable if goods are being shipped out of a country and gold and silver coming in; thus they advocate protectionist government programs to restrict imports of goods.

Balance sheet—a statement of the assets, liabilities and net worth of an individual or a business entity, giving the estimated monetary value of each item as of a specific date. Assets are traditionally listed on the left side of a page, liabilities and net worth on the right. The greater the estimated value of the assets, as compared with that of the liabilities, the more valuable is the property considered to be—and the greater is its net worth or the equity of its owners. And vice versa.

Banknote—a bank's note or promise-to-pay something, usually gold, silver or some other form of money. Banknotes originated as "warehouse receipts" issued as evidence of gold, silver or some other commodity left on deposit by the owner for storage and safekeeping—by the bank, as warehouse custodian—for the owner's account and available for redemption as agreed upon by holders of the notes. As banknotes came into frequent use in trade, without being returned to the bank (warehouse) for redemption, the connection between the banknote itself and the bank's promise to deliver something tangible was gradually forgotten. Banknotes themselves, especially those put out by a government's legally-privileged "Central bank of issue" (see below), came to be considered money, equal to and as good as the commodity it represented, especially when given status as "Legal tender" (see below).

Banks, banking—fundamentally banks are merely depositories, warehouses for storage and safekeeping of other people's money. In the course of fulfilling this role banks usually have substantial funds on hand in their vaults, so that they have traditionally sought to combine their warehousing function with moneylending.

Barter—commodity-for-commodity trade. See "Direct exchange" (below).

Bond—an IOU or promise to repay money borrowed. These pledges, IOUs or promissory notes are frequently traded, i.e., bought and sold, on the market. When the loan falls due, the borrower's obligation is always to repay the money borrowed to whoever owns title to the bond at that time.

Bureaucracy—the system any government uses to administer its various activities. Any government, whether limited, totalitarian or interventionist employs "bureaucrats." The government administrators or bureaucrats are permitted little, if any, discretion but must comply with procedures prescribed in the legislation setting up the programs they administer and defining their duties.

Buyer—it is customary to speak of a trader who gives money in exchange for some other good or service as a "buyer." In this sense, a buyer is contrasted with a seller.

C

Capitalism—the economic system based on private property, including the private ownership of the factors of production. Because property under capitalism is private, its owners may risk it in trying out their new ideas. Thus, capitalism is the only economic system conducive to entrepreneurial experimentation, free and open competition, the accumulation of capitalist savings, the improvement of tools and the development of mass production. Capitalism, with private ownership and control of the factors of production, contrasts with (a) socialism or communism and (b) various forms of interventionism on the basis of the way property is owned and controlled.

Capitalist savings—savings in the form of "Producers' goods" (see below)—raw materials, tools, machines, building, equipment or anything else which is intended —not for consumption directly—but for use in some process of production.

Cartel—a monopolistic combination of domestic producers, made feasible by government protection permitting it to restrict total output and/or sales within the economy so as to charge a monopoly price. (See below). A cartel can come into existence only if the government hampers imports, so that the cartel members are protected from foreign competition. Under a domestic cartel agreement, every member is assigned a definite production quota, those members who restrict production being compensated by the other cartel members according to a definite formula. "Surpluses" produced by cartel members are often disposed of abroad at lower prices. Cartels differ from duopolies and oligopolies (see below) in their greater formality and their being legally sanctioned and protected.

Cash holding—a sum of money an individual keeps on hand so as to be prepared for any expenses that may arise requiring cash payment. The cash holding any particular person will want to have varies in size from time to time, place to place and situation to situation. Everyone continually adjusts the size of his or her cash holding according to the situation. Many persons let their cash holdings decline after pay day, for instance, until another paycheck may be cashed to replenish it. Most persons increase their cash holdings when traveling. In today's money economy few persons permit their cash holdings to decline to zero and remain there for any length of time. To increase a person's cash holding, he or she sells for cash some good or service (labor) at his disposal; to reduce his cash holding, he or she spends or gives money away.

Central Bank of Issue—a legally-privileged bank, authorized by the government to issue banknotes, which are usually declared legal tender for payment of debts within the nation's borders.

Chicago School of Economics—a theoretical school, so named because many of its spokesmen have been associated with the University of Chicago. This "school" is young, having developed as a "school" since the 1920s. Representatives of this "school" attempt to prove theory with statistics. Although they favor many free market ideas, they use statistics as the basis for advocating political reform (the negative income tax, manipulation of the quantity of money and various kinds of government regulations).

Classical School of Economics—a school of thought developed in the 18th and early 19th centuries by thinkers and writers who were among the first to describe business, commerce and market operations in some detail. The philosophy and teachings of its most important representatives laid the basis for free enterprise and the development of limited constitutional government. Yet one of its theories, the fallacious labor theory of value, was taken over by Karl Marx and used as the basis for his theory of communism, the very opposite of free enterprise and limited government.

Closed shop—a business enterprise which has an agreement with a labor union (see below) requiring that only persons who already hold membership in certain unions may be hired. Closed shops are contrasted with (a) open shops and (b) union shops (see below).

Coin clipping or **coin debasement**—processes by which the metallic content of coins is reduced by (1) paring them down in size (clipping) or (2) lowering the ratio of the precious metals in the alloys from which they are made (debasement). In olden times when metallic coins played a significant role as money in the economy, governments clipped and debased coins so as to obtain new stocks of the precious metals from which they could fabricate additional coins to spend for their own accounts. This was their method of spending more than they collected in taxes. Each of the clipped, debased or smaller new coins was legally designated to represent the same nominal denominations as their larger or metallically purer predecessors. Coin clipping and debasement are forms of Inflation (see below).

Collective bargaining—negotiations between an employer's representatives and representatives of the firm's employees' duly authorized unions—on behalf of all the workers under that union's jurisdiction—to try to reach agreement with respect to wages, hours of work, and other conditions of employment. Bargaining effectively precludes individual workers from bargaining personally with their employer or his representatives.

Command society—a community of persons whose actions are controlled and regulated in many respects by officials in authority. Individuals in a command society are not free to pursue their own personal ideas, preferences, choices, values, ends, goals. A command society contrasts with a free market or contract society, where private property is protected and interpersonal relationships are the outcomes of voluntary, peaceful cooperation, exchanges and contractual agreements. A command society is also, inevitably, a status society.

Communism—the term selected by Karl Marx and his friend, Friedrich Engels, to describe the economic and political doctrines they were advocating. A theoretical economic system based on the ideas of Marx and asserted by Lenin to be the ideal toward which the Russian state was aiming. Under communism all property was to be owned and controlled by the people in common and/or local or central government. Because it is physically impossible to do away with private ownership and control of what a person actually consumes (eats up or wears out) the significance of communism arises out of the fact that private persons are not free to own, buy, sell, trade, use or control factors of production. In theory, under communism there would be no markets, no prices, no money. Both production and distribution would be determined by government officials. Everyone would contribute to the general production "according to ability" and receive "according to need." Such a system can never be put into practice on any substantial scale. Attempts to do so must always lead to dictatorship or anarchy and chaos.

Comparative advantage—a theory developed and applied specifically to international trade by the noted English

Classical economist, David Ricardo (1772-1823). Ricardo explained that trade is advantageous to *both* parties, even though one may be superior in *every* field of production and the other superior in none. The resources and talents of the two parties may differ and dovetail so that each enjoys a comparative advantage in a different field. The superior producer may have an *absolute* advantage in *every* field, but a *comparative* advantage only in those fields in which he enjoys super-superior productivity. The inferior producer may have an *absolute* advantage in no field but, nevertheless, he can have a *comparative* advantage in those fields in which the superior producer's productivity is not so pronounced.

Competition—the process in the system of social cooperation by means of which everyone strives to improve his personal situation. In the market economy producers compete by trying to please consumers better; sellers compete by offering better and/or cheaper goods and services; buyers compete by bidding higher prices. As a result, competition in the free market helps to spur production and increase the stocks of goods and services available. Competition on the market contrasts sharply with *biological* competition in nature where plants and animals struggle with one another for shares of the *limited* resources available in order to be able to survive.

Conglomerate—an aggregate; an accumulation of many units to form a new entity. This term has only recently been applied in economics to describe a specific type of business organization created by the merger of several, formerly independent and usually diverse corporations. The formation of conglomerates has become economically worthwhile in recent years primarily because of certain provisions in the tax laws. The 19th century trusts (see below), similar in some respects, usually engaged in the same or similar branches of production, while the interests of conglomerates are often widely diversified.

Consumer sovereignty—the "economic power" consumers exercise on the market by their purchases and refusals to purchase. In a free market, the freedom of consumers to express their preferences, i.e., consumer sovereignty, determines (a) prices, (b) the sums which are saved and invested, (c) the pattern of production, as well as (d) entrepreneurial profits and losses. Consumer sovereignty is a consequence of the freedom of individuals to express their personal (subjective) values in open competition through the market.

Consumers' goods—anything people eat, wear out, use up in the course of daily living. Food, clothing, shelter and also luxury items are consumers' goods. Consumers' goods and producers' goods (see below) are distinguished by their uses.

Consumption—the act of using things up or wearing them out.

Contract society—a society based on peaceful, voluntary interpersonal agreements. Contracts may be between two, or more, parties, written or oral, calling for the performance, or non-performance, of a certain act, or acts. In a contract society, an individual determines to a large extent his own social standing and wealth. Unlike a status society (see below) participants in a contract society may move freely from one economic social group to another insofar as their personal efforts, in cooperation and with the mutual agreement of others, permit. A contract society can endure only when, where and so long as individuals trust one another and the right of individuals to own private property is respected.

Convertible factor of production—something used in production which may be shifted, more or less easily, to another use than that originally intended. A factory that might be remodeled into apartments would be a convertible factor of production. So would a family station wagon that could be converted to truck farm produce to market. See also "Factor of production" and "Inconvertible factor of production" (below).

Cooperation, social or **interpersonal**—the process of working together; an act on the part of two or more persons undertaken for mutual benefit to attain a common goal. Cooperative efforts may be organized in one of two ways—(1) by force, order, decree in a *command society* or (2) by voluntary agreements in a *contract society*.

Corporation—a type of business organization defined by law which enables the company to exist as an independent entity, even if one or all of the persons supplying the original funds should die or sell their interest in the enterprise to someone else. The specific laws regulating corporations have varied from time to time, place to place under different governmental jurisdictions. Under our laws a corporation may take action in many areas, just as an individual can, making contracts, owning, buying and selling property and incurring liabilities. The liability of a corporation shareholder is now limited by law to the extent of his investment, i.e., the shares he holds in *that* firm. The *other* assets of a corporation shareholder cannot be seized in fulfillment of *that* corporation's debts.

Credit expansion—most banks pool the funds of many depositors so as to reduce the risk of lending out funds left with them by depositors for safekeeping, expecting them to be available on demand. Once a bank lends out some of its depositors' money, it no longer has on hand all the reserves it would need if all its depositors should ask at the same time to withdraw all the funds they had left with the bank for safekeeping—in checking accounts and other demand deposits. When a bank increases the number of claims to the money in its vaults in this way by lending, it is expanding credit. To expand credit, it must make it easier for persons to borrow more; it must reduce interest rates below the free market rate or relax the terms for borrowing in other ways. Banks usually justify credit expansion nowadays on the widely-accepted but fallacious theory that they have an obligation to help business firms by making money "easy" to borrow.

Crusades—religious treks to the Mideast undertaken by Christian fanatics (1096-1272) in the attempt to take Jerusalem from the non-Christian "infidels." There were nine distinct Crusades plus the Children's Crusade in 1212-1213.

"Cutthroat" competition—a catchy term used to describe any competition that seems "unfair." It may be applied to cases which appear to represent price discrimination, below cost pricing, predatory pricing, dumping, etc., all of which have been ruled at times to be "in restraint of trade." However, whether such pricing practices actually lessen, or sharpen, competition in a particular instance depends on circumstances.

D

Deduction—the method of developing knowledge and understanding by reasoning logically from *a priori* assumptions, axioms, fundamental principles. This may be graphically described as the "armchair method" of learning.

Direct exchange—barter; commodity-for-commodity trade by persons, each seeking to acquire the various things he wants to use and consume directly in exchange for the particular goods and/or services he himself has available to offer.

"Distribution," economic—in a free market economy, the pattern of ownership which prevails at any instant. Those who contribute to production are compensated in accord with previous agreements or understandings. Thus, goods and services produced under capitalism are dispersed, i.e., "distributed" in the *physical* sense, as they are shipped from person to person and place to place throughout the world. No special "distribution" is necessary. However, when referring to *economic* "distribution" we do not have in mind their actual shipment or transport from one geographical location. *Economic* "distribution" takes place as everyone acquires ownership of that part of production representing his or her particular contribution. Everything that is produced comes into existence as the property of some particular person at a particular place and time, and the ownership is already dispersed—in the course of their production—among the many market participants, geographically scattered far and wide, more or less in proportion to the share each contributed to production. See "Exchange" and "Production."

Disutility of labor—the tedium, discomfort, inconvenience, etc., which comes from having to forego immediate enjoyment, pleasure, fun, leisure, relaxation, etc., in order to work or labor in the effort to attain *other* goals; the dissatisfaction caused because work interferes with doing exactly what one would otherwise have preferred.

Division of labor—a technique of work or labor wherein the production process is divided into many small activities, each intended to accomplish a part or portion of the entire task. Dividing work in this way gives the persons specializing in each separate activity opportunities they wouldn't have had otherwise—to develop speed, efficiency, and even new skills and ideas. The division of labor thus helps speed up production, improve production methods and so make increased production possible.

"Dumping"—disposal of goods or produce, usually across national boundaries, at prices judged to be below their cost. For purposes of legislation, below-cost pricing (dumping) has been defined as selling at less than the market price in the country of origin.

Duopoly or **oligopoly**—collective nouns referring to two, or several, business firms who together effectively control the total supply of a specific item. Duopolists and oligopolists may try, tacitly or by mutual agreement, to act like a real monopoly (see below) by restricting production so as to charge monopoly prices. However, unless they are protected in some way from would-be competitors, such agreements are bound to break down before long.

Duty—a payment due, or tax levied by, government.

E

Economic calculation—the mental process by which the relative importance of any particular good or service may be estimated by comparing units of each individually to a "common denominator" for which any or all of them are exchangeable. Because economic or market values are derived from personal (subjective) values and preferences of individuals, quantitative measurements and comparisons among them are impossible. An individual may know quite well what he prefers, but he cannot measure or weigh his greater preference for one thing over another. Nor can he compare his preferences to those of other persons. However, in a market economy, individuals may make certain comparisons by estimating the importance of something to them personally in terms of another commodity, a "common denominator" for which units of any and every other good or service may be exchanged. This mental process of comparing everything—raw materials, factors of production and finished goods and services—to a single very marketable commodity (money) permits producers and consumers alike to calculate, make plans and undertake business enterprises. This process of estimating the relative importance of all the things we have and all the things we want in terms of a generally-accepted medium of exchange, money, is economic calculation.

Economic goods—things people try to obtain to use or consume in the course of seeking their various personal goals; anything material or non-material which is not available in sufficient quantity to satisfy all demand. Because demand is greater than supply, economic goods are not free for the taking; they are not "free goods" (see below). People must work or pay for economic goods. Thus, economic goods are bought, sold and traded on the market.

"Economic problem"—the conflict arising out of the fact that men whose wishes are limitless live in a world where the things they want are scarce. In the attempt to alleviate this "economic problem," men try to increase their available resources—knowledge, understanding, skills, energy, time, and ideas, as well as their supplies of economic goods and services—so as to better satisfy more of their various wants.

Economic "school" of thought—a set of theories or a body of doctrines proposed as the explanation of economic phenomena. A "school" of thought is an ideology or philosophy, not a physical school building or a legally-recognized educational institution.

Economics—the science of human action; the study of the conscious choices, actions and preferences undertaken purposively by individuals in the attempt to attain their various goals peacefully, as best they can with the time and resources available. Economics does not encompass purposively violent, coercive, destructive, deceitful actions intended to harm others.

Economize—to try to use the easiest, cheapest and most effective means available—all things considered—to accomplish one's ends or goals. This means trying to be frugal with respect to things of great value, saving them for their relatively most urgently-desired purposes only.

Elasticity of demand—the extent to which the demand of consumers for an item is "elastic," i.e., responsive to changes in its unit price.

Embargo—a restriction or prohibition of specific imports.

Empirical knowledge—knowledge acquired from experience, controlled experiment, observation and/or historical study.

Employee—a person hired to perform certain services for another, in accordance with previously agreed upon terms respecting money wages, commissions, bonuses, hours of work, overtime pay if any, fringe benefits and other factors related to working conditions.

Employer—one who hires other persons to perform various services on his behalf, in exchange for wages, salaries or commissions and possibly other benefits also as agreed upon.

Entrepreneur—an idea man and a decision-maker; one who undertakes projects, acts and tries to cope with changes and to bring about further changes. In economics, the entrepreneurs are the ones responsible for an economic enterprise, who decide whether or not to embark on a project and, if so, when, where and how to carry it out. They bear any loss that may result from unanticipated changes or mistakes. They receive "entrepreneurial profit" if their enterprise income is greater than total outgo.

Entrepreneurial profit—the excess of money income over money outgo of a business enterprise. Unless an enterprise recovers from its customers more than the cost of producing and/or reproducing its product, it is not yielding entrepreneurial or monetary (business) profit. Of course, a businessman may also gain a "Psychic profit" (see below) from his enterprise if he *enjoys* what he is doing for reasons other than the money income it yields.

Equity—the net value or net worth of a person's property or share of ownership in a business, i.e., assets minus liabilities. The sum of each stockholder's equity in a corporation is equivalent to the corporation's net worth.

Exchange—this term is usually used to refer to the process of trading one good or service for another. Strictly speaking, however, every conscious action is an exchange. In the process of acting, i.e., consciously seeking to relieve a "felt uneasiness," the actor exchanges or substitutes one situation or condition for another which, under the circumstances, he considers preferable.

Export—the verb meaning to ship out of a geographical area; also a commodity or the produce so shipped.

F

Factors of production—anything used in production. Land, labor and capital are the usual factors of production mentioned in textbooks. However, the term really includes *time* and many other non-physical things such as ideas, knowledge, recipes, etc., that are used to further production. See "Producers' goods" below. It is essential for a free market economy that individuals have the right to acquire ownership of factors of production and to use them as they wish. Unless the owners of factors of production have control over them, they are not free to experiment with new ideas, methods or products in the hope of better satisfying the future demands of consumers.

Federal Reserve System—the nationwide system of banks in the United States set up by legislation passed in 1913. The "Fed," for short, is our central bank. It is administered by a Board of Governors appointed by the President. There are 12 Federal Reserve Districts, each with one Federal Reserve Bank and many commercial member banks. The "Fed's" operations are based on the principles of "Fractional reserve banking" (see below). All member banks are required to keep a fraction of their reserves on deposit with the Federal Reserve Bank in their District. Each of the 12 Federal Reserve Banks issues its own banknotes, known as "Federal Reserve Notes," which are privileged as legal tender.

"Felt uneasiness"—the general economic term for an individual's dissatisfaction with the situation which prevails. Implied in this term is the idea that human beings are not indifferent or neutral to their surroundings; in other words, they have values, preferences and are eager to improve their conditions.

Feudalism—the eight centuries, more or less, of the Middle Ages or Dark Ages, between the fall of the Roman Empire (410 A.D.) and the Renaissance. A feudalistic society is a status society. Under feudalism the majority of the people were peasants or serfs living on autarkic self-sufficient estates in the service of a privileged noble or lord.

Forage—to search for food or provisions. Only the very most primitive peoples depend entirely, for the things they need and want to consume, on finding such natural resources in their own environs.

Foreign exchange—foreign moneys, or promises-to-pay foreign money.

Fractional reserve banking—a system of banking based on pooling the deposits of many depositors so as to permit "Credit expansion" (see above). Banks have traditionally considered they were safe in lending funds that their depositors are entitled to withdraw, maintaining only fractional reserves, on the assumption it is extremely unlikely that *all* their depositors will ask to withdraw *all* the money in *all* their deposits at the same time. However, fractional reserve banking is unsound in principle. A bank that has loaned out more money than it can raise *on demand* from its assets is inherently insolvent.

Free goods—anything, material or non-material, which is available in sufficient quantity to satisfy all demand. Because demand is less than the supply available, free goods are free to anyone who wants them. They have no market price. The items that are free goods may vary from place to place and time to time. Water is a free good beside a lake but a valuable economic good in a dry desert area. Fresh air is a free good in the country, but an economic good to city residents who are willing to pay for fresh air in offices and apartments.

Free market—a market economy where private property is protected, competition is free and open, and the opportunity to trade and to make voluntary contracts is protected, so long as the persons involved do not use force, fraud or threat thereof to interfere with the equal rights of others.

Free port—an area, set apart from all domestic markets, where goods and raw materials may be received, processed and fabricated—before being shipped out once again into world trade—without having to go through a nation's customs and be taxed as imports.

Free trade—international *laissez faire;* an international free market. In a free trade world, individuals would be at liberty to exchange with anyone anywhere who was willing to trade with them. Goods would cross national borders without hindrance. Capital, labor, production, goods and services would tend to go where they were most valuable, i.e., where their marginal utility was highest, where they enjoyed the greatest possible "Comparative advantage" (see above).

Government control or **regulation**—a government imposed and enforced restriction, directive or order.

Government intervention—an act on the part of government which interferes with the market process in some way; a coercive interference which compels peaceful persons to act differently from the way they would have otherwise, even though their actions would not have violated the equal rights of others.

Government, role of—the fundamental obligations of a government are really only two—(a) to protect the lives, property and freedom of all citizens equally from domestic and foreign intruders and (b) to adjudicate (settle through the courts) disputes that arise under its jurisdiction which the persons involved are unable to resolve peacefully among themselves.

Gresham's law—a law of economics, not of governments, named after one of the first persons to note and describe it, Sir Thomas Gresham (1519-1579). Gresham's law points out that when two moneys, valued differently on the market are decreed by law to be equal in value, people will try to use the money they value less (the "bad money") to pay their bills and to keep for themselves the money they value more (the "good money"). The appearance on the market of depreciated, clipped or debased units of money, which have been legally declared to have more value than they actually do, is a signal to traders to use the legally over-valued monetary units in trade whenever possible and to hold for themselves the more valuable, but legally under-valued, monetary units. Thus in popular parlance this law has become "Bad money drives out good." Gresham's law applies to money the general economic law that everyone tries to use the easiest, simplest and cheapest means available to attain his or her various goals.

G

Gambling—an action concerning which one can know nothing in advance about the results except that a certain percentage of the persons gambling will win and a certain percentage will lose. The results depend on pure chance. No amount of knowledge or understanding can improve the odds. A person gambles when he or she bets on the turn of a roulette wheel or the toss of a coin.

Goal, end—the aim of purposive action, selected by the individual actor on the basis of his personal, subjective values, judgment, interpretation and understanding. The ever-present goal or end of every one of us is simply the relief of a "felt uneasiness." Specific goals or ends may be short-, medium-, or long-run. The attainment of a goal or end calls for (a) planning, (b) time, and (c) various resources.

Gold—a metal, units of which have become the world's most widely-used "trading commodity" or medium of exchange. It was gold's popularity for various purposes that made it suitable to use in exchange as "money." Because it is so popular it is known as a "precious metal." Silver enjoys a similar, if lesser, popularity, is also considered a "precious metal" and has been used from time to time as a medium of exchange although not to the same extent as gold.

H

Hampered market economy—a market economy which evolves when various government interventions prevent or hinder certain otherwise peaceful actions of individuals. A hampered market economy cannot operate at maximum potential efficiency because government interventions tend to mislead, delay, sidetrack and discourage voluntary transactions, add to the costs of doing business, reduce production and employment and, thus, bring about different results from those of a free market. Most economies are hampered market economies.

History—past events and/or the record or study of past events; the past actions of individuals and the institutions they established, reported, related and interpreted in the light of available knowledge.

Human action—conscious, purposive, intentional action of individuals; action aimed at definite goals. See also "Action."

"Human rights"—this term is normally used to refer to the freedom of individuals to read, write, speak and worship as they wish. The right to own property, seldom mentioned, should also be included as *the* basic "human right," for the opportunity to own and control property is essential for all other "human rights." If a person does not have the opportunity to acquire private property, he or she must submit as a serf or slave to survive, deprived of "human rights" except as they may be granted by a master.

I

"Idle resources"—produced or semi-produced, more or less inconvertible, factors of production, fabricated for purposes which later proved to have been mistaken. "Idle resources" are usually malinvestments, due to entrepreneurial failures in anticipating consumer demand and market conditions. This term is somewhat misleading for it bears the implication that "idle resources" may be artificially subsidized into activity and, by this simple artifice, rendered non-idle and thus "economic."

Import—the verb meaning to ship into a geographical area from abroad; also a commodity or the produce so shipped.

Inconvertible factor of production—something used in the production of a specific good or service which has only one presently known use. It cannot be shifted or converted to serve another purpose at all, or at least not without incurring such high costs or serious difficulties as to make its conversion appear impossible, impracticable or at least not worthwhile. The huge luxury liners, that became unprofitable with the increase of air travel, and assemblyline machinery, which is geared to producing a certain make or model automobile, are practically inconvertible factors of production. Few, if any, entrepreneurs would be able to conceive of an idea for converting them to uses which would be profitable. See also "Factors of production" and "Convertible factor of production."

Indirect exchange—a market transaction or trade involving a good or service on one side and on the other a "trading commodity," i.e., a medium of exchange or money. Indirect exchange contrasts with barter or direct exchange (see above).

Induction—the method of acquiring knowledge by accumulating data and facts from experience, controlled experiments, observation and/or historical study. The methods of induction may be described in more familiar terms as the "look-see," "trial and error" laboratory experiments and/or research of papers and artifacts.

"Industrial Revolution"—any significant and perhaps especially conspicuous shift or turn-over in production methods. The term is frequently used to refer to the relatively rapid introduction, primarily in England during the 18th and early 19th centuries, of the factory system and mass production, using steam power, replacing the earlier, less efficient and smaller scale handicraft production techniques.

Infant industry—a new industry in an economy. A traditional protectionist argument on behalf of tariffs and other import barriers has been that foreign competition should be restricted to give infant industries a better chance to sell, become established and expand on the domestic market.

Inflation—an increase in the quantity of money. Inflations may be caused by a new discovery of the commodity used as money (whether shells, gold, silver or what-have-you), by a goldsmith's issue of more "warehouse receipts" for gold than he has gold on deposit, an increase of a bank's banknotes over and above the reserves available to redeem them, an increase in the government's issue of printed (fiat) money, etc. Credit expansion (see above) is a variation of inflation.

Interest, interest rate—the price, usually expressed as a ratio or percentage of the sum involved, which a borrower pays for borrowing money. Borrowers are willing to pay such a premium to acquire cash funds promptly, and lenders are ready to forego the use of the funds involved until a later date, in exchange for the payment of interest, because they have different, yet dovetailing time preferences. Interest is a consequence of the fact that events take place over time and that people have values. Interest rates are composed of three factors: (1) *Originary interest,* based on time preference; (2) *Price premium,* based on the expectation of a general shift in prices, due to changes in the quantity of money; (3) *Risk factor,* based on the anticipated chances for success or failure of the specific enterprise concerned. A specific interest rate at a specific time and place is determined, as in the pricing auctions, by competition among prospective lenders and borrowers each bidding or refraining from bidding according to their own personal values and value scales.

"Interstate commerce"—the term used to refer to trade and market transactions carried out within this country but across State boundaries. The term is derived from the provision of the Constitution authorizing the Congress "to regulate Commerce . . . among the several States," as well as from legislation implementing Supreme Court decisions defining this authority.

Interventionist government—a form of government which interferes, regulates, restricts, controls some, not all, peaceful actions of private individuals, even when they were not violating the equal freedom and rights of other persons. Interventionist programs inevitably help some people while hurting others. Because individuals make mistakes, they have seldom come close to the ideal, a strictly limited government, and if they have, they have usually let it deteriorate sooner or later into some form of interventionist government. The economic system associated with interventionist government is a hampered market economy.

Invest, investment—the process of directing savings into specific enterprises set up to engage in production.

"Iron law of wages"—an early economic doctrine which held that the laborers in a society could never receive more than a certain fixed percentage of the wealth produced. If their wages fell below this percent, their numbers would go down as infant mortality, diseases and starvation went up. Their employers would see to it that workers never received more in wages than the percent prescribed by this "iron law," for they would hire fewer workers, compel them to work longer hours, or take higher incomes from the business for themselves.

J

"Just price" idea—the belief, associated primarily with Scholasticism that in any particular situation there was a price, wage, interest rate, profit, etc., which was "right" and "fair."

L

Labor—purposive activity, work, or effort, not necessarily considered pleasurable in and of itself, but valued primarily as a *means* for attaining one or several of a person's *other* goals, ends, wants, needs, etc.

Labor theory of value—the value of a good or service on the market is determined by the work or labor required to produce or obtain it. See "Value theories" (below).

Labor (trade) union—an organization of workers for the purpose of attaining common goals. Membership may be along company, craft or industrial lines. Although unions may be purely voluntary organizations, competing with other voluntary groups and societies for members and financial support, some organizations of workers have been given special recognition by law, entitling them to certain privileges as unions—in obtaining members, excluding non-members from competing for some jobs and bargaining with established and potential employers.

Laissez faire, *French*—a term applied to the political policy of leaving businessmen alone—to "do their own thing," so to speak. If government were to adopt a policy of *laissez faire* this would, in effect, bring about a free market economy. The term is frequently used as a smear word to describe a system under which big business firms would be free to use any tactic, legal or illegal, to gain their own "selfish" ends at the expense of the common man or small consumer. But in fact *laissez faire* does not include allowing anyone the right or privilege to ride roughshod over the equal rights of others. True *laissez faire* would mean freedom.

Legal tender—the commodity or money which the government has recognized by law and which government requires creditors to accept when it is offered them in payment of monetary debts. The U. S. Constitution forbids the States from making "any Thing but gold or silver Coin a Tender in Payment of Debts." The U. S. national government, however, has decreed the paper banknotes of the "Fed" to be legal tender, and their status as legal tender is indicated in print on all Federal Reserve Notes.

Liabilities—the obligations and/or debts of a person or organization.

Limited government—the ideal government, one that is restricted to its legitimate role consisting of two important functions—(a) protecting lives and property from domestic and foreign interference and (b) settling disputes through the courts. A limited government is based on equality under law for all peaceful citizens. Like a night watchman or electrified fence, it guards individuals and their property, without interfering unless provoked into action by someone who uses violence, or threat of violence, to hurt other members of the society and/or their property. A limited government leaves people free and permits them to function in peace. The economic system associated with limited government is capitalism or the free market economy.

Loss—the decline in value resulting from an action when the total yield is insufficient to cover all the costs involved; the opposite of "Profit" (see below).

M

Macro-economics—the name used to describe the study of mass economic phenomena, i.e., the operations and activities of large numbers of persons, groups, collectives, communities, societies, nations, etc.

Madison Avenue—one of the major north-south avenues of New York City which has come to epitomize the advertising industry, because the offices of many advertising agencies are located there.

Margin—an invisible dividing line, in economic terminology, separating (a) those persons who actually buy or sell an item on the market from those who don't and (b) those items that are actually traded on the market from those that aren't. A "sub-marginal" good or service is not traded because potential purchasers value it less than they do the price they would have to pay—in time, money and effort—to acquire it.

Marginal unit—the last unit of a good or service which a person considers worth what it costs to acquire it—in time, money and effort.

Marginal utility—the usefulness or satisfaction which depends on the possession of a single unit of a particular good or service. We may determine the "marginal utility" of any item by ascertaining what we would lose in the way of satisfaction if we had to get along with one less unit of it.

Marginal worker—the worker at the margin. The marginal worker is the person whose productivity just barely covers the costs of hiring him or her. A marginal worker may become sub-marginal (or vice versa) if his productivity or the market demand for his output declines (or increases).

Market—a market is any place or geographical location where two or more persons meet and exchange goods and/or services. The term may also be used as a short cut term for the market economy or market process.

Market economy—any trading area bound into a single unit by the cobweblike network of interpersonal agreements, contracts and exchanges.

Market process—the procedure or arrangement prevailing throughout the market economy which results from the conscious, purposive actions of individuals cooperating, competing and exchanging with one another. The outcome of the market process is production and trade.

Markets, Say's law of—a theory first set forth clearly by Jean Baptiste Say (1767-1832) to the effect that production creates its own market; there can be no widespread business slump on account of general over-production or a general shortage of money. Goods produced become purchasing power for other goods and services. Money prices adjust to help equate supply and demand.

Mass production—the process of production on a large scale for potentially large numbers of consumers; transforming large quantities of raw materials into finished consumers' goods by means of assembly line techniques. Mass production relies heavily on specialization, the division of labor, capitalist savings and the use of tools. Mass production for mass markets takes advantage of the economies of scale made possible by standardizing products and using machines and assembly lines instead of individualistic hand labor.

Means—any resource or tool, material or immaterial, which a person finds useful for seeking a goal. Among the means or resources commonly referred to in economics are raw materials, labor, tools, factories, capital goods, money, and other things used in production.

Medium (media, pl.) of exchange—a "trading commodity" used as money in indirect exchange. As trade increases and the trading area expands, direct exchange or barter becomes cumbersome and impractical. Traders then turn to making trades in terms of some commodity which is in greater demand and thus more readily marketable than the actual items they are seeking to exchange. As a result of countless such transactions, traders may try to arrange trades in terms of several different items. In time one commodity may prove more marketable than others. Then eventually that particular commodity may be transformed from being simply one of several desirable and marketable items into the *most desirable* and *most marketable* commodity and, thus, a suitable medium of exchange. The availability of a medium of exchange contributes substantially to trade, by making transactions easier to arrange, and to production, by making economic calculation possible.

Mercantilism—an economic theory and set of political doctrines based on the concept of artificially stimulating "national wealth" by subsidizing exports of goods and the import of the precious metals (gold and silver). During the 16th, 17th and 18th centuries, quite a few governments enacted various Mercantilist interventions to protect domestic producers from competition. A period of relatively free world trade followed but Mercantilist doctrines have gained popularity in this century and many such programs are now in force in many countries throughout the world.

Micro-economics—the body of economics and economic theory which analyzes, interprets and traces all economic phenomena back to the economic unit, i.e., the individual actor, his individual actions, ideas, choices and preferences.

Money—a commodity used to facilitate trade, thus a "trading commodity" or medium of exchange. Money is the most desirable and most readily marketable commodity in an economy, the commodity which people generally are most willing to accept in trade. Austrian economist Ludwig von Mises defined money as "the most marketable good which people acquire because they want to offer it in later acts of interpersonal exchange." (*Human Action*, 3rd ed., 1966, p. 401)

Money stock—the quantity of money in existence at any one time. Federal Reserve statistics calculate money stock in two ways. What they call M-1 is defined as the total of (1) currency outside of banks plus (2) demand deposits subject to check. Their second calculation of money stock, M-2, includes M-1 PLUS (3) time deposits at commercial banks other than large certificates of deposit. (See Federal Reserve releases for details.) Both M-1 and M-2 have increased substantially in recent decades. The increase in M-2 relative to whatever metallic money has formed its base has been especially spectacular.

Monopoly, monopolist—speaking precisely, this term refers to the *exclusive* control of the *entire* supply of a *specific* good or service. Monopolies may be (a) natural, due to the fact that the quantity of the monopolized item is limited by nature; (b) local, due to the fact that the physical space in which the monopolist operates is strictly limited so that there is actually no room for a competitor; (c) legal, due to the fact that the opportunity to operate depends on a special legal grant, a government license, franchise or privilege. The term monopoly, as well as monopolist, is often used imprecisely to refer to almost any very large firm, or an extremely successful businessman, irrespective of the existence of competitors and potential competitors.

Monopoly price, monopoly gain—a higher unit price than would have appeared on the market under free and open competition; the extra gain, if any, from selling fewer items at such a price. A monopolist may charge a monopoly price for something and reap a monopoly gain *only if the demand for it is such that enough consumers are willing to pay the higher price* and so make the monopolist's net return—from selling a smaller quantity at the higher price—greater than if he sold a larger quantity at the lower, competitive, free market, price. No monopolist, not even one who exercises *exclusive* control over the *entire* supply of a *specific* good or service, is *always* in a position to charge a monopoly price and reap a monopoly gain. This must depend on the wishes of potential consumers, and the existence of alternatives and substitutes. To yield a monopoly gain, the demand on the market for the monopolized item must be *relatively* "inelastic," i.e. consumers must be ready to buy almost as many units at a higher price as they would if its price were lower. See "Elasticity of demand." Yet no monopolist can know with any certainty in advance, when deciding what prices to ask, how "elastic" the demand for his product will be.

Most favored nations—a term used at least since 1922 to refer to those nations whose governments agree to admit each other's products into their respective countries on more favorable terms than they grant imports from less favored nations. Tariffs on imports from most favored nations may be reduced or even eliminated by mutual agreement.

Multinational corporation (MNC)—a corporation with interests and investments in more than one country.

N

Neo-classical School of Economics—a school of thought or set of theories derived from the doctrines of the Classical School, modified somewhat by the marginal utility, subjective value theory. Representatives of this "School" often use mathematical formulae in the attempt to analyze and predict economic phenomena.

Net worth—the estimated market value of the assets of a person or firm, after deducting all liabilities. See also "Equity" (above).

"Niggardly," "niggardliness" of nature—these terms were used by John Stuart Mill (1806-1873) in his *Principles of Political Economy* to describe the fact that the world is not as amply supplied with resources as men would wish. We must struggle to extract, transport and transform raw materials, as they appear on earth, into tools and goods to satisfy our various wants.

Nomadic tribes—small bands of wandering peoples who depend primarily on domesticated animals for the things they need and want to consume. As their livestock require new lands to graze, a nomadic tribe finds it necessary to move from place to place.

Non-tariff barriers (NTB)—governmental regulations, other than direct import taxes (tariffs), which make imports more difficult or more expensive. The purpose of non-tariff barriers—import license requirements, anti-dumping restrictions, Buy American stipulations, etc.—is to hamper trade and/or raise revenue for the government. Some government regulations not intended to hamper imports—domestic health and sanitation standards, trucking restrictions, automobile safety legislation, etc.—may turn out to be unintentional non-tariff barriers.

O

Objective characteristics—the physical or chemical properties or traits of something; its capacity to bring about a definite effect. Contrasts with *subjective* value which depends on the personal ideas and judgments of the individual doing the valuing. See "Value."

Oligopoly—see "Duopoly" (above).

Open shop—a business enterprise which makes no stipulation respecting the union status of employees, both union members and non-members alike being eligible for employment.

Operating statement—a financial statement showing the total receipts and expenditures of a person or firm during a certain period of time.

P

Paradox of value—the apparent contradiction which exists in the statement that some things are very "valuable" in use (air, water) but not very "valuable" in trade; while some things (gold, silver) are very "valuable" in trade, but not very "valuable" in use. This "paradox" was explained when economists realized that market prices were derived from subjective (personal) values of individuals, each of whom was always comparing the relative importance to him of specific *units* of various commodities. Thus the market price of a particular item hinges on the service that depends on a single unit so that when the units of any good are plentiful, relatively less depends on any single unit.

Physiocrats—an economic school of thought based on the concept of "natural order" in production. The Physiocrats' incomplete definition of production, as the result of combining human labor with nature, led them to advocate the granting of special privileges to agricultural producers.

Pickets, picketing, picket lines—terms taken from military tactics where they applied to the posting of guards around a camp to keep out intruders by using force if necessary. This terminology is inappropriate for discussing peaceful and voluntary employer-employee relations. It is perhaps suitable, however, for describing the kind of disputes that arise under current labor legislation. The picketing of an establishment holds the threat of violence if the union pickets are determined to prevent potential workers, who want no more than the opportunity to accept jobs offered them, from crossing picket lines.

Price—an exchange ratio, the ratio at which goods and services are exchanged on the market for one another, or for money. Prices are usually expressed in terms of money, i.e., the medium of exchange, currently in use on the market.

Price, law of—the law that explains market prices. The price of any item on a free market is forced by competition and the pricing process to fall within certain limits, determined by the personal, subjective, value scales of the buyers and sellers at the "margin," (see above), i.e., the invisible dividing line between those who trade and those who don't because they do not consider the exchange to be worth the cost—in time, money and effort.

Primitive societies—the simplest known economic arrangement. People forage, fish and hunt for food and their other necessities. They have only very crude and simple tools to use in production.

Private property—anything, usually physical, which a person may own and dispose of at will. The right of disposal, i.e., the right to *control* the use of a thing, is crucial! Unless a person has control of something, he cannot be said to *own* it. At some times and places persons have been legally treated as private property (slaves) and so bought and sold on the market. Some non-physical things may also be considered private property and so exchangeable on the market—a song, a recipe, a patented idea, a contractual right to acquire an asset, etc.

Producers' goods—anything used in production, to produce consumers' goods and/or other producers' goods. Producers' goods include raw materials, land, labor, as well as produced and partially produced tools, machines, factories and anything else used for further production. Although most people think of producers' goods as applying only to physical things, the term also covers ideas, knowledge and recipes as they too are used to further production. Producers' goods and consumers' goods are distinguished by their uses.

Producers' policy—a deliberate government policy intended to protect less efficient producers from the competition of more efficient producers. Helping some producers in this way must inevitably injure other producers, raise production costs, lower output, increase market prices and, thus, reduce the satisfaction of consumers. Mercantilism and protectionism are specific forms of producers' policies.

Production—the process of combining raw materials, labor and other factors of production or producers' goods over a period of time, in accord with some idea or plan, so as to create goods and/or services consumers want and value more highly than they did its component parts in their previous uses. If the process results in goods and/or services consumers do not want at all, or do not want as much as they would have the component parts in other forms, then the outcome of the process is *not* "production" in its true sense; but rather it is waste and destruction. It might be pointed out here also that any process which helps a product reach the final consumer —transportation, advertising, selling, giving legal advice, etc.—is a step in its production. Even though it may not physically alter the product, it is productive if it contributes in any way to the provision of something a consumer wants.

Profit—the gain derived from an action, the total yield less total costs. There are two kinds of profit: (a) "psychic profit," i.e., personal, subjective, mental or psychological and (b) "entrepreneurial profit," i.e., monetary or business.

Promissory note—a promise-to-pay or an IOU. In the course of doing business, private persons and business firms frequently sign promissory notes—"notes," for short—specifying sums of money, goods or services to be delivered, and the time, terms and conditions of delivery.

Property rights—the freedom and opportunity to acquire, own, hold, use and dispose of private property. This "right" is basic to all market phenomena—exchange, division of labor, specialization, etc. It is an essential element of private property and it is also basic to so-called "human rights."

Protectionism—a deliberate policy on the part of government intended primarily to give domestic producers a competitive advantage on the domestic market as against potential foreign suppliers. Tariffs, import quotas, direct subsidies to domestic producers and the establishment of quality standards which foreigners are unable to meet are typical protectionist devices. Cartels (see above) are feasible only if, as and when some protectionist measures are in force.

Psychic profit—the subjective or psychological gain from an action. If a person receives pleasure from giving a gift, that pleasure is a form of psychic profit. Any time a person trades voluntarily, he or she reaps a psychic profit because the value to him or her of what is received is more than that of what was given in exchange. Thus, whenever a customer buys anything he or she gains psychic profit and if the purchase seems an exceptionally good bargain, something for which he or she would have willingly paid even more, the psychic profit may be substantial. A job that is fun yields a psychic profit as compared with work that is boring. Psychic profits are in the mind. As psychic profits are subjective they cannot be measured.

Purchasing power—the ability to command goods and services through peaceful trading on the market. Purchasing power is the only real manifestation of so-called "economic power." In a free market economy, the only way to acquire purchasing power is to produce, or to receive gifts or loans from someone else who has produced, goods and services others want in exchange. Purchasing power reflects and follows success in serving consumers, the greatest concentrations of purchasing or economic power gravitating into the hands of those who contribute the very most.

Q

Quota—a governmental restriction or limitation of imports or exports, usually stated in terms of physical quantity or monetary value.

R

"Rainy day" (or plain) savings—accumulations of stocks of consumers' goods as reserves to be consumed later—on "rainy days."

Reformation—the religious reforms of the 16th and 17th century. The Renaissance spirit of inquiry led some thinkers to re-examine many accepted religious dogma and practices, including the doctrine of the infallibility of certain church officials. Their doubts led in time to reforms in the Roman Catholic Church and the establishment of a number of Protestant sects.

Renaissance—roughly the three centuries (1300-1600 A.D.) following feudalism when an interest in learning revived as a result of the rediscovery in Europe of the literature and art of the ancient Greeks and Romans. During the Renaissance, a spirit of inquiry among thinkers led to advances in the physical sciences, geographical knowledge, religious philosophy and political theory. Renaissance thinkers contributed to the climate of opinion permitting intellectual inquiry which made possible the evolution of more efficient methods of production.

Resources—any good or service used for production. Raw materials are called *natural* resources because they are natural phenomena, i.e., products of nature. As men refine and fabricate them step-by-step, they become *semi-produced* or *produced* resources, factors of production, or tools. Resources may also be non-material—knowledge, theories, understanding, skills, time, energy, ideas, etc. See "Means."

Restraint of trade—a technical term used, although not clearly defined, in antitrust legislation which refers to activities on the part of businessmen and business firms that ostensibly lead to restricting competition and reducing commercial transactions.

"Right-to-work" laws—laws intended to prevent unions from insisting that employers with whom they have contracts hire only union members. Right-to-work laws preclude closed shops, but not union shops.

"Robber barons"—a name originally applied to some of the more flamboyant and successful 19th century entrepreneurs who extracted raw materials on a large scale, financed or pioneered mass production, amassing large personal fortunes. Implicit in this colorful expression is the idea that their wealth was gained at the expense of workers and consumer.

"Round-about" methods of production—a term sometimes used to describe production with the aid of complex tools, machines and equipment which themselves had to be produced first by a complex, time-consuming process. This term is somewhat misleading. Production is carried on with the aid of previously produced tools and machines of various kinds *precisely because that is the most effective, efficient, fruitful and thus most direct*—not "round-about"—method known to obtain the increased quantities of consumers' goods desired.

S

Saving—the process of refraining from consuming a part of production.

Savings—a surplus of production over consumption. See "'Rainy-day' (or plain) savings" and "Capitalist savings."

Scale of values—the order of importance or urgency according to which every person, consciously or unconsciously, ranks his various needs, wants, goals or ends. Everyone is always necessarily aiming at his most urgently desired, i.e., most important or most valuable, goal or end of the moment—in the light of his personal situation as he views it. See also "Value."

Scholasticism—the doctrine and philosophy of St. Thomas Aquinas (1225-1274) and other Medieval churchmen. With respect to economics, they held that there was a "just price" (see above) and that to charge more or less than that was not right, fair or moral.

Scientific action—an action about which the results may be known in advance. The more a person can learn about the universe, the laws of the physical sciences, cause and effect, the better equipped he or she will be to undertake scientific actions with confidence. A person acts as a scientist, performing scientific actions when he or she follows the proper mechanical steps to start the motor of a car, put it in motion and steer it in a certain direction. To bake a cake according to a proven recipe is also a scientific action. Barring accidents, insufficient knowledge and human error, scientific actions have the results intended.

Seller—it is customary to speak of a trader who gives some specific good or service in exchange for money as a "seller." In this sense, a "seller" is contrasted with a "buyer."

Slavery, serfdom—a form of existence which allows no personal freedom. Serfs and slaves are dependent on a master because they are denied the right to become independent by acquiring private property of their own to use as they wish for their own purposes. Serfs and slaves are considered the property of their owners who have the right to control or dispose of them and/or their product.

Socialism—a theoretical economic system synonymous with communism. Karl Marx and his friend, Friedrich Engels rejected the term socialism because of its association at that time (1848) with a middle class (not workingmen) movement.

Special privileges—benefits granted by government to certain persons, firms, organizations or groups not available to everybody else in the same situation. A special privilege helps some, hurts others and, thus, is not consistent with limited government.

Specialization—the technique of production which uses specialists, each of whom performs one or several separate activities that in combination accomplish a single complex task. See also "Division of Labor."

Specie—monetary coins, usually gold or silver. When banks have found themselves in financial difficulties as a consequence of having inflated or expanded credit (see "Credit expansion," and "Inflation") governments have frequently relieved them of the obligation of fulfilling their pledges to redeem their notes in gold or silver coins. In other words, banks have been permitted at times, with the permission of government, to "suspend specie payment."

Speculation—an action which must be based on only partial knowledge and understanding. A person acts as a speculator when deciding whether, when, how and to what extent to take a specific action. The uncertainty of the future makes every conscious choice a speculation. Deciding whether or not to act—even whether or not to gamble or take a scientific action—is speculating. Entrepreneurial decisions are always speculations, for entrepreneurs can never have complete knowledge concerning the consequences of their actions.

Status society—a social arrangement based on established, government-defined "classes." Every person in a status society is born into a certain status or "class." Some belong to the lower classes of slaves, serfs, peasants, servants or laborers; others to more privileged classes—masters, nobles or lords; except in rare cases no one moves out of the class into which he or she is born. Production in a status society relies to a considerable extent on the use of slave labor. In a status society, both the class structure and the institution of slavery are upheld and strengthened by the superstitious and polytheistic religions of the people.

Stock, common and preferred—a share of ownership in a business firm. Holders of shares of stock are issued stock certificates as evidence of their ownership in the firm. Holders of a company's *common* stock share—according to the terms of their partial ownership—the risk of loss as well as the chance of monetary or entrepreneurial profit. When a company's income declines, the holders of its *preferred* stock are given preference over the owners of its *common* stock in the payment of dividends. Also, if the firm goes out of business, the owners of its *preferred* stock have priority over the holders of its *common* stock if, as and when anything is salvaged from the firm's assets.

Stock exchange—a market place where persons who want to buy or sell shares of ownership in various business firms may meet and trade with one another.

Strike—a tactic used by a group of employees who refuse to work at the jobs they had been holding, but prevent those jobs from being filled by others whom the employer might like to hire for those positions. To quit work in unison is a perfectly legitimate way to try to accomplish a common purpose. However, a strike involves more than simply quitting work in concert. Inherent in the strike concept is the claim that the strikers have a right to use force or threat of force if need be to prevent other would-be workers, known derisively as "strikebreakers" or "scabs," from taking the jobs they had held but which they now reject at the terms being offered. When government sanctions a strike, it backs up the union's threat with force, so that a very few union pickets usually suffice to bar other workers effectively from competing for jobs at the plant being struck and, thus, to protect the privileged position of the strikers.

Subjective value—value depending on the personal ideas and judgment of an individual. See also "Value."

Subsidy—financial aid to some person, persons, businesses, organizations or groups. When government grants subsidies to some, it helps the recipients at the expense of those who are forced to pay the cost.

T

Tariff—a tax levied by government on imports, i.e., goods being brought into the area under its jurisdiction. A tariff is a particular kind of duty.

Time preference—the relative urgency of a person's demand for present goods as compared with future goods. Like personal (subjective) values, different individuals have different time preferences and the same individual has different time preferences at different times and under different circumstances. In the Aesop fable, the Grasshopper's time preference is such that he is probably willing to pay a special premium to enjoy consumers' goods today. On the other hand, the Ant's time preference tempers his desire to consume today; he sets some things aside so he may consume more tomorrow than he otherwise could.

Tool—a term usually applied to physical instruments, i.e., factors of production which are considered useful for attaining a goal—viz. a train to transport goods and people, a hammer to pound nails into a board, a computer to record data and calculate or a warehouse to store merchandise. However, ideas, knowledge and skills are also tools, for they are means we consider useful to help us accomplish our goals. Thus, a tool is any object (material or immaterial) which (a) an individual (b) considers useful (c) for a purpose. Although tools are labor-saving devices, their most important function is to increase production.

Totalitarian government—a government that controls every aspect and action of all persons and things under its jurisdiction. No government manned by fallible human beings will ever really be able to accomplish this very difficult feat. However, many governments have been based on this theory, i.e., that everything which takes place within the country *should* be planned by the central authority. The economic system associated with such a totalitarian government is known as communism, socialism or Nazism, i.e., Hitler's type of National Socialism.

Trade—exchange (see above). Every trade or exchange means giving up something (some good, service or situation, separately or in some combination) to obtain something else (some other good, service or situation, separately or in some combination). It permits people to obtain things from other persons and other parts of the world that they could not acquire otherwise, or at least not as cheaply or as easily. Trade is a product of cooperation. At the same time a trade is very often a step on the road to still further cooperation.

Trust—a specific type of business structure which became important in the late 19th century. The owners of several independent companies in an industry would turn over their stock and control of their firm to "trustees" who then managed and operated the complex of several companies as a single unit under a "trust agreement." The intent of such a "trust agreement" was to try to monopolize the entire production in an industry. (NOTE: This use of the term "trust" is distinct from its use in banking and financial communities to describe a specific legal arrangement under which funds belonging to *one* person are turned over to *another*, a "trustee," to be managed on behalf of a *third* party, the "beneficiary.")

U

Union shop—a business enterprise which has an agreement with a labor union requiring that all employees in certain categories must be, or must become, members of that labor union to retain their jobs; nonunion members may be hired, but only on the condition that they join the specified union within an agreed-upon time. See also "Closed shop."

Usefulness, utility—the capability of a good or service to satisfy a need or serve a purpose. The physical characteristics or properties of a good or service usually form the basis of its utility, but the *subjective* value of a good or service to an individual may have real significance for market prices and pricing. The *subjective* views of individuals concerning the utility of a good or service may make it more or less valuable in the minds of people than its objective characteristics, its physical properties, would seem to warrant.

"Usury"—a term used to describe interest rates. By using this term the speaker implies that the rate of interest referred to is higher than he considers proper under the circumstances.

V

Value—the worth of anything to a specific person or persons. Value is necessarily personal and *subjective*, i.e., it depends on the ideas or judgment of the individuals doing the valuing. A good or service may possess objective (physical or intrinsic) properties or characteristics. However, to speak of its value as being *objective* or *intrinsic* is a contradiction in terms. Values are always personal, *subjective*, in the minds of the individual valuer.

Value theories—several theoretical explanations have been suggested as to why some goods and services are wanted or needed more than others and considered desirable enough for people to be willing to work or give up something else to get them. The most significant theories advanced over the centuries to explain economic and/or market values have been:

1. Goods or services are *valued the same* as what is given in trade for them. (Aristotle and Aquinas)
2. Goods or services are *valued at their cost of production.* (Adam Smith and Karl Marx)
3. Goods or services are *valued at what they will bring in trade or "exchange."* (Adam Smith and others)
4. Goods and services are *valued by individuals, as judged from their personal (subjective) viewpoints.* Adam Smith recognized one form of personal evaluation, "use value." But Smith's concept of "use" was too narrow. Only later was full recognition, for the determination of economic value, given to the importance of *individual, personal evaluations* of *specific units* of a good or service under *specific circumstances.* Individuals always believe what they have, and are not trying to dispose of, is more valuable in "use" to them personally, under the circumstances, then it would be in "exchange." Thus when they *do* decide to make a trade, it is because they believe what they are offering to exchange is worth *less* to them personally than what they expect to receive in return. Barring force, fraud and mistakes in judgment then, both parties will consider themselves to have gained as the result of a voluntary trade. (Menger, Jevons, Walras and the subjective value "Austrian" theoreticians)

W

Wage, wage rates—the market price paid a person for performing a service or certain amount of labor. Wages, like prices, are exchange ratios between money and the item under consideration. A wage is simply a specific term used to describe the price—usually expressed in money terms—paid at a particular place and time for a certain amount of labor or service, as opposed to a physical good or commodity.

Wall Street—a New York City street which has become almost synonymous with the stock market, "big business," and financial speculation. The offices of the New York Stock Exchange and of many large banks and investment firms are located there.

"Welfare economics"—the government policy of granting special privileges or subsidies to favored groups or persons. Advocates of such "welfare" programs usually ignore, or at least fail to mention, that their policies are helping some persons only at the expense of others, those who must pay their financial cost and those whose plans and activities are adversely affected.

"Wild cat" banking—a colorful phrase for describing fractional reserve banking. A "wild cat bank" is one which expands its issue of notes and loans more, on the basis of lower reserves, than more cautious bankers of its day generally consider wise. No "wild cat bank" can survive very long—its shortage of funds will become apparent as soon as a substantial number of its depositors try to withdraw their money from the bank.

Y

"Yellow-dog" contract—an employment contract which forbids employees from joining a union, or requires them to resign their jobs if they are, or ever should become, union members. The opposite of a closed shop (see above).

Annotated Index of Authors